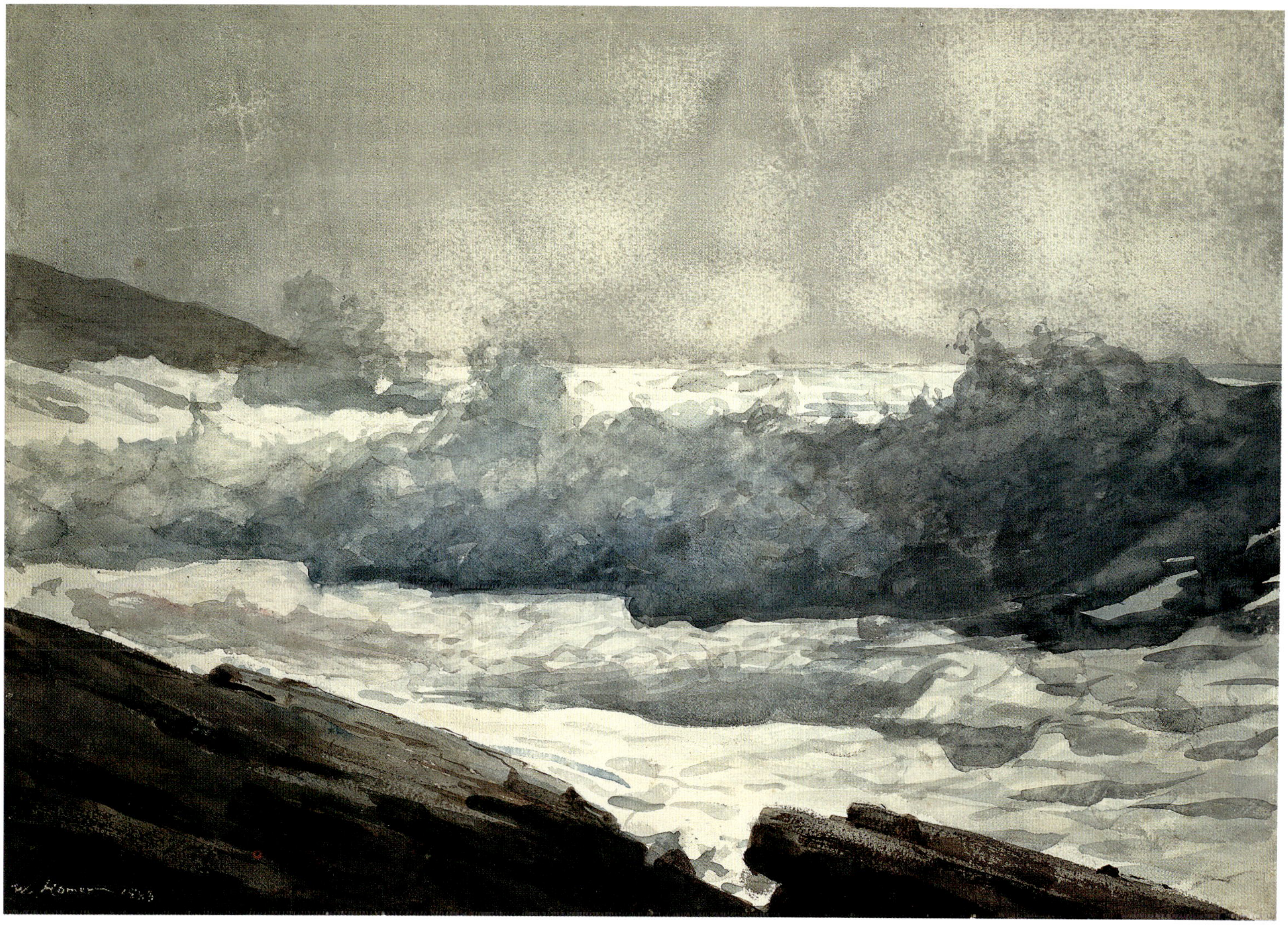
W. Homer 1883

(preceding page)

PROUT'S NECK, BREAKERS 1883

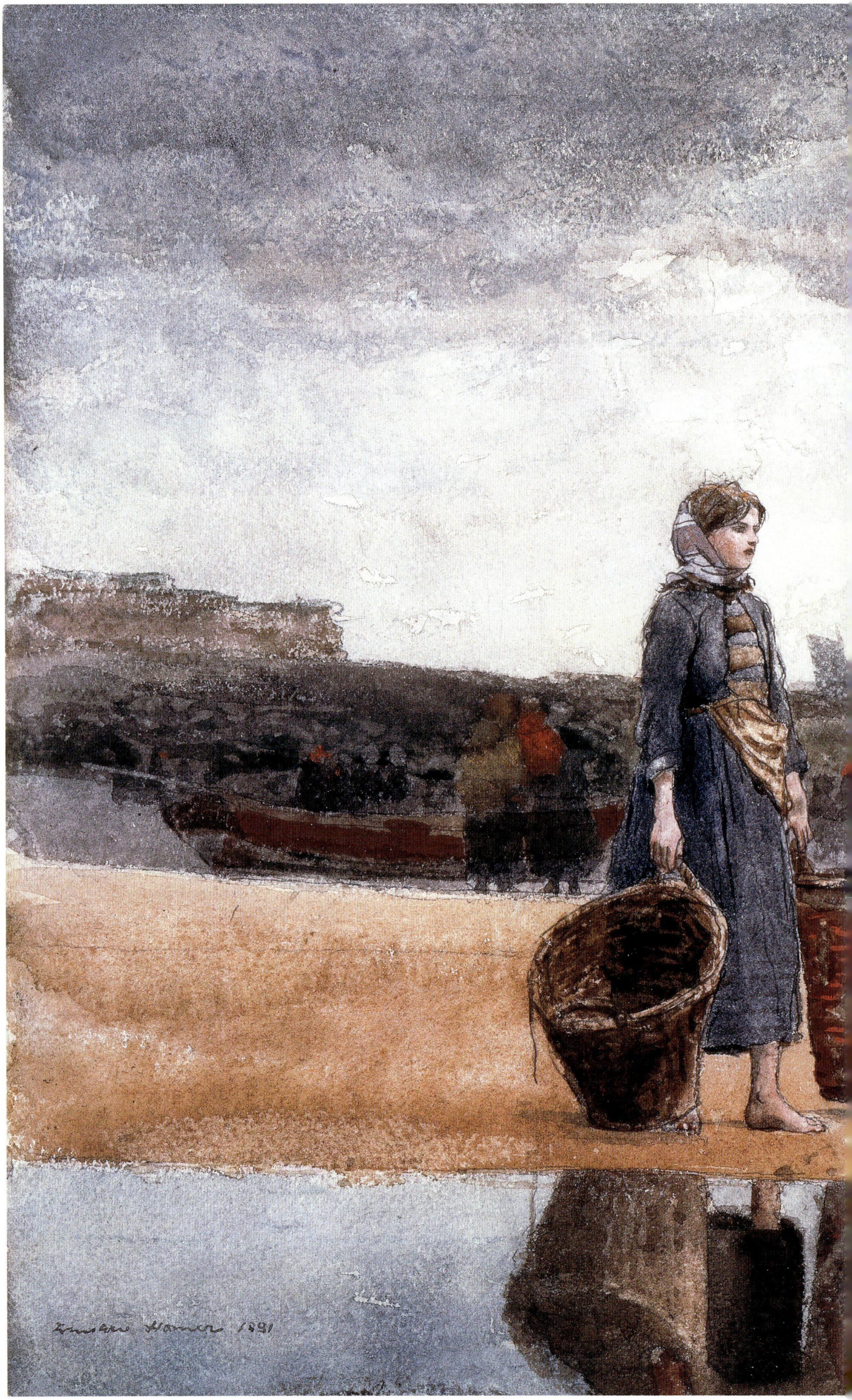

FISHER GIRLS ON THE BEACH, TYNEMOUTH 1881

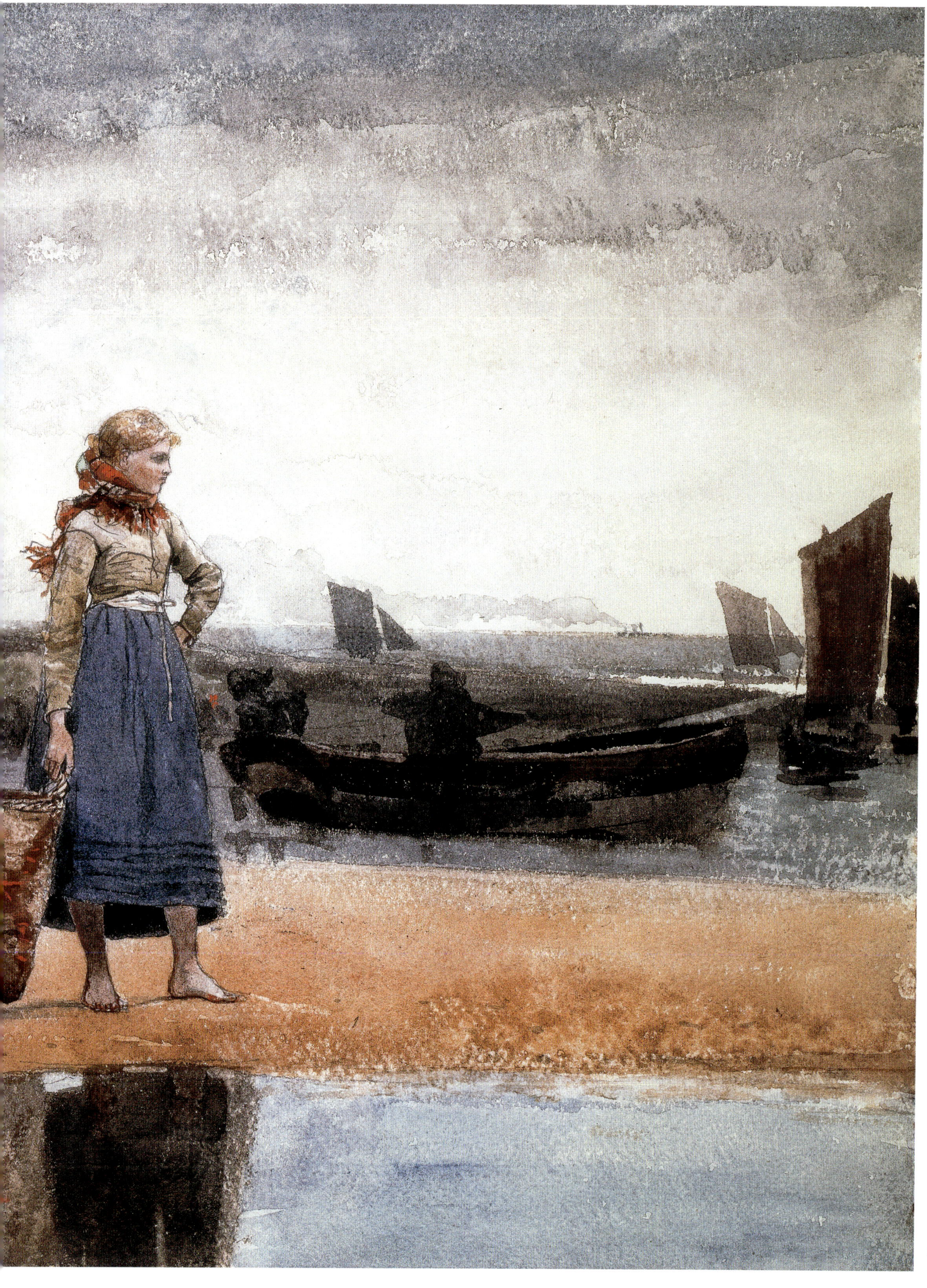

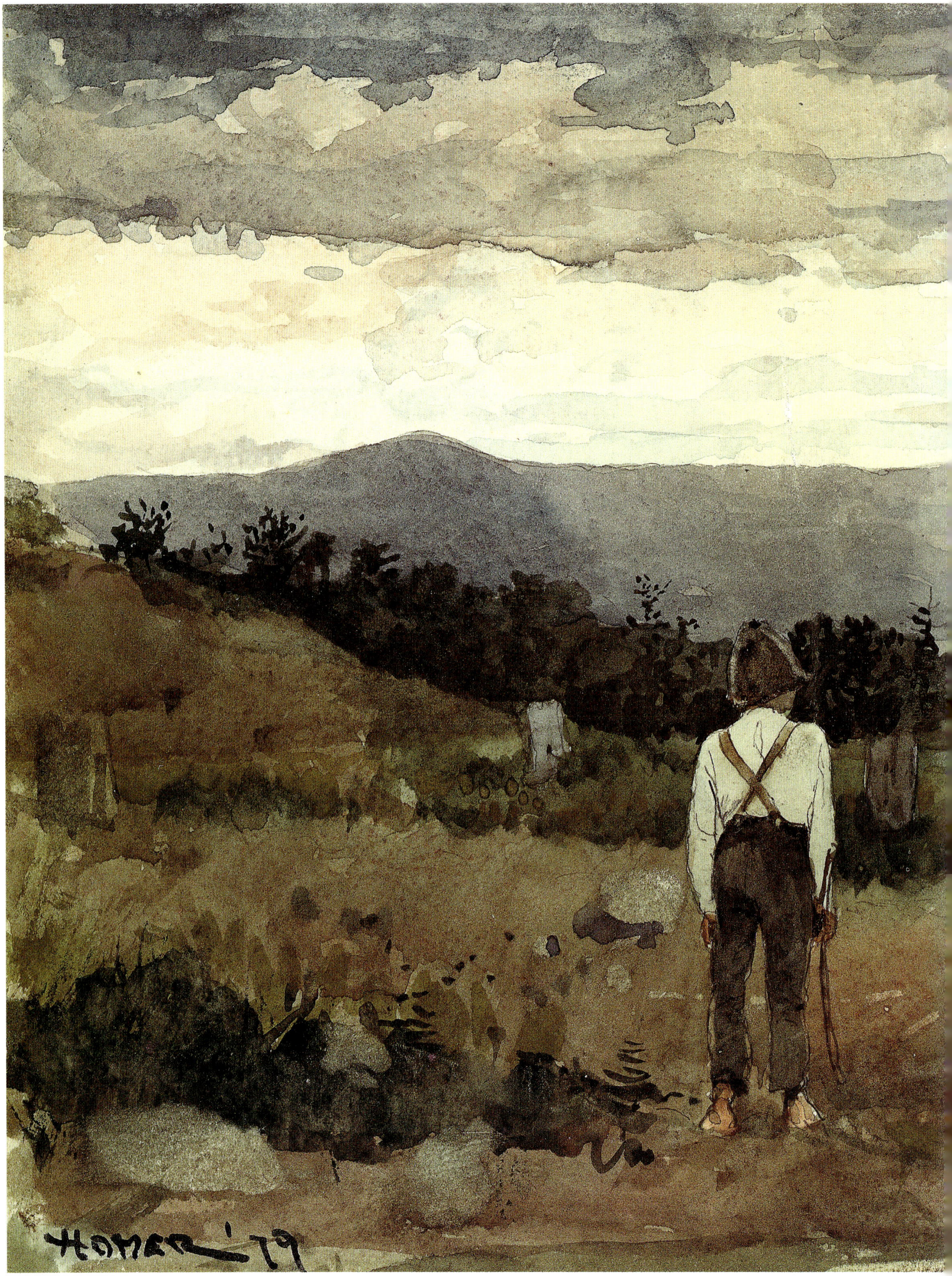

Driving Cows to Pasture 1879

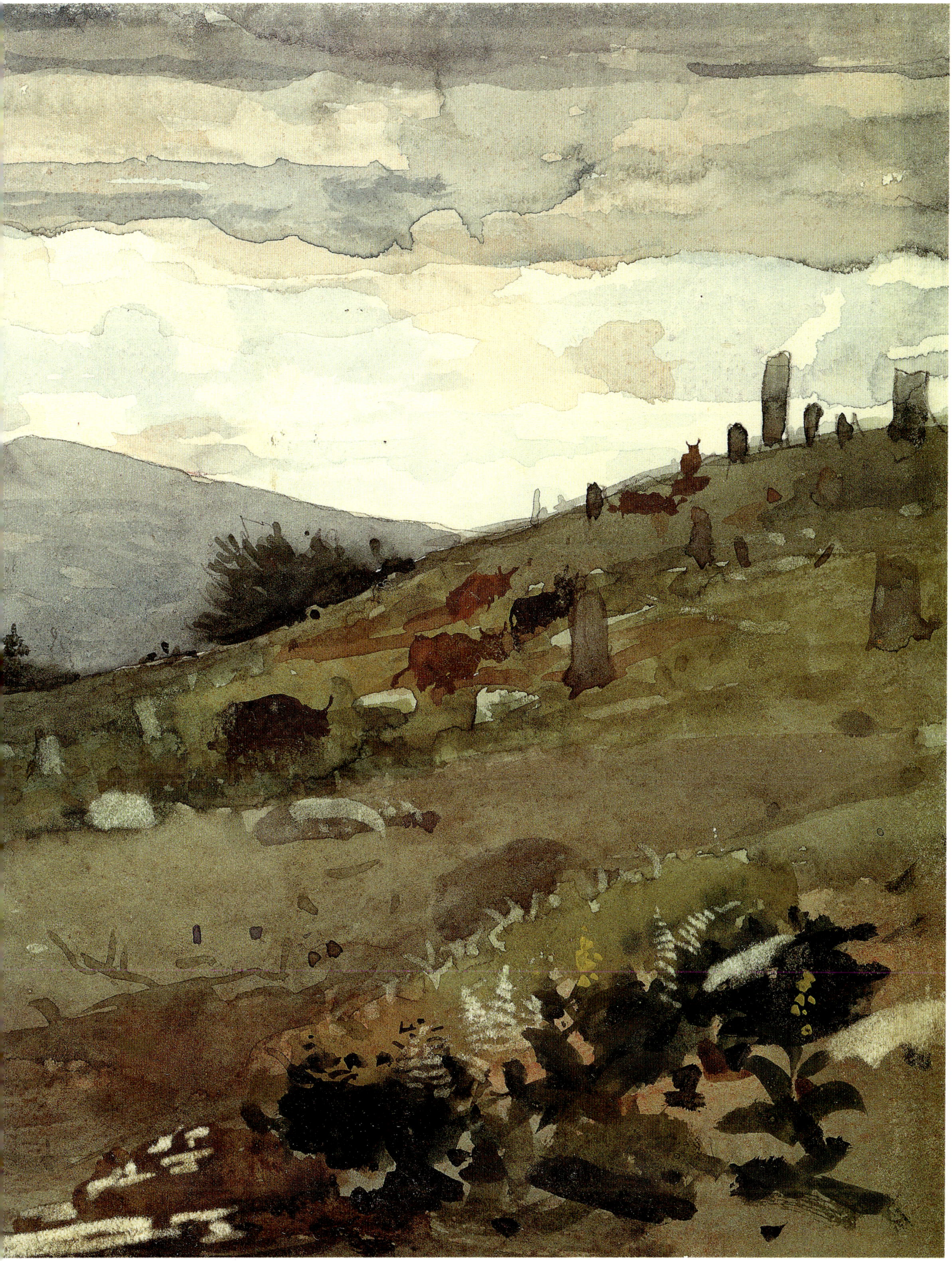

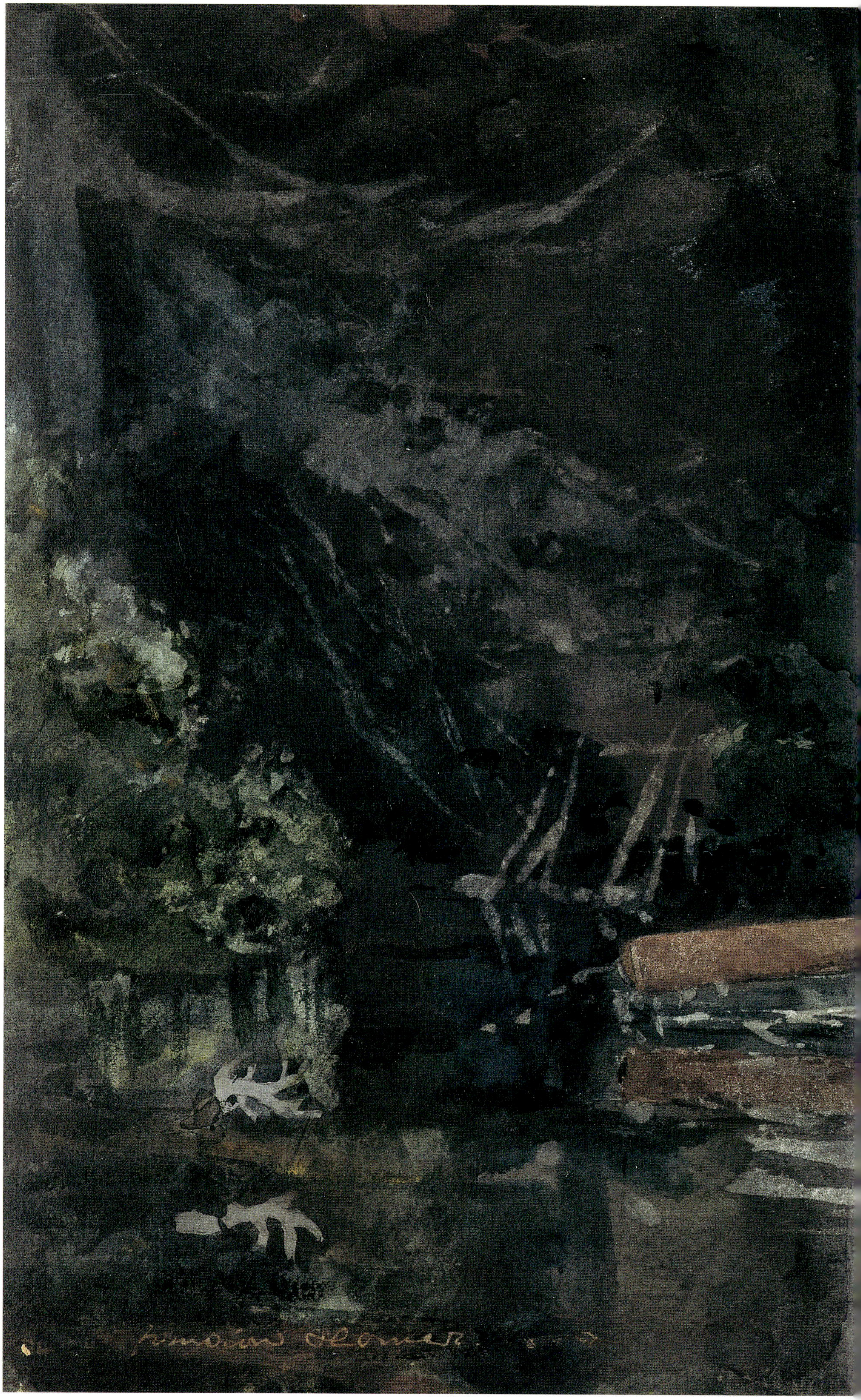

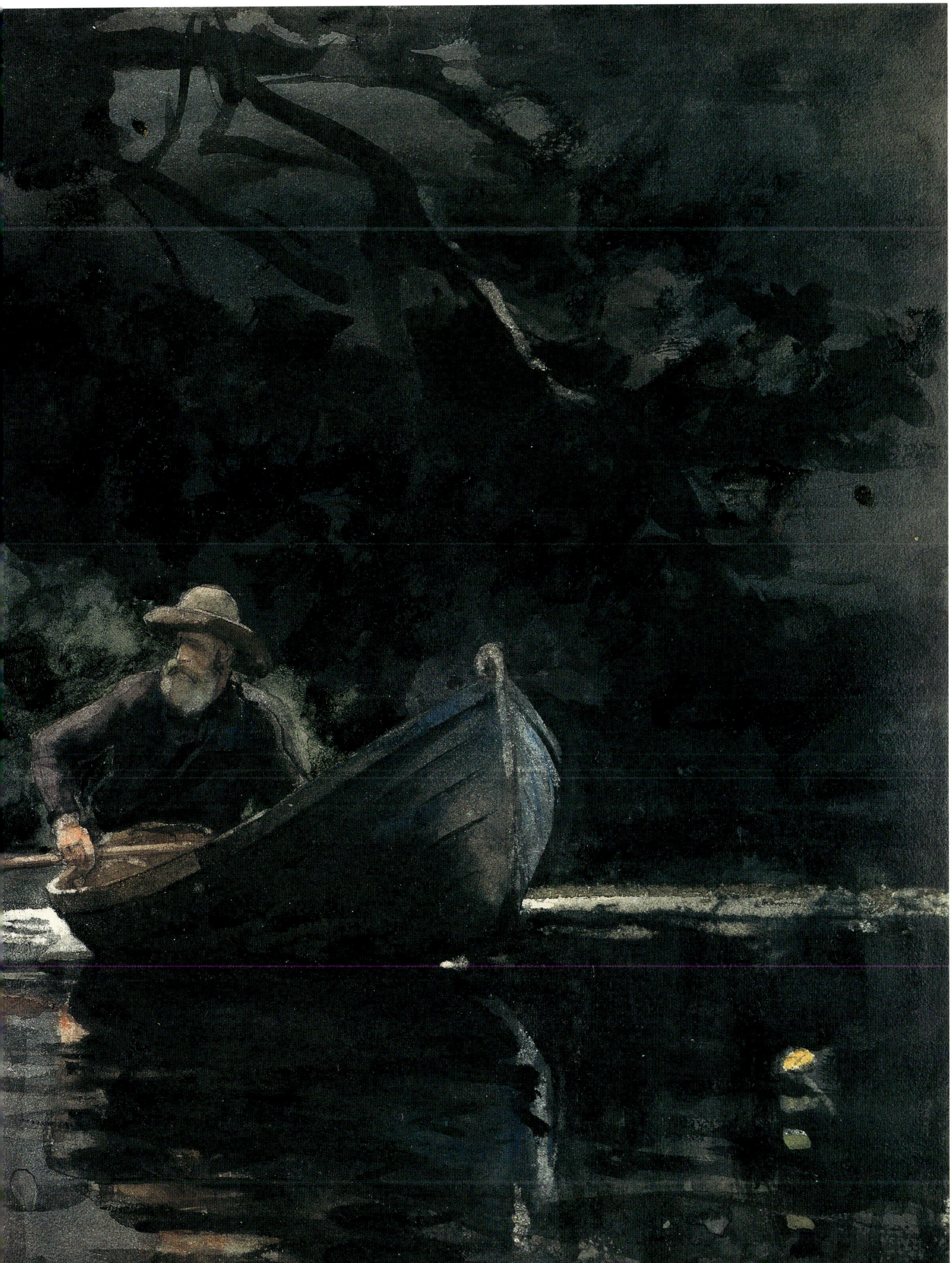

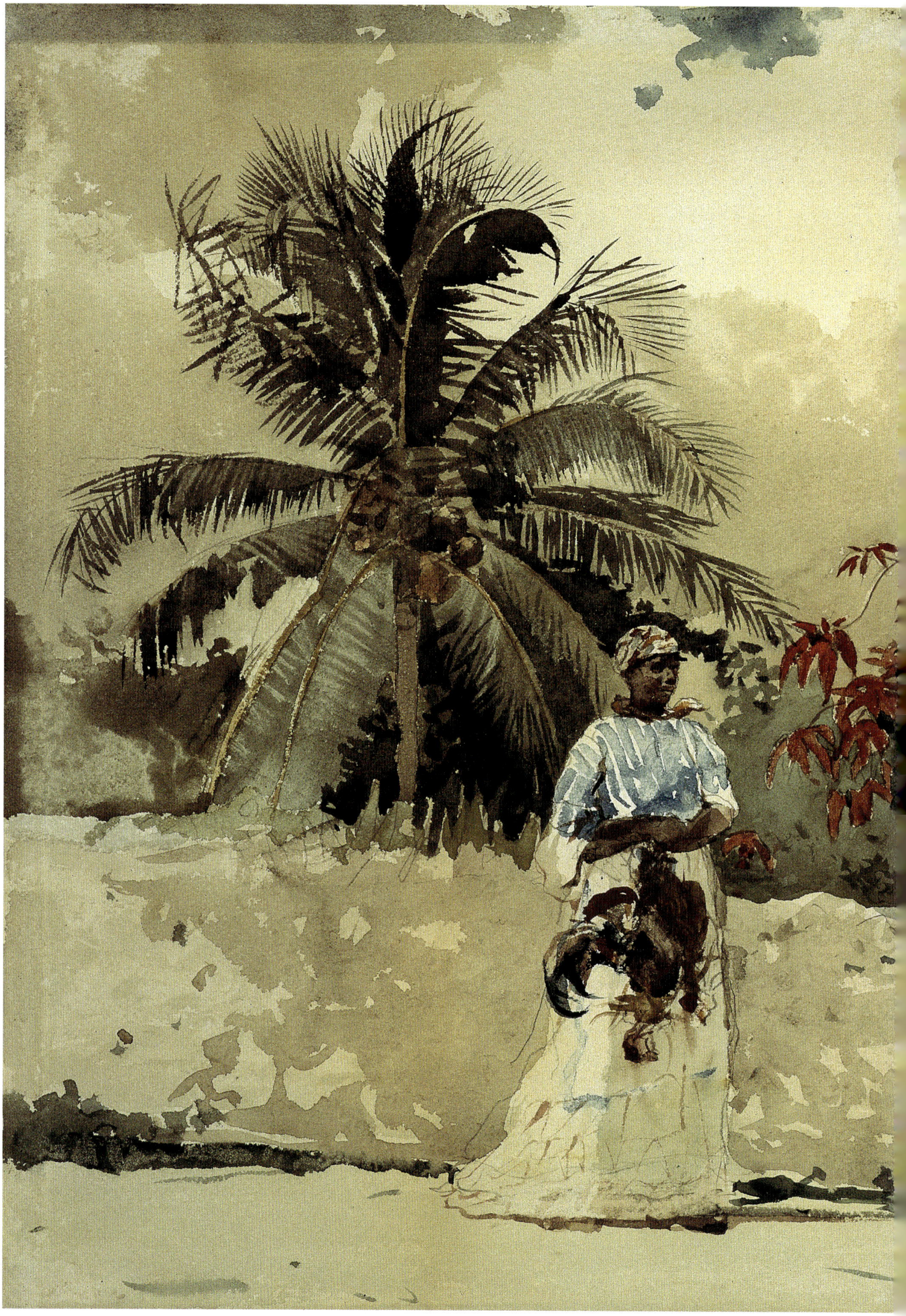

ON THE WAY TO MARKET, BAHAMAS 1885

By **MILES UNGER** Picture Editor & Designer **ARNOLD SKOLNICK**

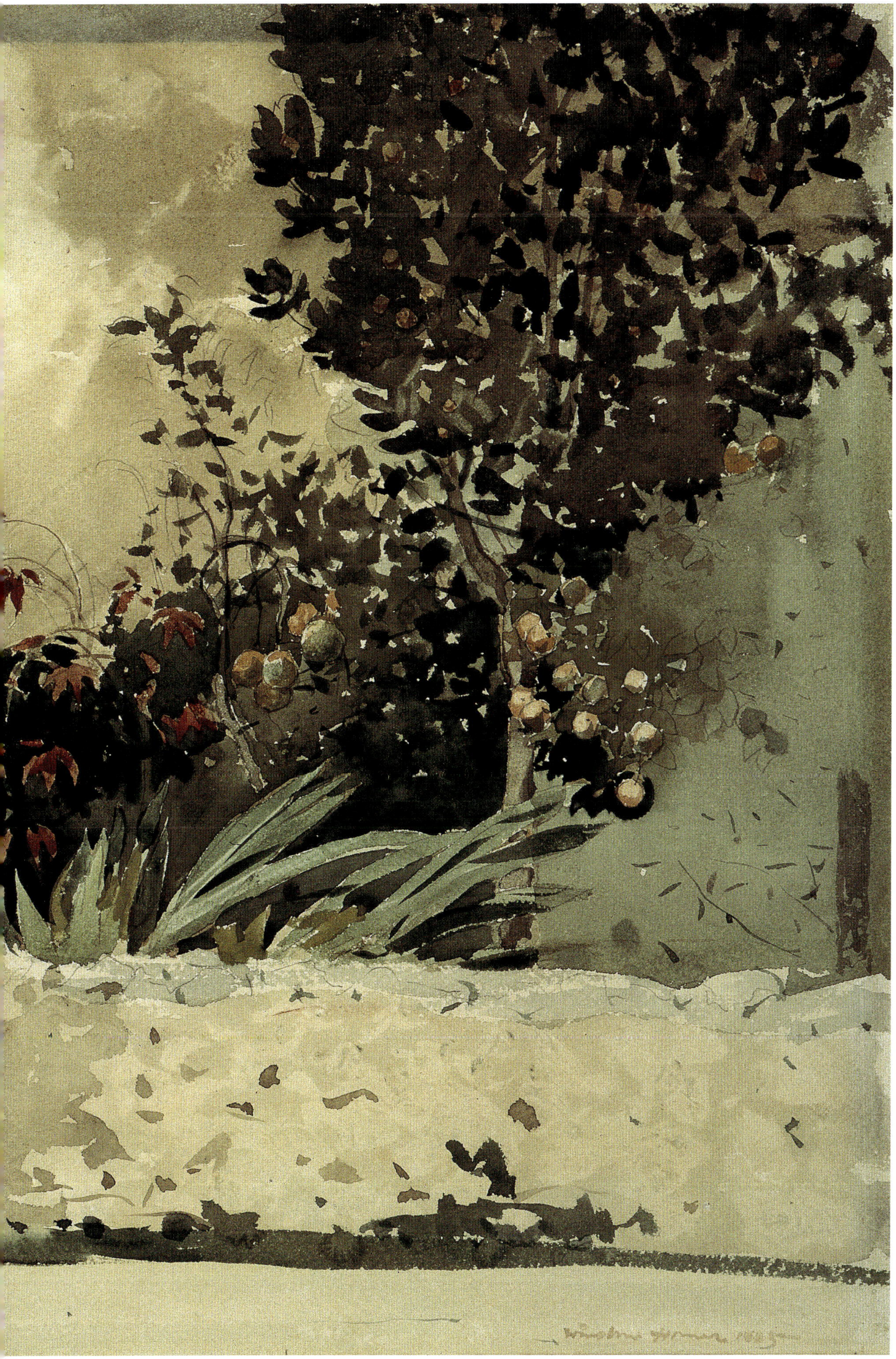

W.W. NORTON & COMPANY NEW YORK • LONDON

Produced by Chameleon Books, Inc.
31 Smith Road, Chesterfield, MA 01012

Book design / production: Arnold Skolnick

Design associate: KC Scott
Production assistant: Judy Lyons
Printed in China

The text of this book is composed in Filosofia
with the display set in Franklin Gothic ITC Heavy Bold

Library of Congress Cataloging-in-Publication Data

Unger, Miles.
The Watercolors of Winslow Homer / Miles Unger.
p. cm.
ISBN 0-393-02047-9
1. Homer, Winslow, 1836–1910—Criticism and Interpretation.
I. Homer, Winslow, 1836–1910. II. Title.

ND1839.H6 U54 2001
759.13—dc21

2001030914

W. W. Norton & Company, Inc.
500 Fifth Avenue, New York, N.Y. 10110
www.wwnorton.com

W. W. Norton & Company Ltd.
Castle House, 75/76 Wells Street, London W1T 3QT

1 2 3 4 5 6 7 8 9 0

ACKNOWLEDGMENTS

In writing this book I am indebted to the work of the many scholars who have sifted through the primary sources relating to Homer's life and art. Lloyd Goodrich's early biography of the artist and Nicolai Cikovsky Jr.'s more recent studies have been invaluable resources. Anyone who loves Homer's watercolors owes a debt of gratitude to Helen A. Cooper, whose groundbreaking exhibition and catalog of Homer's watercolors must form the basis of all subsequent investigations.

I would also like to express my appreciation to the staffs of the Worcester Art Museum, the Fogg Art Museum, the Museum of Fine Arts, Boston, and the Addison Gallery of American Art, without whose assistance this book would not have been possible.

—Miles Unger

Chameleon Books wishes to thank all the public institutions that have supplied the images found in this book: Addison Gallery of American Art; Albright-Knox Art Gallery; The Art Institute of Chicago; The Art Museum, Princeton University; The Baltimore Museum of Art; Bowdoin College Museum of Art; The Brooklyn Museum of Art; The Butler Institute of American Art; Canajoharie Library and Art Gallery; The Carnegie Institute Museum of Art; Cooper-Hewitt, National Design Museum; The Corcoran Gallery of Art; Cummer Gallery of Art and Gardens; The Currier Gallery of Art; The Fine Arts Museums of San Francisco; The Fogg Art Museum; Georgia Museum of Art; Hirshhorn Museum and Sculpture Garden; The Hyde Collection; Los Angeles County Museum of Art; Memorial Art Gallery of the University of Rochester; The Metropolitan Museum of Art; Mills College Art Museum; Milwaukee Art Museum; Museum of Fine Arts, Boston; Museum of Fine Arts, Springfield; National Gallery of Art; New Britain Museum of American Art; Norton Museum of Art; The New York Historical Society; Philadelphia Museum of Art; Plainfield Public Library; Portland Museum of Art, Maine; San Antonio Museum of Art; Scripps College; Spencer Museum of Art; Sterling and Francine Clark Art Institute; Terra Foundation for the Arts; Wadsworth Atheneum; Westmoreland County Museum of Art; Worcester Art Museum, and Yale University Art Gallery.

We are also greatful to all the galleries for their assistance: Vance Jordan Fine Art; Caldwell Gallery, Ltd. Inc; Questroyal Fine Art, New York; Kennedy Galleries, New York; Meredith Long & Company, Houston, Texas.

We are also indebted to the private collectors who were willing to share their Homers with the public: Mr. and Mrs. Arthur G. Altschul; Joe Ann and Julian Ganz Jr.; Mrs. Wellington Henderson; Mr. and Mrs. George M. Kaufman; Cornelia and Meredith Long; Christopher May; Mr. and Mrs. Paul Mellon; Jean Pennau; Mr. A. Alfred Taubman; Sam and Robbie Vickers; and the private collectors who wanted to remain anonymous.

My warm and special thanks to Heidi Applegate and Franklin Kelly at the National Gallery of Art; Ruth Jenson at the Brooklyn Museum; and Jennifer Doyle at Christie's Images, whose contribution to this book was enormous.

I am very greatful to Jim Mairs and the staff at W. W. Norton and to Martha Hoppin for their help.

—Arnold Skolnick

To Jody

The Life and Art of Winslow Homer

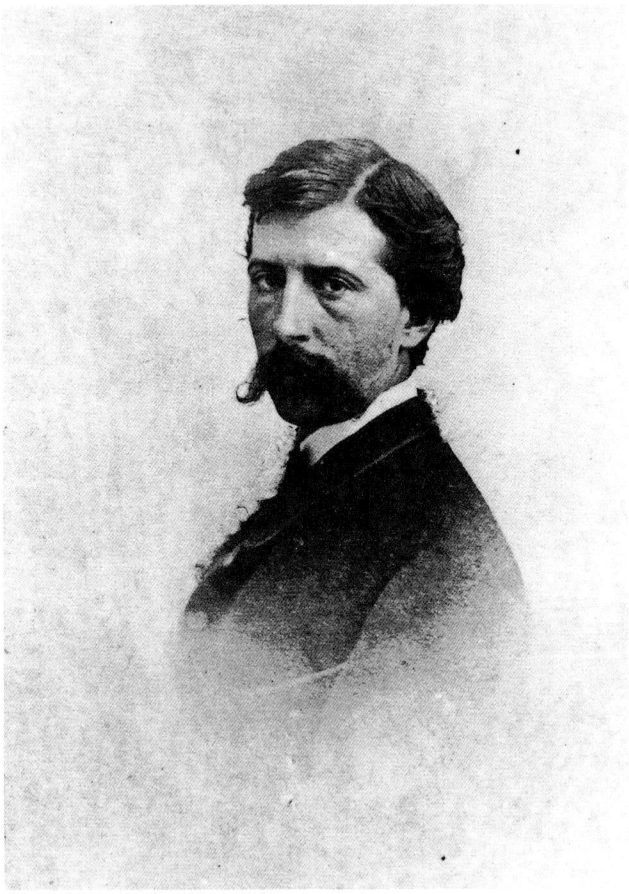

Winslow Homer as a Young Man in Paris, 1867

The close to seven hundred works in watercolor that have survived from Winslow Homer's hand constitute perhaps the single most important body of work ever created in the medium. These works, now among the prized possessions of many of America's finest museums, represent a remarkable achievement for an artist who came to the medium only after his career was well underway and who regarded them, at least initially, largely as a means of earning a steady income while he labored over his oil paintings. They remain unmatched in the variety of themes they tackle, the range of techniques they employ, and the scope of expressive possibilities they reveal. From charming scenes of a Gloucester, Massachusetts, childhood to the heart of a forest where man and beast engage in an unrelenting struggle for survival, from the troubled waters and rain-dark skies of the English North Sea coast to the glare of a tropical paradise, Homer's brush described with both precision and poetry the many moods of nature and wove a compelling narrative of mankind's place in the world.

Using materials widely available to both professional and amateur artists of the time, Homer managed to coax an enormous range of visual and expressive effects from a notoriously unforgiving form. To serve his restless imagination, he deployed almost every weapon in the watercolorist's arsenal, scraping, dabbing, sponging, or otherwise reworking an image until it met with his exacting standards. Never a purist, he would sometimes add touches of opaque gouache to pick out a telling detail, while at other times he would achieve his effects through the most transparent of washes. He was capable of both vanishing delicacy and almost brutal directness, and a single image can embrace approaches that to a less resourceful artist might have seemed contradictory.

Although the decision to take up watercolor was largely practical, once taken, Homer applied himself with gusto. As was typically the case with this dour, hardheaded New Englander, a sound business decision elicited unsuspected depths of feeling. Such poetry, and his restless searching out of new artistic horizons, belies the image that he presents in his own letters of a man who saw art primarily in terms of dollars and cents. The truth is that no artist whose goal was simply to earn a living would have been so willing to confound his audience and defy the critics. To an often bewildered public, Homer appeared to reinvent himself with each new exhibition. He had an almost perverse capacity to change course, and no sooner had popular taste caught up with him than he was offering up something new and equally difficult to digest. Who would suspect a kinship between the barefoot boys of the early 1870s and the grizzled woodsmen of the 1890s? Or that the same man who was praised for painting genteel ladies engaged in genteel pursuits would in the space of a year or two fill his paintings with robust fishwives monumental enough to pit their strength against the fury of the elements?

It was through the medium of watercolor that Homer charted new paths in his art. Unlike the oils, which took months or even years to complete, Homer tended to make his watercolors in bunches during working vacations so that each series was tied to a particular time and locale. These works, usually painted outdoors directly in front of the scenes they depict, were a great source of pictorial ideas that often found their way into the more comprehensive statement of the studio oil painting. In fact, many of his most famous paintings began as watercolors: *Breezing Up* is an almost exact translation in oil of the watercolor *Sailing the Catboat* [pp. 40–41], while one of his last and greatest oil paintings, *The Gulf Stream*, combines motifs culled from a series of watercolors painted in the Bahamas fourteen years earlier.

Once Homer had made watercolor part of his repertoire, the announcement of a new theme in his work almost always appeared first in this medium: the elegiac quality that marks much of the late work found an early expression in the sunset watercolors painted in Gloucester in 1880; the storm-churned sea that threatens to overwhelm the men who dare to test themselves against its might made its first appearance in the watercolors he painted along the English coast in 1881; and the new, vibrant palette that followed the artist's first encounter with the tropics was announced in a brilliant series of watercolors he painted in 1885 while on vacation in Nassau.

Watercolor was for Homer the medium of experimentation, where he allowed himself to try new things and admitted the possibility of failure. There is a refreshing sense of contingency in these works, an immediacy sometimes lacking in the oil paintings. But these are not mere sketches, tentative thoughts invested with deeper meaning only when translated into a weightier medium. As Homer's career progressed, and as his understanding of the unique properties of watercolor deepened, his work in this form began to take on a life of its own. There are no equivalents in oil to the poetic evocations of the deep forest achieved in his Adirondacks watercolors or the coloristic exuberance that marked his first trip to the Bahamas. Certainly there are oil paintings that derive from the same material, but they are fundamentally different from the watercolors with which they are associated. As Homer's confidence in both mediums grew, the character and function of the watercolors changed. What had begun as a casual form suitable for sketching first impressions of a scene became the preferred form for recording his most intense and intimate responses to the natural world. There is nothing casual about Homer's fluent late watercolors, where he homes in on the precise qualities of a single moment in nature: the stillness of a mountain lake shrouded by fog; the rush of cold water between chattering rocks; the sheen of salt water on the back of a diver rising to the surface. Each moment is set down not only with visual exactitude but also with a profound understanding of the emotions such moments arouse. If the oil paintings tend toward grand public pronouncements, the watercolors are deeply personal expressions.

Homer's career as a painter in watercolor coincided with and contributed crucially to the maturing of the medium as a serious form of artistic expression. During the early years of his career, watercolor was just beginning to gain acceptance among professional artists as something worthy of their attention. By the end of his life, watercolor was firmly established as a major art form in its own right and one that represented perhaps the United States's most original contribution to the visual arts. While it would be overstating the case to say that Homer alone was responsible for this remarkable growth, it is certain that the ambition, thematic range, and emotional power of his work provided an example and inspiration for those who followed. It was an accomplishment that the artist himself seemed to recognize. "You will see," he declared late in life in a letter to his beloved older brother, Charles, "in the future I will live by my water-colors."

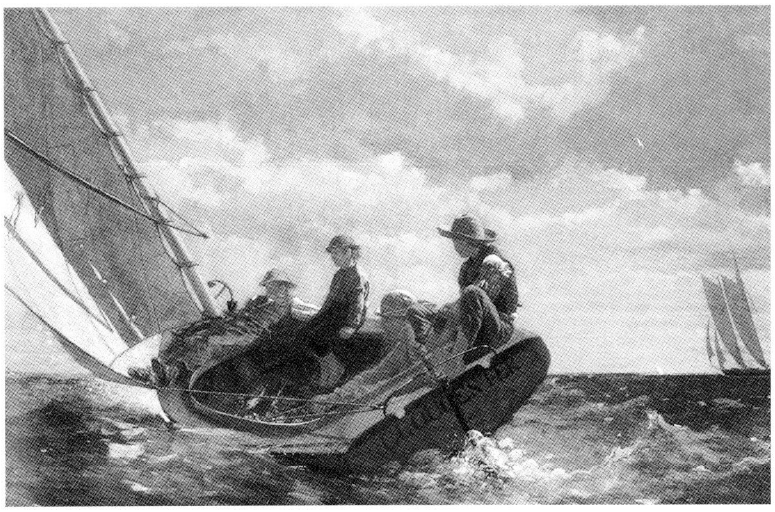

BREEZING UP (A FAIR WIND) 1878–1879

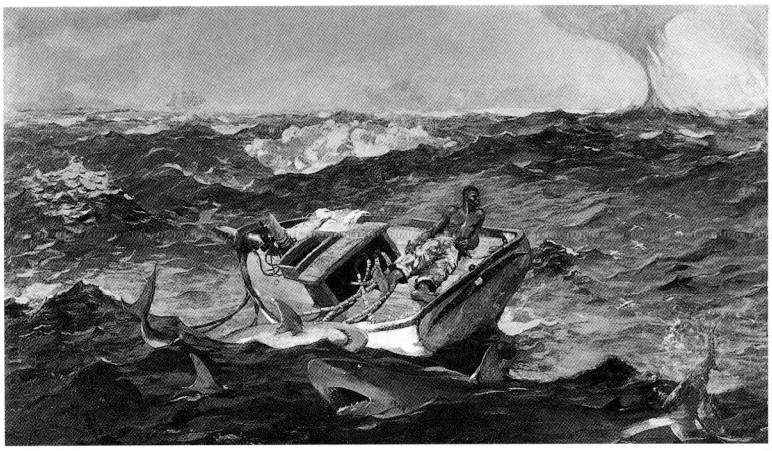

THE GULF STREAM 1899

EARLY YEARS

Winslow Homer was born in Boston in 1836, the second of three boys, and raised in the then rural town of

Cambridge, Massachusetts. His father, Charles Savage Homer, Sr., was an unsuccessful businessman, and the family depended from time to time on the moral and financial support of better-off relatives. Despite these somewhat precarious circumstances, Winslow's was by all accounts a happy childhood, one in which his artistic inclinations were encouraged by both parents. His mother, Henrietta Maria Benson Homer, was herself a talented amateur watercolorist, a fact that certainly influenced the future course of her son's career.

Homer's older brother, Charles, attended Harvard—ultimately going on to become a chemist and a successful business executive—but the family's financial situation would not permit putting a second son through college. (After spending the war in the navy, Winslow's younger brother, Arthur Benson Homer, also went into business, establishing a lumber company in Galveston, Texas.) Instead, Charles Senior sought a career path for this son that would combine his evident talent for drawing with the practical need to earn a living. It was through his father's efforts that the eighteen-year-old Winslow landed his first professional job as an apprentice at John Bufford's lithography shop in Boston. Despite grim memories of his two years at the shop, where he worked primarily drawing covers for sheet music, commercial illustration gave the young artist valuable experience at a time when America offered to its talented sons and daughters few opportunities for training or earning a living as a fine artist. Homer would later describe his life at Bufford's as a form of slavery, but the mix of practical and artistic considerations that led to his apprenticeship was to characterize his entire career. For Homer, art was both a passion and a means of supporting himself. If he later cherished his independence, he never pursued art as a dilettante who worked only when the spirit moved him, but as a job demanding diligence and the skill that could only be gained through hard work.

Homer left Bufford's after two years to set up as a freelance illustrator, first for the local magazine *Ballou's Pictorial* and soon for the larger New York–based *Harper's Weekly*. By 1859, he had moved to New York City to pursue the greater opportunities available to a freelance illustrator in what was then, as now, the nation's cultural capital. It was at this time that Homer first took steps that revealed his ambition to remake himself as a fine artist. In 1861, he signed up for lessons from the landscape painter Frederick Rondel, who, according to one contemporary account, "once a week, on Saturdays, taught him to handle his brush, set his palette, & c." Although Rondel may have taught him the rudiments of painting, his contribution to Homer's development as an artist was minimal. Neither Rondel nor any other figure played the role of mentor to the budding artist. Homer's formal training as a painter was scant, and his insistence that he was self-taught appears largely accurate.

It was as a commercial illustrator that he trained his eye and his hand. The discipline of commercial work was crucial in honing his skills as a storyteller, and during these early years his twin roles as a fine artist and an illustrator were mutually reinforcing. In fact, Homer's first oil painting, *A Sharpshooter on Picket-Duty* from 1863—based on his experiences accompanying the Army of the Potomac during the siege of Yorktown while on assignment for *Harper's Weekly*—first saw light as an engraving for the magazine. This work not only marked the launching of Homer's career as a painter; it demonstrates his capacity to distill a subject as complex as modern warfare

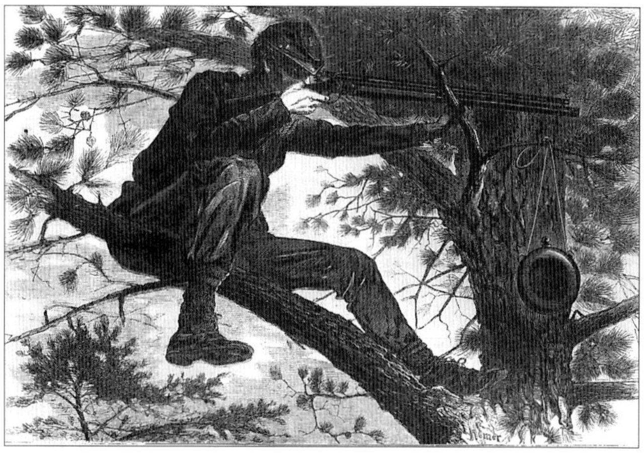

THE ARMY OF THE POTOMAC—
A SHARP-SHOOTER ON PICKET DUTY 1862

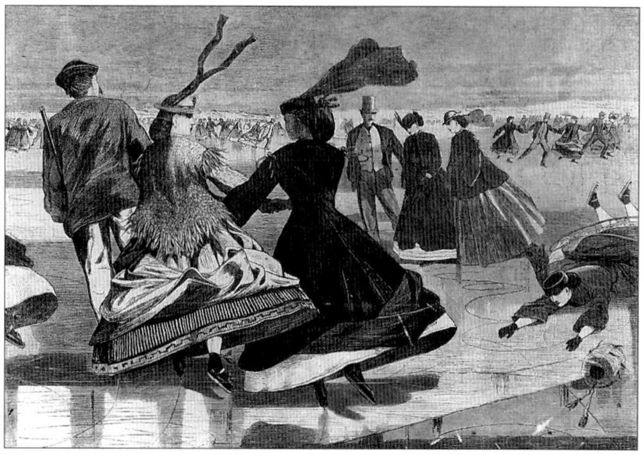

OUR NATIONAL WINTER EXERCISE—SKATING 1866

into a single compressed image whose meaning is instantly legible. It is revealing that for his first oil painting Homer should choose a subject with none of the heroism or pageantry normally associated with military themes. He showed from the start a willingness to confront uncomfortable truths rather than cater to conventional expectations. This is the anonymous face of modern warfare—cold, calculating, the perfect hybrid of man and killing machine. Later in life, Homer described the sharpshooter's job as "being as near murder as anything I could think of in connection with the army & and always had a horror of that branch of the service."

Homer's success as an illustrator depended on his ability to sum up a situation with a few well-chosen figures and telling gestures. This narrative compression characterizes his finest painting. One of his great gifts as an artist was his ability to give palpable substance to visual facts and to make each fact an essential element in the overall pictorial and narrative scheme. Details like the rifle's telescopic site are precisely observed but included only when they further the thrust of the story.

Working for the popular magazines of the day, Homer was essentially a reporter, capturing the passing scene for readers hungry for information and detailed vignettes of daily life. Whether depicting elegant couples skating on a frozen pond or the tedium and danger of army life, he relied on his visual memory and acute powers of observation. While these illustrations are marvels of clarity, his paintings are deliberately open-ended. The storytelling prowess is still evident, but these are stories without clear-cut resolutions—and the artist was notoriously reluctant to reveal his intentions. When asked to explain the meaning of *The Gulf Stream* to a squeamish audience, Homer responded with sarcasm: "You ask me for a full description of my picture of the 'Gulf Stream.' I regret very much that I have painted a picture that requires any description. . . . You can tell these ladies that the unfortunate negro who now is so dazed and parboiled, will be rescued & returned to his friends and home, & ever after live happily."

A Desperate Plunge

In the summer of 1873, Winslow Homer, then thirty-seven, took what one contemporary writer described as "a sudden and desperate plunge into water color painting." If this immersion in a new medium was something less than an act of desperation, it came at what was clearly a frustrating time in the artist's life. In 1867, he had received widespread critical acclaim for the Civil War painting *Prisoners from the Front*, a scene drawn from America's great national trauma that brought the young artist to the attention of the public and led to his election as a full member of the prestigious National Academy of Design. This success at the beginning of his career as a professional artist meant that Homer never lacked for critical attention, but when his work was discussed in the press it was often to scold him for failing to live up to that early promise. Critics complained his paintings lacked refinement; they were too crude, his subjects too prosaic. Many were offended that he had the audacity to exhibit rough sketches as finished works. For a nation now eager to wrap itself in the mantle of sophisticated European culture, the naturalistic scenes from Homer's brush, bluntly painted and with evidently little patience for subtleties of technique or natural grace, could appear coarse and provincial. Worse, as far as Homer himself was concerned, they did not sell, condemning him to the drudgery of commercial work that he once described as a "treadmill existence" and a kind of "bondage."

Rapidly executed, these early watercolors, modest in scale and casual in their conception, could be produced more quickly and sold more cheaply than the oils, and had the potential to provide a more reliable source of income. As late as 1900, Homer could write: "My work for the past two or three years has been mostly in water colors. . . . I have . . . paid expenses in that way, while I have at times painted an oil picture." It is significant that despite recurrent money woes, he abandoned the security of commercial work in 1875, one year after he began to exhibit his watercolors. The painter John F. Weir, a neighbor of Homer's during this period at the Tenth Street Studio Building in New York, recalled that "he was then drawing for *Harper's Weekly*, and struggling to get out of it to take up more important work."

That work would from this point on include the sub-

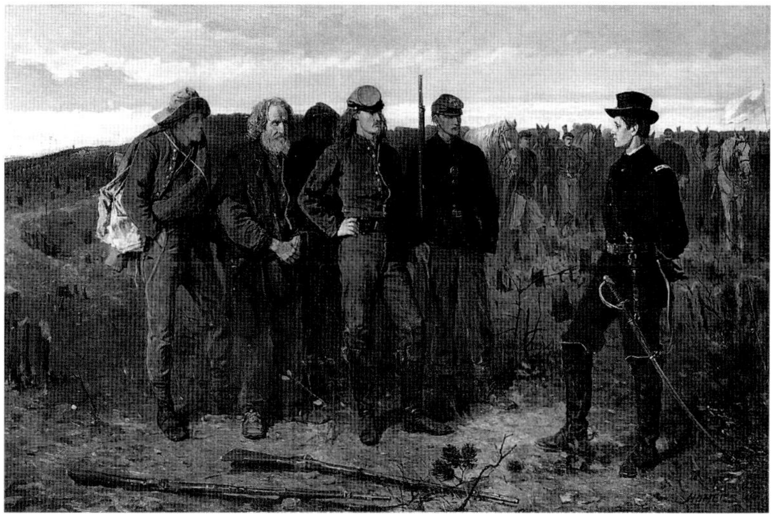

PRISONERS FROM THE FRONT 1866

stantial production of watercolors. Watercolor offered Homer a compromise between the higher calling of oil painting and the hackwork of commercial illustration, but it is clear from the outset that he discovered in it a form wholly in keeping with his artistic aims. The decision was psychologically important as well, signaling his wholehearted commitment to a career as a fine artist. For this Yankee descended from a long line of merchants and businessmen, it could not have been an easy choice, and for the remainder of his life—even in his old age when he was famous and financially secure—Homer would grumble about the prices his works were fetching and act as if he were on the brink of financial ruin. The commitment, in any case, was not instantaneous. Homer continued to contribute to such popular magazines as *Harper's Weekly*, *The Galaxy*, and *Every Saturday* for a full year after the first successful showing of his watercolors.

The subject he explored in his first concentrated effort in the medium was the carefree life of children at play in and about the busy harbor of Gloucester, Massachusetts. It was a theme that demanded an intimate scale and lightness of touch. The barefoot boys and sun-bonneted girls, echoing in their freedom from adult supervision the youths of Mark Twain's novels, were calculated to appeal to a nation yearning for familiar, reassuring themes after the upheavals of the Civil War and Reconstruction. But his approach already bore the marks of a distinctive artistic personality, combining keen powers of observation and directness, even bluntness, of application. As an avowed realist, the fact that watercolor allowed Homer to complete paintings on the spot, *en plein*

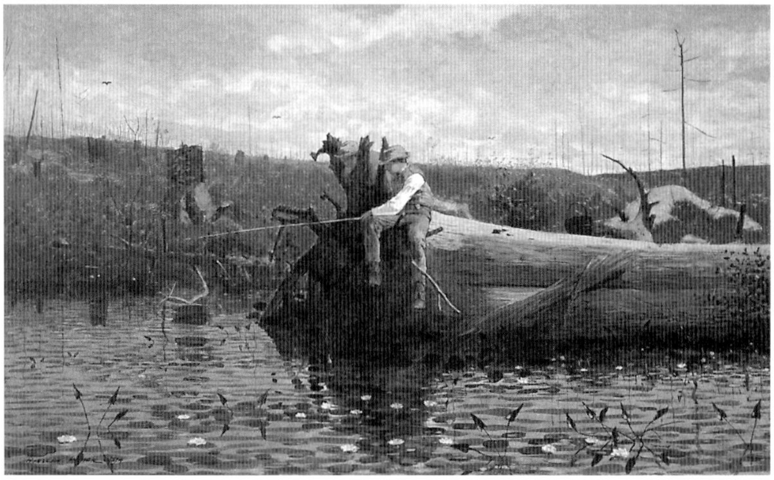

Waiting for a Bite 1874

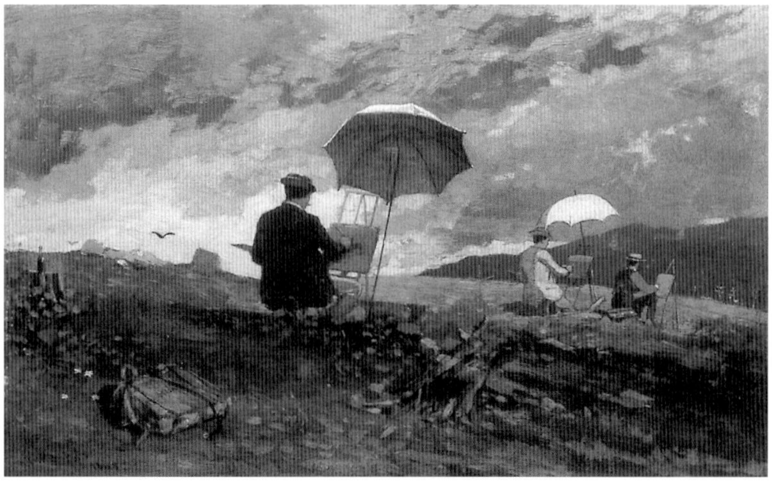

Artists Sketching in the White Mountains 1868

air, meant they possessed an immediacy and an authenticity sometimes lacking in the studio paintings.

The liveliness with which he set these images down on paper was perfectly attuned to the ease of summer and the sparkling light of sea and sand. With a few rapid strokes of the pencil he would lay in the basic elements of the composition, next applying color in broad, transparent washes and "reserving" areas of white paper for the highlights (see *The Berry Pickers* pp. 30–31). There is here a firm grasp of the essentials of an image that will remain a hallmark of Homer's art. He demonstrated from the beginning an instinctive understanding of how transparent colors on paper quickly applied could capture the sparkle of the noonday sun on sand, the salt tang of an offshore breeze. If his oils were sometimes labored, he was clearly seduced by watercolor's ability to capture life on the wing.

An examination of Homer's art from this period provides a fascinating glimpse into the strategies he used to meet the challenges imposed by each of the mediums in which he worked. Throughout his early career, his paintings nourished his commercial work; the reverse was also true. There are numerous images that he executed in watercolor, in oil, and as magazine illustrations, including an image of boys fishing from 1874. Of the three versions, the watercolor *Waiting for a Bite* [p. 52] seems the most spontaneous, giving the impression of a scene happened upon and set down on the spot. Both the engraving and the oil painting are more studied; the engraving [p. 53] closely follows the composition and setting of the watercolor, while in the oil Homer eliminated one of the figures and changed the background to create a more desolate scene. The graphic clarity of the engraving is instructive, revealing how carefully composed the watercolor actually is, despite its initial impression of casualness. In Homer's time, the job of the commercial illustrator was to render an image on the wooden block and hand it off to a professional who would do the engraving. It was a discipline that demanded clarity of design and precise delineation of form, qualities that are apparent in most of the early watercolors. As Homer's mastery of materials grew, and as he left the world of magazine illustration behind, precisely delineated forms would be replaced by luminous washes that suggest rather than describe.

This recycling and reworking of images from one medium to another influenced how Homer, particularly early in his career, composed his paintings. He not only created different versions of the same scene, but took apart and reassembled elements from different works to fashion entirely new compositions. In making the oil painting *Milking Time* (see the drawing for the painting, p. 58), Homer borrowed the figure from the watercolor *In the Garden* [p. 58]. The artist has simply turned the figure around and placed in her hands a pail and stool that explain her presence in the pasture. An 1878 watercolor titled *The Milkmaid* [p. 59] shows this same girl accompanied by a colorful rooster.

Homer scholar Nicolai Cikovsky, Jr., compares the artist's mixing and matching of compositional elements to Eli Whitney's "American System" of industrial production through interchangeable parts. These artistic shortcuts were related to Homer's experience as a commercial illustrator, where such recycling aided in the invention of new compositions. Having drawn from life a particularly satisfying pose, the artist was determined to get the most out of it. What is remarkable, however, is not that Homer recycled his images but that he could extract from the same motif such a wide variety of feelings and meanings. The addition of the plank fence in the oil painting turns a conventional composition into a radical experiment in two-dimensional design that one contemporary critic sarcastically described as possessing "the tender grace of a gridiron." The inclusion of the fence gives a psychological tension to the half turn of the girl's body and distracted gaze, now directed across what seems an impenetrable barrier. Recycling motifs from one image to another was a strategy Homer used less frequently as he left the rigors of commercial work behind and struck out on his own.

Waiting for a Bite is a modest work, but it anticipates in important ways the later career. The subject—the dropping of a baited line into the water and the bond this simple act establishes between man and the natural environment—introduces a theme that lies at the heart of many of his greatest watercolors. Throughout his life Homer was an avid fisherman, and many of his watercolors were made on trips planned as much to indulge this

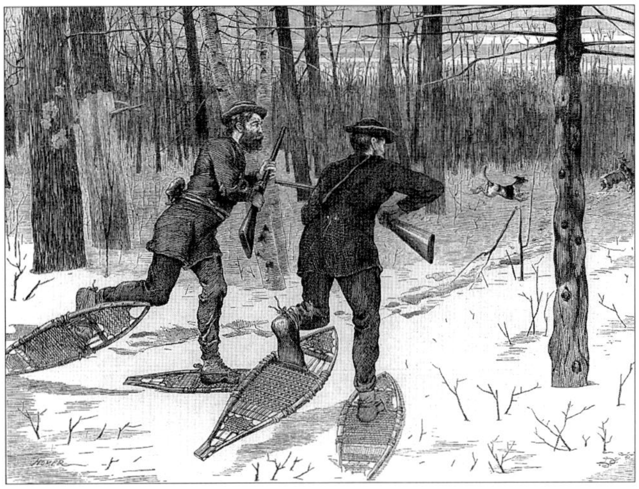

DEER-STALKING IN THE ADIRONDACKS IN WINTER 1871

passion as to provide subjects for his paintings. His early biographer William Howe Downes describes how during his years of apprenticeship, the artist would wake up at 3 A.M. to fish at nearby Fresh Pond in Cambridge before reporting to work. The setting of *Waiting for a Bite* too is significant, providing an early glimpse of a locale that will become the scene of some of his greatest artistic triumphs. The work was sketched in the Adirondacks in upstate New York whose lakes and woods would be the scene not only of a number of early engravings but of many of his finest watercolors.

Homer spent most of the 1860s and '70s in New York City, but it is clear that he was ill suited to an urban existence. A love of the outdoors remained with him throughout his life and is an essential ingredient of his art. It was a love he shared with his older brother Charles, who often accompanied him on his fishing expeditions, and letters between the two are as likely to dwell on the hobby they shared as on artistic matters. An 1878 biographical sketch of the artist in the *The Art Journal* observed: "He has a great liking for country life—a liking which he thinks had its origin in the meadows, ponds, fishing, and beautiful surroundings of that suburban place [Cambridge]. To this day there is no recreation that Mr. Homer prefers to an excursion into the country."

If Homer's illustrations often focus on the life of the city street, in his own paintings he almost never touched on urban themes. During the two decades he spent in New York City, the setting for his paintings remained exclusively the rustic farmyard, the seacoast, or the manicured lawn where fashionable young ladies indulge in the latest craze, a game of croquet. This clearly reflects the artist's own inclinations: when he had to please no one but himself, it was the life of the country that appealed to him.

Of course, Homer was not unique in favoring rural over urban scenes. This was an era when the public preferred to lose itself in the charm of country life rather than confront the often grim reality of factories and slums that surrounded them. Art journals of the day describe the typical routine of the New York artist, spending the summer months in the countryside making sketches that would then be turned into finished oil paintings during the winter season. Homer amusingly captures the life of the artist in pursuit of the scenic vista in the oil painting *Artists Sketching in the White Mountains*. Instead of focusing on the spectacular scenery that has brought artists to this spot, Homer draws our attention to the foreground crowded with easels and strewn with the makings of picnic lunches. Although Homer clearly preferred to breathe the country air, his vision remained largely unclouded by sentiment.

During the two decades the artist lived in New York City, his favorite getaways included trips to Gloucester, Massachusetts, a locale he seemed to have selected for its picturesque possibilities, and upstate New York, where Charles's business partner Lawson Valentine maintained a summer home. This rural area will be the setting for his early series of watercolors depicting farm life.

Homer's watercolors are intimately bound up with these working vacations. Easily transported and well suited to sketching outdoors, watercolor was for him the perfect traveling companion. One can easily correlate the early seaside watercolors with a Gloucester sojourn, and a trip to Virginia is hypothesized primarily on the basis of a group of paintings that depict the lives of southern blacks. The twenty months he spent in the English fishing hamlet of Cullercoats in northern England are chronicled in his most concentrated efforts in the watercolor medium, a body of work whose somber tones reflect the gloom of the North European clime. After 1883, by which time Homer had settled permanently in Prout's Neck, a remote spot on the Maine coast, fishing expeditions to the Adirondacks and Quebec punctuated the warmer months and vacations in the tropics served to relieve the harsh New England winter. Each of these places is recorded in watercolors made on the spot, works filled with the vitality that only comes from direct observation.

An American Realist

From the promising beginning he made in the summer of 1873, watercolor played an increasingly important role in Homer's career. He found in the medium that direct contact with nature that underpins all his best work. Henry James, in a decidedly mixed review of Homer's early watercolors, declared that his greatest virtue as an artist was to see everything in "its natural envelope of light." This sen-

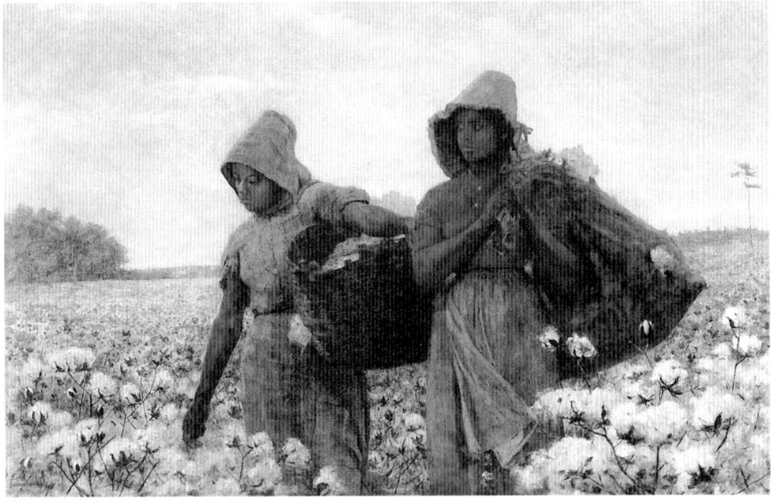

The Cotton Pickers 1876

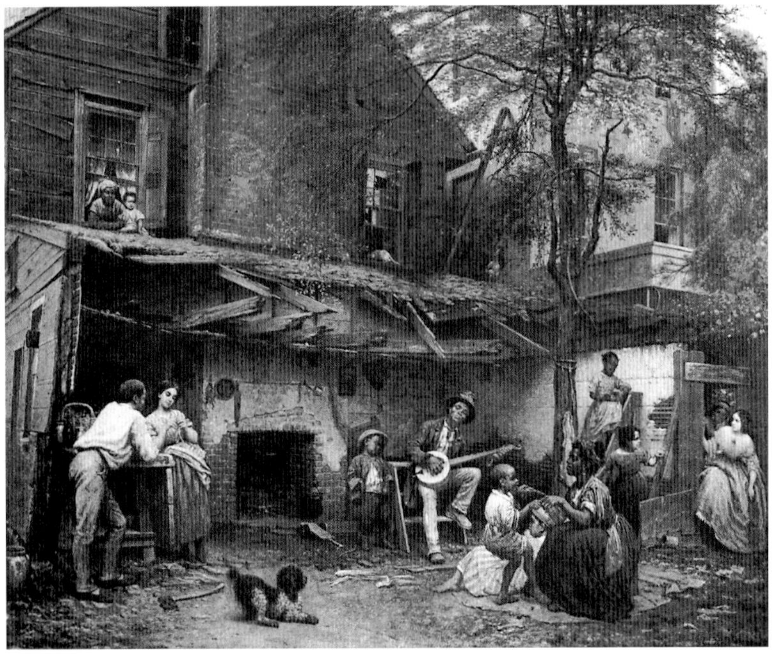

Negro Life in the South, 1859 by Eastman Johnson

sitivity to the ever-changing qualities of natural light and atmosphere is most keenly felt in his watercolors, though the lessons learned carried over into his oil paintings. Toting brushes, pad, and paintbox into the woods and onto the beach allowed him the most direct means to transmit to his viewers the experience of actually being there.

In searching out suitable material in the rural byways of the country, Homer was far from unique, but the honesty of his vision gives to these accounts an immediacy often lacking in the work of his colleagues. Eastman Johnson, Homer's enormously popular contemporary, also based many of his most famous works on rural scenes captured far from his New York studio; but at least in the works he exhibited publicly, there is a slightly contrived quality that makes them less firsthand accounts of his travels than sentimental evocations of a rustic never-never-land. One need only compare a work like *The Cotton Pickers* with Johnson's *Negro Life in the South* to realize how closely Homer's art hews to what he could actually observe.

Winslow Homer has often been regarded as the quintessential American artist, independent, plainspoken, and firmly wedded to the notion of art as something that reproduces faithfully the blunt facts of life. Such a disdain for metaphysics and firm commitment to the evidence of the eyes goes back to the beginnings of American art. This is the sensibility manifest in the paintings of the colonial-era master John Singleton Copley—like Homer a native of Boston—and elaborated by artists like Thomas Eakins. The equation of Americanness with simple realism has a literary parallel as well, from the "Plain style" of the Puritan sermon to the vernacular of Mark Twain and Walt Whitman and later the spare prose of Ernest Hemingway. Homer's apparent lack of polish fed the stereotype of the American artist as someone who was largely untutored and impatient with anything overly refined. This was homespun art—plain, coarse, and uncompromisingly honest.

Contemporaries certainly saw him in this light, and no doubt this is how Homer would have characterized himself. Art was for him a form of fact finding, an objective, almost scientific calling. His friend John W. Beatty summed up the conventional wisdom on Homer when he claimed, "The basis of his art, I think, was simple truth." He goes on to describe the following conversation with the artist:

> "Mr. Homer, do you ever take the liberty, in painting nature, of modifying the color of any part?"
>
> "Never! Never! When I have selected the thing carefully, I paint it exactly as it appears."

This is a telling passage, not only because of Homer's insistence that he recorded only what he could observe, but because he states his conviction that art was above all a process of selection, of deciding what to include and what to leave out. For Homer, as with most artists who don the realist mantle, the term conceals as much as it reveals. Homer had a keen eye for the telling fact and in his best work he pared down the elements to the bare essentials, creating narratives of concentrated power. Through his choice of subject, and through the firm editing of all that distracts from the main expression of the idea, he elevates the commonplace to something timeless and profound. As his art evolves, his eye becomes more selective, until the facts become not ends in themselves but the means to tell larger truths of the natural world and the human place within its scheme.

Although this is especially true of late oil paintings like *The Gulf Stream* or *Kissing the Moon*, the sense of reality distilled to its essentials also infuses many of the late watercolors. In watercolors like *Leaping Trout* [pp. 166–167], one is convinced that the image is completely true to nature, yet in describing the arc of the bounding fish, Homer has somehow captured a deeper truth about the rhythms of all living things. To apply the term "realism" to this work or *Mink Pond* [pp. 168–169] tells us little about the magical effect these paintings have on us; there is, indeed, something exactly right about the way Homer has painted this small corner of the world, but this fidelity to nature goes beyond prosaic fact to embrace a wider constellation of ethical and perceptual meanings.

Even those who decried Homer's lack of polish recognized the distinctive Americanness of his art. A critic for the *The Art Journal* wrote in 1877:

> He paints the life that he sees as he sees it; he never softens a line nor modifies a feature, nor yields for a moment to any soft seduction of beauty. He is wholly in sympathy with the rude and uncouth conditions of American life; he likes the men, the women, the boys, the girls, of the rustic by-ways of our land—and he likes them as they are, awkward in dress, spare in form, tanned and freckled by the sun, with no sensuous warmth, no dream of beauty.

This assessment was echoed in 1880 by another writer: "The freshness, the crudity, and the solid worth of American civilization are well typified in the thoroughly native art of Mr. Homer." But the apparent "freshness" and "crudity" of these works is a little deceptive, masking the extent to which they are conventional, even romanticized, evocations of a rural idyll. A capacity to render figures convincingly in real sunlight and in their natural setting lends a degree of plausibility to what might otherwise appear artificial. Even in the more calculated oil paintings, like *Snap the Whip*, Homer achieved through his sparkling light and no-nonsense application of paint a truth to life his contemporaries could seldom match.

These are qualities that Homer shared with the French Impressionists, who at exactly the same moment were shaking up academic conventions across the Atlantic. Though many scholars have tried to trace a direct impact of Impressionism on Homer's work, it seems likely that similarities depend more on parallel aims than on direct influence. Homer did in fact spend the better part of 1867 in France, a trip made initially to view the Exposition Universelle in Paris, where two of his paintings hung in the American section. But there is no indication that he took an interest in the aesthetic controversies sparked by the work of artists like Gustave Courbet and Edouard Manet, or that he knew any of the radical young artists who were to follow their lead and create a new movement in art.

Like the Impressionists, Homer preferred to suggest forms with his brush rather than delineate them precisely. This sketchy finish, which often disturbed contemporary viewers, gives to his works a feeling of immediacy lacking in paintings where every detail is crisply rendered. But Homer, unlike his French colleagues, never abandoned the tradition of tonal painting. Even in his later tropical watercolors, dominated by bright colors, his forms are never dissolved in light but remain solidly modeled.

Homer's commitment to realism led him to complete as much of his paintings as possible out of doors, an approach still inconsistently applied in the era before the followers of Monet and Renoir made such practices commonplace. An early account of Homer at work describes him "out upon the roof [of his studio] . . . painting what he sees . . . real things, instinct with life and warm with the glory of God's sunshine." While one wonders what exactly Homer could see from the roof of his New York studio that he would have wished to paint, there is no need to doubt his preference for painting in "God's sunshine." Painting *en plein air* was part of the philosophic underpinnings of his work but, particularly in his oil painting, it was more an ideal to be strived for than a hard and fast rule. He told the critic George W. Sheldon in 1880, "I prefer

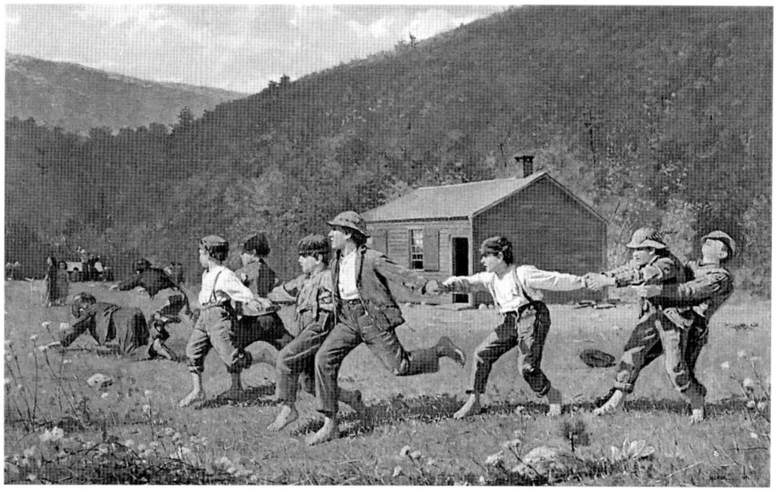

SNAP THE WHIP 1872

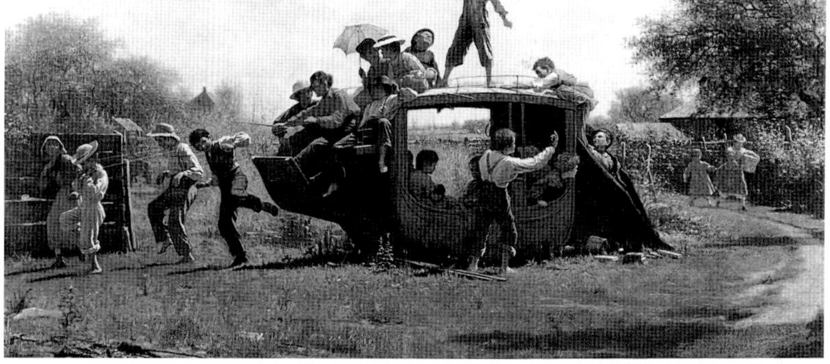

The Old Stage Coach, 1871 by Eastman Johnson

every time a picture composed and painted out-doors. . . . This making studies and then taking them home to use them is only half right. You get composition, but you lose freshness; you miss the subtle and, to the artist, the finer characteristics of the scene itself." Earlier in the same article, Sheldon declared:

> Almost everything that he has shown to the public as a result of his professional efforts has been drawn directly from Nature, and under the impression made by it upon his mind at the time when he committed it to paper or canvas. No painter in this country, probably, has a profounder respect for such out-door work, a more lively apprehension of its value, or a sincerer and more serious aversion to manufactured and conventional studio-pictures. He paints what he has seen; he tells what he has felt; he records what he knows. Now, a painter who begins and finishes indoors a figure of a man, woman, or child, that is outdoors, misses a hundred little facts, the absence of which is sure to convict him of his offense against truth—a hundred little accidental effects of sunshine and shadow that can be reproduced only in the immediate presence of Nature.

This commitment to painting *en plein air* is most clearly felt in the watercolors, rapidly executed in front of the scene itself. Not only do these works provide source material for the oil paintings, they serve as a yardstick against which he could measure the truth of his more studied compositions. In painting watercolor, Homer schooled his eyes in the lessons of light and shadow, in the complexity of color reflected and refracted. These are the lessons upon which all his art depends.

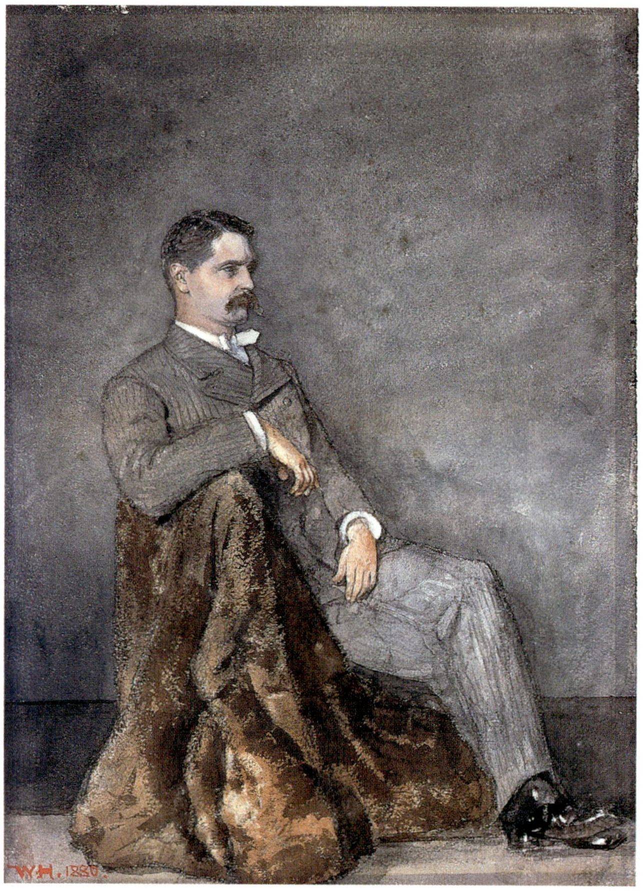

THE ARTIST'S BROTHER, CHARLES SAVAGE HOMER, JR.
1880

A PORTRAIT OF THE ARTIST

If Homer liked to portray himself as a hardheaded realist, his paintings suggest a far more passionate and complex nature. He was notoriously uncommunicative, forcing biographers to supplement scant documentary evidence of his personal life with clues gleaned from his art. Homer once told his dealer, M. Knoedler & Co., "Don't let the public poke its nose into my picture." Far from discouraging would-be biographers, such statements have tempted those seeking to understand the man to probe beneath the surface of his art. But the paintings are as enigmatic as the person who made them, concealing as much as they reveal.

The artist's character appears at first to be full of contradictions. He was simultaneously reserved and passionate, both a sensible man of business and a starry-eyed dreamer. But a consistent picture emerges if one assumes that a gruff, no-nonsense facade served to disguise a highly emotional nature that he was uncomfortable expressing. Typical of his business letters is one he wrote to the Chicago dealers O'Brien & Son in 1893: "At present and for some time past I see no reason why I should paint any pictures. P.S. I will paint for money at any

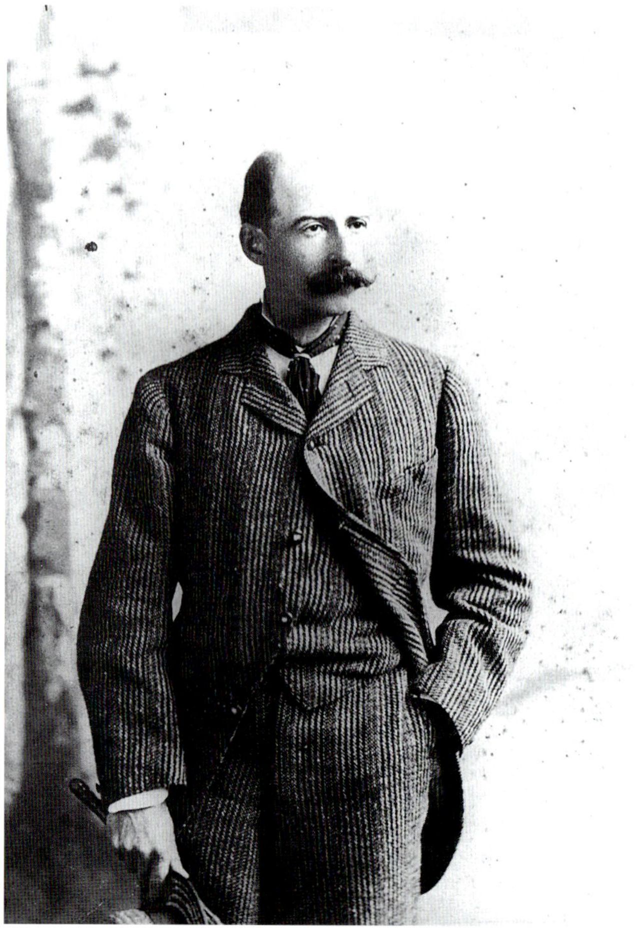

Winslow Homer Taken in New York, 1880

time. Any subject, any size." If missives like this imply a bottom-line mentality, the artistic choices Homer made throughout his career lead to a far different assessment. Unlike some of his colleagues who were only too eager to please, Homer was a man who stubbornly followed his own vision. It was a quality all the more difficult for someone as sensitive to criticism as he was. The biting sarcasm of his letters was actually a reflection of the artist's thin skin, and a perceived setback or critical rebuff usually met with a similarly bristling response.

Homer was fastidious in dress and habits. He was once described by his acquaintance William J. Bixbee as having "the appearance of a well to do business man. No affectation." Contemporary accounts suggest a reserved, shy man, capable of great warmth with those close to him but suspicious of the motives of strangers. Above all, Homer was an intensely private man, who resented any intrusion into his affairs. His life, he insisted, was nobody's business but his own. Asked by a would-be biographer for information about his life, he responded: "It may seem ungrateful to you that after your twenty-five years of hard work in booming my pictures that I should not agree with you in regard to that proposed sketch of my life. But I think that it would probably kill me to have such a thing appear, and as the most interesting part of my life is of no concern to the public I must decline to give you any particulars in regard to it."

There is much one would like to know about the artist's personal life, particularly for the light it might shed on the evolution of his work. A transformation in the circumstances of his life and the mood of his art at the beginning of the 1880s suggests a profound personal crisis, but the evidence for such an event remains circumstantial. Whatever lay behind the change, the break with his former mode of living was dramatic. From being a well-connected figure on the New York art scene throughout the 1870s, Homer by 1883 had begun to lead a solitary existence on the remote Maine coast. This shift in circumstances, which occurred following a twenty-month stay in the English fishing village of Cullercoats, also marked a watershed in his art. Before the sojourn in England, one finds an artist of a serious but generally optimistic bent, who chronicles with affection and occasional irony the native scenery, customs, and mores. There is a gentleness and conviviality to his images of children at play — including such masterpieces as *Snap the Whip* and *Breezing Up*—and fashionable young ladies engaged in ladylike pursuits that suggests a generally sunny disposition.

But with the images of the storm-swept English coast that Homer painted between 1881 and 1883, the tone of his art became decidedly darker. In the Cullercoats watercolors, women continue to play a prominent role, but they are no longer the society girls of the 1870s. They are instead robust working girls with rough hands and indomitable spirits. Crucially, his view of the natural world also underwent a dramatic transformation. From this point on, Homer ceased to see nature as merely a pleasant backdrop for his rustic idylls, but as a dynamic and often threatening force. After 1883, Homer depicted what is almost exclusively a man's world. His heroes are fishermen, hunters, and guides, each of whom is defined by his relationship with the natural world. The virtues he celebrates are of the traditionally virile sort: courage, strength, stoic acceptance, and a competence born of hard experience.

Many biographers have posited a failed love affair as the basis for the change in Homer's art. The best evidence lies in a series of accomplished watercolors he made in the late 1870s, most featuring an attractive redheaded young lady; these are as frankly sensuous images as Homer ever brushed. According to one of Homer's biographers, Lloyd Goodrich, Homer's failure to win this young lady's hand was due to his precarious financial situation, a story which if true might help explain his constant concern, often voiced in his letters, over money.

The story is persuasive if not conclusive, but it is also probable that no single explanation accounts for all the changes Homer made in his life and his art. His last decades were not spent as the irascible hermit of Prout's Neck that legend has made him out to be, yet it is clear that he deliberately cut himself off from the cosmopolitan circles in which he had been accustomed to travel. Perhaps it was simply that he finally had the opportunity to adopt a lifestyle more suited to his taciturn nature. And while not yet firmly established, either financially or critically, he was committed to being an artist, so that practical considerations may have led him to adopt a simpler and less costly lifestyle.

Even in the years that he maintained a studio in New York, Homer was notorious for resenting interruptions while he worked, and the new arrangements certainly suited his need for privacy. An article —significantly written in 1880, at just the time when his supposed love affair had come to an unhappy end—includes the following comment about the artist: "Mr. Homer's strength as an artist is only equaled by his roughness when he does not happen to be just in the humor of being approached." It is this picture of Homer, as gruff and unfriendly, that has come down through the years, perhaps less because it is the truest picture of the man but because it fulfills our expectations of the creative genius isolated from society.

THE ARTIST AT HOME

In 1882, Homer's brother Charles, by then a top executive in a varnish manufacturing company, had purchased a large house in Prout's Neck, Maine—a small peninsula ten miles south of Portland separating Saco Bay from the open Atlantic Ocean—to be used as a summer rendezvous for the entire Homer clan. By 1884, Winslow had converted the adjacent carriage house to serve as his home and studio. This modest building, to which he added the wide balcony where he spent countless hours gazing at the surf pounding the rocky shore, remained his home and primary workplace until his death in 1910.

Homer was invariably described by neighbors as generous and kind, though visitors from the city wishing to look in on the famous artist were likely to be turned away, often rudely. A contemporary biographical sketch provides a rather romantic view of the solitary artist:

> Like Thoreau, Winslow Homer is a recluse, for the reason that art of the sort he lives for is incompatible with the amenities of society. He lives in a lonesome spot on the coast of Maine. His sole companions are natural and unsophisticated beings, outdoor folk, hunters, fishermen, sailors, farmers. No artificial refinements, no etiquette of the drawing-room, no afternoon tea chatter, no club gossip, for this hermit of the brush.

But this picture, if not entirely false, is incomplete. At Prout's Neck, at least in the warmer months, Homer was surrounded by family, and letters to and from his parents, brothers, and sister-in-law Mattie, Charles's wife, with whom he was particularly close, attest to his warmth and capacity to give and receive affection. Homer's notorious gruffness was no doubt the product of

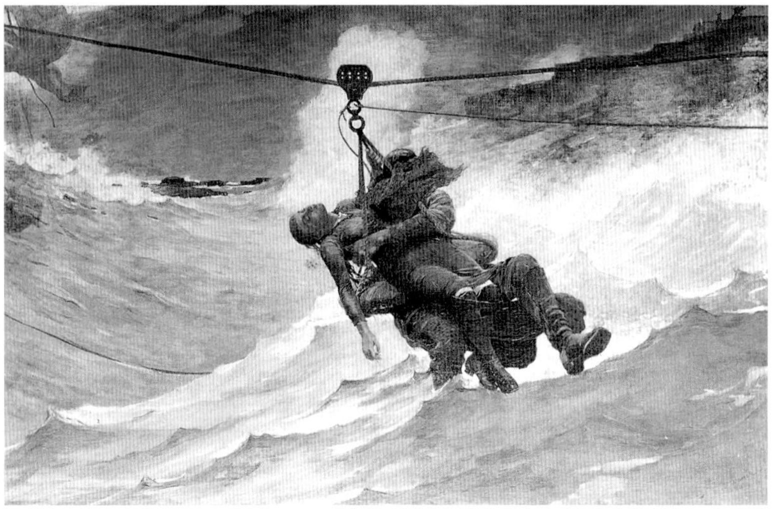

THE LIFE LINE 1884

an intensely shy nature. For such a man, the guides and fishermen with whom he consorted may have been more congenial company than the sophisticated socialites of New York. In his letters, Homer clearly identifies with those who work for a living, portraying the life of the artist as more perspiration than inspiration.

Homer was one of those rare people at ease with solitude. He wrote to Charles in 1884, "I like my home more than ever as people thin out." He was also not averse to poking fun at himself. In a letter to the engraver Louis Prang, he defends himself with humor while still managing to confirm by protesting too much the assessment he purports to reject: "I deny that I am a recluse as is generally understood by the term. Neither am I an unsociable hog.

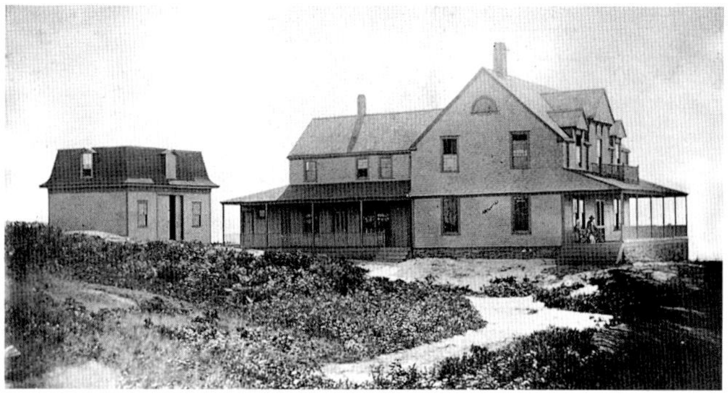

The Charles Savage Homer House in Prout's Neck, Maine, with Winslow Homer's Studio (left), 1883

. . . I do my own work. No other man or woman within half a mile & four miles from railroad & P.O. This is the only life in which I am permitted to mind my own business. I suppose I am today the only man in New England who can do it. I am perfectly happy & contented. Happy New Year."

At Prout's Neck, Homer led a Spartan existence, though the bitter climate sometimes got too much even for this hardy soul. A typical letter to his father, dated December 1886, reveals something of his life there and provides a telling rationale for his frequent tropical vacations: "I made a mistake in not getting a larger stove. It is very comfortable within ten feet of it. It heats the room within two feet of the floor, & water freezes up anywhere within that space. I wear rubber boots & two pair of drawers."

It was during these years at Prout's Neck that Homer began to receive the critical acclaim and financial security that had eluded him early in his career. A breakthrough was the exhibition to almost universal praise of the oil painting *The Life Line* in 1884, and its subsequent sale at the generous price of $2,500. (The *New York Herald* commented, "This purchase shows that the tide is turning, and our richer collectors are beginning to patronize American as well as foreign art.") This painting of a daring rescue at sea was one of a series of classic marine images painted in the mid-1880s—others in the group include such famous works as *The Herring Net*, *Undertow*, and *Eight Bells*—that in both subject and mood evolved from the Cullercoats watercolors. To many critics, *The Life Line* was the artist's finest achievement since his early *Prisoners From the Front*, and from this point on Homer was consistently included among the nation's leading painters.

But despite the satisfaction this success—hard-won and on his own terms—might have brought, the artist's life changed little. As honors and money came his way, Homer continued to live the life to which he had become accustomed and that seemed to suit his introspective nature. Here by the ocean's edge, alone with his thoughts and in close contact with the natural environment from which he always drew his strength, he created some of his greatest works. As he wrote to Charles in 1895, "The life that I have chosen gives me my full hours of enjoyment for the balance of my life. The Sun will not rise, or set, without my notice, and thanks."

Homer and the American Watercolor Tradition

Watercolor in America has deep roots, but it was only in the mid-nineteenth century that it came to be regarded as an independent vehicle for artistic expression. As far back as the sixteenth century, artists who accompanied the early explorers set down their observations on the native customs and local flora in a medium that was both portable and easy to handle. The tradition of the artist-explorer setting out with his box of watercolors continued well into the nineteenth century, when artists like George Catlin and Karl Bodmer used the medium to record the vanishing way of life of the western Indians. To some extent Homer belongs to this tradition, discovering in watercolor the perfect accompaniment for his rustic get-aways, but he elevates this modest craft to new heights. His object was less to record interesting or exotic details for the folks back home than to capture on paper the many moods and meanings of nature itself.

Homer belonged to a generation that fundamentally transformed the watercolorist's art. For much of the nineteenth century, even such accomplished artists as John James Audubon regarded watercolor as little more than a form of tinted drawing, with thin washes of color contained within precisely defined borders. Writing in 1873, one critic summed up the situation: "Until recently, watercolors have not found much favor in this country. They have been looked upon as pretty fancy work, fit for girls and amateurs, and the terms 'washy' and 'weak' have been almost universally applied to them." Homer, along with colleagues like his friend John La Farge, used watercolor expressively, relying on the medium's natural luminosity to suggest light and atmosphere rather than simply to describe a local hue. In their watercolors, paint is not limited by the drawing but freely applied in bold strokes and broad washes, often over the most rudimentary of graphite skeletons. As Homer's art matured, even this spare armature began to dissolve. In the late watercolors, minimal notations in pencil serve less to define form than to accent and give coherence to floating veils of saturated color.

Unlike James Abbott McNeill Whistler and John Singer Sargent [p. 24], each of whom also produced important work in watercolor, Homer's influence on his contemporaries and on later generations was almost entirely dependent on the paintings themselves. Because he remained a willing exile from the centers of culture, and because he cared little for the company of other artists—and even less for hobnobbing with the smart set—Homer founded no movements and left no disciples. Whistler's influence was attributable as much to his dandyish poses and often outrageous pronouncements as to his art, while no one was better connected socially than Sargent, who was welcome in the finest homes on either side of the Atlantic. Homer's influence was pervasive yet difficult to pin down. It is known that in 1892 Sargent payed

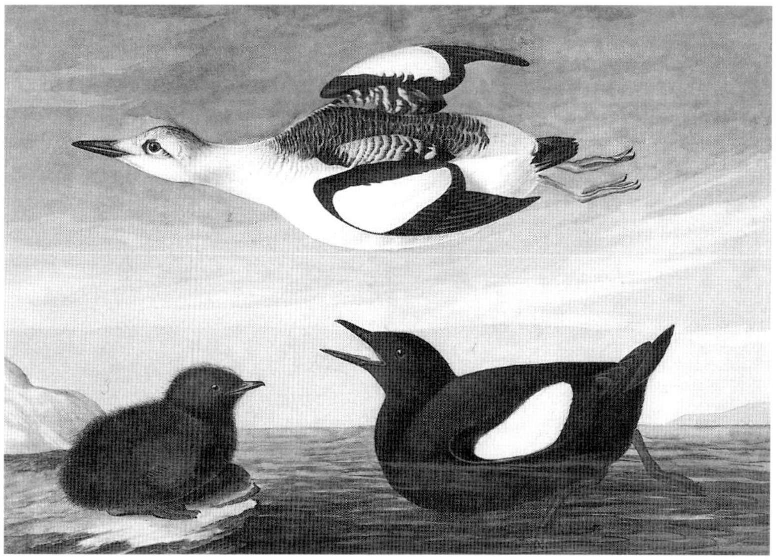

Black Guillemot, 1833 by John James Audubon

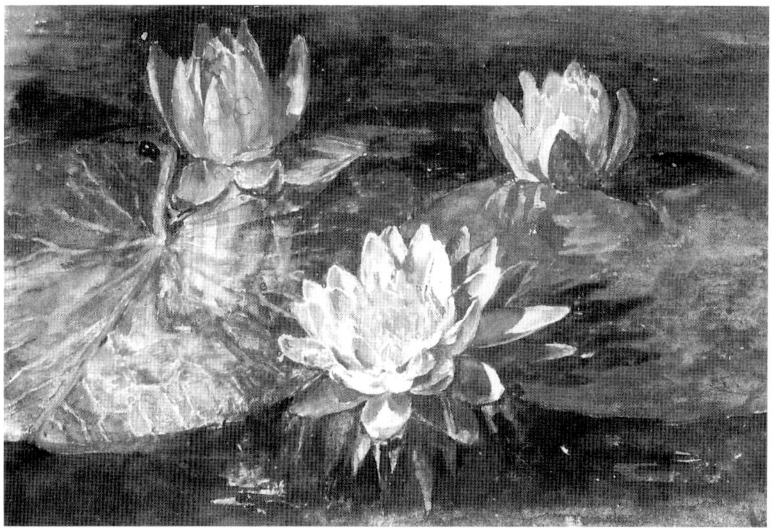

Water-Lillies, Red and Green Pads. Study from Nature, 1883 by John La Farge

a visit to the home of the collector T. B. Clarke, who showed him around the room he called his "Homer gallery," perhaps the finest contemporary gathering of the artist's work; but by then Sargent was already an accomplished master of the medium. Sargent undoubtedly admired Homer's work, yet his own dazzling brushwork and superficial display owed little to Homer's intensity and fidelity to nature.

Homer's most important legacy to future generations of watercolor painters was his unflagging commitment to the medium as a serious art form. Not only was he remarkably productive as a watercolorist. He clearly saw these works as an important part of his profile as an artist. Homer often devoted his exhibitions exclusively to work in watercolor; to him, the watercolors were not merely studies for other paintings but self-sufficient works of art in their own right. The significance of his achievement in the medium was affirmed in the years following his death

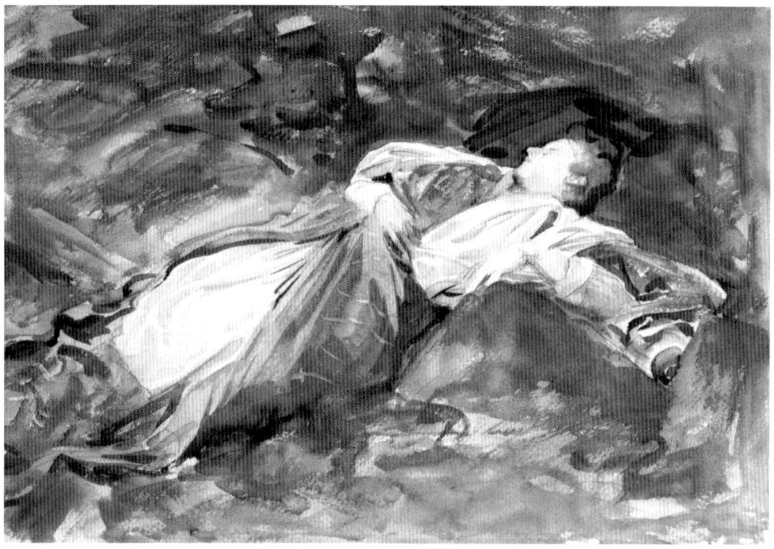

Violet Sleeping, *c.* 1907–1910 by John Singer Sargent

when major American museums like the Metropolitan, the Brooklyn Museum, and Boston's Museum of Fine Arts snatched up large groups of Homer's watercolors. In 1917, the Worcester Art Museum purchased one watercolor, *The Turkey Buzzard* of 1904, for $2,200, an astonishing sum for an artist who had begun his career asking between $30 and $75. (*Waiting for a Bite* could be had in the 1880s for the paltry sum of $50.)

During the artist's lifetime, prices for his watercolors remained modest and he continued to rely on the quantity of sales to provide a steady income. The largest of the Cullercoats watercolors were priced between $300 and $500 in the early 1880s. And as late as the 1890s, while his reputation as one of the country's leading artists was being solidified, his watercolors could still be had relatively cheaply. *The Sun*, reporting on an exhibition of the Adirondacks watercolors in 1890, noted: "Mr. Homer has met with a success which, if pecuniary outcome is any test, could hardly have been greater. . . . But it is a pity that he rates himself below his proper worth. Not only for his own sake, but for the sake of art and American artists in general, Mr. Homer ought to have asked more for these admirable water colors than $125 apiece."

The dramatic increase in prices in the years after his death reflects Homer's growing fame and also the greater esteem in which the medium was now held, a transformation his own genius surely helped bring about. By demonstrating what was possible using water-based pigments and paper, Homer helped to usher in the era when painters like Maurice Prendergast and John Marin could establish themselves as major artists primarily on the basis of their watercolors.

Critics, while not always comfortable with the daring of Homer's watercolors, were quick to recognize the seriousness of his endeavor. As far back as 1881, a critic for *The Nation* wrote: "Mr. Homer goes as far as anyone has ever done in demonstrating the value of watercolors as a serious means of expressing dignified artistic impressions, and does it wholly in his own way."

Homer was only one of many artists riding the wave of popularity in watercolor painting that began around midcentury. The American Society of Painters in Water Colors—which changed its name in 1877 to the American Watercolor Society—had been founded in 1866 as a venue for the exhibition and promotion of works in the medium, and included, in addition to Homer himself, such distinguished figures as William Trost Richards, Jasper Cropsey, and John La Farge. The inspiration came largely from across the Atlantic, where English artists like J. M. W. Turner and the Pre-Raphaelites had already shown that watercolor could yield works of great ambition. A landmark exhibition of British Art, held in 1857–58 in Philadelphia and New York, included 188 watercolors; and it was the popularity of the 1873 international exhibition sponsored by the American Society of Painters in Water Colors, which featured works by prominent British artists, that almost certainly motivated Homer to take his own "desperate plunge" later that summer.

Like many of his contemporaries, Homer was profoundly influenced by the bold compositional devices of Japanese prints, and no one of his generation, particularly with his realist ideology, could have been immune to the impact of photography. But each technique borrowed, each influence absorbed, was transformed under the intensity of the artist's singular vision. Though Homer's art gave rise to no movements and promulgated no theories, in their ambition, richness, and truth to nature, his watercolors served as a model for coming generations.

TOOLS AND TECHNIQUES

Few of the methods that Homer employed in his watercolors originated with him. His contribution to the craft of watercolor painting lies not so much in pioneering new techniques—in fact the techniques he adopted were often thought old-fashioned even at the time—as in making tried-and-true methods serve new expressive ends. One would be hard-pressed to discover a trick or device used in one of his paintings that is not to be found in the work of his lesser contemporaries. The materials he used, including Winsor & Newton moist watercolors and J. Whatman's paper of medium or heavy weight, were widely available to amateurs and professionals alike. But in the end, guided by a deft hand and a uniquely perceptive eye, Homer's watercolors reveal a powerful and original voice.

Homer absorbed what he needed from a variety of sources: the color theories of the French scientist Michel-Eugène Chevreul, whose *The Laws of Contrast of Color* he once referred to as his bible; contemporary manuals on watercolor that proliferated at midcentury and that were filled with both practical advice and stylistic recommendations; and the firsthand study of fellow artists, particularly the works of the great English masters. Such influences must be inferred from the paintings themselves since Homer rarely spoke about other artists, preferring to view himself as self-taught and beholden only to nature as he saw it. While still at Bufford's he was reported to have said to another apprentice, "If a man wants to be an artist, he should never look at pictures."

What distinguished Homer's approach from the beginning was the freedom with which he put brush to paper. Writing in 1875 for *The Art Journal*, one critic complained: "Mr. Homer's style is wonderfully vigorous and original; with a few dashes of the brush, he suggests a picture, but a mere suggestion only, and it is a mistaken eccentricity which prevents finish." In language that was to be echoed frequently in his lifetime, another critic described his watercolors as "mere memorandum blots and exclamation points," though he went on to say, with an ambivalence typical of contemporary responses, that the artist's pictures were "so pleasant to look at, we are almost content not to ask Mr. Homer for a finished piece." Unlike many of his colleagues—particularly those like John William Hill or Henry Roderick Newman who subscribed to John Ruskin's formulation of art as a faithful and detailed reproduction of natural form—Homer did not build up his images in thousands of stippled strokes, but in broad washes rapidly applied. When he wished, as in some of the large-scale watercolors he made in Cullercoats, he was capable of achieving a high degree of finish; but usually he favored a more spontaneous approach. For Homer, watercolor was the medium of light and atmosphere, perfect for establishing a feeling of being immersed in nature.

In the early watercolors, the paint is usually applied on dry paper in quick strokes. A graphite underdrawing serves to block out the major forms and to pick out details. This initial drawing often remains an important element in the final composition. The graphite lines that define the folds of the man's shirt in *Driving Cows to Pasture* [pp. 4–5] or the hound's neck and chest in *Dog on a Log* [p. 152] are not simply artifacts of the working process but critical elements in guiding our eyes to the key element in the scene.

That he was not in his earliest watercolors entirely at ease with the new medium is attested to in these works by the liberal application of opaque gouache, often used in areas already washed in dark colors where he wished to add lighter accents. It is a technique that more closely mirrors painting in oils, where darks tend to be thin and transparent and highlights thick and opaque. In the charming *Boys and Kitten* [p. 33], the lighter green of the sun-dappled leaves is created by mixing small amounts of opaque white into the darker pigment. Even at this early date, however, Homer tends to combine different techniques as needed. In *The Berry Pickers* [pp. 30–31], light areas on the back of the girl's dress and the boy's shirtsleeves are created by reserving areas of white paper, while the flowers in the foreground are dabbed over the

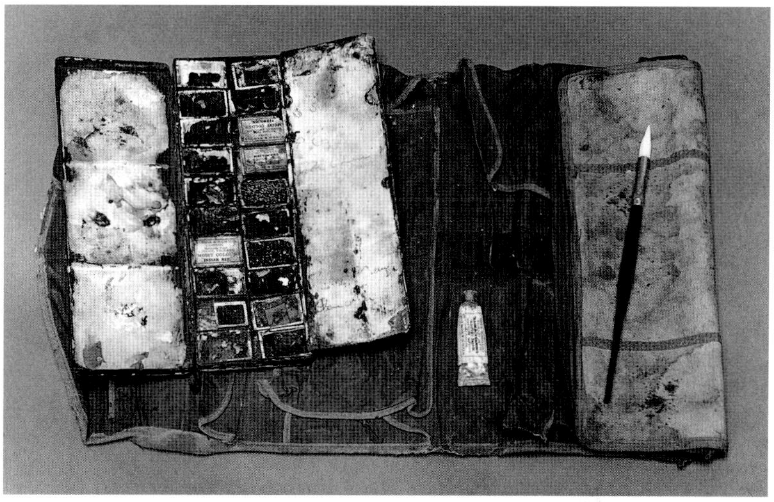

Winslow Homer's Watercolor Box.

dark wash with lighter, opaque paint.

Homer was never finicky about process, using whatever was required to achieve the desired result. Unlike Sargent, who cultivated an aristocratic sense of ease in his watercolors—often with great, but concealed, labor—Homer allowed his audience to see each step of the journey as he changed his mind or composed on the fly. One can often find traces of an earlier composition showing through in the finished work, as in the 1885–86 *In a Florida Jungle* [pp. 198–199] where the alligator, now placed in the water where he looks menacingly at his intended prey, has a ghostly twin from an earlier composition sitting on the beach. Watercolor is often regarded as the most unforgiving of media, requiring careful planning and rapid execution; but while Homer was clearly capable of painting quickly and with an assured hand, he was willing to rework a passage to achieve a more satisfying image. In *An Afterglow* [pp. 94–95], a monumental watercolor from Cullercoats, the changes that he made in the composition—including scraping out the prows of the boats to give them a lower profile—are clearly visible. What could have been a rather formal image is made more lively by the artist's permitting us a glimpse into his working method.

Even in his early works Homer applied varying degrees of finish to suit the particular subject, from the almost offhand execution of *Boys and Kitten* [p. 33] to the more carefully composed *Boy in a Boatyard* [p. 39]. For Homer, the approach is calibrated to the overall mood, carefree in the former and graver, almost ominous, in the latter. Over the next few years Homer demonstrated his versatility in the medium, going from the luminous veils of brilliant color of *In the Garden* [p. 58] to the solid modeling and reductive palette of *Blackboard* [p. 65].

But it is with the works begun in Cullercoats— some of which were actually completed in his studio upon his return to America in 1883— that we see Homer mastering the full range of techniques available to the nineteenth-century watercolor painter. His increased ambition is signaled as well in the larger scale of these works. The early watercolors typically had been painted on sheets measuring 10 by 14 inches, but in Cullercoats he began to work on sheets measuring 20 by 15 or 22 by 17 inches. These works show the influence of English models not only in their subjects but in technique as well. Following artists like Turner, Homer now worked "wet into wet," layering translucent veils of color on dampened paper to achieve subtle atmospheric effects. In these works, Homer was striving for monumentality, which he conveyed through solidly modeled figures and a somber palette. An unusually large number of preparatory drawings exist for the Cullercoats watercolors—particularly for *Perils of the Sea* and *The Wreck of the Iron Crown* [pp. 101, 102–103]—confirming that these compositions were not completed on the spot but in the studio. Unlike some of his early Gloucester watercolors—which were conceived as fleeting impressions, a moment caught on the wing and set down effortlessly—the Cullercoats watercolors approach the solemn grandeur of his oil paintings.

The Cullercoats paintings are the most European of Homer's works, clearly indebted to depictions by Jules Breton and Jean-François Millet of heroic peasants and the Anglo-Dutch tradition of marine painting. Carefully crafted, they fit comfortably within the English tradition of the "exhibition watercolor," an elaborate work meant to compete in impact with large-scale oil paintings. He also used the "subtractive" techniques favored by British artists, where subtle gradations were achieved by re-wetting and then lifting out pigment from the paper. The solid modeling of the figures in *Mending the Nets* [p. 105] was achieved through careful lifting out of pigment in the lighter areas. The same technique is used to wonderful effect to create highlights in the foliage of the highly finished watercolor *In a Florida Jungle* [pp. 198–199]. In his Cullercoats watercolors, he sometimes employed masking agents—which prevent pigments from adhering to the

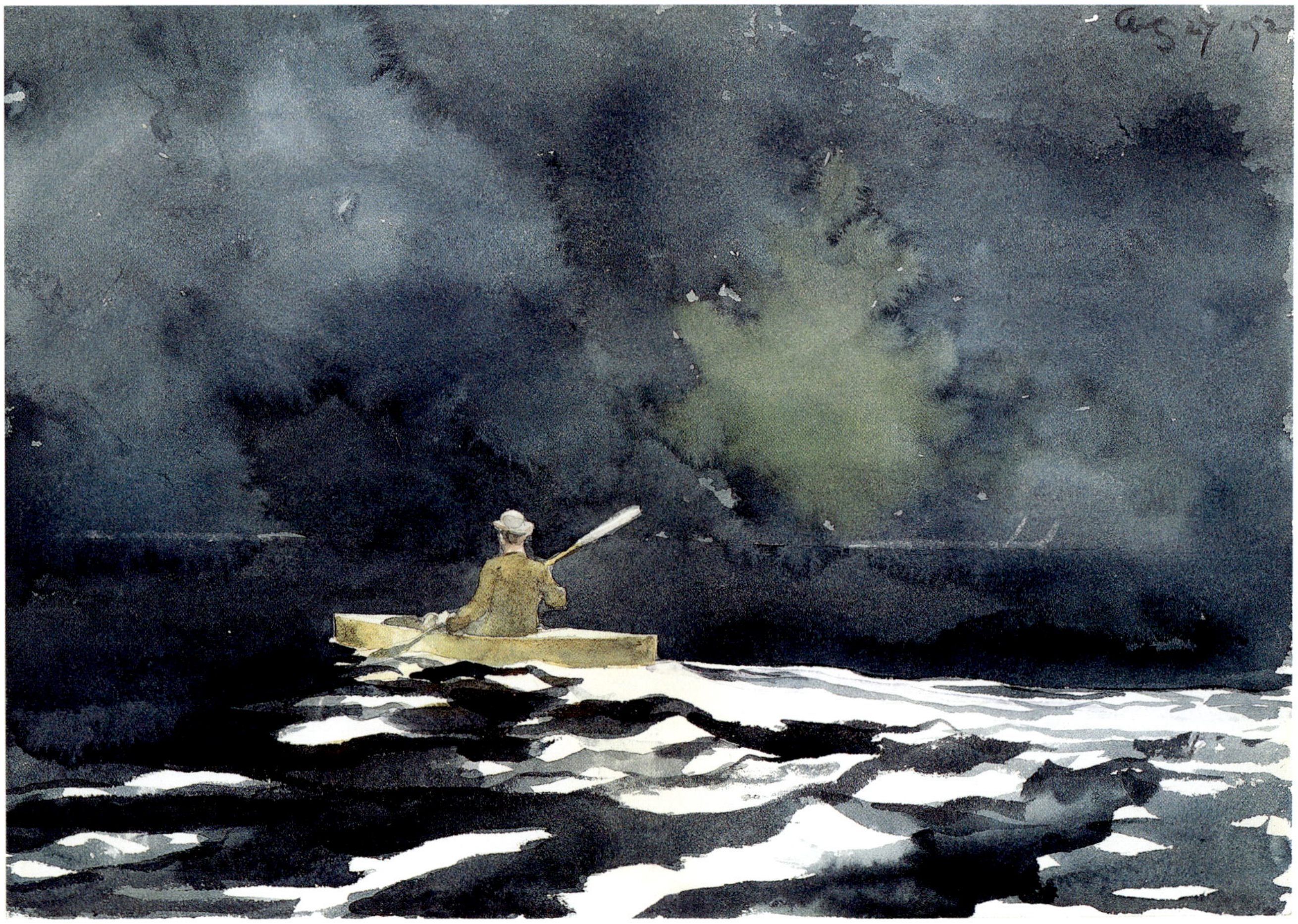

PADDLING AT DUSK 1892

paper in selected areas—that permitted a degree of painterly freedom in the application of washes without the risk of losing the lightest areas. This technique can be observed in the foam at the center of the *The Wreck of the Iron Crown*, where the eerie whiteness of the paper serves to draw the eye into the heart of the action. Another method used to correct a composition or to add highlights was to scrape the paper—usually with the pointed end of the brush handle or a knife—a technique that gives to the surface of many of Homer's watercolors a rough, worked look. The streaks of white in the puddle in the foreground of *Inside the Bar, Cullercoats* [pp. 92–93] were achieved by scraping through to the white paper below, as were the fine lines of the bent fishing rod and the streak of the boat's wake in *Adirondack Lake* [pp. 162–163].

Homer knew the value of both spontaneity and more deliberate methods. In his earliest watercolors, the effect of the rapid, apparently spontaneous brushwork served to emphasize lightness of mood and the immediacy of the moment. In the later watercolors, he became a master of the controlled accident as a means of expressing deeper truths about nature. Looseness or sketchiness of application can, in the hands of a master, convey much more than is actually there. In *Paddling at Dusk*, the line of trees is indicated only by the dark mass of dripped and sponged paint, its very indistinctness evoking the gloom of the gathering night. In *Dog on a Log* [p. 152], the soft light of the forest interior is conjured by repeated washing and staining with thin colors, which are then lifted up so that they leave only the most delicate of tints behind. The indistinctness of the background foliage contrasts with the carefully drawn figure of the dog, who stands out in bold relief.

The increasingly sophisticated layering of translucent colors to achieve subtle nuances of light and tone is a hallmark of Homer's late watercolors. In *The Blue Boat* [pp. 140–141], as in many of the late watercolors, an atmospheric landscape is conjured with strict economy of means. A variegated landscape of earth and foliage is suggested through the simple device of applying a rust-colored wash over mottled green shapes, a lushness that would be lost by an artist who felt the need to pick out every leaf and branch.

Dark, neutral tones often turn out to be the product of superimposed, contrasting hues that, here and there, pull apart to reveal unsuspected brilliance. In *Deer Drinking* [p. 156], the dark green water is formed by blues layered over yellow to create the effect of deep shade and dappled sunlight reflected from the surface of a pond. The richness Homer achieves in his dark tones is apparent in works like *Leaping Trout*, [pp. 166–167] where layered washes of warm and cool tones evoke the murk of a forest pond drenched in humid vapors.

From the beginning, Homer was content to allow his hesitations and corrections to show through. As his work matured, he permitted the natural qualities of the medium to play a greater and more expressive role. In addition to re-wetting and lifting up precisely defined areas of paint—essentially drawing in negative—he would also puddle water on the paper, allowing pigment to dissolve and flow freely across the surface. In *Fishing Boats, Key West* [pp. 214–215], he submerged already painted passages in the foreground, allowing the water to pick up and redeposit the pigment. One can clearly make out in the lower left of the painting the ridge of darker color left behind, a free-flowing line that captures perfectly the ripple of windswept waves in the moments preceding a storm.

Ultimately, however, technique meant little to Homer except as a means of expressing an idea or feeling. He is not one of those artists who astounds us with his technical facility. The wonder we feel standing in front of one of Homer's watercolors has little to do with painterly pyrotechnics, but instead comes from their capacity to conjure the natural world with unprecedented truth and vividness. Viewing works like *The Blue Boat*, we have the sensation not merely of being transported to some scenic spot but of witnessing nature in a privileged moment when it reveals itself most fully. Homer himself seemed particularly pleased with this work, writing under his signature the cryptic phrase: "This will do the business." It is a rare moment of self-revelation, but one that seems entirely appropriate, for it is in such works that Homer drops the protective cloak of the unsentimental realist to expose the heart of a true visionary.

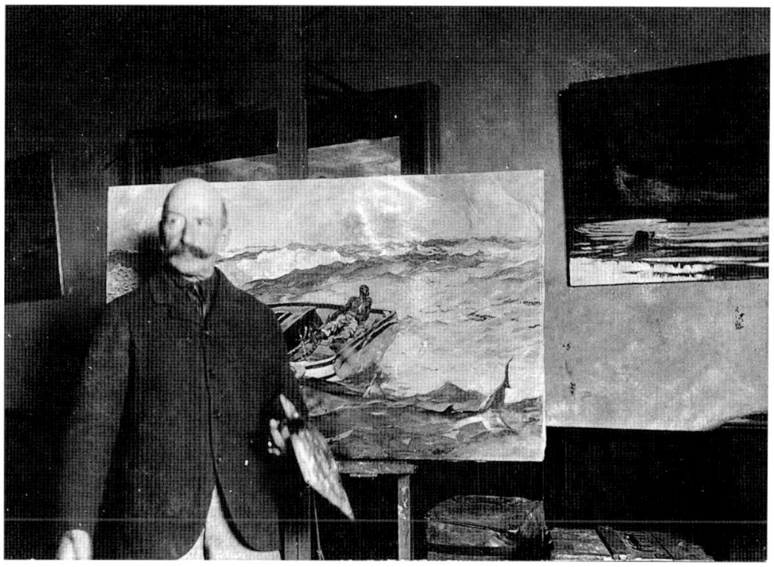

Winslow Homer with "The Gulf Stream," in hisPainting Room at Prout's Neck, c. 1900

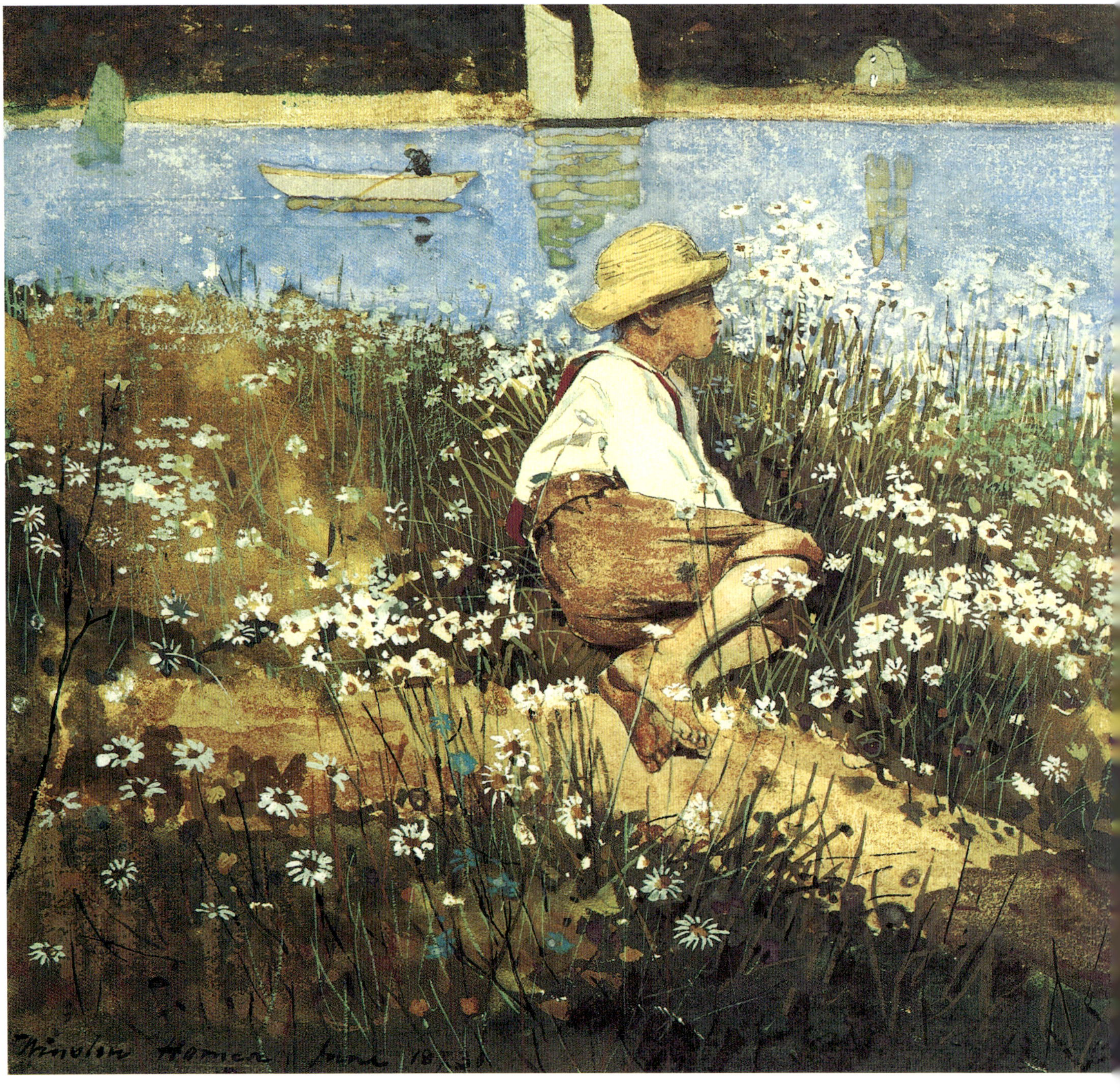

I.
Summer at the Shore: Gloucester, 1873

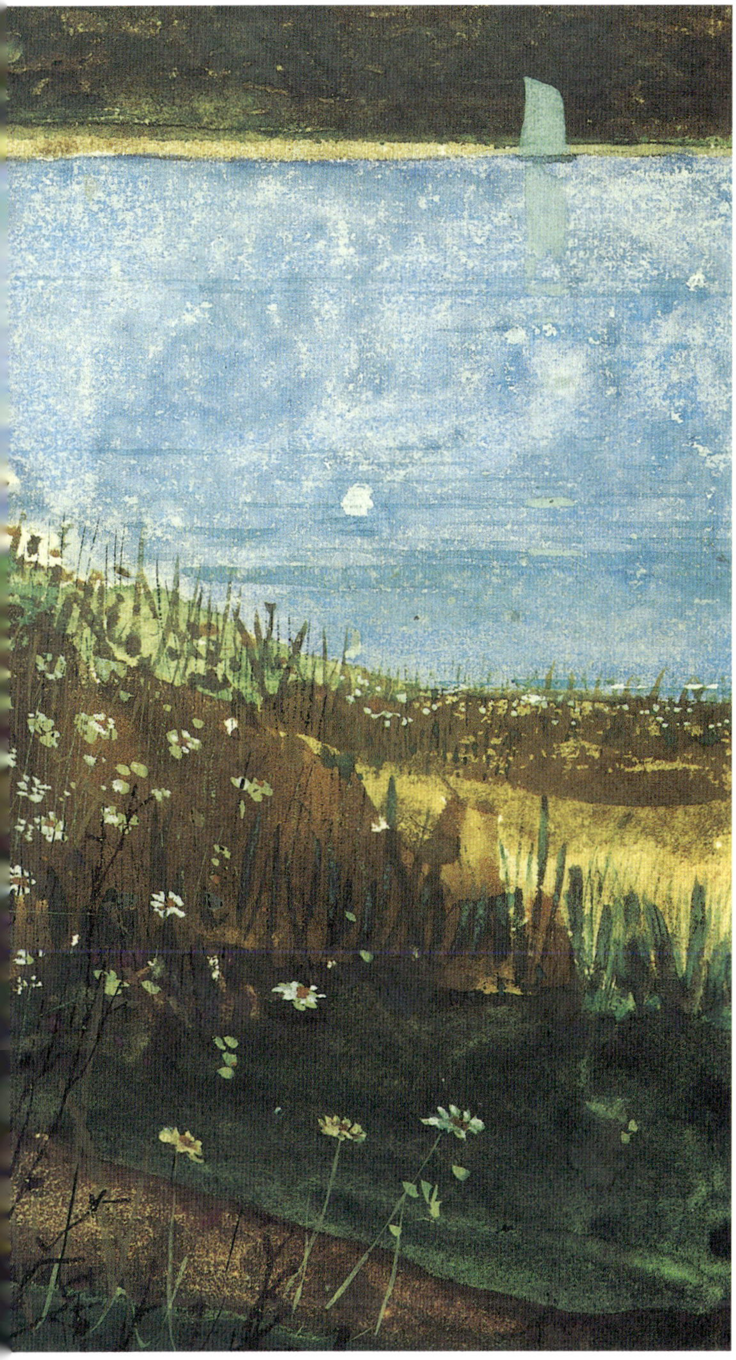

Watching the Harbor 1873

When Homer set out for the busy fishing port of Gloucester, Massachusetts, in the summer of 1873 to find picturesque material to paint in watercolor, he was not entirely unfamiliar with the medium. His work as a commercial illustrator had already given him considerable experience handling water-based media; the drawings that served as the basis for his illustrations were essentially monochrome watercolors executed in line and washes made from white gouache and thinned-out ink. A work like *Windy Day, Cullercoats* [p. 93], in chalk highlighted with white paint, recalls the drawings Homer was making on his engraving blocks.

But the summer of 1873 marked Homer's first in-depth exploration of watercolor as an independent form of artistic expression. Over the next couple of years the work in watercolor was closely linked to his commercial illustrations. Many of the early watercolors—including *The Berry Pickers*, *How Many Eggs?*, and *Waiting for a Bite*—led a second life as illustrations for *Harper's Weekly*, but Homer considered them to be legitimate works of art in their own right and marketed them as such. Despite the fact that he took up watercolor at least in part in the hope of establishing a reliable source of income, he did not simply repeat himself in shifting from one medium to another. Even when using almost identical compositions, he made significant changes that revealed an appreciation for the unique qualities of each. From the beginning he brought to his watercolors a sensibility entirely different from—one might almost say at odds with—his work as a commercial illustrator.

The Berry Pickers is one of those works that Homer executed as both a watercolor and an engraving. It is a delightful scene that celebrates the simple joys of childhood. A popular contemporary poem by Lucy Larcom describing a similar scene reveals the constellation of ideas that gave these scenes their universal appeal—childhood, health, and the simple pleasures of being in nature:

THE BERRY PICKERS 1873

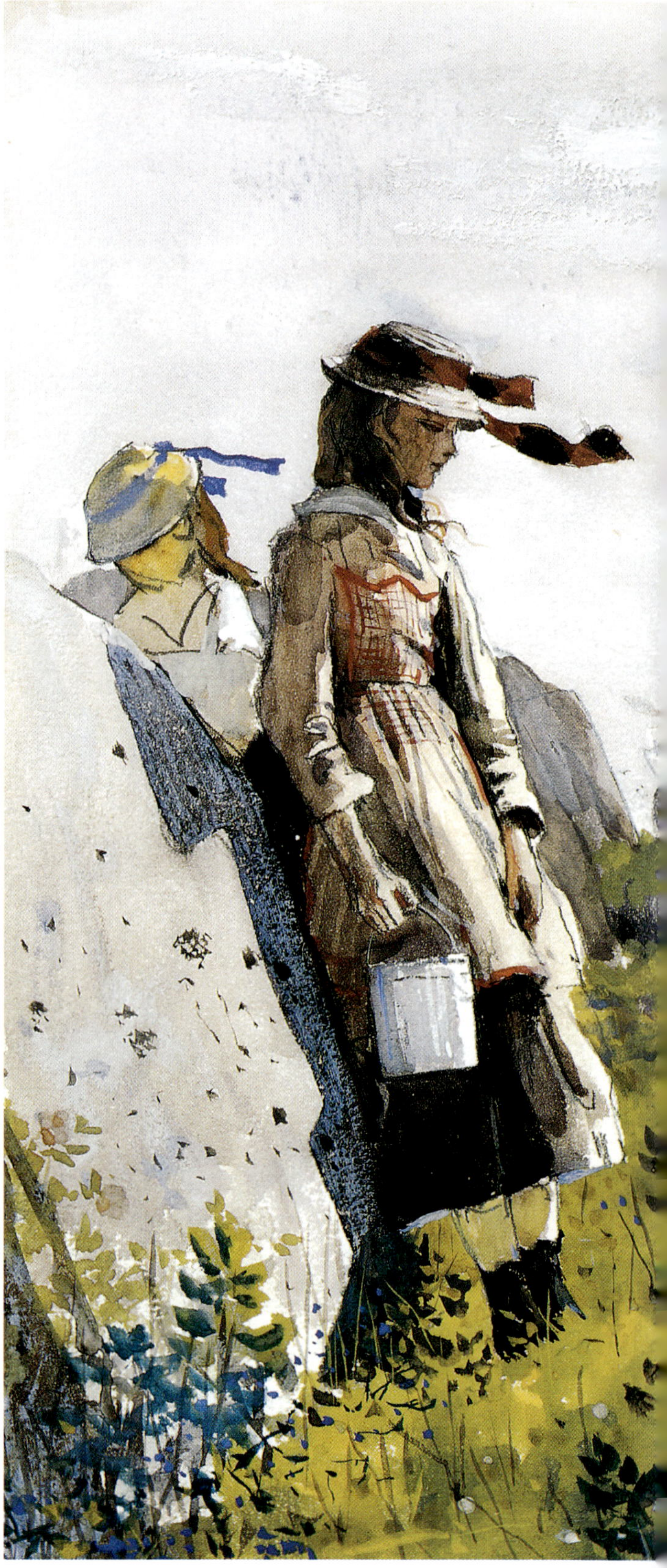

Red lilies blaze out of the thicket
Wild roses blush here and there:
There's sweetness in all the breezes,
There's health in each breath of air.
Hark to the wind in the pine-trees!
Hark to the tinkling rill!
O, pleasant it is a-berrying
In the pastures on the hill!

Despite the conventional subject matter of the artist's image, he manages to infuse each version with a vitality all its own. A comparison of the engraving with the watercolor on which it is based reveals myriad changes, large and small, that ultimately transform our experience of the scene. The most obvious, and most superficial, is the reversing of the composition that took place when the drawing was turned into an engraving. More important, the scene takes on an entirely different character in the black-and-white version. The overall tone is muted. A lively scene has become static, like an ancient frieze commemorating a timeless childhood ritual. The engraving's success depends on crisply rendered details and abstract linear patterns. The girl in the checked dress that Homer placed in the foreground adds an element of visual interest that compensates for the print's lack of color and atmospheric sparkle.

In contrast to the engraving, the watercolor *The Berry Pickers* relies on the apparent spontaneity of its execution. Using bright colors and exploiting the white of the paper, Homer emphasizes light and atmosphere over firm contour and immediacy over studied compositional devices. What in the engraving seems like a rite of summer endlessly repeated is in the watercolor a keenly observed and

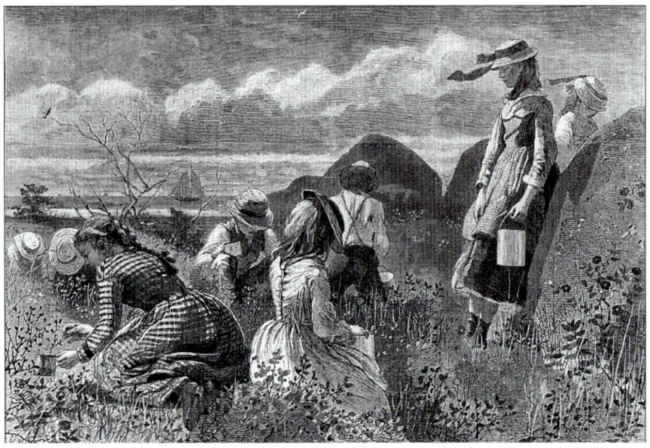

GATHERING BERRIES 1874

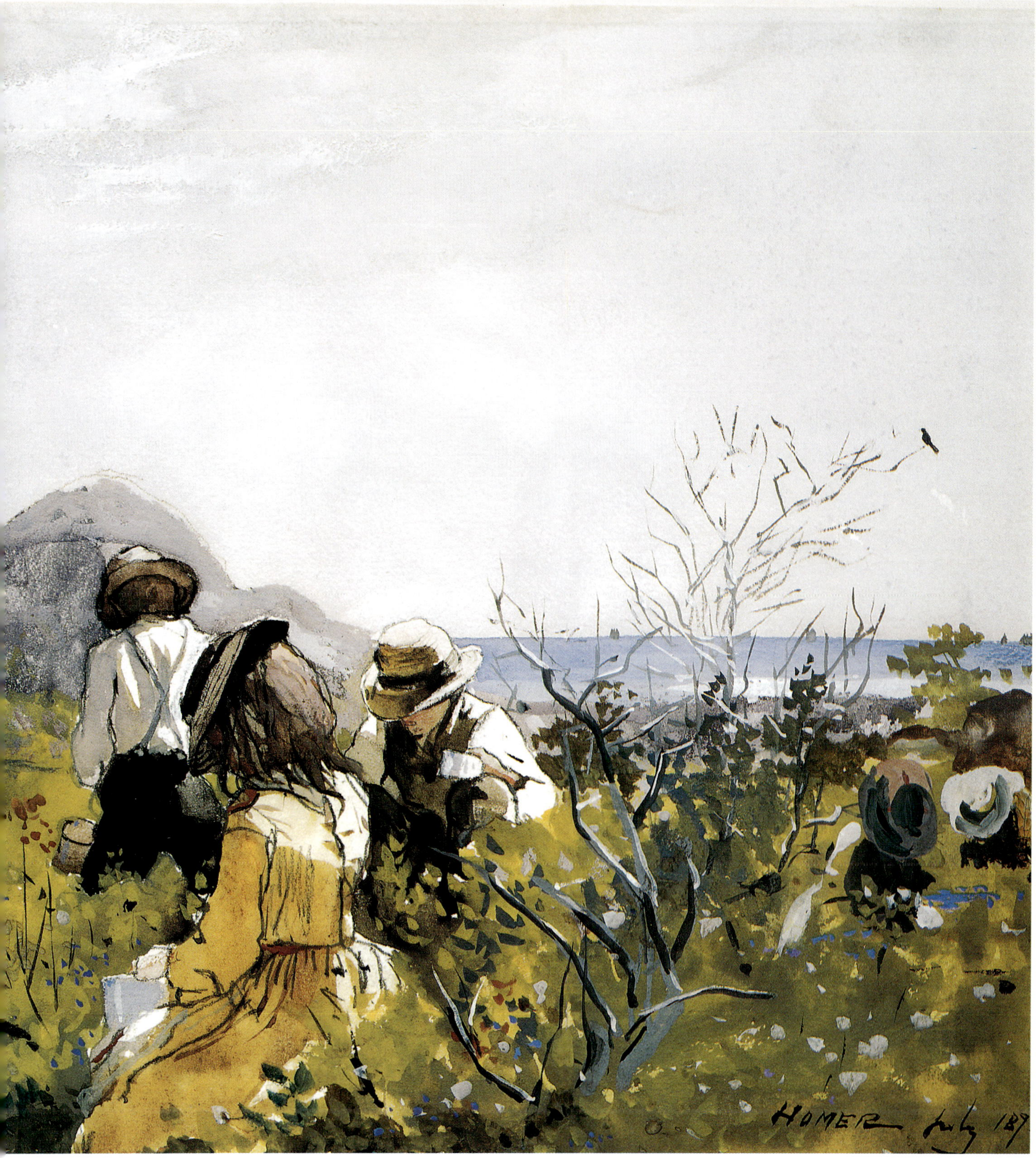
HOMER July 187

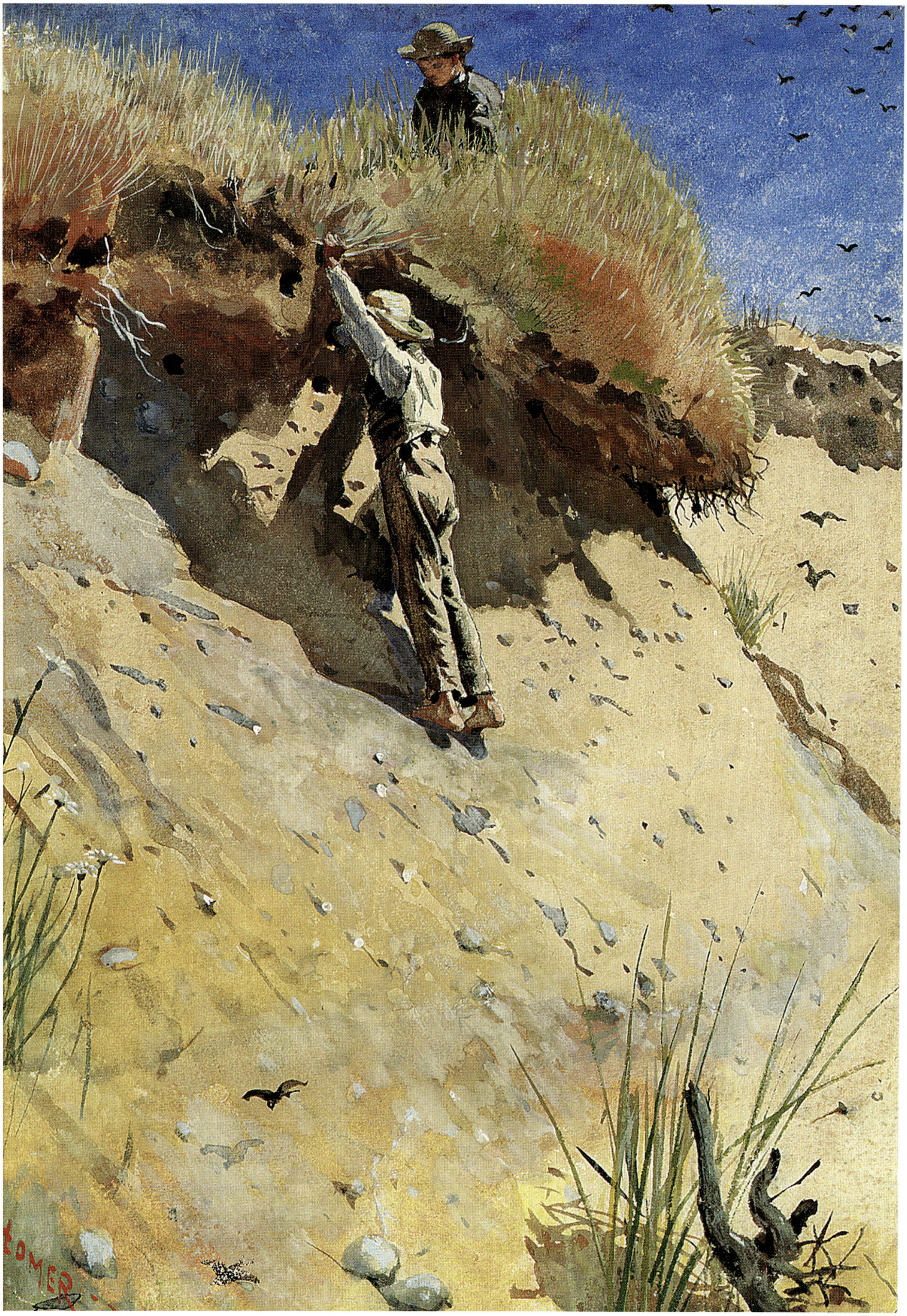

How Many Eggs? 1873

deeply felt moment without past or future. Whereas the engraving is carefully calibrated, the watercolor represents the artist's immediate response to his surroundings. Through dappled sun and shade, through buds and branches rendered with mere dabs and flicks of the brush as if dancing in the breeze, Homer brings to life the ever-changing scene.

It is in such unassuming works that the artist began to explore the properties unique to watercolor, explorations that opened up new vistas in his work and, ultimately, expanded the possibilities of the medium itself. He was also capable at this early stage of greater firmness of design and psychological penetration. Although many of these images are lighthearted vignettes of outdoor activities—fishing, picnicking, digging for clams, or searching for swallows' eggs—others strike a more introspective note. *Boy in a Boatyard* [p. 39] is a composition startling for its abstract geometry—the slashing diagonal of the white sail playing off the roundness of the empty barrel—and sense of melancholy. The boy, his face hidden in shadow beneath his straw hat, is the first of many images Homer will create throughout his career of solitary figures lost in silent revery.

BOYS AND KITTEN 1873

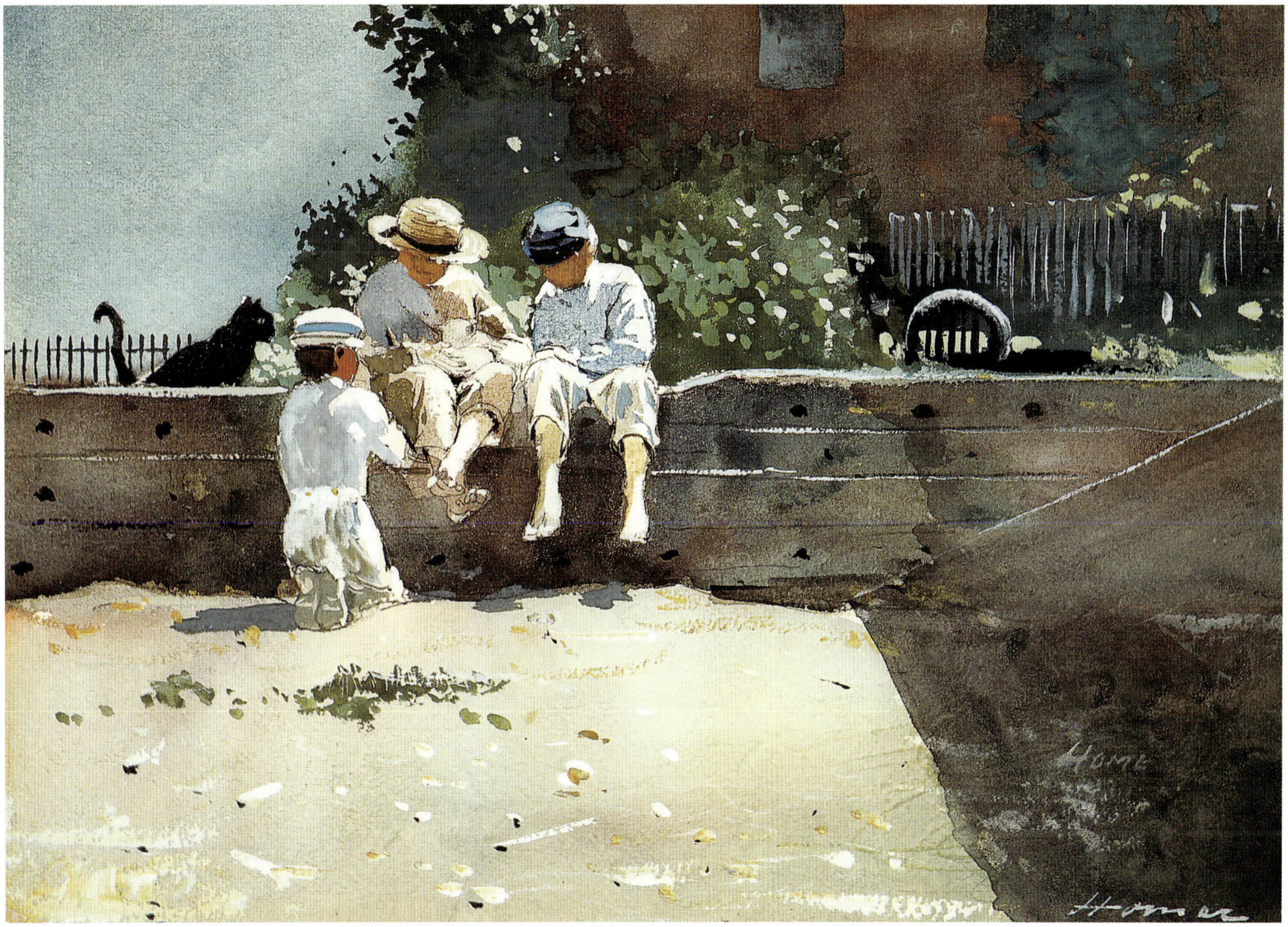

Many of the Gloucester watercolors feature children looking out to sea, anticipating the more explicitly tragic narratives of the Cullercoats paintings from the decade to follow. In *Watching the Harbor* [pp. 28–29], a work painted largely in opaque gouache, a young boy looks expectantly over the water. Is he awaiting the return of his father's ship or perhaps merely dreaming of a time when he will be old enough to sail himself to distant shores? Typically, Homer sets up a strong but open-ended narrative. Though we cannot know the thoughts that fill the boy's head, the daisy-strewn hillside on which he lounges strikes an optimistic chord. In *Waiting for Dad*, [p. 39] the

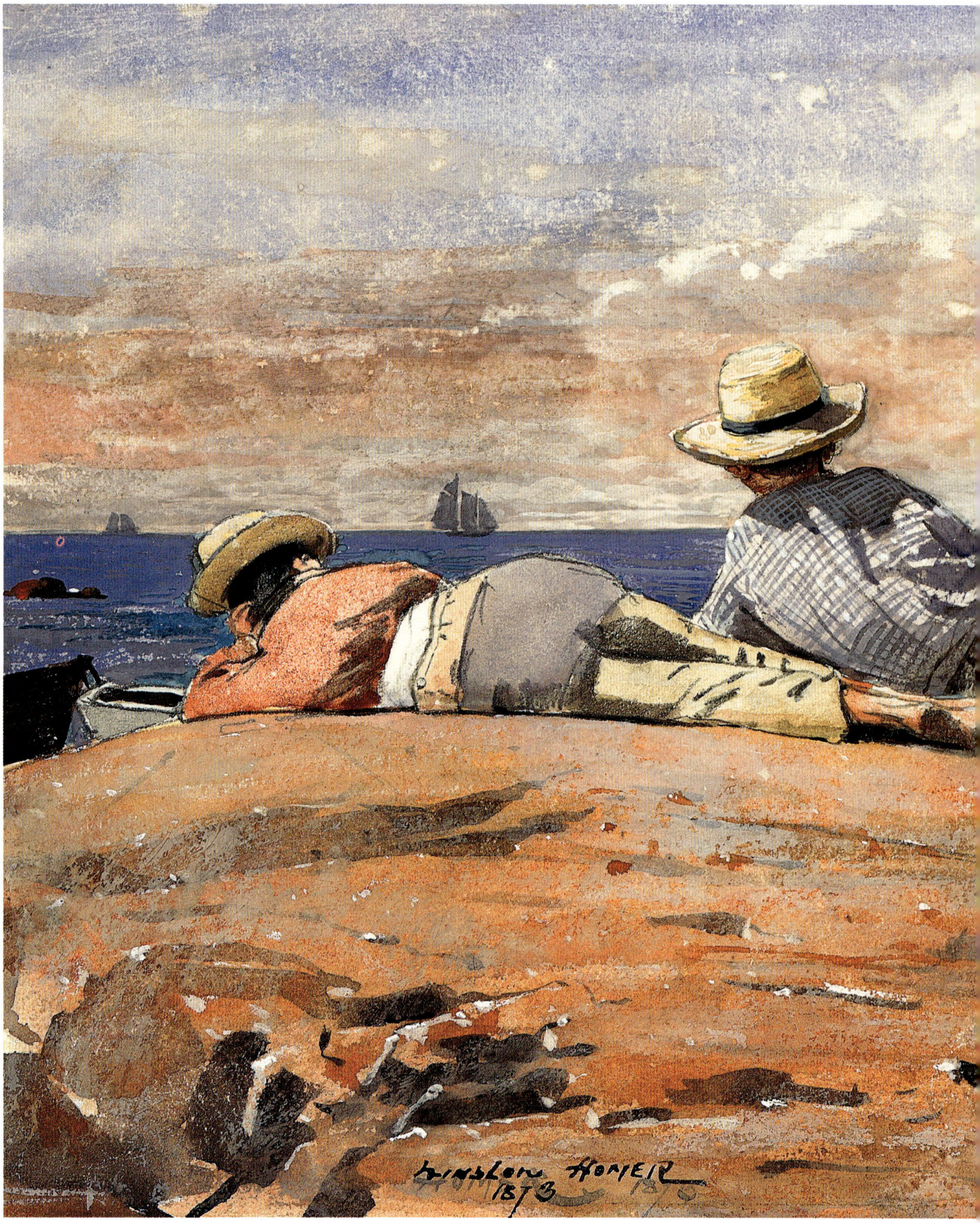

work's title allows us to share the thoughts of the boy whose face is turned away from us. Homer added a Madonna-like mother and child to the oil painting based on the same composition that transforms this slice of life into a scene with religious and metaphysical overtones. Even in the charming scene *Boys Wading,* [p. 38] where the figures' gaze is transfixed by some hidden object on the sandy bottom, the mood is contemplative rather than boisterous.

In fact, despite a superficially carefree atmosphere, there is a wistfulness to many of these images, a sense of longing or anxiety embodied in the motif of a young boy,

THREE BOYS ON THE SHORE 1873

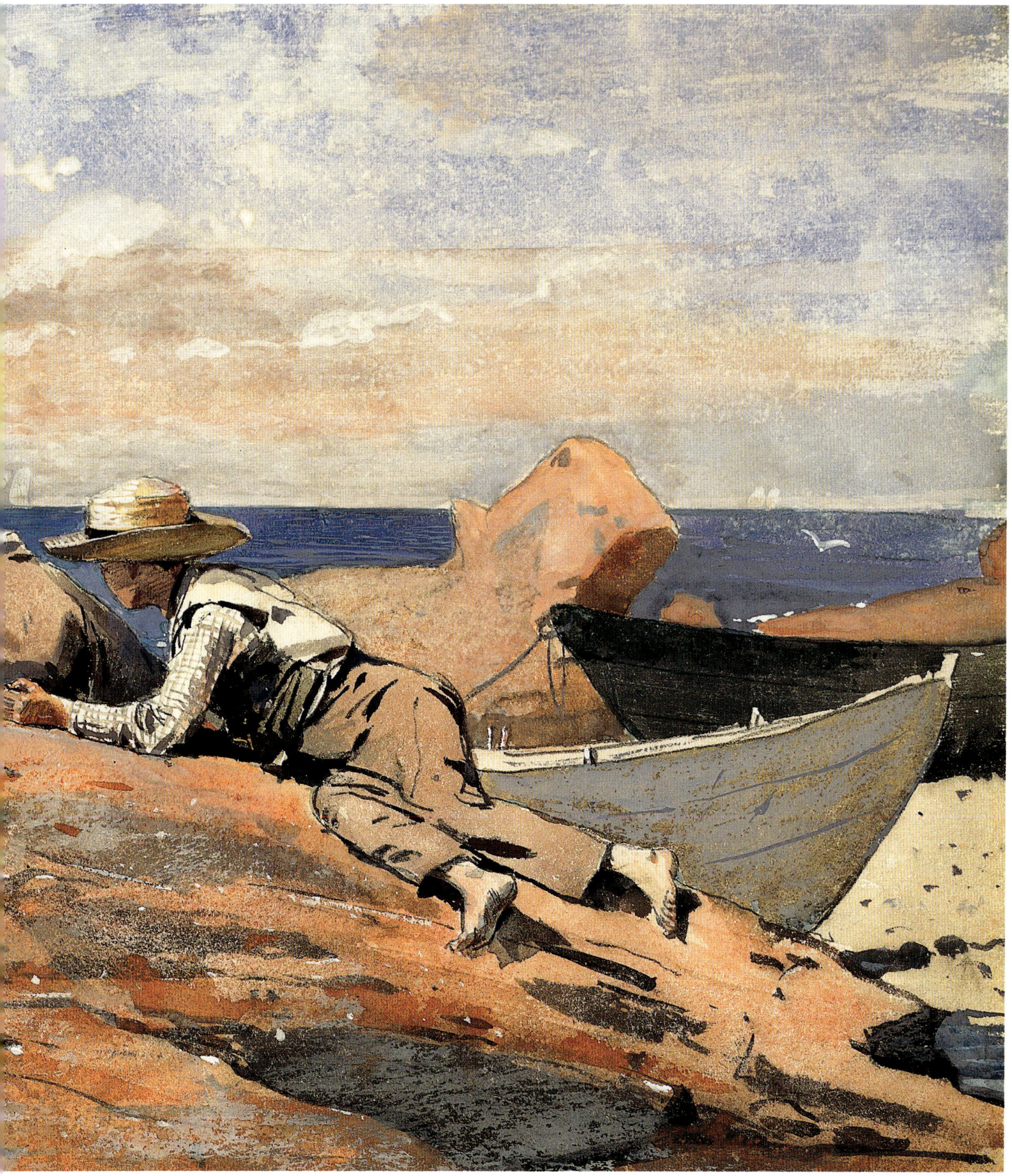

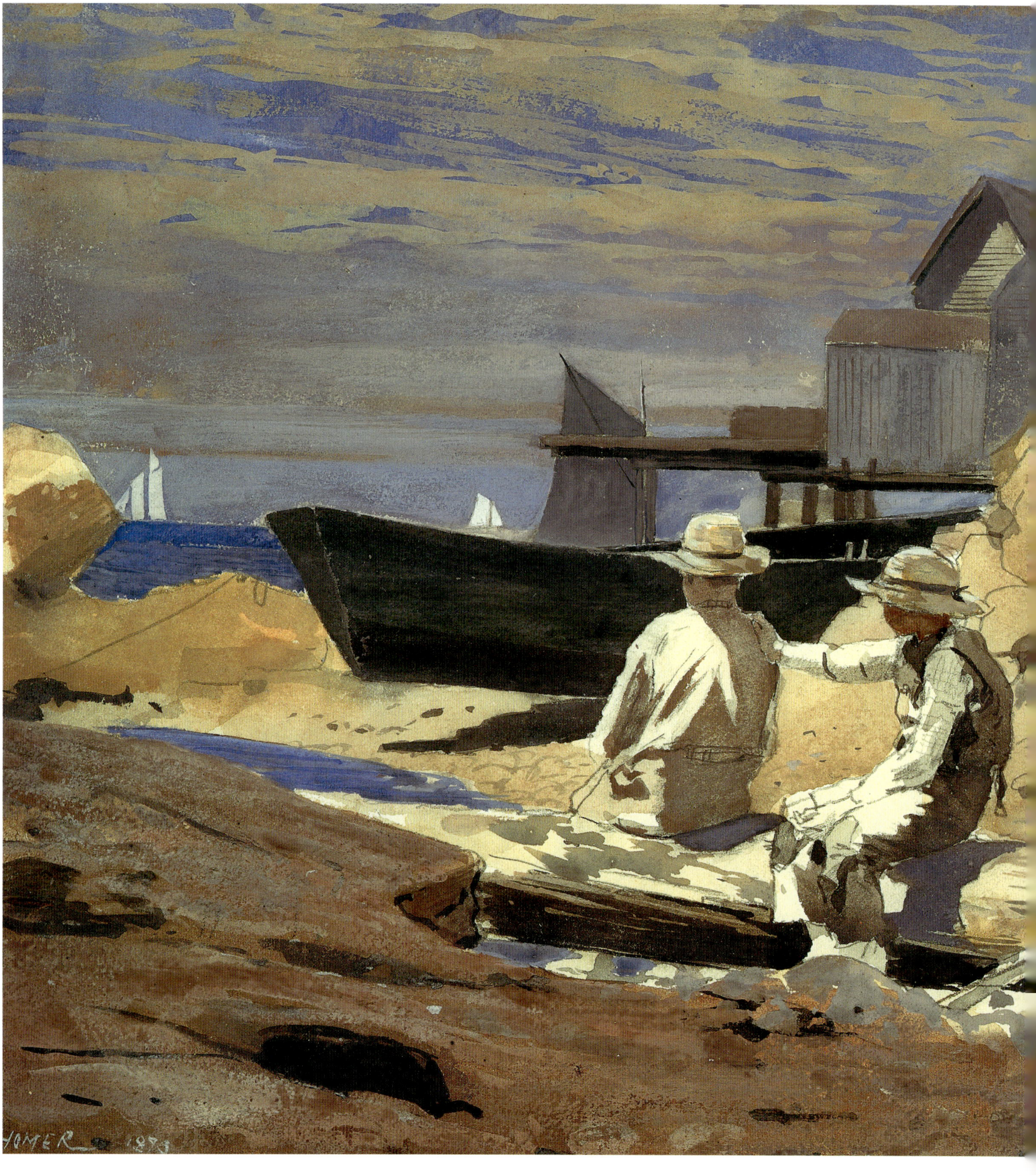

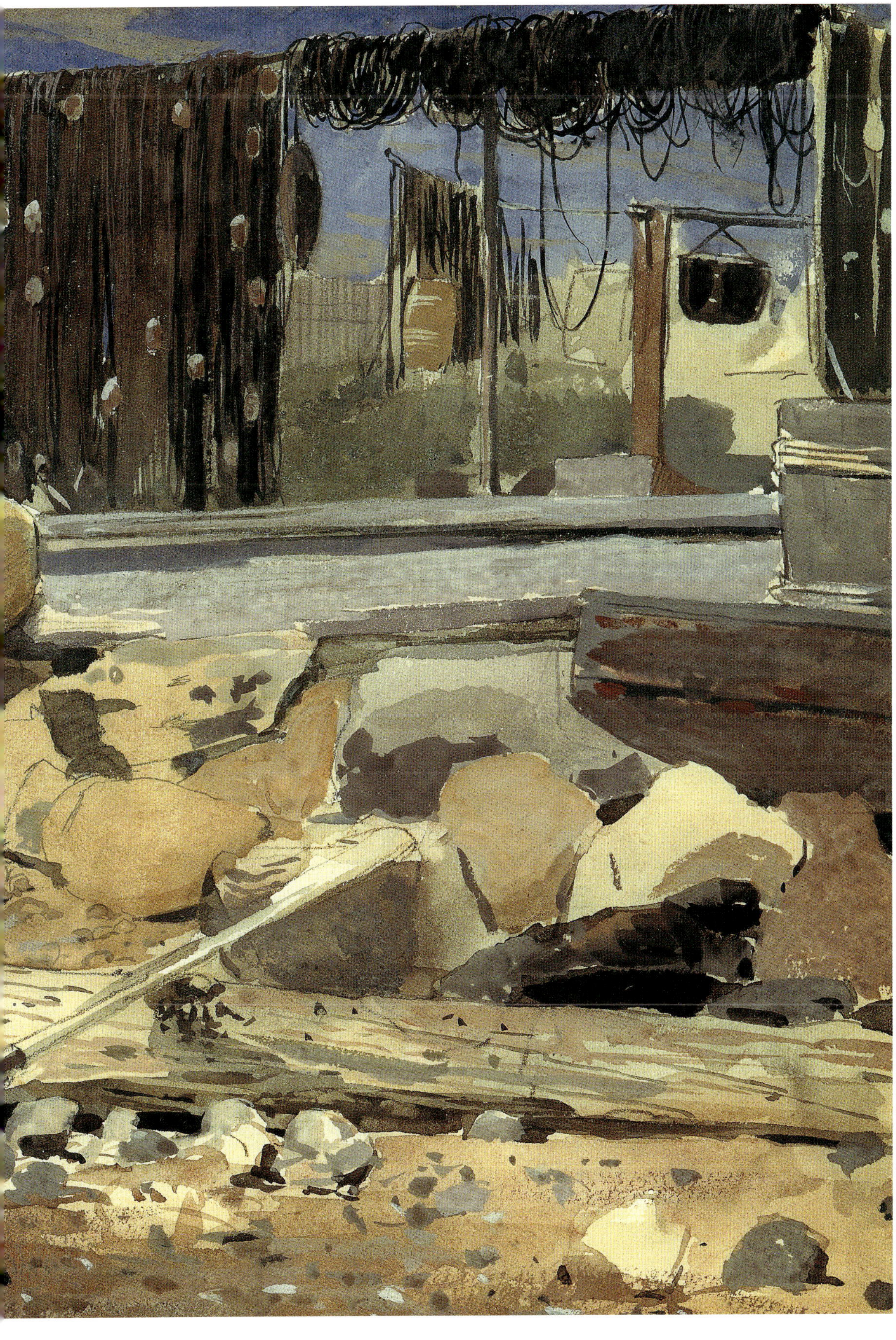

Waiting for the Boats 1873

or boys, staring out into the distance as if into an uncertain future. Watching and waiting are the activities most often depicted in these scenes. An introspective mood, a state of mind not usually associated with a boy's summer, also distinguishes *Three Boys on the Shore*, and *Waiting for the Boats*. This last painting in particular, where one boy rests his arm consolingly on the shoulder of his companion, is filled with intimations of mortality. The dangers of the seafaring life, which will become explicit in the watercolors of the 1880s, are only hinted at obliquely, but hope and fear are currents that flow just beneath the placid surface and give all these works a deeper resonance.

It would not be implausible to view these boys as symbolic representatives of a youthful nation. Like boys everywhere, they are filled with optimism, but these youngsters seem to recognize that they are about to enter uncharted waters. Homer made such metaphorical links

BOYS WADING 1873

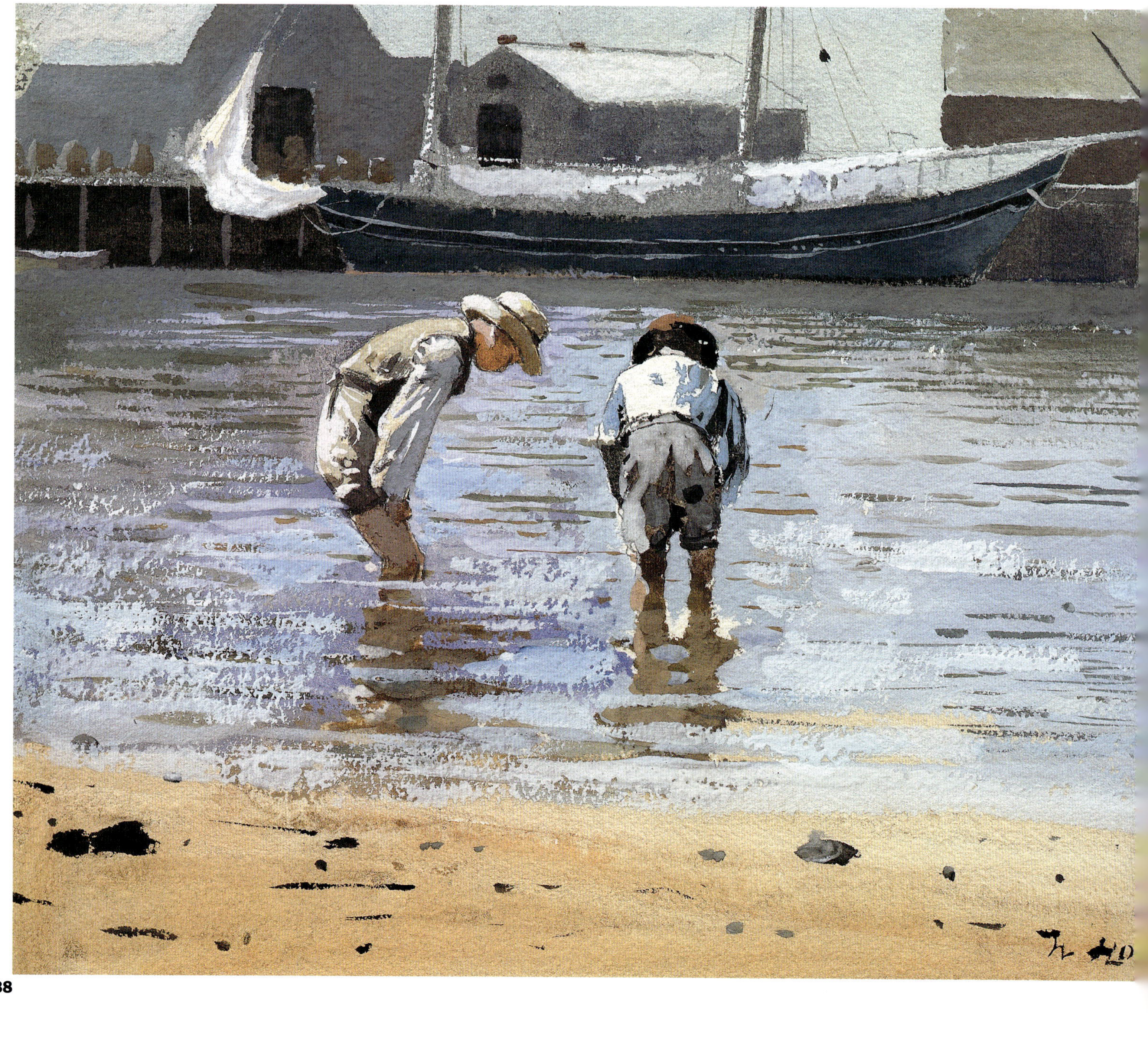

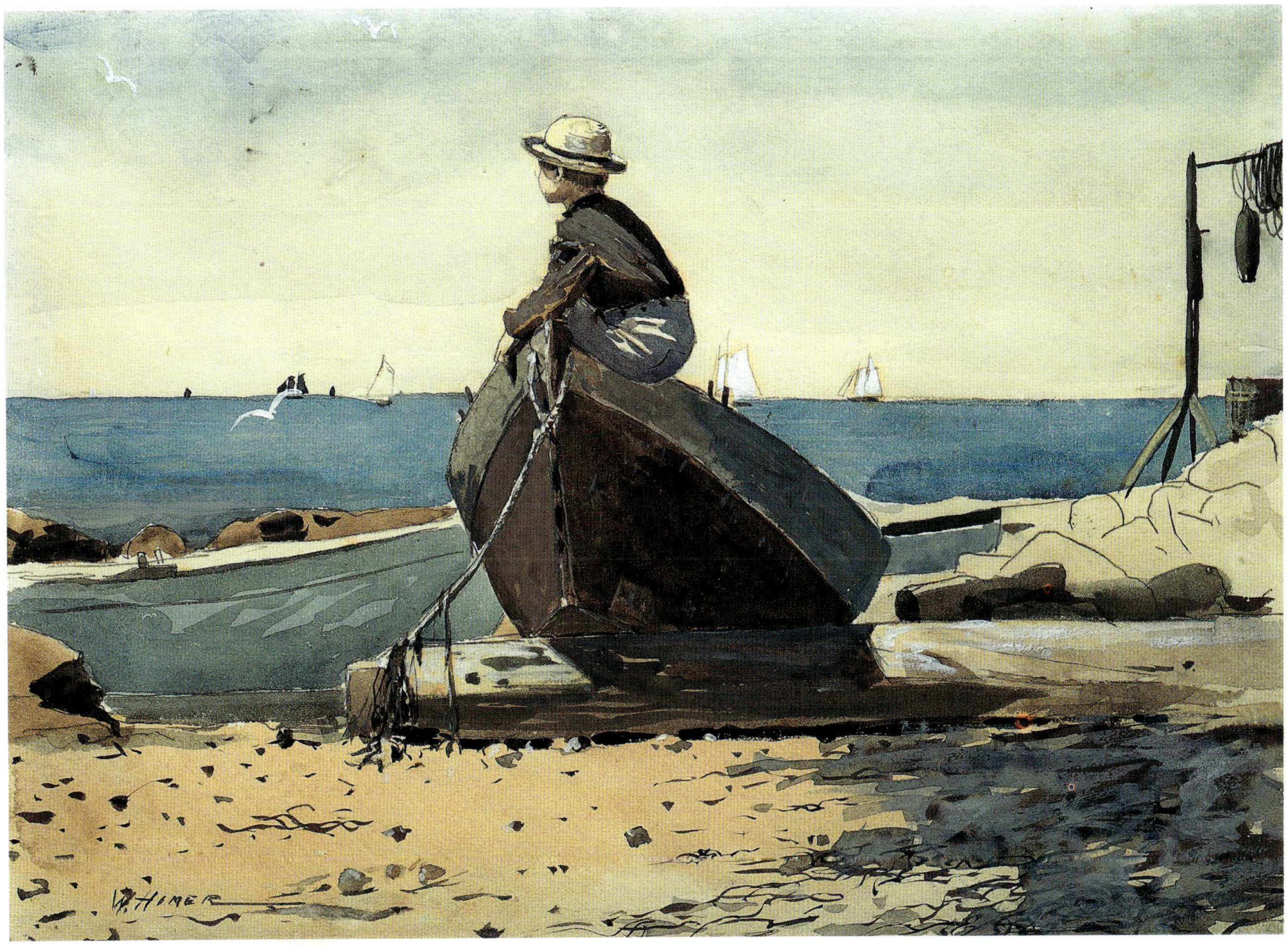

Waiting for Dad 1873

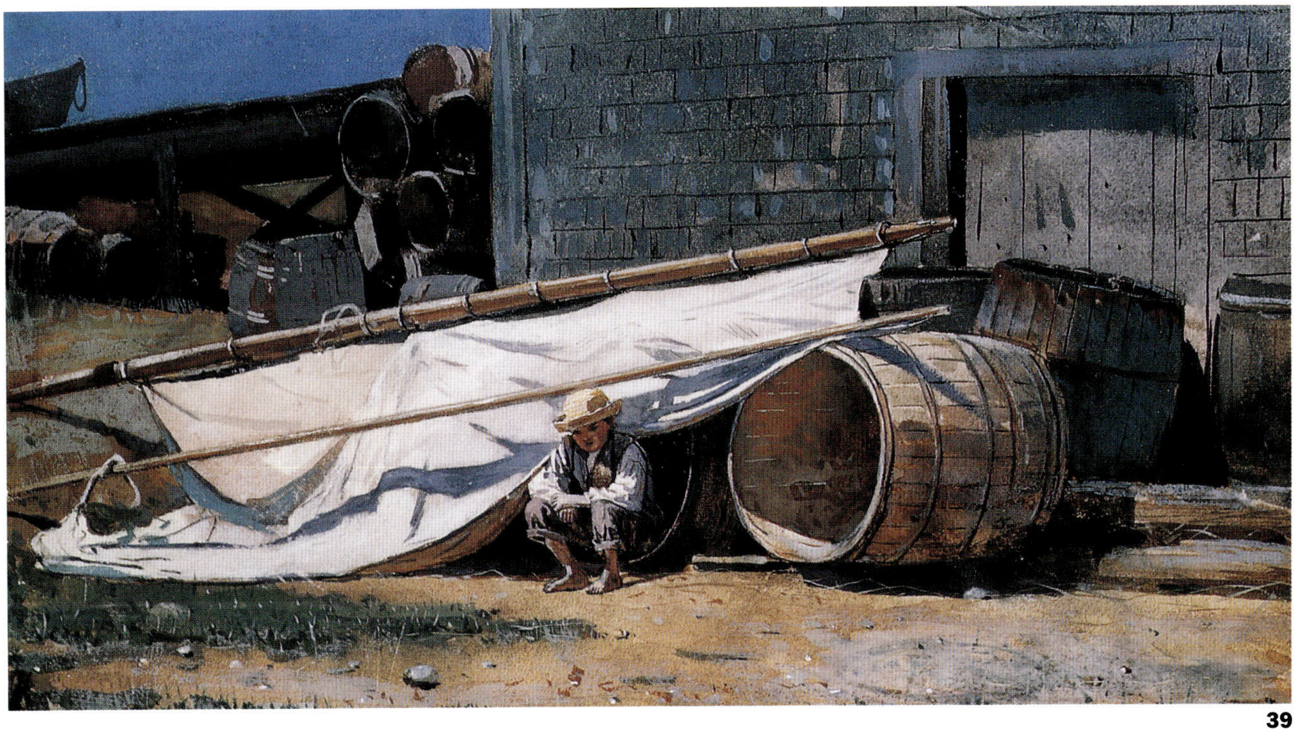

Boy in a Boatyard 1873

explicit in paintings he completed immediately after the Civil War, works like *Veteran in a New Field*, where the returning soldier lays down the implements of war and picks up those of peace. A similar interpretation seems in order here. For a nation emerging battered but unbroken from the horror of civil war, these images offered an affirmation of innocence regained. But these paintings of idle summer days are not merely escapist. They acknowledge in their wistful tone that troubled times may lie ahead.

Sailing the Catboat c. 1873

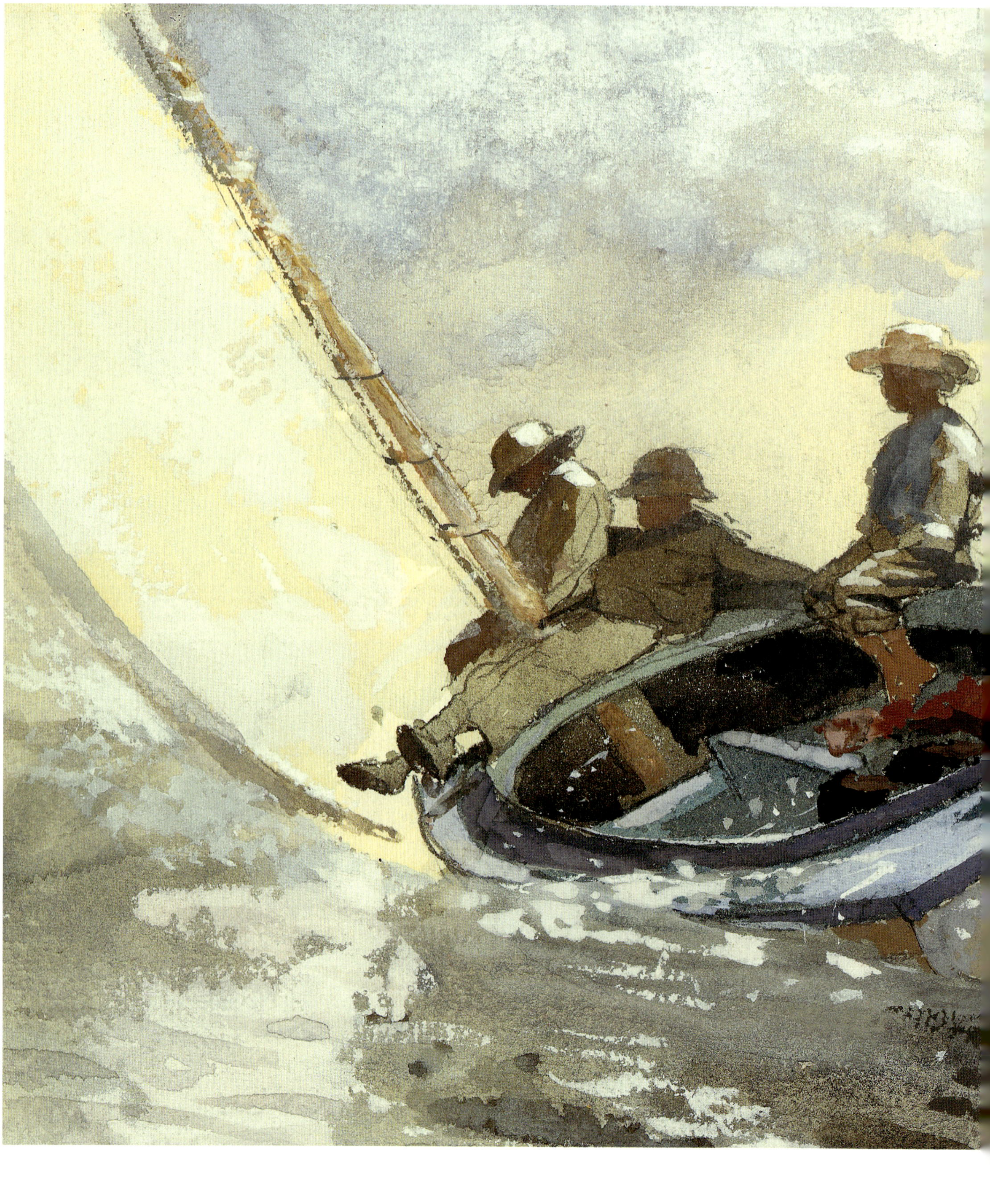

Sailing the Catboat, which served as the basis for the famous oil painting *Breezing Up* [p. 13], also features young boys staring out to a distant horizon; only here their taut, active postures suggest not anxiety but the excitement of the voyage. They do not wait by the shore but seize the rudder and sail boldly toward the horizon. Hopefulness and a sense of adventure are the keynotes of this work. Significantly, the oil painting dates to 1876, and its buoyant mood may reflect the good feelings engendered by the nation's Centennial. In depicting a boat manned by a youthful crew and speeding before a freshening breeze, Homer perfectly captures the celebratory spirit of a country anxious to put the past behind it and look toward a bright tomorrow.

Sailing the Catboat reveals as well Homer's mastery of abstract composition. The asymmetry of design, the massing of forms in the foreground to create bold silhouettes, and a preference for diagonal lines, all suggest the

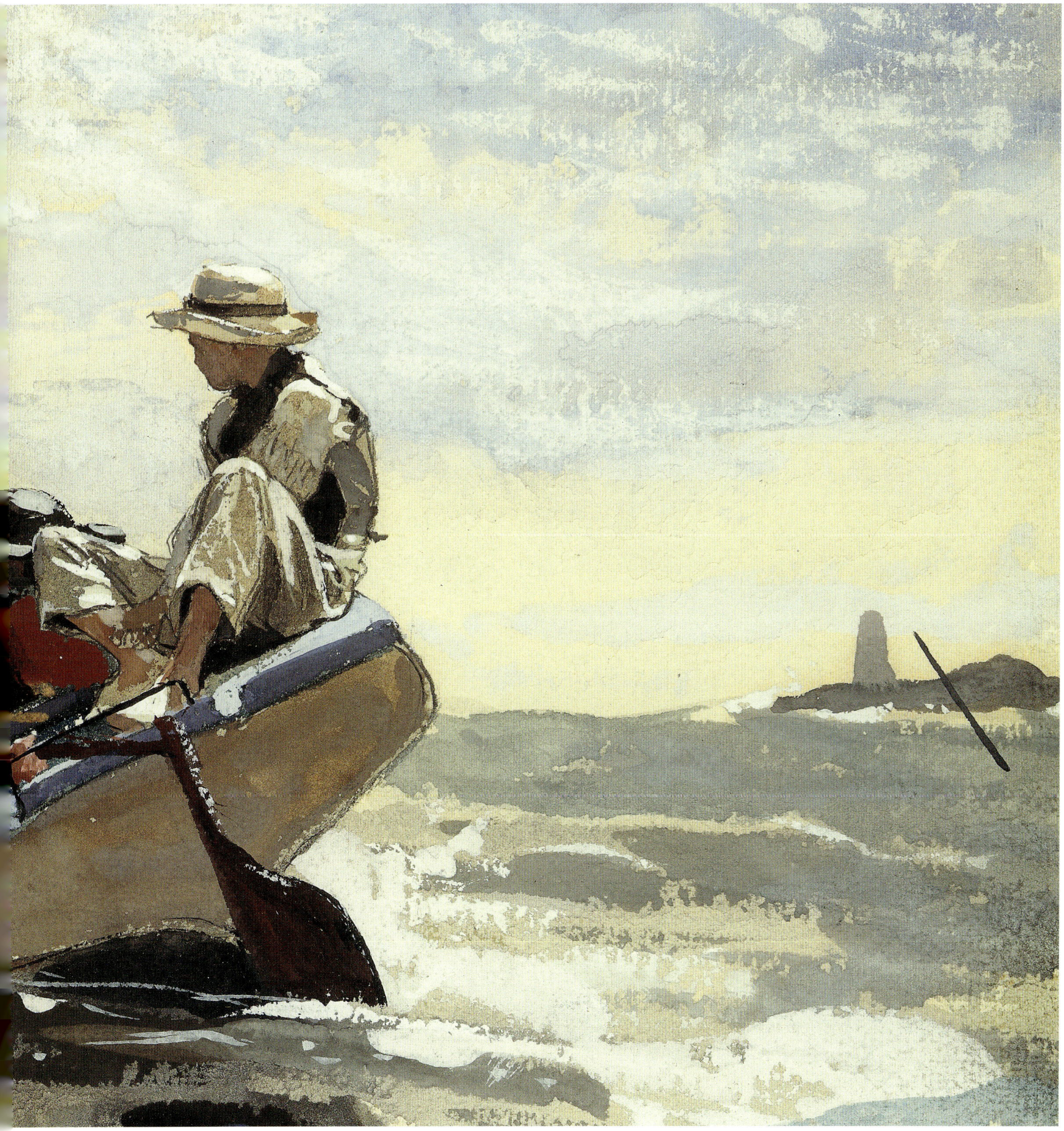

influence of Japanese art that was much in vogue in these years on both sides of the Atlantic. The rectilinear grid of the pier that fills the foreground of *In Charge of Baby*—emphasizing two-dimensional design at the expense of a fully realized illusion of three-dimensional space—likewise recalls the daring contrasts and collapsing perspective used to such great effect by Japanese printmakers like Hiroshige and Hokusai, artists who had an enormous impact as well on the evolution of Impressionism. In works like these, Homer showed himself to be as willing to experiment and as open to non-Western influences as his European colleagues. Despite their distinctly American flavor, *Sailing the Catboat* and *In Charge of Baby* come remarkably close to contemporary works by Manet, Degas, and Whistler.

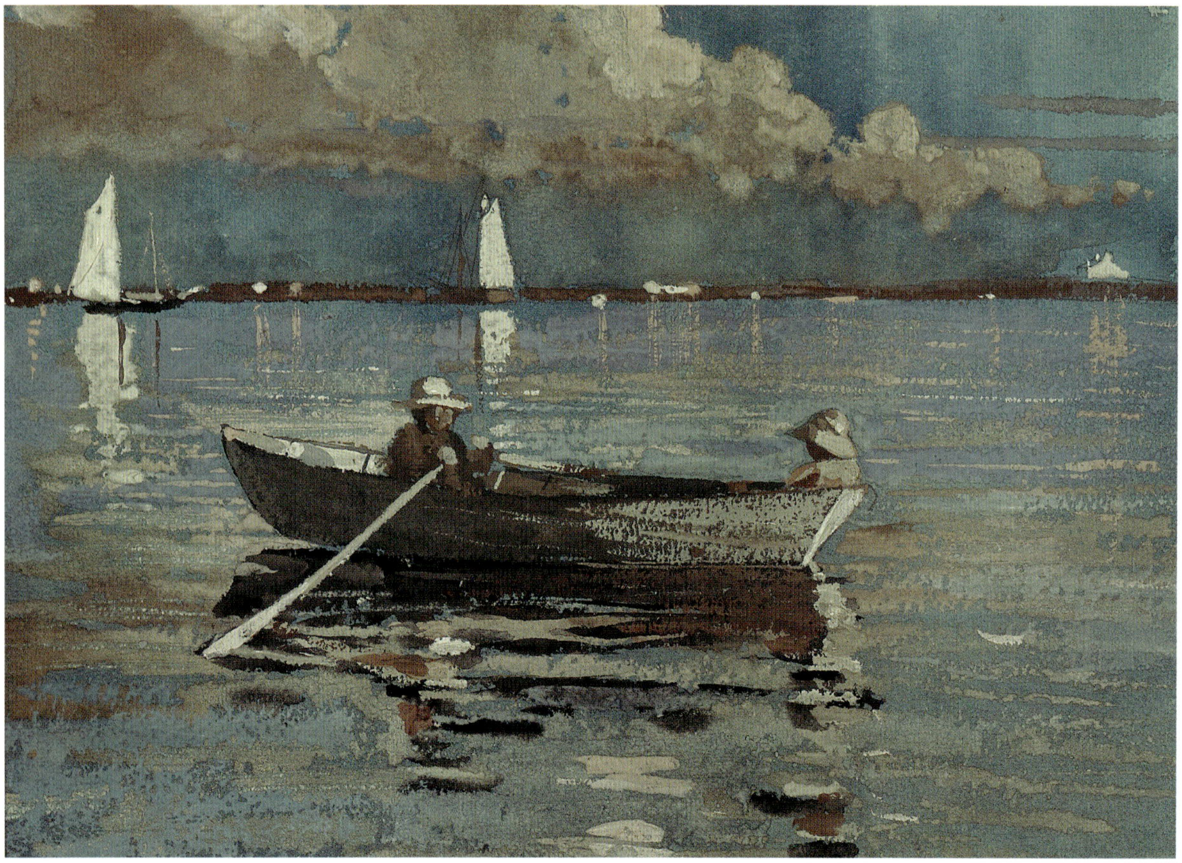

GLOUCESTER HARBOR 1873

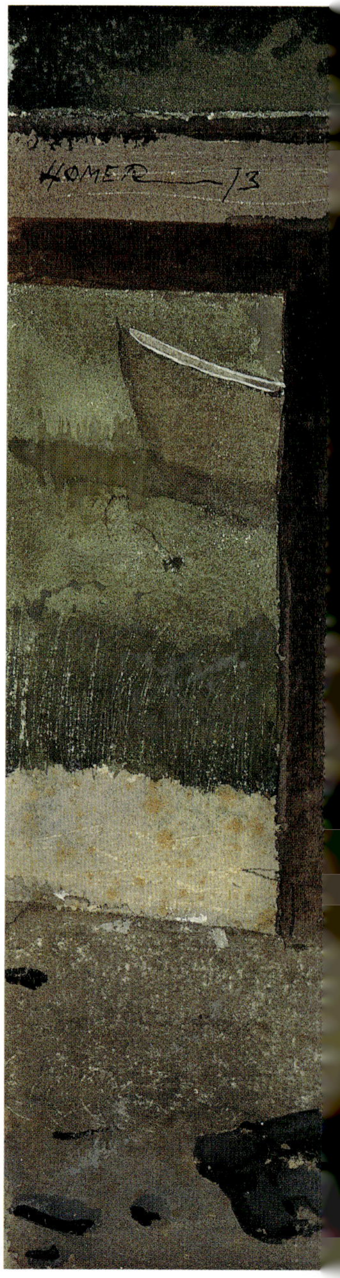

IN CHARGE OF BABY 1873

The Gloucester sojourn of the summer of 1873 was the first of many working vacations in which Homer produced a body of watercolors associated with a particular time and place. Throughout his life, these frequent trips served as a means of relaxation and an opportunity to gather new material for his art. Though he sometimes completed his more ambitious watercolors in the studio far from the original scene, they are intimately linked to his travels and capture the distinctive flavor of the locale that inspired them.

This summer also marked Homer's deepening involvement with the sea as a subject for his art. Many of his magazine illustrations depict the popular oceanside resorts of the day (see p. 69), as do a few of his early oil paintings, but these watercolors are the first works of art to explore in a concerted way the distinctive rhythms and atmosphere of the sea and the lives of the people along its shore. His focus has shifted in the watercolors from the oceanside resort to the working fishing port. In picturing the world of children Homer avoids confronting some of the harsh realities of the seafaring life, but even as these boys and girls clamber amid the rocks and dunes he intimates that their fate is tied to the unpredictable sea.

The ocean for Homer was the inspiration for his deepest meditations about mankind's place in the universe. And while the scene in these early watercolors seems relatively benign, there are hints of stormier weather to come. These light-filled images of sea and strand represent Homer's first bold foray into a territory that he will ultimately claim as his own undisputed domain.

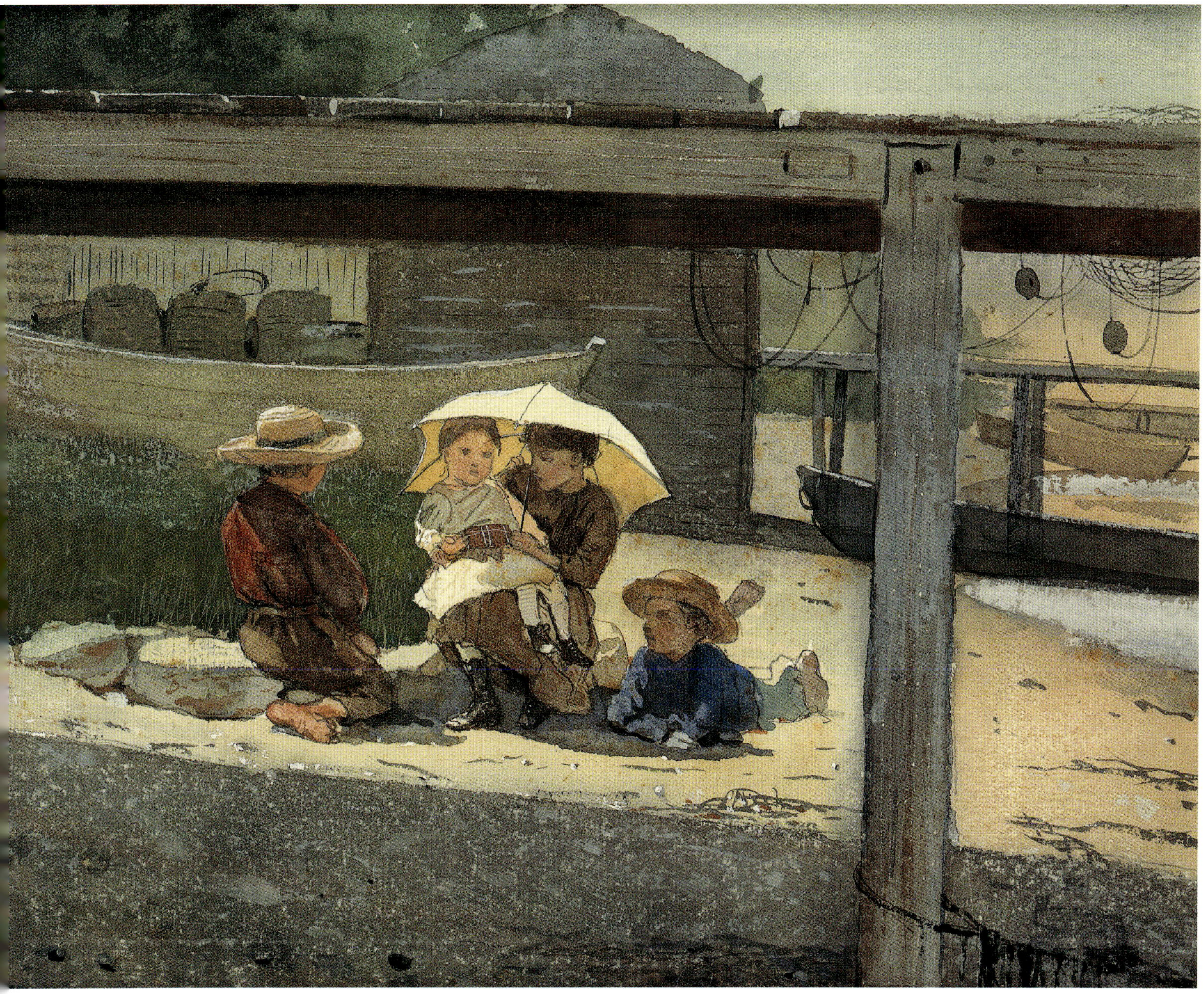

FEEDING TIME 1878

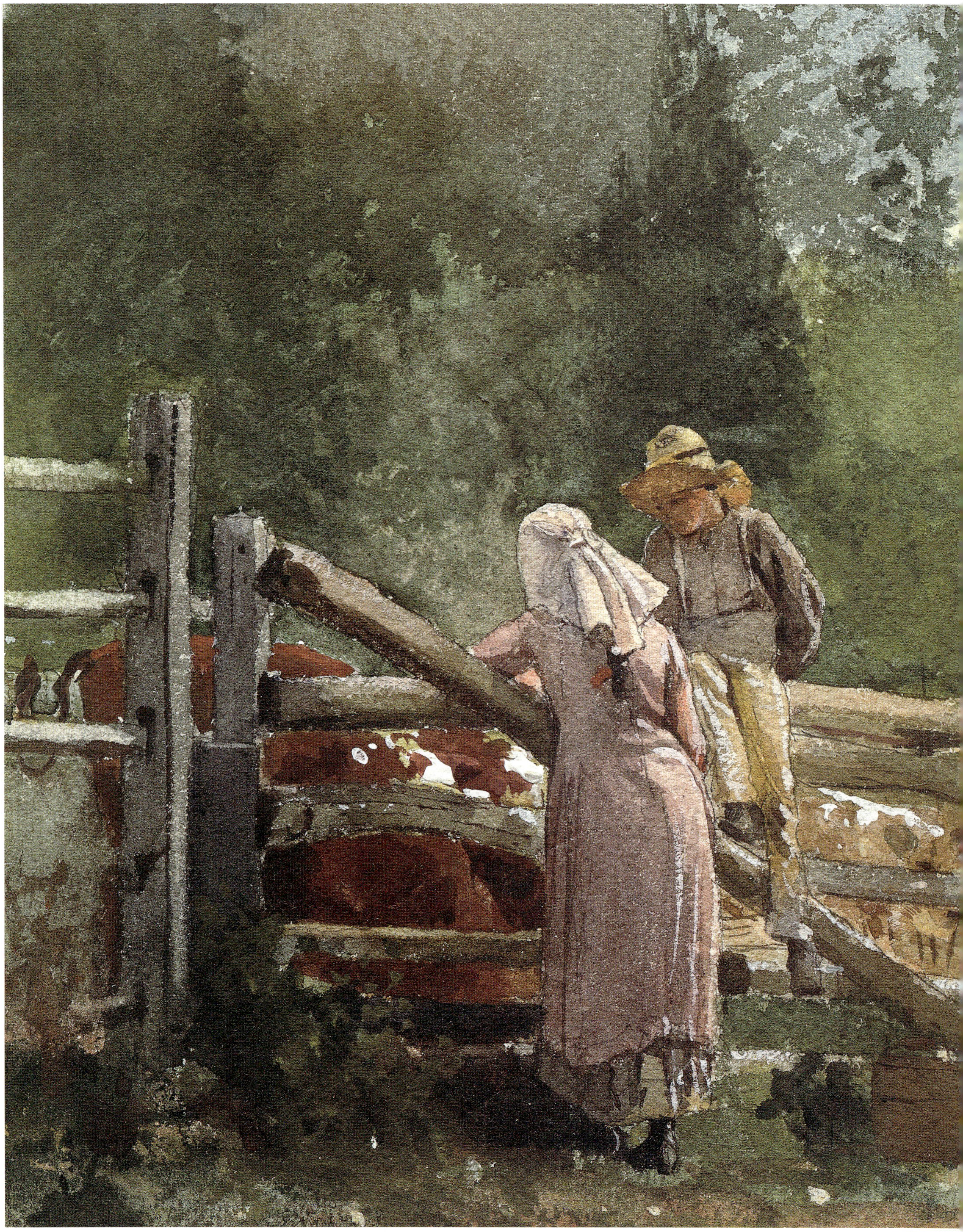

II.
Rustic Idyll: Upstate New York, Virginia, 1874–1878

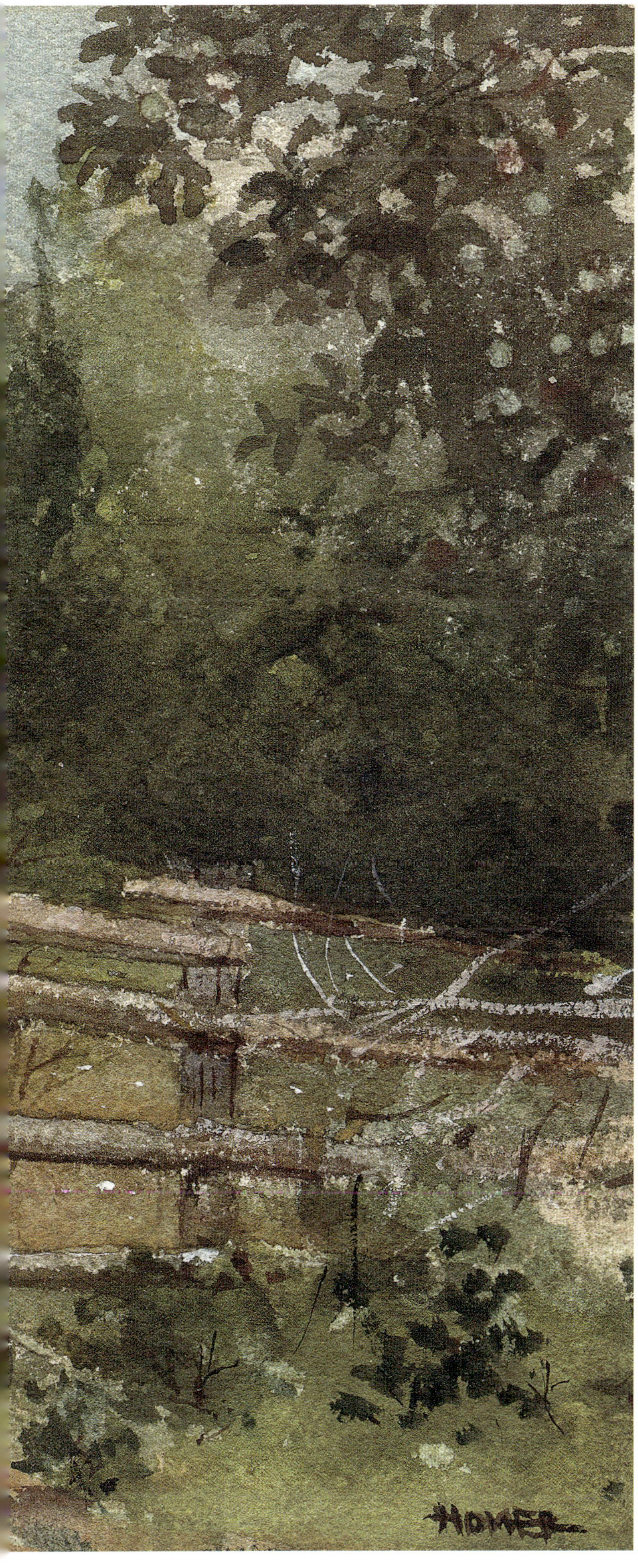

Scenes of rural childhood dominate the artist's work from the 1870s. This is the subject of his watercolors populated with rustic lads and lasses, shepherds and shepherdesses, and also of such famous oil paintings of the time as *Snap the Whip* [p. 19], *Crossing the Pasture*, and *The Nooning*. In depicting this world of youthful games and lazy summer afternoons, Homer was entirely in step with contemporary taste. These paintings were made just as Mark Twain was completing *The Adventures of Tom Sawyer* and Louisa May Alcott was enjoying her first great success with *Little Women*. Scenes of childhood struck a reassuring note at a time when the wounds of war had yet to heal and as the rapid changes brought about by industrialization meant that many Americans looked to the future with anxiety and to the past with longing.

As Twain did in his writing, Homer adopted in his paintings a distinctly vernacular idiom. Not only are the themes rustic but the manner of painting them is rough; these are paintings dressed in homespun wool rather than fancy silk. Homer's depictions of one-room schoolhouses and shepherd girls tending their flocks are not factual documents of rural scenery but emblems of a way of life under siege by the forces of modernity.

The paintings of this period are imbued with feelings of nostalgia. Some of Homer's shepherd girls, like the one pictured in *Fresh Air* [p. 60], are actually dressed in eighteenth-century garb, actors in a costume drama celebrating simpler times. These sentimental works demonstrate how difficult it is to pin the realist label on Homer. He was but one of many artists of the time participating in the genre of the rustic idyll, a paean to the rural way of life that goes back at least as far as the writings of the Roman poet Virgil. Eastman Johnson's *The Old Stage Coach* [p. 19], at the time perhaps the most celebrated American work to depict rural childhood, follows a similar formula. Commenting on this work, a critic's words in the *New York Evening Post* could apply equally to Homer's paintings: "Does not as much glee, so much pure spirit, communicate itself to our own jaded or inert being so that life springs anew, and we drink again from the pure sources of existence—childhood and summer in the country!"

As later with the regionalist painters of the 1930s, there is a distinctly nationalist message to these depictions of country life. One critic wrote of works like *Flock of Sheep, Houghton Farm* [p. 61] and *Weary* [p.57], "Here are American shepherdesses which only Mr. Homer paints—self-possessed, serious, independent; not French peasants who till the soil; not Swiss slaves who watch cows, knitting stockings meanwhile with eyes downcast; not German *frauen* . . . but free-born American women on

RUSTIC COURTSHIP 1874

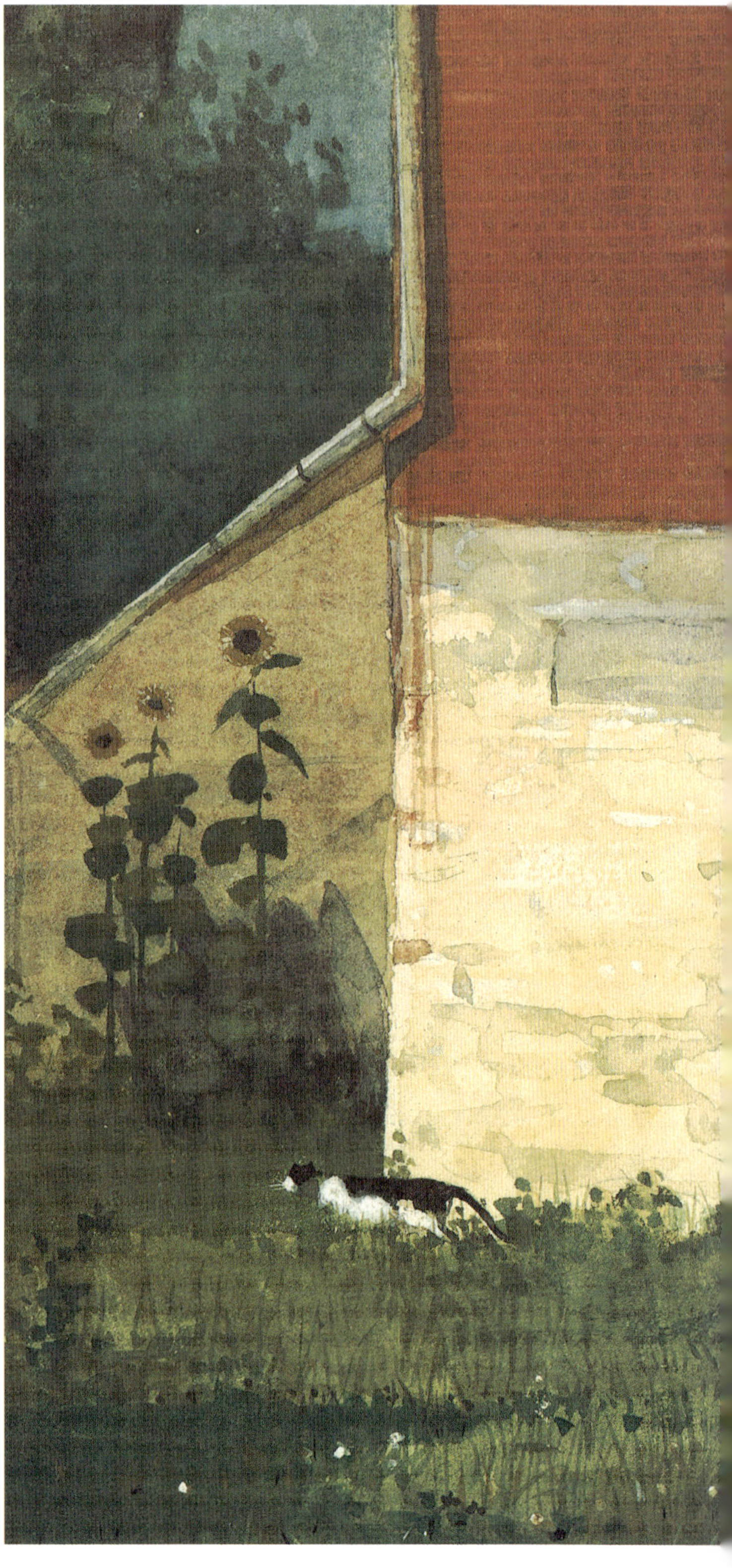

free-soil farms...." This despite the fact that Homer's watercolors of this period owe a good deal to the paintings of the French Barbizon School, whose leading lights, painters like Millet and Breton, did much to stimulate a taste for peasant genre scenes in America. The influence of these artists can be felt particularly in works like *Fresh Air* [p. 60], where the figure, viewed from a low angle so that she looms against a cloud-flecked sky, possesses a monumentality and rhetorical flourish that is more French than American.

In every time and every place, native soil inspires nationalist feeling. Homer's rustic scenes are no exception. Rural life in America, however, carried a unique set of associations. In Millet's work, the peasant was a symbol of the heroic but downtrodden underclass; for native genre painters like Homer, the simple country lad or lass was an emblem of a democratic, classless society. The religious piety of Millet is replaced by faith in a democratic system of government. Eugene Benson, a painter, writer, and friend of Homer's in the 1860s, and a figure who has been regarded as a spokesman for the artist in these years, wrote of "[t]he gospel of modern art as it must be developed in America . . . free from tradition, [and] based wholly on the common life of the democratic man, who develops his own being on a free soil, and in the midst of a vast country."

In these watercolors Homer shifts the scene from seashore to rolling countryside, but the mood is the same—largely carefree, with interludes of quiet introspection. Labor is present in these works, but it is not the harsh toil of the factories that were changing the face of America. What Homer depicted instead were pleasant chores rendered all the more delightful by being performed in the fragrant country air. Homer rarely played the role of social crusader in his art. He doesn't show us the grim face of rural poverty, preferring to dwell on the more picturesque aspects of life. These are simple folk in a land of plenty, contented and in harmony with their environment.

An 1874 stay at the Walden, New York, farm of Lawson Valentine, Charles Homer's business partner, accounts for the delightful *Fresh Eggs*, as well as the more carefully wrought *Rustic Courtship*, whose obvious narrative appeal and careful design form a link with his illustrations of the time. This flirtatious exchange between housemaid and farmhand takes on wider implications as Homer turns an amorous moment into a negotiation between

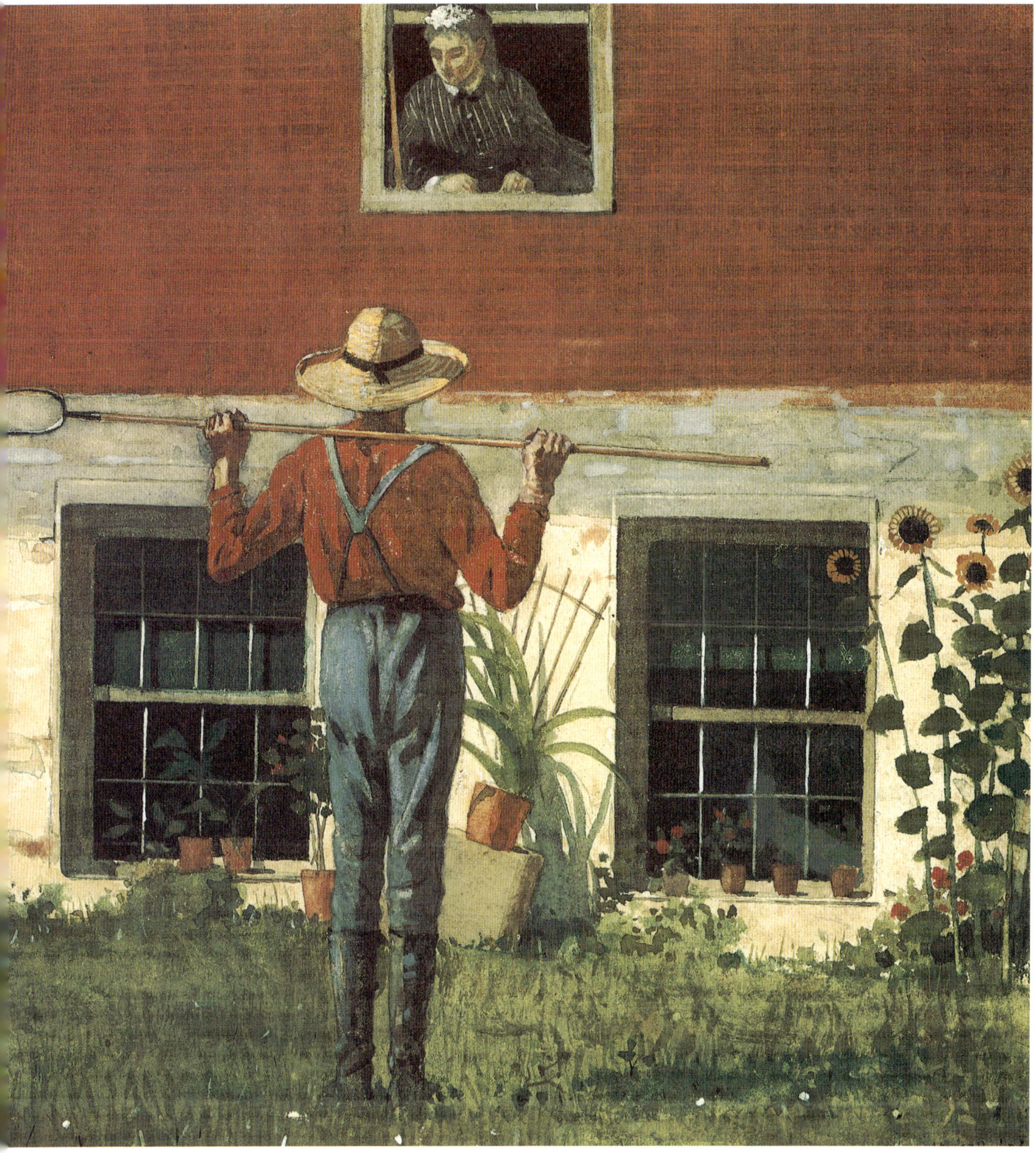

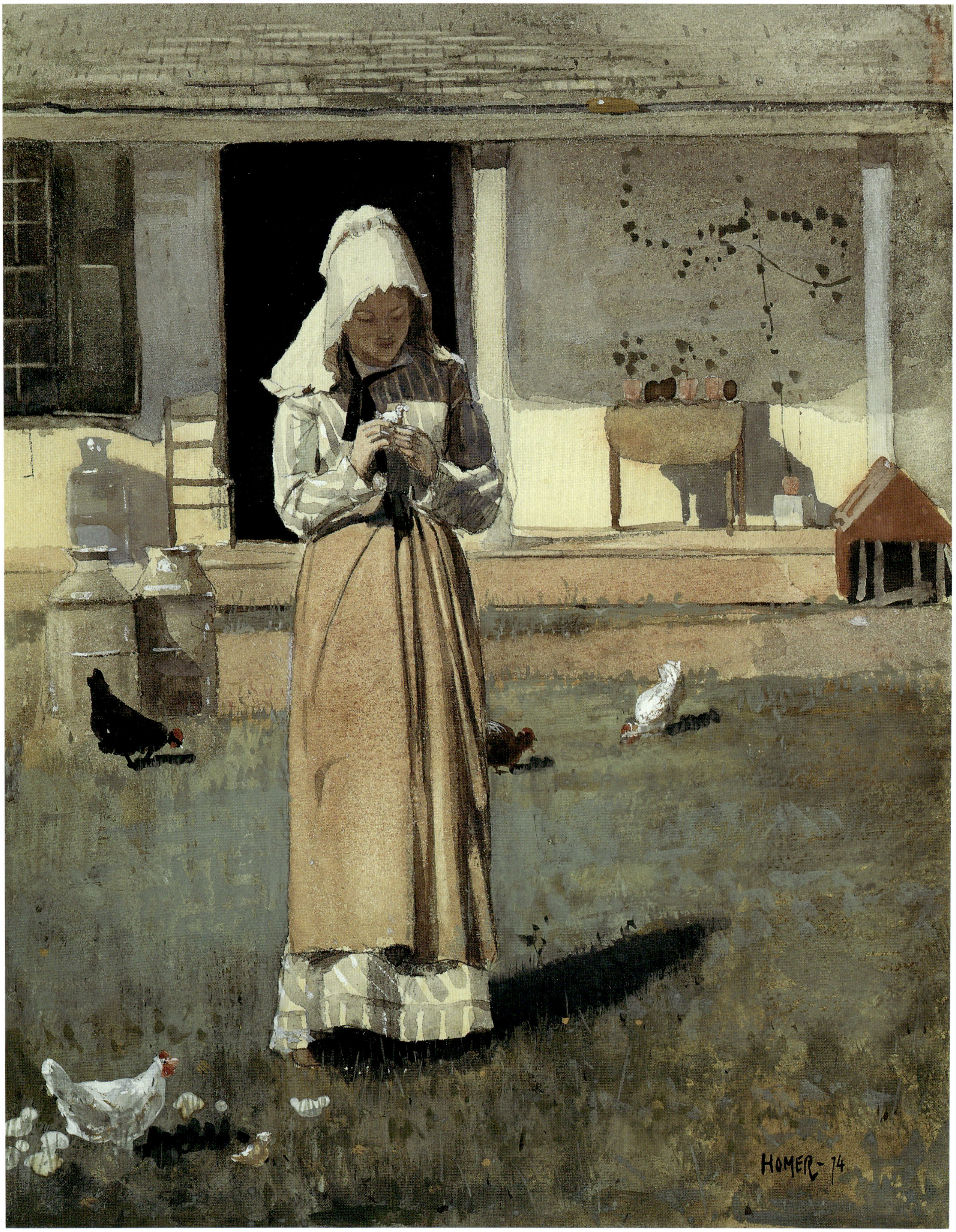

The Sick Chicken 1874

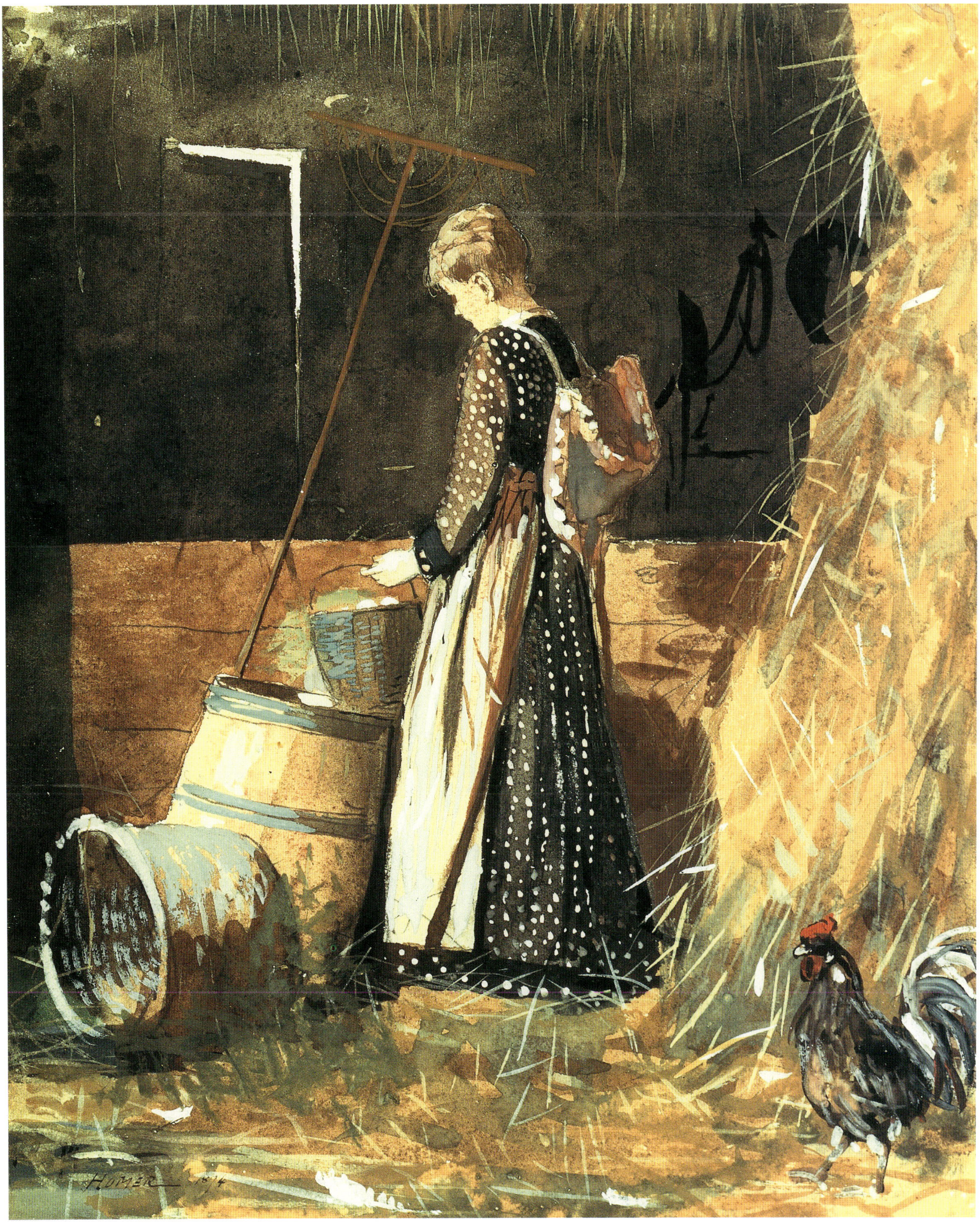

FRESH EGGS 1874

HOMEWORK 1874

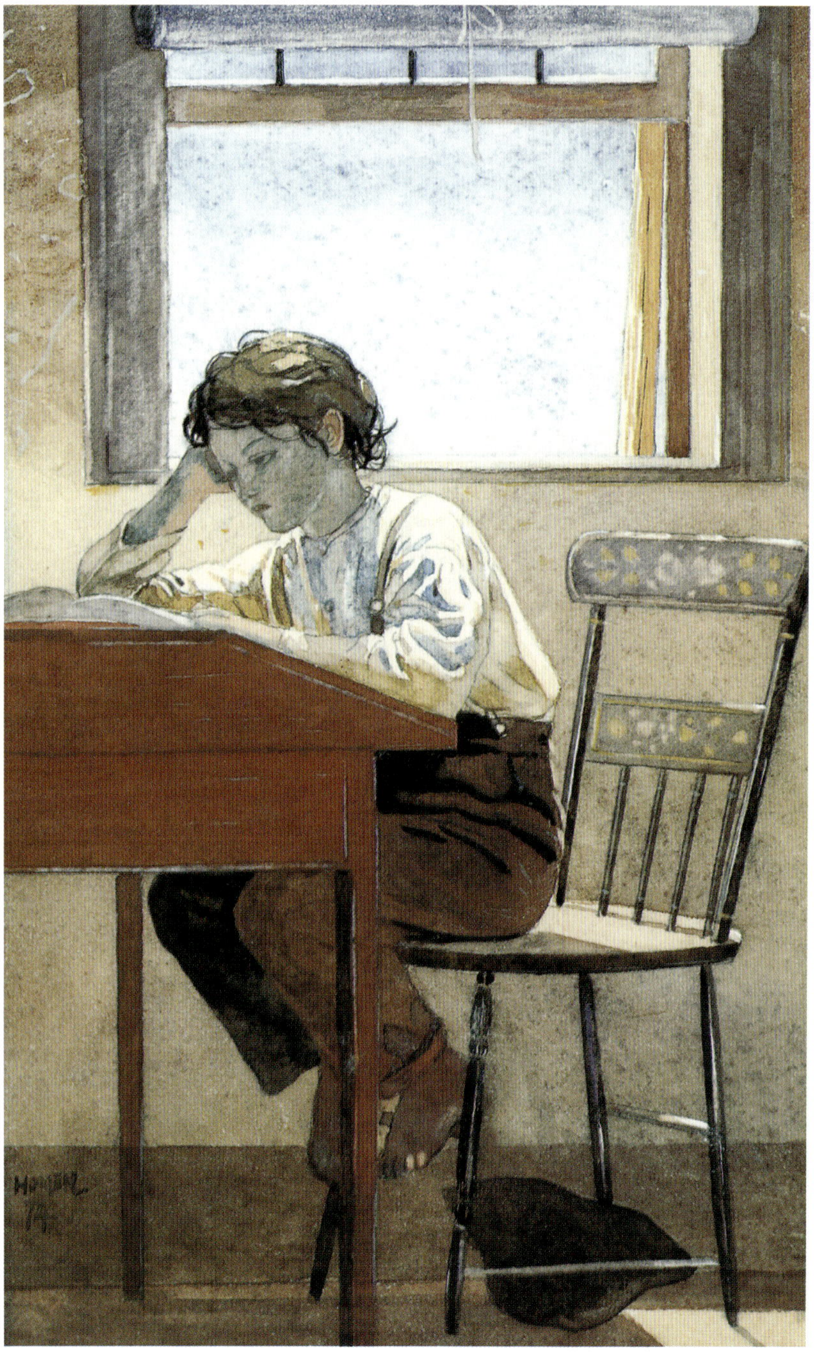

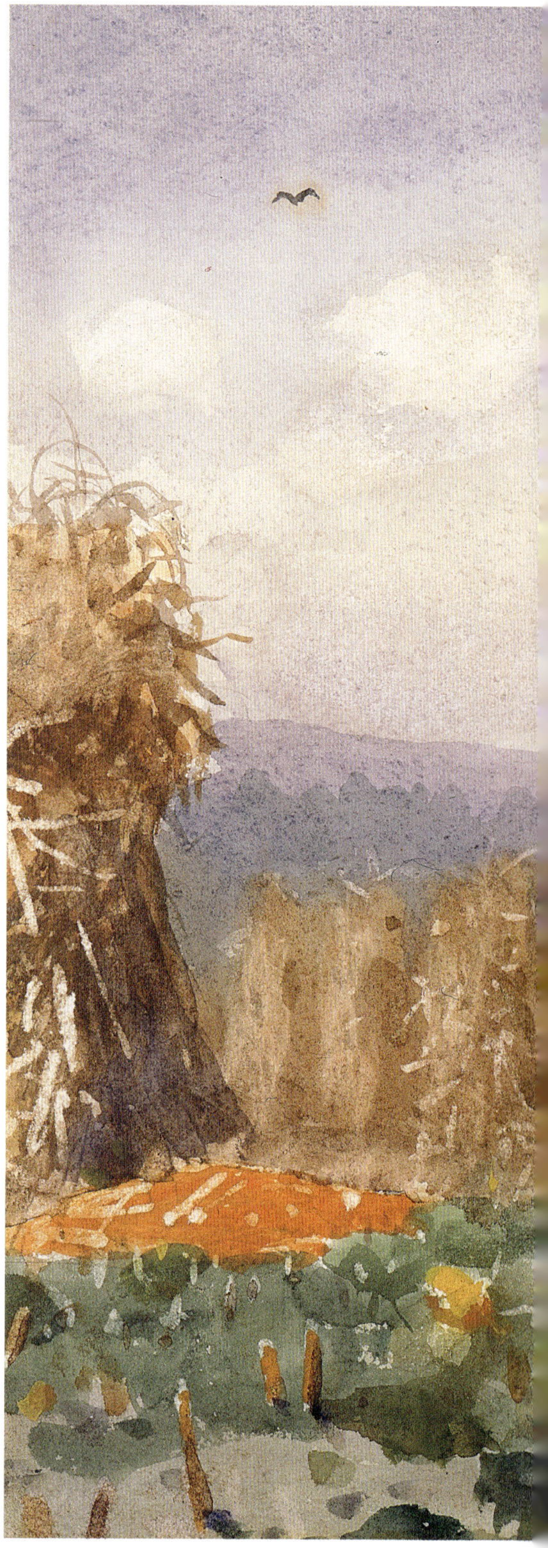

THE PUMPKIN PATCH 1878

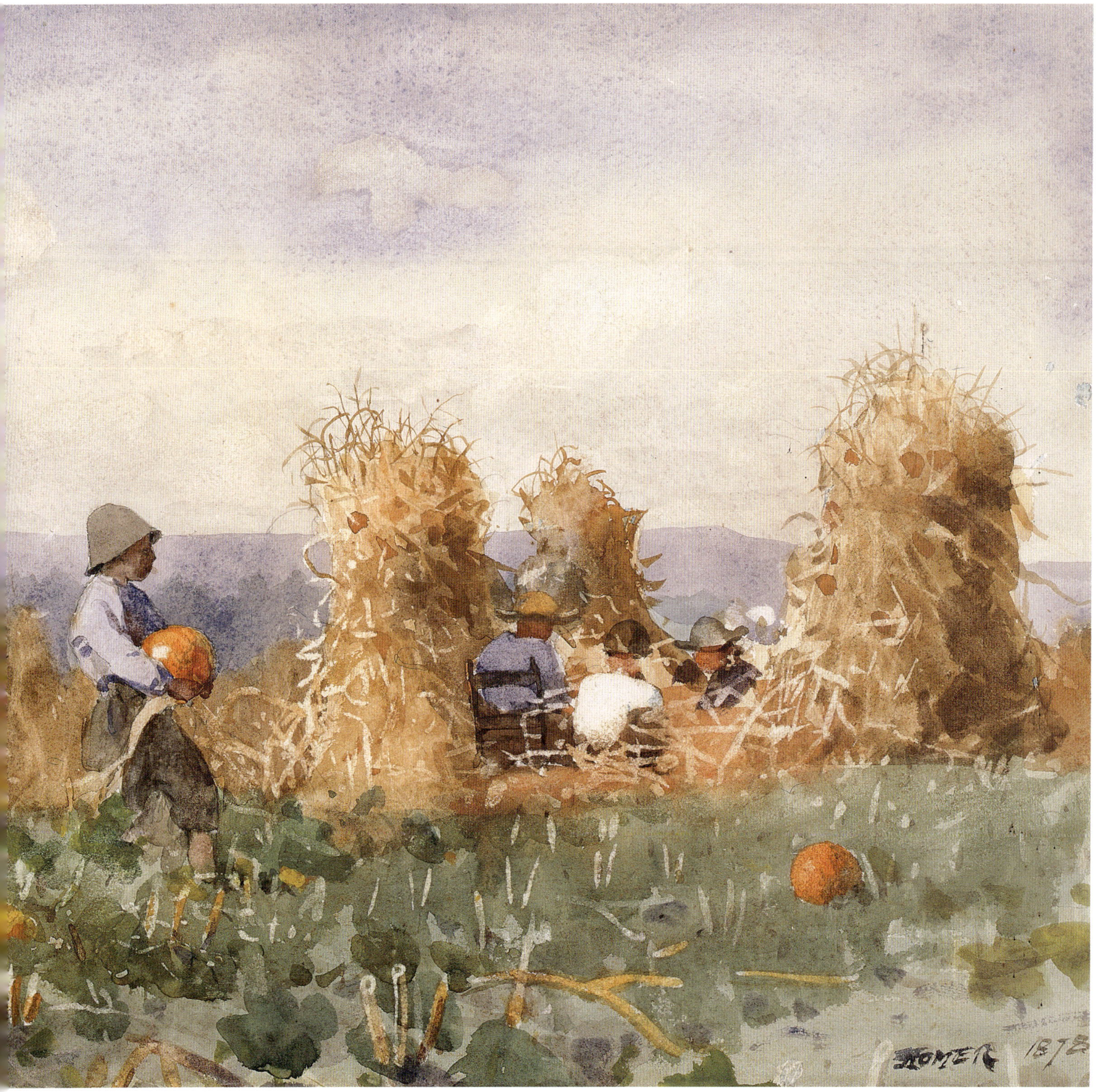

separate worlds—male and female, outdoors and indoors, rustic and genteel.

A beautiful, if inelegantly titled, work, *The Sick Chicken*, also dates to this trip. With its muted palette of browns and deft accents of white and brilliant crimson, it demonstrates Homer's sense of abstract design and consummate control of tone and color. The grid of the farmhouse porch serves, like the pier in *In Charge of Baby*, as the geometric underpinning of the composition. Homer artfully frames the girl's white bonnet in the darkened doorway, and contrasts the wedge of the red coop and round profile of the jugs with the rectilinear grid of the house. But such is the freshness of his vision that we are hardly aware of the careful planning that went into the watercolor's construction, perfectly content instead to lose ourselves in the simple charm of the scene.

Homework is a rare interior and one of the few watercolors to pick up the theme of the one-room schoolhouse that Homer treated in numerous oil paintings of the time. Here the geometry of the setting emphasizes the oppressive routine of school. In contrast to the straight-backed chair and sharp-angled desk, the barefoot boys slouches,

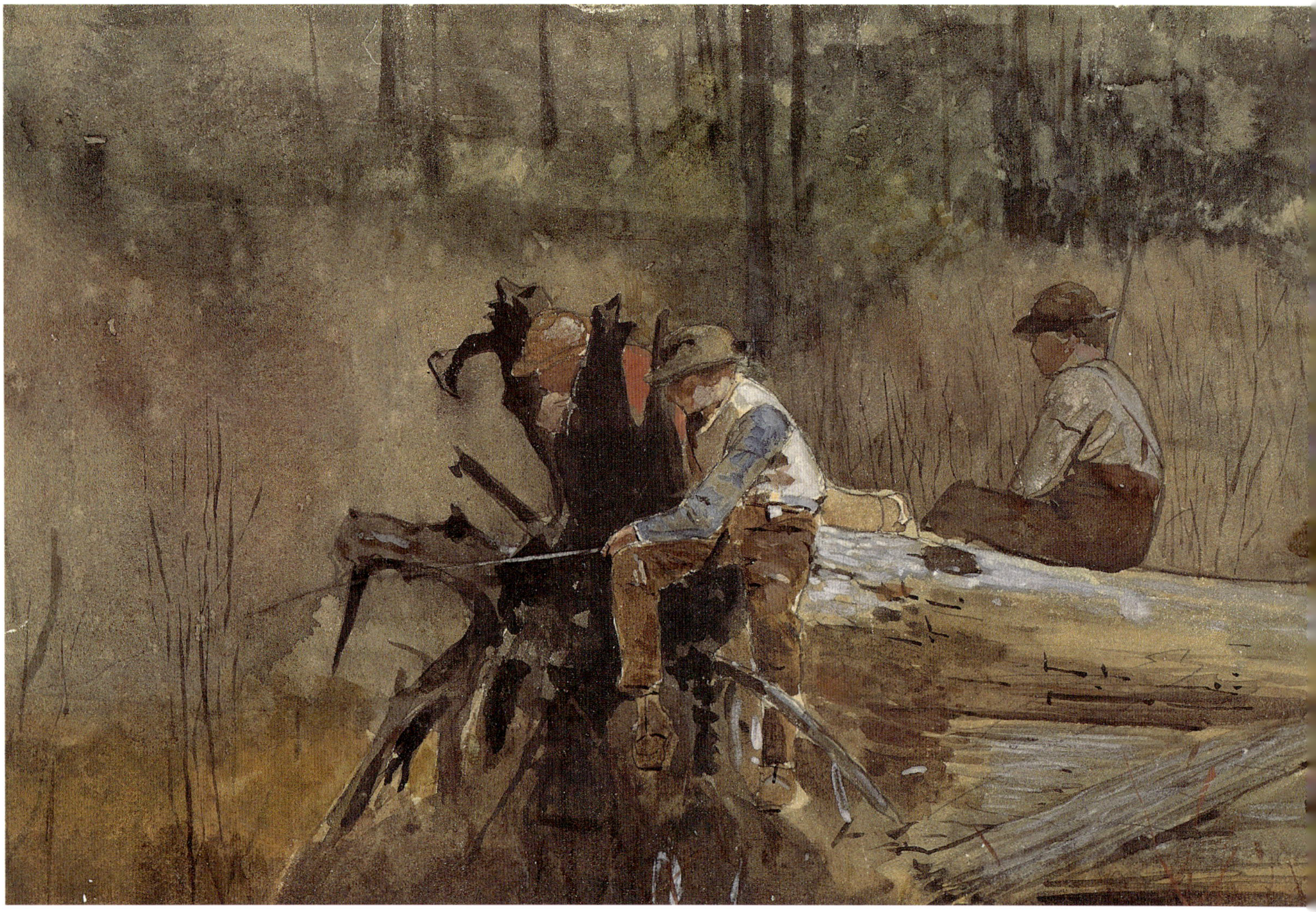

his back arched, head resting wearily on his hand. Though he dutifully faces his lesson, the open window beckons, promising freedom to come.

Even when Homer's paintings appear spontaneous, closer study often reveals an underlying order. Homer cited the importance of Chevreul's *Laws of Contrast of Color* in deepening his understanding of the uses of color harmonies and dissonances, and the influence of this treatise can be discerned in many of the early works. In *The Pumpkin Patch*, Homer wove into a tapestry of rich autumnal tones threads of brighter hue. The painting is a study in chromatic contrasts, beginning with the basic opposition between the warm browns of the dried stalks and the cool purplish hue of the overcast sky. The artist draws out this theme and variation in bolder contrasts: between the glistening orange skin of the pumpkins and purple shirts of the workers; and, in the foreground, a single squash set off by the green grass is a clash of complementaries that reveals his strategic deployment of opposing hues.

The watercolors *In the Garden* and *The Milkmaid* [pp. 58–59] reveal Homer's tendency at this stage of his career to reuse identical figures and motifs in a variety of different settings. *In the Garden* shows a girl in a pink flowered dress and dark collar seen from the back. *The Milkmaid* shows the same girl seen from the front and in a new setting. The addition of a couple of props and a change in setting drastically alters the meaning of the original: the dreamy girl lost in thought among the flowers has become a sturdy country lass, though she still retains something of the original's mysterious, otherworldly air.

What troubled Homer's contemporaries more than this recycling, and was to them a surer sign of slovenliness, was his apparently slapdash manner of painting. Some approved of his methods, one critic explaining that "Mr. Homer's subjects are such that elaborate finish would be out of place"; others dismissed these watercolors as "art stenography." Even his admirers urged him to bring a higher degreee of finish to what were held to be "mere sketches."

Still others took him to task for the crudeness of his subjects. Henry James, in an early review of Homer's work, deplored his "barren plank fences, his glaring, bald blue skies, his big, dreary vacant lots of meadows, his freckled straight-haired Yankee urchins, his flat-breasted maidens, suggestive of a dish of rural doughnuts and pie, his calico sun-bonnets, his flannel shirts, his cow-hide boots." James continues in a vein that pays grudging respect to Homer's evident virtues while revealing the European

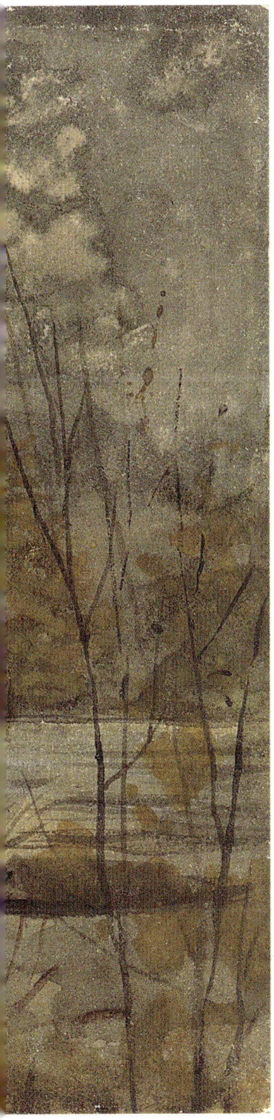

WAITING FOR A BITE c 1874

WAITING FOR A BITE 1874

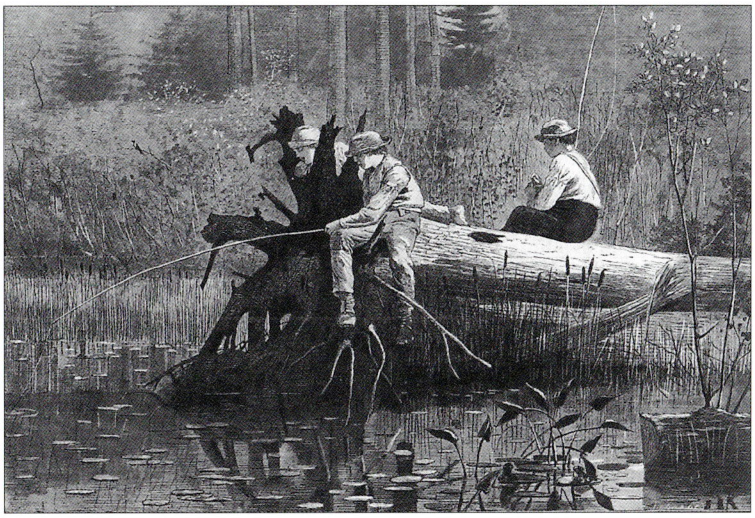

MAN IN A PUNT, FISHING 1874

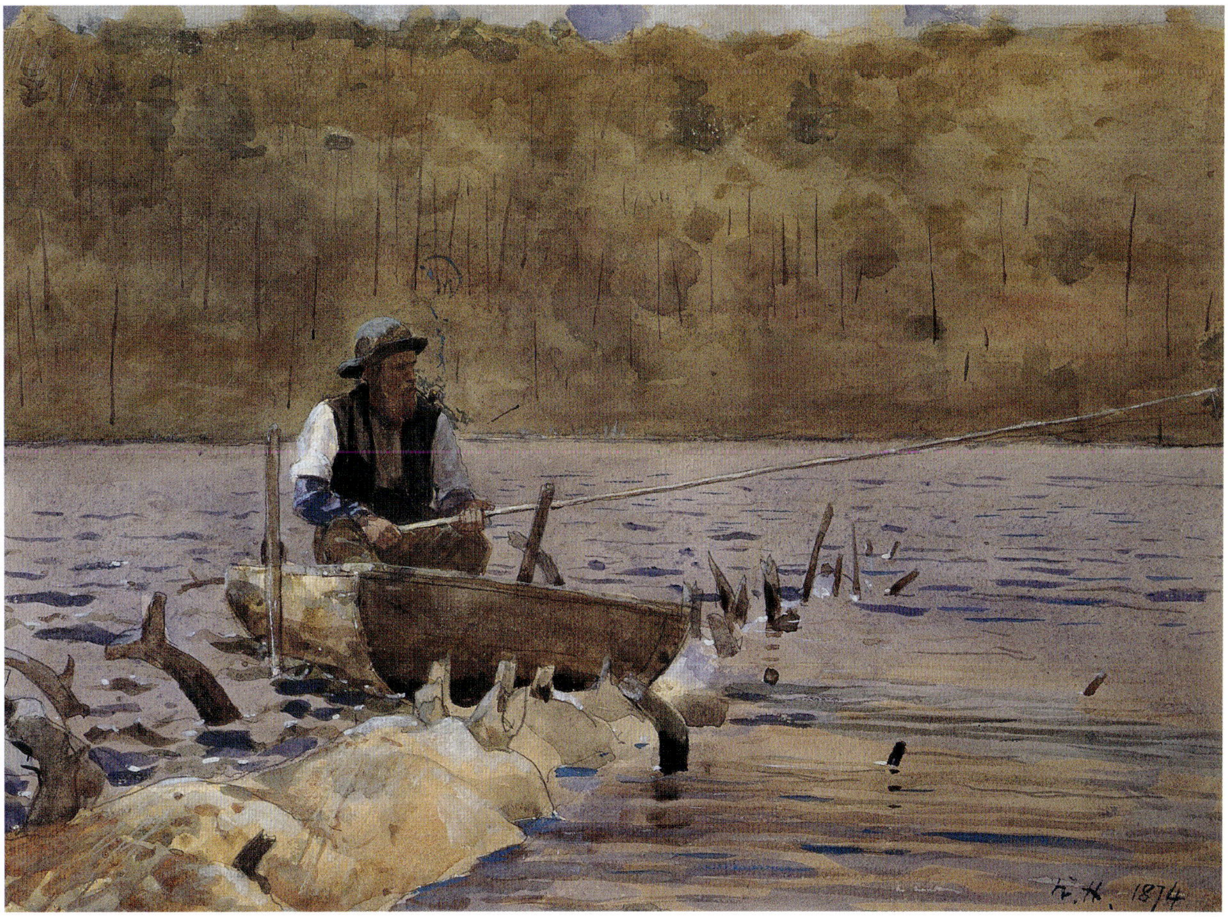

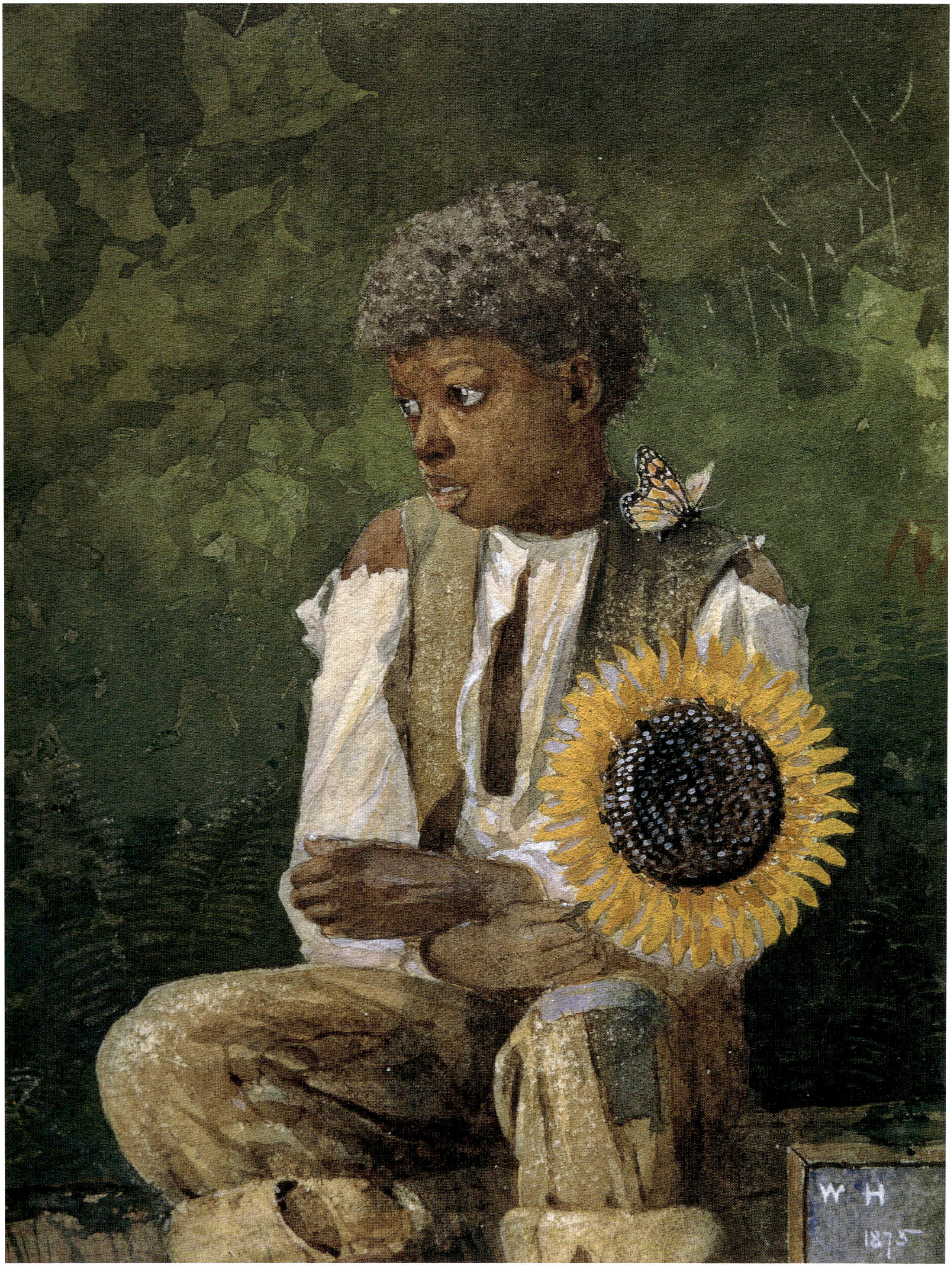

Taking a Sunflower to the teacher 1875

bias of much of the cultural elite at this time: "He has chosen the least pictorial features of the least pictorial range of scenery and civilization; he has resolutely treated them as if they *were* pictorial, as if they were every inch as good as Capri and Tangiers; and, to reward his audacity, he has incontestably succeeded."

James's comments reflect a cultural rift between those who looked to Europe for cultural guidance and those who wished to promote a native school with its own distinctive language that could speak to a young, democratic nation. The contours of this debate and Homer's leading role as an exponent of the native school are reflected in an 1877 review in the *New York Evening Post*: "Winslow Homer and Eastman Johnson . . . deserve mention, because of conscientious endeavors in a right direction, because of efforts impelled by a desire to render picturesque, not only the natural features, but also the life of our country, by portraying its incidents and their surroundings. These artists prove to us . . . better than many others, perhaps, that such scenes are capable of being rendered equally interesting with scenes from German, French, Italian or Spanish life. . . ." The debate over whether American artists should look to Europe for inspiration or consciously strive to develop a native genre has been a permanent feature of U.S. culture, but it was particularly acute in the decades following the Civil War. The ebb and flow of this argument had profound consequences for Homer, caught as he was between his instinct for native realism and a public that often clamored for works that spoke in a more refined, cosmopolitan tongue.

Sometime in the mid-1870s Homer took a trip to Virginia that served as the inspiration for a number of oils and watercolors depicting the lives of southern blacks. This subject—which he elaborated more fully in his oil paintings of the time— was natural for any artist whose mission was to record the rich variety of American life. At

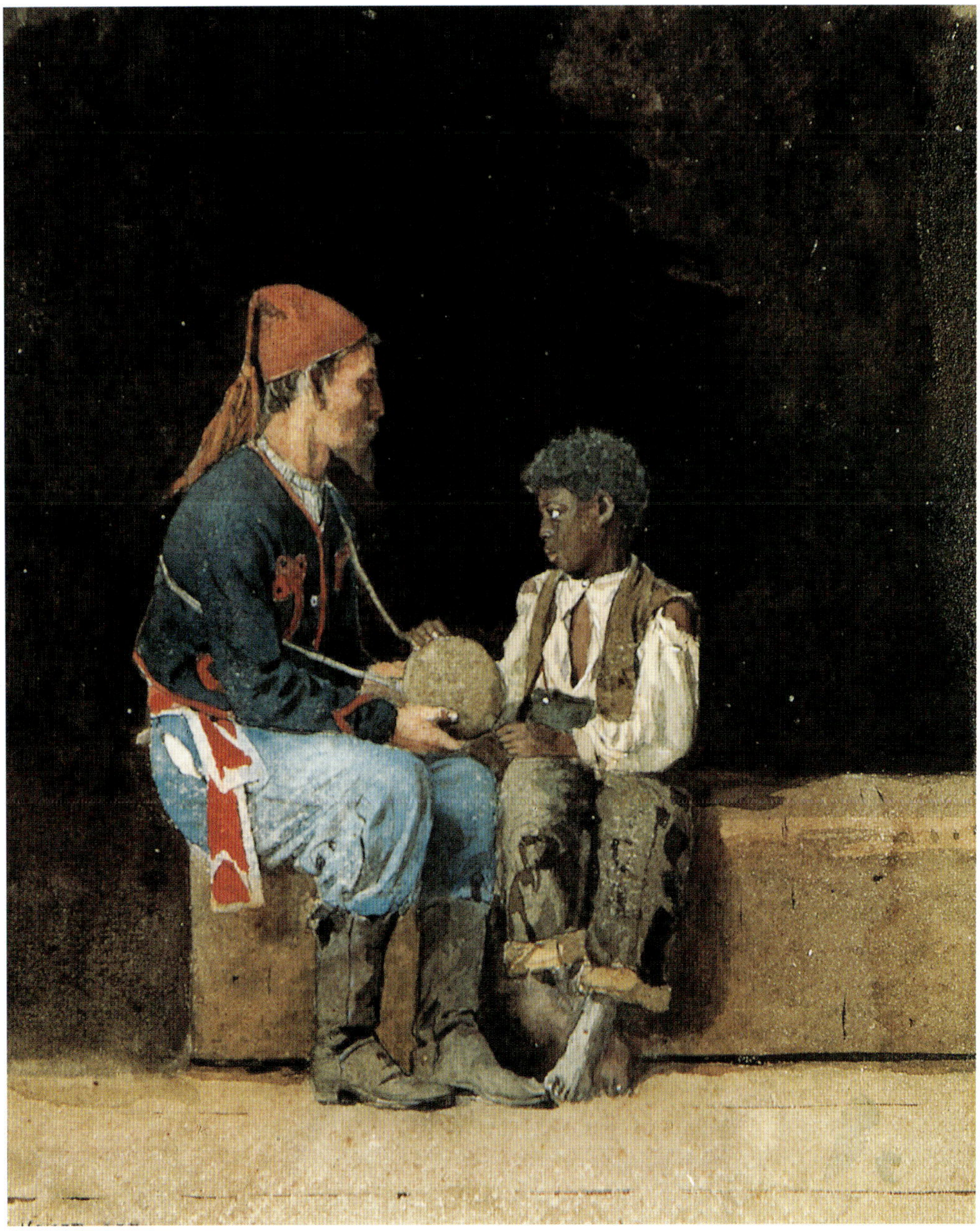

CONTRABAND 1875

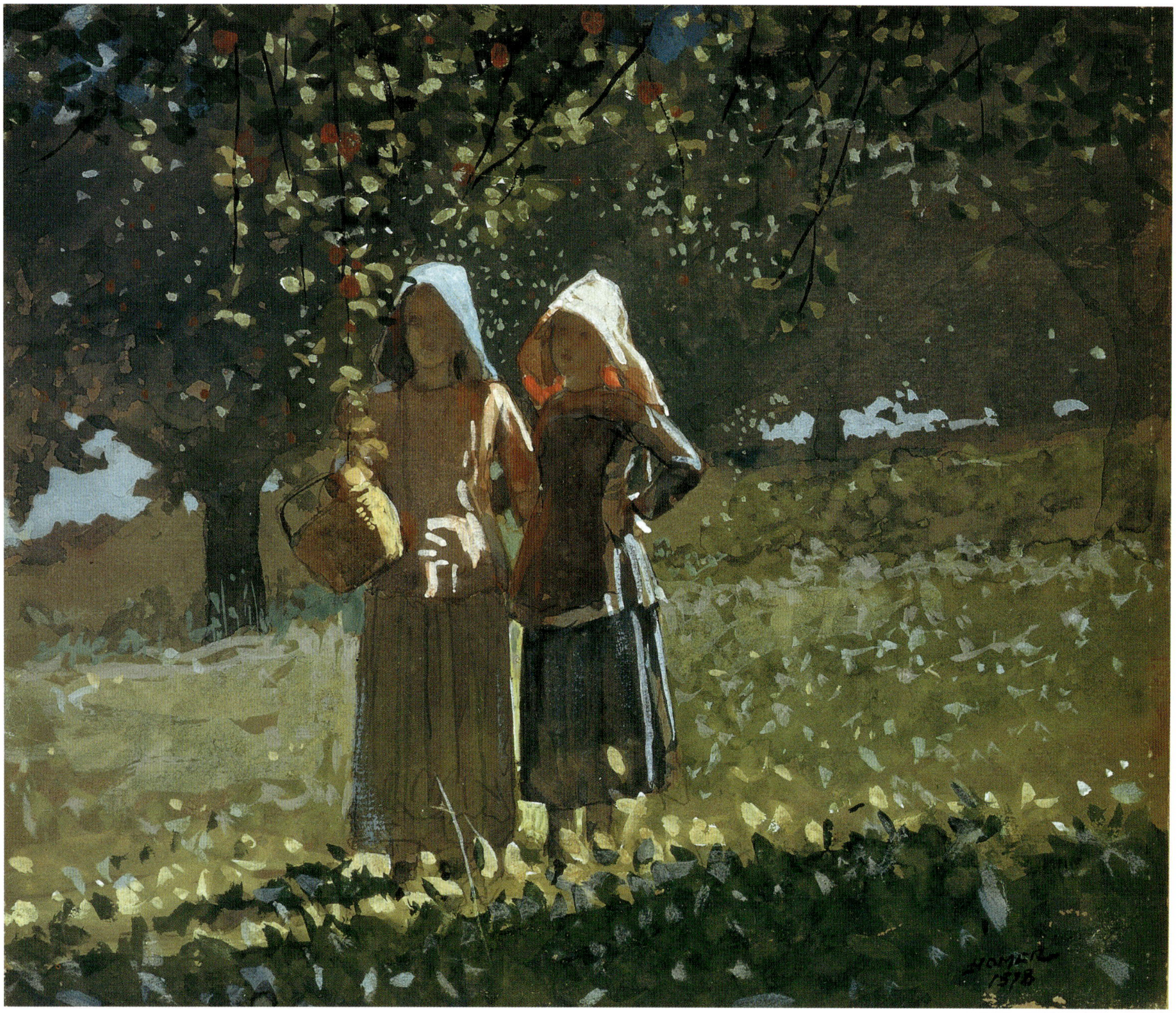

least three watercolors, including *The Busy Bee*, *Contraband*, and *Taking a Sunflower to the Teacher*, depict the same young boy and appear to be studio concoctions that recall rather than record that earlier trip. Though the position of African Americans in southern society was still very much at issue in these years—Reconstruction officially came to an end in 1877—Homer's watercolors largely avoided overt social commentary, stressing simple pleasures and rural charm. Homer seemed to feel that oil painting was the appropriate medium in which to address the larger political and social issues of the day, which he did in works like *Sunday Morning in Virginia* (1876), dealing with the issue of literacy among the former slaves, and *The Cotton Pickers* [p. 18] Even here, however, the tone is largely sentimental rather than confrontational. The exception among the watercolors is *Contraband*; significantly, this scene, which depicts a moment of understanding between a young black boy and a Union soldier, deals with the war many years past rather than the bitter controversies of the current moment.

But if Homer does not confront directly the wrenching issues of the day, his portrayal of African Americans is largely sympathetic and free from caricature. *Taking a Sunflower to the Teacher* presents us with a deliberately artificial design. Of more concern to the artist than the social position of his subject is the visual echo created by juxtaposing the boy's head with the dark center of the flower. The calculated artfulness of the painting is emphasized by the butterfly that alights on the boy's shoulder, repeating the yellow-black color scheme of the flower—perhaps another instance of Chevreul's influence. Homer, by focusing as in his Gloucester pictures almost exclusively on the world of children, is able to soften the harsh edges of life, even on an issue as fraught as relations between the races.

A third group of rustic watercolors stems from an

Apple Picking 1878

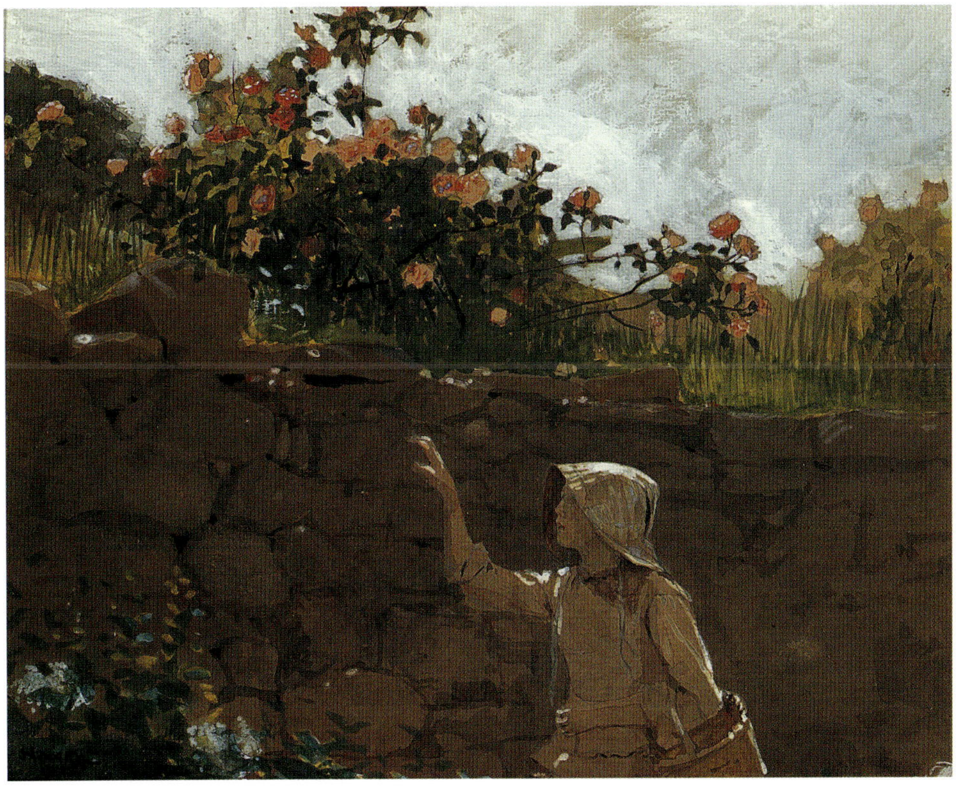

GIRL IN A GARDEN 1878

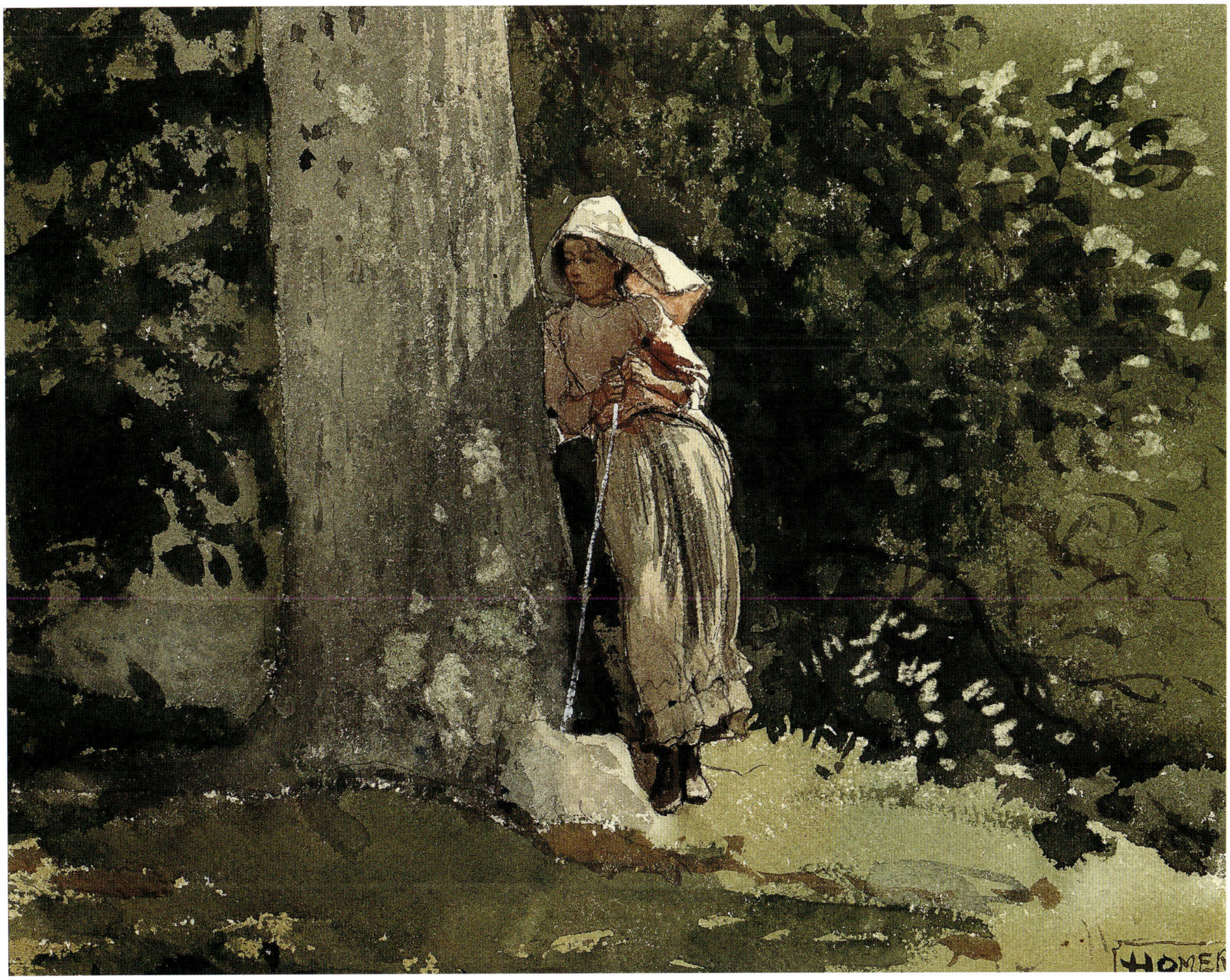

WEARY c. 1878

In the Garden 1874

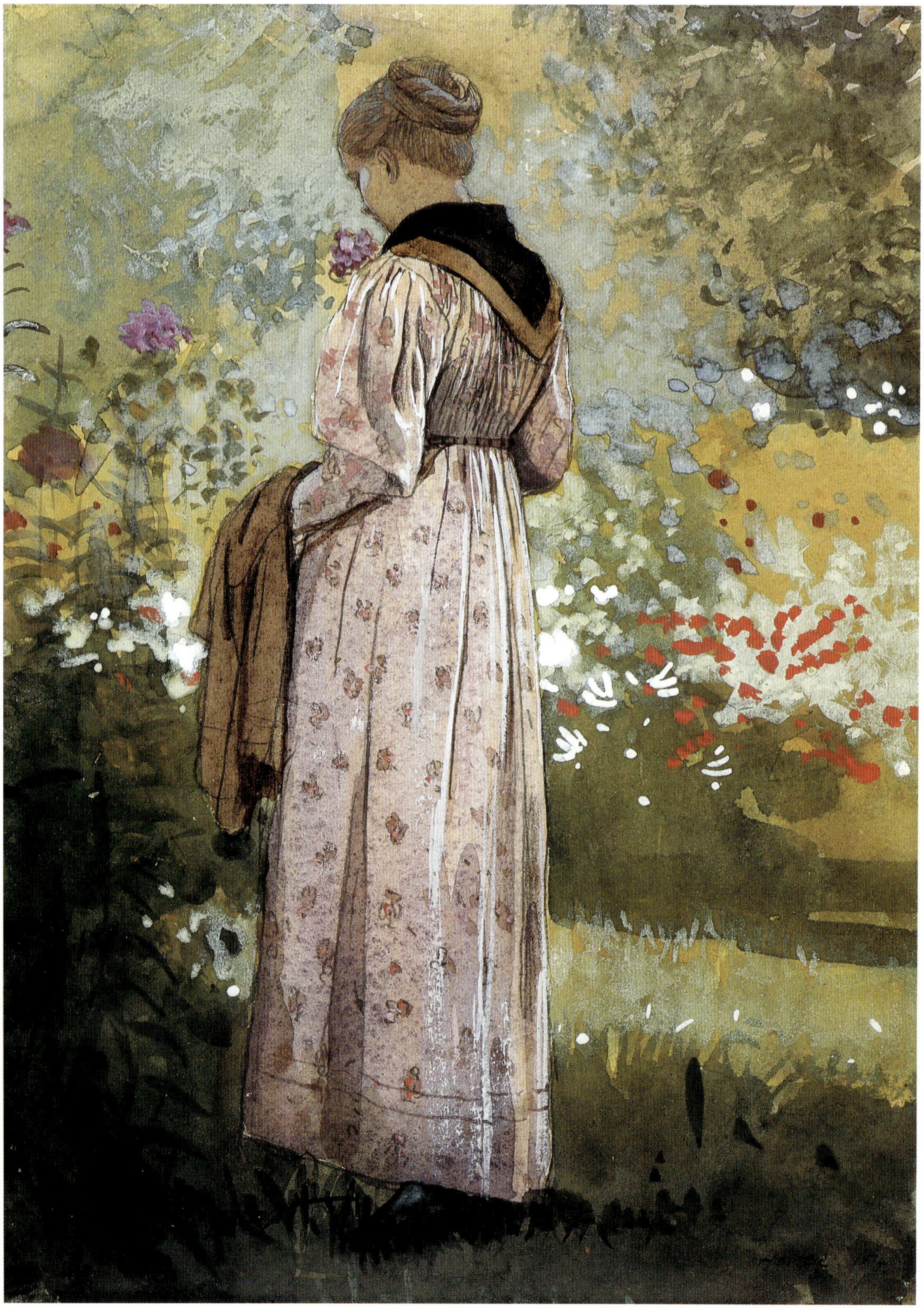

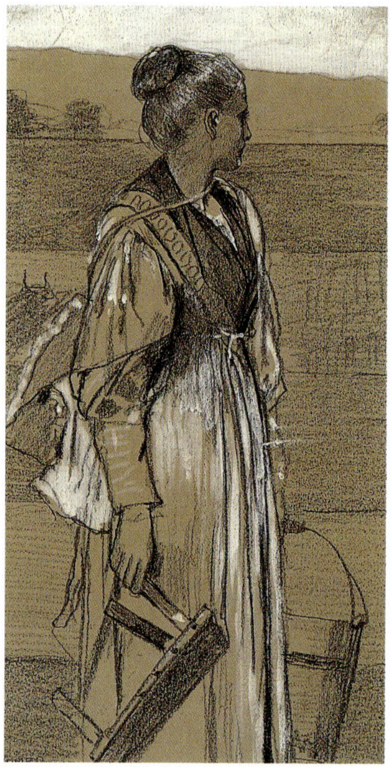

A Milkmaid 1875

The Milkmaid 1878

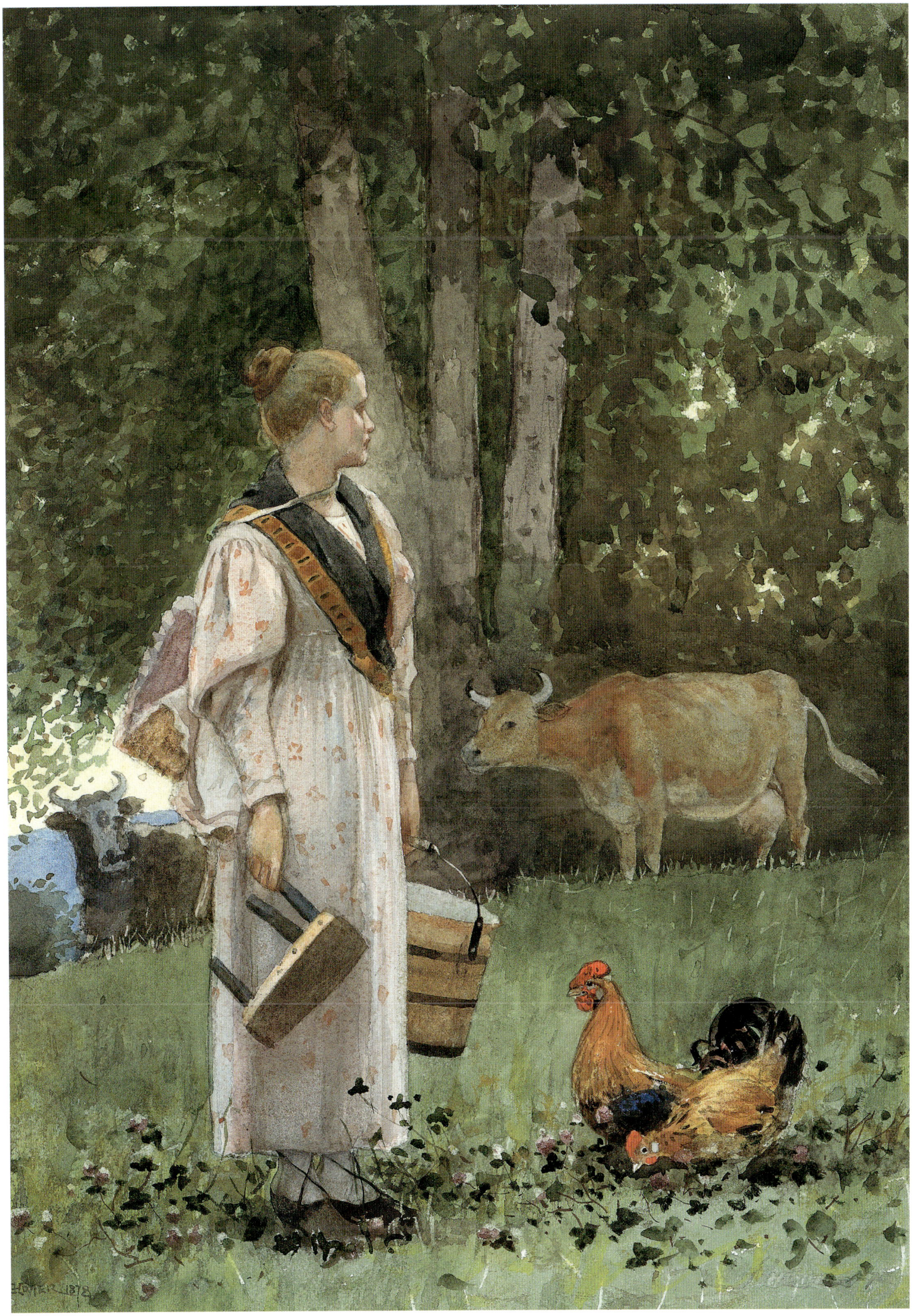

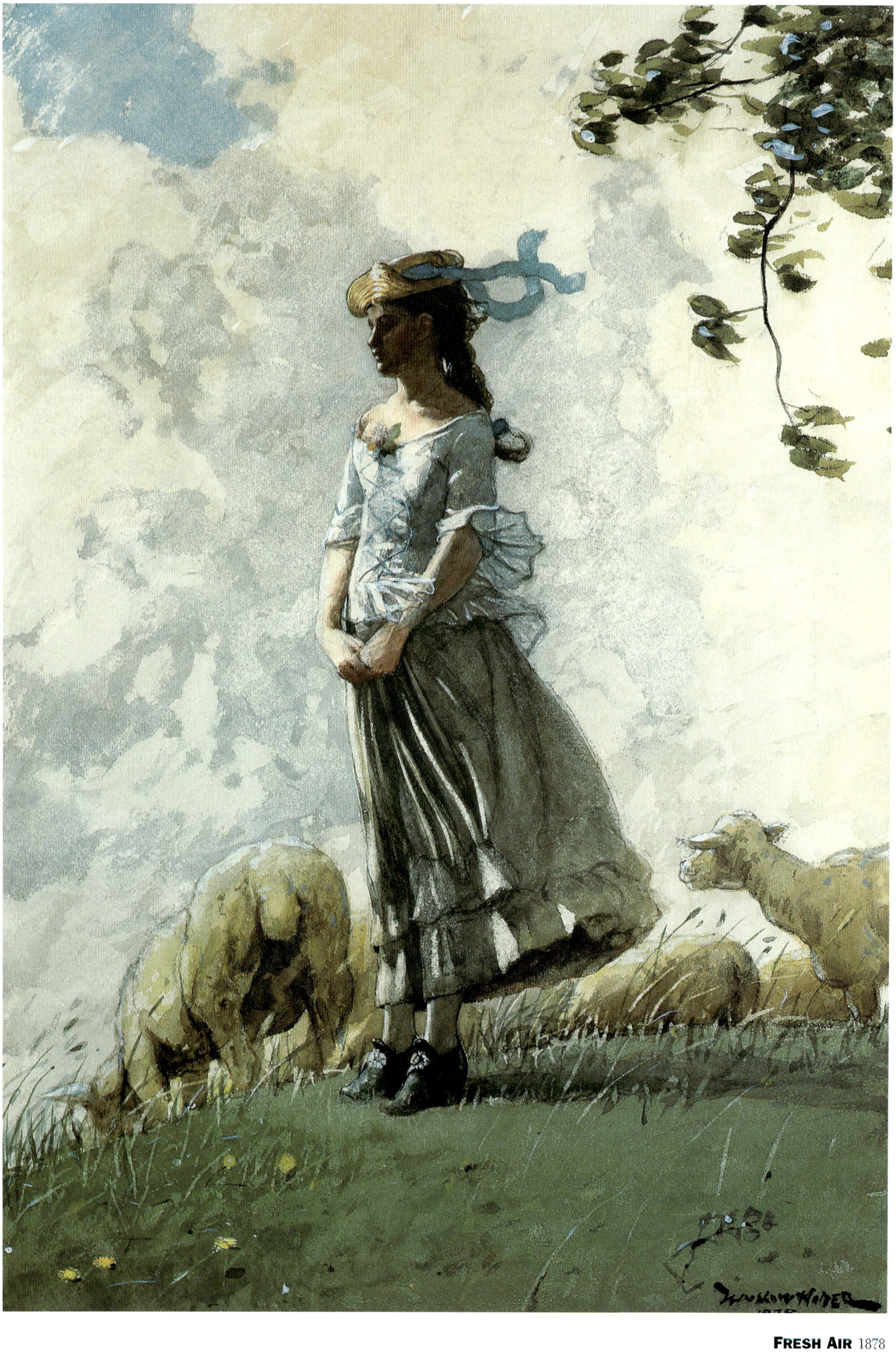

FRESH AIR 1878

1878 visit to Houghton Farm in Mountainville, New York, which Lawson Valentine had recently purchased as his country home. From this visit comes a series of watercolors depicting children in rural settings. Some, including *Apple Picking*, are painted largely in opaque gouache on tinted paper. While full of charm and impressionist sparkle, these works look backward in terms of technique. The denser pigments, created by mixing opaque Chinese white into the water-based paints, do not permit those luminous veils of color that Homer will exploit to great effect in his later works. Works that point to the future include *Flock of Sheep, Houghton Farm*; *Weary*; and *Feeding Time*. These more atmospheric watercolors were executed in transparent washes that demonstrate his increasingly confident and experimental approach to the medium.

The critic for *The New York Sun* summed up the appeal of such pastoral images: "To Mr. Homer belongs the distinction of having discovered the American shepherdess and introduced her to the public in studies that are more essentially and distinctly pastoral than anything that any American artist has yet attempted. . . . [They] convey the idea of wholesome, hearty and artless youngsters." In artless youth, embodied in these healthy rural maidens dressed in calico, most Americans saw their own national character reflected.

The pensive mood of *Flock of Sheep, Houghton Farm* recalls Gloucester paintings such as *Boy in a Boatyard* and *Waiting for the Boats*, but the rendering is even looser. The dark woods are sketched in with the only the briefest notations to indicate trunks and branches. A similar mood is evoked in *Feeding Time*, a work that reveals Homer's capacity to use mottled stains and blotches to suggest dense foliage and softly filtered light. Homer manages to convey with amazing fidelity the dappled light and shade of the verdant countryside in alternating patches of warm and cool tones—greens, roses, and pale yellows. Here, in the shade of a summer afternoon, we see nature in its most gentle guise. The looseness of the drawing and the delicacy of the paint handling contribute to the idyllic mood, part realistic scene, part Arcadian dream.

FLOCK OF SHEEP, HOUGHTON FARM 1878

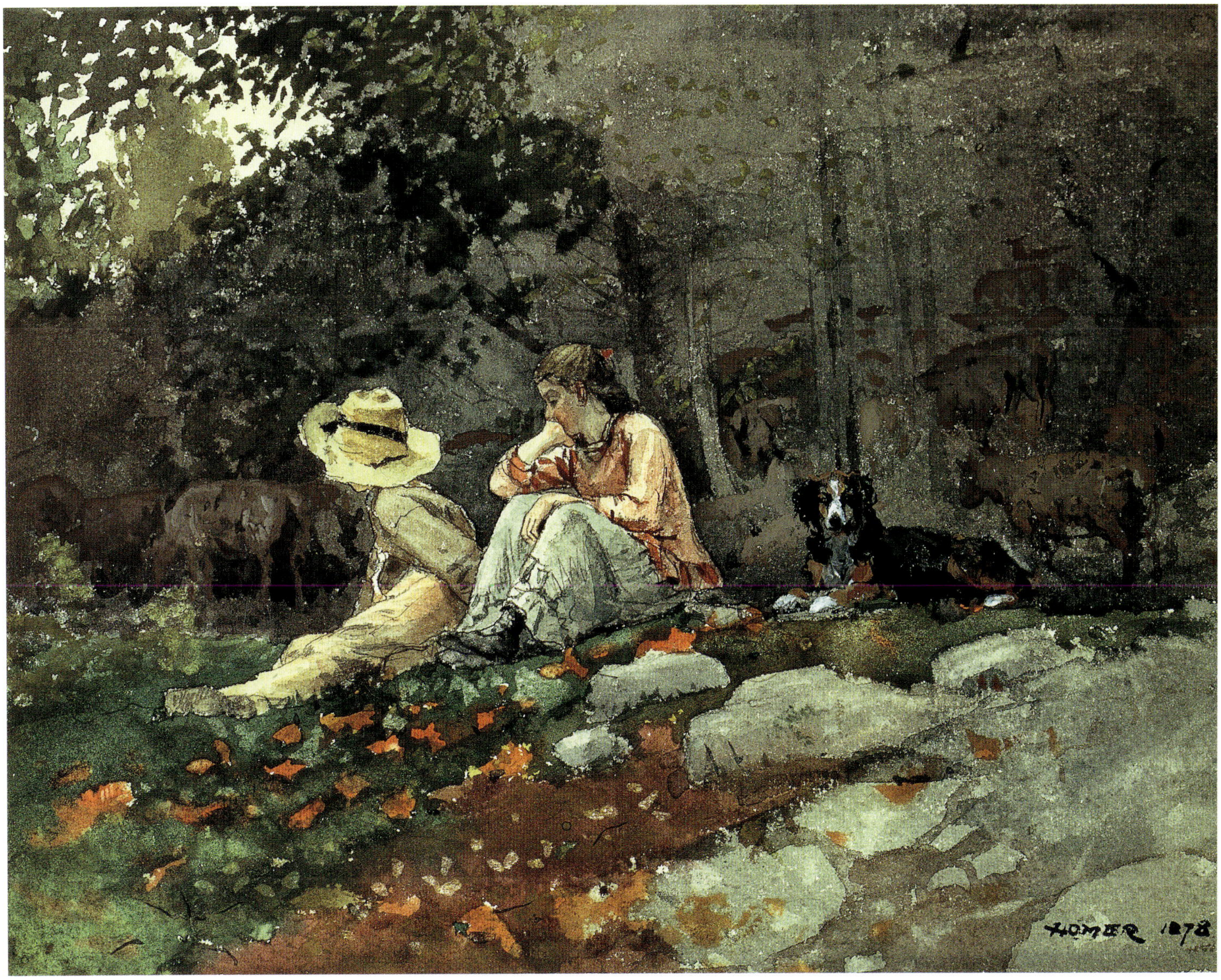

III.
Homer in Love: 1874–1879

At the same time that Homer was limning his rustics lads and lasses, he was also creating a very different kind of watercolor painting. These watercolors depicting genteel young ladies—a theme not usually associated with this artist—are set apart in terms of their subject matter and by the greater sense of refinement he brought to them. As always for Homer, the mode of painting was suited to the theme, and the higher degree of finish is in keeping with their well-bred subjects.

Direct evidence is scant, but most scholars accept the probability of an unhappy love affair to account, at least in part, for the romantic mood of these works and the transformations that took place in Homer's art and lifestyle at the beginning of the 1880s. Yet one need not explain the subject of these works entirely, or even principally, in terms of Homer's private life. Artists like John George Brown, William John Hennessy, and Eastman Johnson were painting similarly sentimental scenes of women in garden settings, emphasizing the gentle nature of the gentle sex. Such paintings reveal Homer's willingness at this point in his career to make concessions to public taste, and perhaps even some uncertainty as to the direction his own art ought to take. If his depictions of rustic children were deliberately provincial in tone, these works have a more sophisticated, more European, veneer.

The watercolors from the mid-1870s reveal the extent to which Homer in these years was waging his artistic battle on traditional turf. The themes of his work from this period—rustic childhood and genteel womanhood—fall well within the norms of sentimental Victorian culture. For those who criticized his pictures of country folk as coarse or unpolished, these finely crafted paintings of decorous young ladies offered a response. Even the paintings of Cullercoats fishwives in the next decade fall within the orbit of traditional Victorian attitudes, though in these latter works a woman's worth is measured not by her grace but by her heroic fortitude.

In some of the earlier oil paintings, like those in which women play croquet, bathe at the seashore, or go riding in the White Mountains, Homer portrays a distinctly modern type: active, confident, at ease in company of men with whom she consorts on an equal footing. These figures could illustrate Walt Whitman's lines from *Leaves of Grass*: "They know how to swim, row, wrestle, shoot run . . . /They are ultimate in their own right—they are calm, /clear, well possess'd of themselves." In an 1867 essay titled "Democracy," Whitman makes clear the social and political tensions that swirled around the meaning of womanhood, and where his own sympathies lie:

> The idea of the women of America (extricated from this daze, this fossil and unhealthy air which hangs about the word, Lady), developed, raised to become the robust equals, workers . . . with the men—greater than man . . . capable of being so, soon as they realize

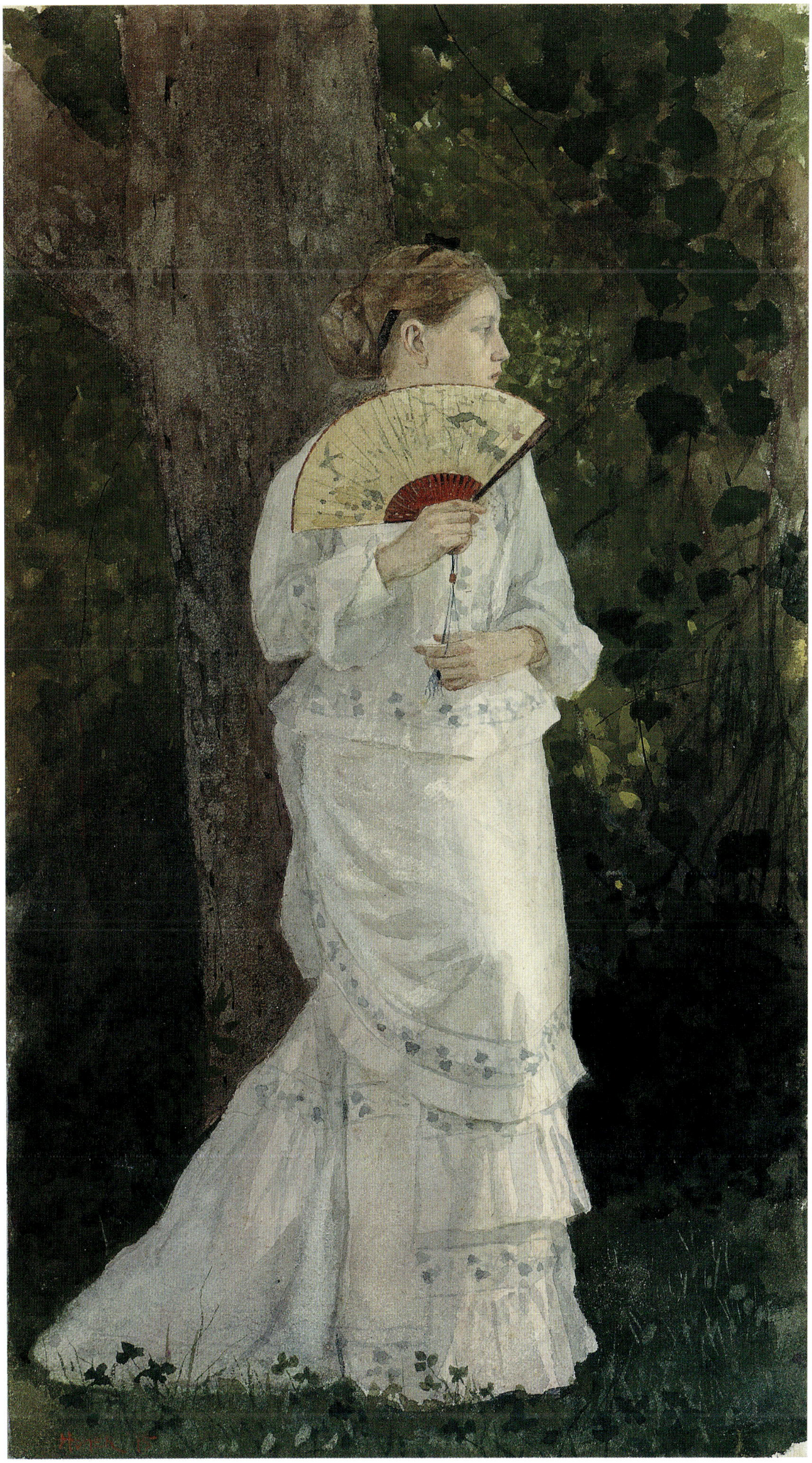

The Trysting Place 1875

WOMAN AND ELEPHANT 1877

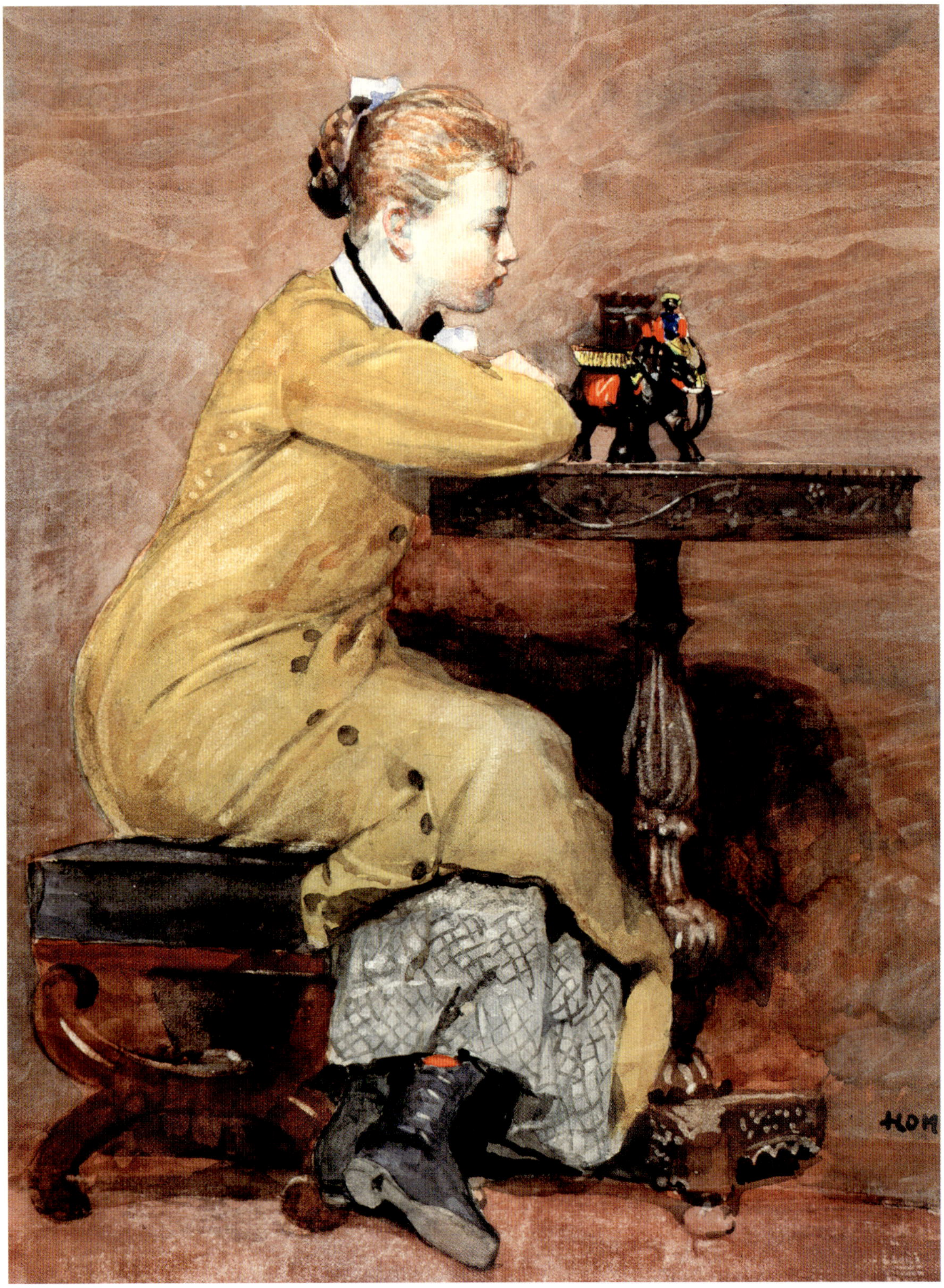

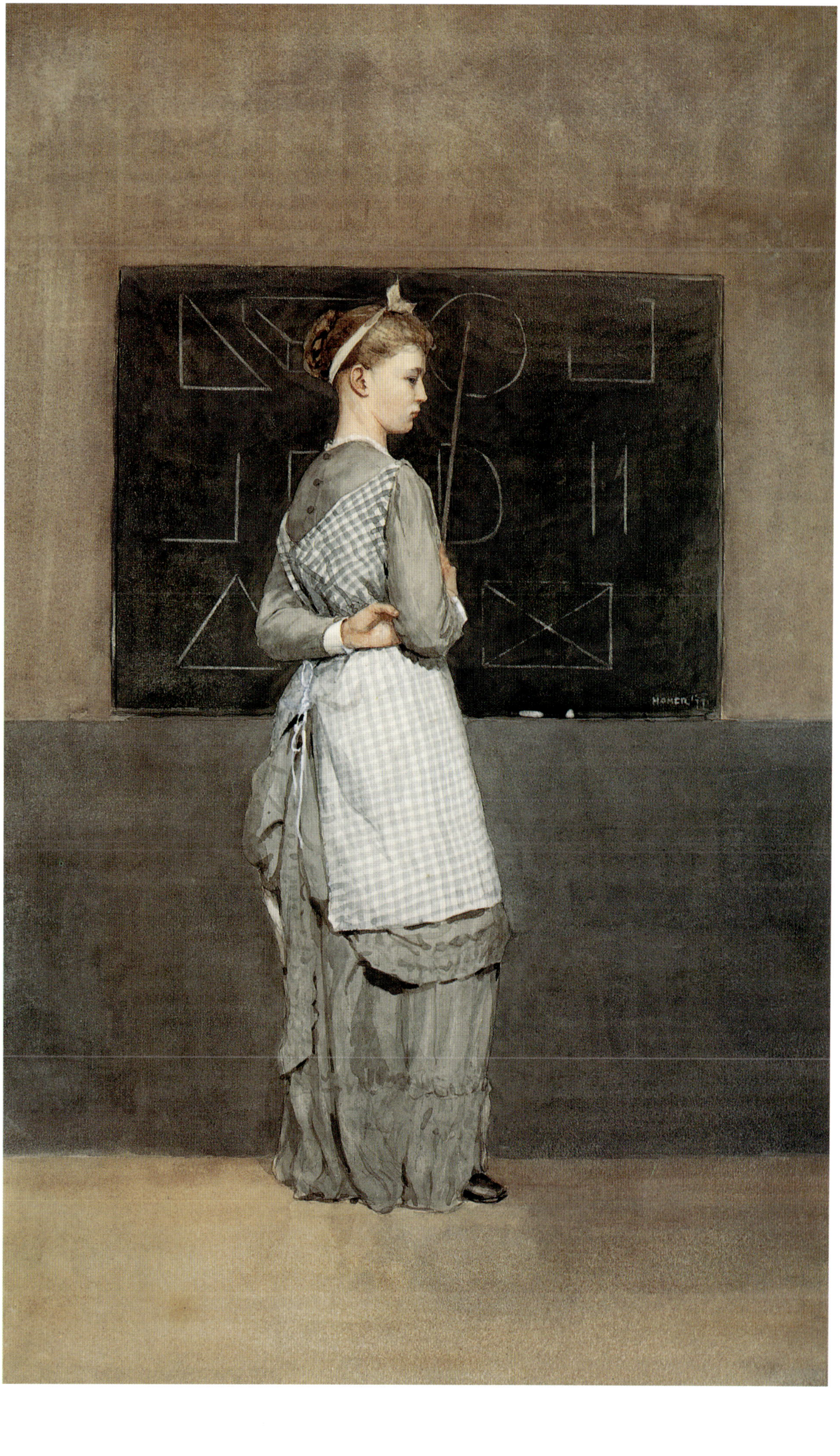

BLACKBOARD 1877

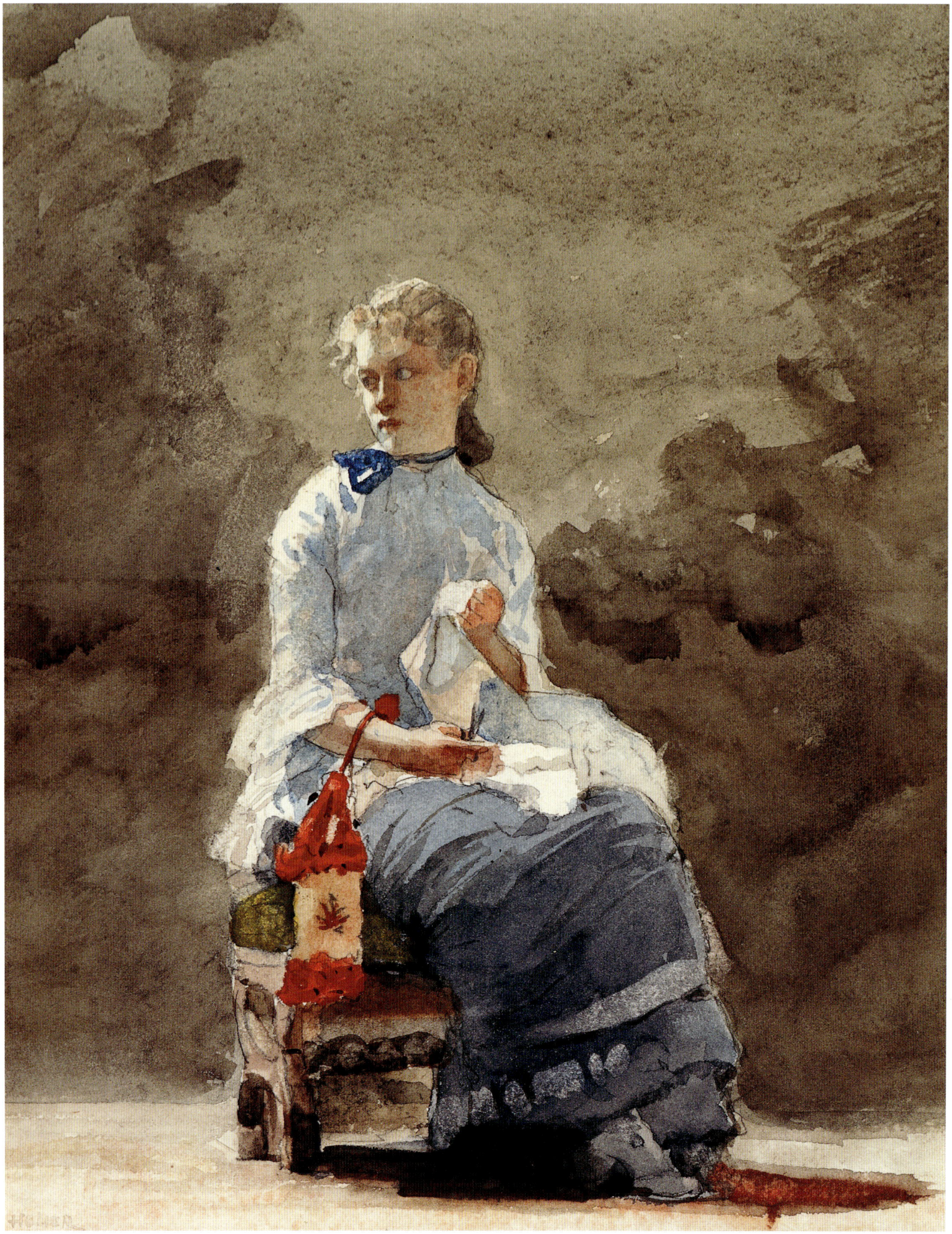

WOMAN SEWING 1879

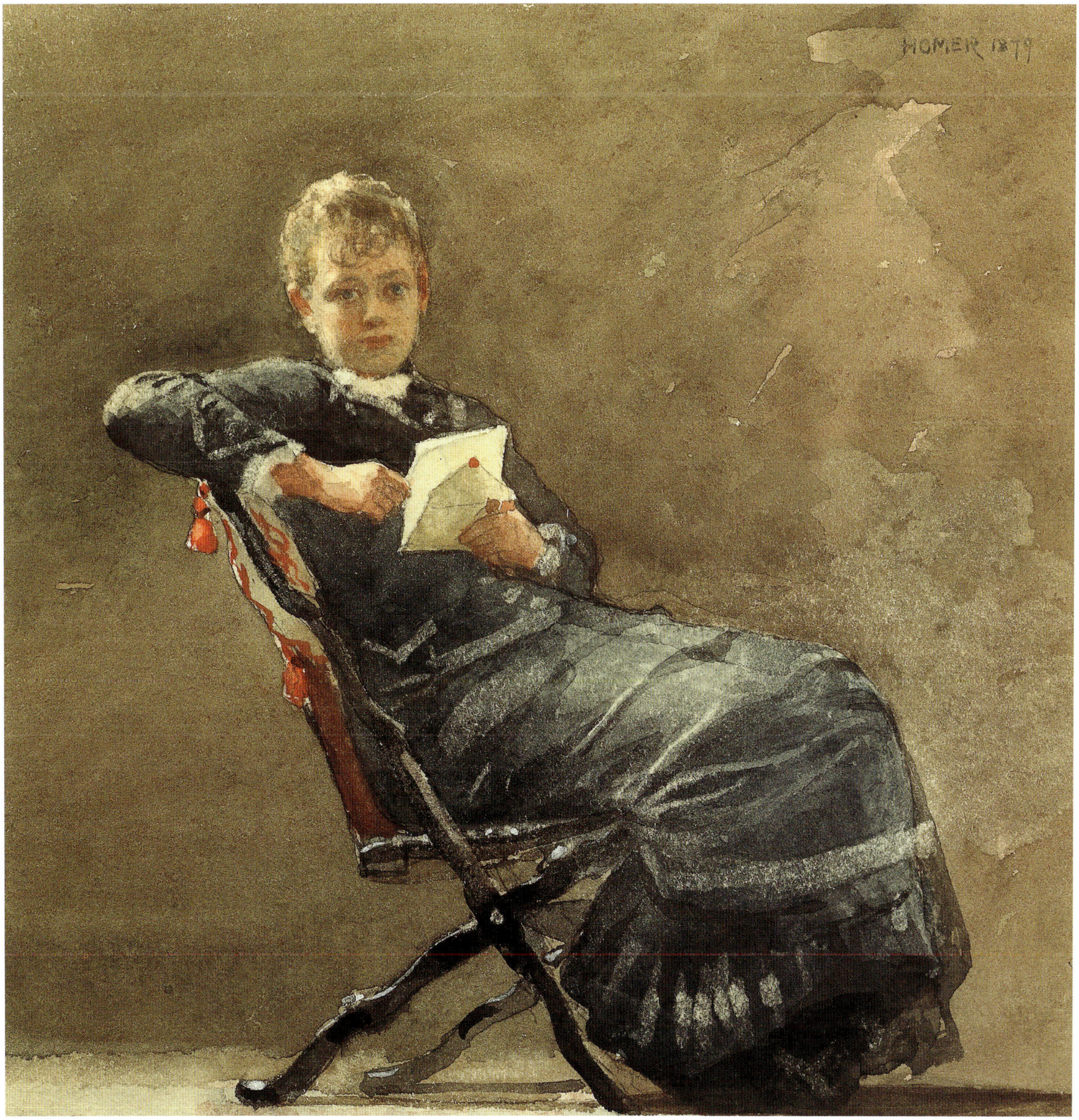

GIRL SEATED 1879

> it, and can bring themselves to give up toys and fictions, and launch forth, as men do, amid real, independent, stormy life.

Homer's depictions of women in the 1870s have, in contrast to some of the earlier illustrations, a hint of that "fossil and unhealthy air." In works like *The New Novel*, *Portrait of a Lady*, and *The Trysting Place*, Homer presents a rather conventional view as if, as is often the case in such matters, a romantic interest clouded his judgment. These women are lovely, elegant, and largely passive, engaged in quiet pursuits and often emotionally withdrawn as if pining for an absent lover.

The decorative quality is reinforced by compositions that seem far more studied than his loosely brushed images of rural youths. Set against largely monochrome backgrounds, the figures form strong two-dimensional designs reminiscent of Japanese art, a link made more explicit by such Orientalizing details as the fan carried by the woman in *The Trysting Place*. Homer's self-conscious *Japonism* was noted by contemporary critics. Commenting on an oil painting of this period, *The Nation* wrote: "His breadth of view becomes breadth of flatness; and the present picture, highly characteristic of a large class of Mr. Homer's work, suggests that if he could represent his hill on a Japanese box with two lacquers, upon which the women should be inlaid . . . his secret ideal would be satisfied."

The Trysting Place is an image that delights in artifice, like a society belle who cultivates a look that is as much a product of art as of nature. The pale yellow fan, with its crescent of vermilion drawing our eyes to the woman's hand, plays off the pale shades of her dress and the variegated greens of the background that evoke a hidden copse, perfect for a secret rendezvous. It is a lovely image, but one that lacks the strength of observation and muscularity we usually associate with the artist. *Blackboard* is an equally contrived image, though Homer's aims here are less overtly sentimental. The image, which depicts a teacher conducting a drawing lesson, is a study in muted tones and spare geometry as self-consciously aesthetic as anything ever painted by Whistler. Typically, however, Homer never sacrifices the plausible reality of the scene to achieve his rigorously abstract results. *The New Novel* is composed around a contrapuntal play of red and green contrasts that recalls Chevreul's emphasis on structuring a work around

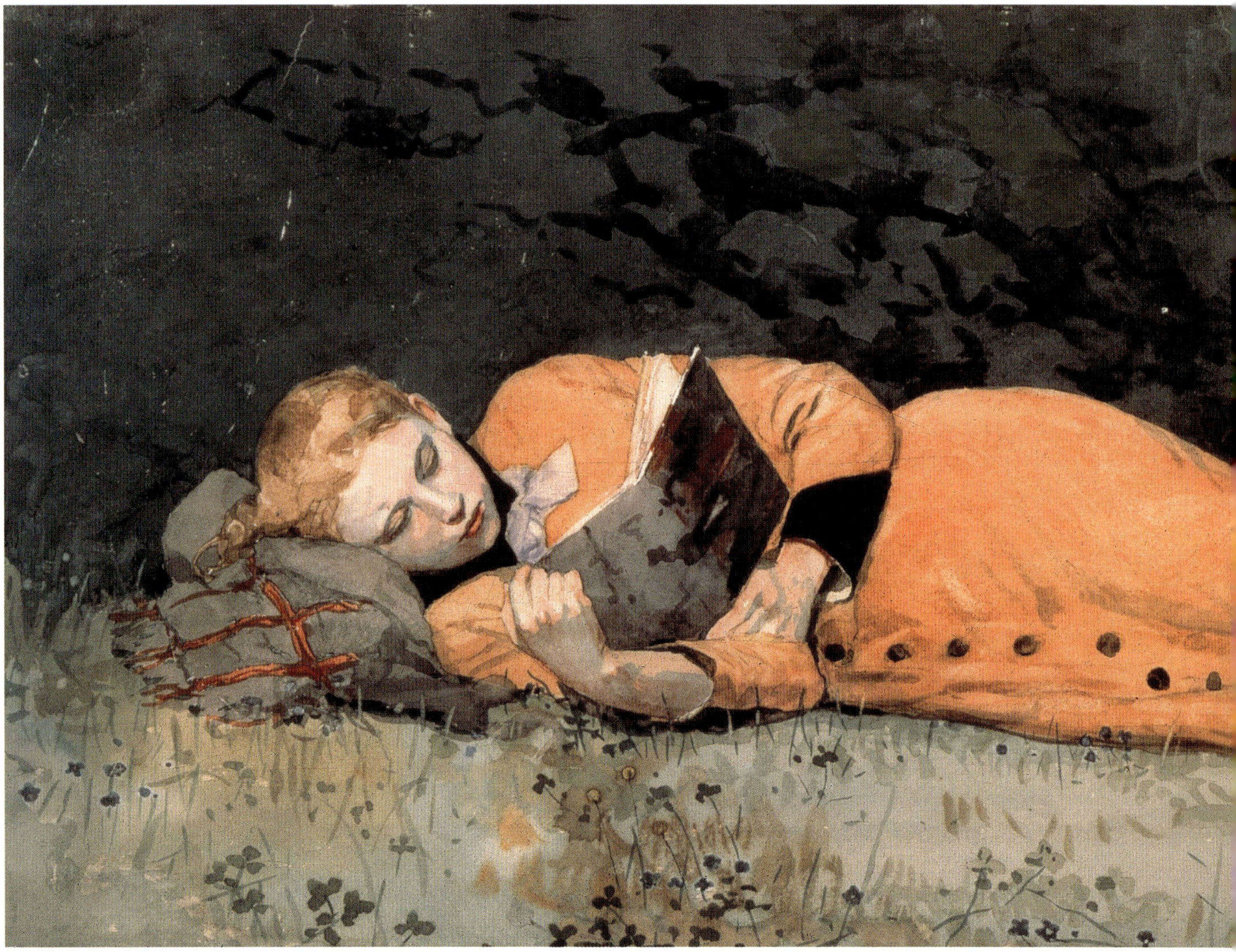

complementaries. Like *The Trysting Place* and *Blackboard*, it is a decorative work that delights in artifice.

In *Rustic Courtship* [pp. 46–47], Homer drew a distinction between the masculine outdoors and a feminine interior setting. The Victorian attitude that the proper place for women was within the home makes such distinctions inevitable. And while he was perfectly willing, as his Cullercoats watercolors demonstrate, to include women within a more rugged setting, when it came to those of his own bourgeois background, Homer shared the prejudices of his time and class. In *Woman Sewing*, he depicts the figure in an interior setting. And even when he places her outdoors, as in *The New Novel*, it is in the domesticated setting of a well-manicured garden.

On those few occasions when Homer depicted intimacy between the sexes, the scene is filled with tension. An intriguing watercolor from 1874 titled *Moonlight* is typical. Against a moonlit backdrop of sand and pounding surf, the artist has silhouetted the figures of a man—who very much resembles contemporary photographs of Homer himself— and a woman; as the man leans toward his companion, the woman turns away. Although the narrative is not explicit, her pose hints at a less than happy outcome to the nocturnal rendezvous. The seaside setting is also suggestive of the symbolic role the ocean will play in Homer's work. An 1869 illustration that appeared in *Appleton's Journal*, titled *The Beach at Long Branch*, reinforces the sexual associations of the ocean. In this engraving, a pretty young lady inscribes the artist's initials in the sand. The original text that accompanied the picture read in part:

> The shallow film of water, which washes away so many letters in the sand, is a very suggestive symbol of coquetry. Many a name, however, has been written "on the beach in Long Branch" which has never been effaced—the beach has gladdened more hearts than it has saddened, despite its reputation—it has made more matches than it has broken.

Given this evidence, it would not be too far-fetched to view Homer's late seascapes as a reflection of a turbulent and thwarted emotional life. The early date of *Moonlight* does not allow us to read it as a token of his own unhappy affair, but it perhaps suggests something melancholy in the makeup of this reserved and solitary man.

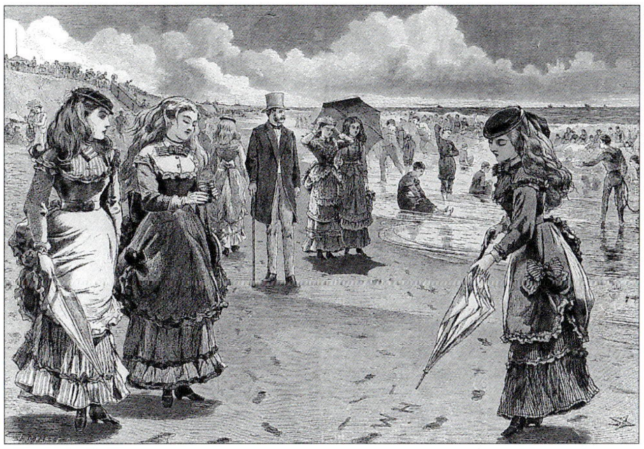

THE BEACH AT LONG BRANCH 1869

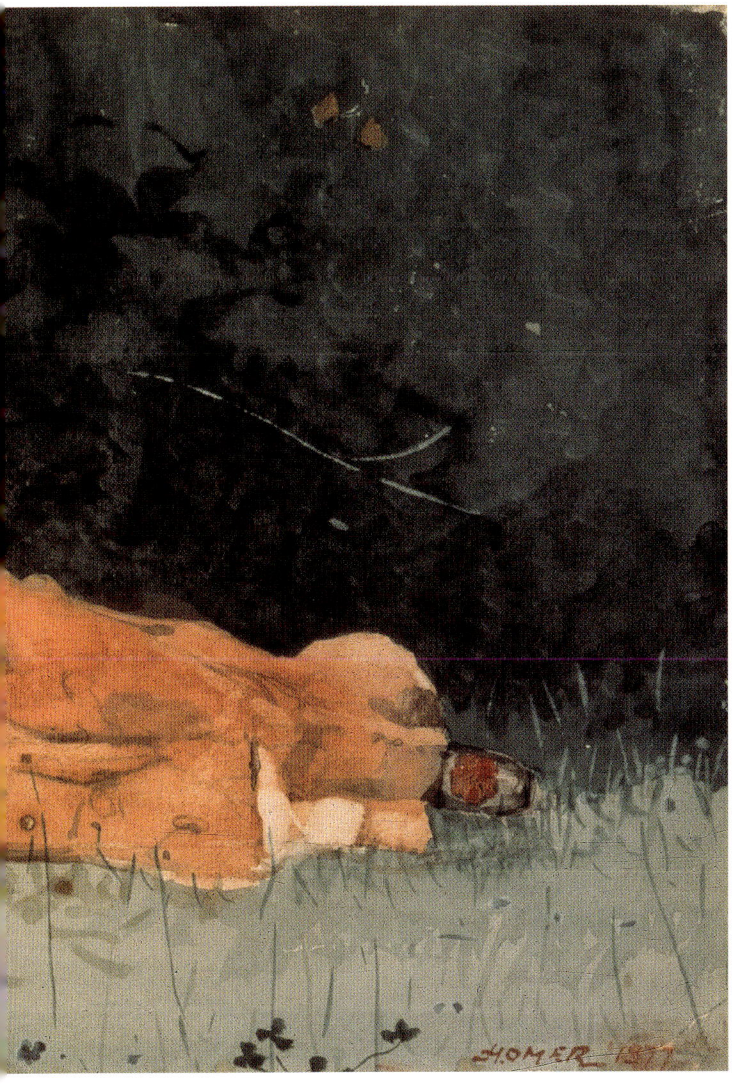

THE NEW NOVEL 1877

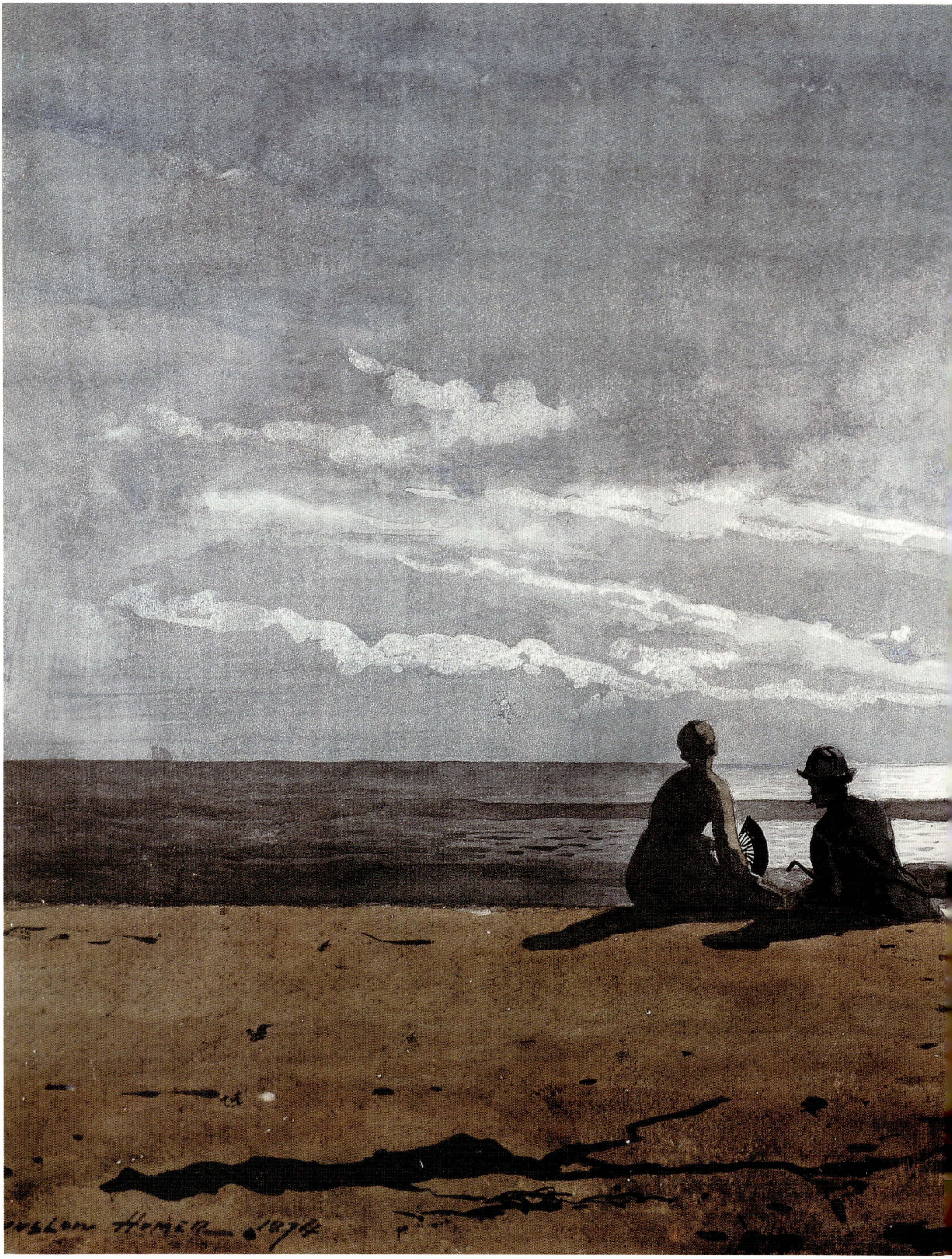

MOONLIGHT 1874

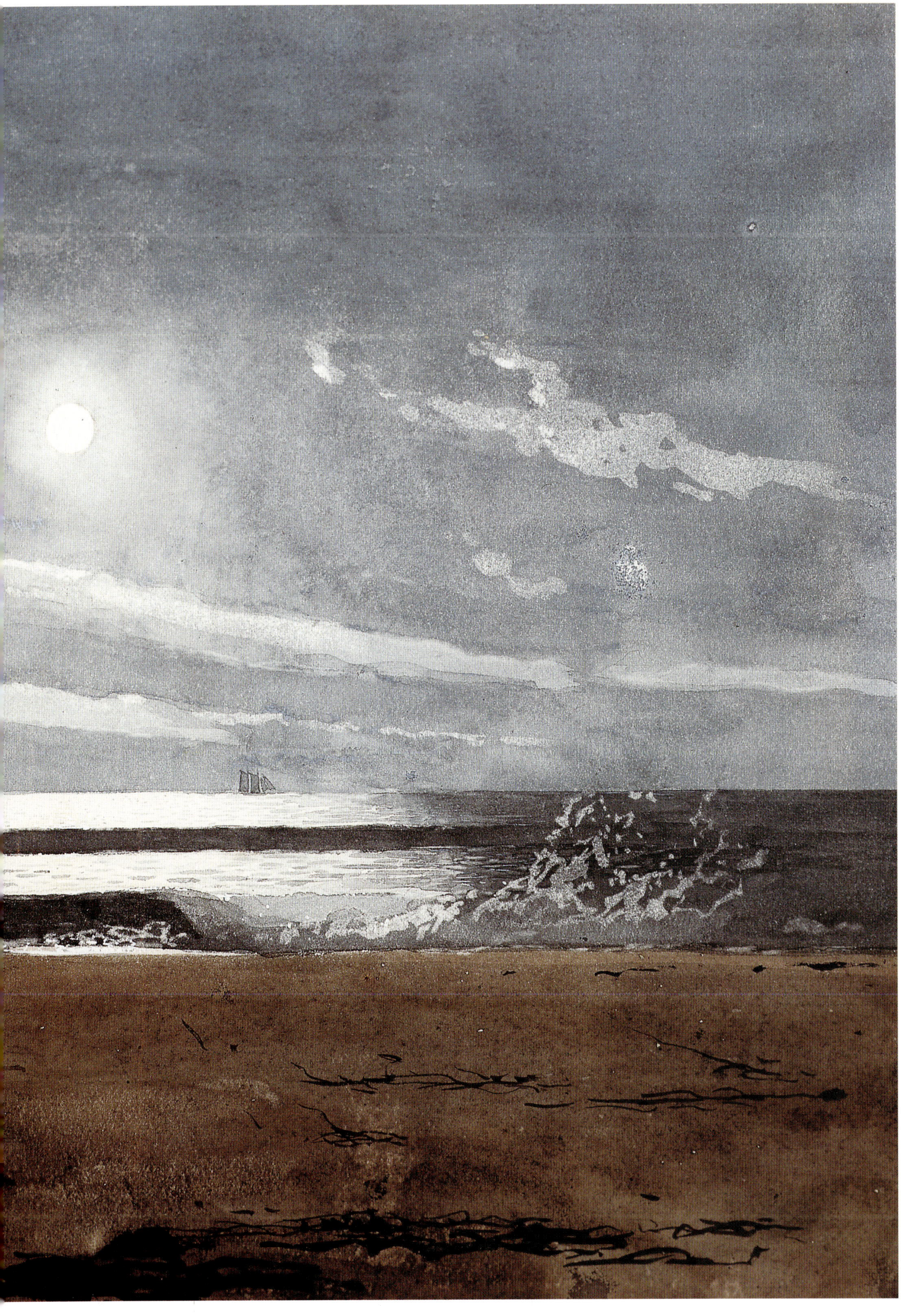

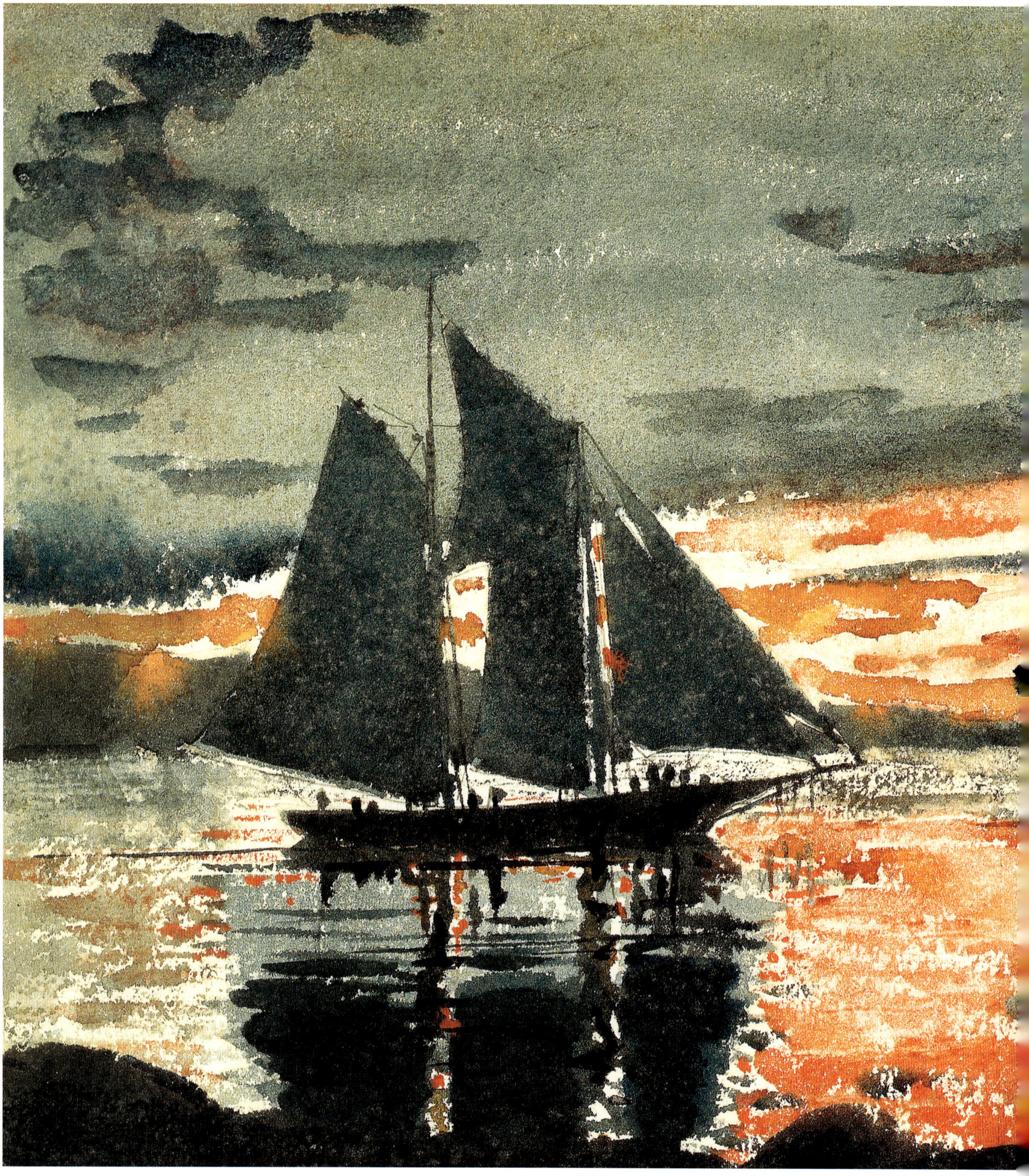

IV.
Sunset: Gloucester, 1880

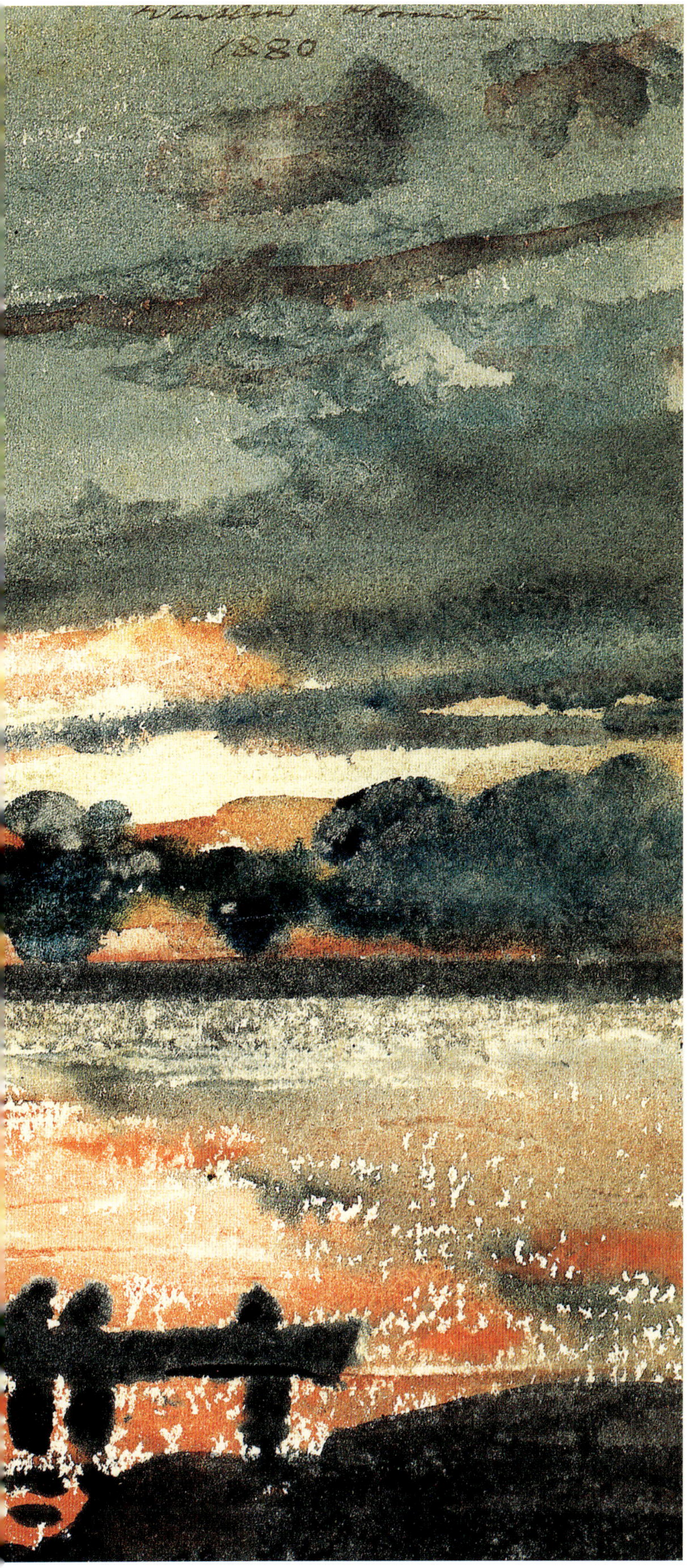

Sunset Fires 1880

The summer of 1880 marked a turning point in Homer's career. Returning to the place where he had undertaken his first serious exploration of watercolor, he now began to shed the lifestyle of a fashionable New York artist and to exhibit those traits of rugged individualism that we associate with the artist. He also began at this time to shed the conventional elements that smoothed the rough edges of his art. As Homer's vision of the world became harsher, the children and genteel young ladies who had dominated his work in the 1870s were replaced by more robust types, capable of holding their own in threatening circumstances. Had Homer died before this summer, he might have been judged by history as a gifted painter of genre scenes showing undeniable strength but not a singular artistic genius. Following this summer in Gloucester, Homer's art begins to fall less comfortably within conventional norms. It is here that he starts to assert his own stubborn personality, suppressed but not invisible in the earlier work, and where the legend of the dour, visionary hermit of the sea begins to emerge.

The change was signaled by the altered circumstances of his residence in the fishing port. In that earlier summer he had lodged at the Atlantic Hotel, in the heart of the bustling downtown; in 1880, by contrast, he sought out the isolation of Ten Pound Island in the center of the harbor, where he boarded with the lighthouse keeper. A friend of the artist remembered that at the time he "knew plenty of nice people, but he associated with two fishermen, and preferred their company." From this point in his life, Homer could more often be found in the company of such uncomplicated men than with his social equals.

Equally significant for his art, Homer from this moment spent the remainder of his life in close proximity to the sea. With the exception of fishing trips to the wilderness of the Adirondacks or Quebec, he was rarely far from the ocean that became an increasingly important spiritual force in his life and the subject of most of his major oil paintings.

A new mood has also crept into this work from the summer of 1880. In some of these watercolors, Homer seemed to seek out a more epic language, focusing on extraordinary moments unmoored from quotidian realities. It would be tempting for the sake of a clearer narrative to focus exclusively on his most innovative work of the summer—depictions of isolated boats against flaming sunsets or moonlit vistas whose visionary quality stands comparison to the work of Turner, Whistler, and Albert Pinkham Ryder. But it is clear that these images are part of a larger pattern of experimentation that pushed in

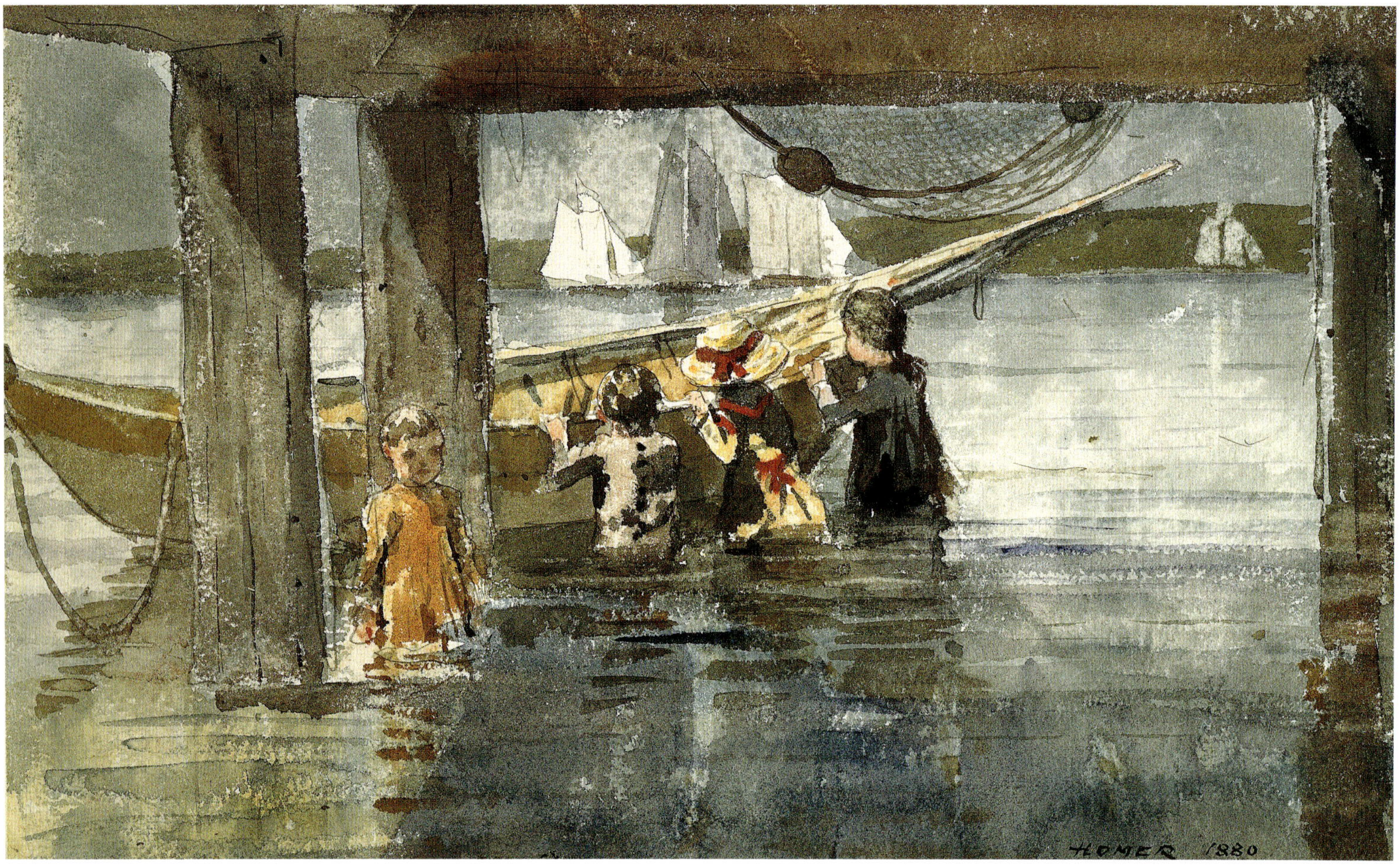

CHILDREN PLAYING UNDER A GLOUCESTER WHARF 1880

more than one direction. In addition to works like *Sailboat and Fourth of July Fireworks* and *Eastern Point Light*, which seem all raw emotion, or the coloristic explosions of *Sunset Fires* and *Gloucester Sunset*, there are numerous paintings in a more lighthearted vein. *Children Playing Under a Gloucester Wharf* possesses some of the playfulness and lightness of touch of the 1873 work, though the "impressionistic" looseness of the brushwork is even bolder than in those earlier watercolors. Sketching quickly with the brush on dry, rough-textured paper, Homer allows the white to show through the patchwork of color, contributing to the overall luminous tone. He contains the almost chaotic brushwork within a rigorous geometric composition imposed by the boxy frame of the wharf, a composition that recalls *In Charge of Baby*. *Boys in a Dory* also echoes the themes of his earlier Gloucester stay, but particularly in the prismatic colors of red and deep blue that seep into the reflections on the water one can glimpse Homer striving for bolder effects and a more intense mode of expression. His technique in this work runs the gamut, from thickly applied strokes in the foreground—with a good deal of opaque white used to create the play of the low sun across the rippling water—to the most delicate of washes used for the ghostly silhouettes of the distant sailboats that are the focus of the boys' attention.

Given the more careful finish and muted tones of the watercolors that followed during his twenty-month Cullercoats stay, it is possible to view the summer of 1880 as a time in which Homer deliberately tested out new directions that would yield results only later. One work that did bear more immediate fruit is *A Wreck Near Gloucester*, the first image in the artist's oeuvre to acknowledge explicitly the destructive fury of the ocean. This theme, which was to play an important role in Homer's art over the coming years, here makes a rather tame debut: in depicting men unloading cargo from the wreck, he shows us not the storm that stranded the boat but its aftermath. The awesome power of nature that is here only implied will become the central theme of his Cullercoats watercolors.

The boldest works Homer produced this summer are his sunset and moonlit views of Gloucester Harbor. These are works without traditional narrative or figurative elements. Their power comes from their emotional intensity, conveyed through jarring contrasts of color and the rigor of their two-dimensional design. In *Eastern Point Light*, Homer lightly brushes veils of somber gray over a dry surface, allowing the pigment to soak into some areas while in other areas leaving the paper almost completely exposed to indicate the bright reflection of moonlight on water. By working on a dry surface, he allows thousands of pinpricks of white to show through the dark washes, imparting velvety shimmer to the night sky and water.

BOYS IN A DORY 1880

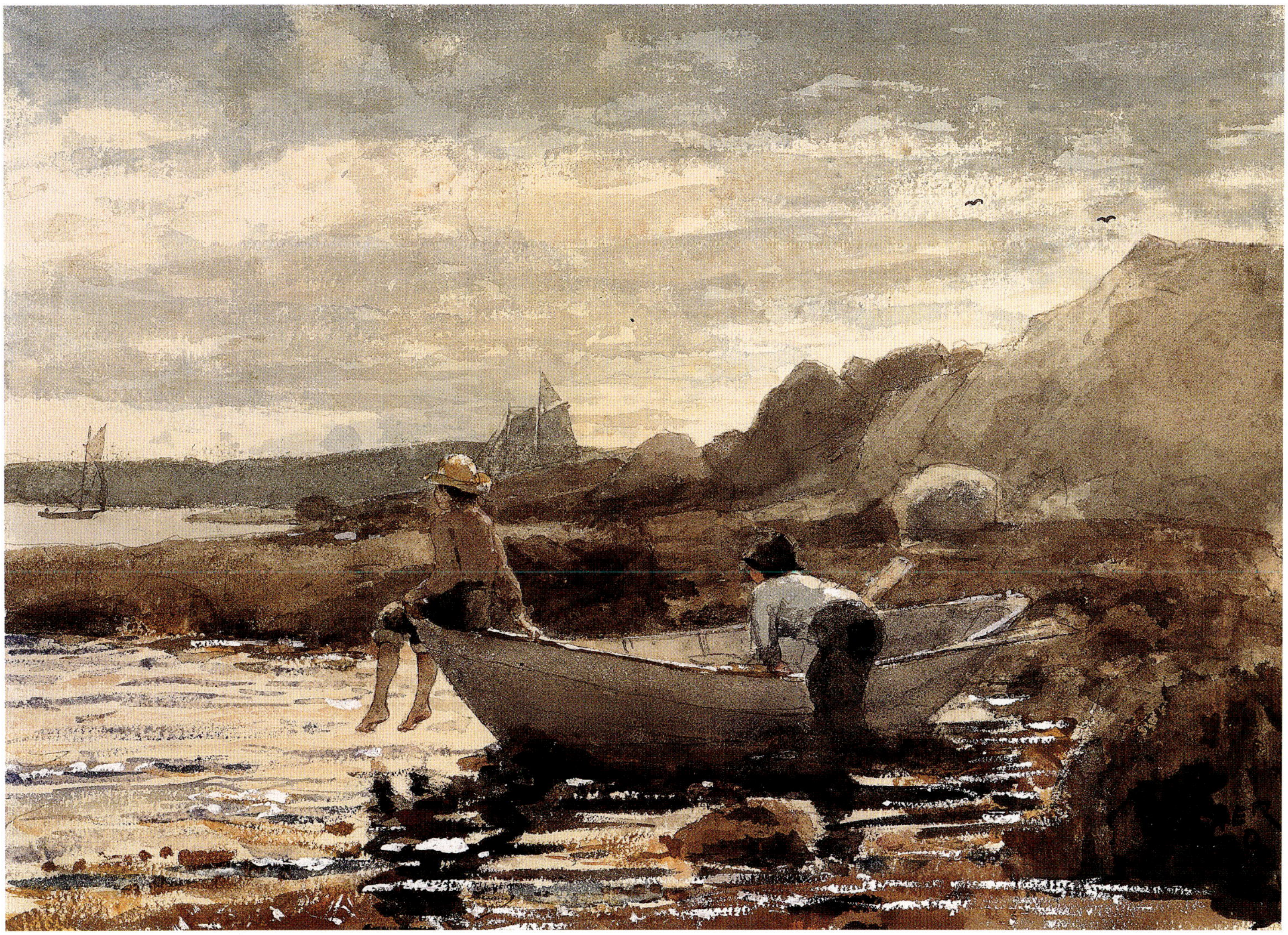

Sailboat and Fourth of July Fireworks is painted on saturated paper, creating the soft blooms of pigment that evoke the night sky illuminated by fiery explosions. It is an early example of Homer working wet into wet, a technique he explored more fully in the Cullercoats paintings. An article in *The Nation* from 1879 described how many artists were "experimenting with simple clouds of color floated on wet paper," exactly the technique Homer employed in this work. Lighter areas were achieved by a variety of means: reserving areas of paper that were then washed in light tones; scraping through dark washes to expose the paper below; and using touches of opaque white. Homer employed this last technique to frame the dark hull and sails, bringing the greatest tonal contrast to the most important element in the composition.

Sunset Fires and *Sunset at Gloucester* have a brooding intensity new in Homer's art. Based on simple chromatic contrasts—red and black, blue and orange—they demonstrate in the starkest possible terms the expressive power of pure color. More significant than the specific techniques employed in these works is the greater ambition they reflect. Even in these modest formats—despite their apparent expansiveness, none is much larger than a standard piece of typing paper—one feels the artist striving to express some timeless truth about man's place in the universe. Gone is the rustic charm of much of the earlier works. There are no stories on which to hang our hats, little to engage our natural sympathies. Instead, Homer seems to be confronting nature at its most elemental and to be grappling with the most profound issues of life and death. One critic wrote eloquently of these works in which the artist had "boldly omitted everything that could not serve his purpose,—which was to show the demoniac splendor of stormy sunset skies and waters,—and then, unsatisfied by the brilliant hues of nature, had keyed them to deeper force, made them doubly powerful, the reds stronger, the blacks blacker,—insisting upon and emphasizing a theme which another artist would have already thought too pronounced and too emphatic for artistic use." The ambition of the paintings from the summer of 1880 looks forward to the more monumental paintings of the coming years, announcing the larger stage upon which Homer's art will now unfold.

Wreck Near Gloucester 1880

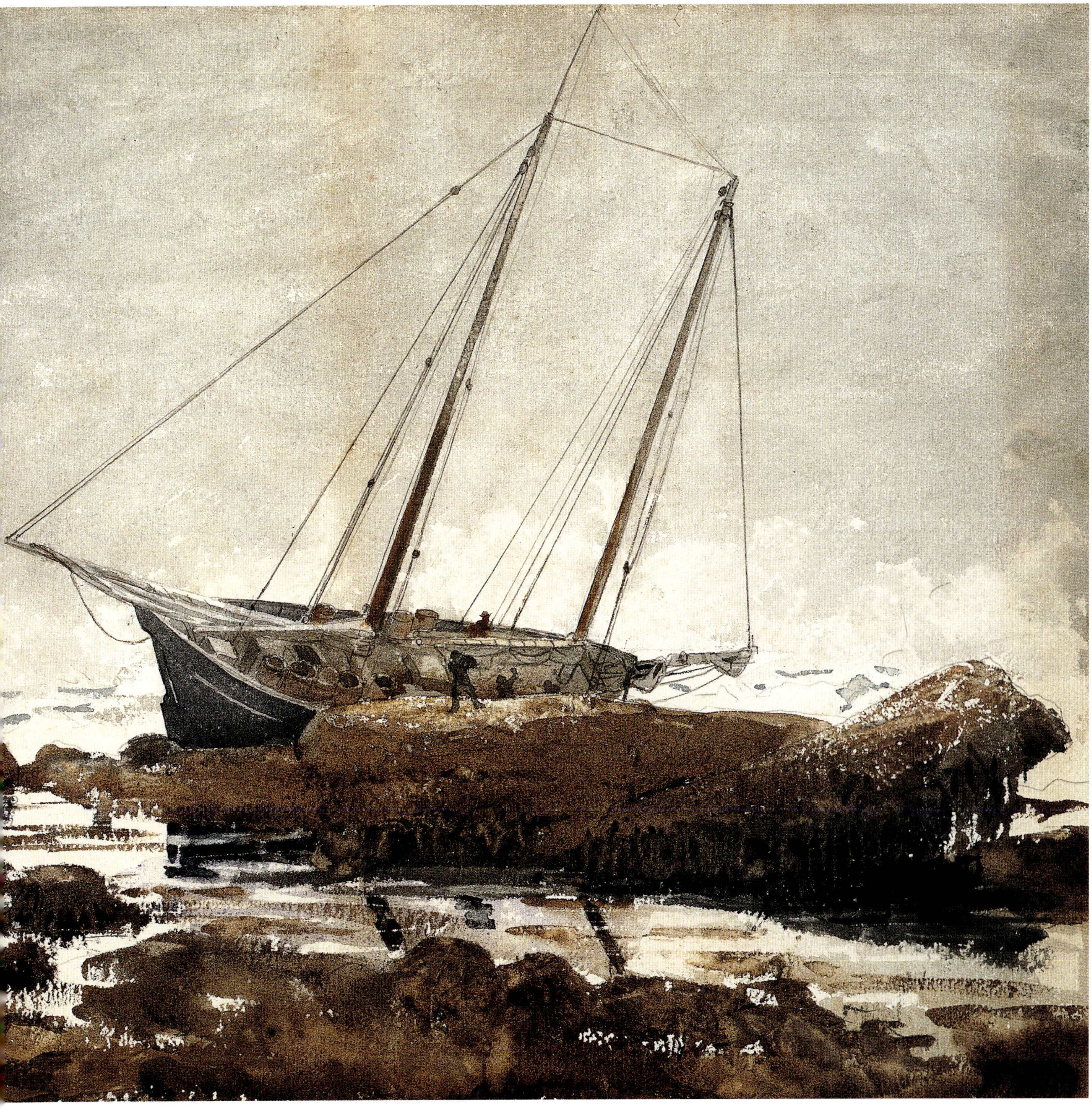

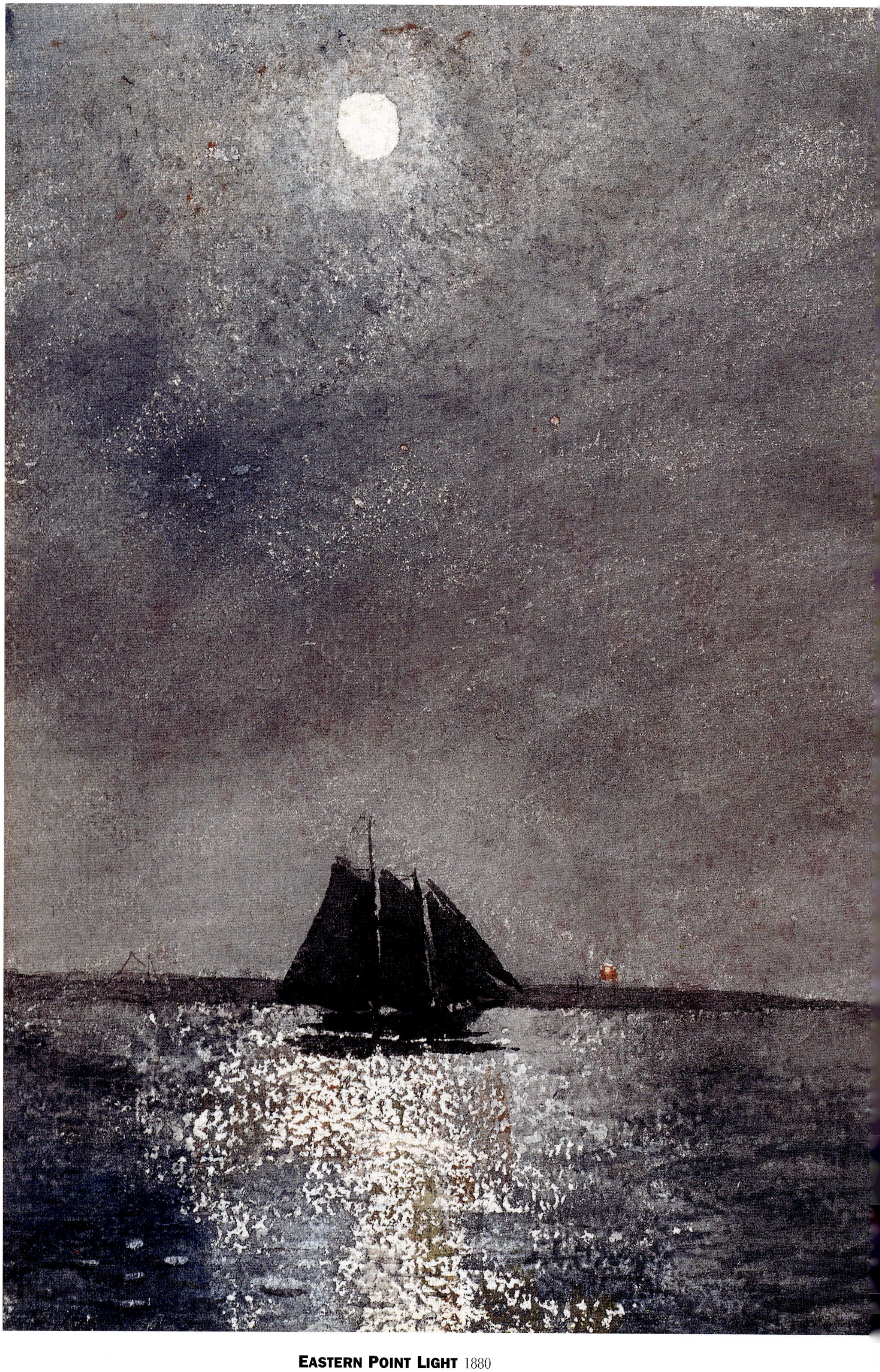

Eastern Point Light 1880

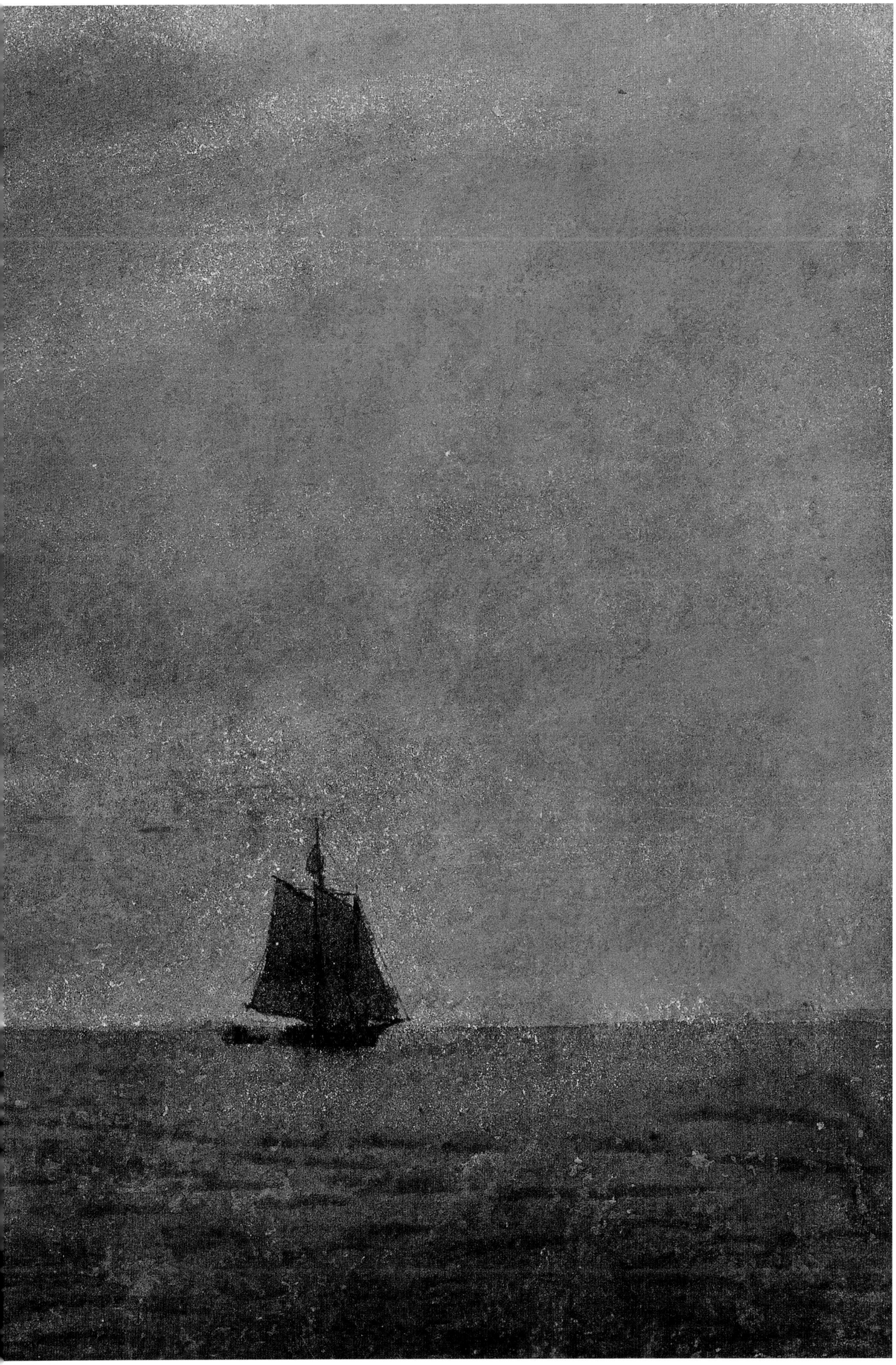

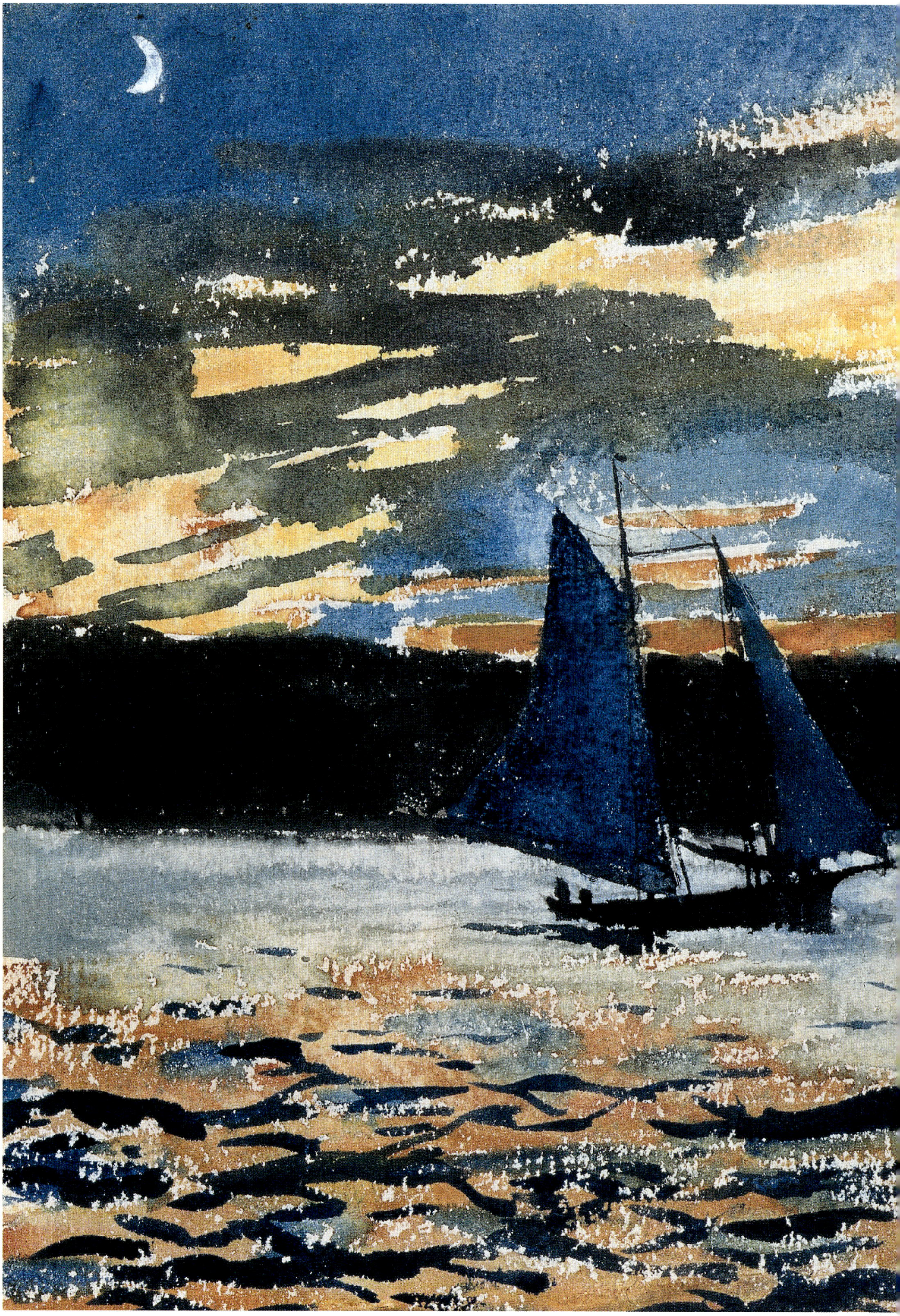

Gloucester Sunset 1880

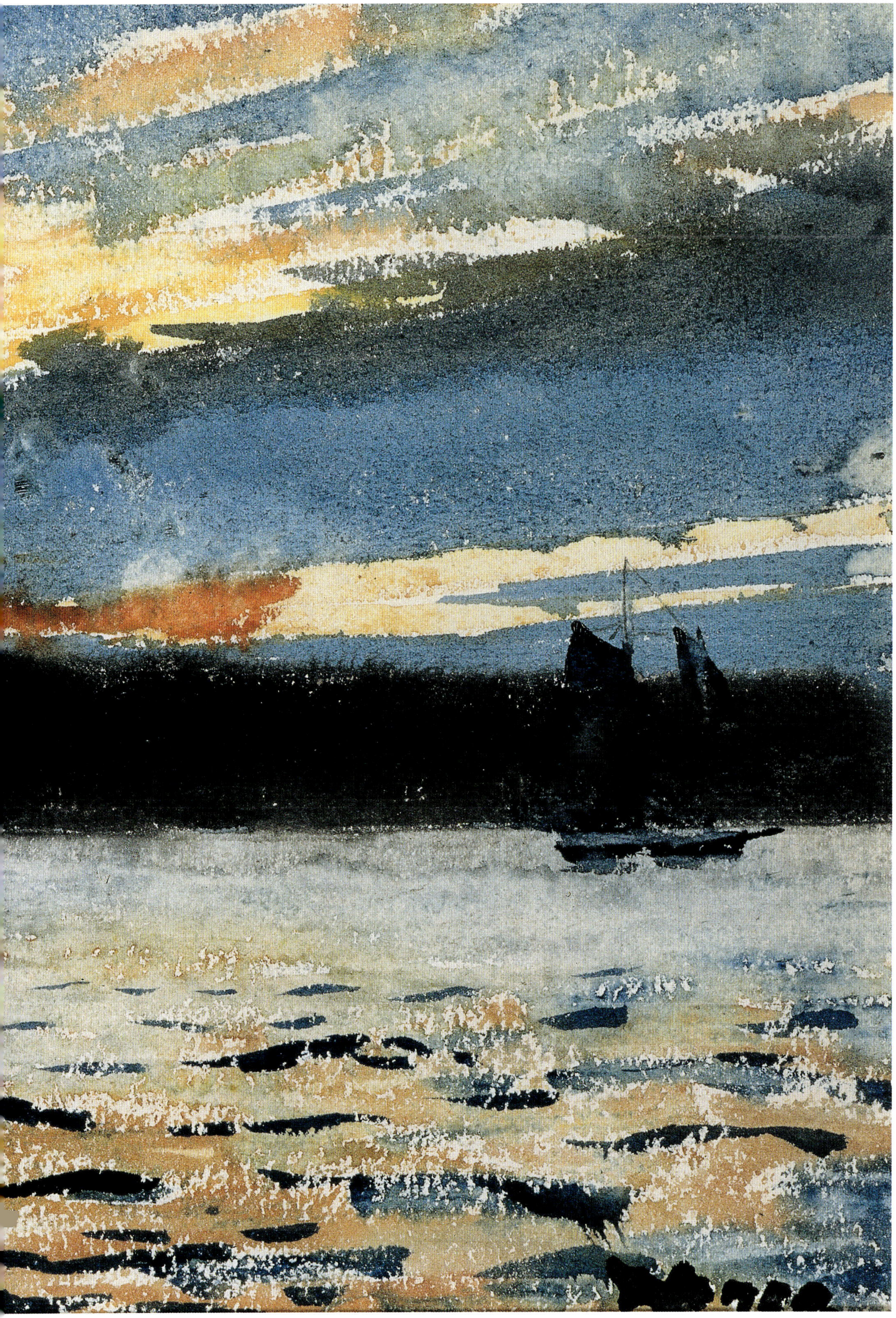

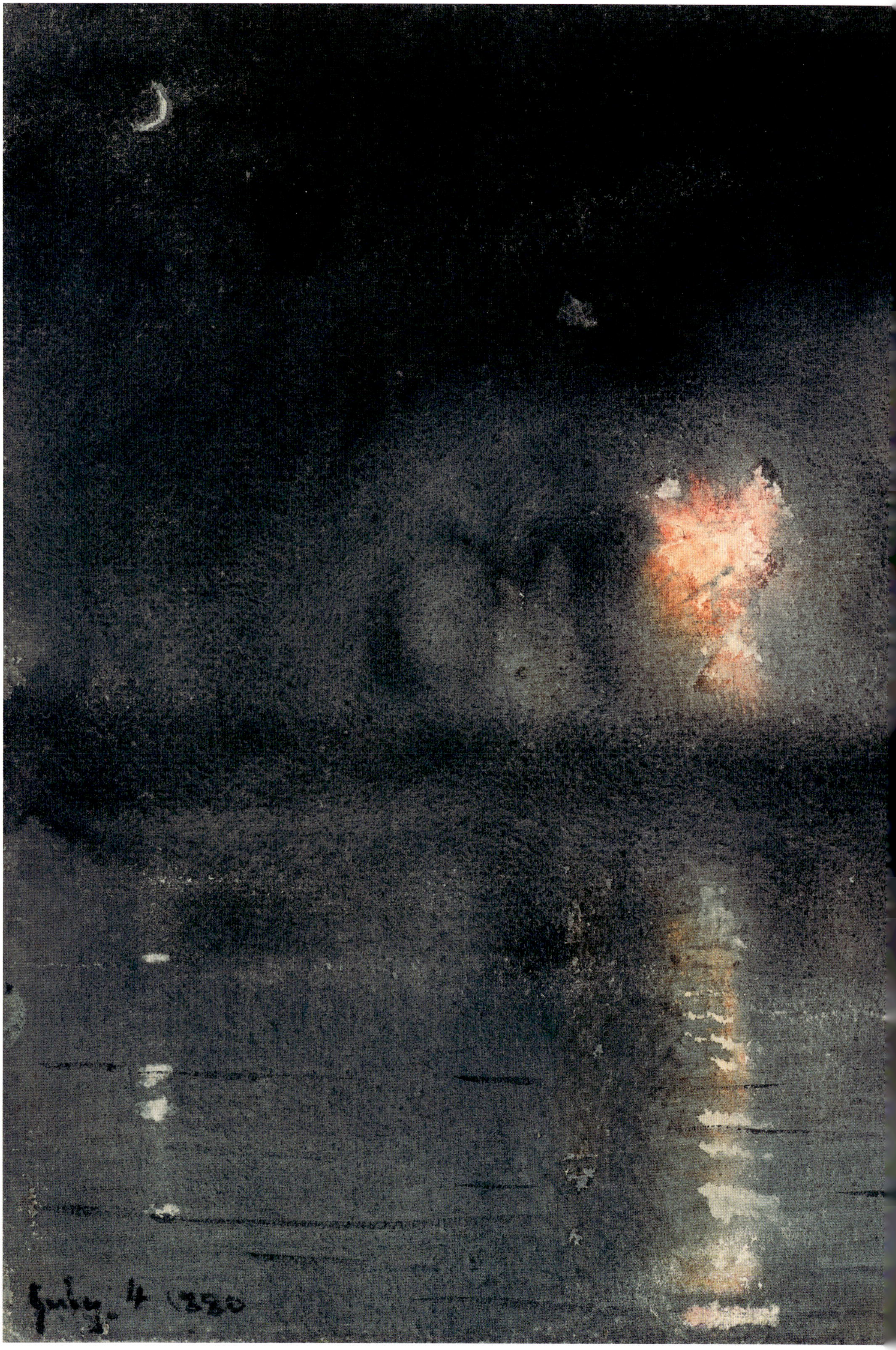
July 4 1880

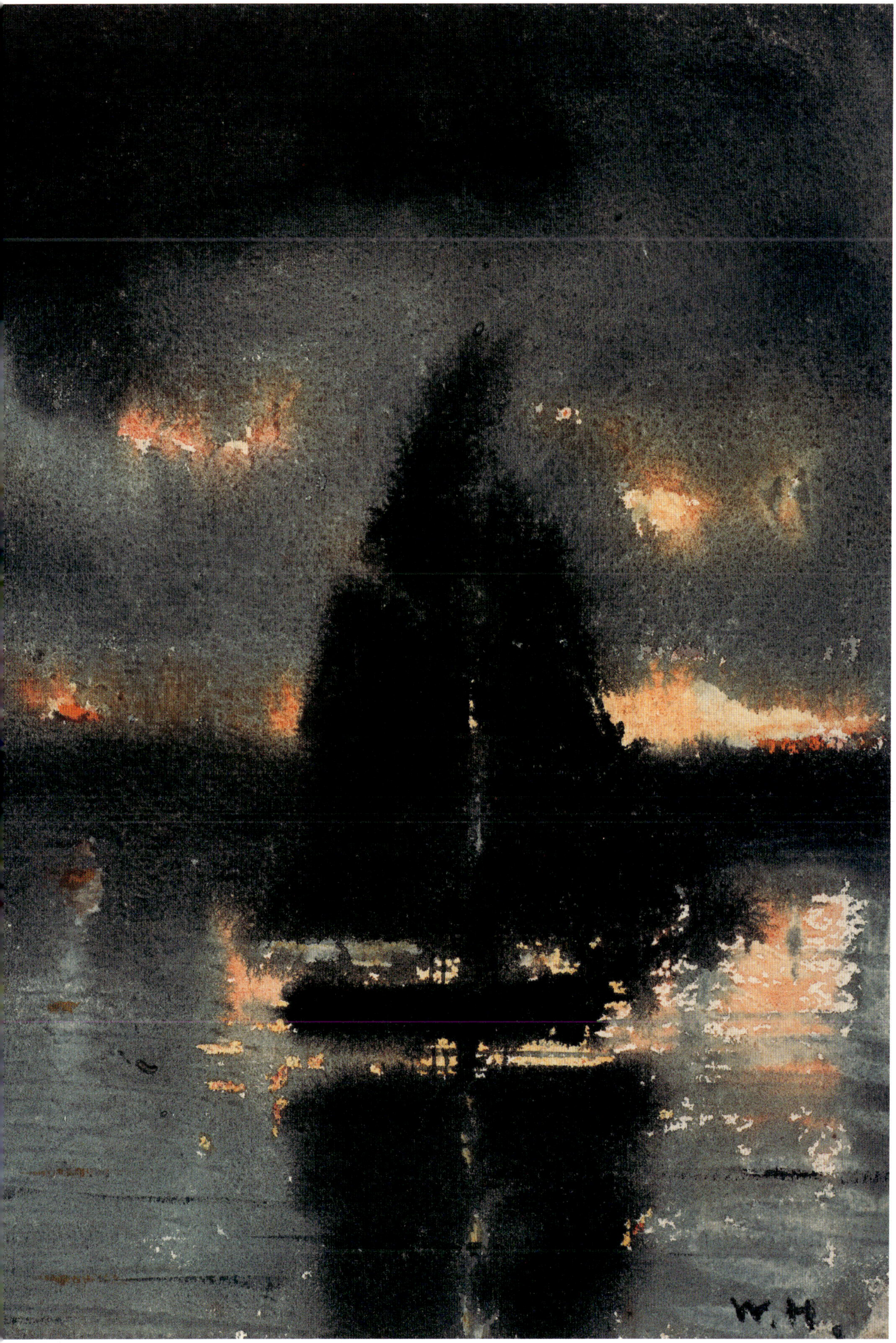

Sailboat and Fourth of July Fireworks 1880

V.
The Angry Sea: Cullercoats, England, 1881–1883

In March 1881, Homer set out for the village of Cullercoats on the North Sea coast of England. It is unclear whether Cullercoats was Homer's original destination or if he only heard about the picturesque fishing village while en route to Liverpool. In any case, when he arrived, his intention was to remain just a few months. That his stay lasted twenty months, including a storm-swept winter season, is an indication that he regarded this interlude as an important moment in his professional life. Unlike his earlier trip to France in 1866–67, Homer's second European stay was immensely productive and had a lasting impact on his life and art.

Cullercoats in Homer's time was a small village near the larger port of Tynemouth. It numbered fewer than fifteen hundred full-time residents, most of whom were involved in the fishing industry. But like many coastal towns in the late nineteenth century, Cullercoats was adding tourism to the traditional salt-water economy. In addition to full-time residents, Cullercoats boasted a significant colony of artists, attracted by the dramatic scenery and picturesque natives, and it had already become a popular destination for city folk hoping to escape the summer heat. Thus, Homer's exclusive focus on the fishermen and fishwives who earned their living from the treacherous sea is selective. It is instructive to compare this approach to that of the Impressionists, who also painted *en plein air* and often in similar seaside locales. Whereas the Impressionists focused on tourists and other pleasure seekers—men and women of their own class who were engaged in a similar pursuit of pleasant prospects—Homer was attracted to more timeless themes. In Cullercoats, and later in his Caribbean paintings, Homer painted the inhabitants of the place and edited out anything that might remind the viewer of the sightseeing that the artist and his prosperous compatriots were engaged in. If the Impressionists were sophisticated urbanites, who looked at their subjects with an almost ironic detachment, Homer was more deeply—and, one might say, more naively—invested in his picturesque subjects.

It was not that he was unaware of the pictorial possibilities of more modern scenes. Many of his illustrations described the seaside resort as a place where different classes and the young of both sexes could mix with free-

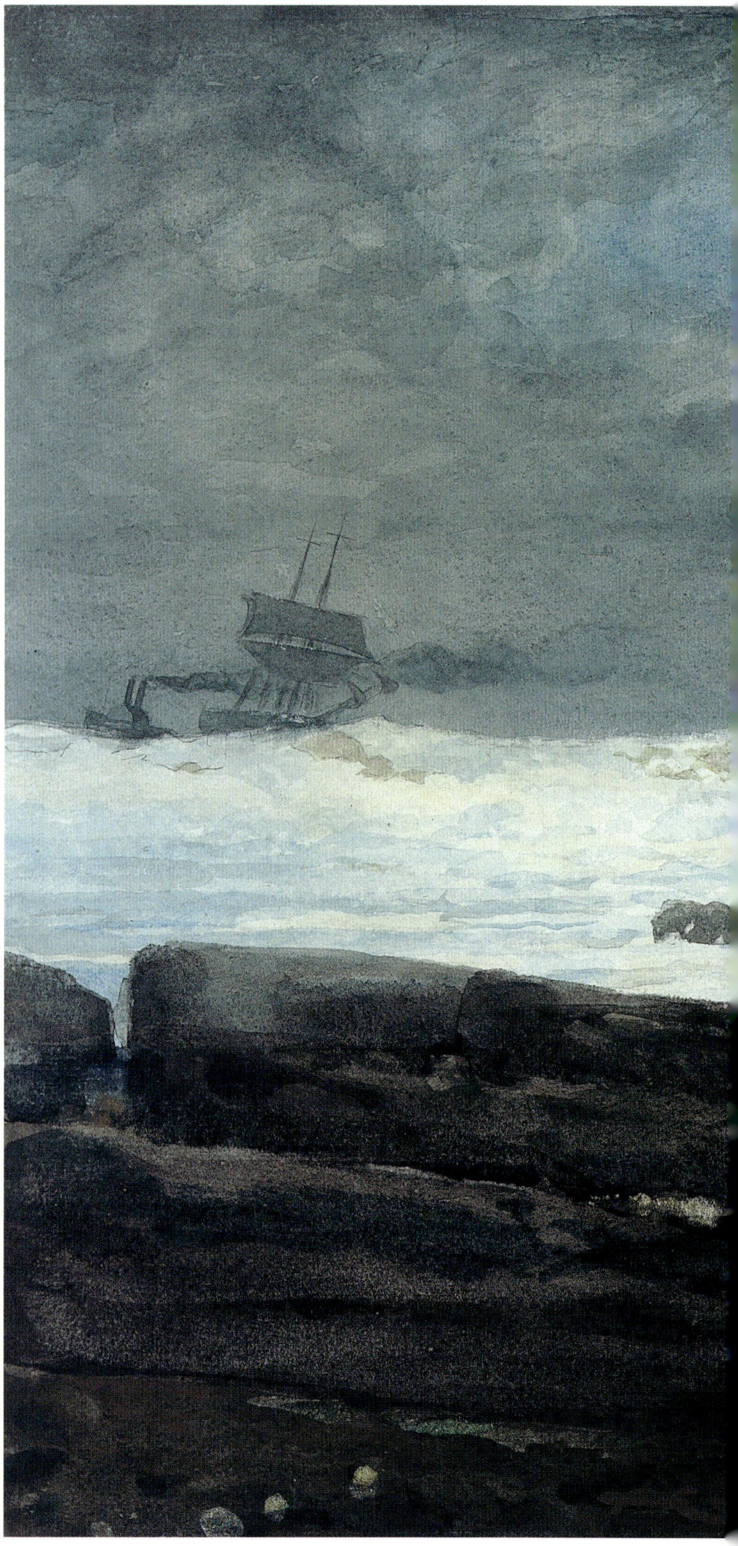

Fishwives 1883

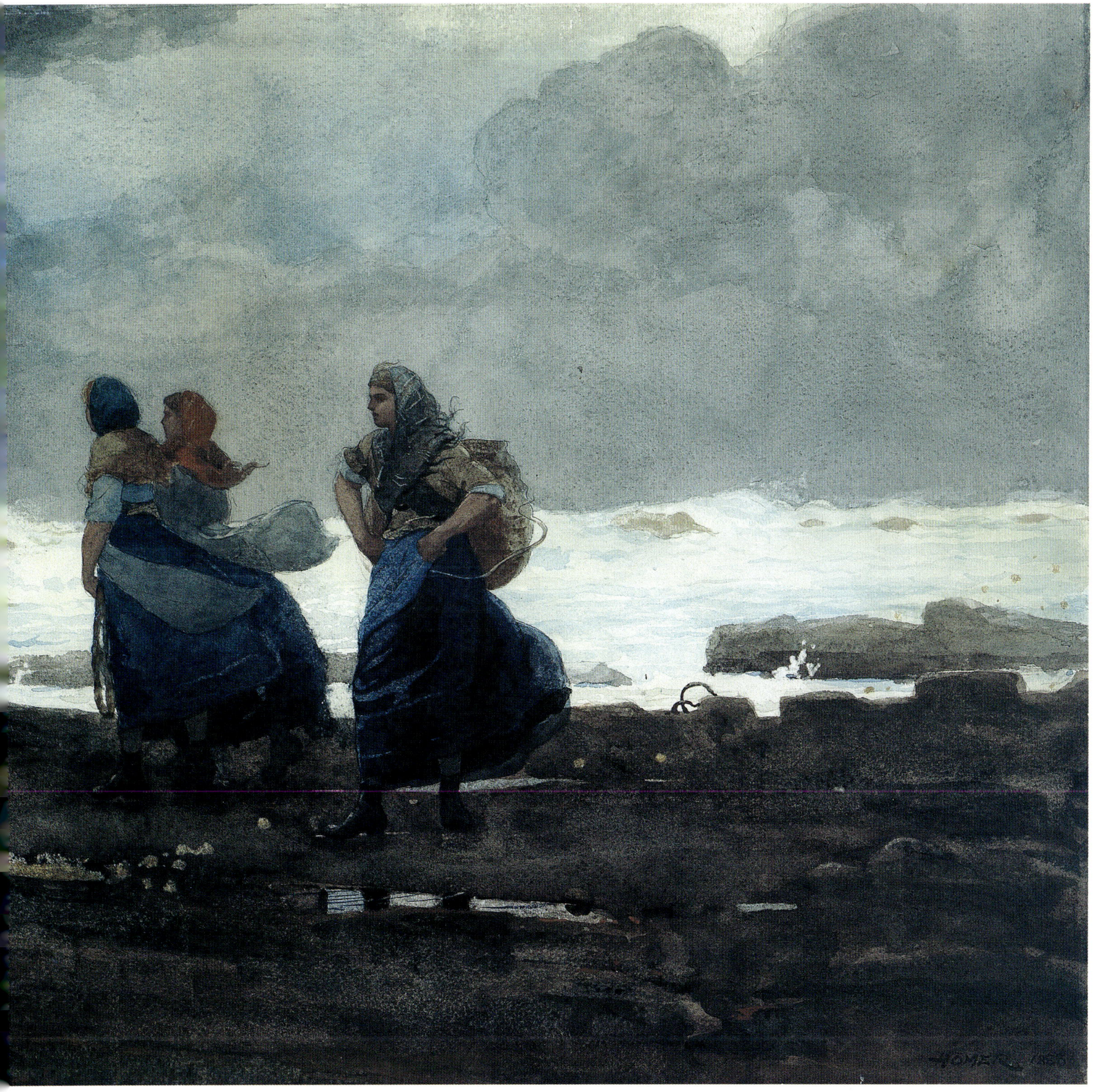

dom in a relaxed atmosphere encouraged by the sun and sea air. In the magazine engravings, he did not depict the ocean as a threatening element but as a place to frolic and to flirt. Early oil paintings like *Low Tide* and *Long Branch, New Jersey* also picture popular seaside resorts. But as Homer's career progressed, he abandoned these modern slice-of-life scenes—the very subjects that fascinated artists like Eugène Boudin, Edouard Manet, and Claude Monet—as too trivial a subject for serious art. Homer's mature art did not point, like that of his French colleagues, in the direction of modernism, but returned to the grand themes and intense emotionalism of the Romantic era.

This is particularly evident in the Cullercoats watercolors. There are few hints of the encroachment of contemporary life in these works. The men and women who populate these paintings live as they have always done, facing the same dangers and hardships as their forebears.

In these watercolors Homer defined what would become a key theme of his art: the stark confrontation of man—and in this case also woman—and unforgiving nature. These works possess all the epic sweep of Herman Melville's writing and a somewhat old-fashioned earnestness,

SUMMER CLOUD 1881

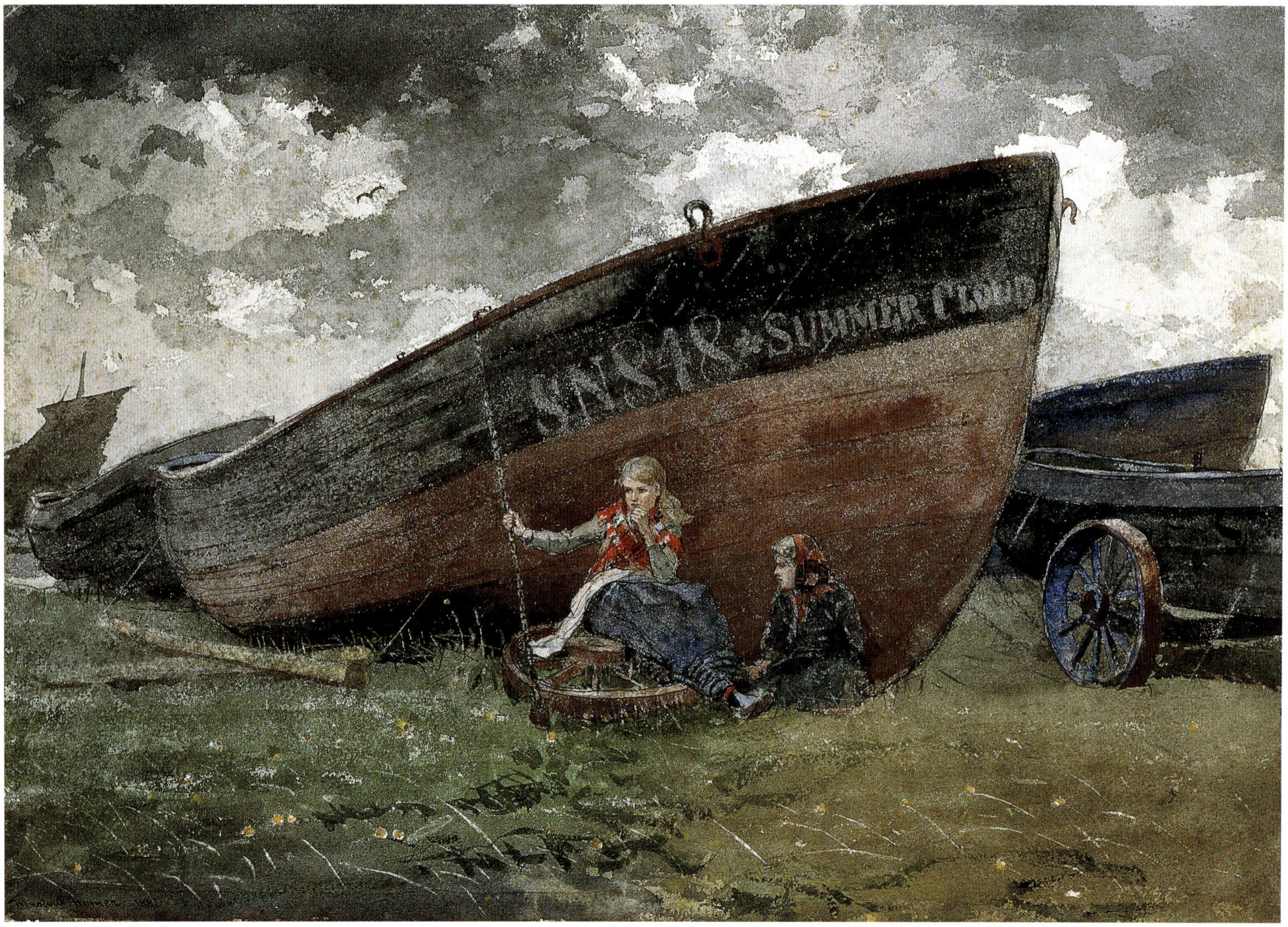

though, as always in Homer's art, they employ a down-to-earth language that grounds them in reality. There is little place in this world for the gentle humor that marked his *Artists Sketching in the White Mountains* [p. 16], where the confrontation of man and nature is eased somewhat by the bottle of Beaujolais and the ham sandwich.

The young girls looking out to sea in *On the Cliff* recall earlier Gloucester watercolors like *The Berry Pickers* [pp. 30–31]. This is a light, airy work, full of sparkle and redolent of salt breezes. *Looking Over the Cliff* is a far different work, more somber and more monumental. The composition has been simplified and the figures isolated against a cloudy sky so that they possess the imposing grandeur of classical statues. These girls are not simple fishing girls enjoying an afternoon off, but pillars of strength, able to withstand the vicissitudes of life.

Four Fisherwives is a highly finished work whose larger scale—at more than 28 inches its width is double that of many of the earlier watercolors—signals Homer's greater ambitions. In painting the four young ladies who stride purposefully across the beach, Homer was taking his cue from painters like the Dutchman Jozef Israëls and the Englishman James Clarke Hook, who celebrated

On the Cliff 1881

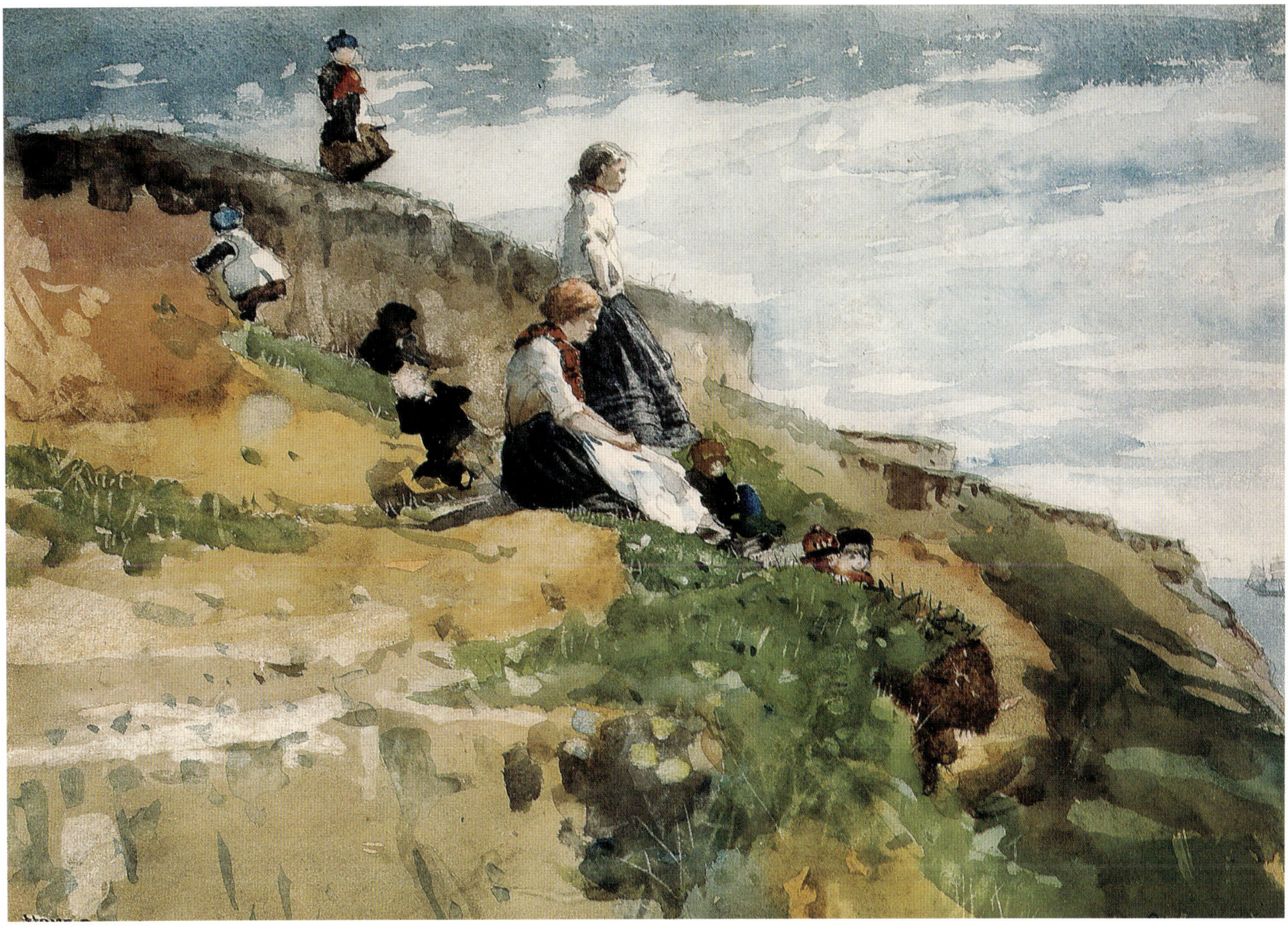

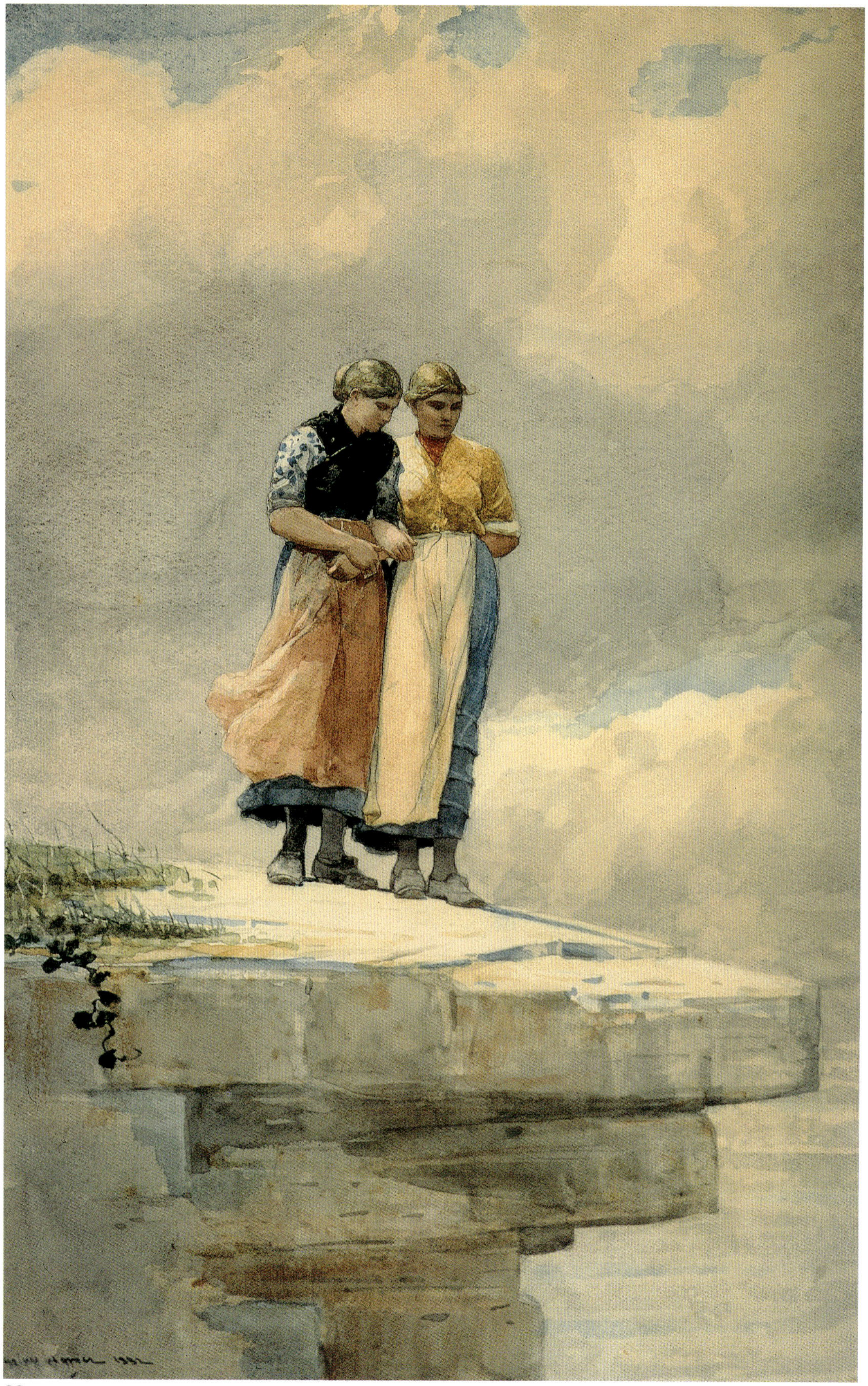

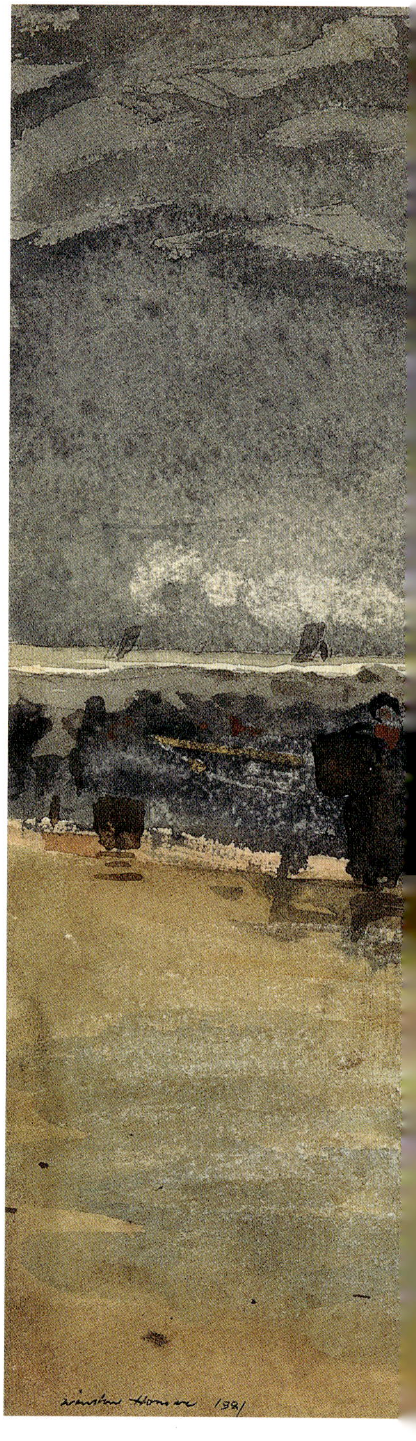

Looking over the Cliff 1882

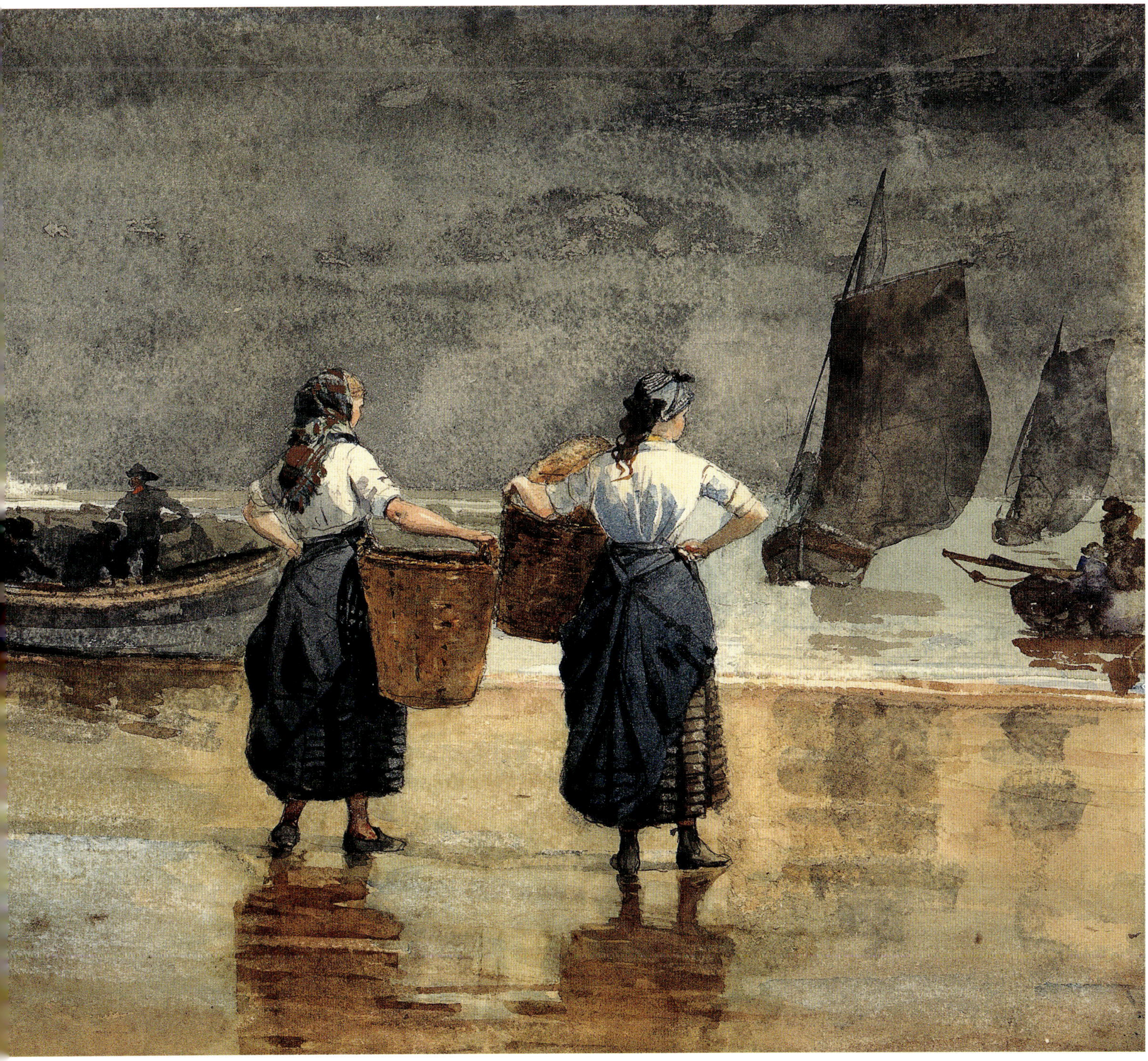

FISHER GIRLS ON THE BEACH, CULLERCOATS 1881

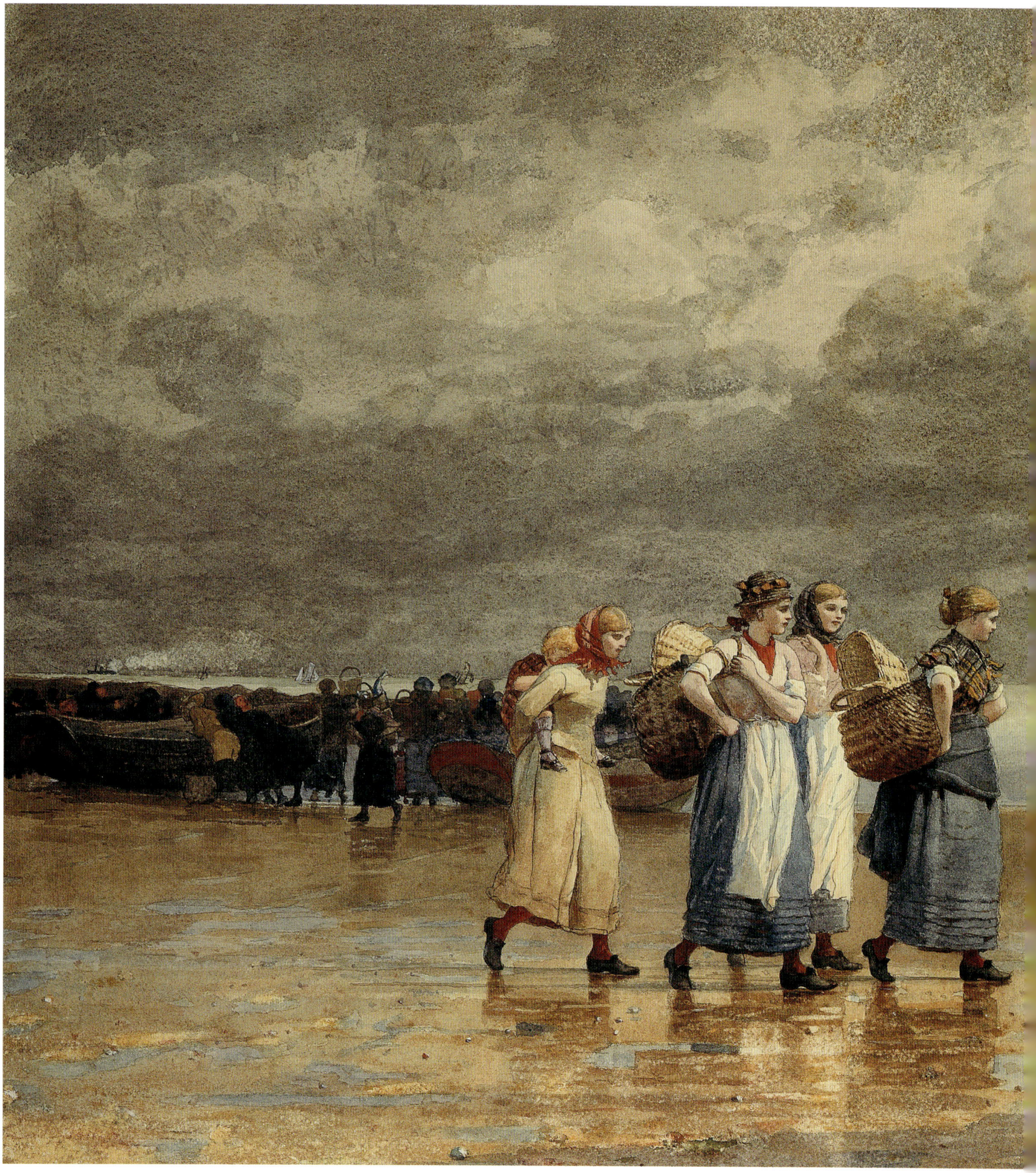

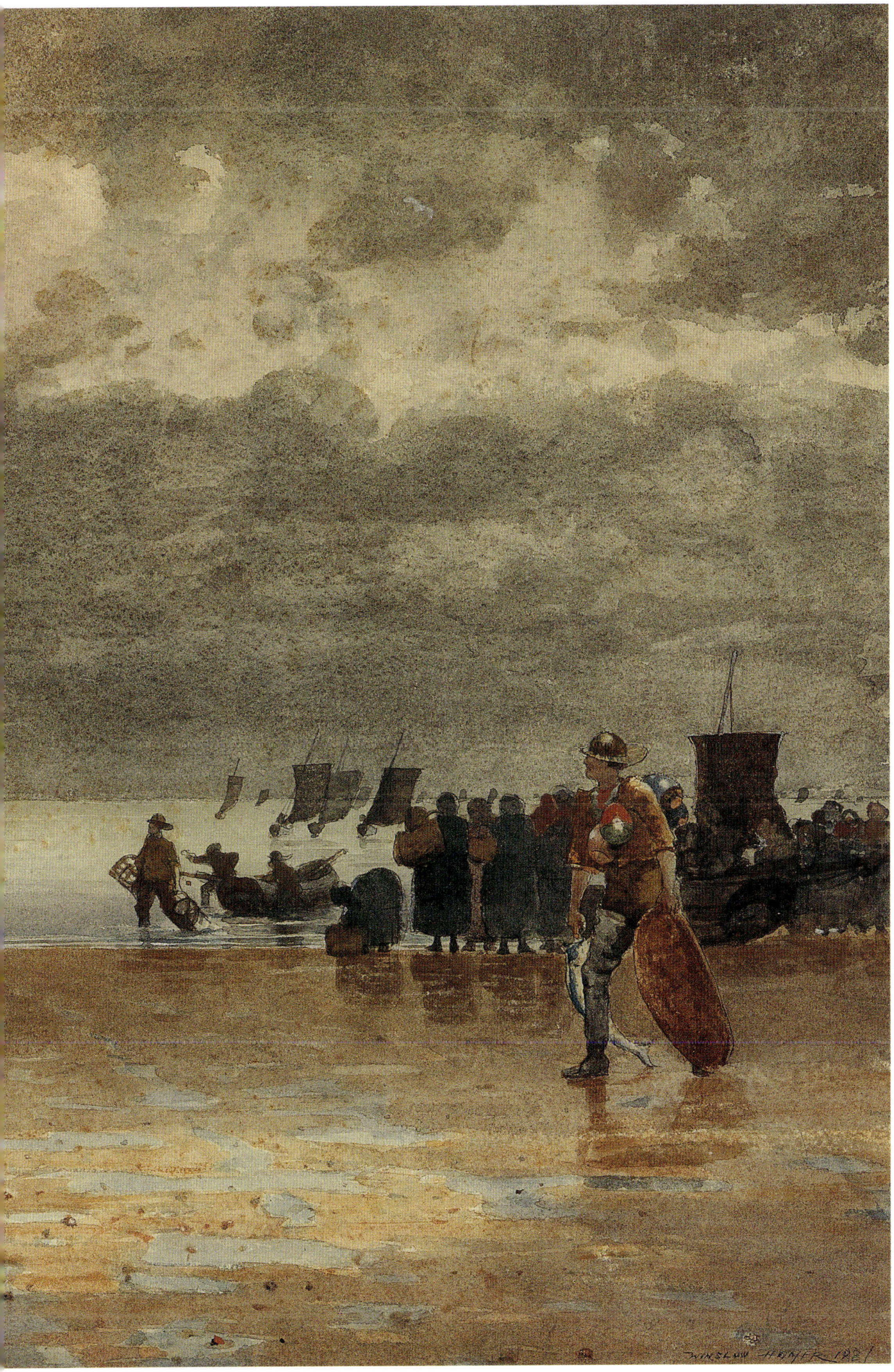

Four Fisherwives 1881

hardworking fishwives for their picturesque beauty and as embodiments of simple virtues. He may also have had in mind a popular contemporary English novel, *Christie Johnstone* by Charles Reade, whose heroine is a poor fisherwoman admired by a young lord. Reade describes such women in words that could apply equally to Homer's heroic figures: "Their supple persons moved as Nature intended; every gesture was ease, grace, and freedom. What with their own radiance, and the snowy cleanliness and brightness of their costume, they came like meteors. . . ." Unlike the carefree inhabitants of his Gloucester watercolors—and his rustic lasses who seem merely to play at being shepherdesses—these are working girls with strong arms and wind-burned cheeks. One contemporary

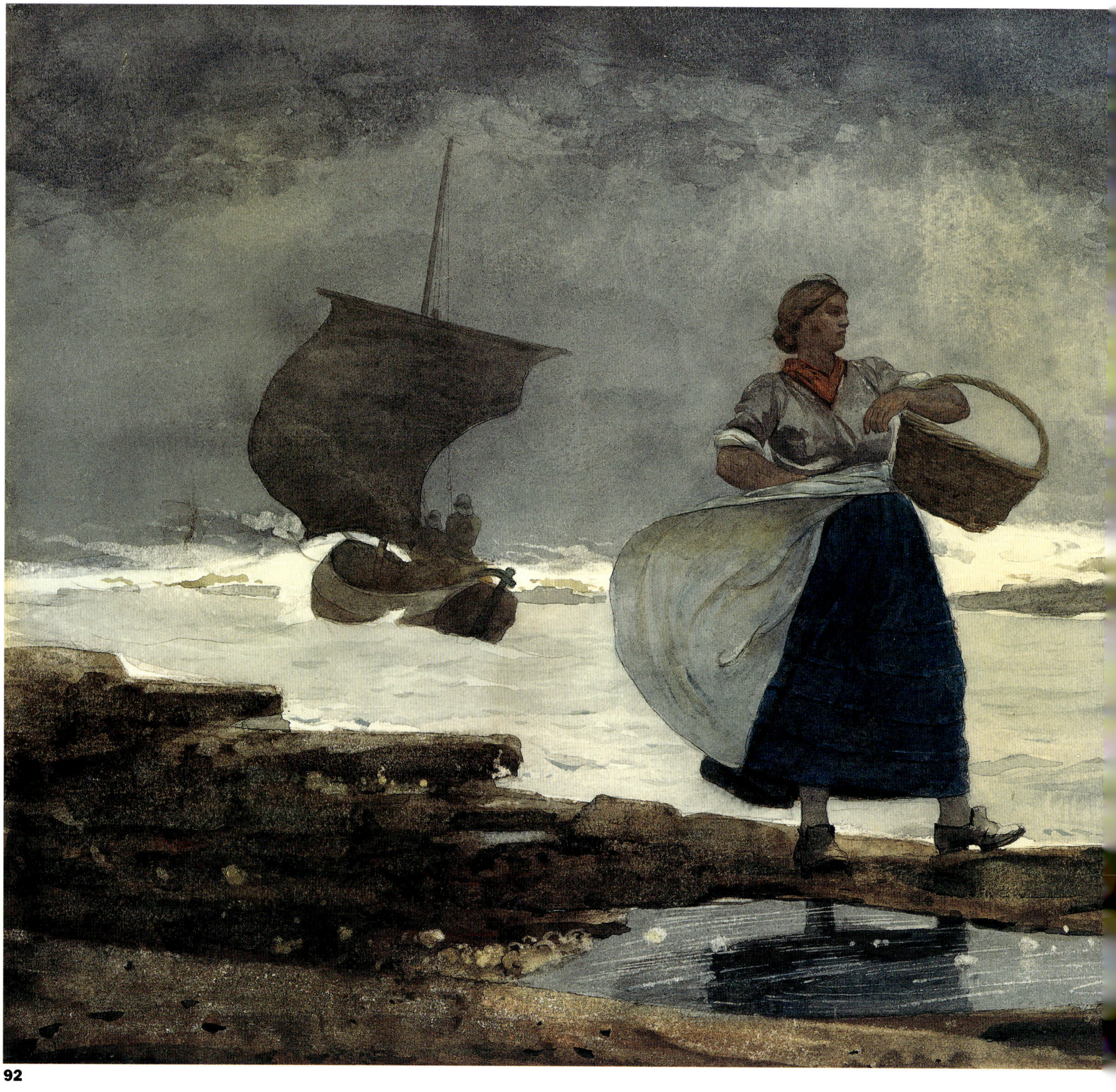

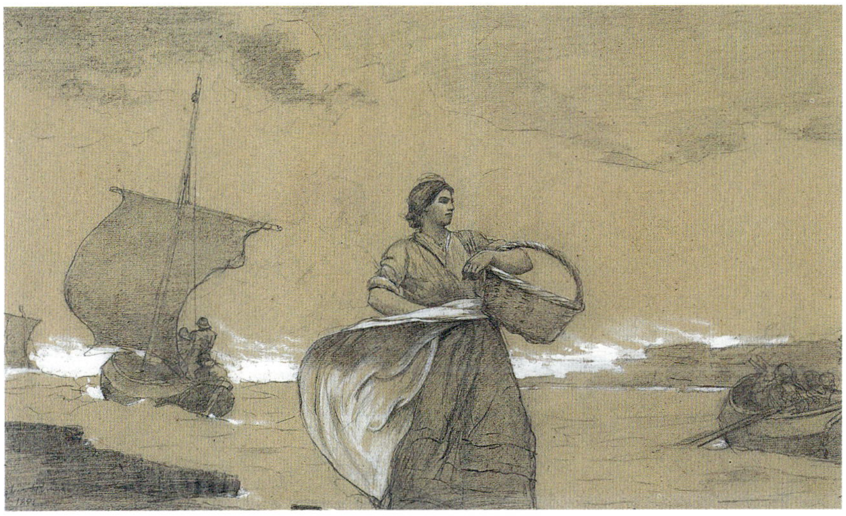

Windy Day, Cullercoats 1881

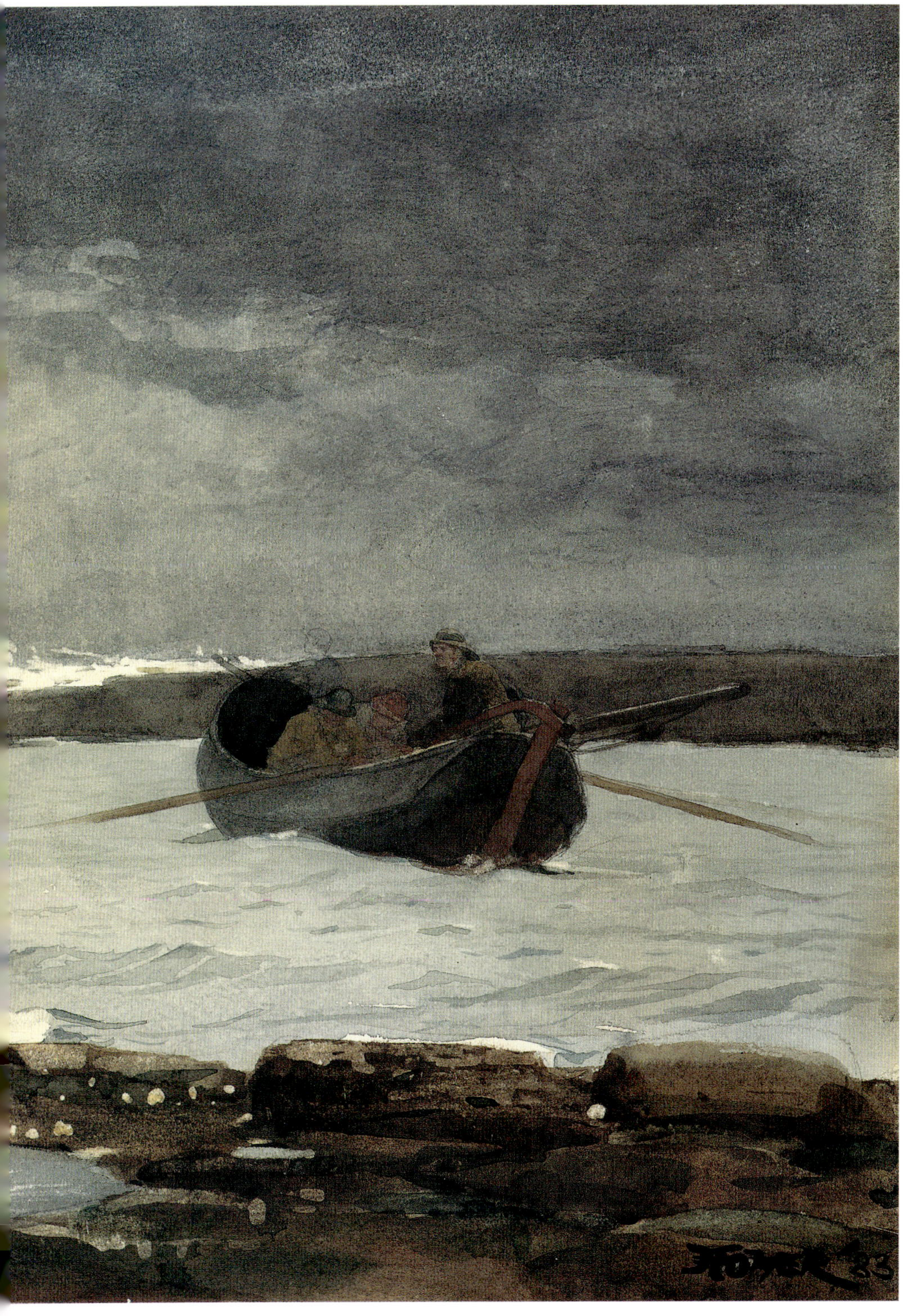

Inside the Bar, Cullercoats 1883

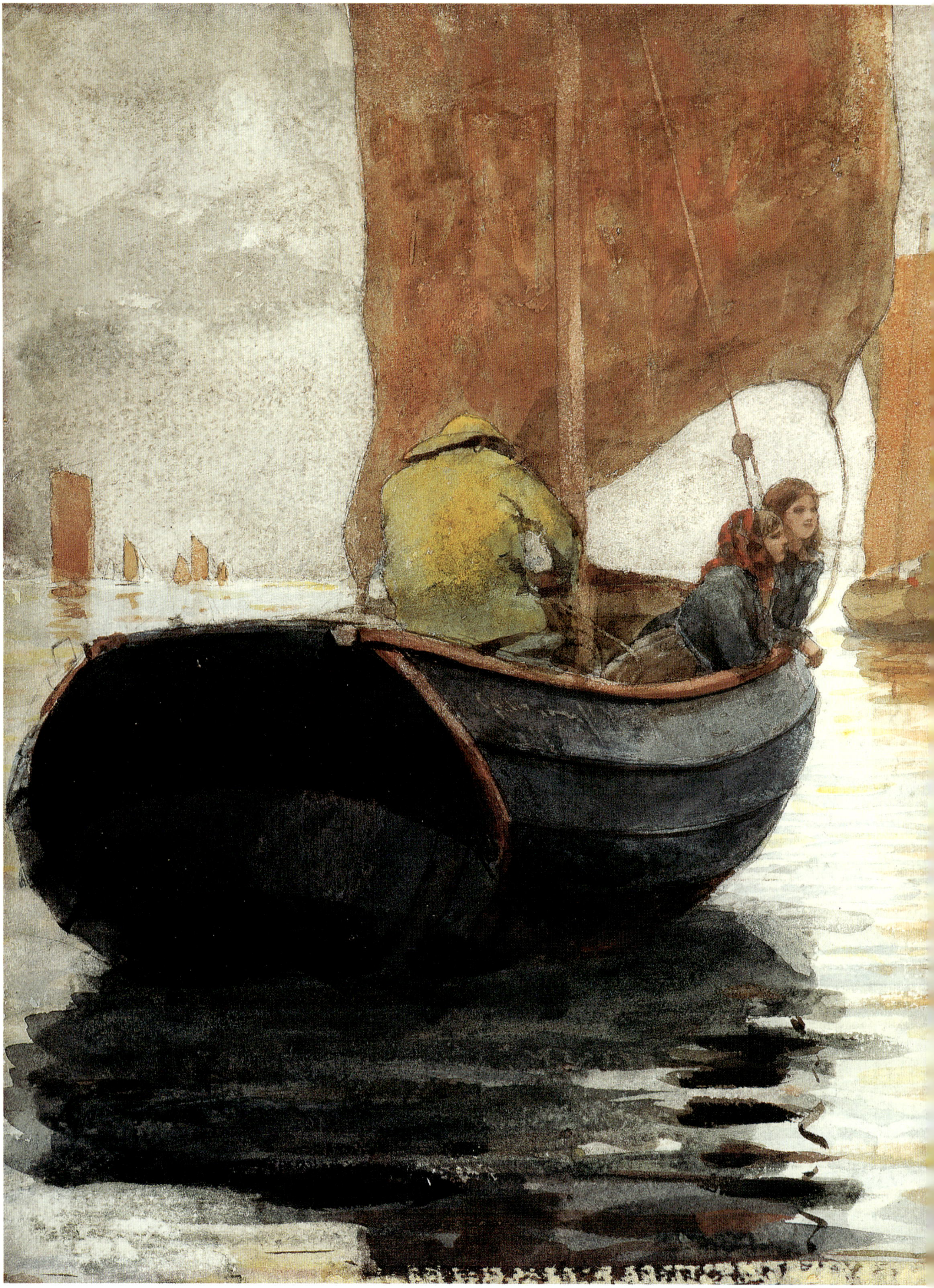

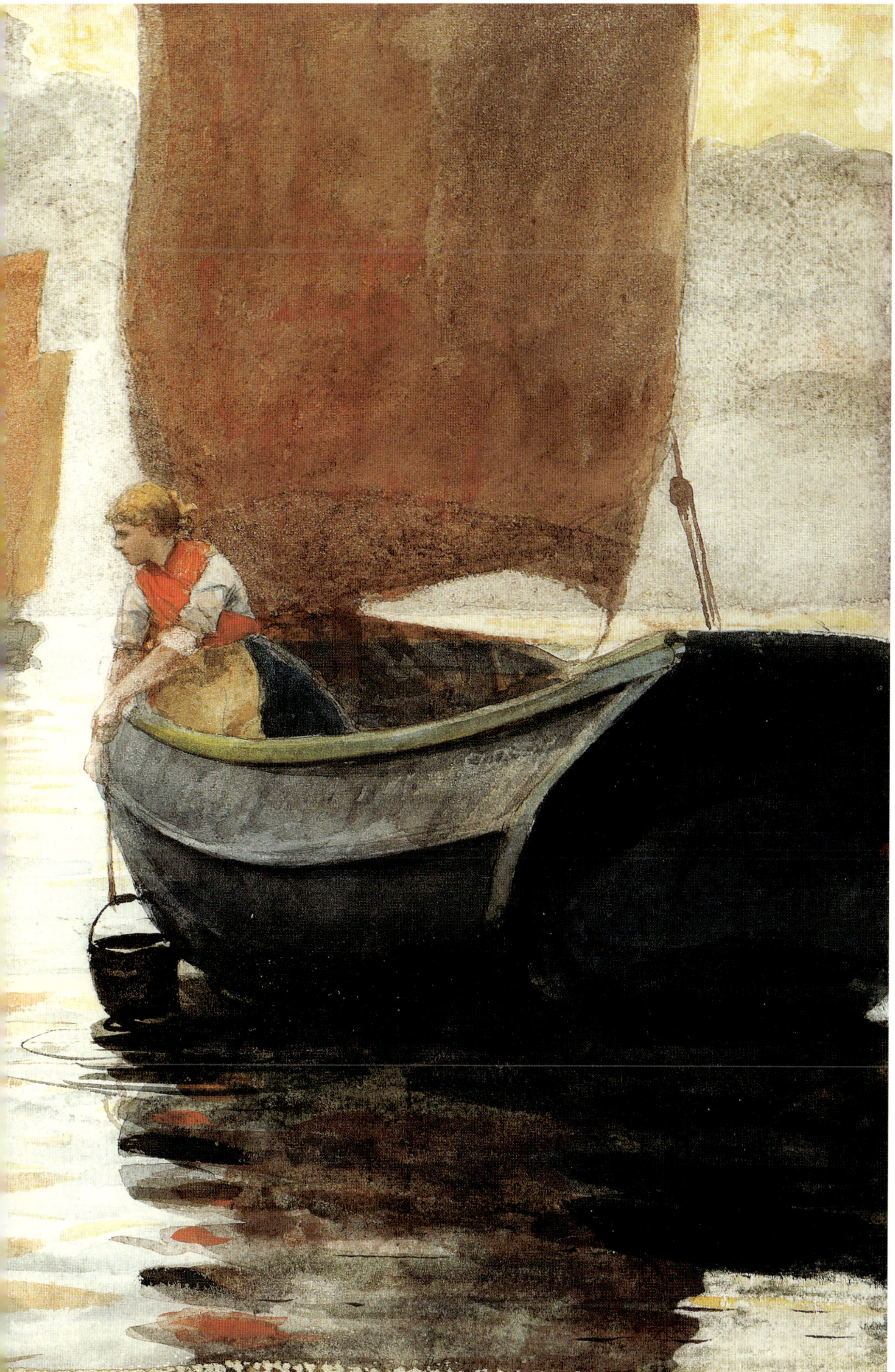

An Afterglow 1883

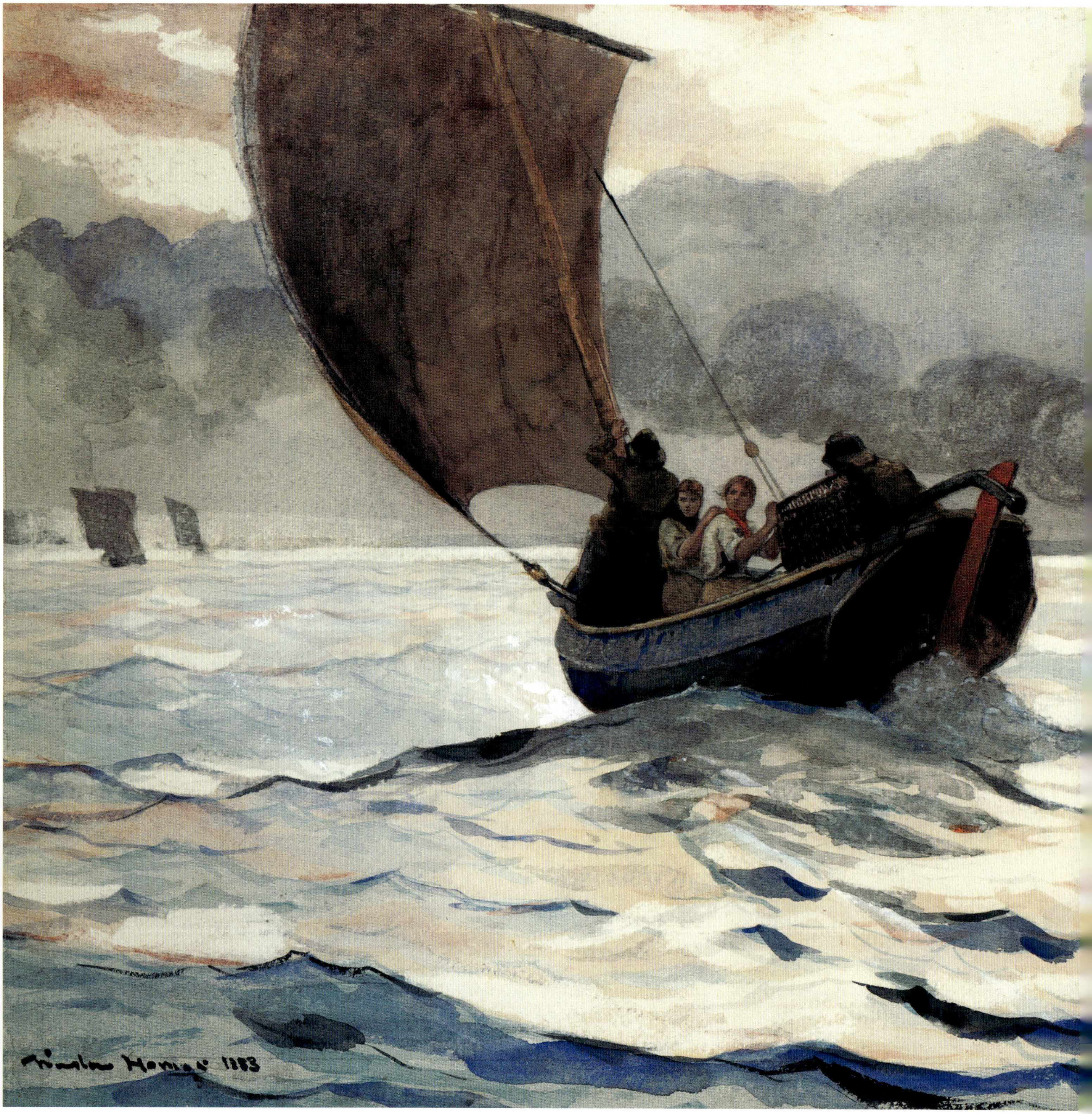
Winslow Homer 1883

RETURNING FISHING BOATS 1883

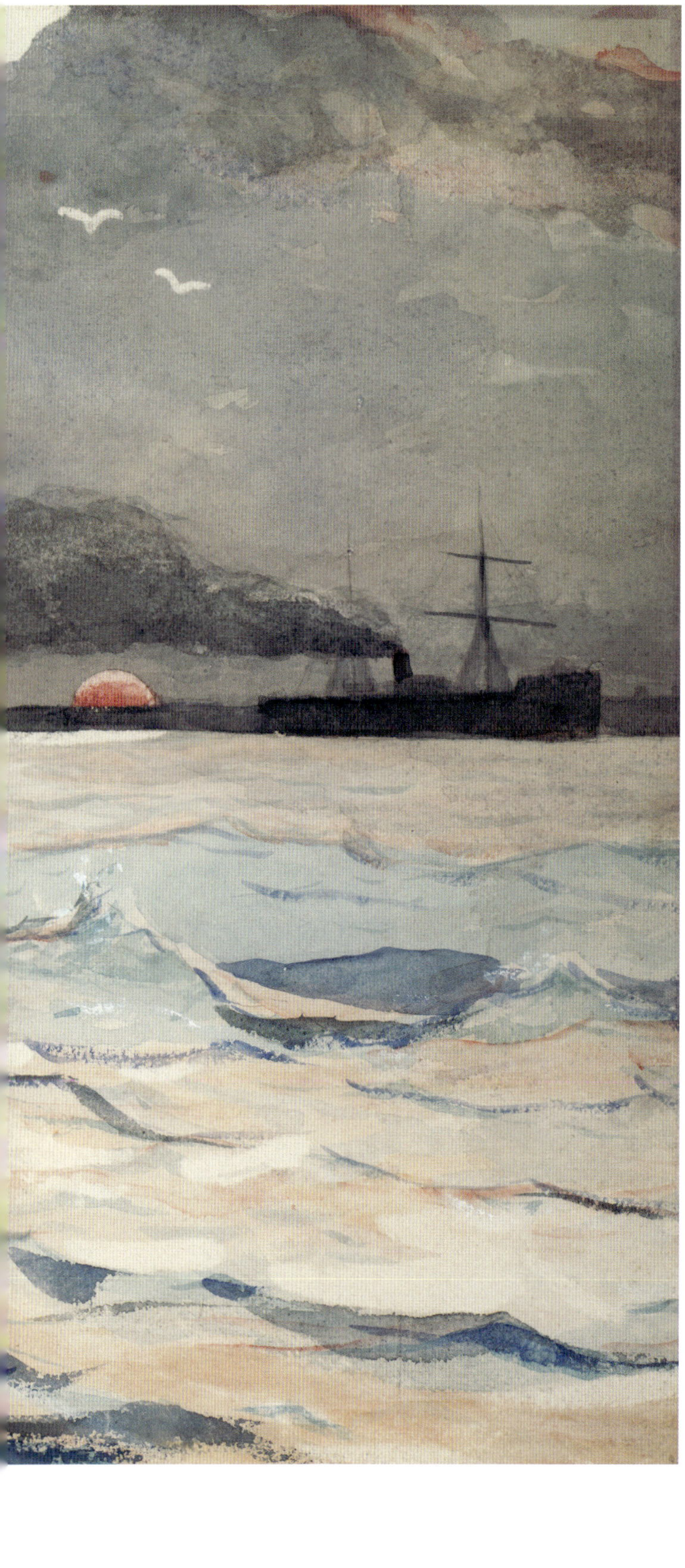

FISHING OFF SCARBOROUGH 1882

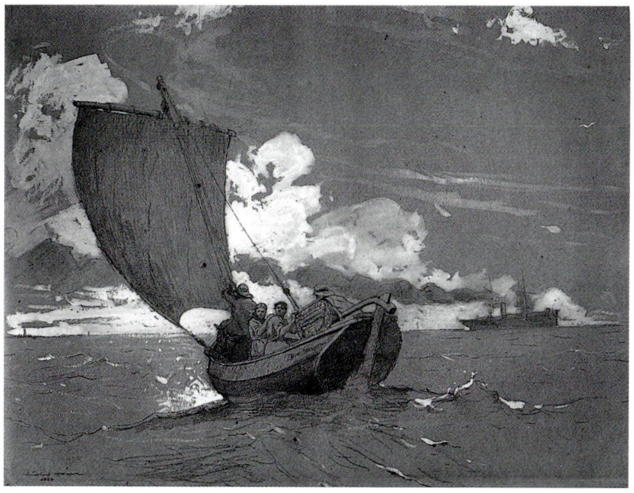

observer noted of such women: "They work harder than the men, ashore. Poor things! But then the men are almost always afloat, you see. They are big strong lasses, with hands and arms 'very large.' . . ."

In Homer's English watercolors, the delicate creatures of the 1870s have been replaced by figures whose beauty derives from strength of body and character. Set against the broad horizontal bands of sea, sand, and sky, these women dominate the scene. Their costumes provide accents of red, blue, and white in an otherwise somber palette that intimates more tempestuous scenes to come. Also banished is that sense of a moment caught on the wing characteristic of Homer's earliest watercolors. Through careful finish and composition, *Four Fisherwives* is calculated to achieve a more monumental effect that would stand comparison with the great art of the past.

The care with which these works were composed is revealed again in *Inside the Bar, Cullercoats*, where the curve of a woman's billowing apron is repeated in the wind-filled sail; even the rounded bow of the oncoming vessel and the basket's handle echo this basic shape, giving the work an insistent, almost musical rhythm. Even more monumental is *An Afterglow*—one of the works completed back in his New York studio in 1883—in which the two nearly symmetrical forms of the boats surround a central void. There is a sense of repose rare among the Cullercoats works: the water has stilled in the waning day and women lean from boat to boat, completing their chores and catching up on the day's news. Such a scene is described in a

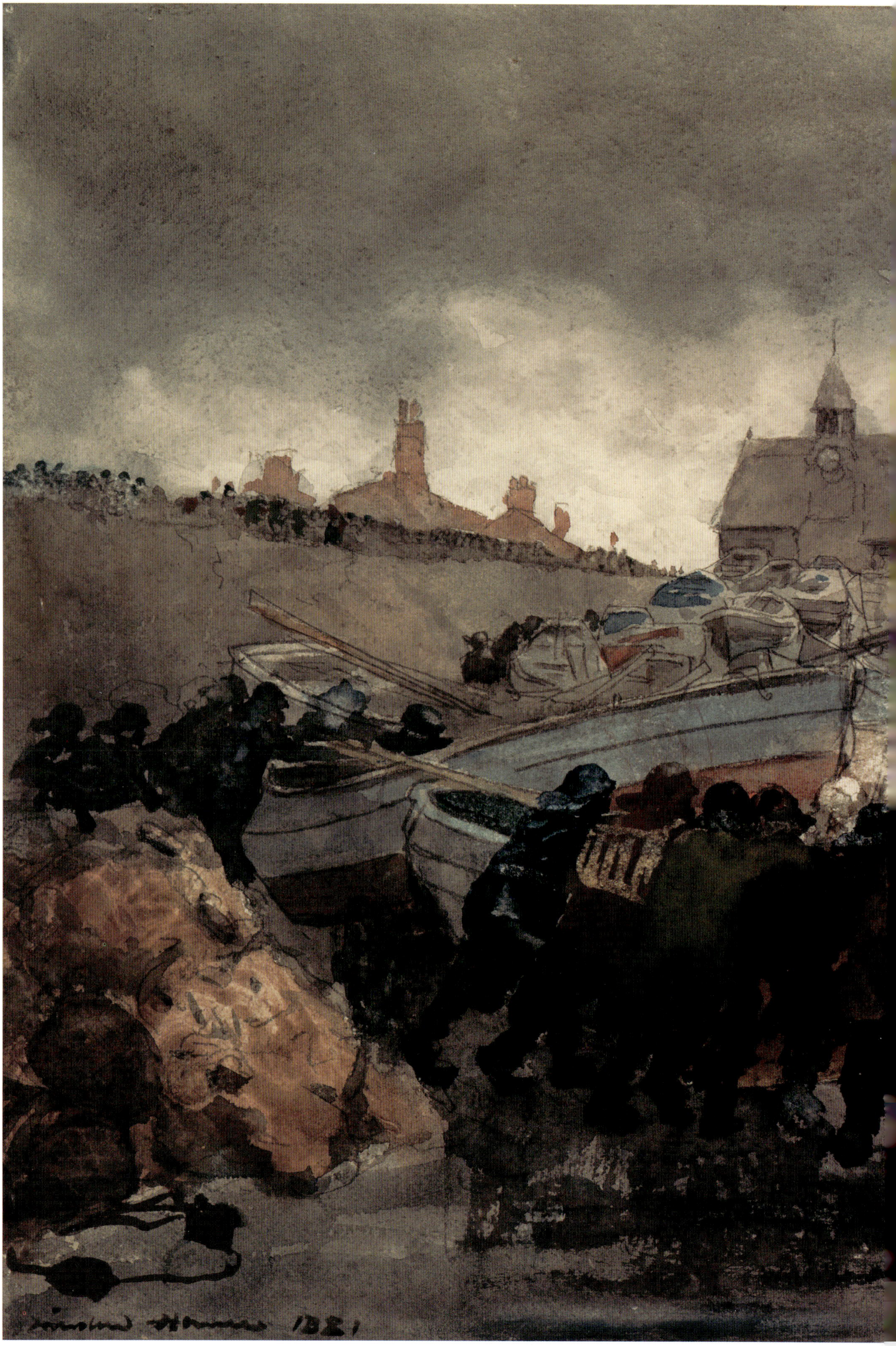

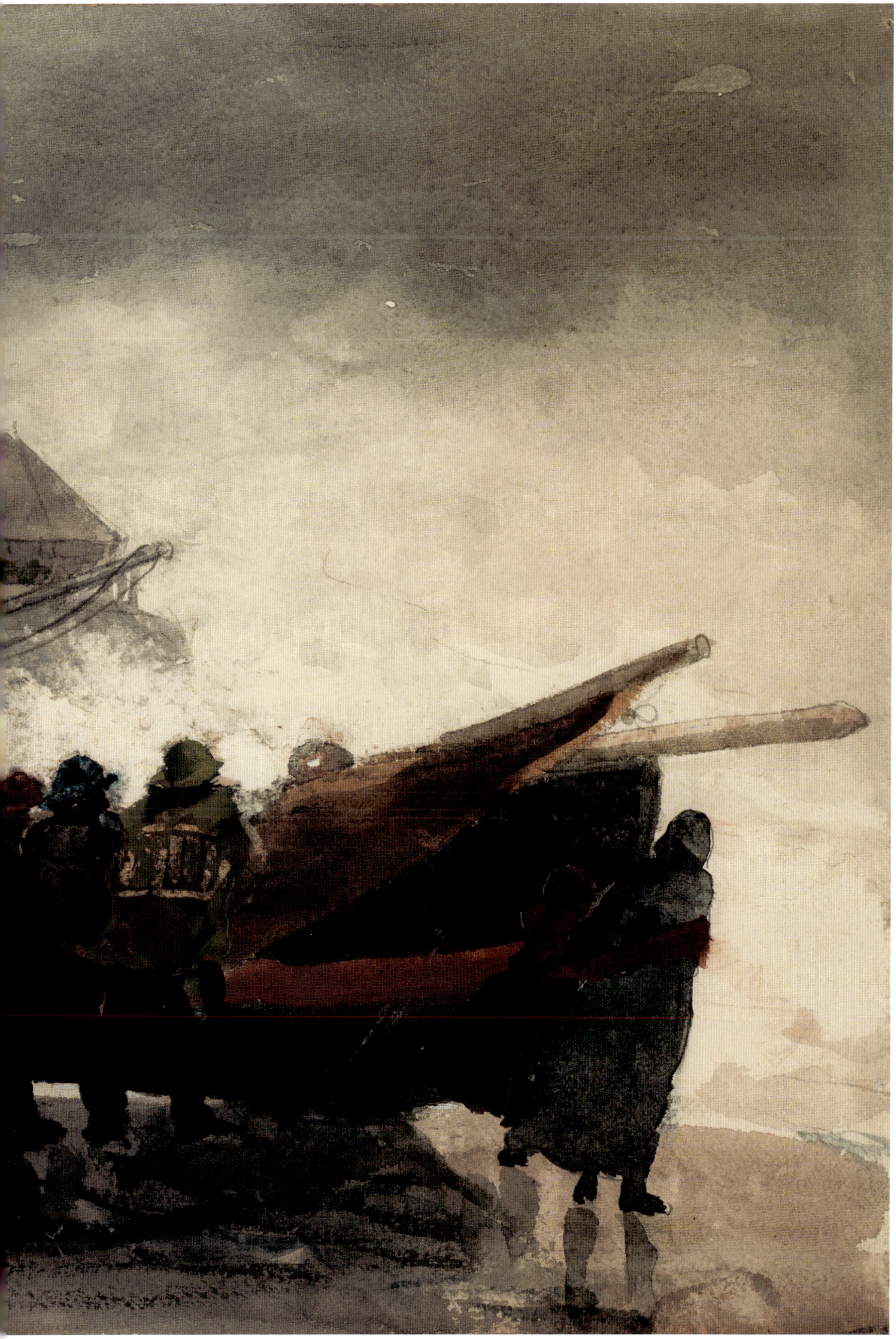

Watching the Tempest 1881

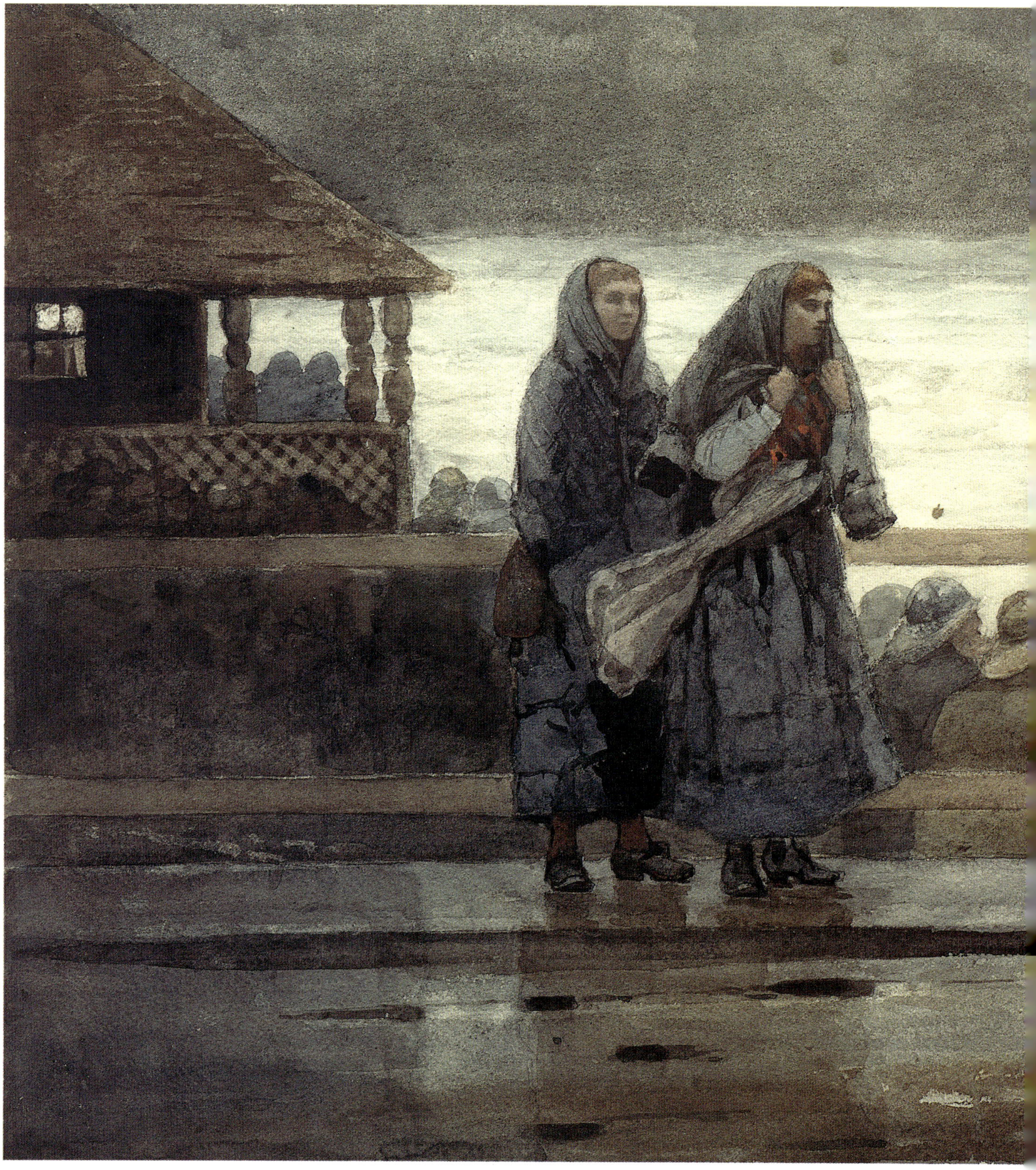

contemporary account: "When the boats are coming in the crowd in the haven is one to delight an artist: the cobles nearing shore one after another, their brown sails flapping, lowering, furling, as they come to land; the men splashing about in the water with gaily-painted oilskins and huge sea-boots; the women in their blue flannel dresses, standing in groups, waiting and gossiping."

An Afterglow, like many of the Cullercoats works, confirms that Homer was not doctrinaire about completing his paintings outdoors. Extensive alterations to the profiles of the boats and sails reveal how carefully he worked in this medium usually unforgiving of correction. Most of the larger English watercolors were not painted on the spot but completed in the studio from sketches made on site. Numerous drawings exist for paintings like *The Wreck of the Iron Crown* and *Perils of the Sea*, ranging from quick sketches—complete with Homer's color notations—to finished pieces suitable for exhibition.

Thematically, the Cullercoats paintings tread new ground. With the notable exception of *An Afterglow*, nature is no longer seen as benign; the gentle landscape that nurtures youthful escapades has become an active and threatening force. The lives of fishermen and their families was, as Homer well knew from his Gloucester days, a perilous one. Any sudden change in the weather could spell disaster for the crew aboard fragile boats and for the families who depended on them. Charles Dickens describes in *David Copperfield* the fury of a coastal storm

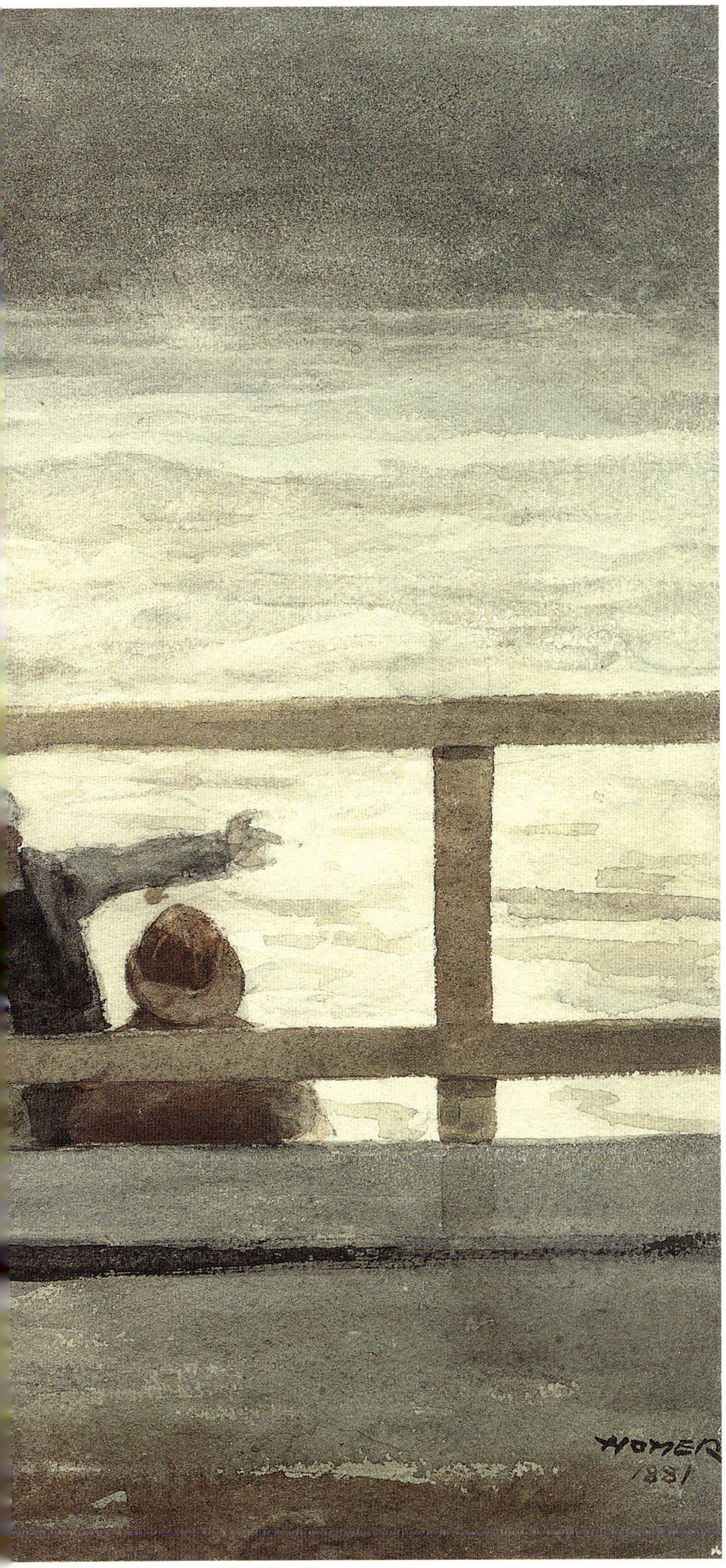

PERILS OF THE SEA 1881

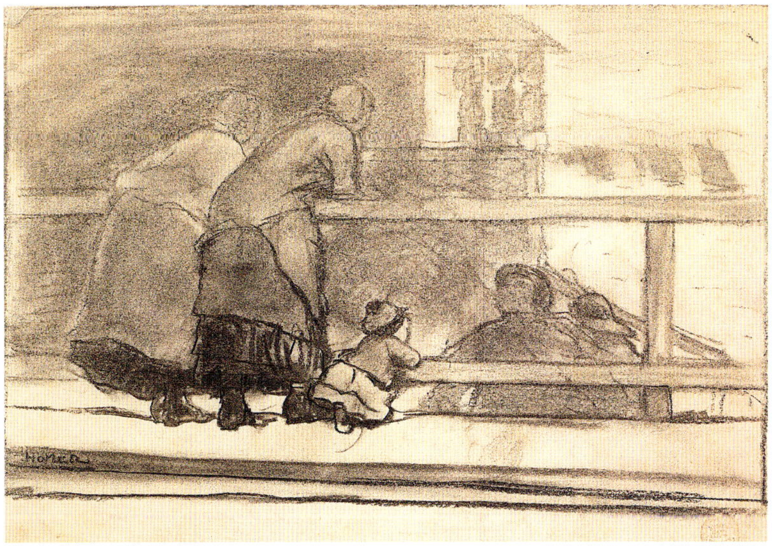

TWO WOMEN AND A CHILD AT A RAIL, OVERLOOKING THE BEACH AT CULLERCOATS 1881

and the terror it strikes in the hearts of those left on shore: "Joining these groups, I found bewailing women whose husbands were away in herring or oyster boats, which there was too much reason to think might have foundered before they could run in anywhere for safety . . . even stout mariners, disturbed and anxious, leveling their glasses at the sea from behind places of shelter, as if they were surveying an enemy."

The marine disaster, first hinted at in *A Wreck Near Gloucester*, takes center stage in *The Wreck of the Iron Crown*, one of the largest and most elaborate watercolors of Homer's career. The painting originated in a daring rescue that the artist actually witnessed; but the many preparatory drawings attest that the final work was completed in the studio. Despite, or perhaps because of, the careful preparation, this painting is strangely inert, stifled perhaps by the amount of time and labor Homer invested in it. More successful is *Watching the Tempest*. Here the sense of impending disaster is made all the more acute by the blinding surge of white foam—an effect produced by extensive scraping of the paper—that rolls over the men and women who peer out to sea and that hides from us the source of their anxiety.

Typically, Homer sets up a contrast in these works between the world of women and the world of men. Though the women are sturdy and clearly capable, having shed that "fossil and unhealthy air" that characterized his female figures of the 1870s, they are still largely passive, unable to change the outcome of events. In *Perils of the Sea*, he erects a physical barrier between the two groups: the men stand ready below in their foul-weather gear, poised to leap into action, while the women above can only wait and worry. A contemporary visitor to Cullercoats described just such a scene: "On stormy nights a great fire burns in the grate; and brown-bearded fishermen from Cullercoats and brave shop-keepers from Shields—clad in sea-boots and guernseys and sou'-westers, with their life-belts close to their hands—lounge in groups at the hearth or stand looking out into the storm, ready, whenever the guns of the *Castor* are heard, to leap into their boat and for other lives do battle with the perilous sea."

For Homer, however, it is not clear who plays the more heroic part. In his Cullercoats paintings, it is more often the stoic endurance of the women than the courage of the men that draws his attention. It is not simply their

The Wreck of the Iron Crown 1881

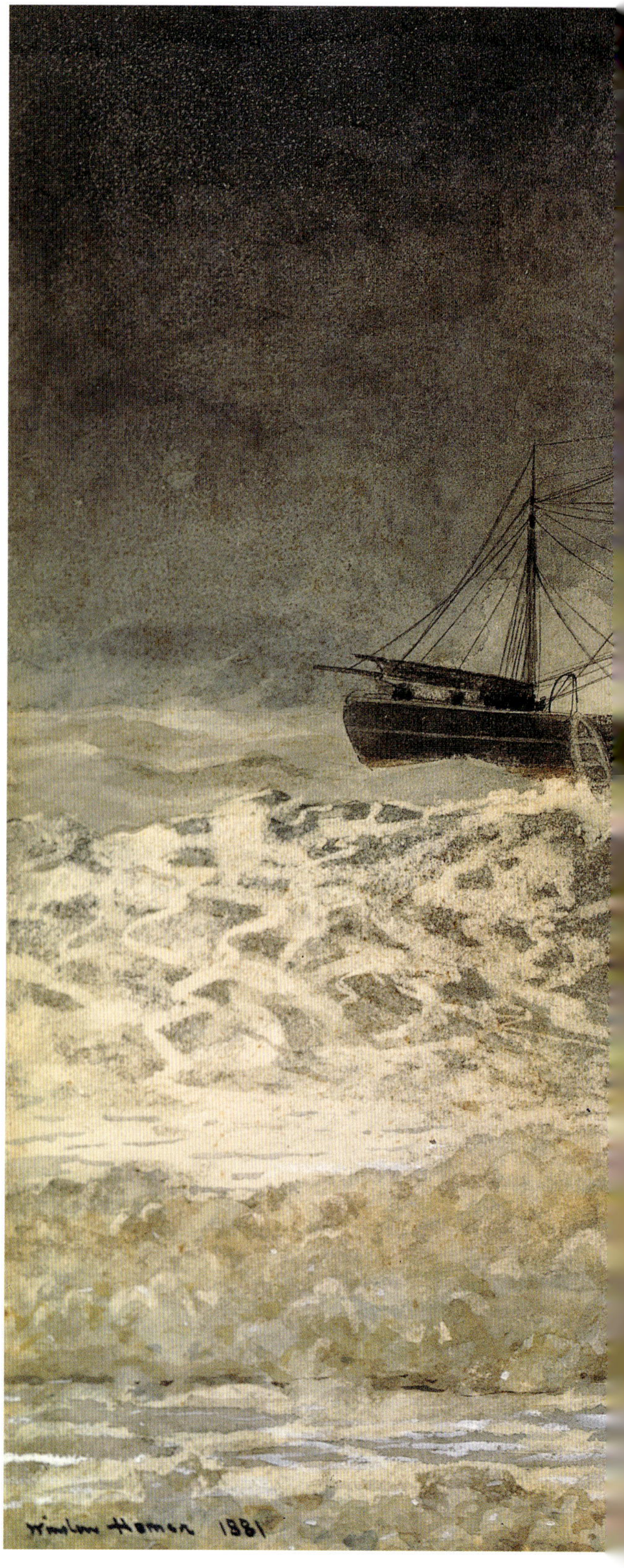

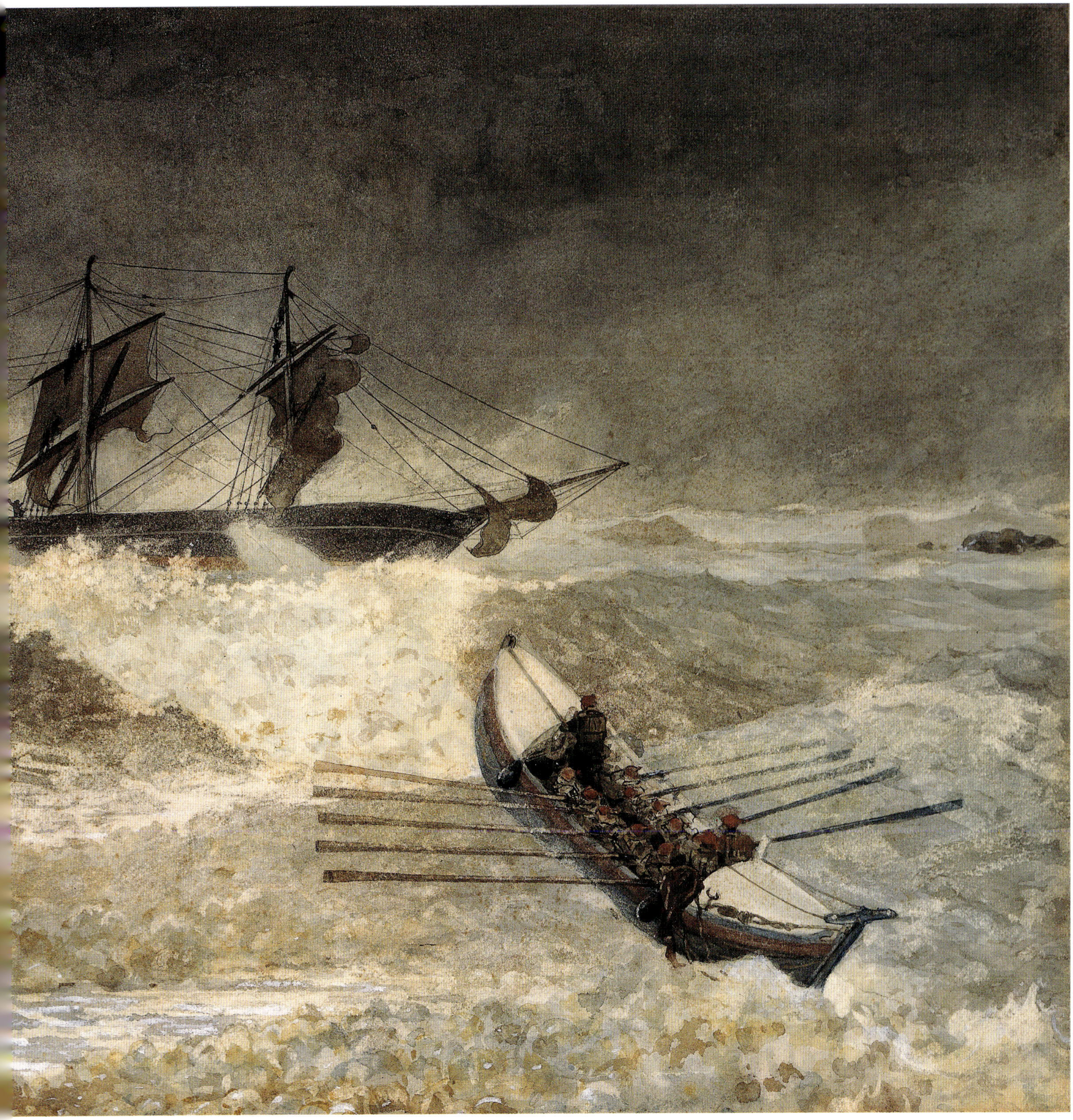

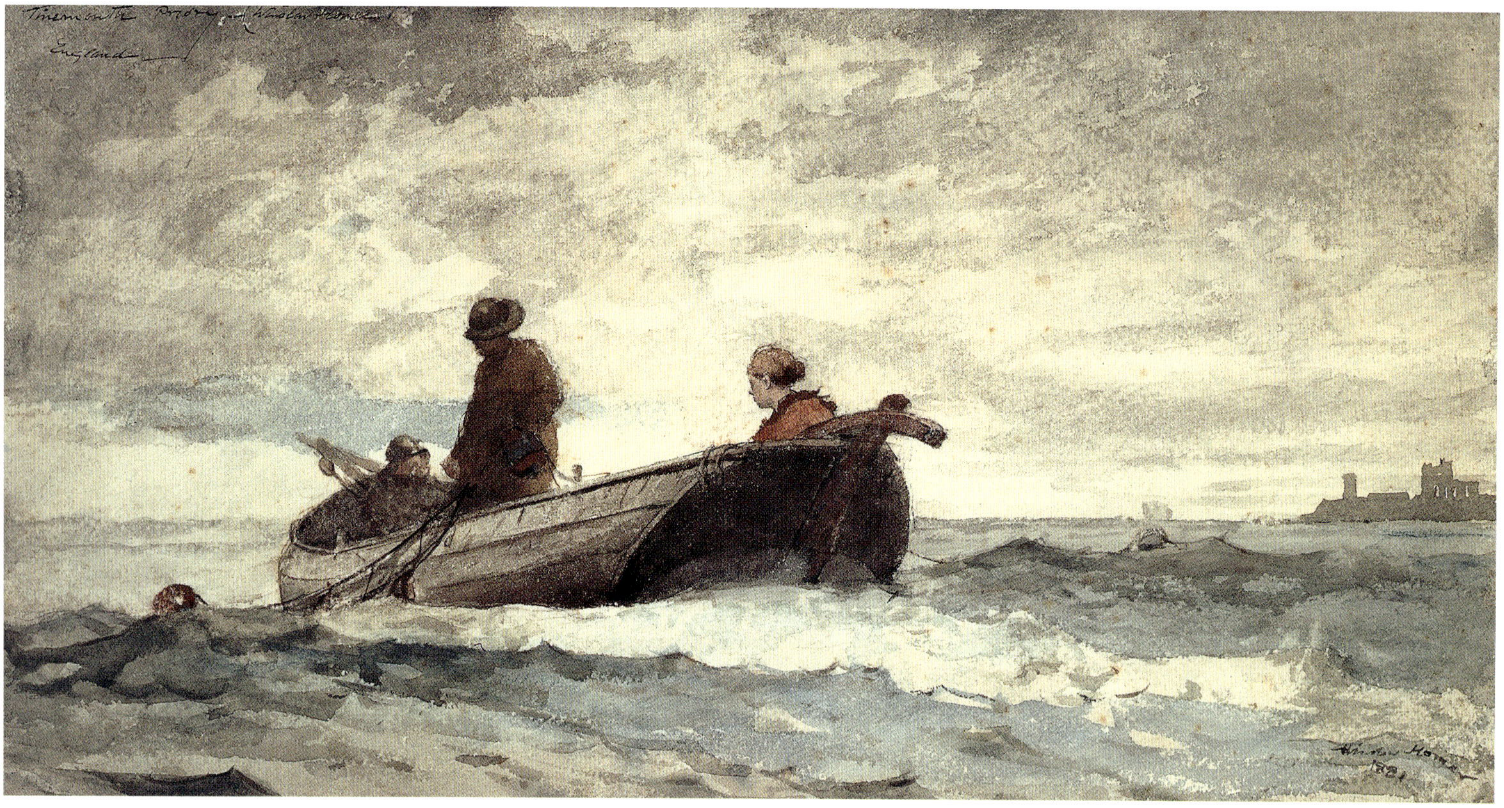

TYNEMOUTH PRIORY, ENGLAND 1881

capacity to endure that Homer admires, but their strength and quiet dignity. Even in a tamer environment, such as the cobblestone courtyard depicted in *Mending the Nets*, the women possess a grandeur that is in no way lessened by the mundane task in which they are absorbed. These watercolors are not portraits of particular women but depict archetypal figures who embody the universal ideal of womanhood. Scholars have remarked on the resemblance between these women and ancient statues of Greek goddesses, positing perhaps the influence of the *Elgin Marbles* that Homer could have seen at the British Museum during his London stay. Whether or not such a direct inspiration can be found for his Cullercoats women, it is clear that in these works he was seeking a place within the grand tradition of Western art.

A work unique among Homer's watercolors is *The Houses of Parliament*. Although his first magazine illustrations depicted the bustle of a busy Boston street, urban scenes were uncongenial to Homer and rarely found their way into his paintings. In this lovely work, made near the beginning of his stay in England, the artist minimizes the harsher angles of the city by focusing on the wide river and bathing distant buildings in a softening fog. He manages in the end to turn the English capital into an atmospheric vision in rose and silver and the seat of government into a fairy castle.

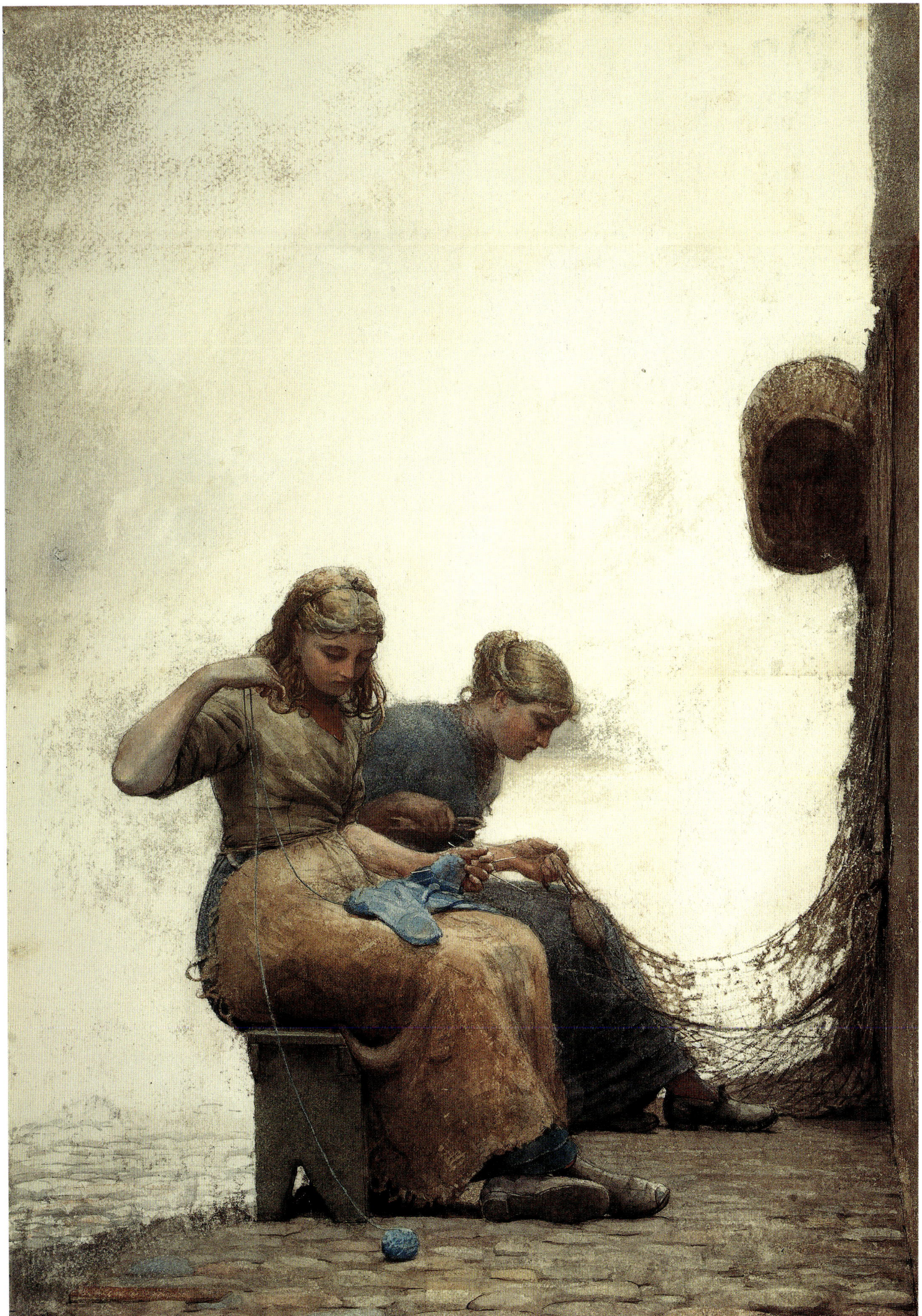

Mending the Nets 1882

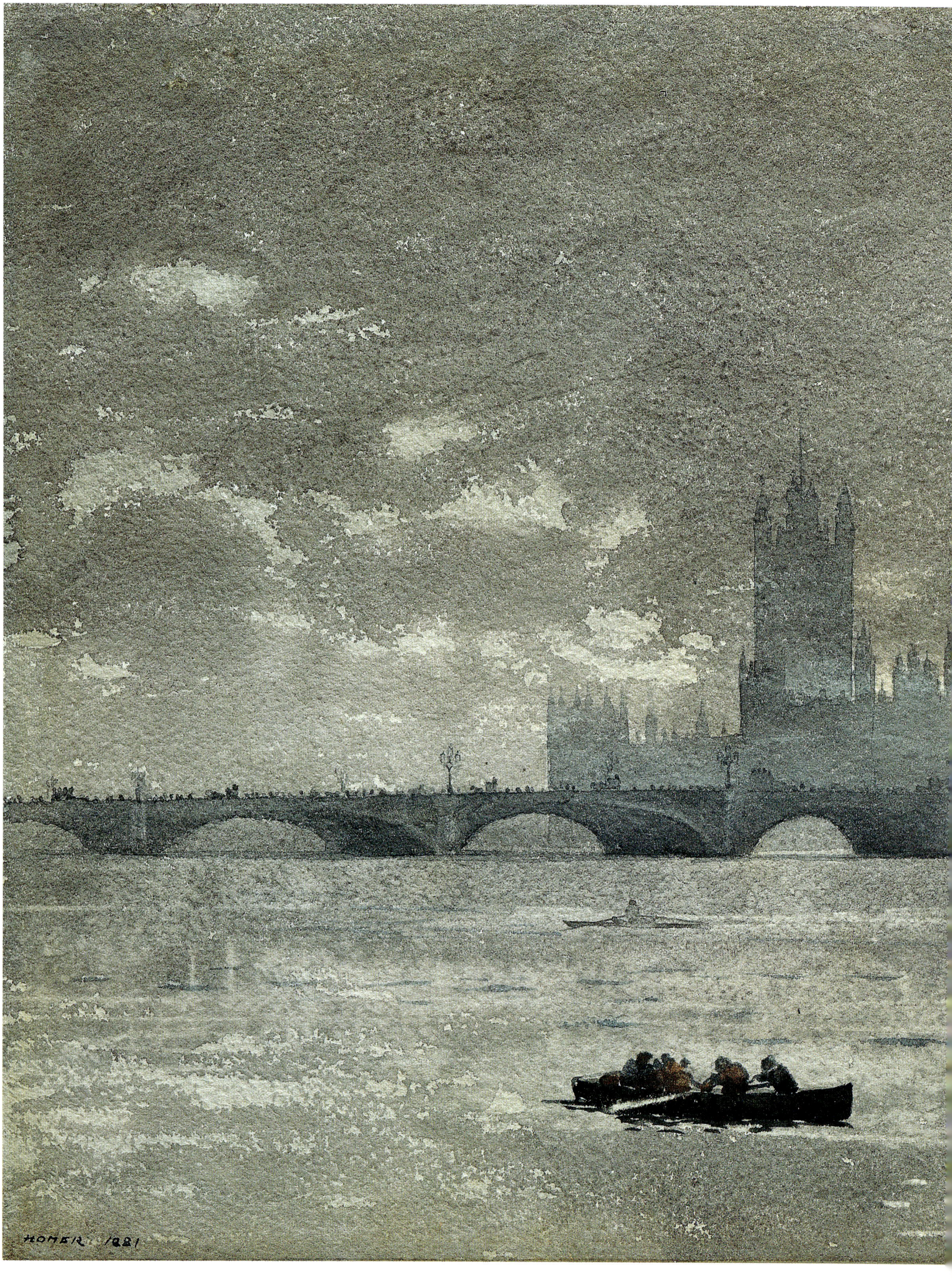
HOMER 1881

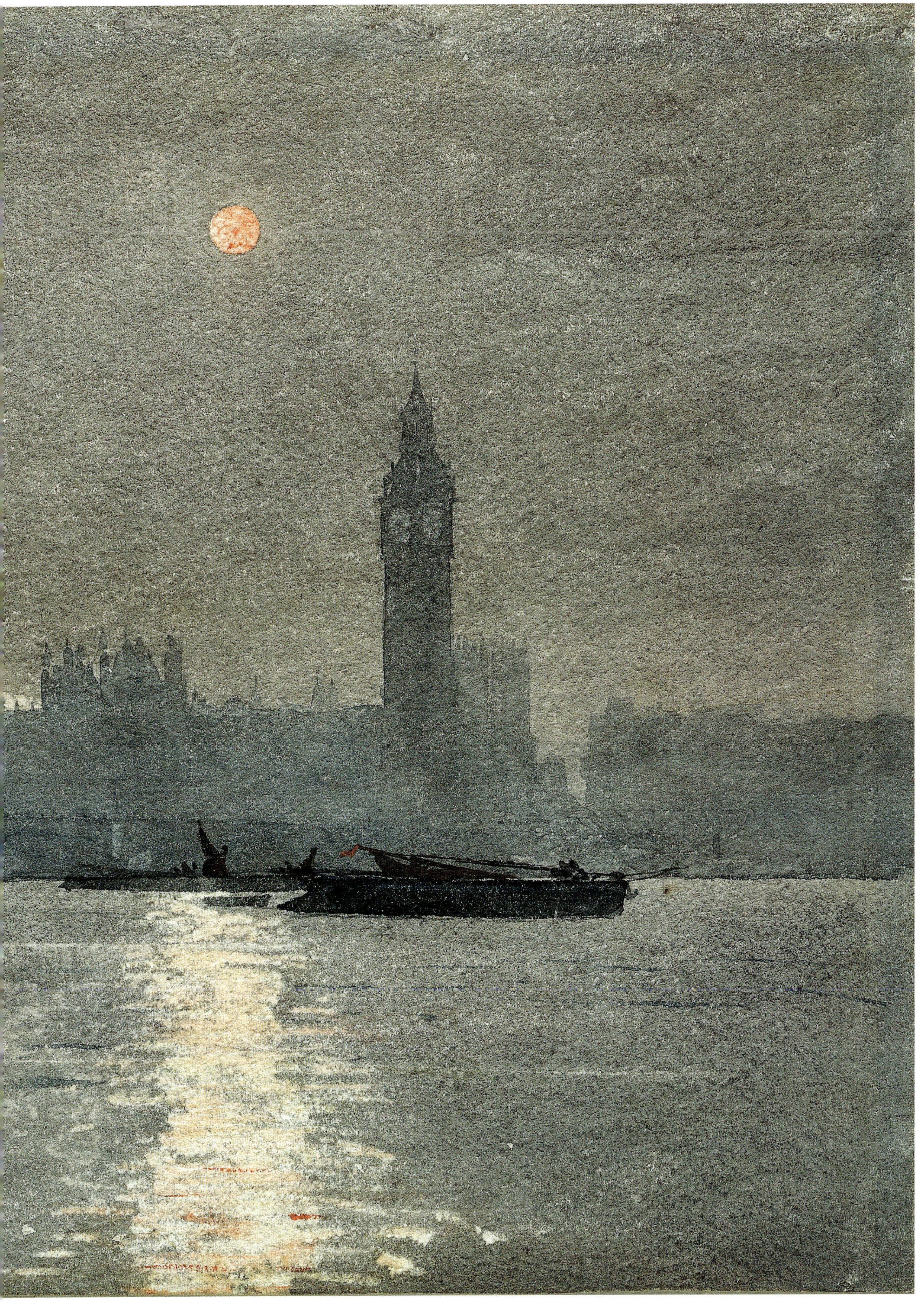

The Houses of Parliament 1881

Blown Away c. 1888

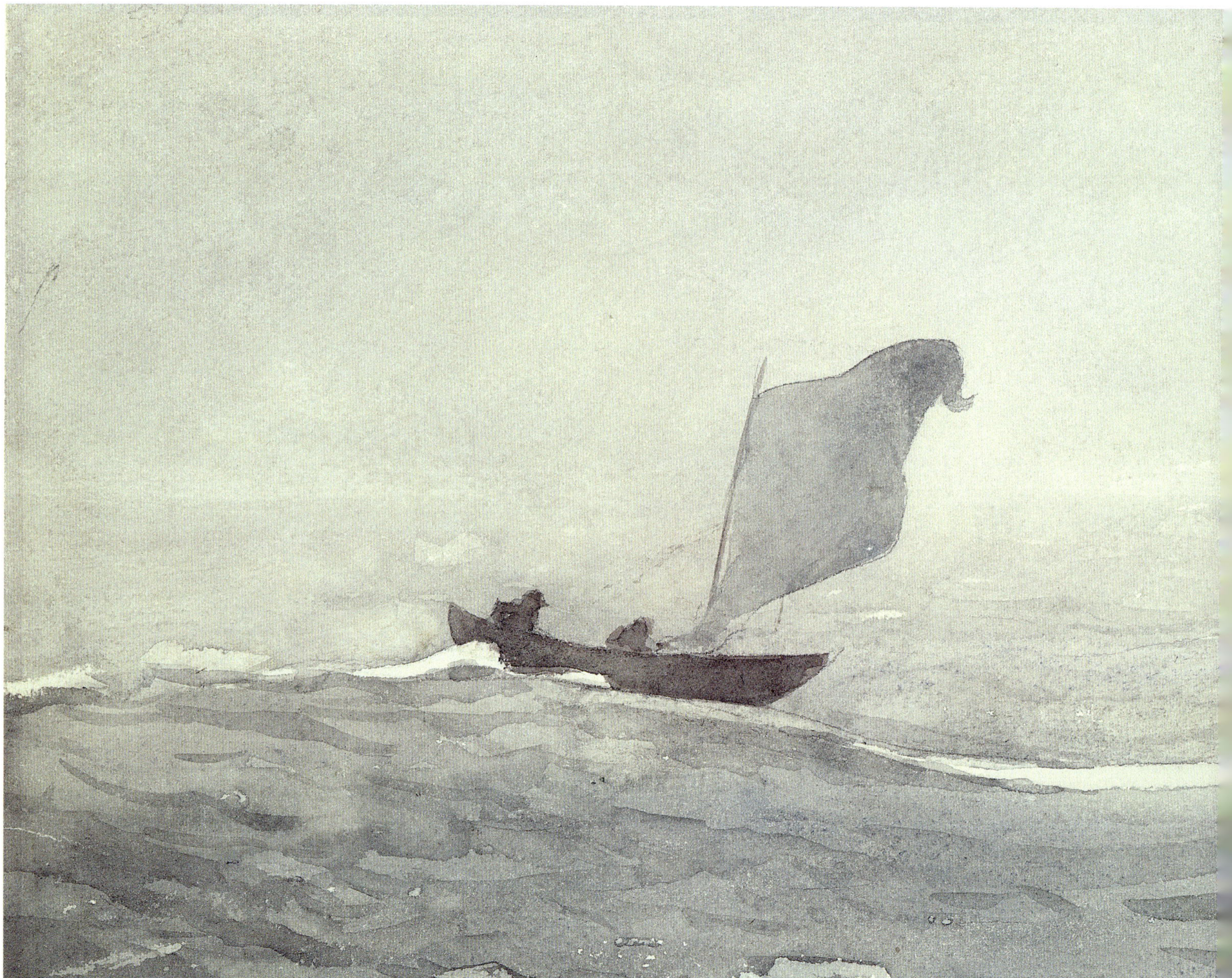

VI.
Isolation: Prout's Neck, 1883–1896

After a twenty-month absence, Homer returned to America in November 1882, briefly setting up shop again in New York City. But he was no longer at ease in the New York society in which he once traveled, and by May 1883 he had settled permanently in Prout's Neck, Maine. It is likely that his time in Cullercoats confirmed in Homer a taste for isolation and a love for the tempestuous regions where land and ocean meet. From this point on, he would be known as America's foremost chronicler of the life of the sea whose dramatic potential he first began to tap in his English watercolors.

If Homer hoped to boost his reputation as a watercolorist with his Cullercoats works, by and large he succeeded. They offered a rebuttal to the criticism often leveled at his work in the medium that they were merely unfinished sketches. Yet to twenty-first-century eyes, something is lost in these works—a freshness and sparkle that convey the feeling of being present at the scene. It is only in his later watercolors that Homer will find the means to combine the vividness and truth to nature of his early watercolors with the grandeur of his Cullercoats work.

Upon his return to America, the new watercolors were widely praised, though his major oil paintings based on English subjects—including *The Coming Away of the Gale*, which he later repainted—fared less well. Typical of the positive reception of his watercolors is this review from the *Boston Evening Transcript*: "Homer is both the historian and poet of the sea and sea-coast life. . . . The whole gamut of watercolor power, from the richness of elemental life depth and vividness to the density of storm darkness and human woe, and thence again to life light, joyousness, delicacy and subtle glow, is here run with a strength and accuracy that few not seeing will believe it capable of. Indeed it seems to proclaim its capacity to be perhaps the most artistic of all mediums when adequately handled."

THE SHIP'S BOAT 1883

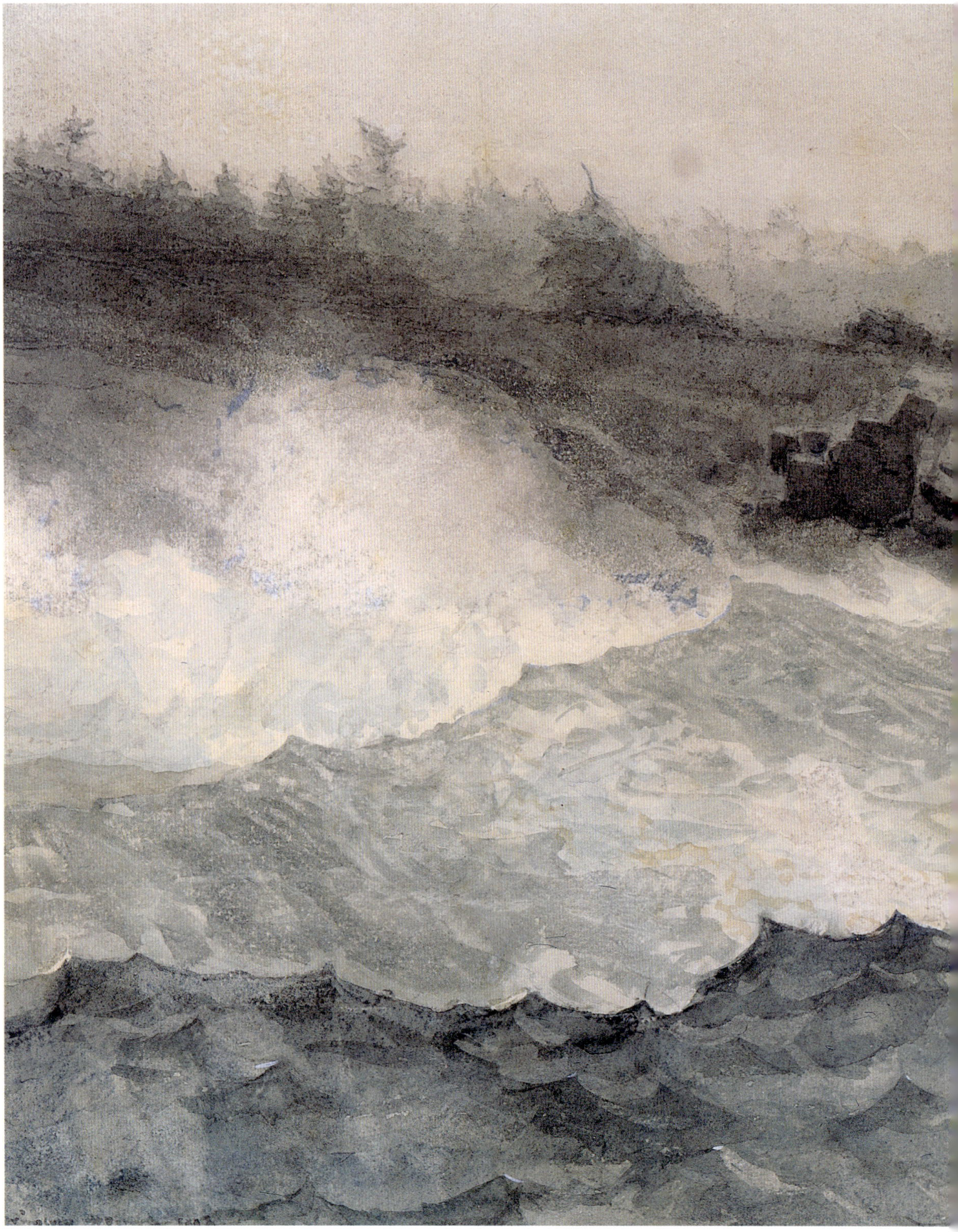

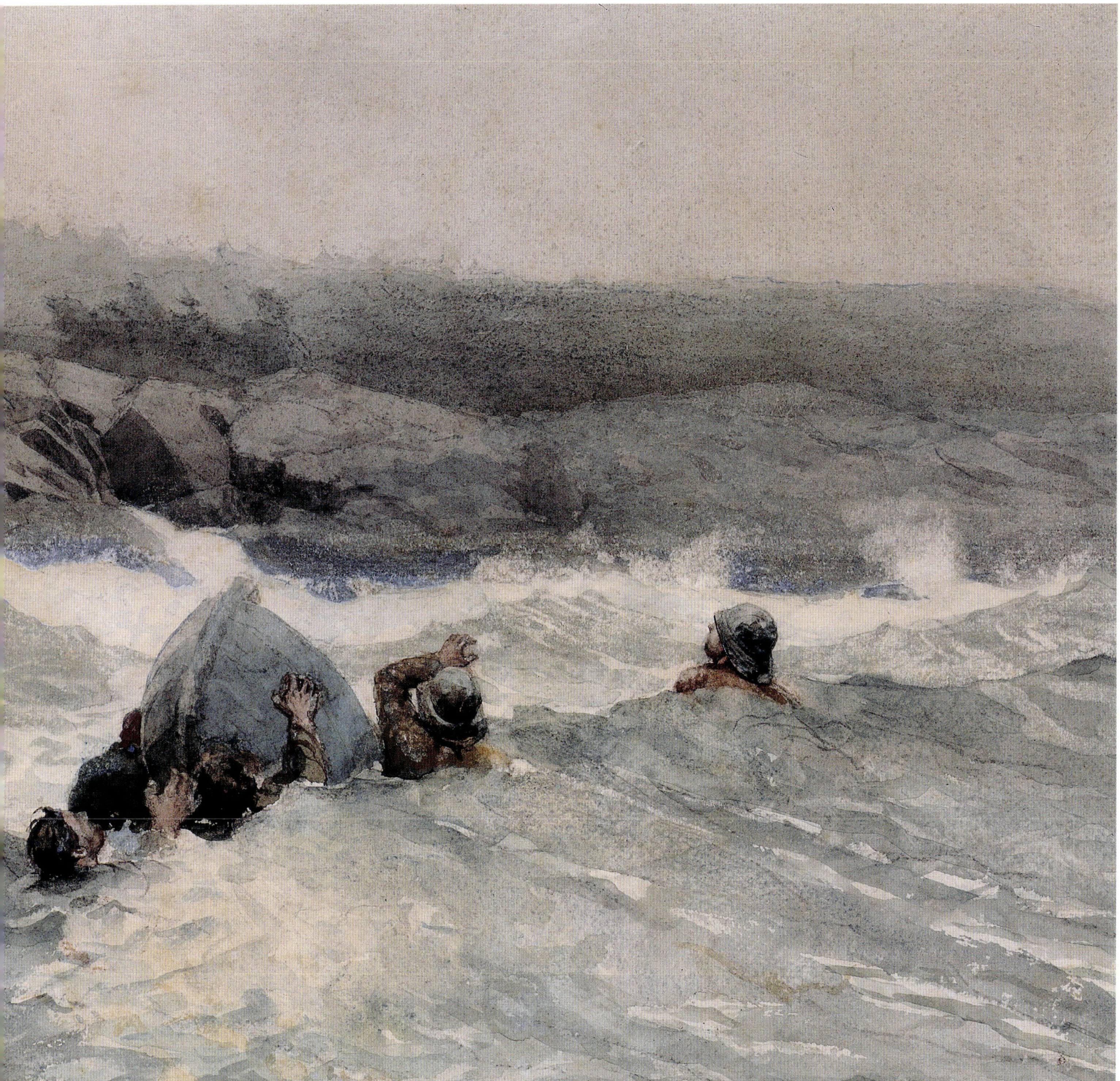

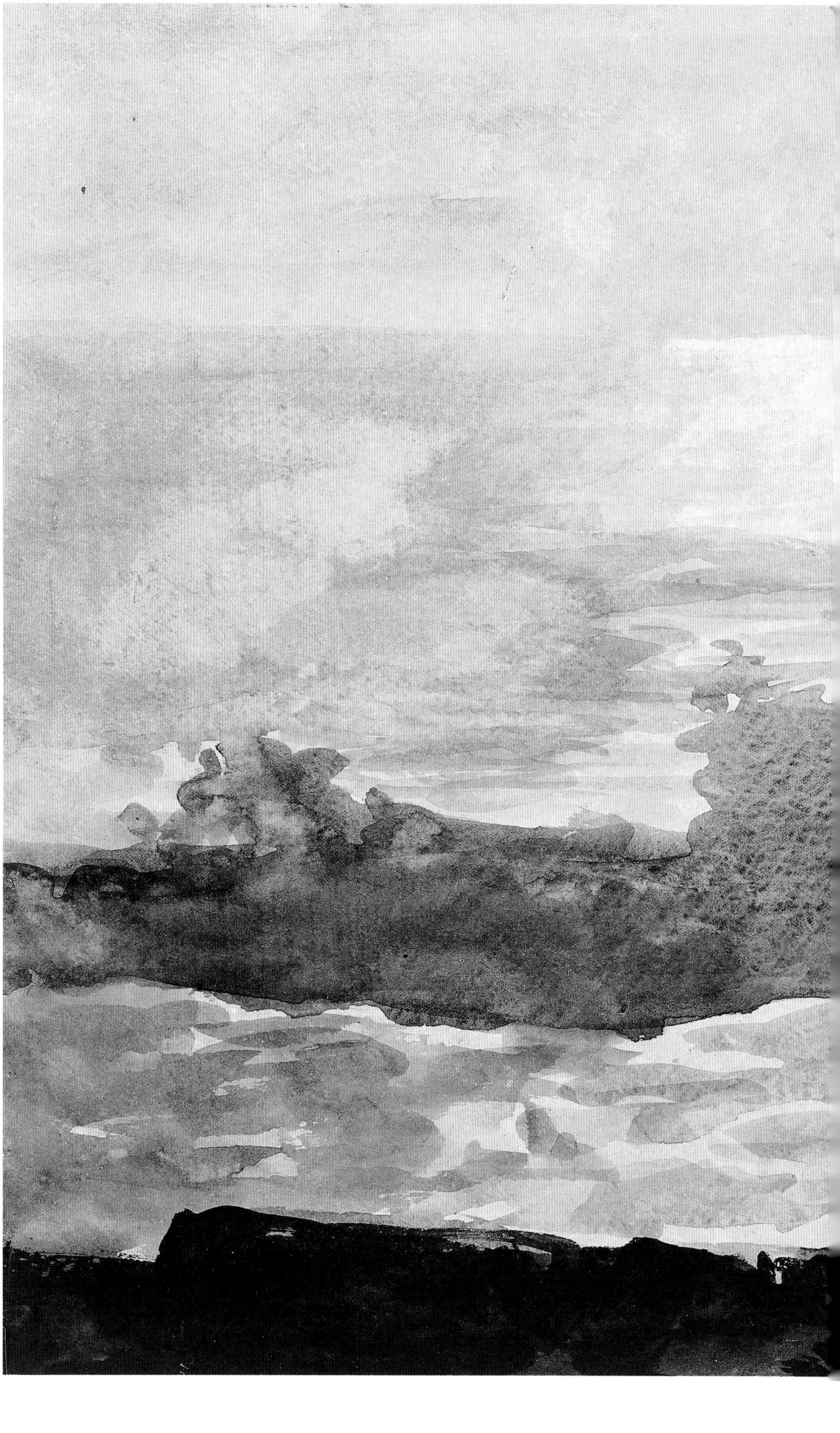

A SUMMER NIGHT 1890

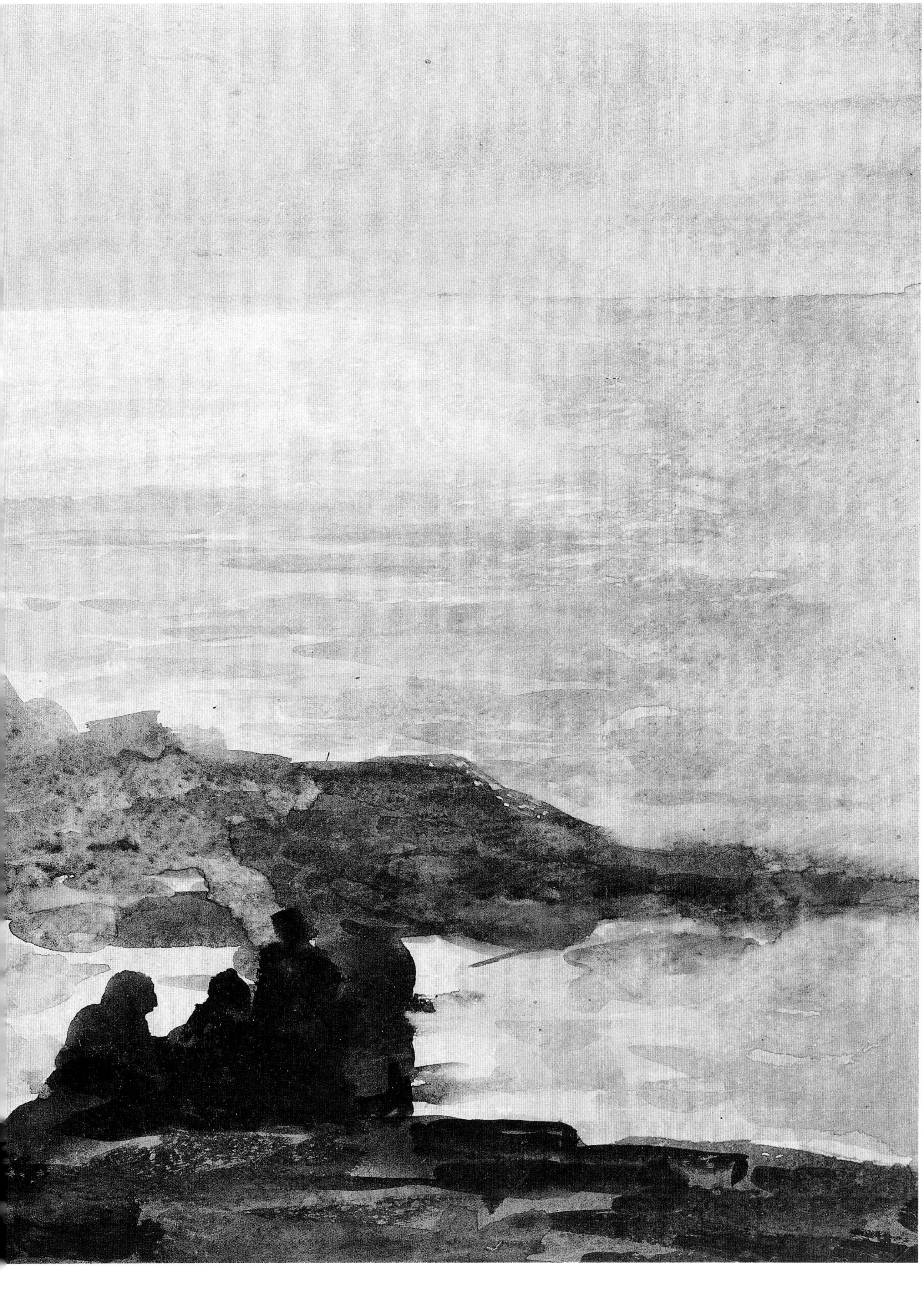

The Northeaster 1883

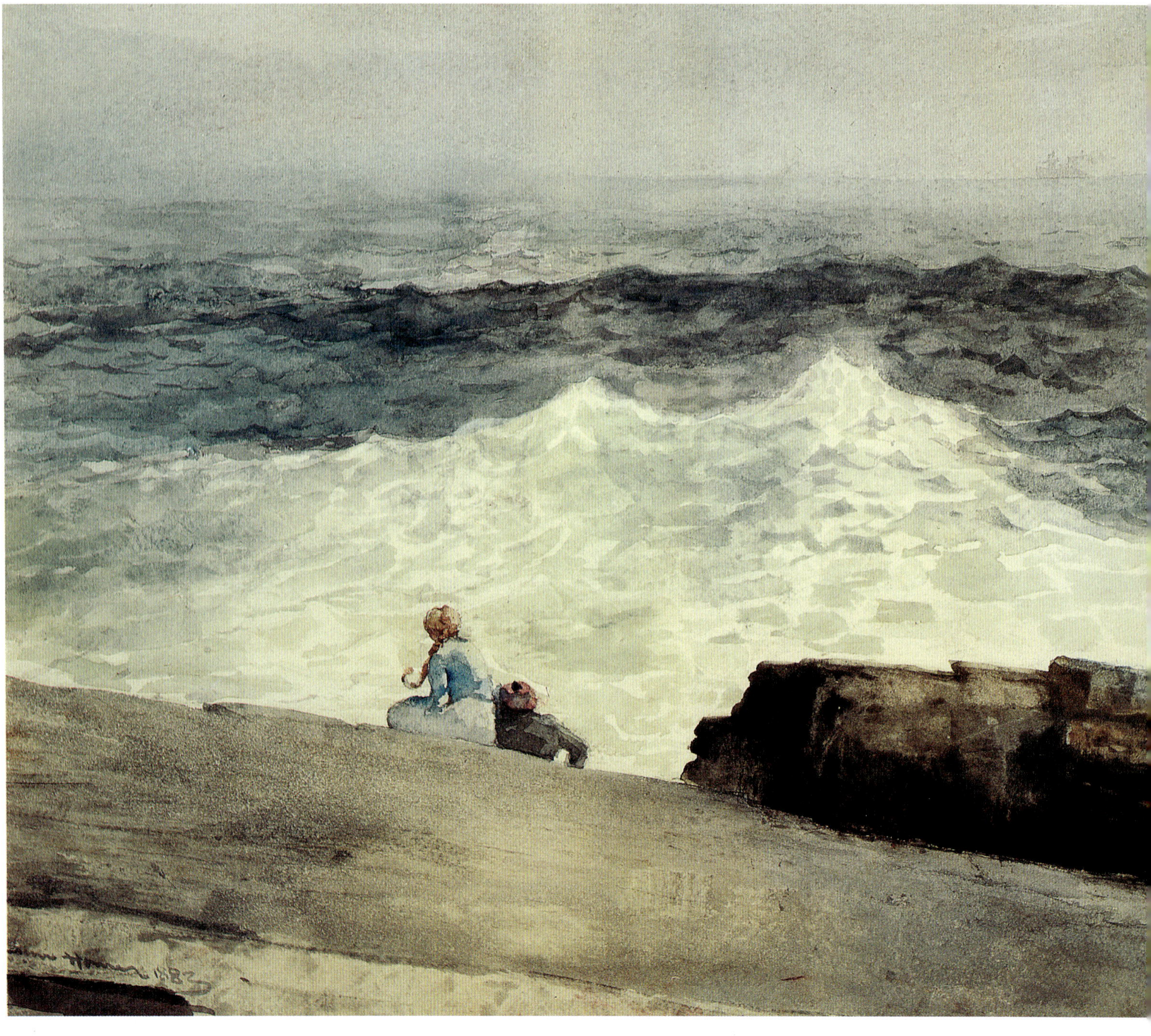

After the success of the Cullercoats watercolors, Homer produced a series of oil paintings in a similar vein—including *The Life Line* [p. 22], *The Herring Net*, and *Undertow*—that were an immediate hit with critics and public alike, and that remain today among his most famous paintings. It was these marine paintings that finally solidified Homer's reputation as one of America's leading artists. The threatening mood of these works is in keeping with his English watercolors, as is their core theme: the perpetual struggle to survive in an unforgiving environment.

The watercolors Homer produced in and around his home in Prout's Neck do not form a cohesive body of work. There are moments of real poetry, such as *A Summer Night*, with its almost abstract forms and surreal light, and the harrowing *Blown Away*, which condenses the horrific narratives of works like *The Wreck of the Iron Crown* into a few spare washes. In *The Ship's Boat*, Homer comes closest

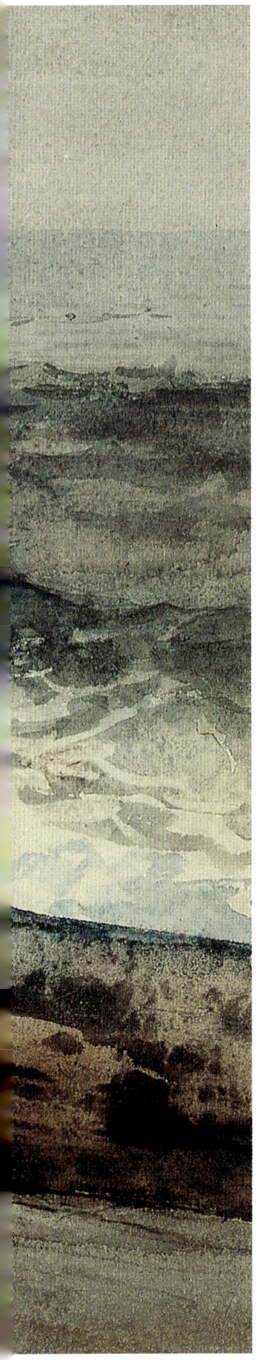

MAINE CLIFFS 1883

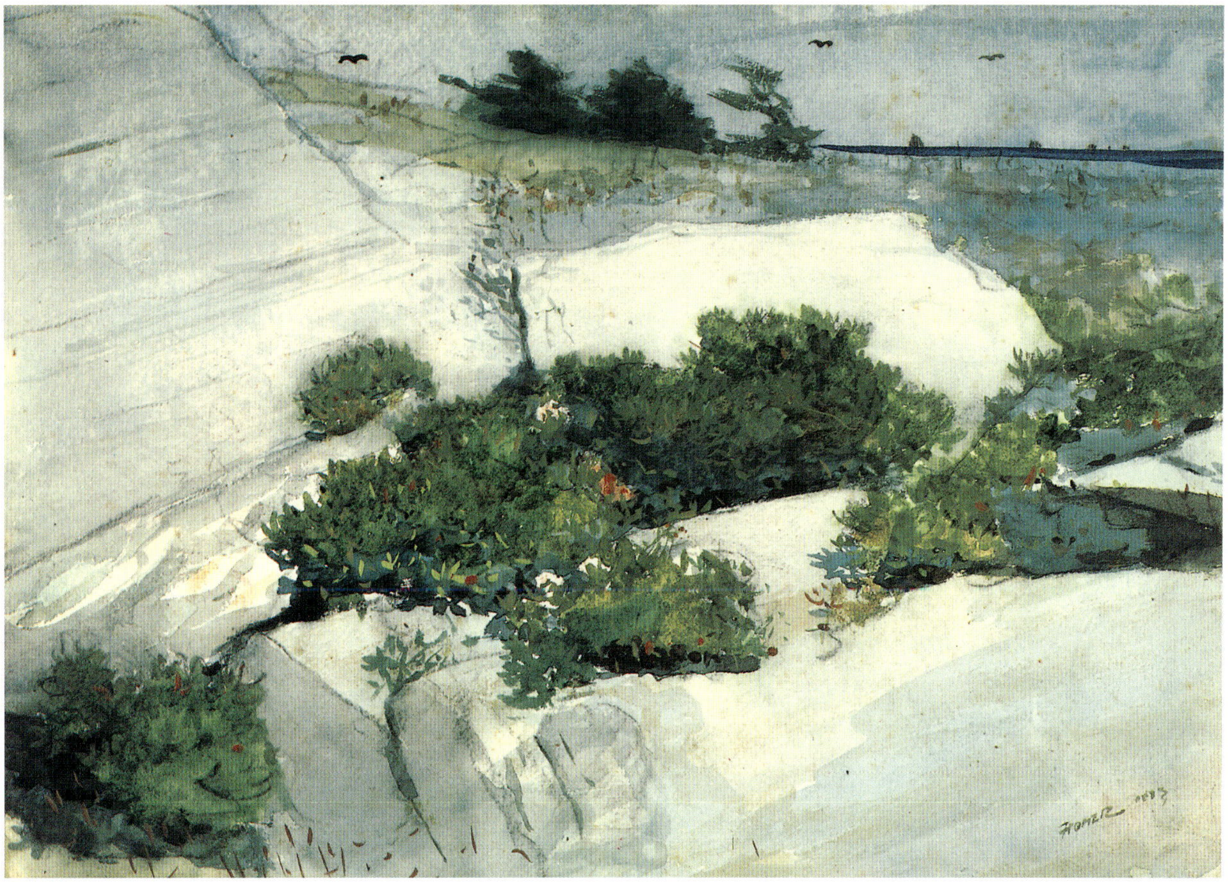

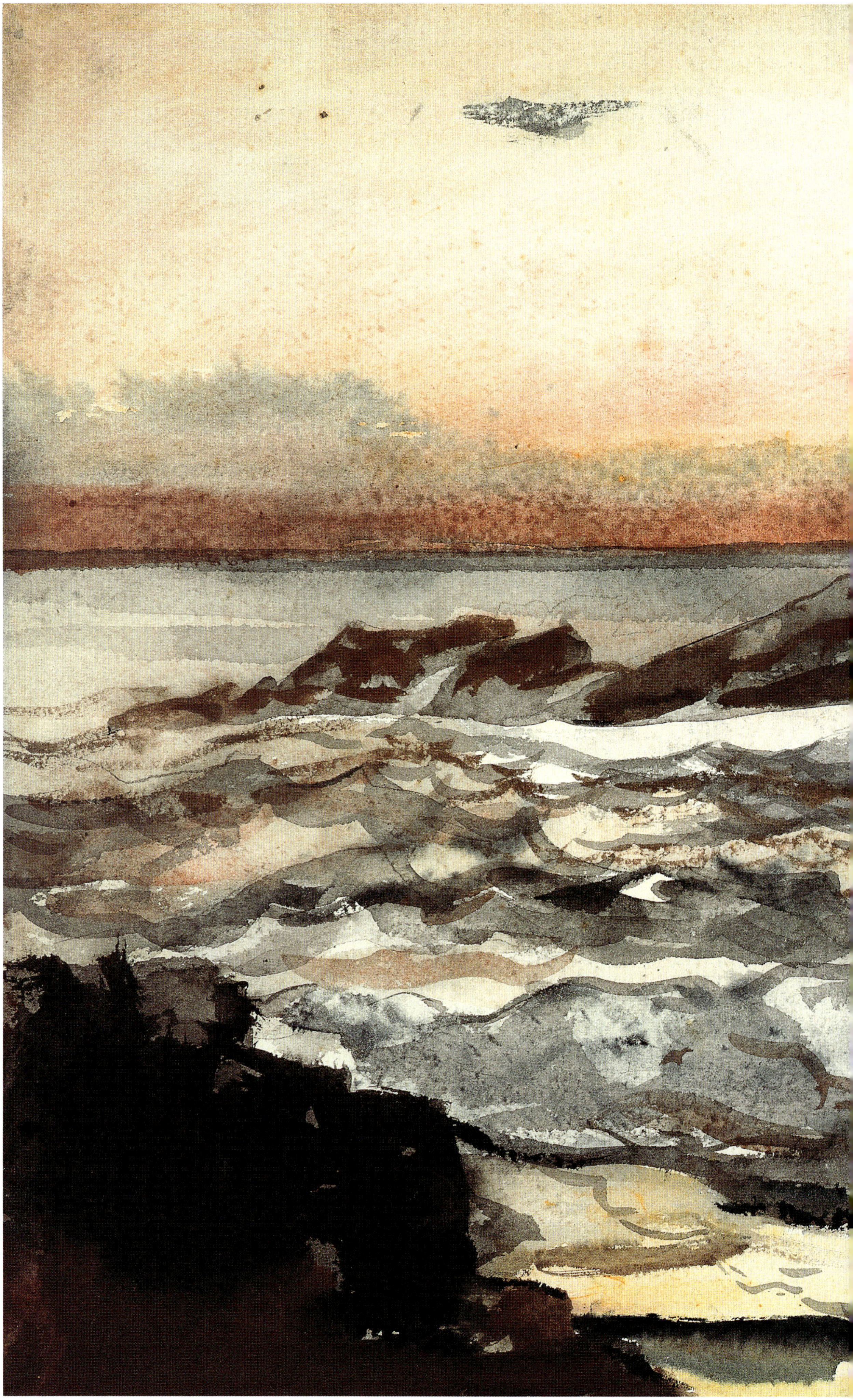

PROUT'S NECK, SURF ON ROCKS 1895

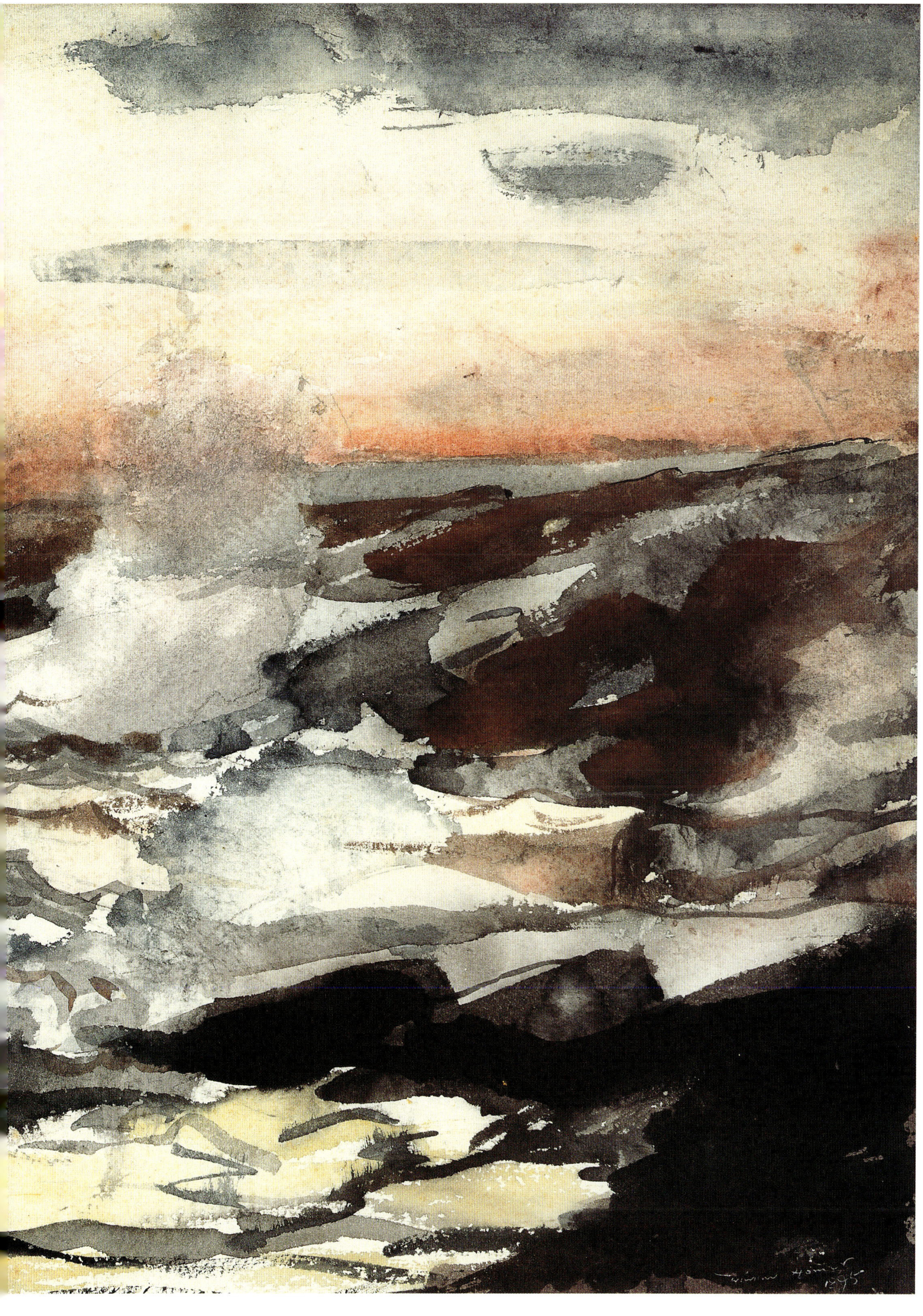

to repeating the successful formula of the Cullercoats watercolors. This dramatic scene of sailors fighting for their lives in a stormy sea has the dramatic sweep of the English watercolors, but Homer has reversed his usual point of view. Now he has selected a vantage point that places the viewer in the waves along with the imperiled sailors so that we seem to share their fate. We no longer identify, as in the Cullercoats watercolors, with the spectators of the tragedy but with the victims themselves.

Though in many respects this work resembles his English watercolors, the bleak shoreline with its rocky cliffs and conifers clearly places the scene of this tragedy along the Maine coast where the artist now made his home. This rugged coast, with its ceaseless battle between wave and rock, forms the central motif of the watercolors and oil paintings Homer made in Prout's Neck. For the most part, Prout's Neck for Homer meant oil painting, and his greatest works on this theme were done in that more substantial medium. The watercolors he produced at home were mostly afterthoughts to fill in between the important work of completing his major oils. Created

DEEP SEA FISHING 1894

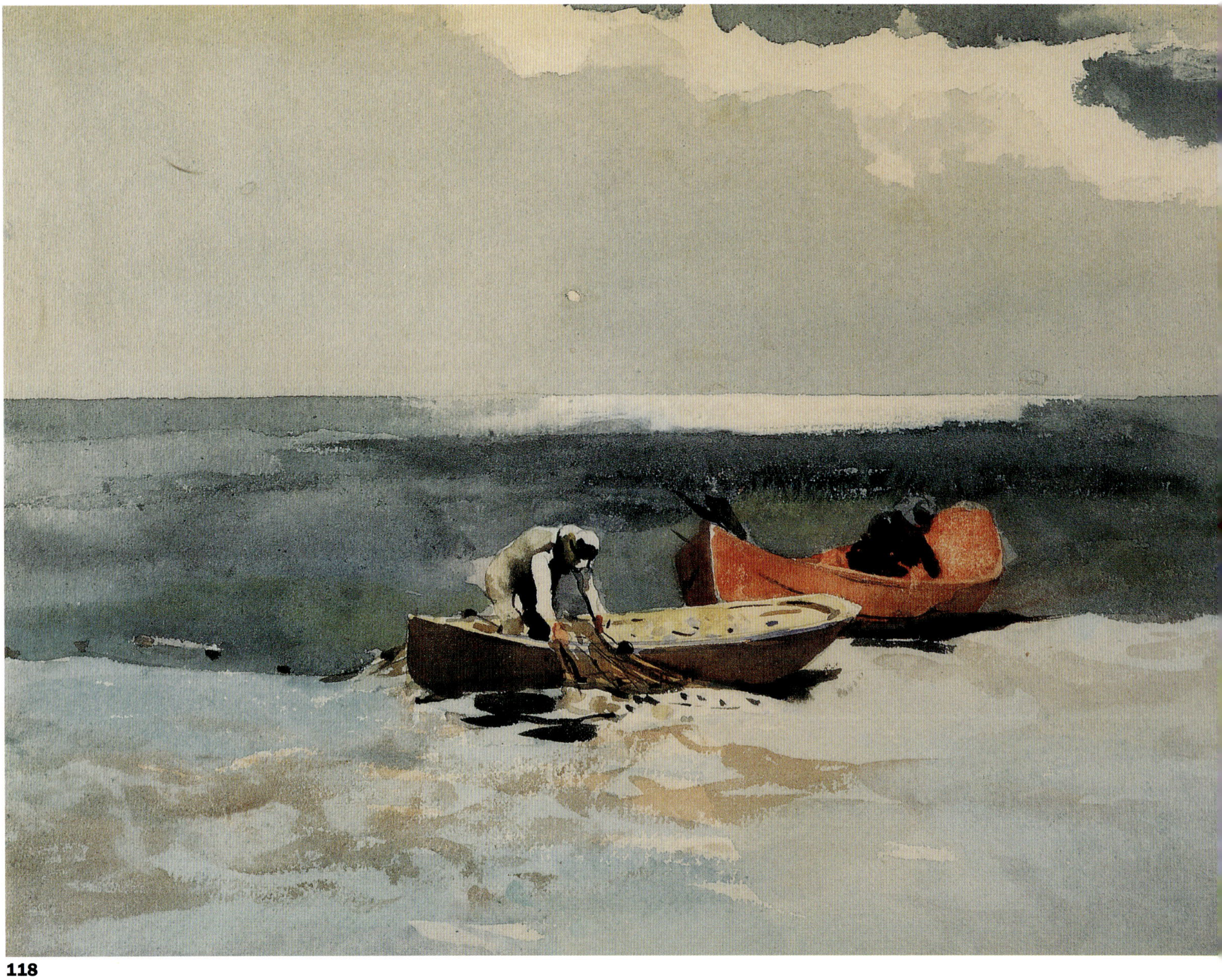

HERRING FISHING 1894

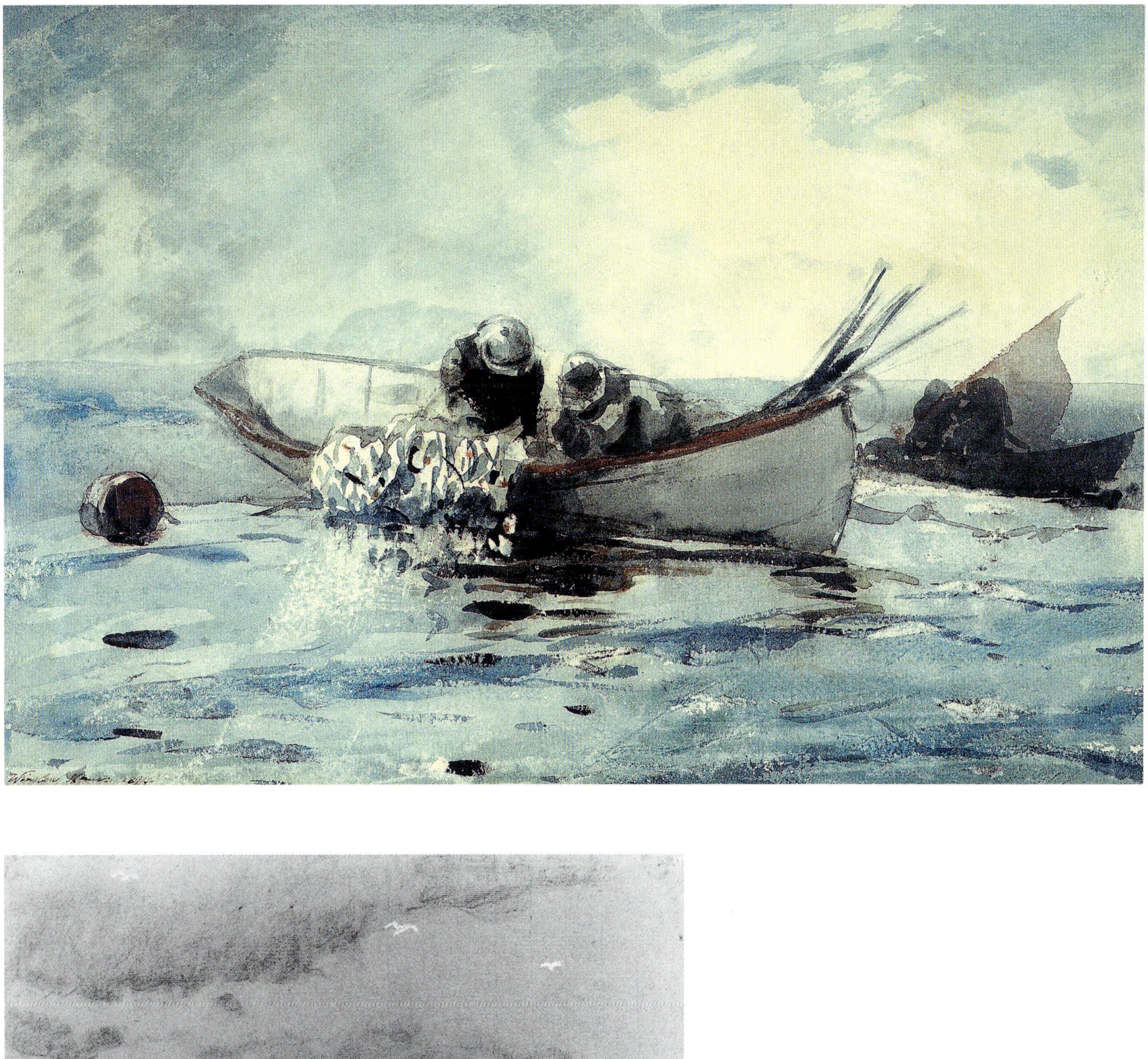

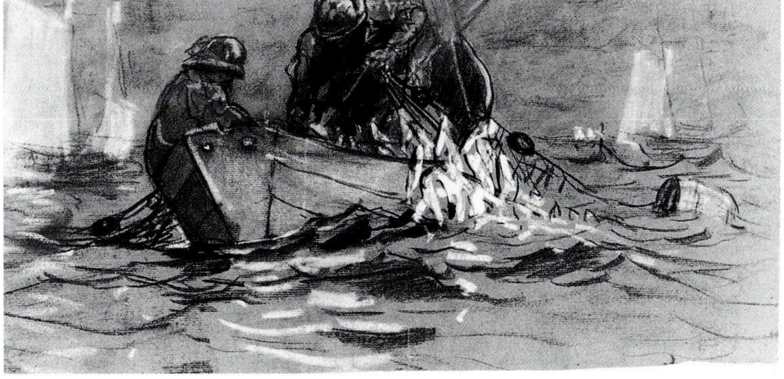

STUDY FOR THE HERRING NET 1884–1885

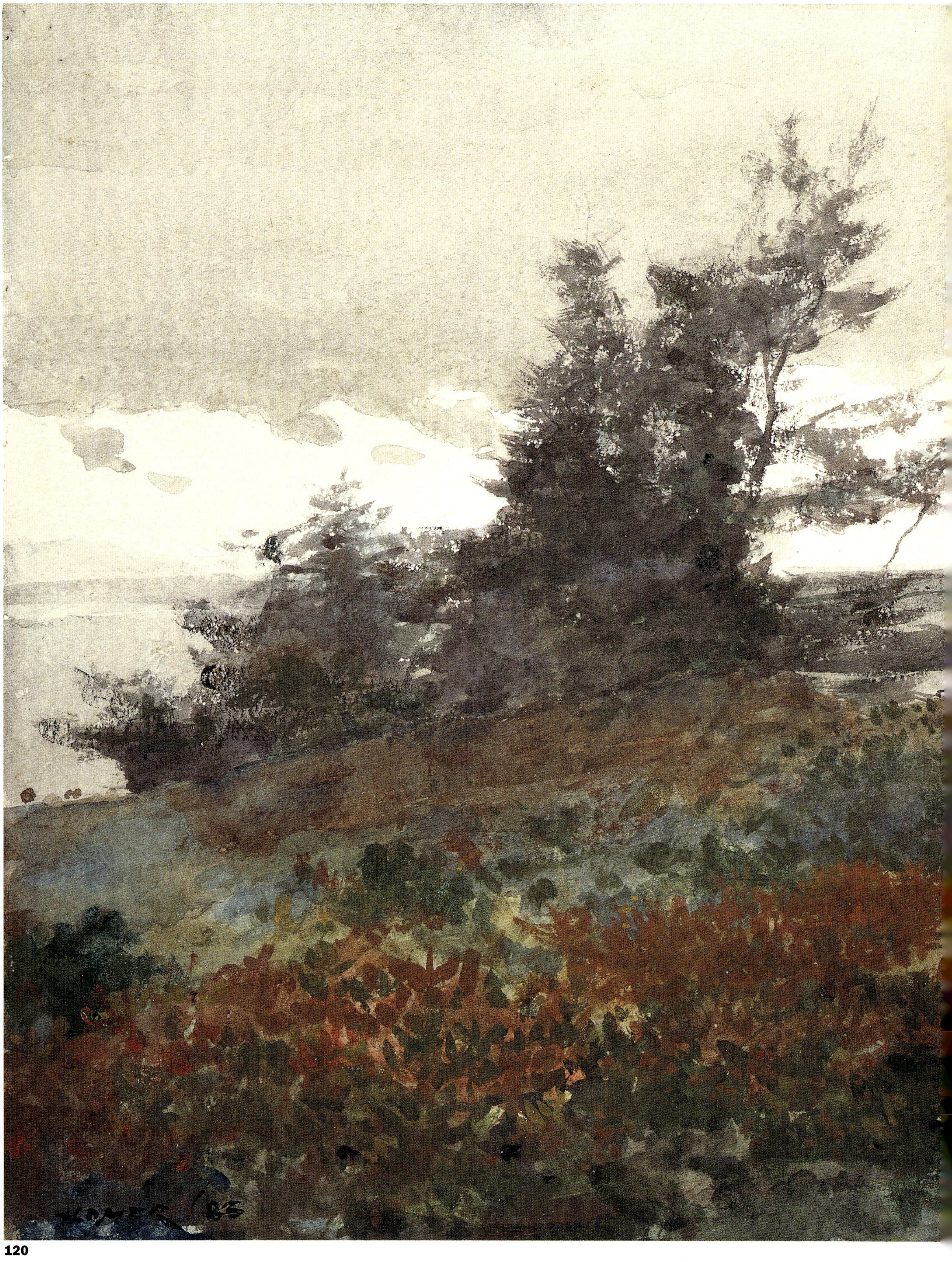
HOMER '85

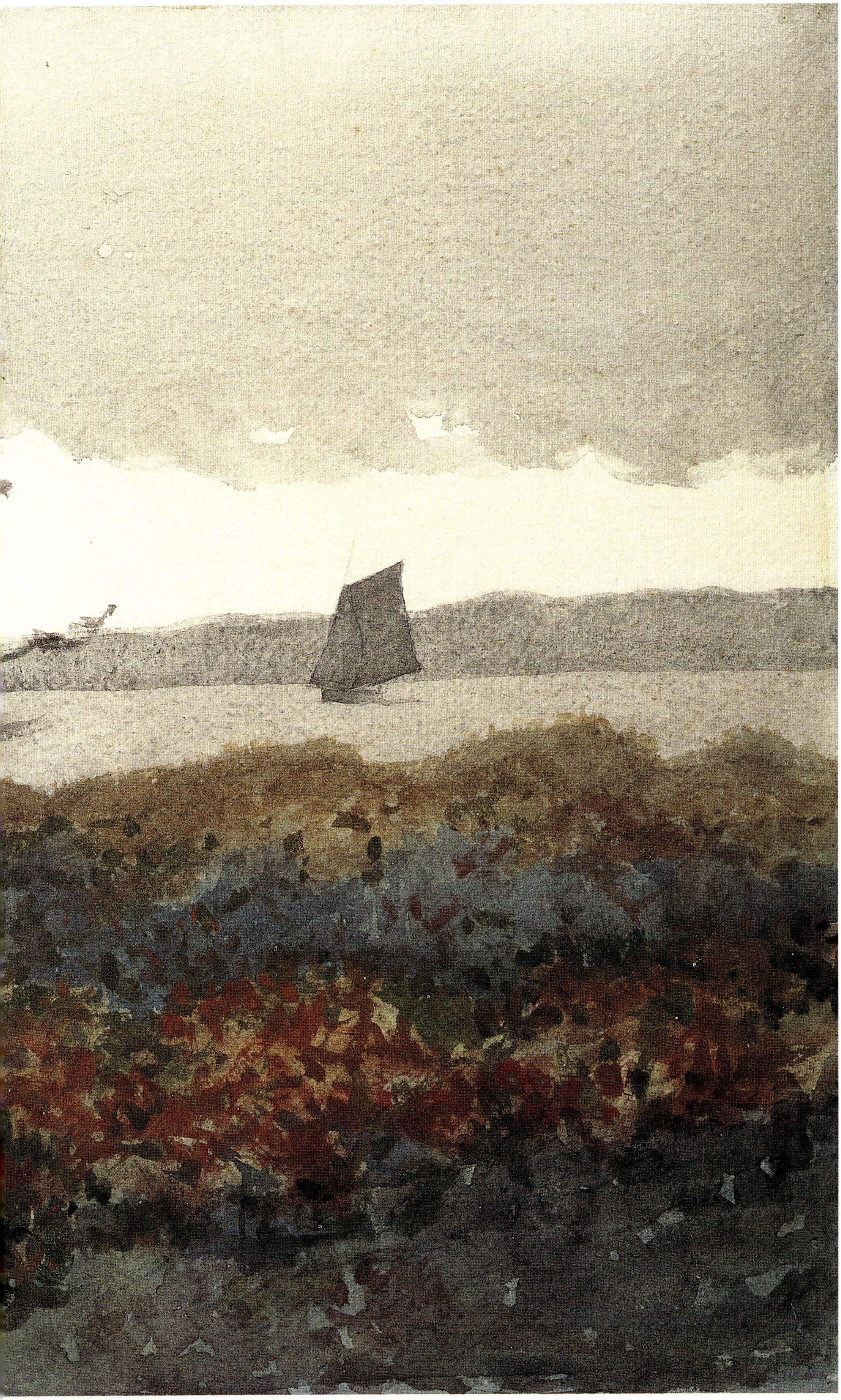

PROUT'S NECK, LOOKING TOWARD OLD ORCHARD 1883

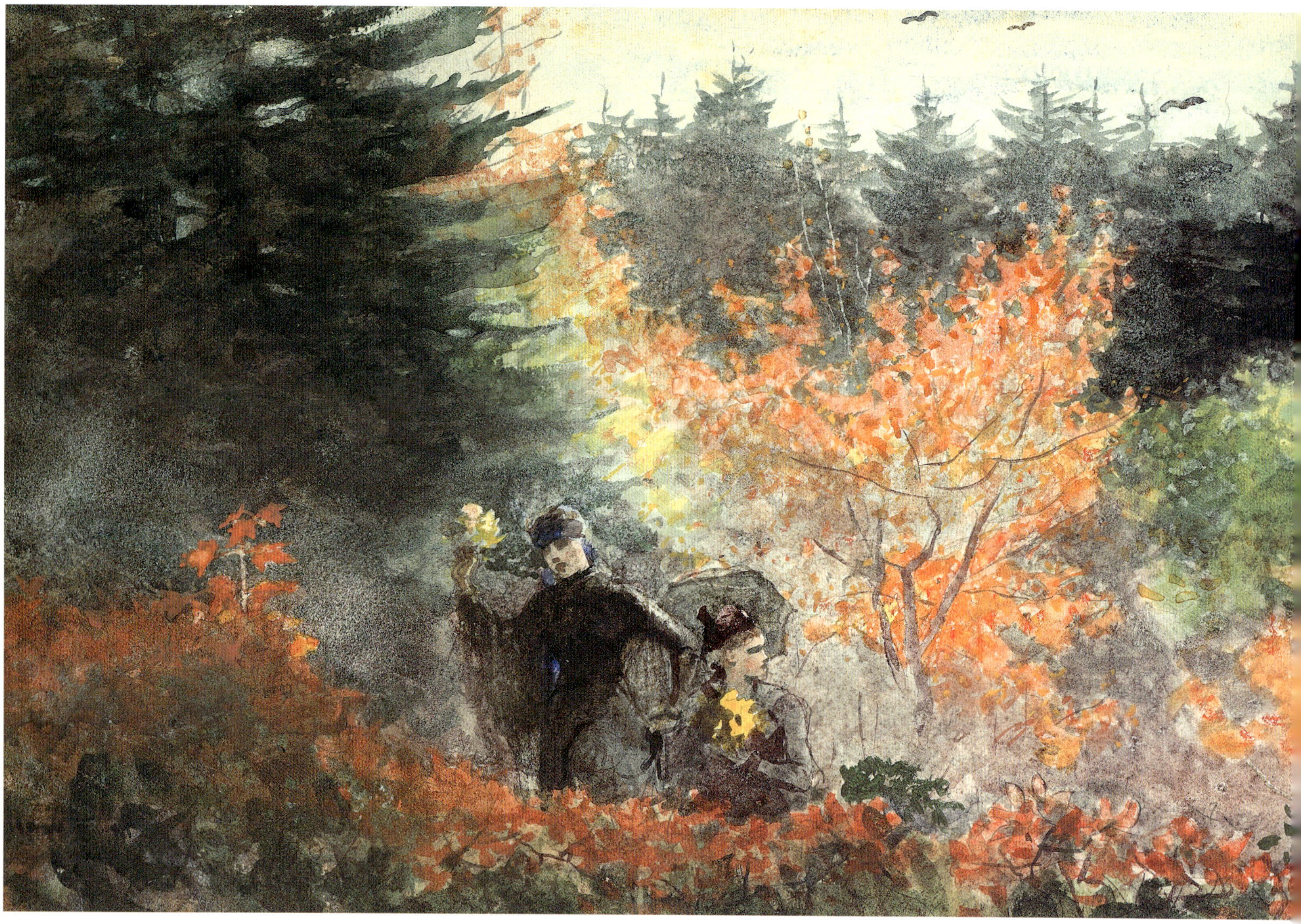

WOMEN IN AUTUMN WOODS c. 1887

sporadically over more than a decade, they are diverse in technique and mood, ranging from the calm of *Maine Cliffs*, a study in almost abstract harmonies of gray and green, to the suppressed fury of *Prout's Neck, Surf on Rocks*. After Cullercoats, Homer became something of a connoisseur of foul weather. His friend John W. Beatty recalled: "[W]hen I knew him he was comparatively indifferent to the ordinary and peaceful aspects of the ocean. . . . But when the lowering clouds gathered above the horizon, and tumultuous waves ran along the rockbound coast and up the shelving, precipitous rocks, his interest became intense." But the contrast between obdurate rock and foaming surf, so successfully rendered in Homer's great marine paintings, seemed ill suited to the lighter medium of watercolor. No watercolor, with the possible exception of *Diamond Shoal* [pp. 216–217], the last he ever painted, conveys the ocean's violent temper with the power of oil paintings like *Northeaster* or *Winter Coast*.

In 1884, Homer spent some time with the herring fleets that worked the New England coasts, and these experiences are recalled in watercolors like *Herring Fishing* and *Deep Sea Fishing*, as well as the famous oil painting *The Herring Net*. Despite the obvious similarities in subject and composition, the later date of the watercolors indi-

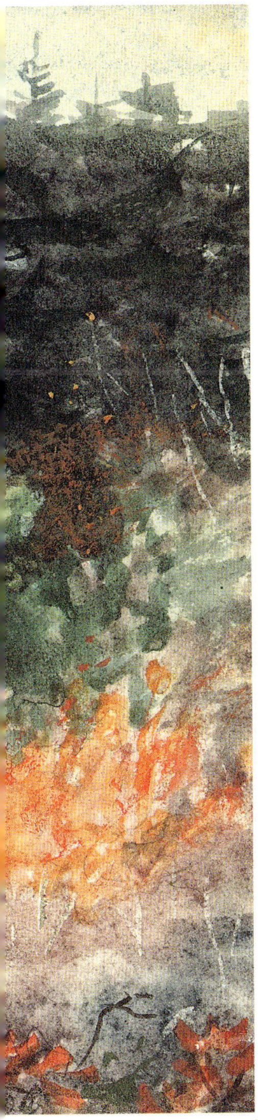

cates that they were not preperatory sketches for the oil painting but rather a further exploration of a theme that fascinated the artist. The watercolors are less overtly dramatic and monumental than the oil painting or the study, where the low vantage point allows the figures to loom above the horizon. The watercolors are marked instead by a greater coloristic and painterly freedom. The loose brushwork and spare washes are characteristic of Homer's late watercolor technique, where detail is sacrificed for the sake of the overall mood and atmosphere. Homer managed in these works to say a great deal with very little.

There are as well watercolors he painted near his Maine home that, at least in terms of their subjects, recall his earlier rural scenes. Works like *"For to be a Farmer's Boy" (Old English Song)* and *Women in Autumn Woods*, both from 1887, reveal a new intensity of color and an enigmatic tone that distinguishes them from those more narrative vignettes. These later works are marked by a stringent economy of means. The freedom in the handling of paint is even more pronounced than in works like *Feeding Time* [pp. 44–45] and *Flock of Sheep, Houghton Farm* [p. 61], where foliage and filtered light are suggested through mottled stains of saturated color. In *"For to be a Farmer's Boy"* and *Women in Autumn Woods*, the artist provides even fewer visual clues to anchor the scenes in reality. In saturated colors and with a minimum of detail, Homer evokes, rather than depicts, his melancholy autumnal scenes.

"For to be a Farmer's Boy" (Old English Song) 1887

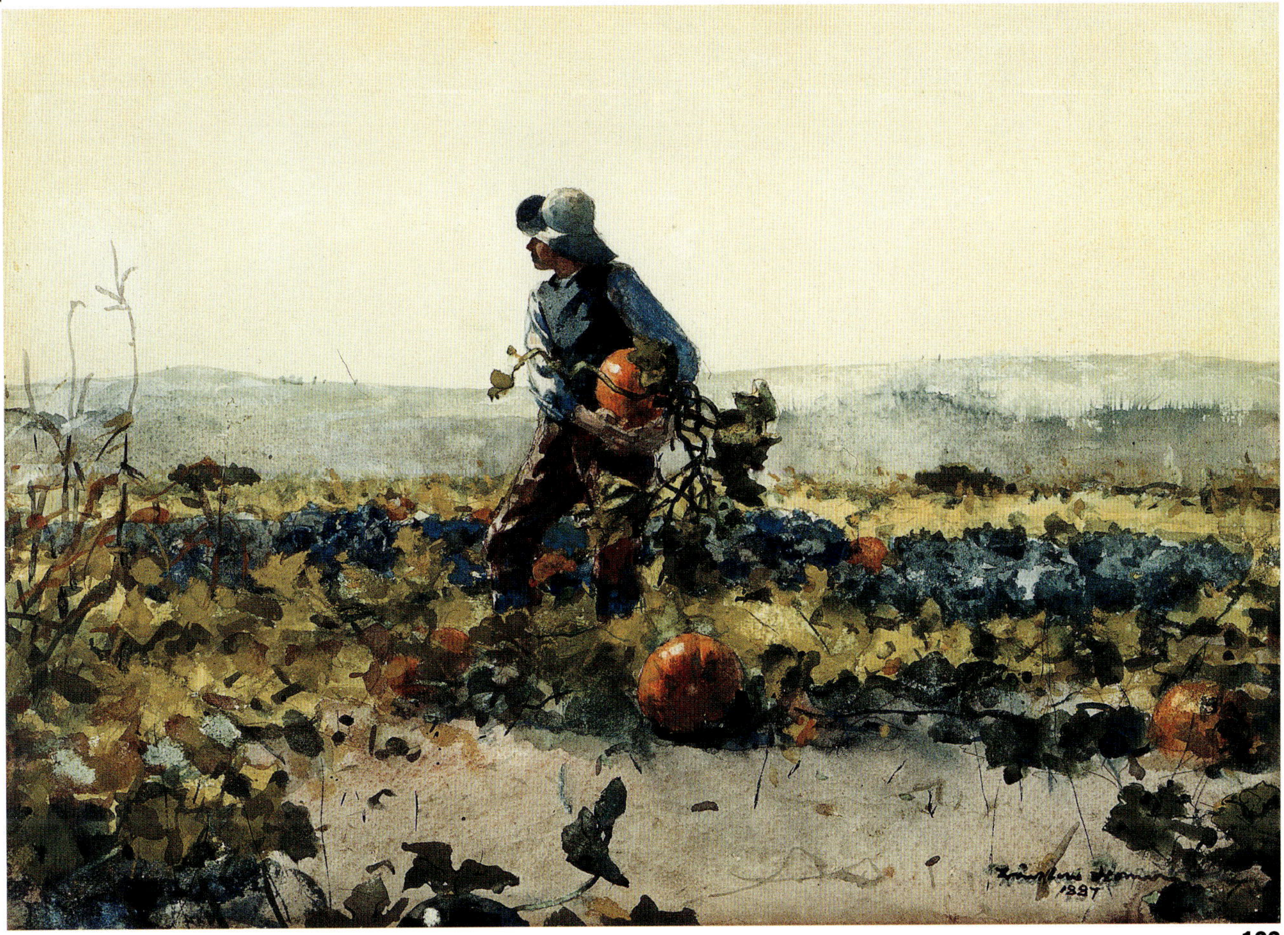

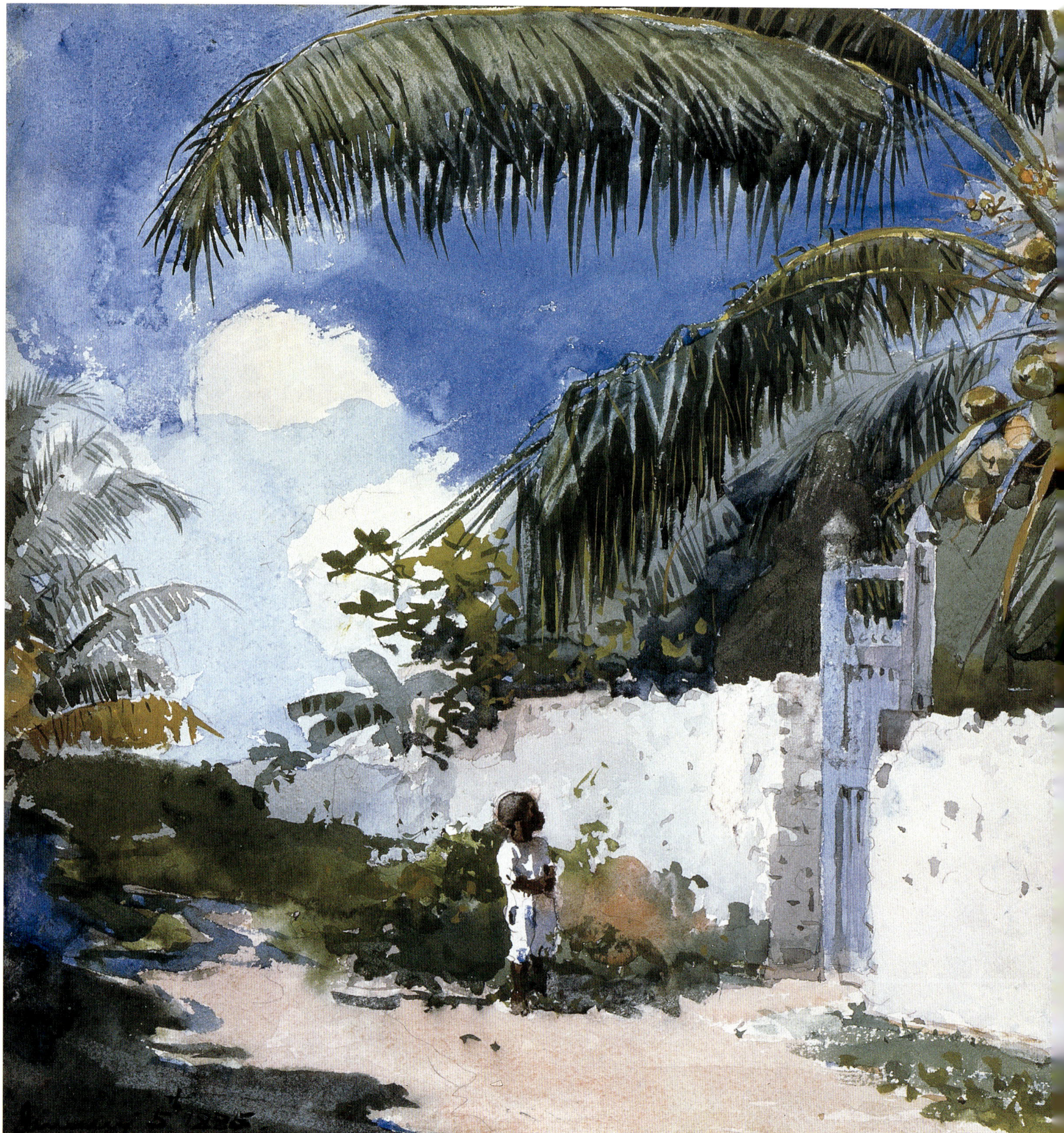

VII.
Tropical Interlude: Bahamas, Cuba, 1884–1885

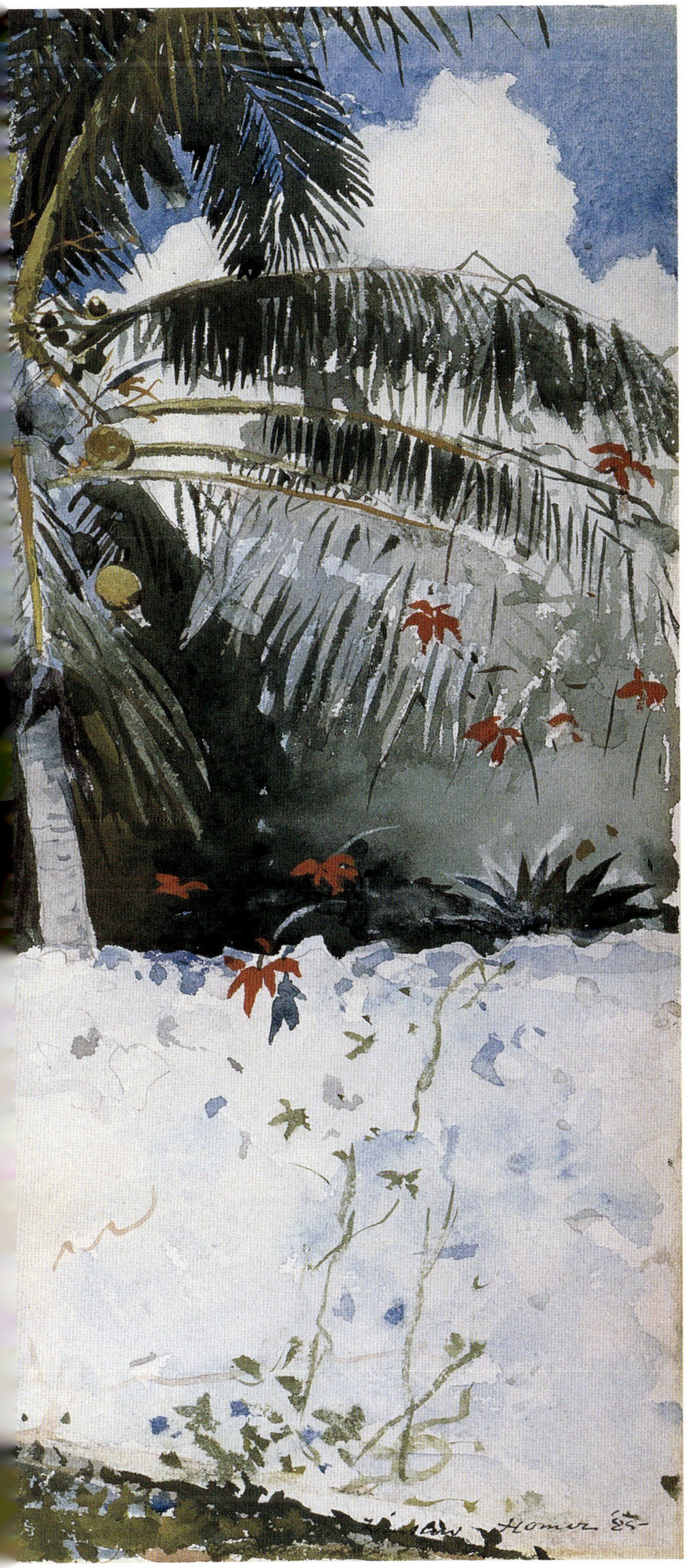

A Garden in Nassau 1885

By 1875, Homer had ceased to make his living as a commercial illustrator, so it is a little surprising that in 1884 he accepted a commission from *Century Magazine* to make a series of watercolors to accompany an article on Nassau in the Bahamas. The allure of the warm Caribbean, just then beginning to attract large numbers of American tourists, was apparently sufficient to overcome his aversion to working on commission. In any case, as an established artist, he was in a much stronger position to do as he pleased than he had been at the outset of his career. And on the evidence of the work he produced, he felt fully at liberty to pursue his own vision. Homer arrived in Nassau in December 1884. He spent two months on the island, painting more than thirty watercolors, nine of which were ultimately used to illustrate the article.

It was not unusual that something begun for eminently practical reasons should have called forth some of his most creative efforts. These tropical watercolors, spanning a full two decades and encompassing a wide variety of scenery and themes, constitute a remarkable new phase in Homer's art. If the gloomy North Sea clime could best be captured in browns and grays, the blazing light and vibrant colors of the tropics called for a whole new palette and approach to the medium. The Cullercoats paintings depend on subtle modulations of tone to create forms with sculptural volume. In the searing light of the Bahamas, form tends to flatten out, bright accents against a blue sky or white wall. Two-dimensional design takes precedence over the convincing rendering of three-dimensional form, so that in their broad areas of vivid colors some of these watercolors approach once more the qualities of Japanese prints. Succulent oranges framed by dark leaves, lush blossoms overtopping whitewashed walls, the bronzed backs of native divers against the cerulean ocean: all these drew from the artist vivid colors and a previously unsuspected joyousness. The contrast between the sensual vitality of these works and the somber tonalities of the Cullercoats watercolors could not be greater.

Still, as always in Homer's work, an ominous undercurrent flows beneath the bright surface of this tropical paradise. Homer was a white-skinned tourist from the prosperous mainland; the world he depicts, however, is that of the dark-skinned natives who first came to these islands as slaves and who still led lives of hardship and unceasing toil. In *Rest* [p. 128], a woman briefly sets down her burden, a basket of fruit perhaps intended for her white employers residing in luxury behind the walls of

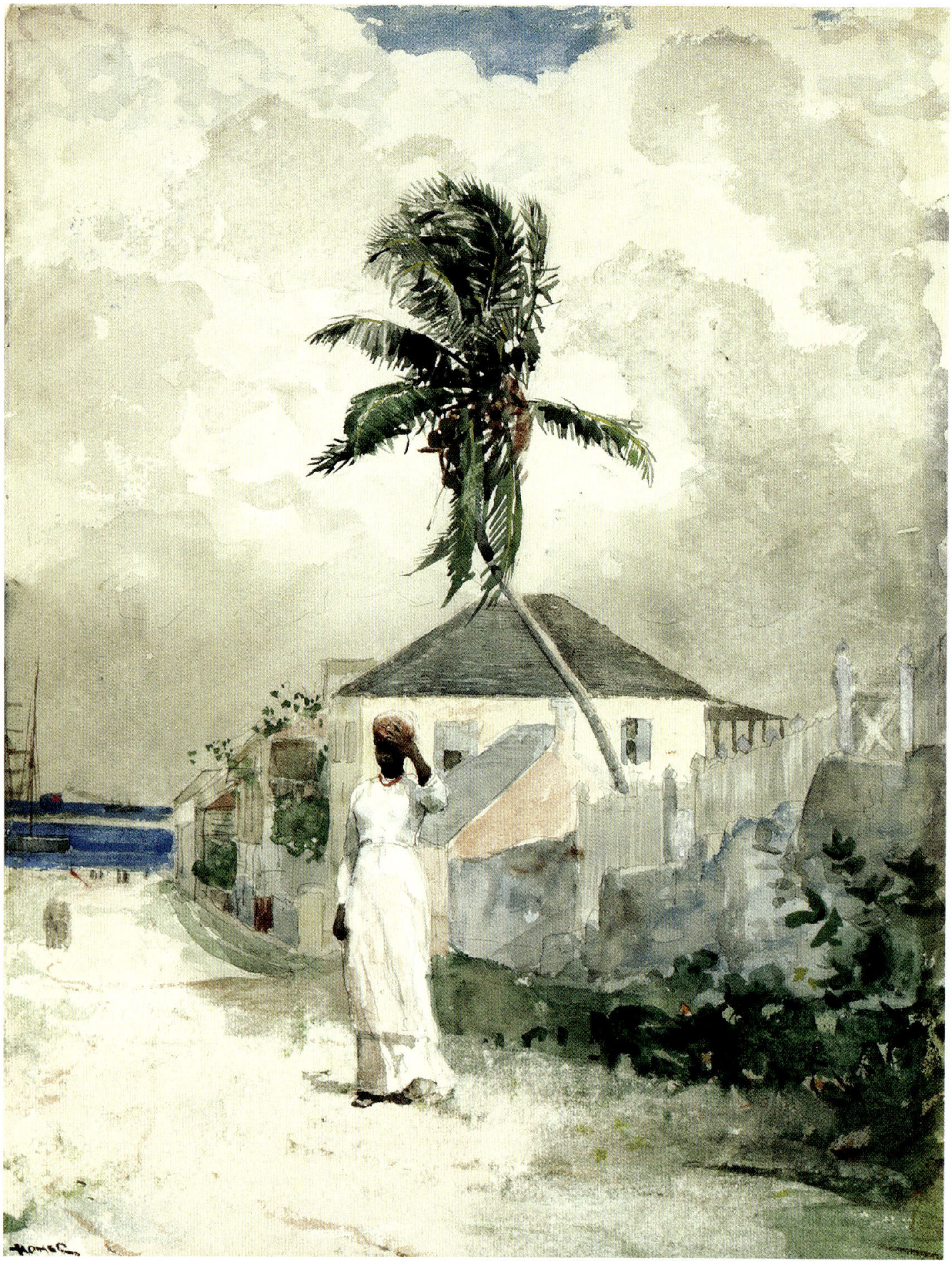

ALONG THE ROAD, BAHAMAS 1885

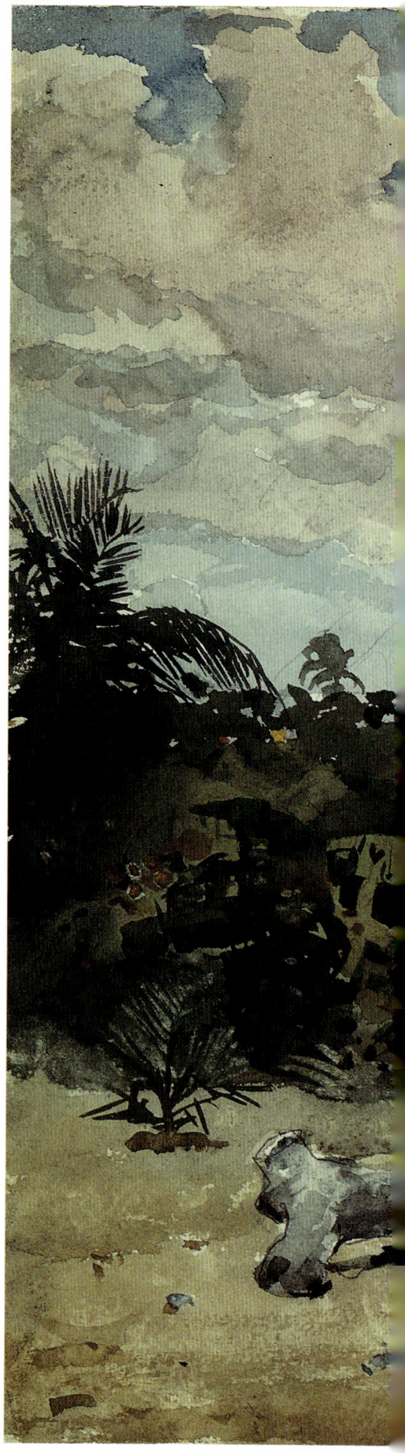

NATIVE HUTS, NASSAU 1885

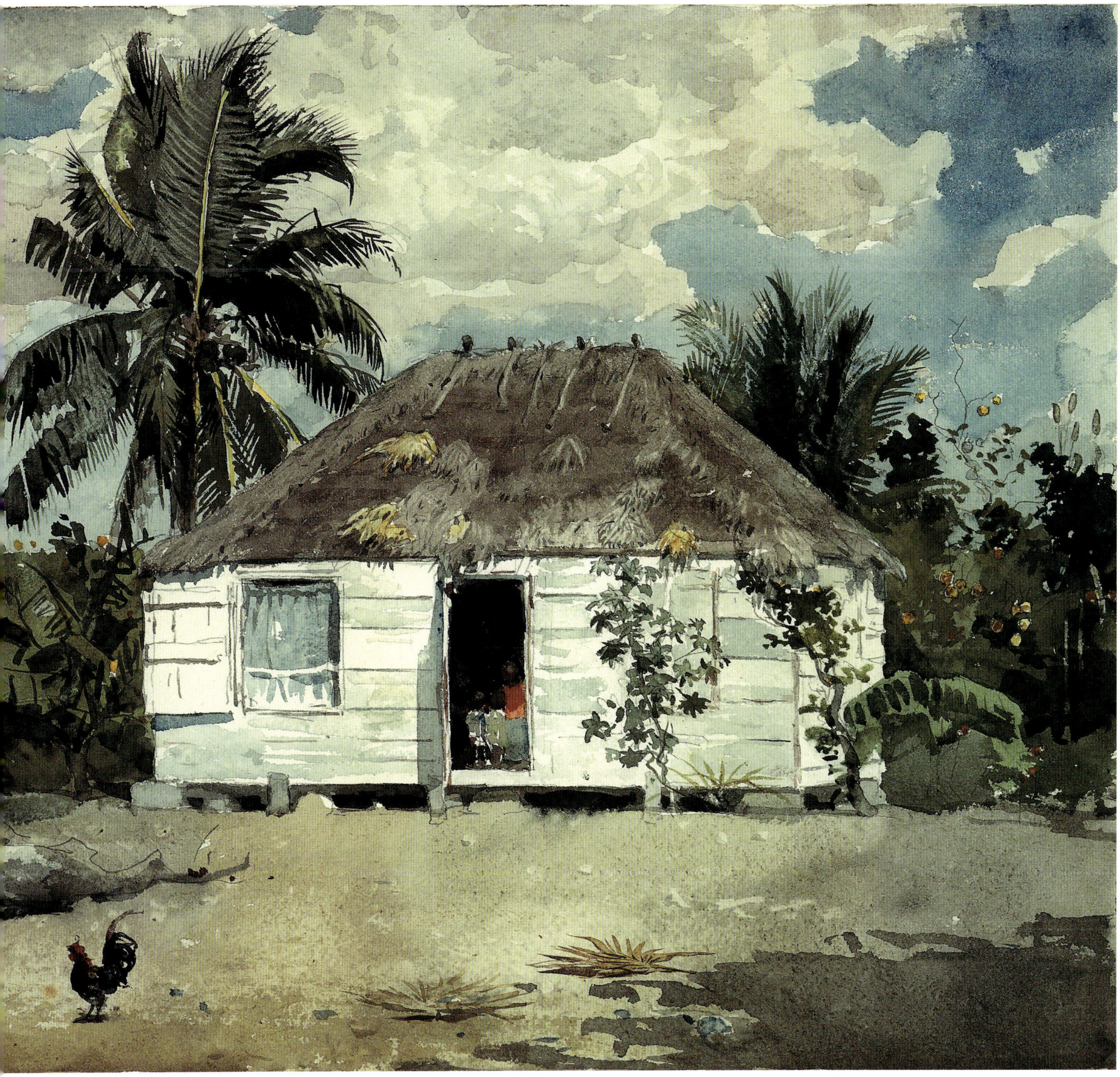

whitewashed coral limestone. Such women, like the Cullercoats fishwives, are characterized by heroic endurance, though their stoicism is disguised somewhat by the beauty of the scenery and the bright colors of their costumes. Even in the sumptuous *A Garden in Nassau*, there is an element of racial tension. Here a young black boy pauses to look into a lush garden to which he is denied entrance by the wall and closed gate. There is a paradox to Homer's depictions of the black natives: they belong to and are identified with the landscape, but they are in important ways excluded from the best these tropical islands offered. Homer never shows us the owners of these exclusive mansions, who are of little interest to the artist. Instead, he turns a sympathetic eye to those on the outside looking in.

As with his earlier depictions of rural blacks in the American South, it is not necessary to read into these works a modern egalitarian social conscience. In works like *Native Huts, Nassau* Homer clearly meant us to enjoy the picturesque details of the shack's thatched roof and the chickens pecking in the yard rather than to cry out against the poverty they represent. He did not condemn upper-class privilege, choosing instead to ignore it as a subject with few pictorial possibilities. His attitude toward the native inhabitants was one of instinctive sympathy rather than moral outrage. He was attracted to them, as he

ORANGES ON A BRANCH 1885

REST 1885

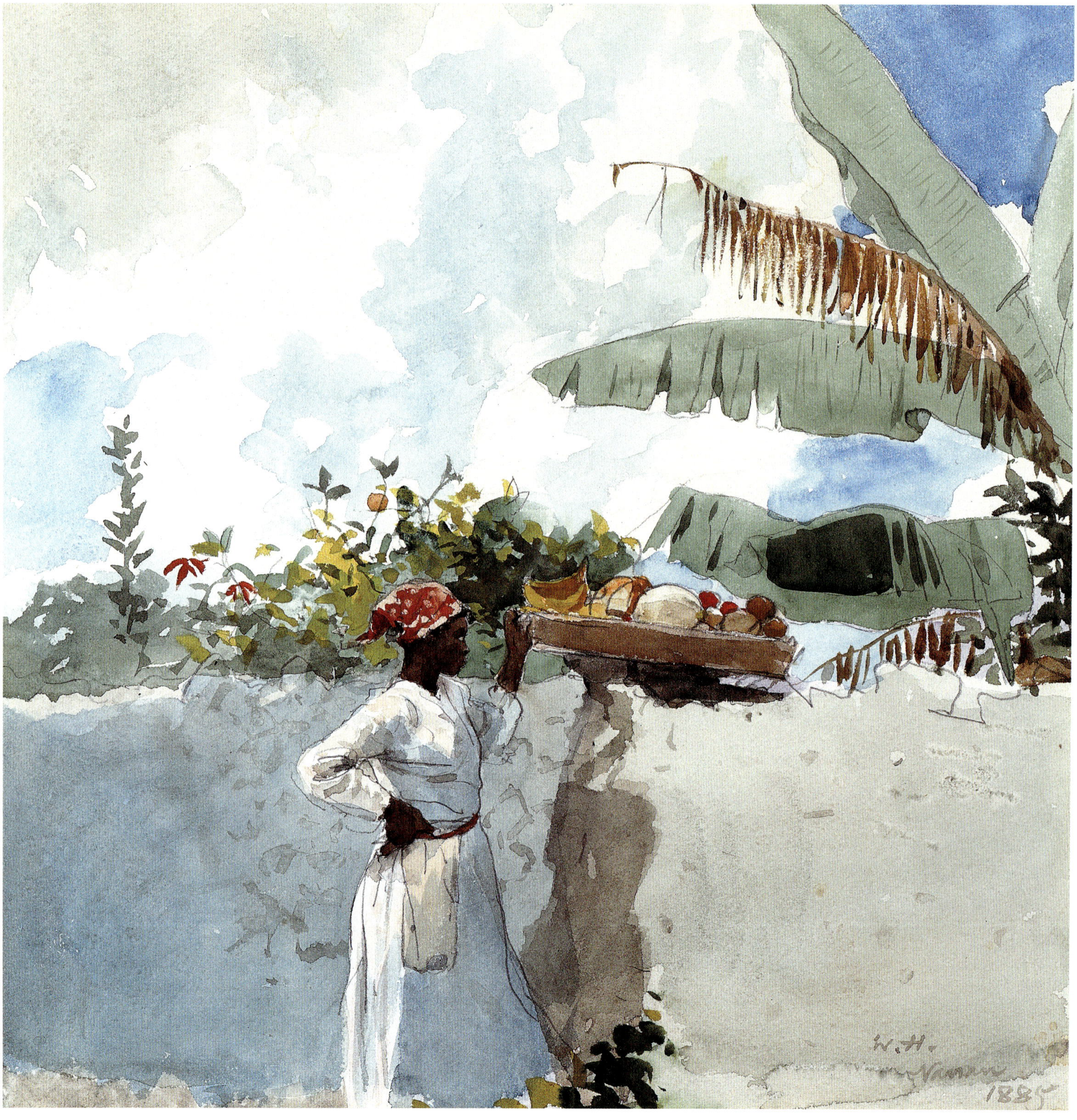

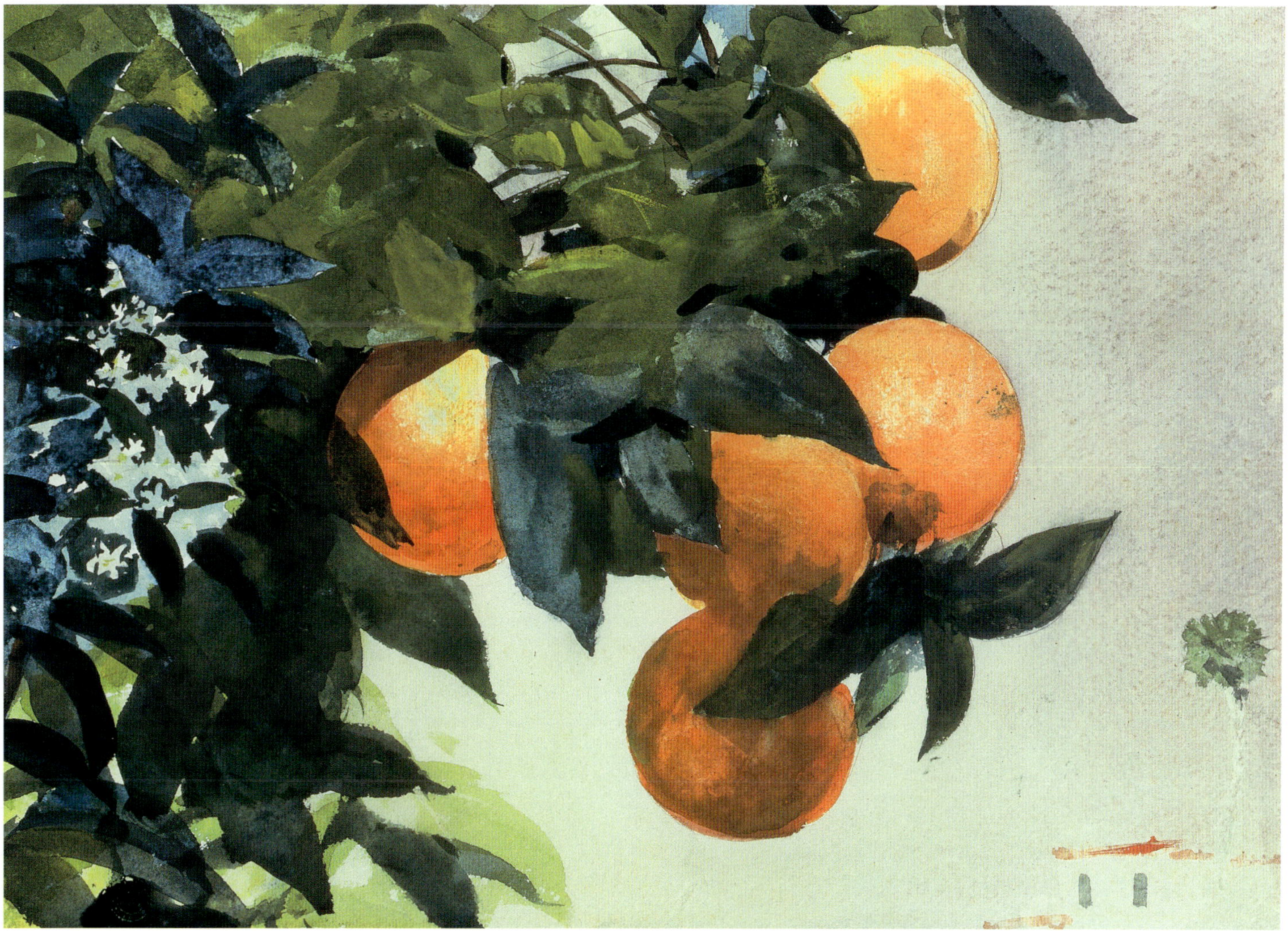

was to the fishwives of Cullercoats and the grizzled guides of his Adirondacks paintings, as embodiments of the honest virtues of hard work and respect for the natural world. One might almost say that Homer was attracted to them because in his mind they belonged to the natural world rather than civilization.

In terms of technique, the Nassau watercolors mark yet another chapter in Homer's approach to watercolor. To some extent they represent a return to his pre-Cullercoats work in their freedom of execution. Contemporaries noted this as well, using language that echoes earlier criticism of his work. The *Boston Evening Transcript* judged that "Life, vigor, fire—all are here, and the sketch is masterly. . . . In no respect are they pictures, only sketches, and as such they are unusually notable."

But these works do not simply return to the earlier sketchy style. Homer is now in full command of his tools, laying in saturated washes with complete confidence, homing in on telling details only when they add to the impact of the image. In *Oranges on a Branch*, the fruit's glistening peel and succulent roundness are palpable yet achieved with miraculous economy; white blossoms are crisply rendered against dark leaves by masking and lifting out. By contrast, the tree and house in the distance are mere wisps, forms eaten away by the acid light of a hot afternoon. There is no fussiness or hesitation here. Henry James's observation that Homer "sees everything at one with its envelope of light and air" is completely vindicated in these works painted beneath the hot tropical sun.

In *Sponge Fishing, the Bahamas*, Homer employs an impressionist technique, with gestural blots of color suggesting a vessel crowded with goods and passengers. More monumental and more soldly painted is *Sharks (also The Derelict)*. This is an ominous work and one that reveals yet another facet of Homer's tropical paintings, an apocalyptic tone whose most famous expression comes in the oil painting *The Gulf Stream* [p. 13]. The subject of the wreck at sea is not new to Homer's work, having dominated the images he painted in England, but now he gives to this tragic tale a new context. The stormy sea of earlier works seems an almost abstract force, but the shark-infested waters of the tropics make the threat seem more savage and more personal. Nature is no longer simply indifferent to man's fate but, as embodied in the thrashing fish who surround the shattered vessel, actively malevolent. In the tropics, even these harbingers of death possess a fierce vitality.

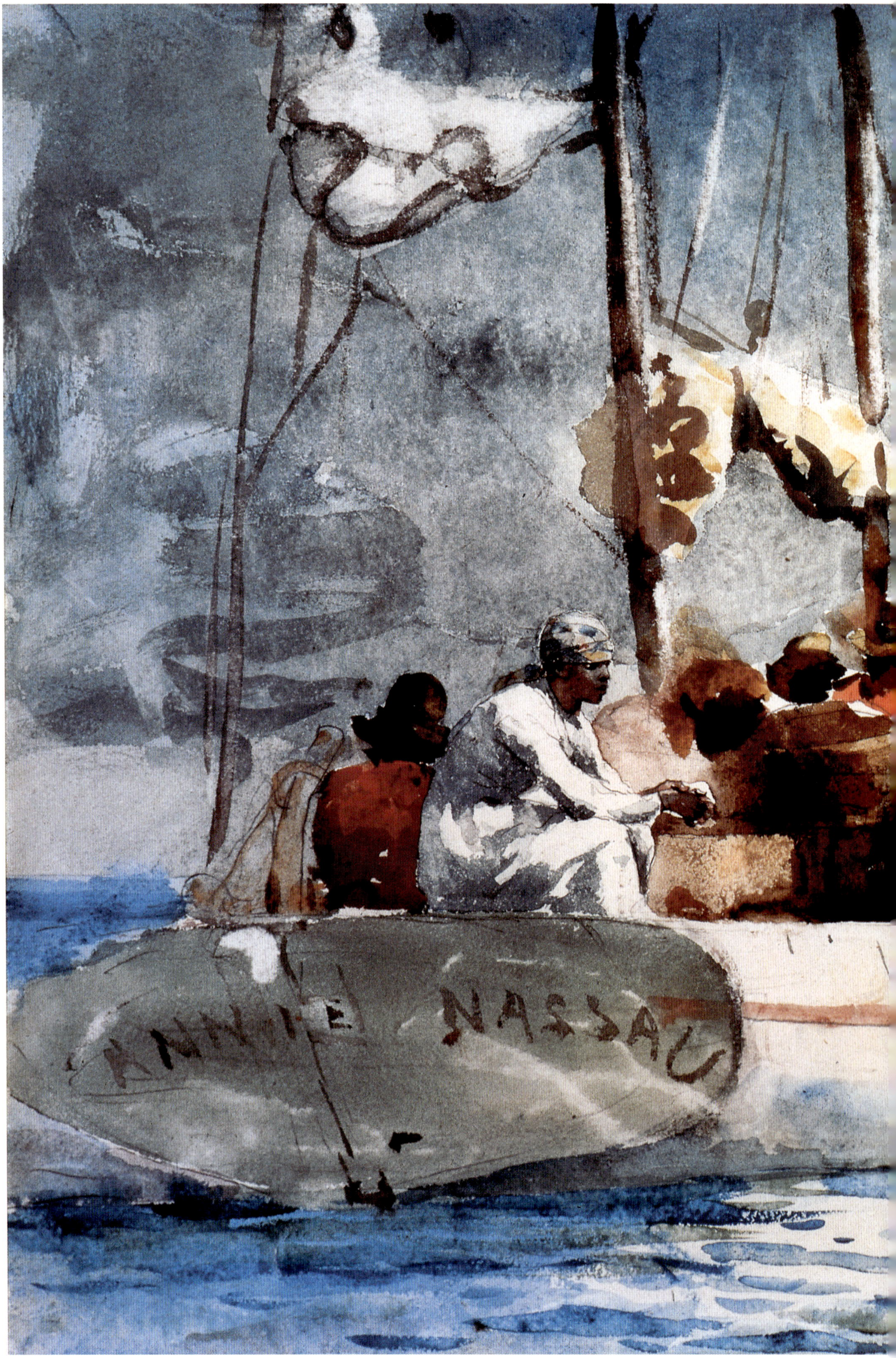

Sponge Fishing, The Bahamas 1885

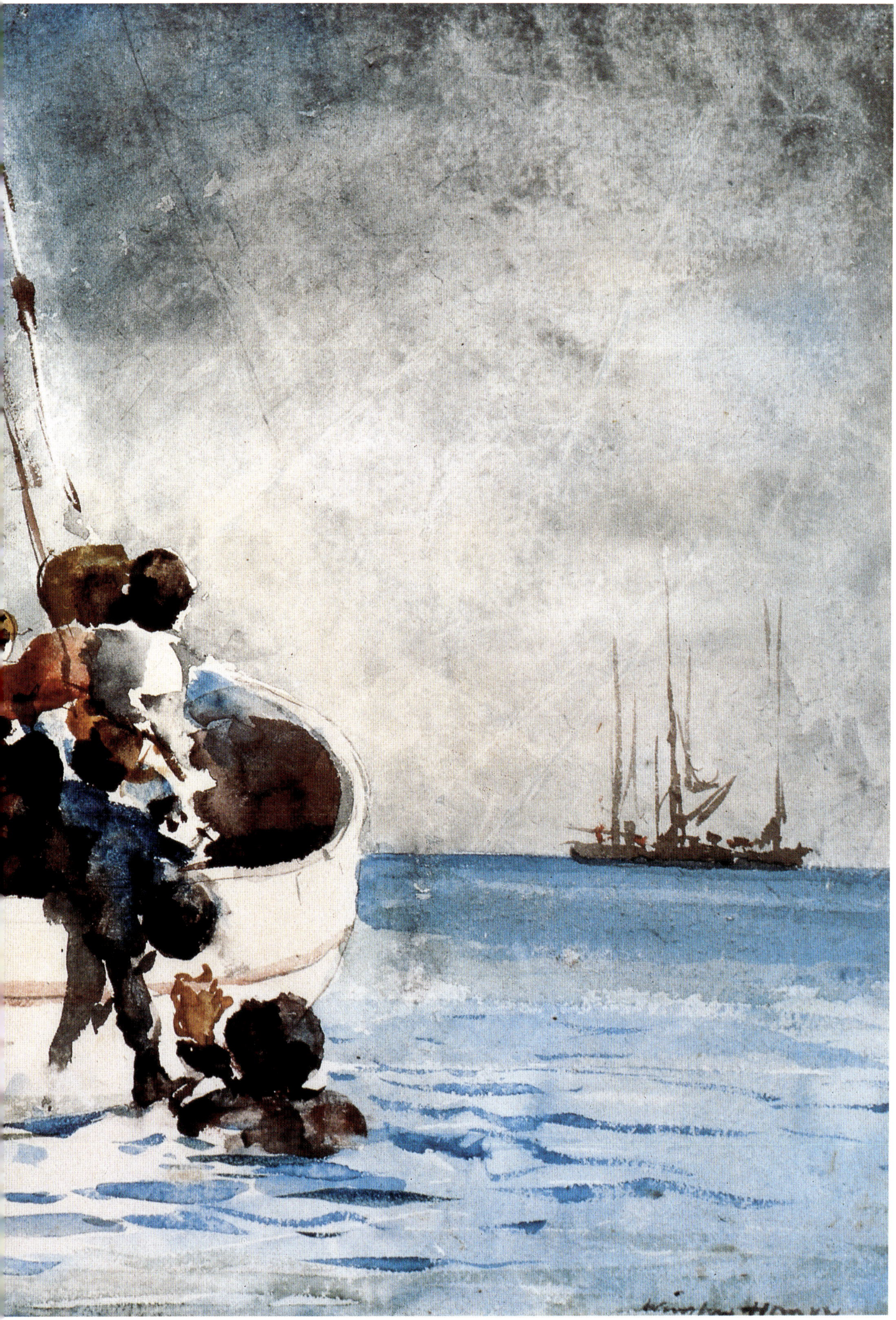

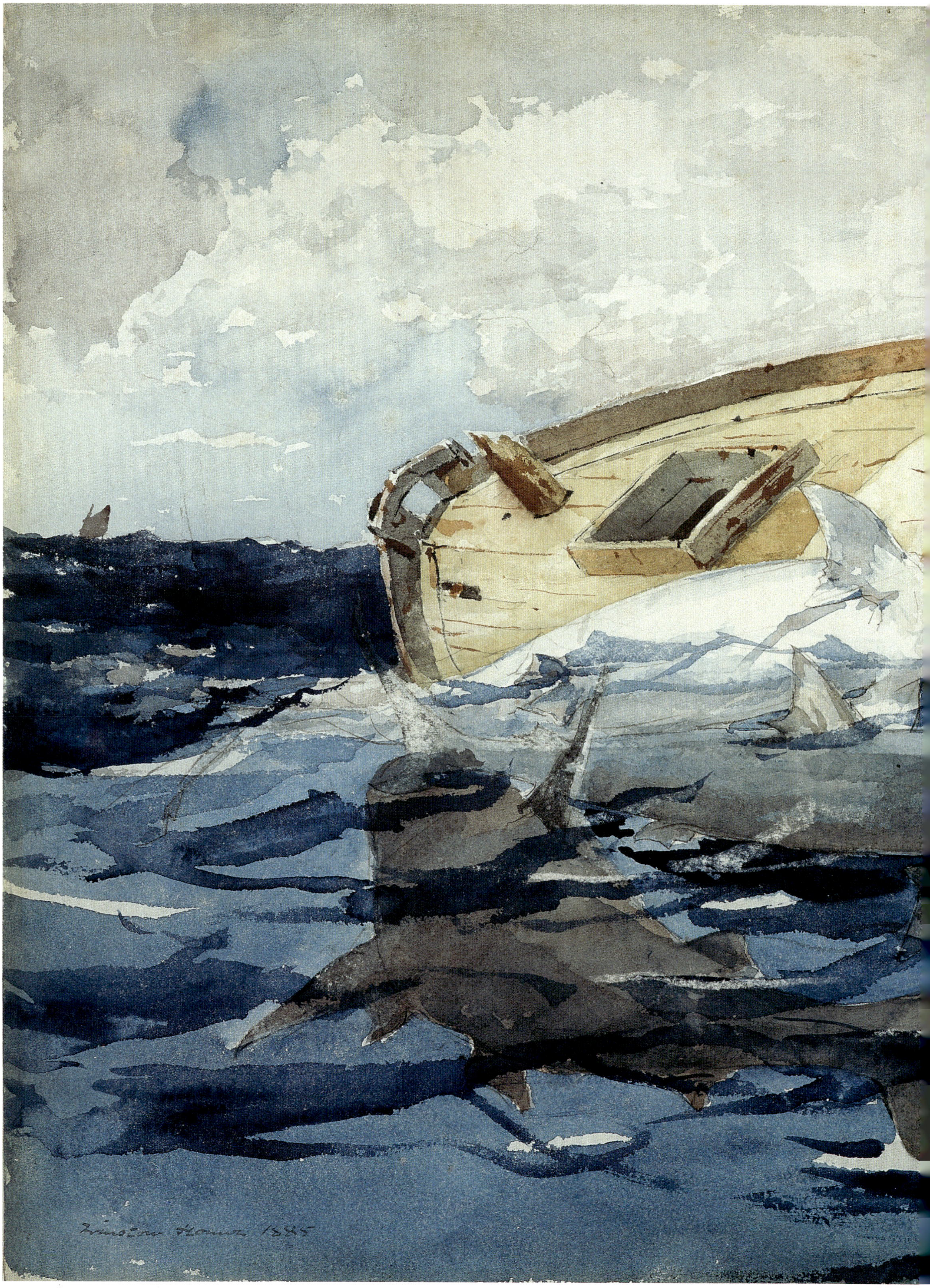
Winslow Homer 1885

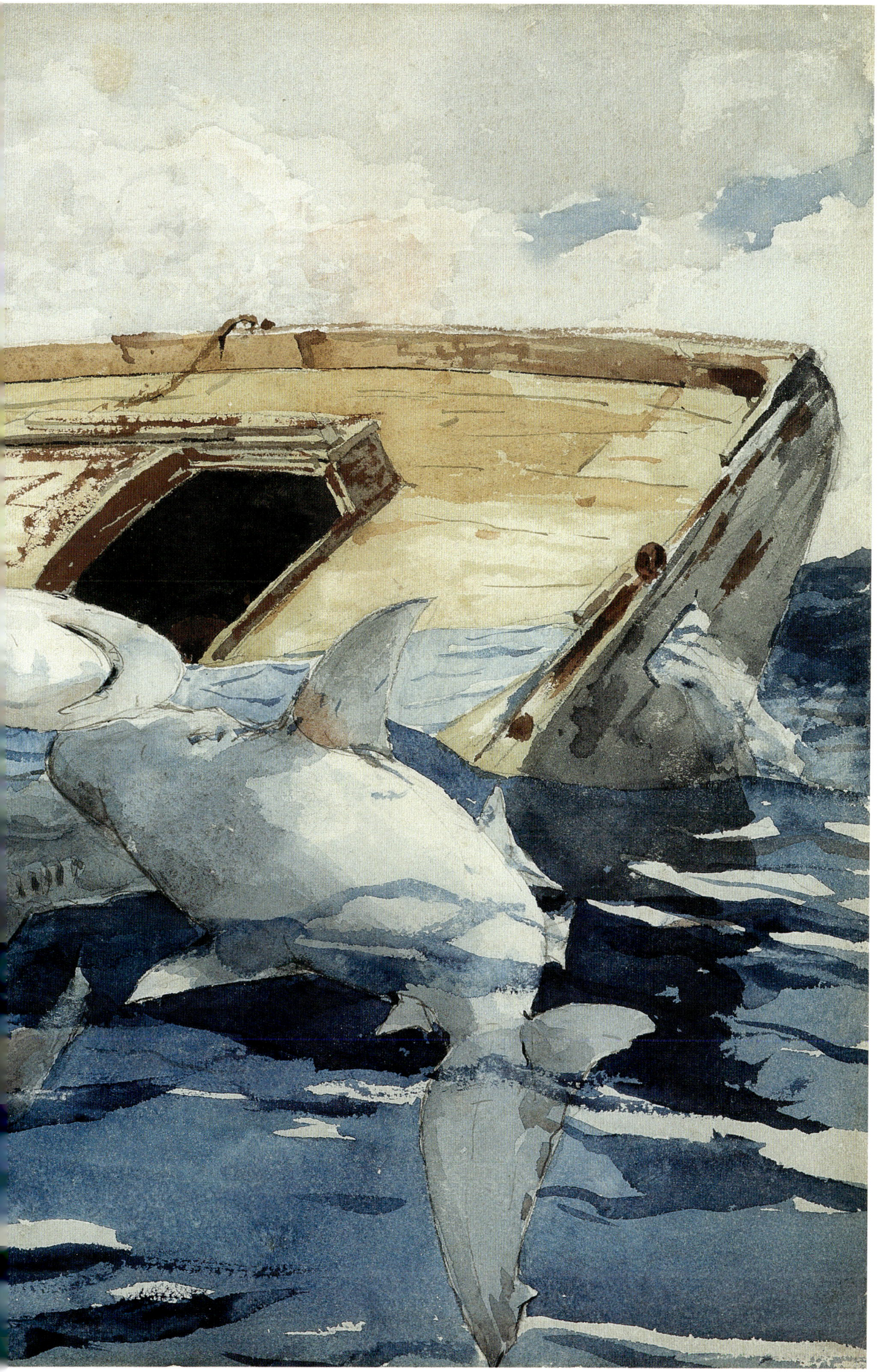

SHARKS; ALSO
THE DERELICT 1885

On his return journey in February 1885, Homer stopped off in Cuba, anticipating in a letter to Charles: "I expect some fine things—it is certainly the richest field for an Artist that I have seen." His prediction turned out to be overly optimistic; the paintings from this portion of the trip are few and among the least successful of his mature career. Homer was always more at home depicting figures in a natural setting. Ironically, the natural arch depicted in *Glass Windows, Bahamas* feels far more architectural than his views of Cuban buildings. Works like *Street Corner, Santiago de Cuba* have a certain charm, but the view of crumbling walls and narrow streets lacks the luminosity and sureness of his Bahamas work.

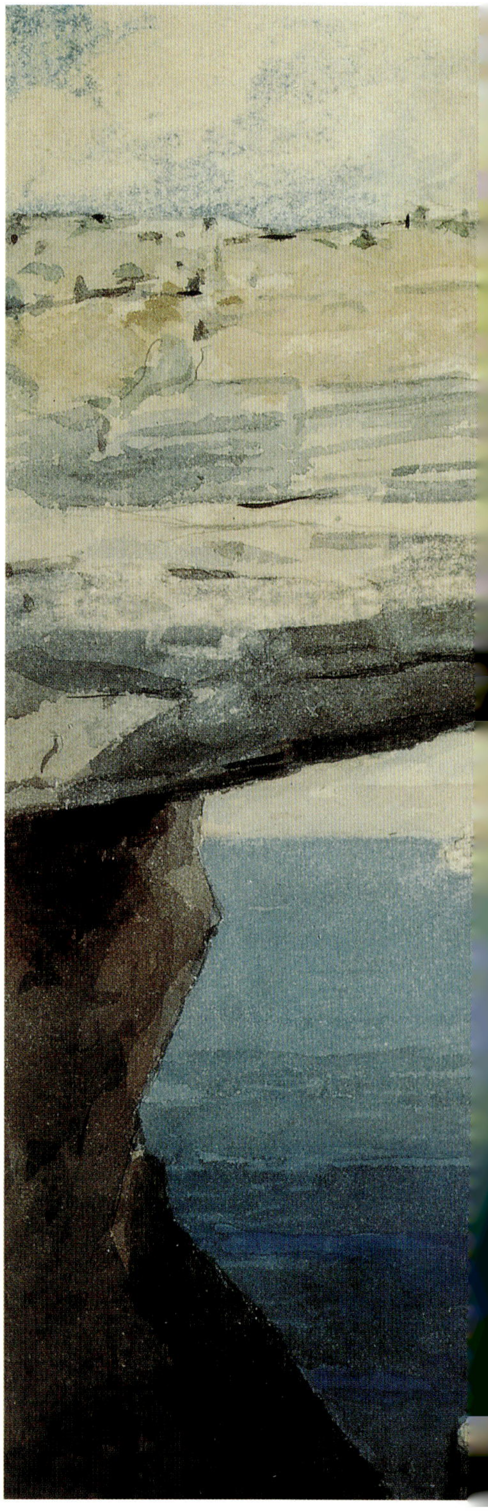

STREET CORNER, SANTIAGO DE CUBA 1885

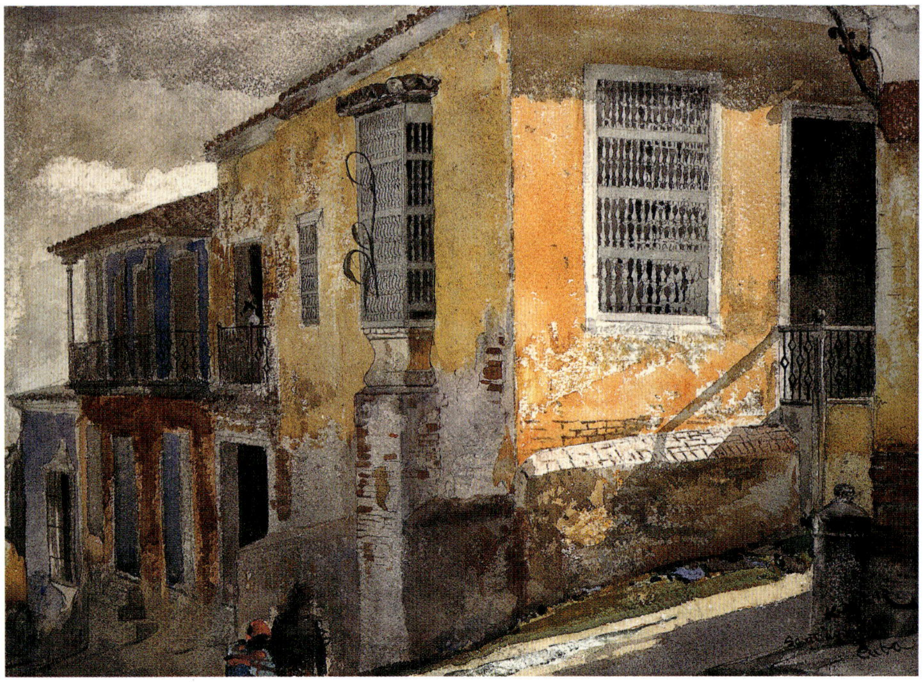

Glass Windows, Bahamas 1885

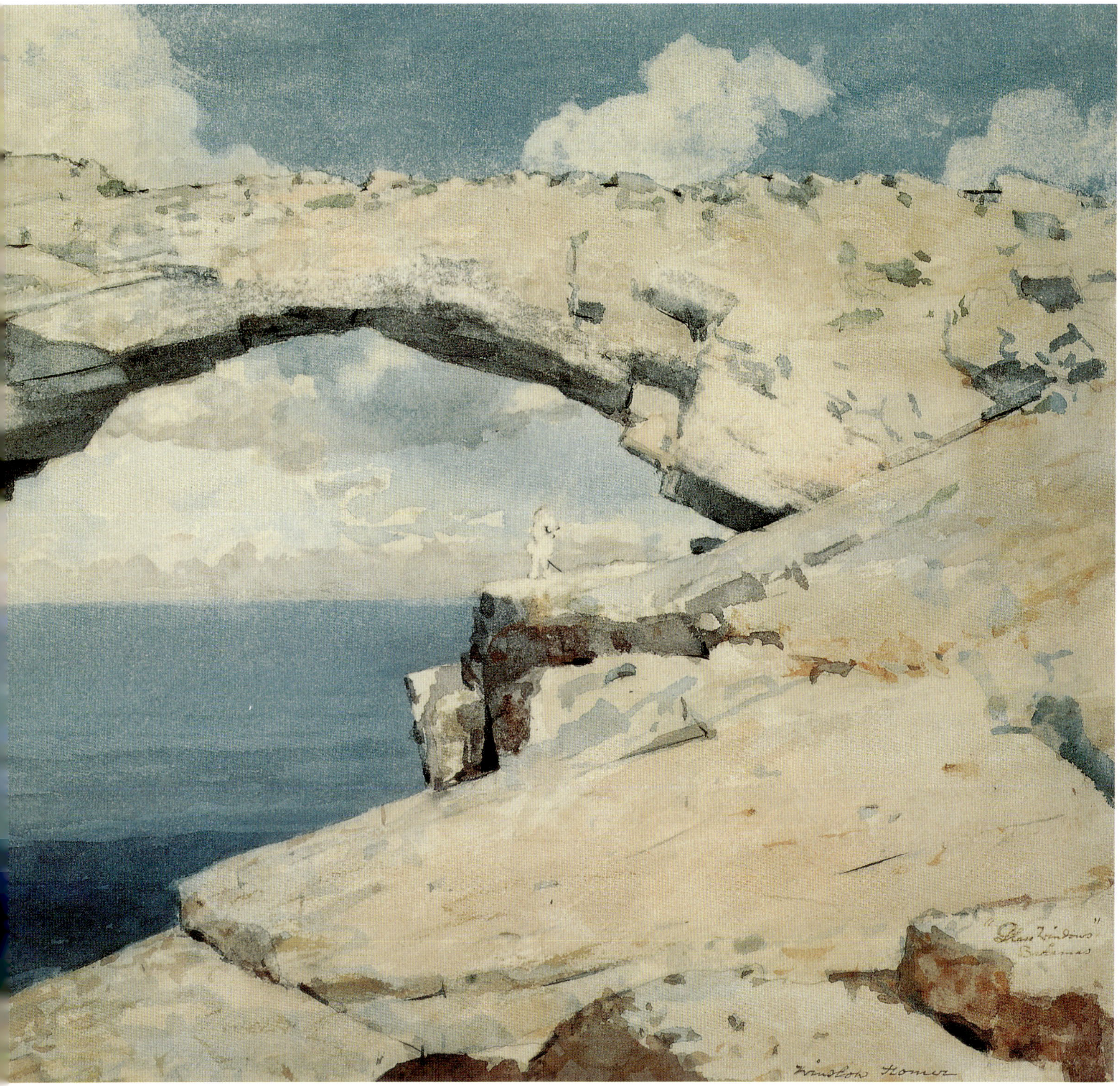

VIII.
Hunters and Hunted: The Adirondacks, 1874–1900

Among Homer's greatest watercolors are those he painted in the deep woods of the Adirondacks in upstate New York. Homer came to the woods not simply as an artist gathering material but as a confirmed outdoorsman, drawn by his passion for fishing to the streams and hidden lakes of the forest. Not for him the sweeping vistas of contemporaries like Frederic Church or Albert Bierstadt, whose panoramic works took in entire mountain ranges in a single canvas. Homer knew the forest from the inside out, from loamy floor with its dense undergrowth to the dappled canopy above. This is not a view of nature as something that dwarfs man. The forest for Homer is crucially different from the sea, whose vastness and indifference to humanity's fate make it an object of terror. Its scale is human. The woods are a stage on which a man may act on equal terms with his environment. And because that person is to some extent the master of his own fate in the woods, a different moral order applies. The ocean reveals human helplessness in the face of things infinitely larger—survival is the only imperative. The forest, more vulnerable than the eternal sea, demands that we behave responsibly.

The bulk of Homer's Adirondacks watercolors date to the last decade of the nineteenth century, but his engagement with the theme goes back as far as 1870 and to such important early oil paintings as *Adirondack Lake* and *The Two Guides*. A month-long stay at the Thomas Baker farm in Minerva, New York, during the spring of 1874 produced such early watercolors as *Waiting for a Bite* [p. 52] and *Trappers Resting*. These loosely brushed, atmospheric watercolors prefigure the subjects that dominate his later work. The same narrative concerns find their way into commercial illustrations of the period: *Trapping in the Adirondacks* is a composition he later reworked as *The Blue Boat*, one of the masterpieces of his mature years; *Deer-Stalking in the Adirondacks in Winter* [p. 17] is an early treatment of the teamwork between hound and hunter that Homer will explore fully in the watercolors after 1889.

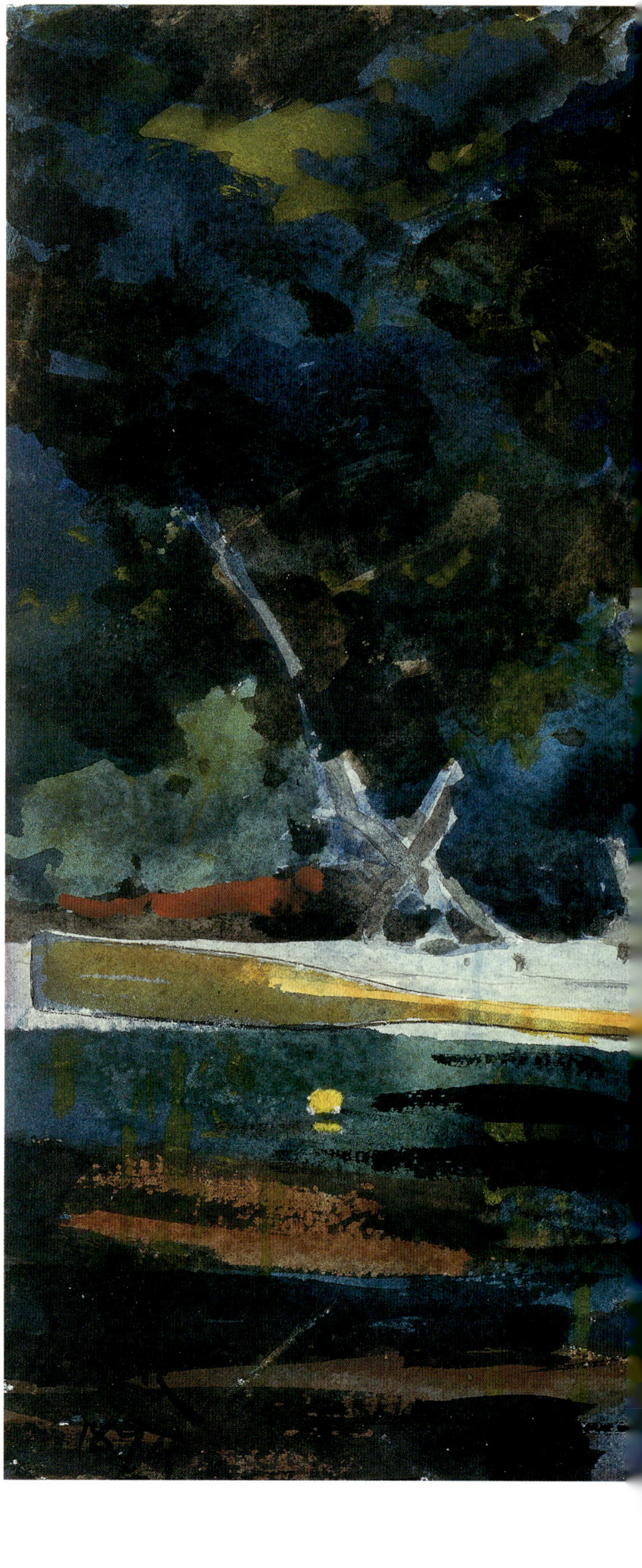

The Adirondack Guide 1894

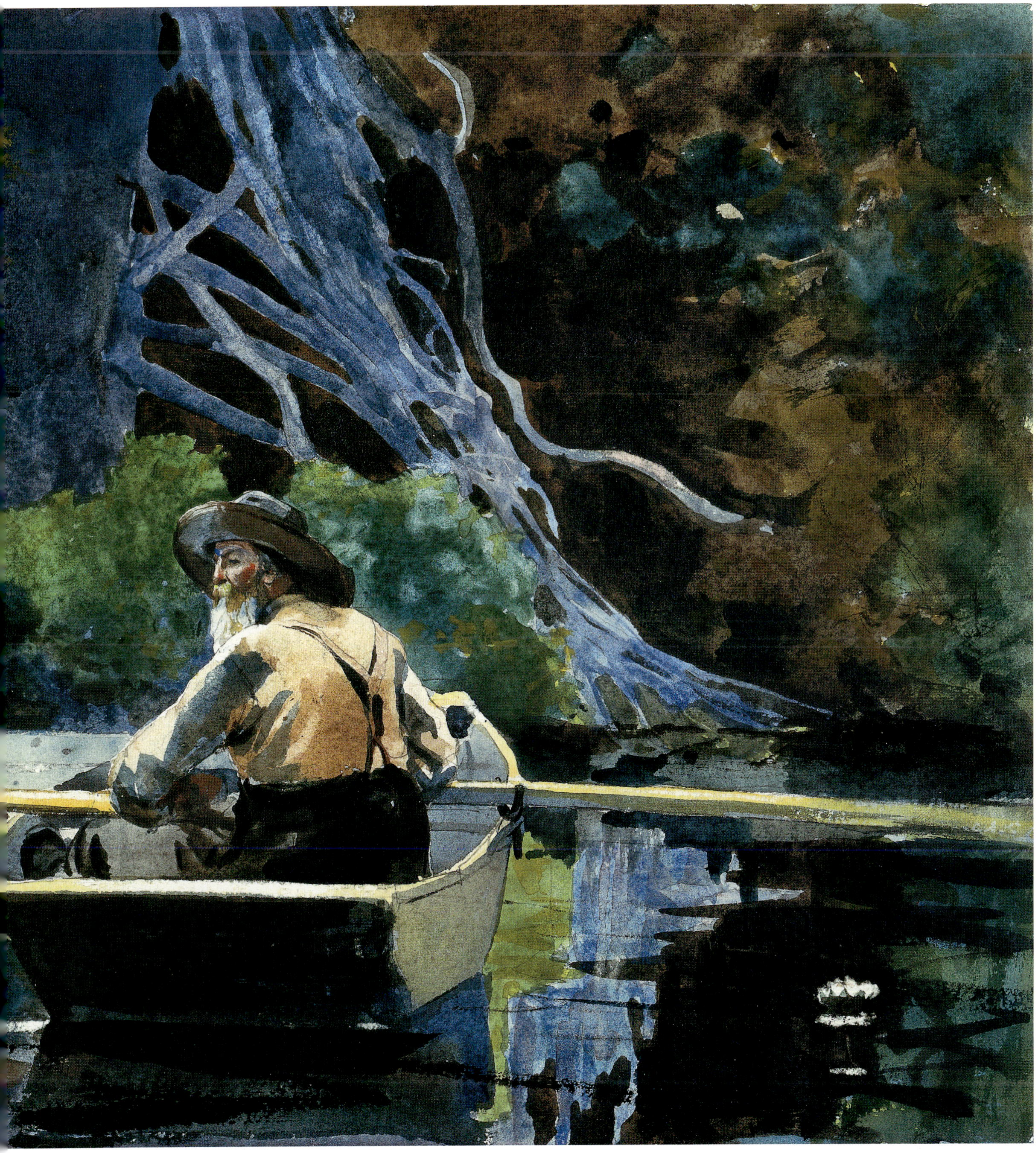

Homer was not the only artist of the time to create images of hunting and fishing. The popular prints of Currier & Ives include numerous images based on exactly the same themes. Homer, as so often with one eye on the bottom line, was catering to a well-established market of fellow fishermen who were among the most avid collectors of these watercolors. Thomas B. Clarke, Homer's greatest patron, was an avid angler.

The late nineteenth century saw an explosive growth in nature tourism as an increasingly urbanized society began to appreciate the wilderness as a place in which to restore the soul and soothe nerves frayed by the fast pace of modern life. Ironically, the popularity of such wilderness sites, and the ease of access provided by extensions of the railway lines, placed in jeopardy the fragile ecosystems so recently "discovered." Homer was not alone in recognizing the danger of the situation. *The New York Times* complained that the Adirondacks "has fallen from that estate of fish and solitude for which it was originally celebrated. . . . The desert has blossomed with parasols and the waste places are filled with picnic parties, reveling in lemonade and *sardines*." George P. Marsh, whose pleas for wilderness conservation were influential in establishing the 700,000-acre Adirondack State Park in 1885, was keenly aware of the threat people posed to the natural environment. In his influential environmental tract *Man and Nature*, he wrote: "The preservation of existing woods, and the far more costly extension of them where they have been unduly reduced, are among the most obvious of the duties which this age owes to those that are to come."

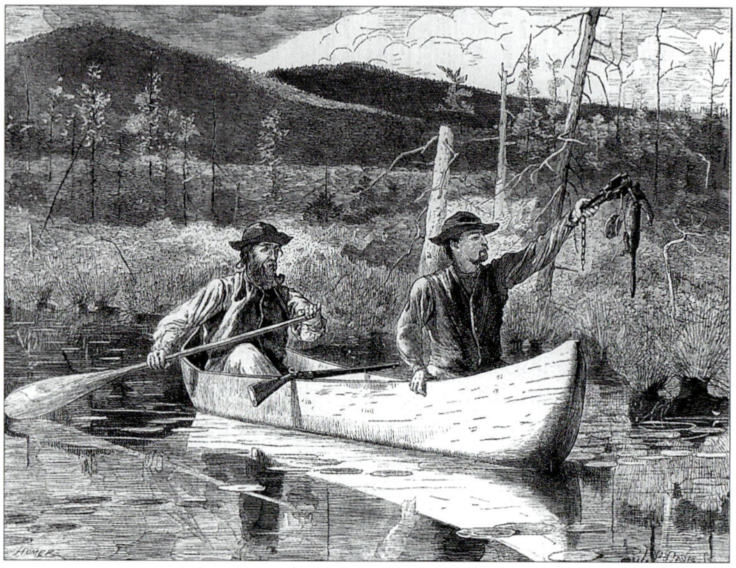

TRAPPING IN THE ADIRONDACKS 1870

TRAPPERS RESTING 1874

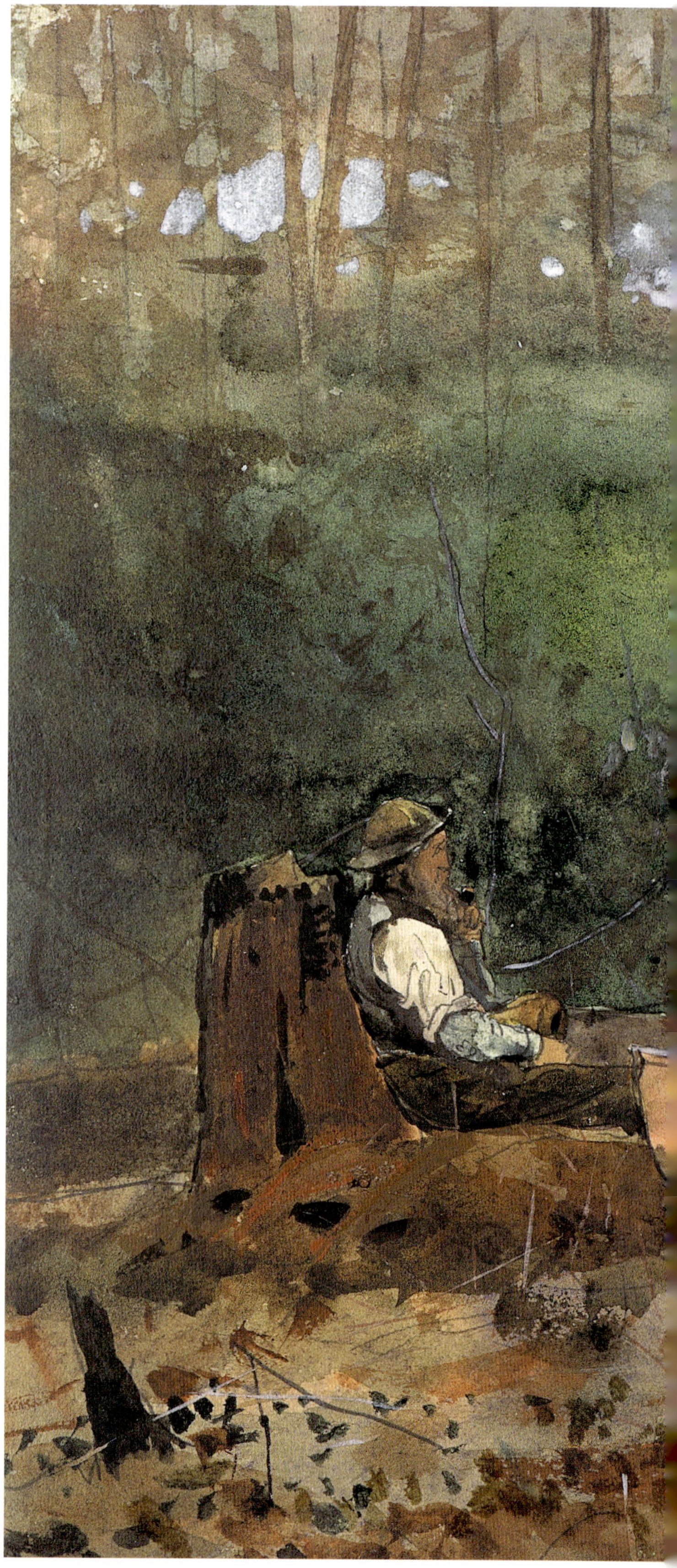

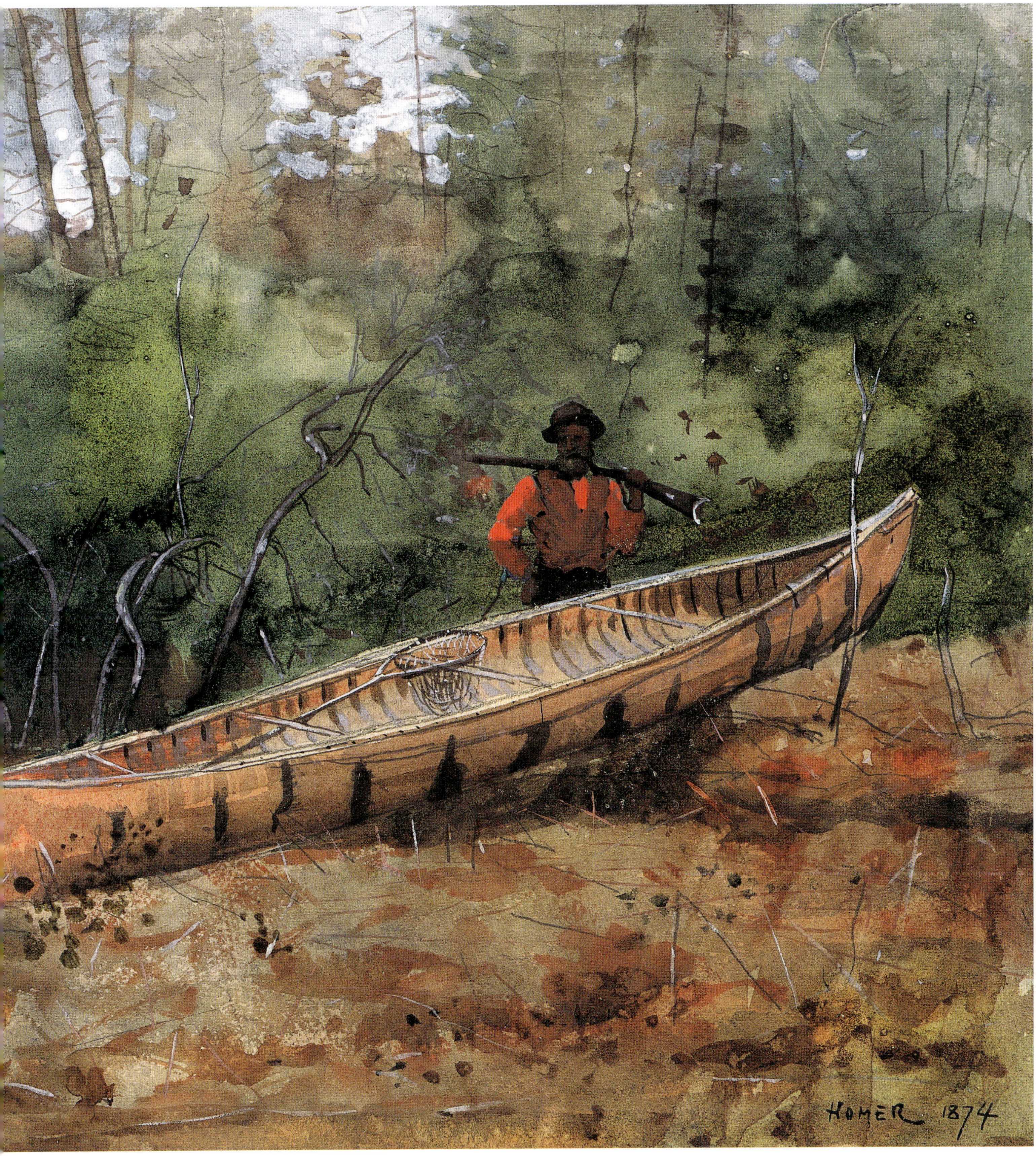
HOMER 1874

Homer treated such ecological concerns explicitly in a series of works depicting logging in the Adirondacks. In *The Woodcutter*, the lumberman surveys the woods below like a general seeking new lands to conquer; the hilltop on which he stands is desolate, a reminder of what happens when land is stripped of its timber. He is a figure of heroic proportions, but one associated with death and destruction. *Hudson River, Logging* [p. 145] treats the business of plundering the forest for timber in less apocalyptic terms. The lumbermen portrayed here are, like the guides and trappers, hardworking fellows earning a living from the natural environment. There is little here to suggest an impending ecological disaster.

More poignant is *Old Friends* [p. 149], where the grizzled figure gazes up at an ancient tree as if wishing a fond farewell to a relic of an earlier age. In works like this and *Hunter in the Adirondacks* [pp. 150–151], we feel Homer's reverence and love for the deep forest. In both watercolors Homer describes a cycle of growth and decay, of life born anew from death. Both tree and woodsman in *Old Friends* are survivors and possess the dignity of all things that have withstood the ravages of time. In *Hunter in the Adirondacks*, the younger man strides over a dead tree like David over a fallen Goliath. He stands tall and straight like the vigorous young saplings that have sprung up from the forest floor made fertile by the decay of older generations. Youth's triumph, Homer seems to say, is shortlived; wisdom comes from recognizing and accepting one's place in the cycles of nature. It is a Darwinian view of nature as a constant struggle, but one that offers its own consolations.

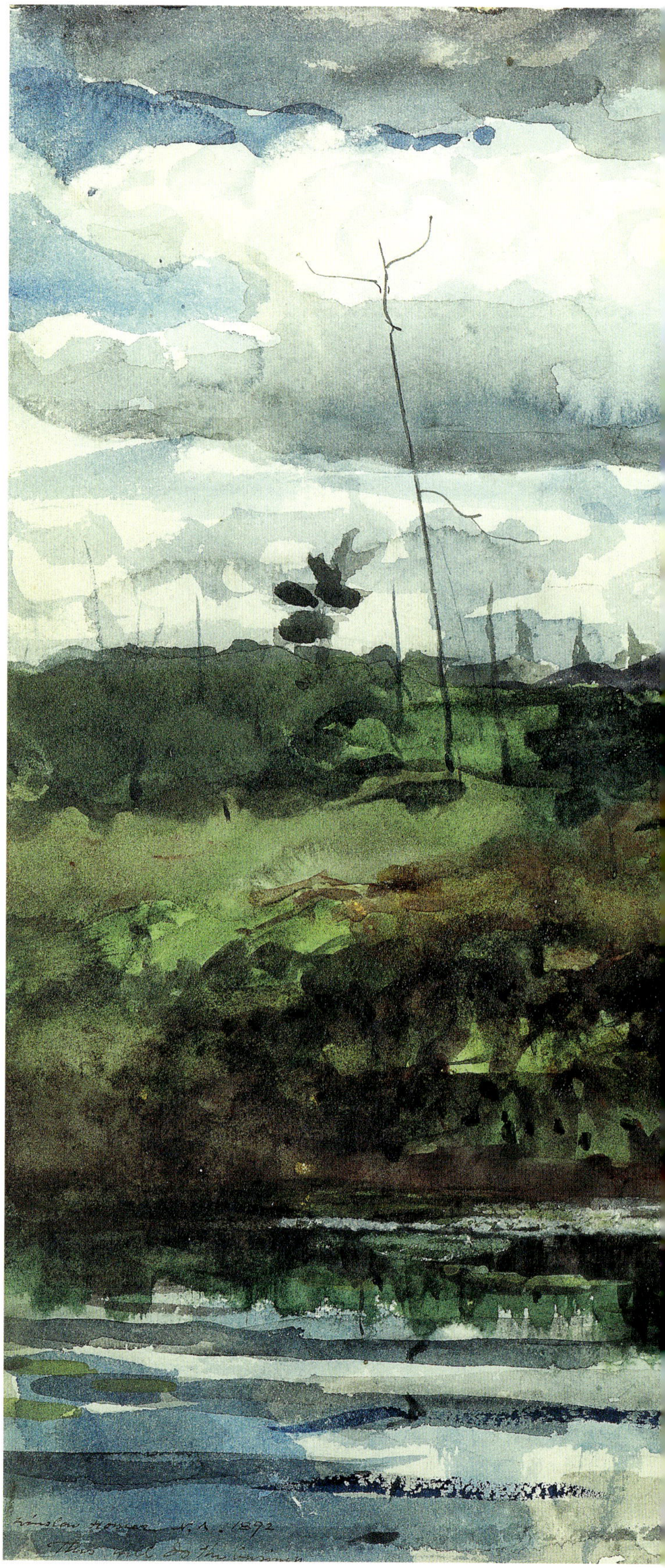

THE BLUE BOAT 1892

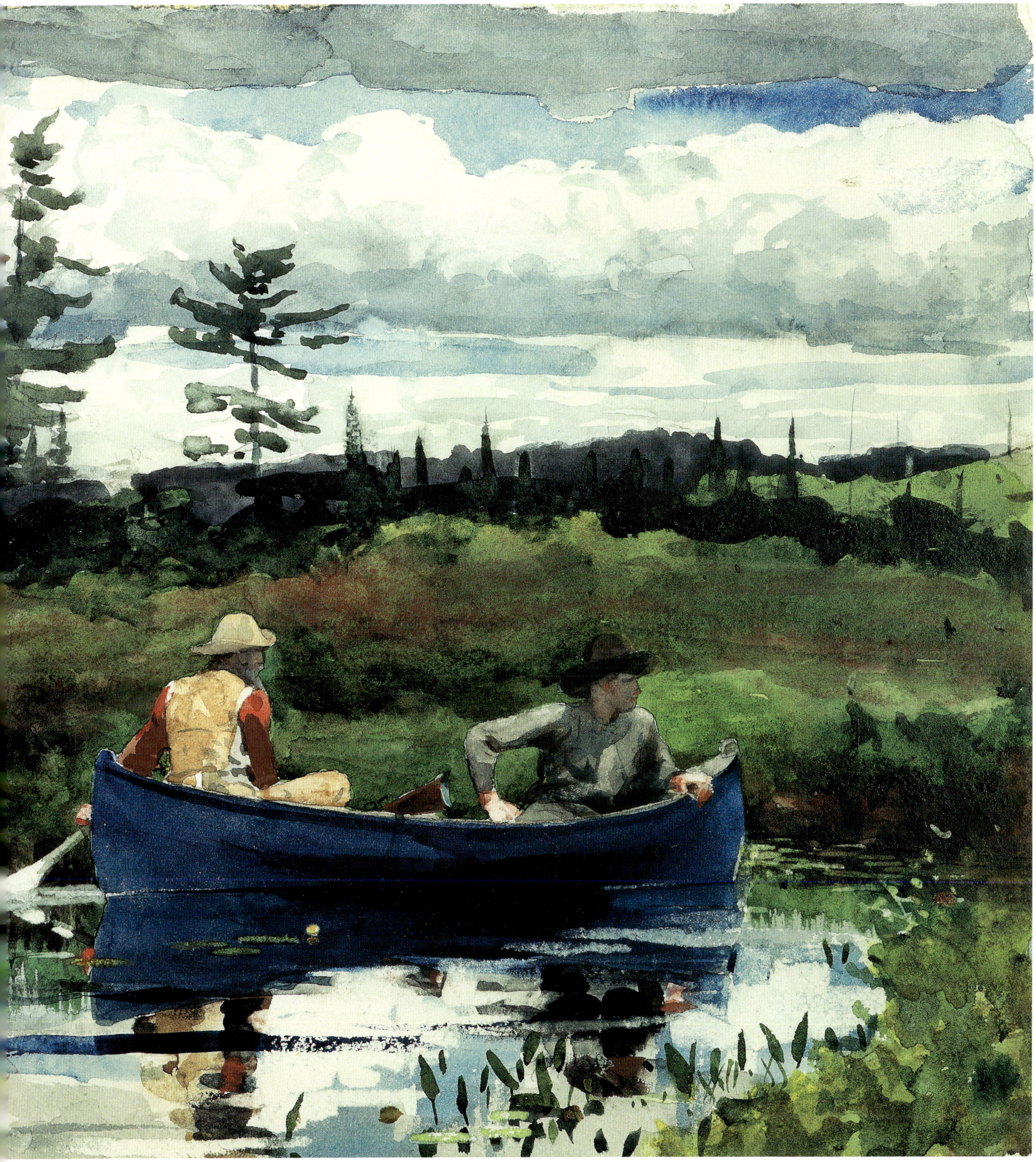

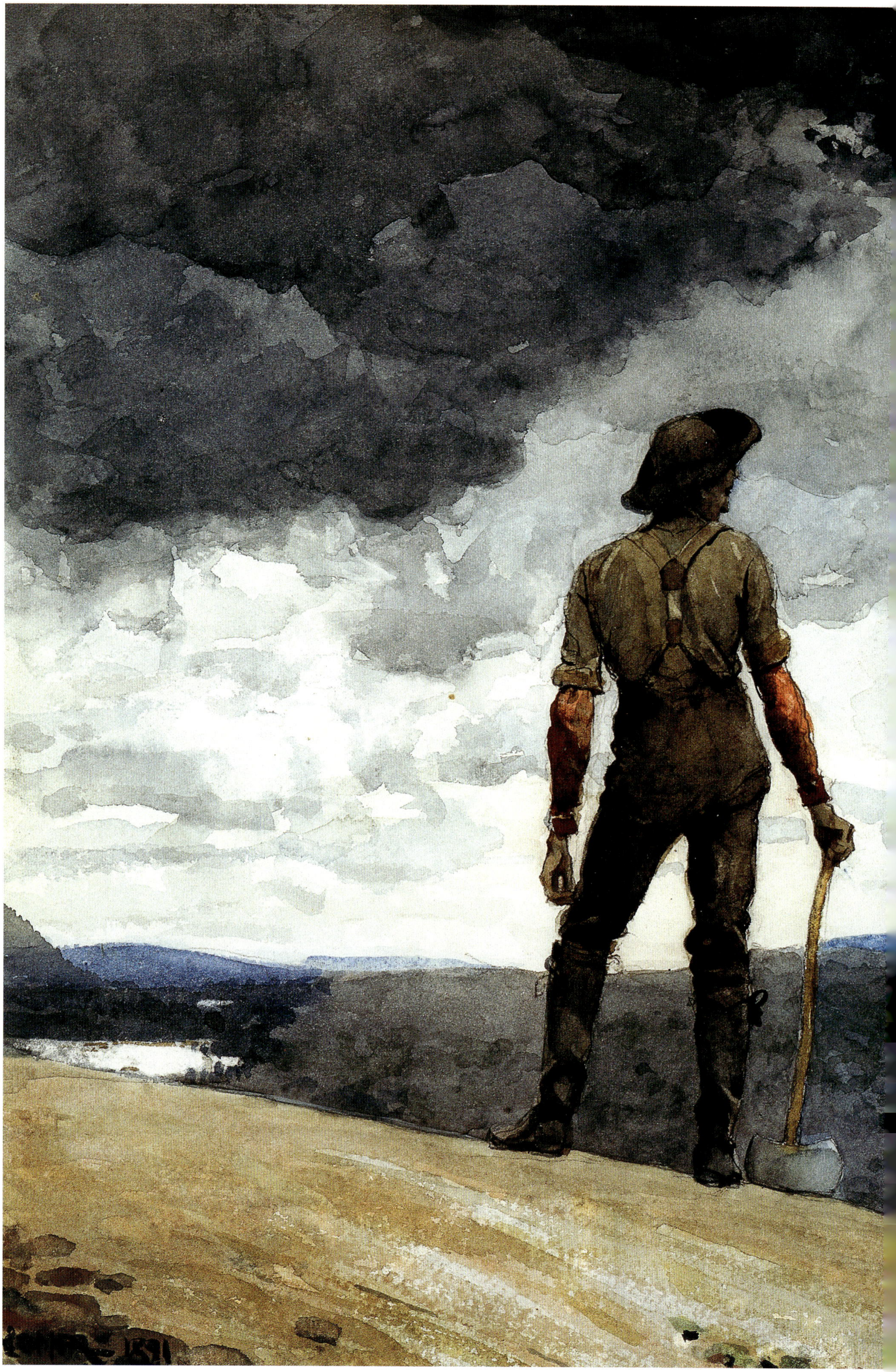

THE WOODCUTTER 1891

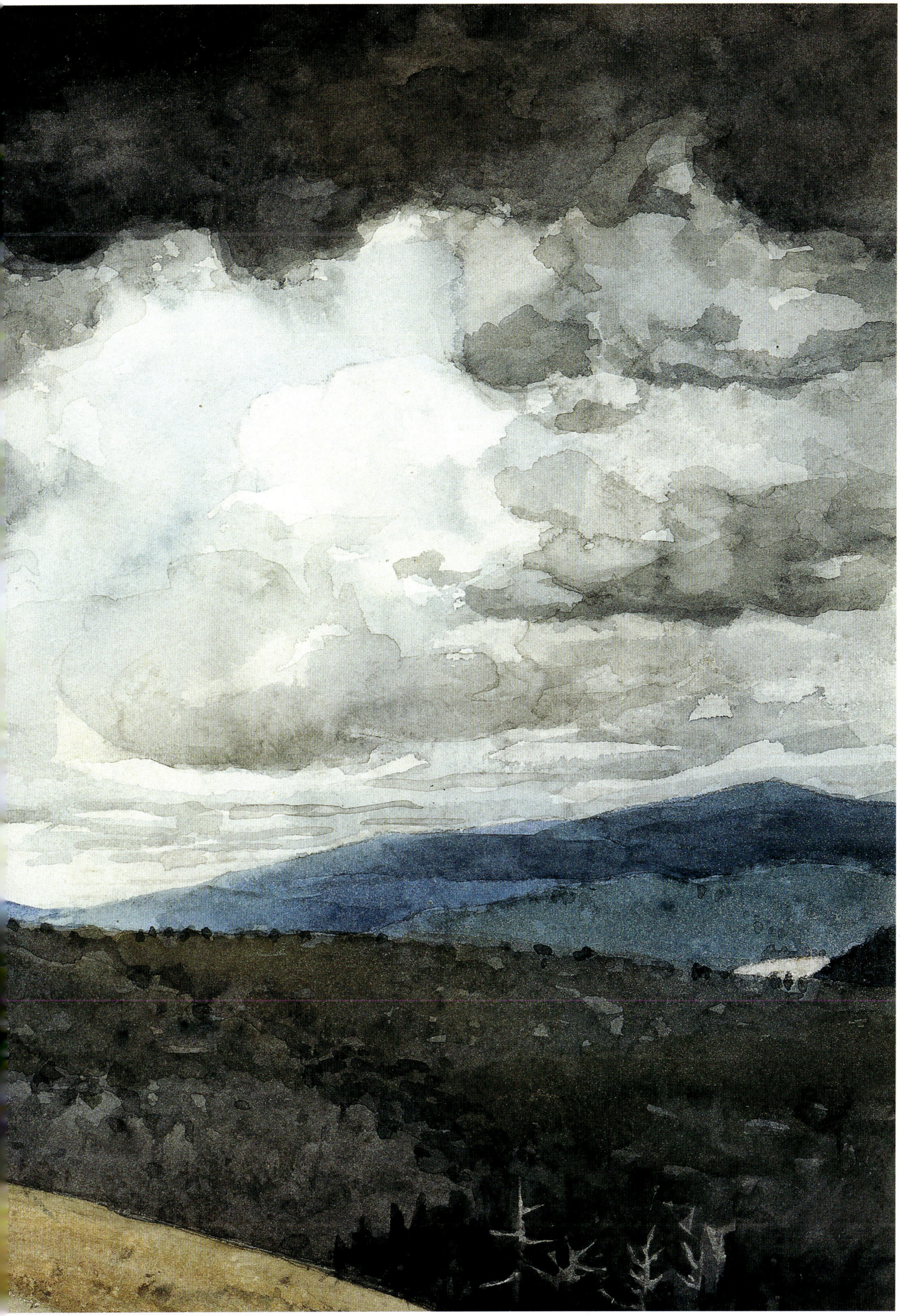

Old Settlers [p. 148] is one of the few works where the main actors are animal rather than human. As the title implies, the black bears who blunder through the undergrowth are the true denizens of the deep forest. Unlike *Hunter in the Adirondacks* and *Old Friends*, Homer now shows us a broad panorama with distant mountains surrounding a shimmering lake—made by scratching through to the white paper. Instead of a narrow range of tones that captures the half-light of the shaded forest, he uses sharper contrasts that convey the feeling of broad expanses and varied terrain. The flattened silhouettes of the tall pines that form a decorative pattern against the sky owe a clear debt to Japanese art. But even when the artist emphasizes the two-dimensional surface of the image, he combines it with a view into deep space; abstract elements, however prominent, never undermine the reality of the scene.

Homer's Adirondacks watercolors encompass an ecosystem that has both a literal and an ethical dimension. The hunters, fishermen, trappers, and lumbermen who ply their trades in the woods are those with the greatest sympathy for and understanding of the natural environment. But they are also its most ruthless exploiters. These are men who know the woods with an intimacy born of lifelong experience but who also often act merely in the interest of profit. The artist's ambivalence toward these people is apparent throughout. He admires their courage and cunning while deploring their cruelty and selfishness. Ultimately, Homer's vision is clear-eyed and unsentimental, recognizing that cruelty and selfishness are, along with heartbreaking beauty, firmly inscribed in the natural order.

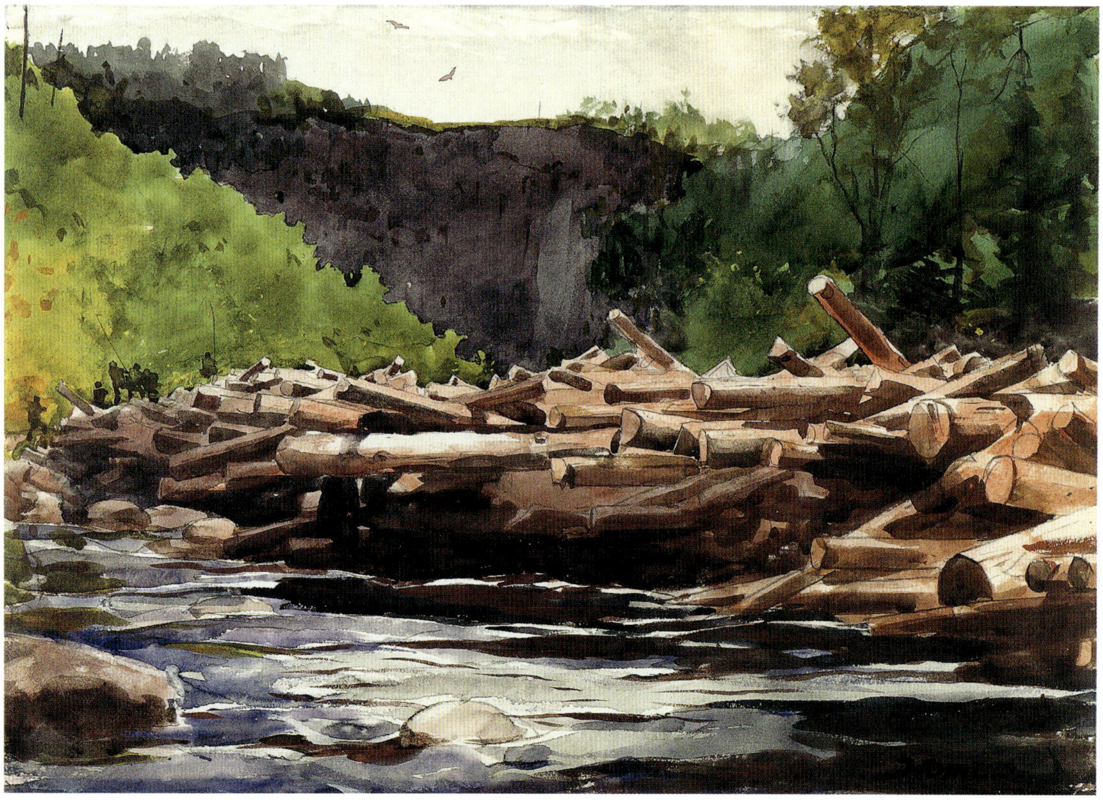

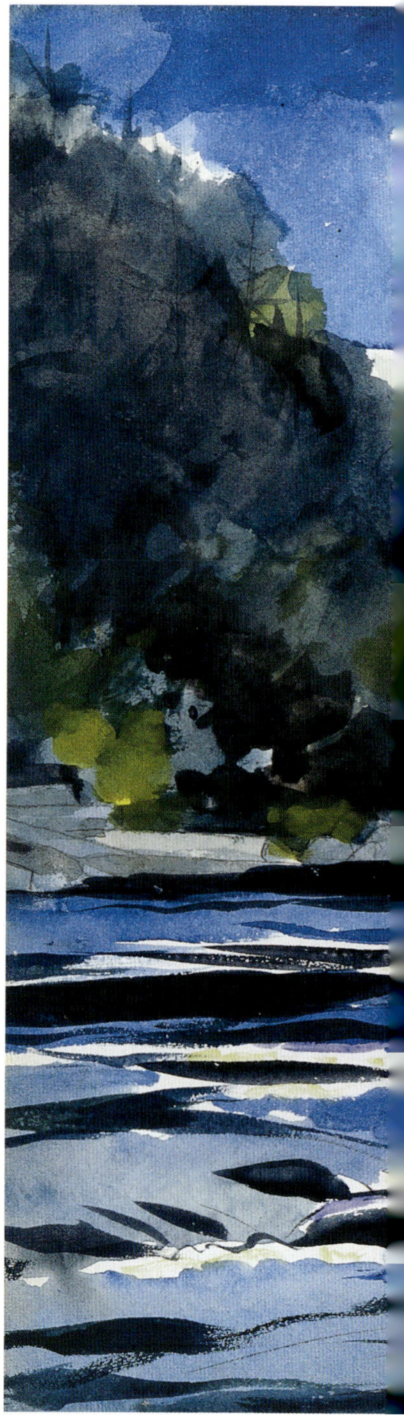

Hudson River at Blue Ledge, Essex County (The Log Jam) 1889

HUDSON RIVER, LOGGING 1892

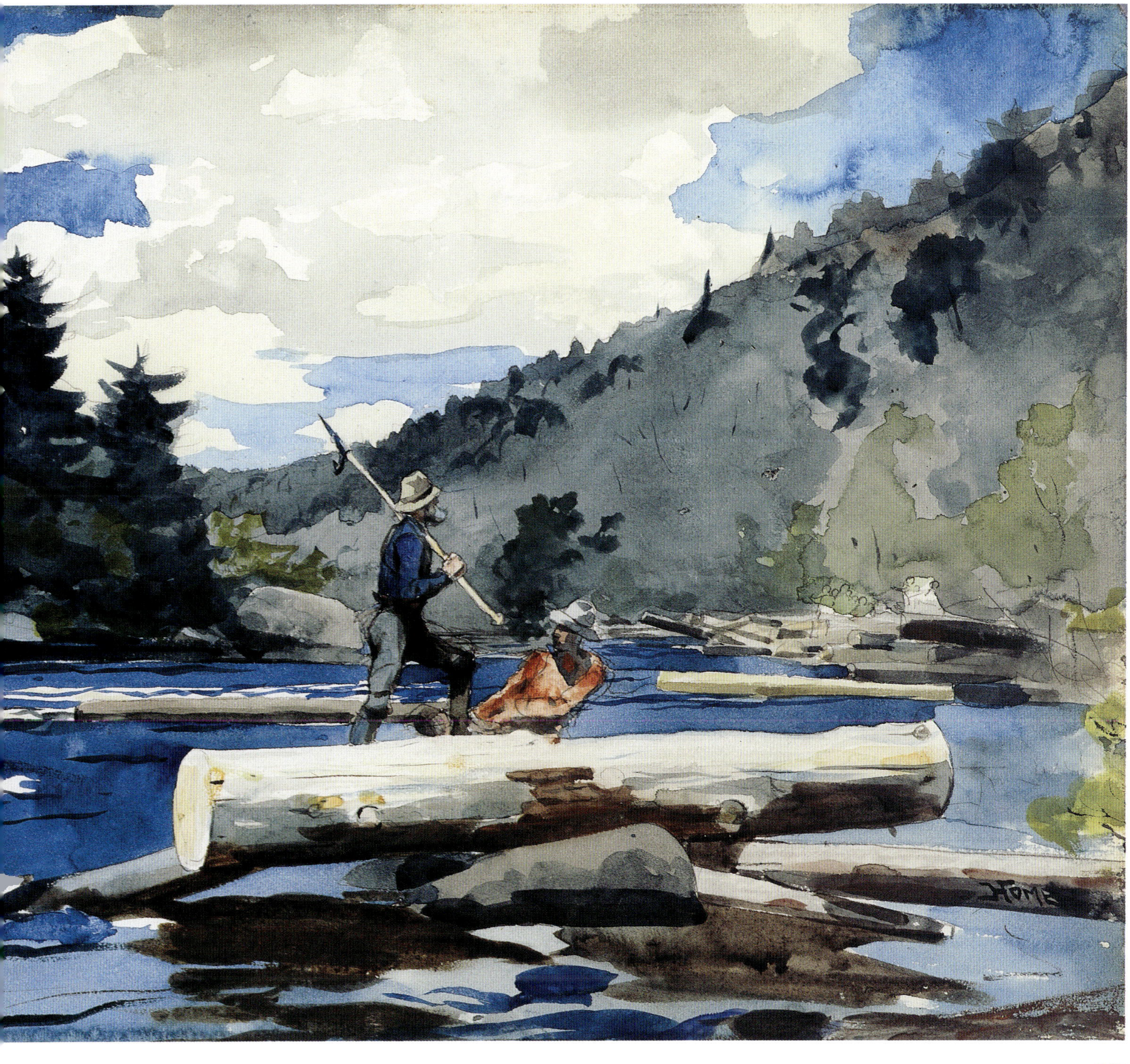

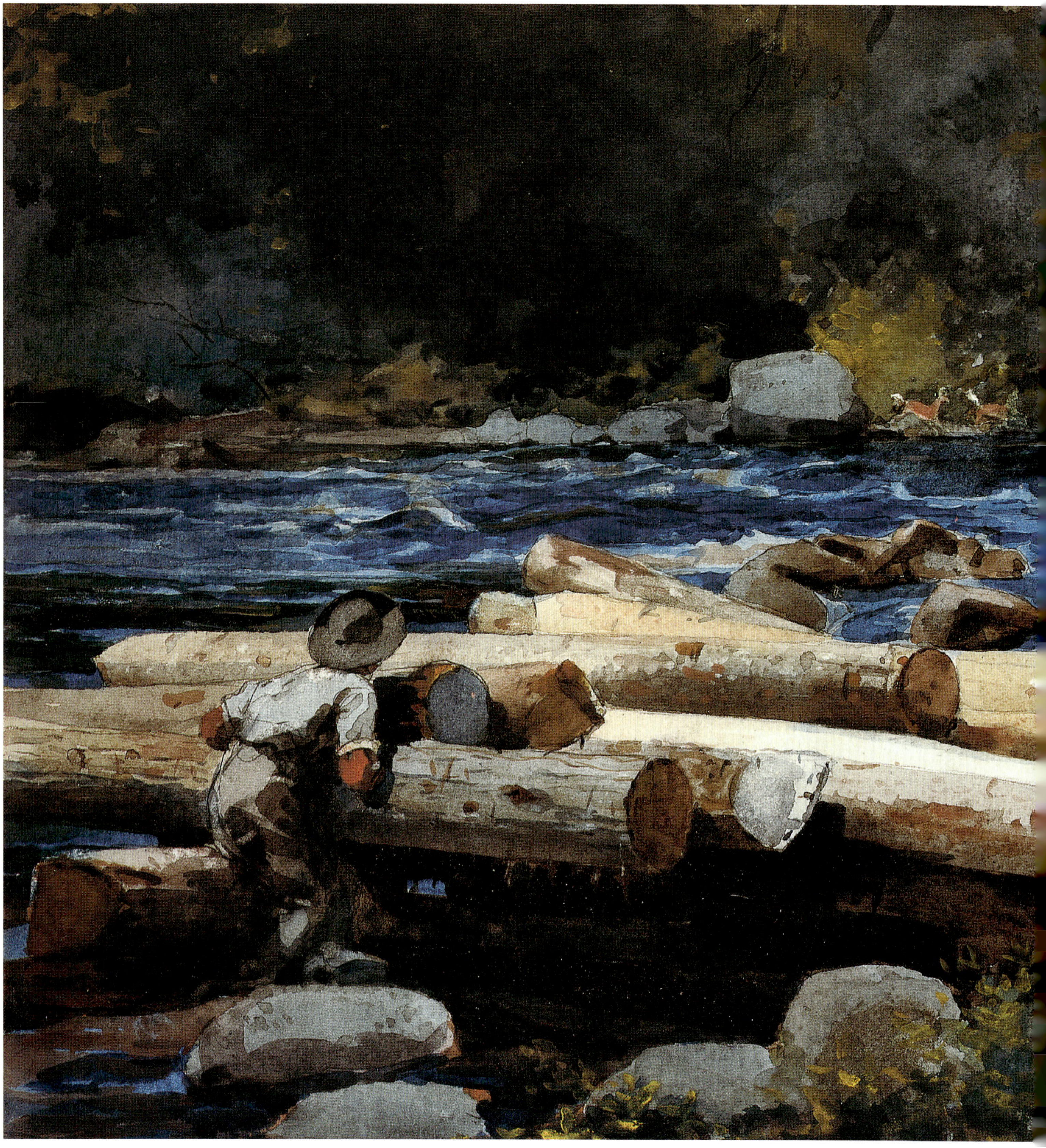

HUDSON RIVER 1892

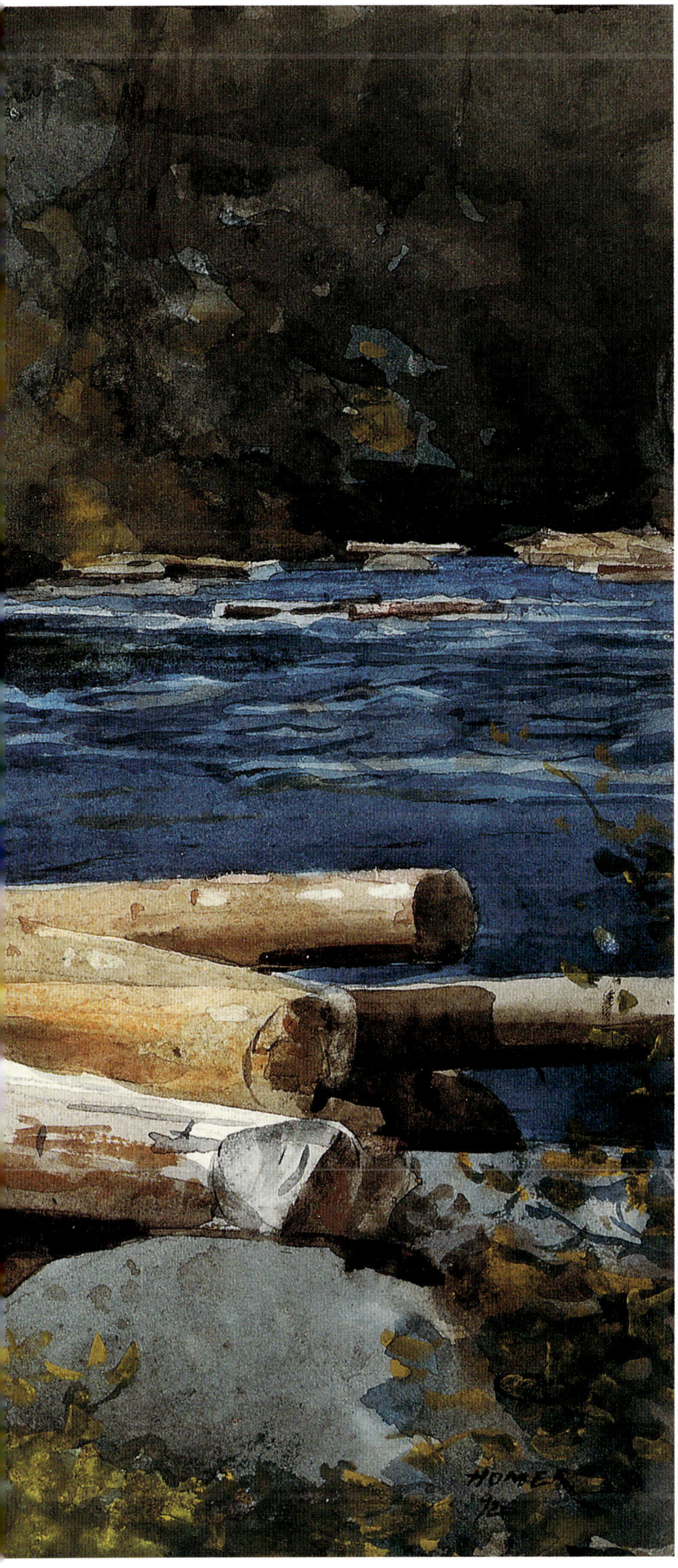

Homer was almost never a pure landscape painter. The prettiest or most dramatic scenes held little interest for him unless they served as the proving ground of human endeavor. Many of the late seascapes minimize the human element, but there the drama of pounding surf and obdurate rock replaces a more overt narrative. Everywhere in the Adirondacks watercolors we see the evidence of man, even when no human figures are present. This is not the pristine wilderness but one under often unbearable pressure. The landscape, however, is not merely a passive backdrop but an active player in the drama. Its very fragility allows it to test the character of those who enter its twilight realm and to pass judgment on their actions.

This ethical dimension of the woods is most dramatically illustrated by the deer-hunting scenes that form one of the central narratives of these works. Homer, though not a hunter himself, was intimately acquainted with hunters and their methods and was unsparing in his depictions. From the eagerness of the hounds catching a scent to the look of terror in the eyes of an exhausted stag barely able to keep afloat as he seeks the safety of deep water, Homer had a keen sympathy and observant eye for his animal subjects. The humans often fare less well. Sometimes they are anonymous killers, a mere puff of white in the distance indicating the fatal shot; at other times, as in *An October Day* [pp. 154–155], the relentlessness of the hunter pursuing his quarry highlights the sport's cruelty. The man who has set out after the stag in his boat and the dog who has driven the creature into the deep water and now waits expectantly by the shore are not immediately apparent; once noticed, they give the scene its narrative tension. Set against an autumnal backdrop whose breathtaking beauty marks the dying of the season, *An October Day* unfolds like a Greek tragedy toward its inevitable conclusion.

The most dramatic example of Homer's censure of the sport of hunting comes in the twin images *Deer Drinking* and *The Fallen Deer* [pp. 156–157]. It is the same doe in each picture, shown moments apart. In the first image, we see her straddling a log to drink from the cool water of the lake; in the second, she is sprawled over that same log, mortally wounded. On the back of the second image, Homer wrote: "just shot . . . A miserable . . . Pot hunter," a rare instance in which the artist vented his feelings on a subject he painted. Despite these angry words, Homer does not dwell in the image itself on the human role.

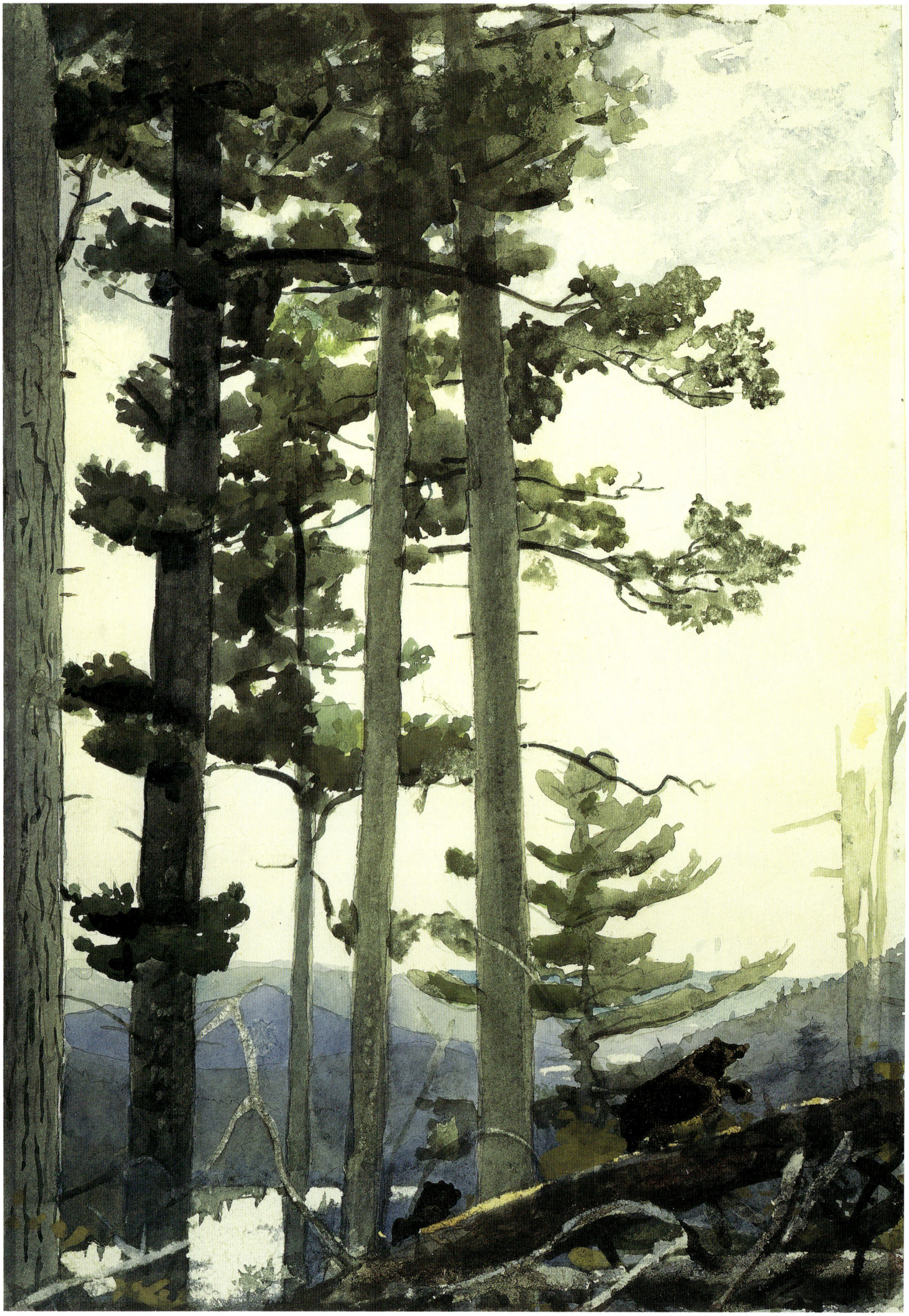

OLD SETTLERS 1892

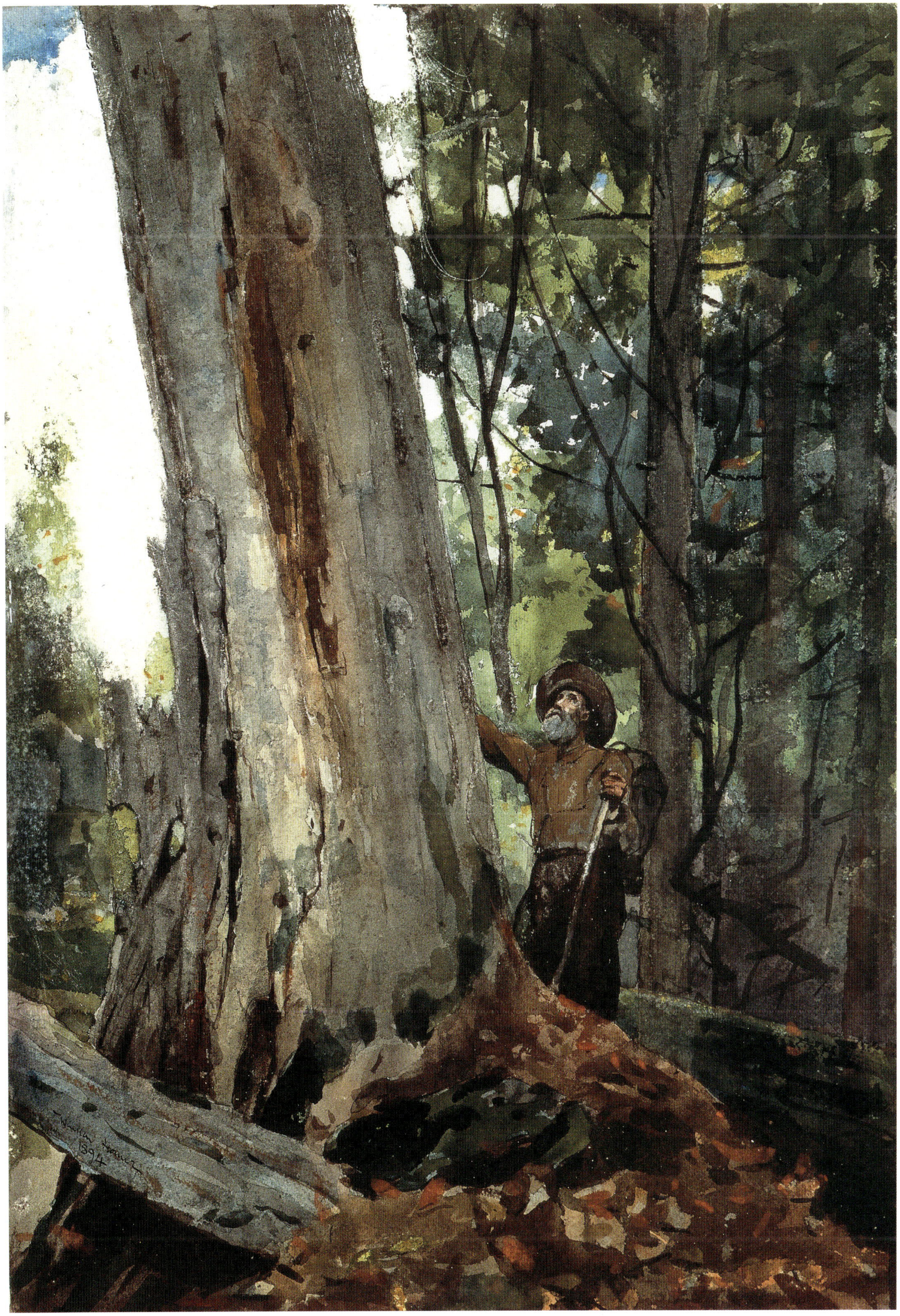

OLD FRIENDS 1894

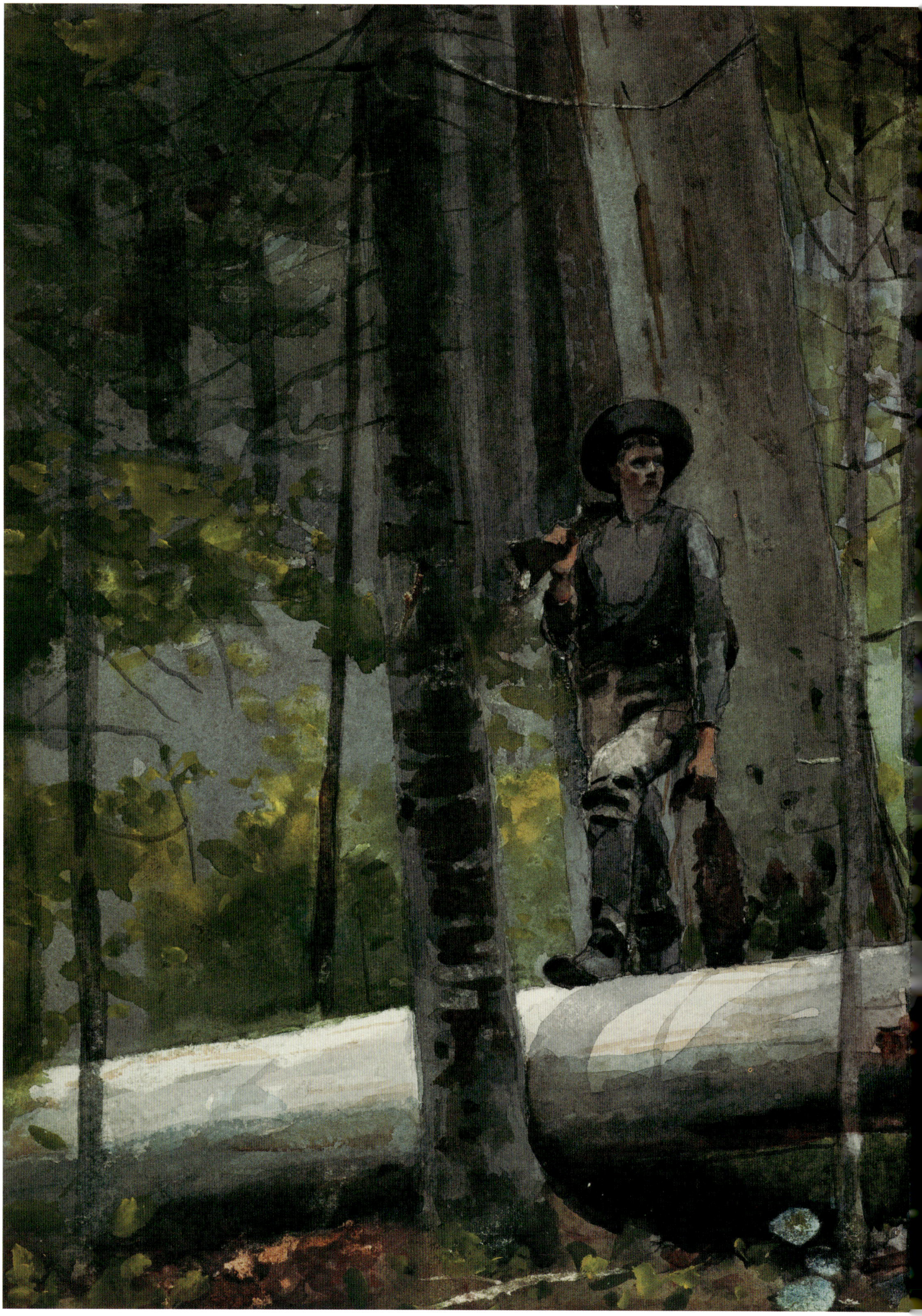

Hunter in the Adirondacks 1892

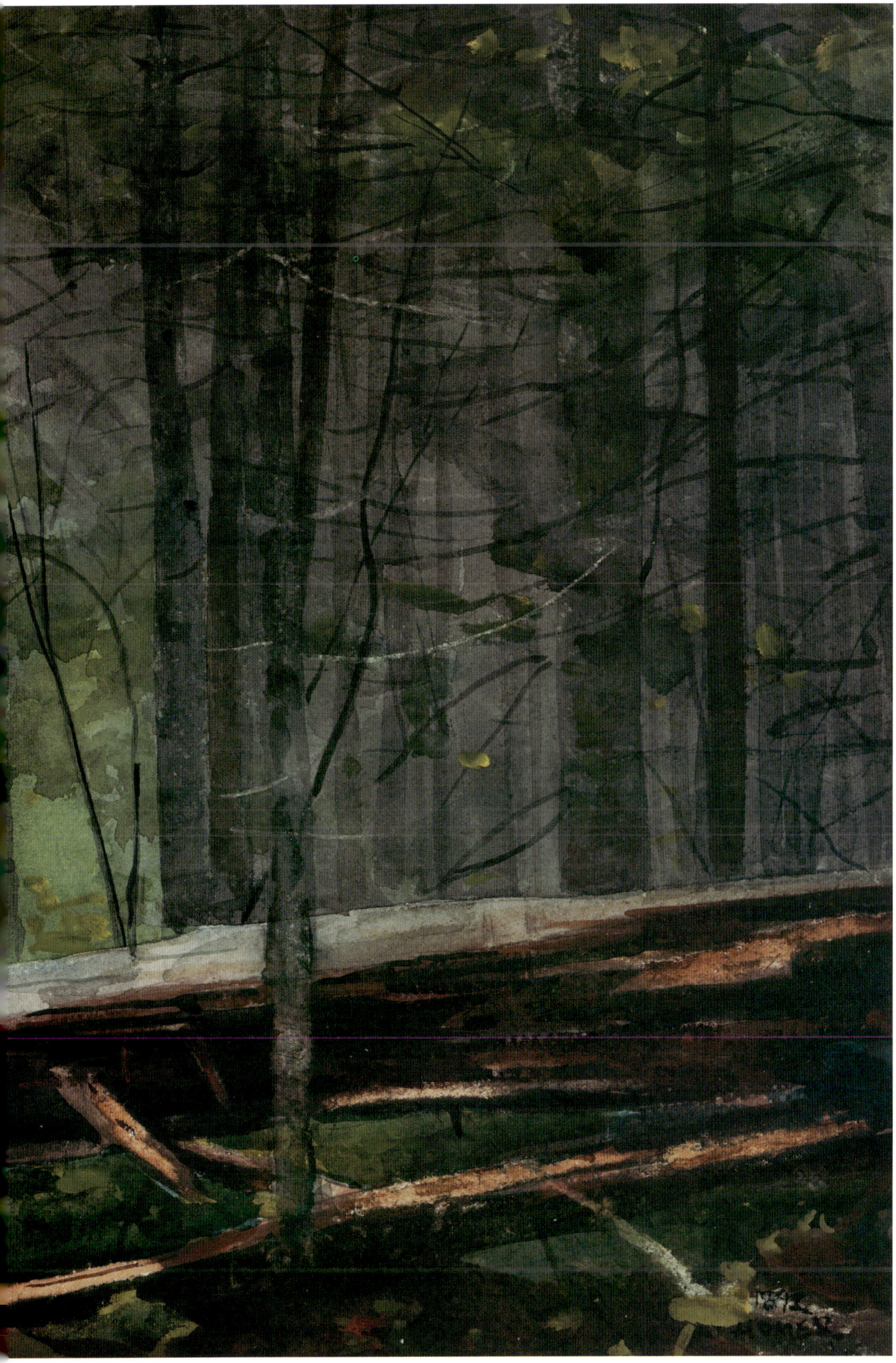

Though the agency of death is a human act, he focuses on the moment of death itself, seen as an essential part of the natural order with or without human presence. It would be unwise to ascribe to these works any explicit reference to the controversial ideas of Charles Darwin that dominated scientific and religious debate in the late nineteenth century, but it is clear that Homer's conception of the natural order is in keeping with this harsh vision.

Homer's narrative is not simply a parable of good and evil. He does not spare us the cruelty of the sport, but he also recognizes that death is the prerequisite for new life. The landscape itself, as he clearly shows us through the fallen tree the doe straddles, is built up in a continuing process in which decay leads to new life. He makes the point again in *Guide Carrying a Deer* [pp. 158–159], in which the figure from *Hunter in the Adirondacks* now poses with his trophy while resting his leg on the stump of a felled tree. In this gorgeous watercolor—which he turned into the oil painting *Huntsman with Dogs*—Homer compresses the life cycle within a single memorable image, from the vitality of youth to the helplessness of death. The ravaged, if still beautiful, landscape reinforces the meaning of the central motif, revealing how firmly woven we are into the natural order.

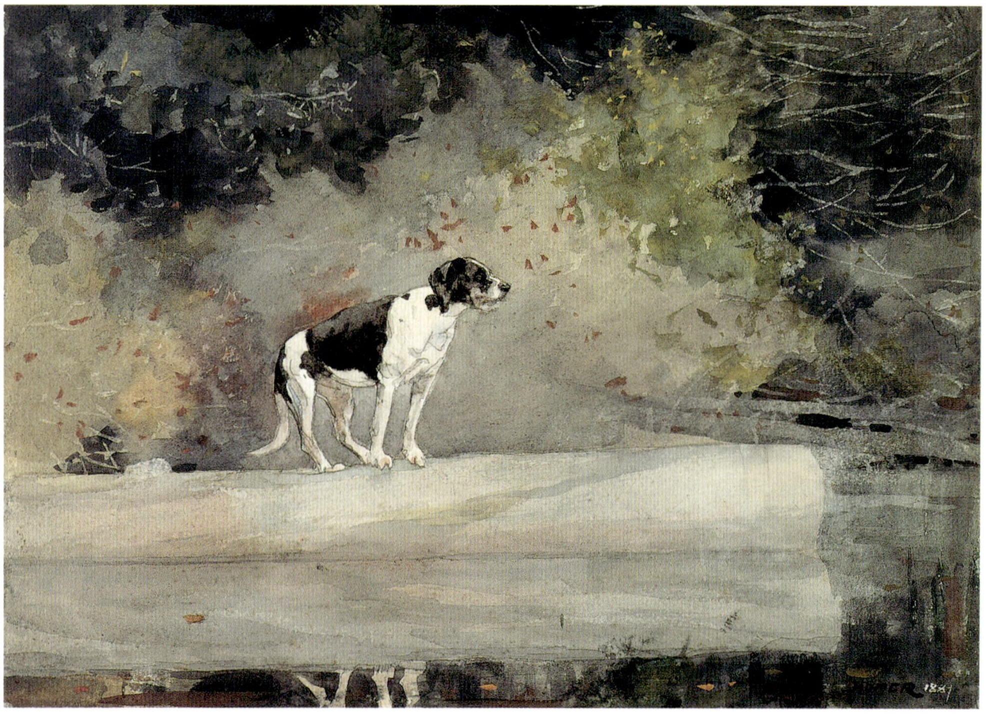

Dog on a Log 1889

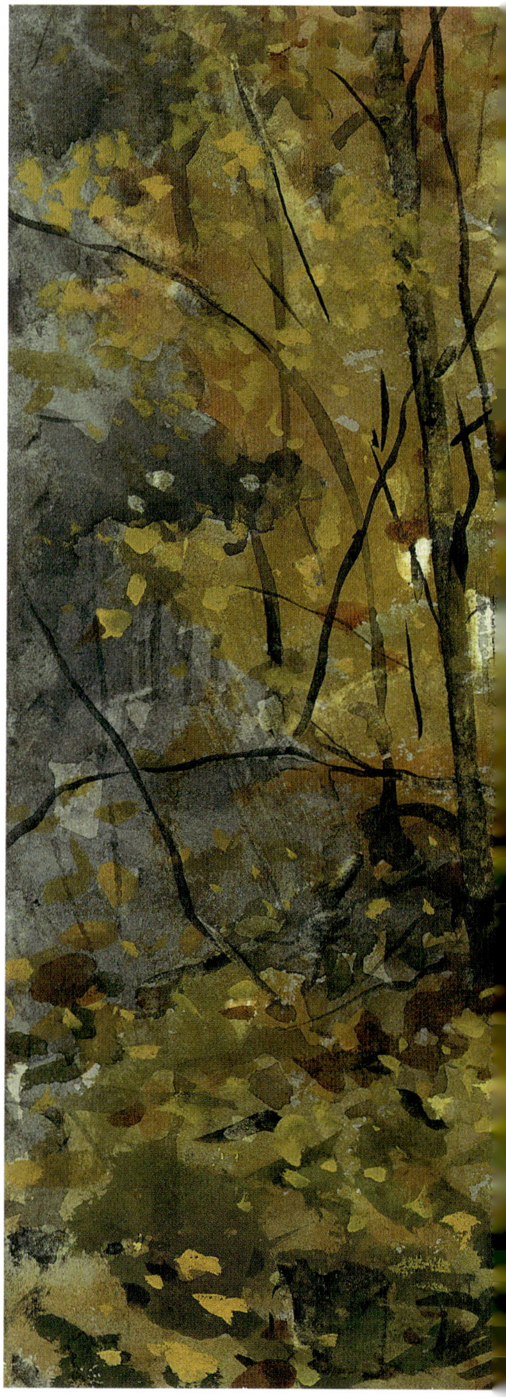

On the Trail c. 1892

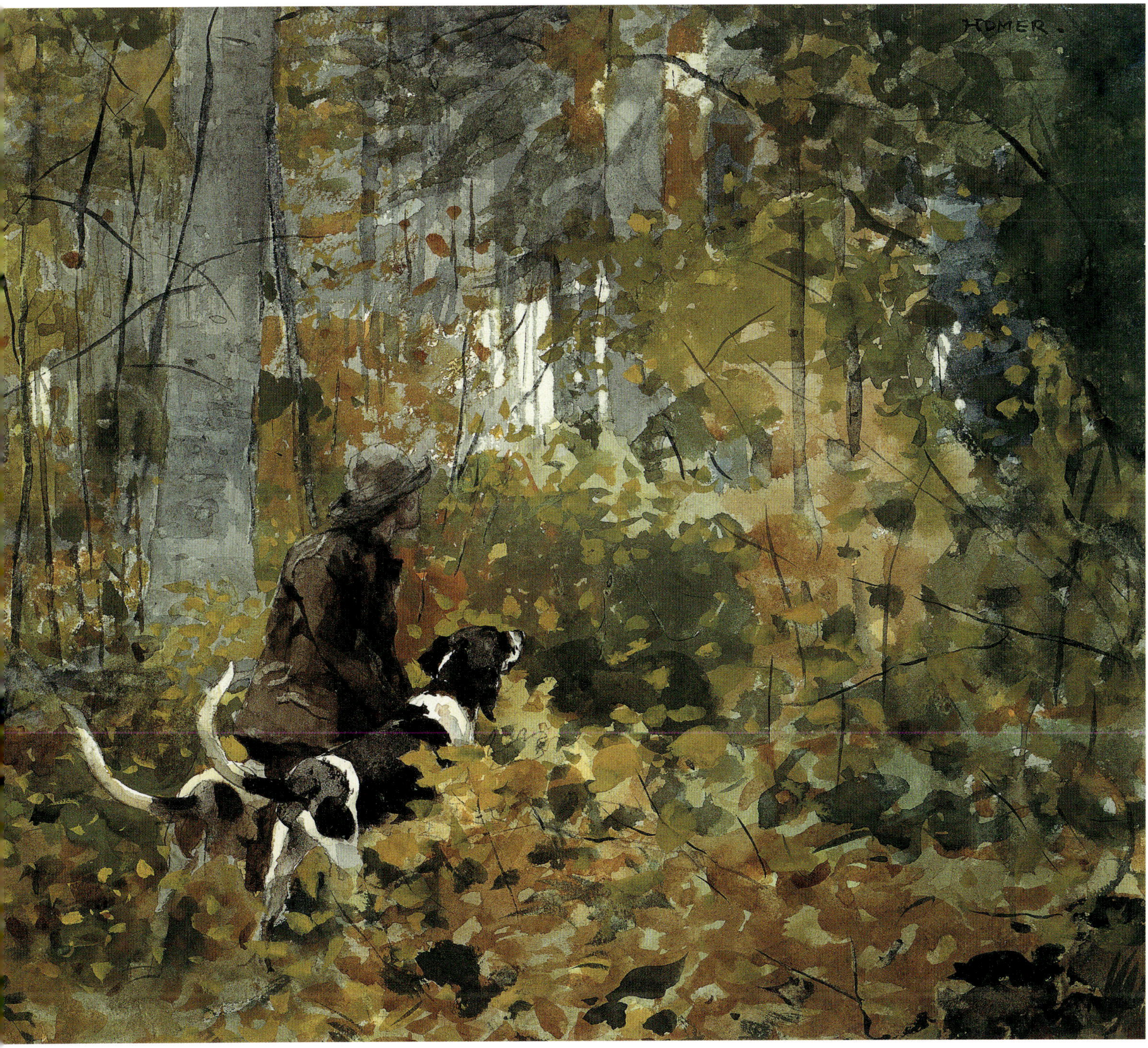
HOMER

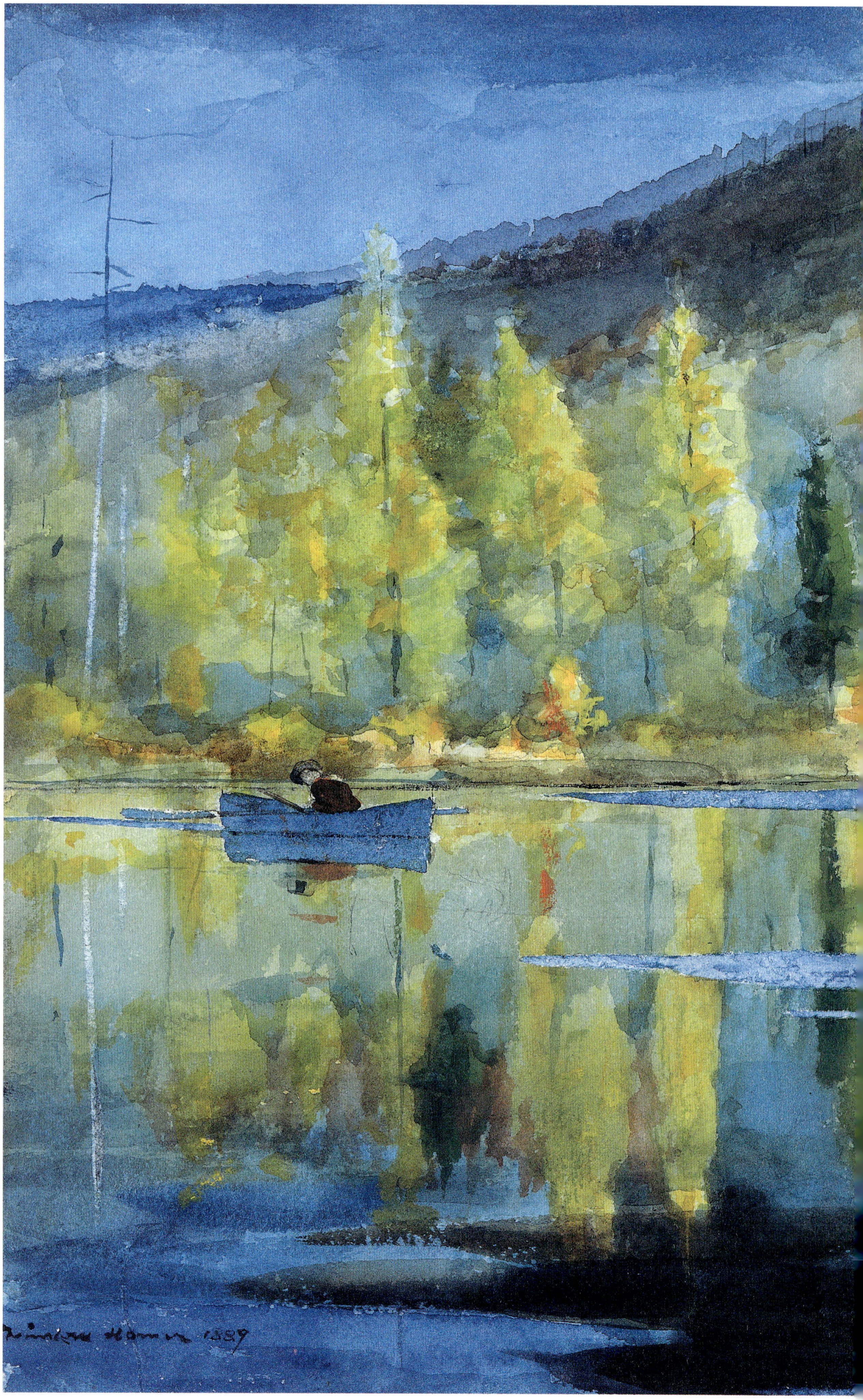

An October Day 1889

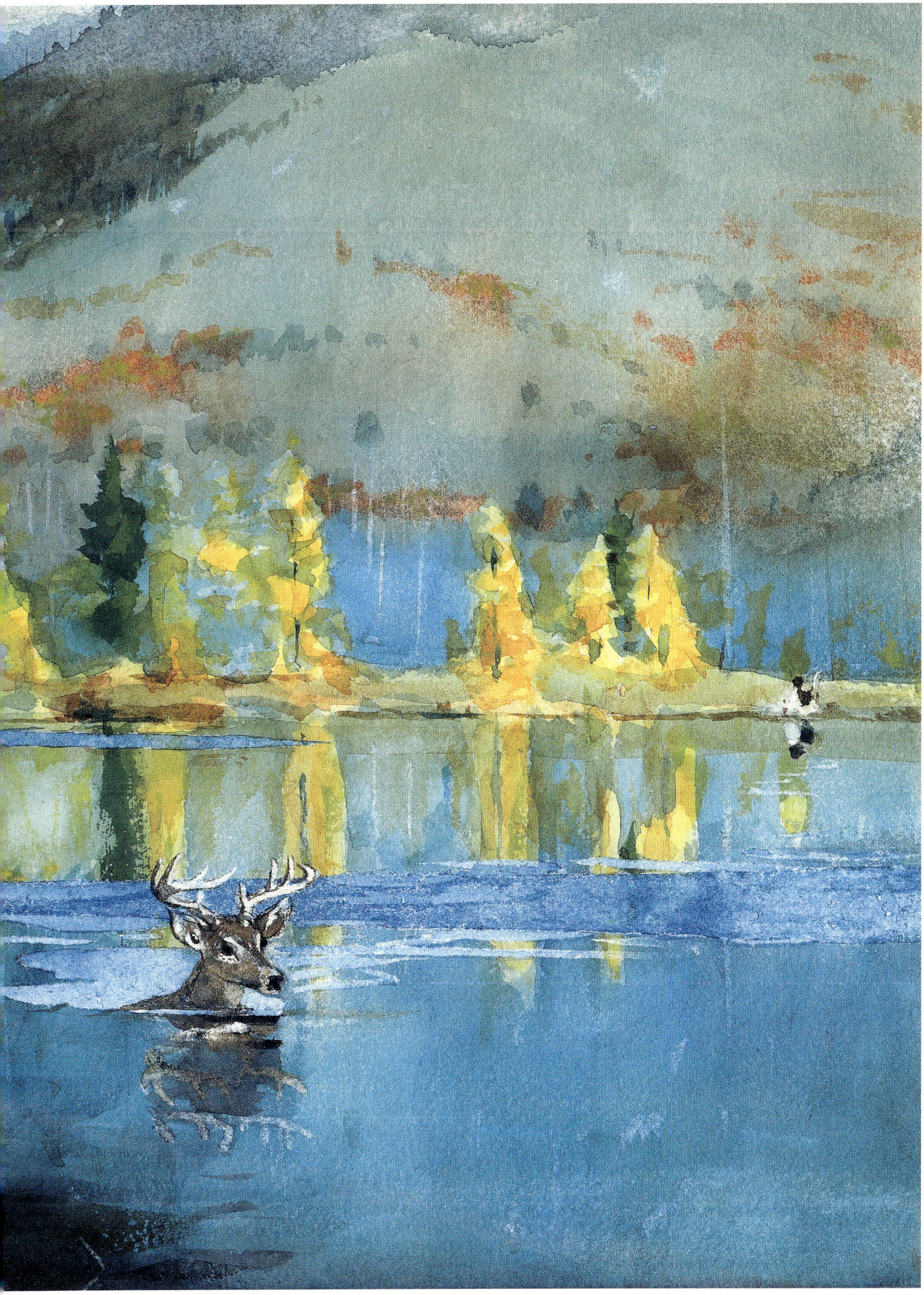

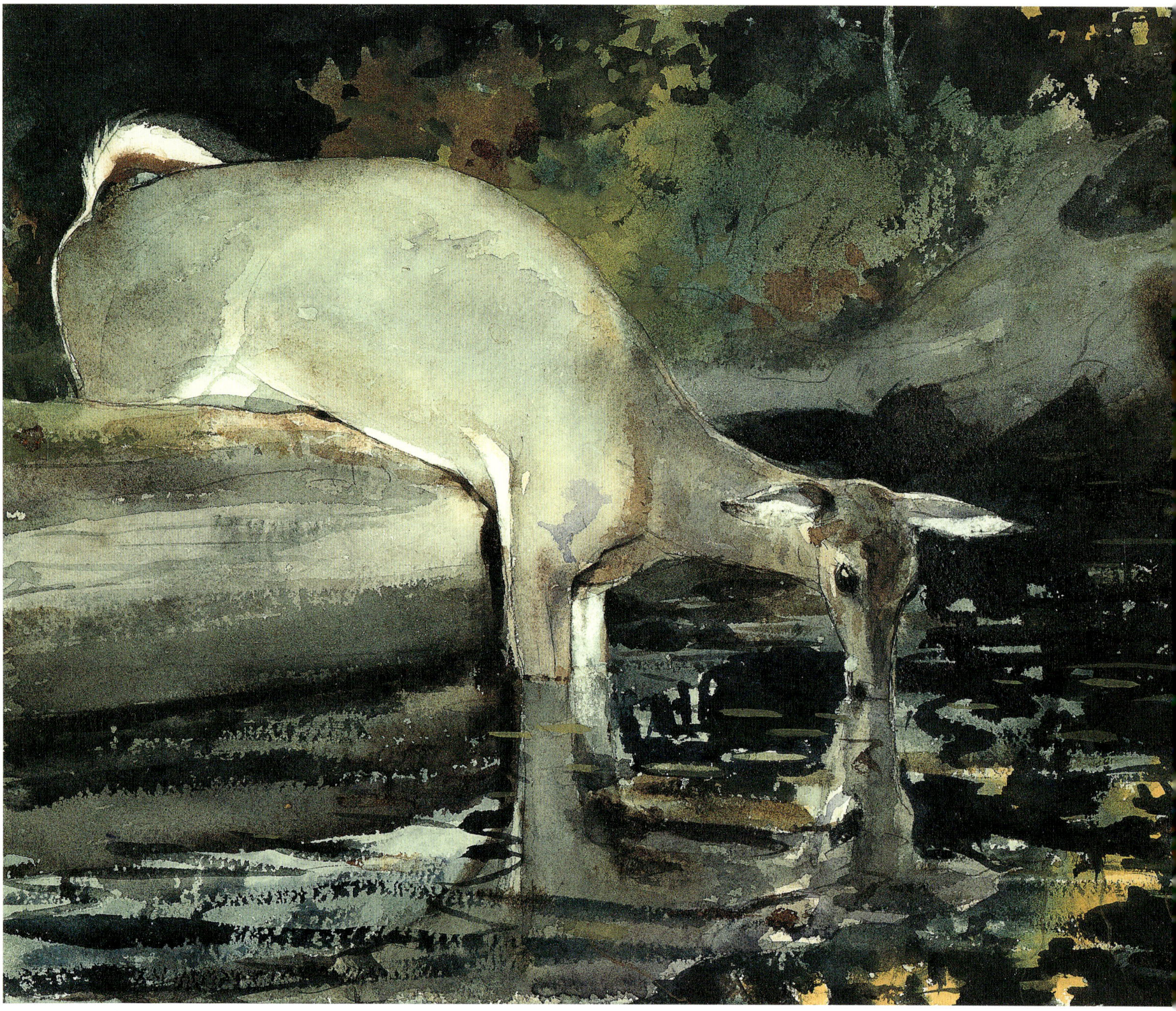

Deer Drinking 1892

The Fallen Deer 1892

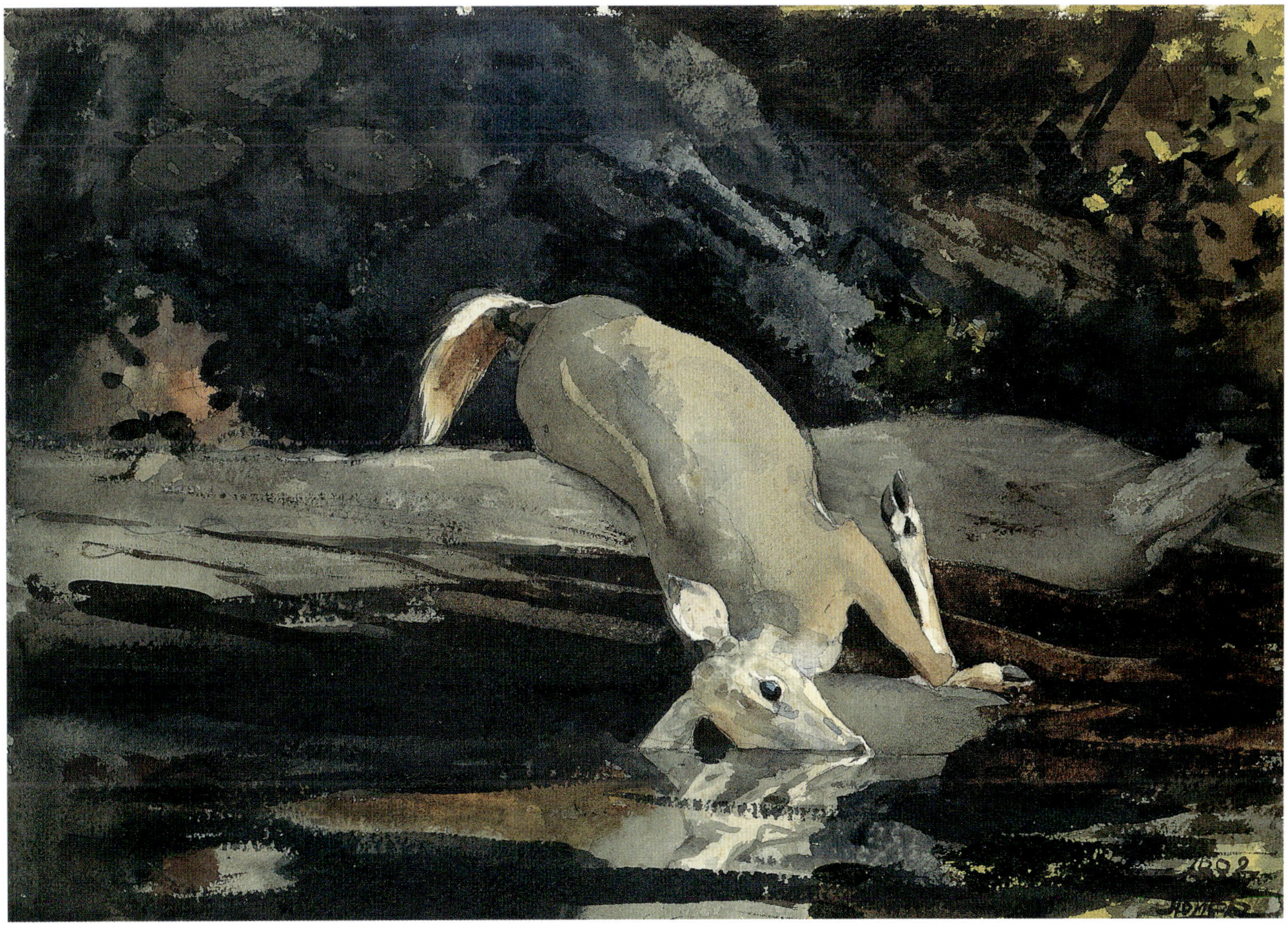

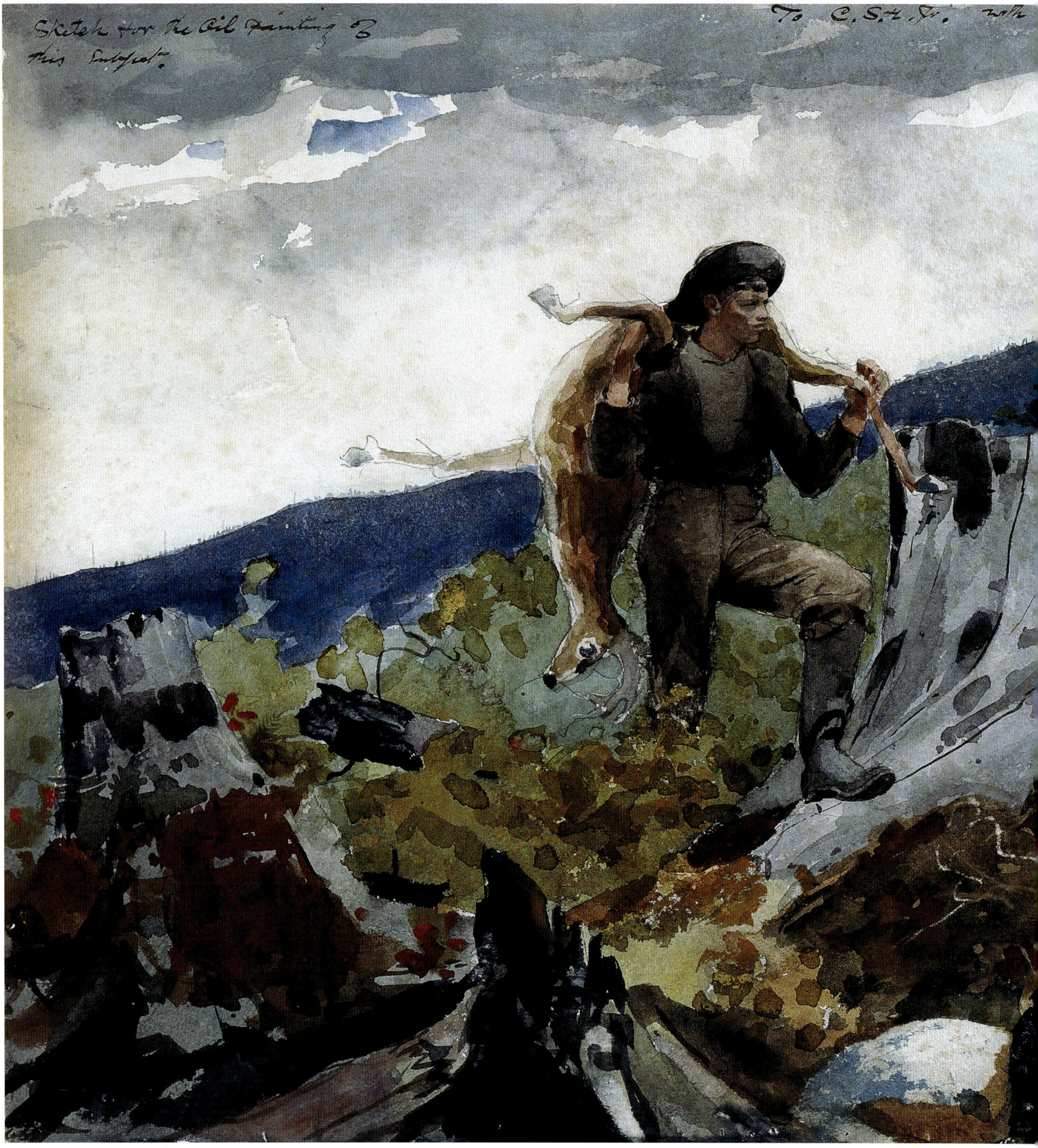
Sketch for the Oil Painting of
this Subject.
To C.S.H. Jr. with

Guide Carrying a Deer 1891

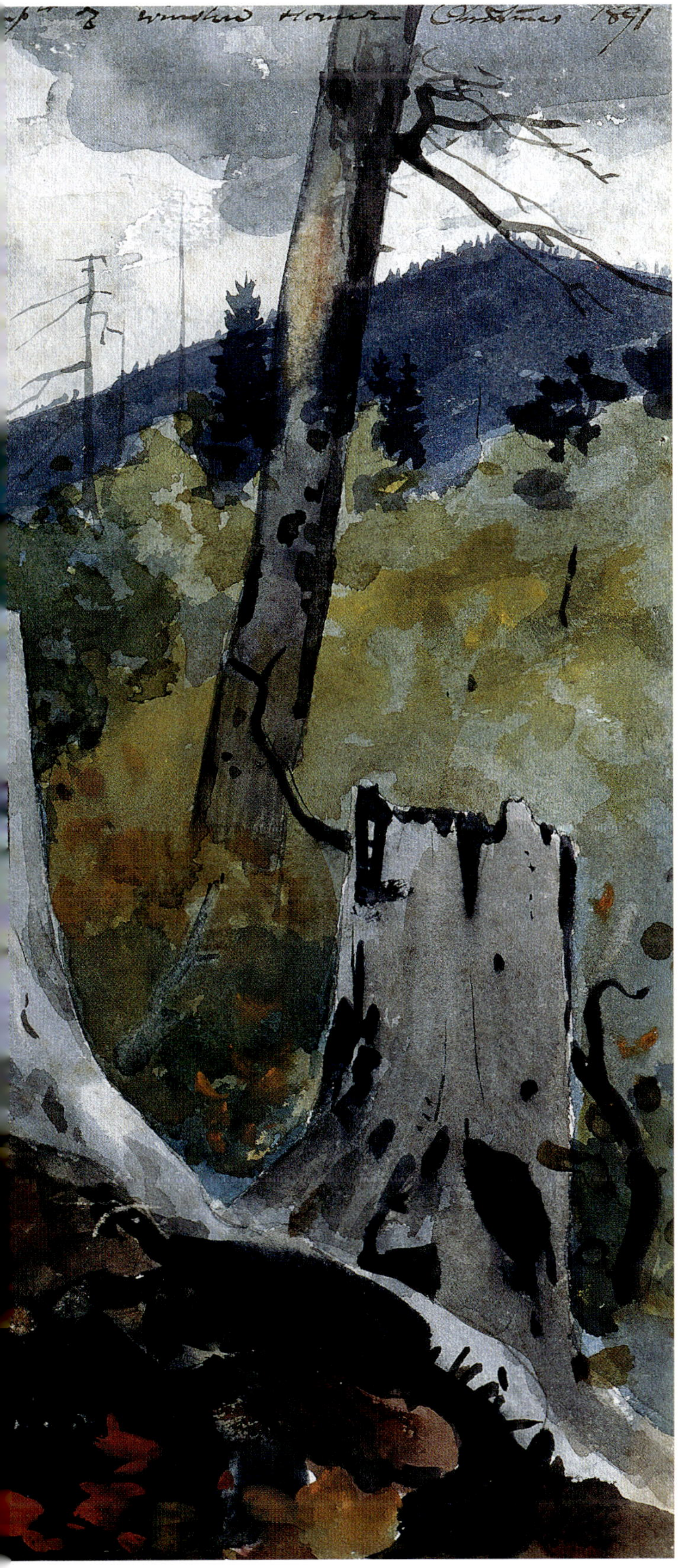

Although the young hunter featured in these works is often seen as callow, the older, bearded guide provides an example of a properly respectful attitude toward nature (see pp. 6–7). Like Natty Bumppo, hero of James Fenimore Cooper's *Leatherstocking Tales*, this is a man who belongs to the forest; he seems as much a creature of the woods as the deer themselves. Homer based this figure on Rufus Wallace, a guide employed by the North Woods Club that he and his brother Charles belonged to; but he clearly represents a type of forest sage, a man half wild but embodying simple virtues. Homer's figure mirrors closely Charles Dudley Warner's description of the famous guide Old Mountain Phelps:

> He was a true citizen of the wilderness. Thoreau would have liked him. . . . His tawny hair was long and tangled, matted now many years past the possibility of being entered by a comb. His features were small and delicate, and set in the frame of a reddish beard. . . . His clothes seemed to have been put on him once for all, like the bark of a tree, a long time ago. . . . This woodsman, this trapper, this hunter, this fisherman, this sitter on a log, and philosopher, was the real proprietor of the region over which he was willing to guide the stranger. . . . In all that country, he alone had noticed the sunsets, and observed the delightful processes of the seasons, taken pleasure in the woods for themselves, and climbed mountains solely for the sake of the prospect.

Not only does Phelps possess more practical knowledge than those who come to the woods for recreation; he is in fact more attuned to the poetry of the natural world.

Unlike the young man who is often explicitly linked with scenes of violence, the older man usually plays the role of mentor and backwoods philosopher. The scenes in which he figures prominently are contemplative in mood. Death has not been banished from these scenes, though there is little or no overt violence. In *Adirondack Guide*, the bearded guide is depicted as a solitary figure in a boat, a traditional symbol in art of the soul on its journey through life. As he nears the darkened shore, both beautiful and mysterious—despite the figure's pose, his destination is indicated by the direction of the boat— he casts his eyes back as if recalling the earlier stages of his life's journey. This is not a allegory in the tradition of Thomas Cole's *Voyage of Life*—it is much more firmly grounded in the here and now—but within a realistic setting Homer still conveys the spiritual dimension of the journey.

AN UNEXPECTED CATCH 1890

BOY FISHING 1892

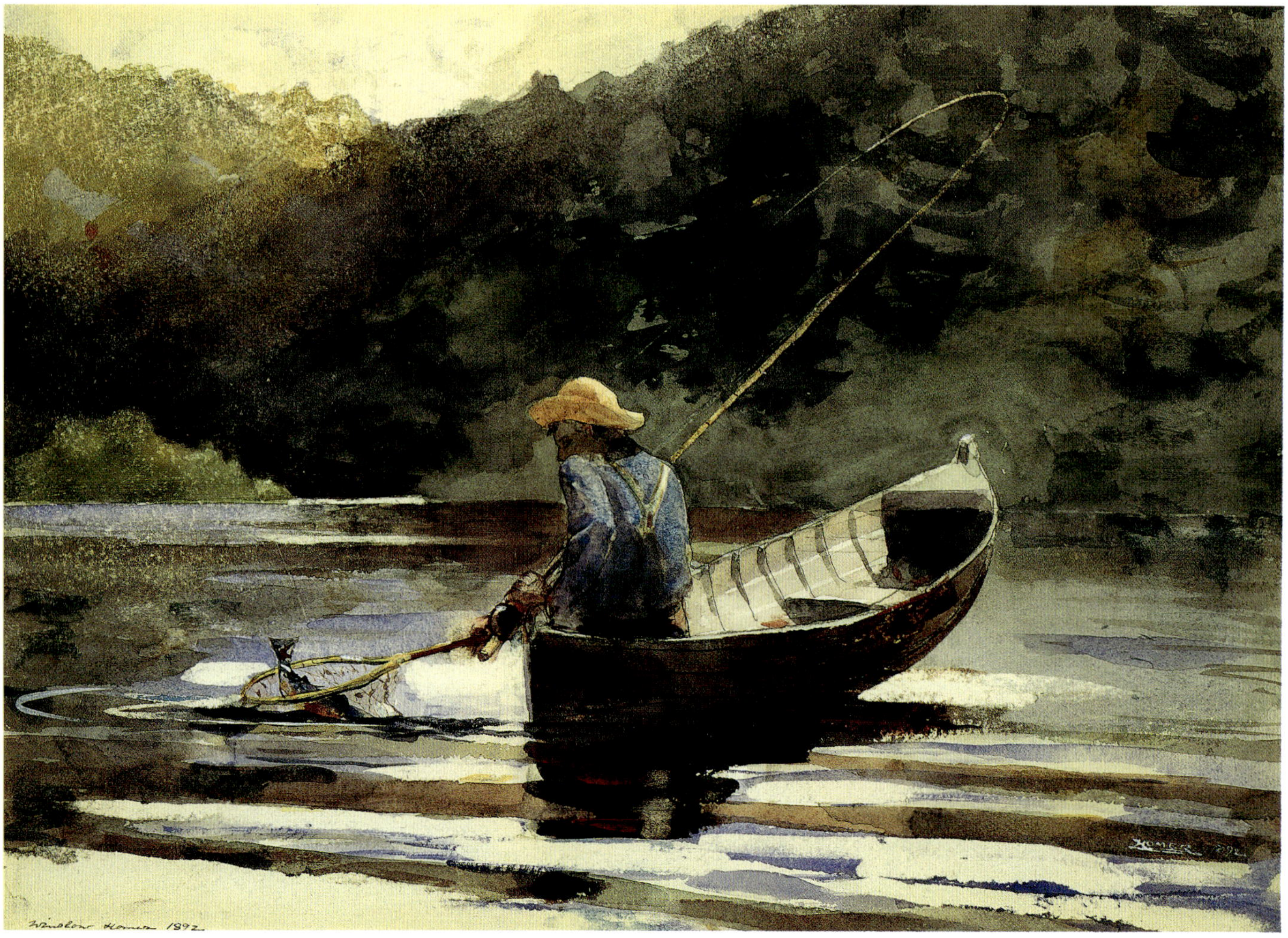

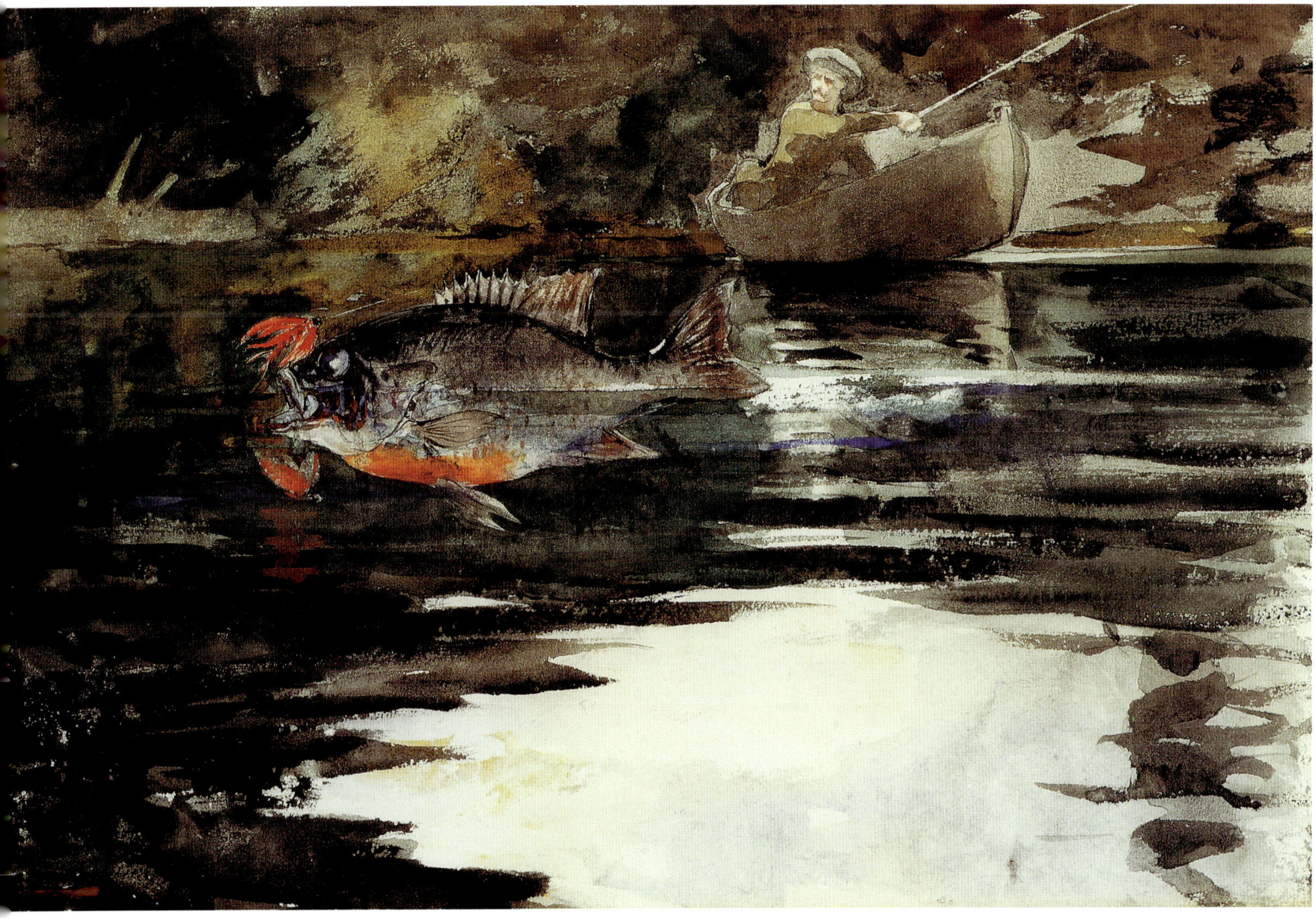

The bearded guide is frailer than his youthful companion, but this is a world where wisdom gained from years of experience is of more value than brute strength. Works featuring this woodland sage are among Homer's most poetic. The guide stands in for the artist, sharing his reverence for nature's beauty and unfathomable mystery.

It was the artist's passion for fishing that led him in 1886 to join the North Woods Club, a private hunting and fishing preserve on Mink Pond near Minerva, New York. No one has ever depicted the allure of this sport more effectively than Winslow Homer, who captures both the stillness of the mountain lake in the first light of day and the excitement of the catch. Works like *Adirondack Lake* and *Sunrise, Fishing in the Adirondacks* depict moments of complete serenity. Homer records subtle changes of light and atmosphere with all the precision of Monet, but he was less interested in conveying nature's transitoriness than he was in revealing its underlying unity. Nowhere is the suggestive power of his brush more in evidence than in these works where a few well-chosen blots and stains give complete expression to the natural world's most fleeting moments.

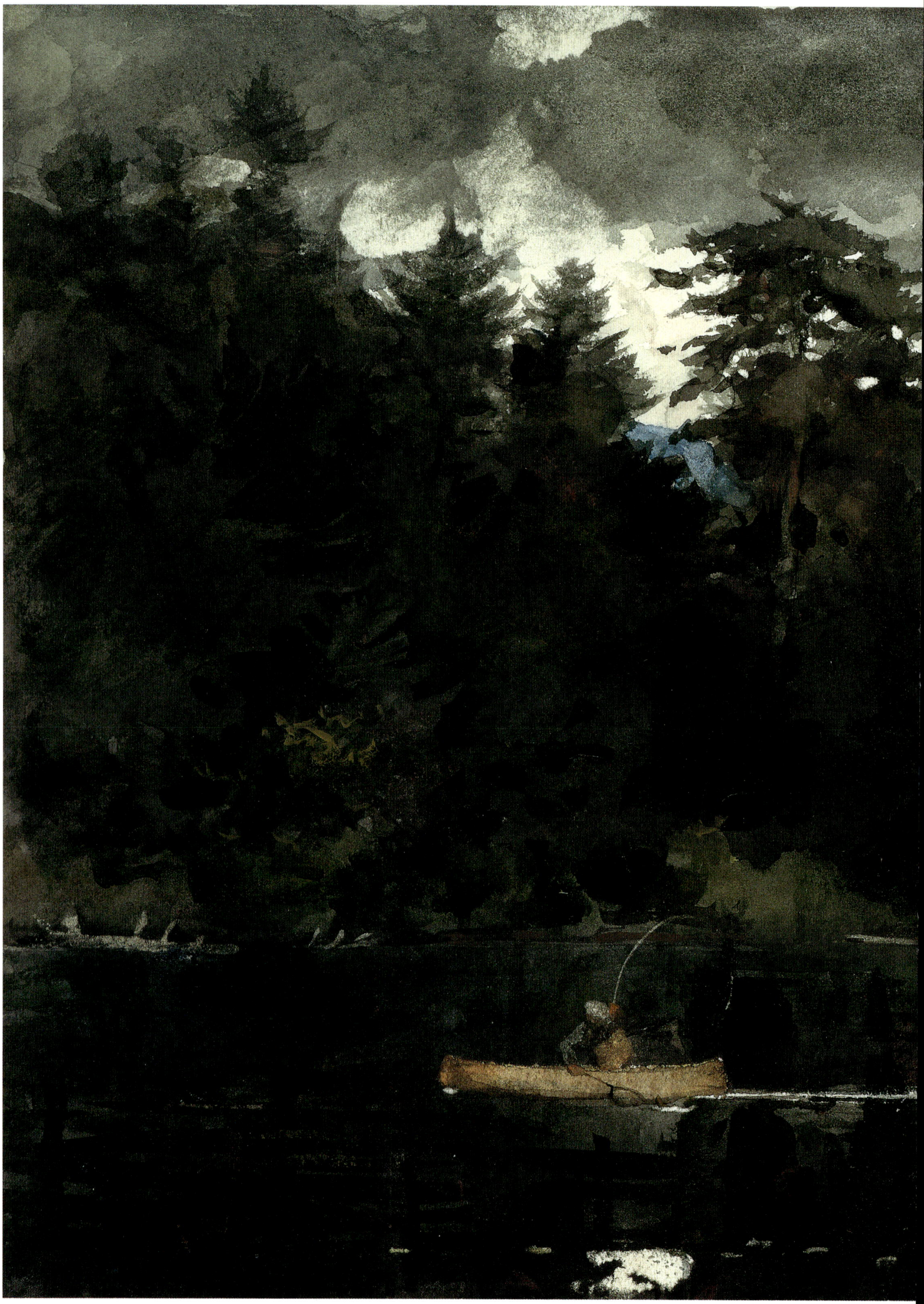

Adirondack Lake 1889

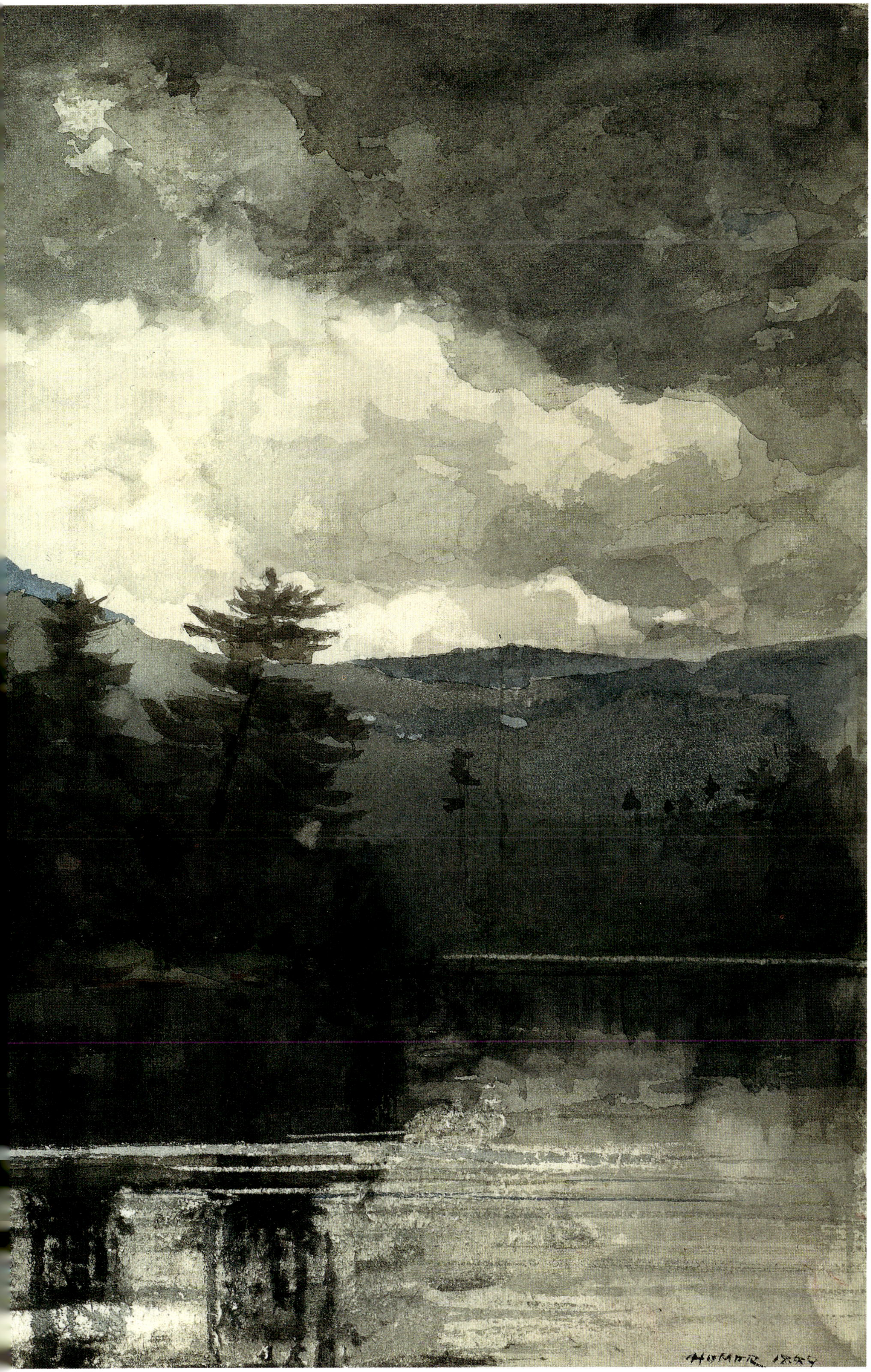
HOMER 1889

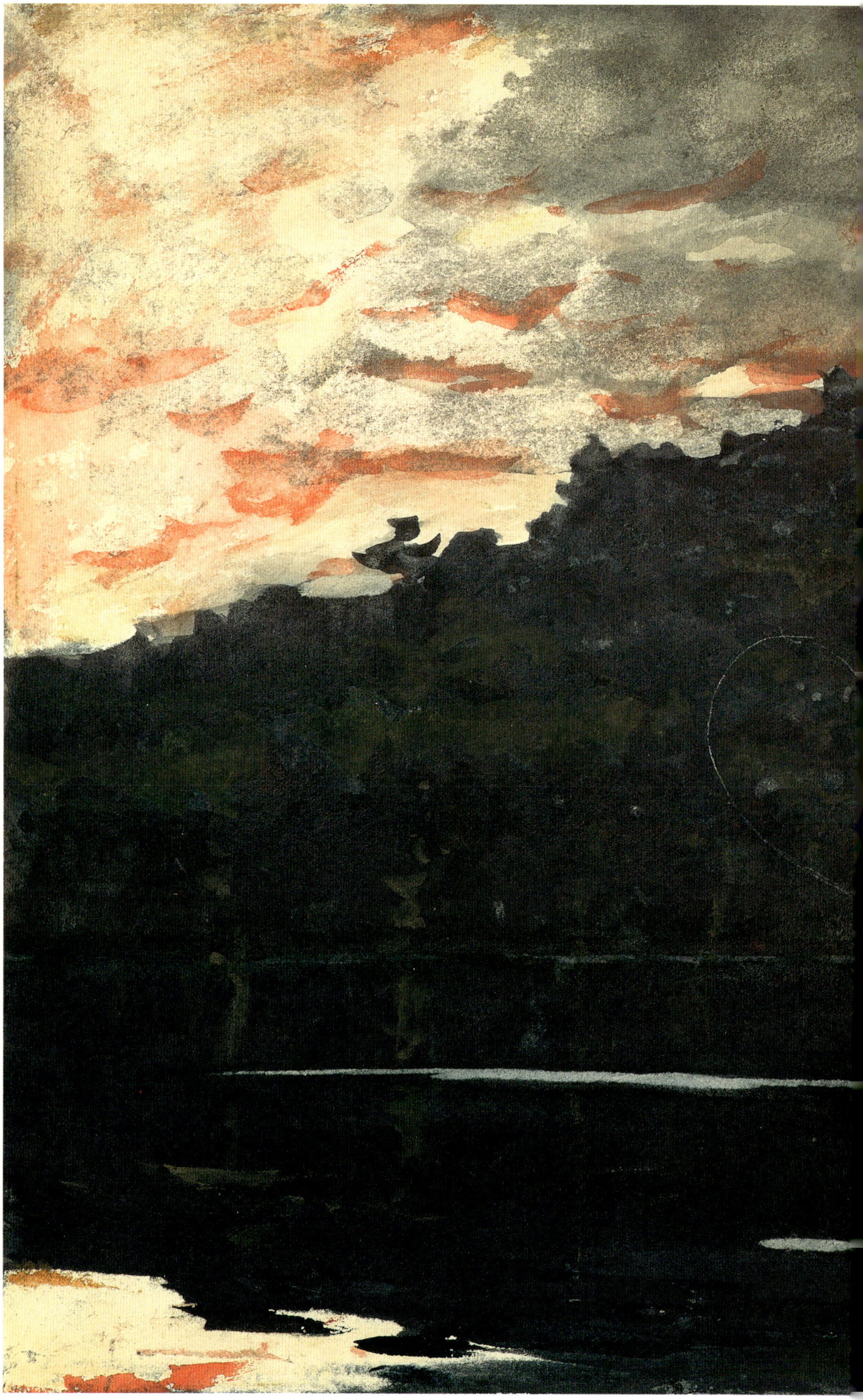

Sunrise, Fishing in the Adirondacks 1892

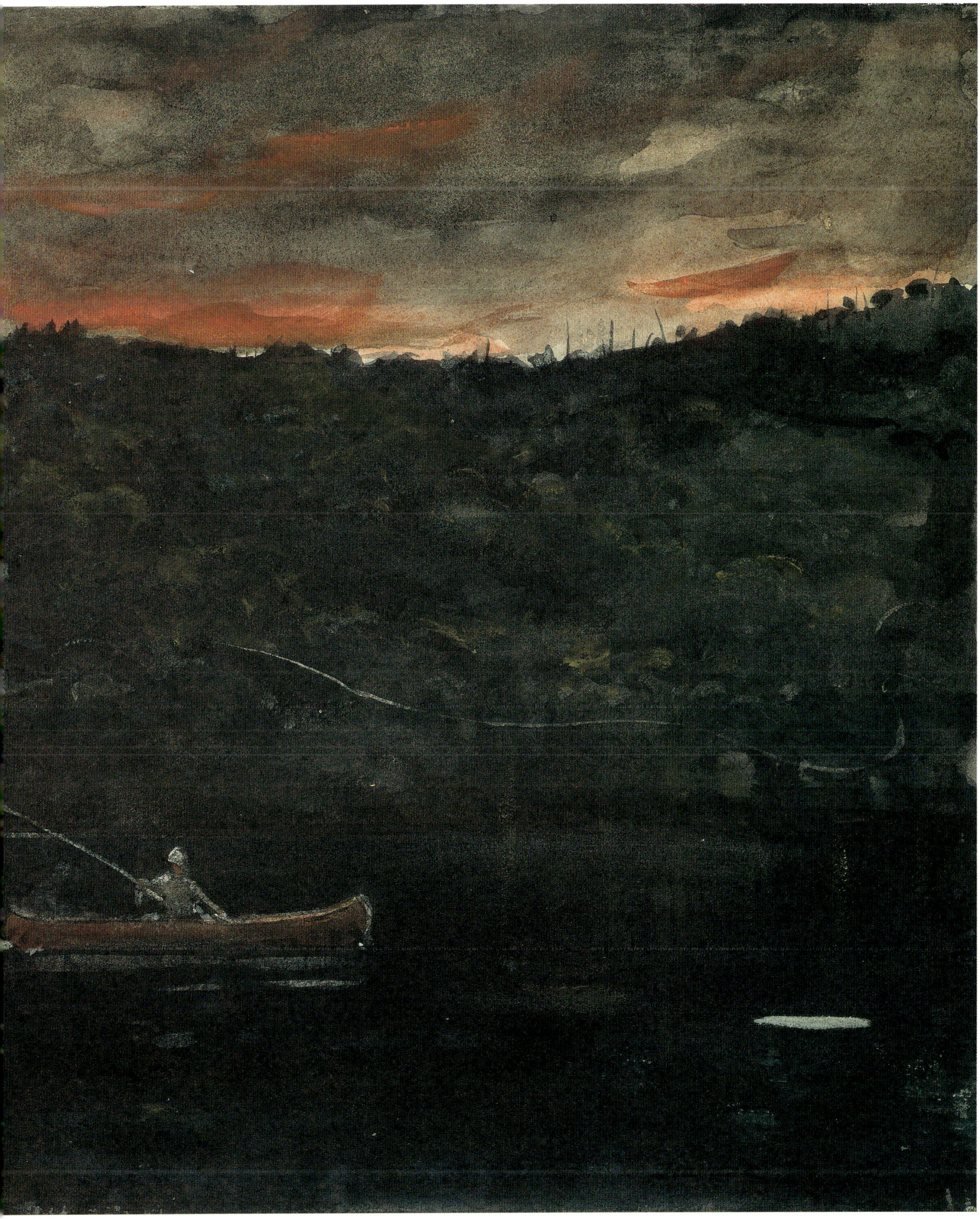

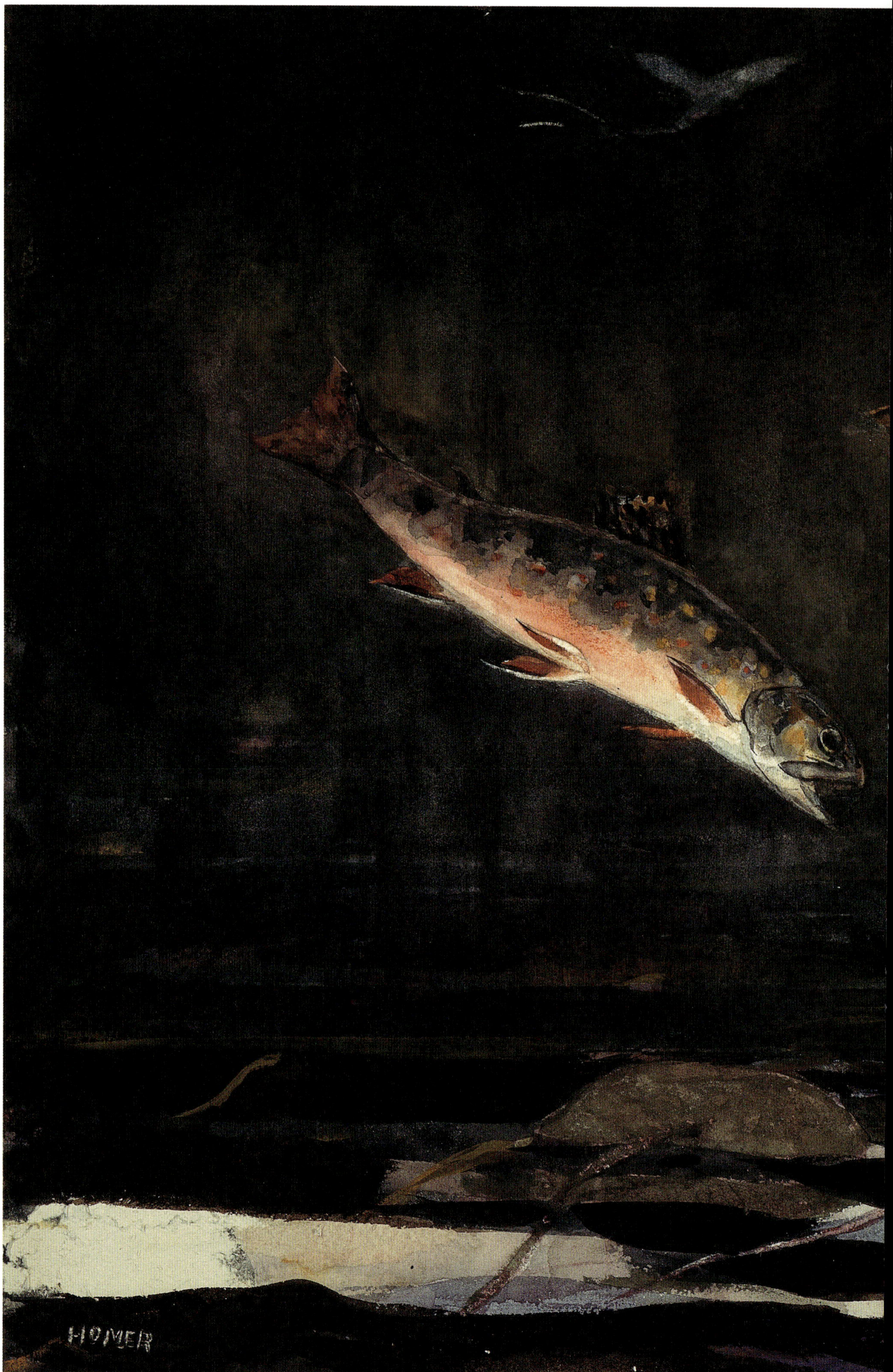
HOMER

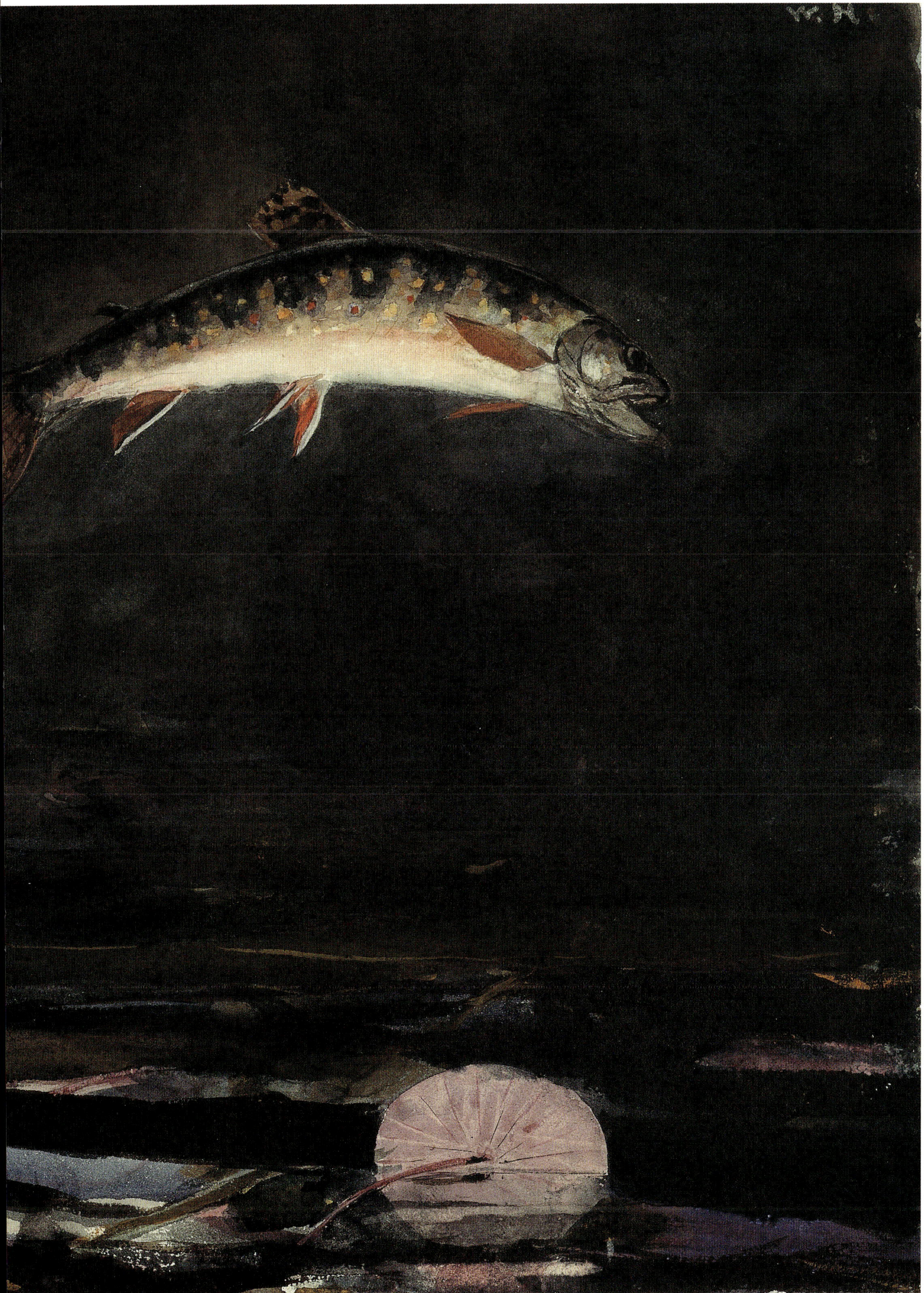

Leaping Trout 1889

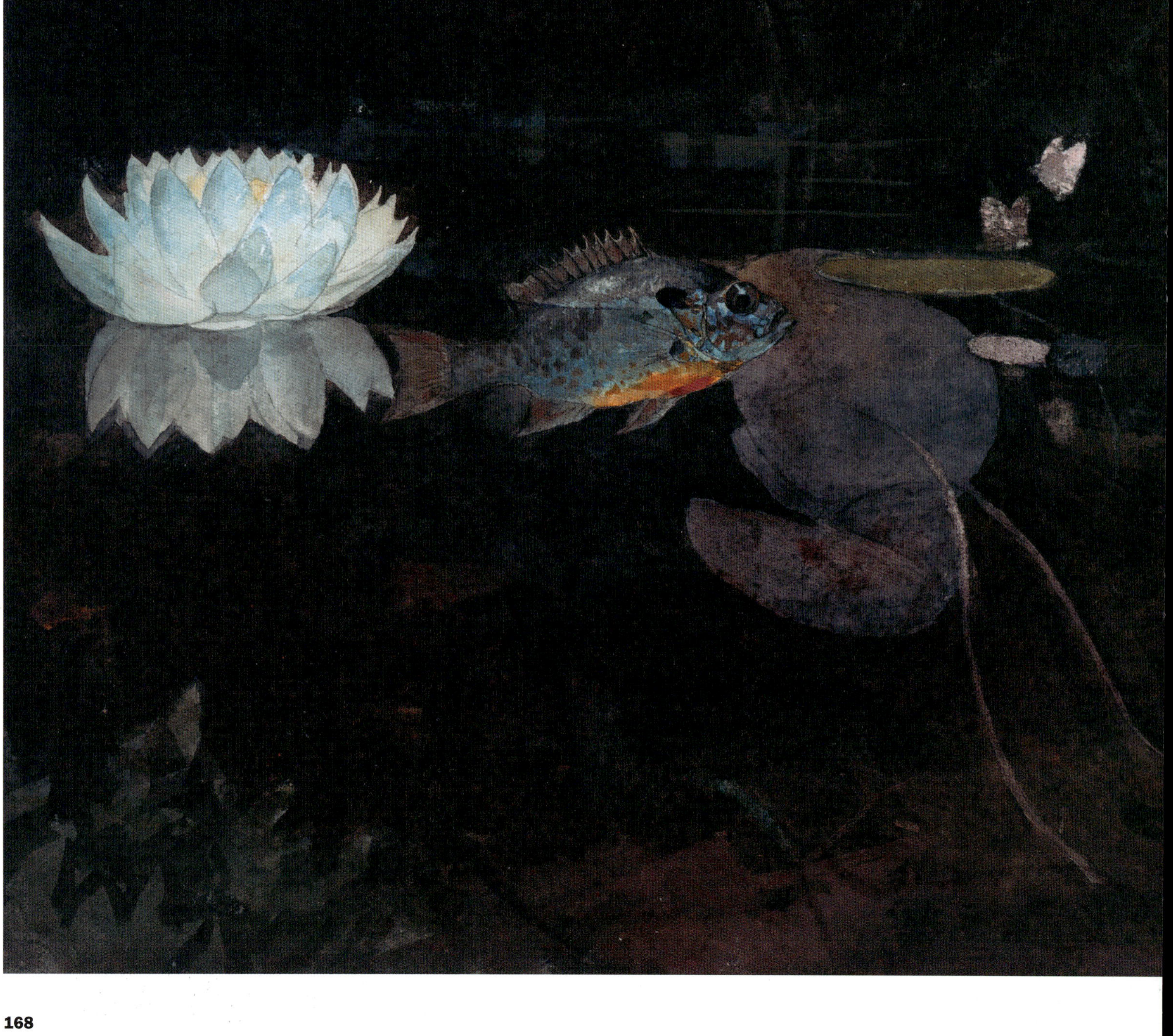

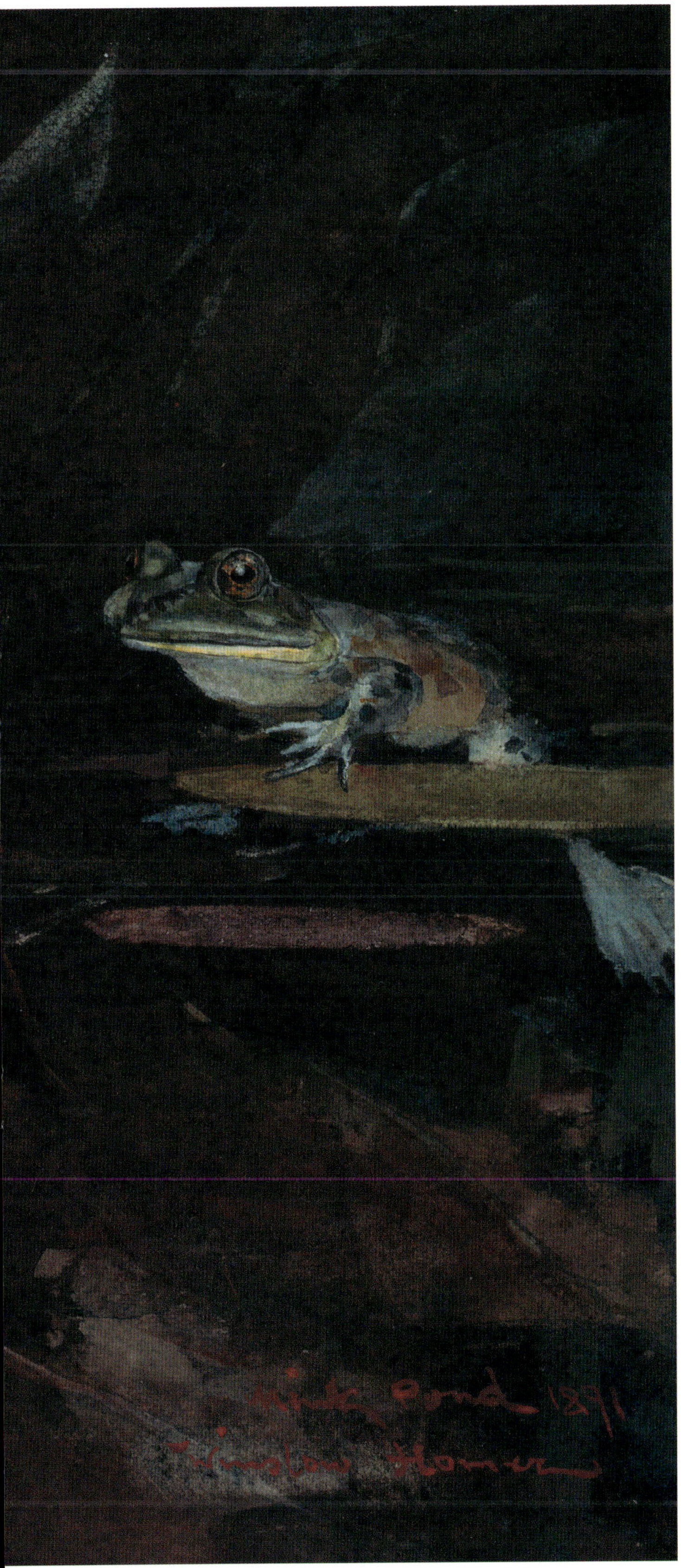

Homer painted both the fishermen and their prey, describing accurately the delicate beauty of the silvery trout that drew sportsmen to these mountain lakes. *Leaping Trout* and *Mink Pond* are among the most heartfelt tributes to nature's savage beauty ever painted. In the murky depths of the humid pond Homer discovers a primeval world of strange creatures and impossible blossoms. Man is never distant from these scenes—witness the fisherman's fly at the top of *Leaping Trout* that has urged the fish to these acrobatic feats—but in these works the artist gives the greater role to the creatures of the woods and ponds. The bullfrog in *Mink Pond*, poised on his lilypad and hungrily eying the moths who flutter nearby, embodies an age-old Darwinian struggle of hunter and hunted that goes back well before the time when humans first walked the earth.

These are among Homer's most unabashedly gorgeous and decorative works. Jewel-like colors of rose, yellow and blue gleam against dark backgrounds. Their effect has often been compared to stained-glass windows, a form for which Homer at the time, influenced by the success in the medium of his friend John La Farge, expressed some interest. These close-ups of the natural world have a slightly hallucinatory feel, as if the artist had grown intoxicated in drinking deeply from nature's rejuvenating spring.

MINK POND 1891

IX.
Swift River: Quebec 1893–1902

Homer's passion for fishing and the wilderness sent him in search of more pristine vistas than the crowded Adirondacks. In the early 1890s, he and Charles joined the Tourilli Fish and Game Club, near Lake St. John and the Saguenay River, about 100 miles north of Quebec City. For one who, like Homer, preferred nature to society, the unspoiled woods of northern Canada held an elemental appeal. He wrote to Charles: "The place suits me as if it was made for me by a kind of providence."

On occasion, Homer captured on paper a bit of local color. But the Quebec watercolors are dominated by scenes depicting the sport that drew him to the Canadian wilderness. In *End of the Portage*, Homer's unsurpassed skill in rendering the complexities of light and shade in a woodland setting gives to an otherwise prosaic task a kind of grandeur. But in most of the Quebec paintings, the main protagonist is the river. Unlike the calm that pervades the Adirondacks fishing pictures, the pulse of the Quebec pictures is quickened by the churning waters of the Saguenay River and the high-flying ouananiche salmon, described by one sportsman as "the grandest game fish that has yet fallen to the fisherman's lure." *A Good Pool, Saguenay River* reprises the device used in *Leaping Trout* of placing the fish in the foreground of the painting, but the tug-of-war between man and fish is more urgent. Here fishing is not a matter of communing with serene nature, but an aerobic sport requiring quickness and muscle.

Homer's brushwork becomes more fluent in these works, moving as swiftly as the water rushing over the rocks and swirling in frothy pools. The whitewater is conjured in areas of reserved paper, often tinted by washes of reddish brown that describe the iron-rich sediments churned up by the river. These compositions accentuate the exhilaration and danger that drew canoeists to what one traveler dubbed "The River of Death." In *Canoe in the Rapids*, Homer places our viewpoint at the water's surface, right behind the boat headed for some unseen obstacle, maximizing the drama of the moment. In *Shooting the Rapids*, the low viewpoint again emphasizes the nervous agitation of the water. Homer treats the background with utmost simplicity, the better to focus our attention on the action. He has depicted the dramatic moment when the river drops away, exposing the prow of the canoe. The figures, while simply rendered,

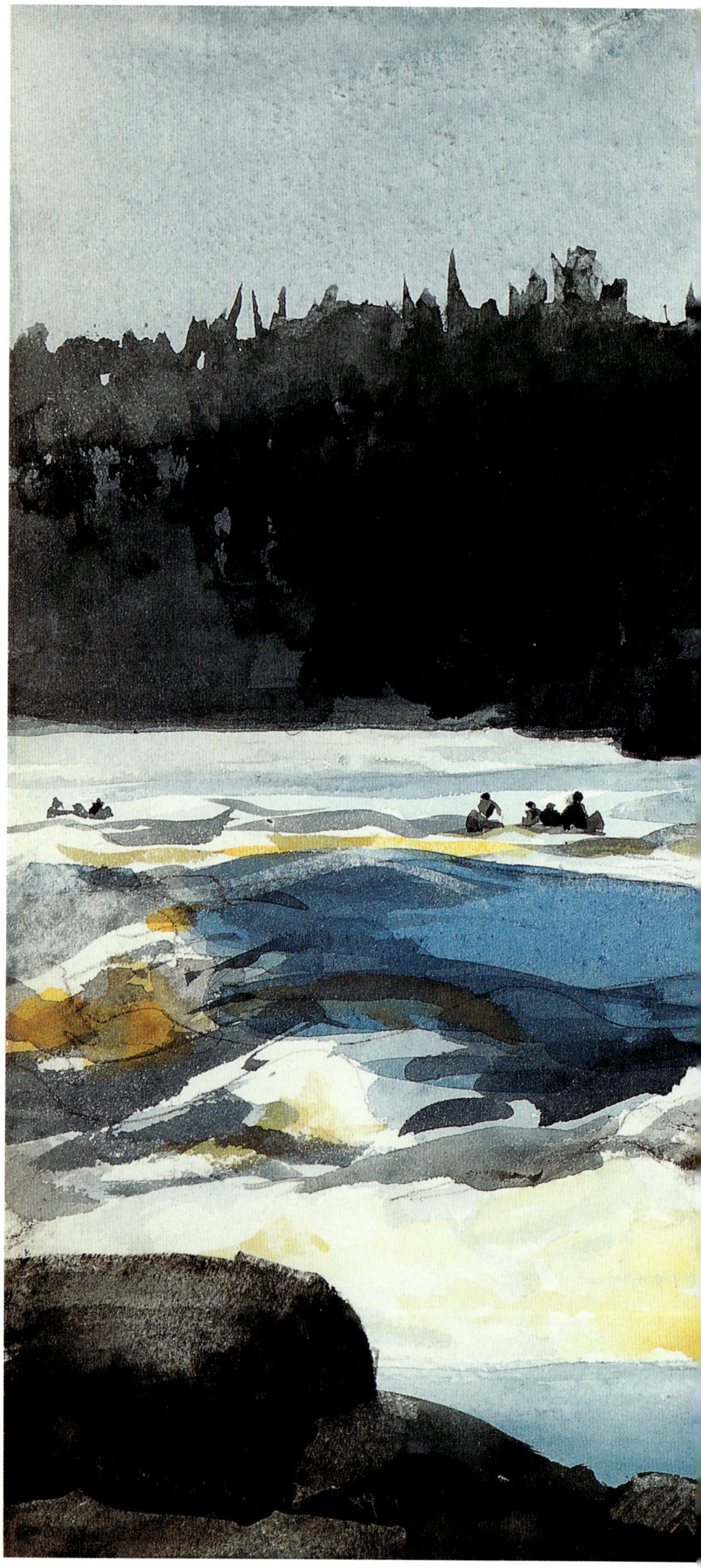

Saguenay River, Lower Rapids 1897

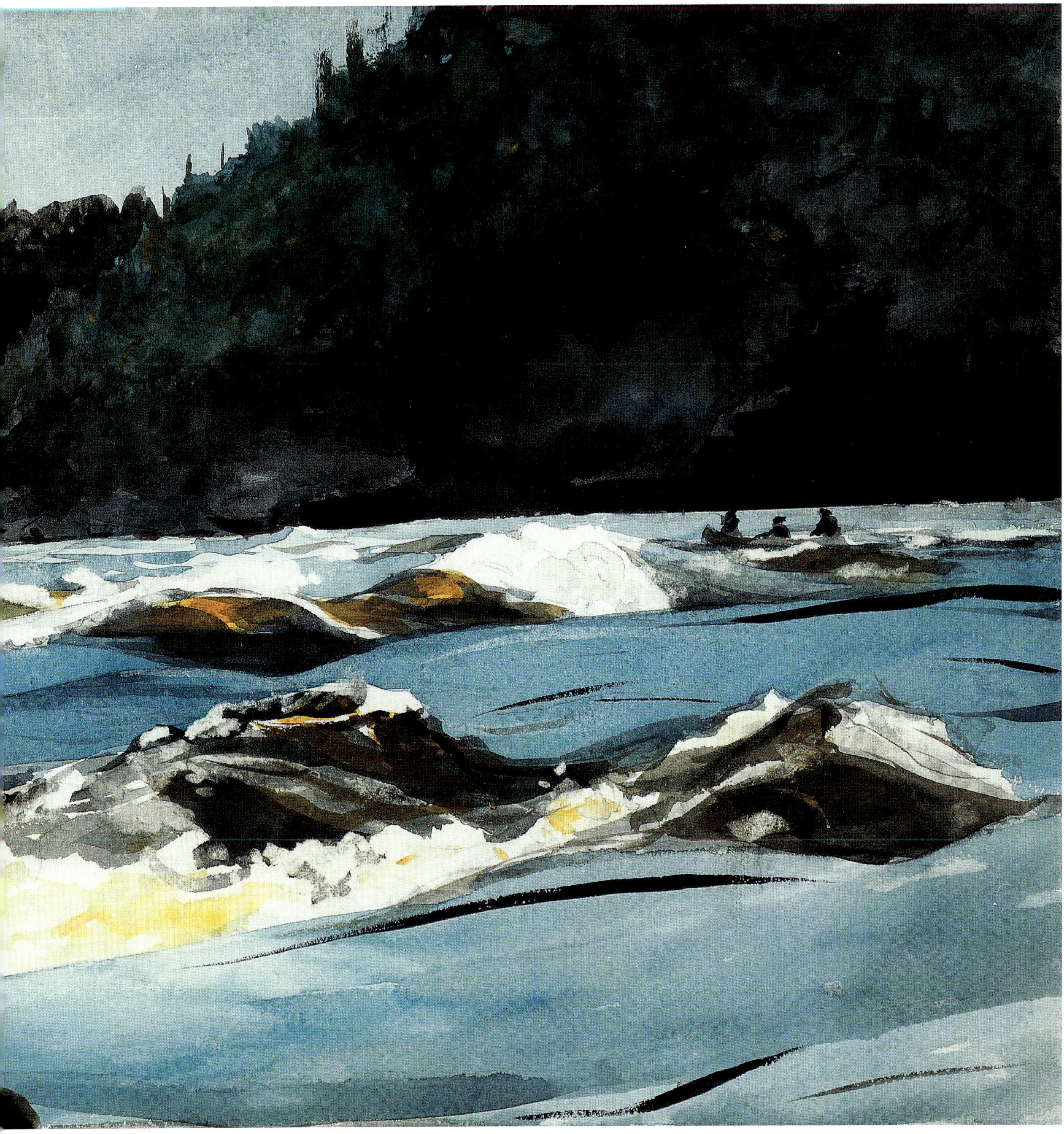

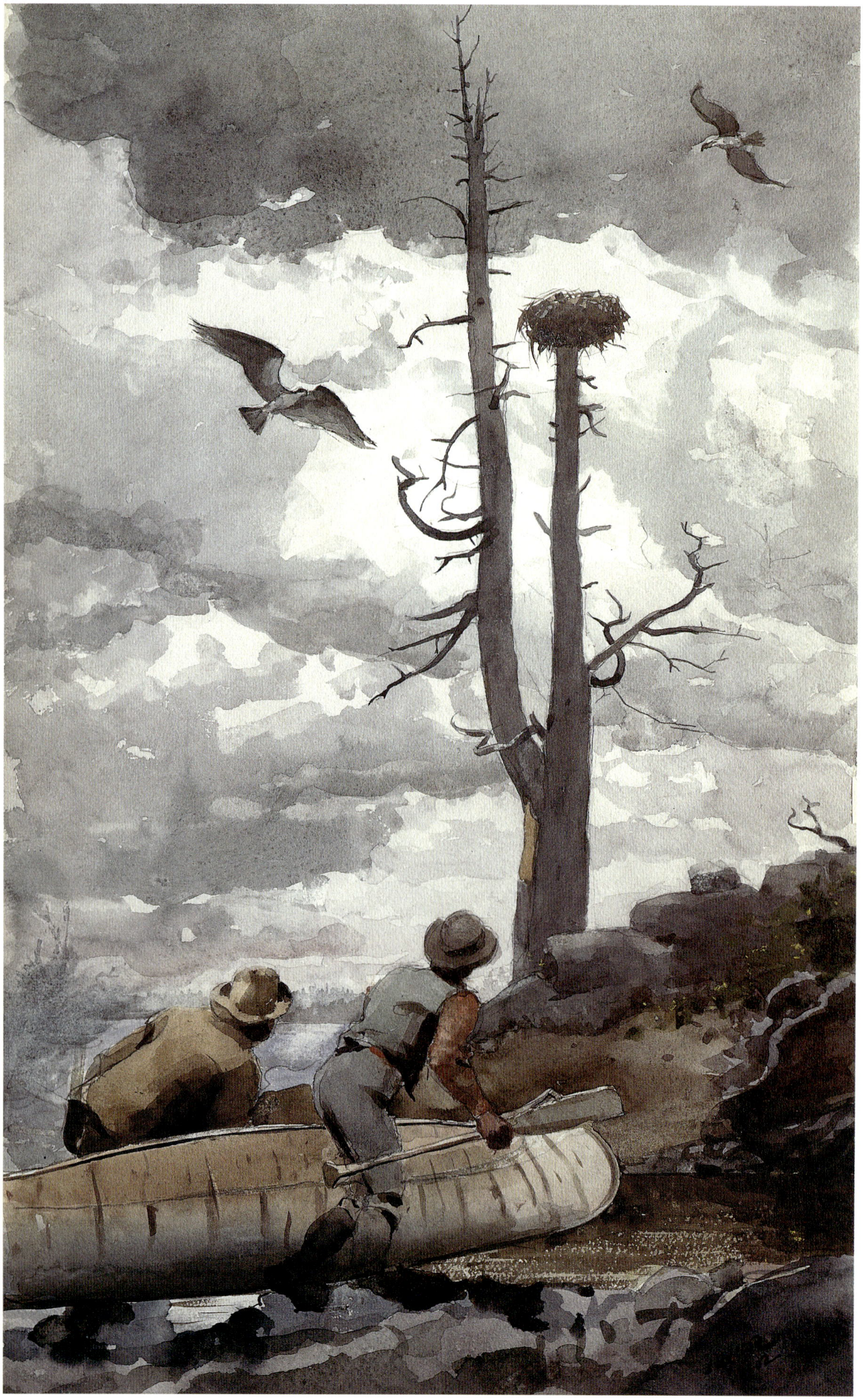

OSPREY'S NEST 1902

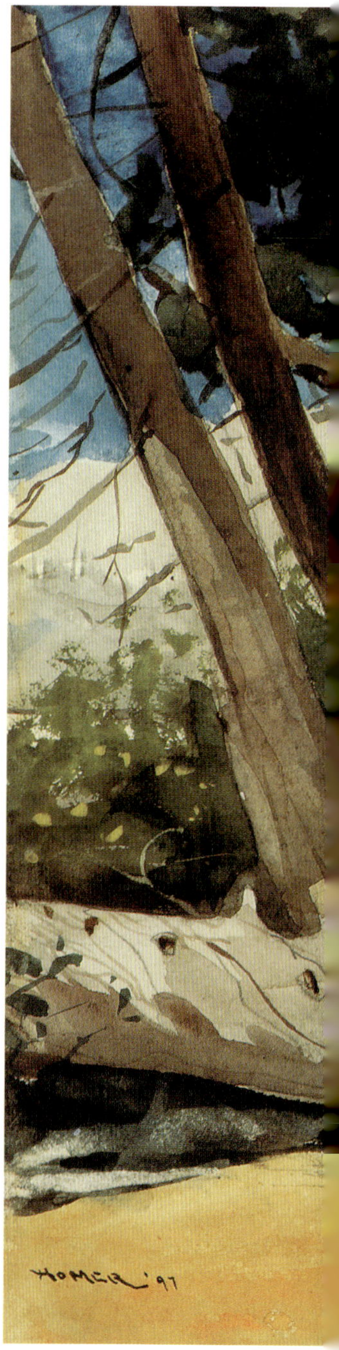

END OF THE PORTAGE 1897

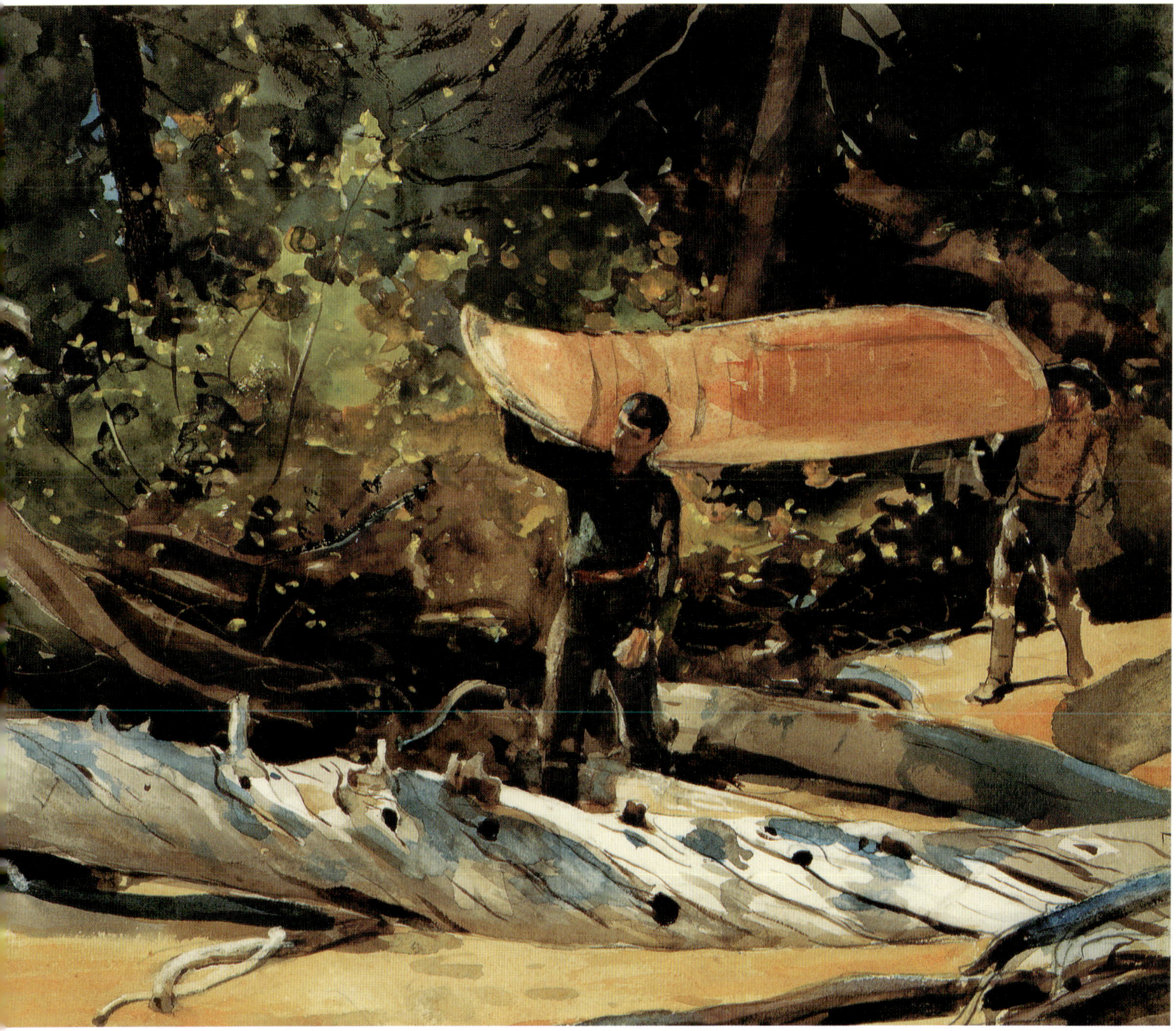

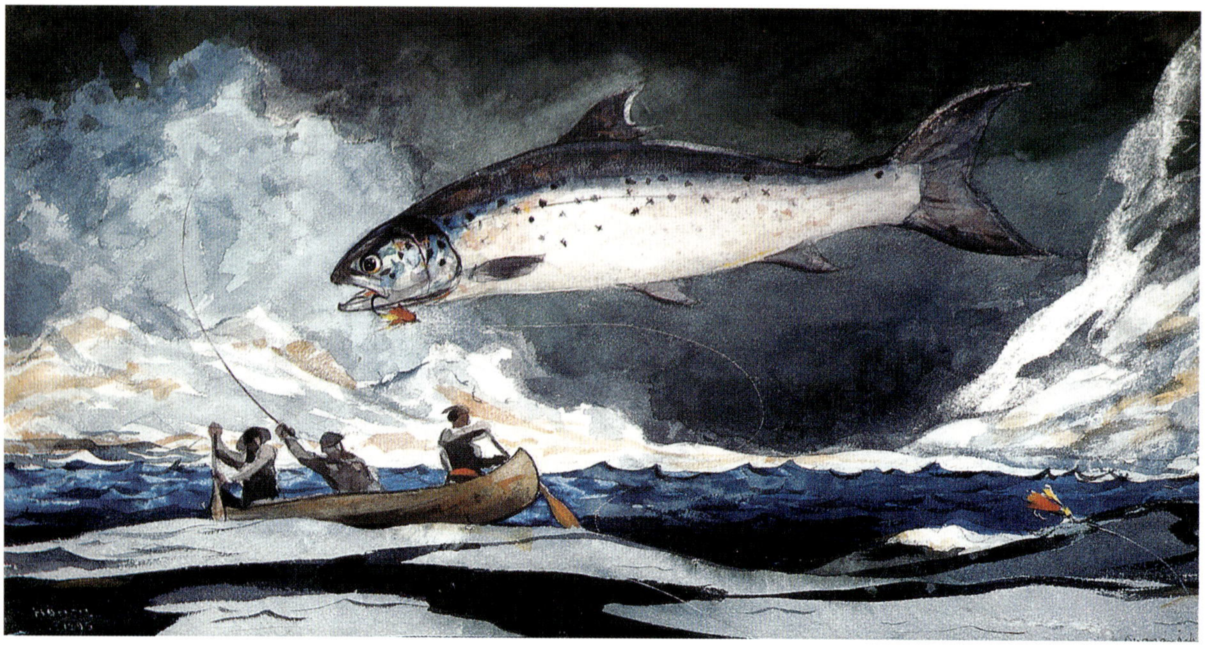

A Good Pool, Saguenay River 1895

show a complete understanding of the physical demands of the sport. The leader propels the boat forward with his oar, his gaze searching out possible obstacles ahead, while his companion pulls back on his oar to steer the boat between the rocks.

The pulsing energy of these paintings is a far cry from the serenity of works like *The Blue Boat* or *Adirondack Guide*. Frederic Remington, a fellow artist and outdoorsman, wrote of the kind of man attracted to these sports: ". . . faster—faster into the boil of the waters, he hears the roar and boom ahead, and the black rocks crop up in thickening masses to dispute his way. He is fighting a game battle with the elements, and they are remorseless. He may break his leg or lose his life in the tipover which is imminent, but the fool is happy—let him die." It was to these hardy souls, businessmen and professionals who eased the stress of their daily lives through such wilderness adventures, that Homer's watercolors were calculated to appeal.

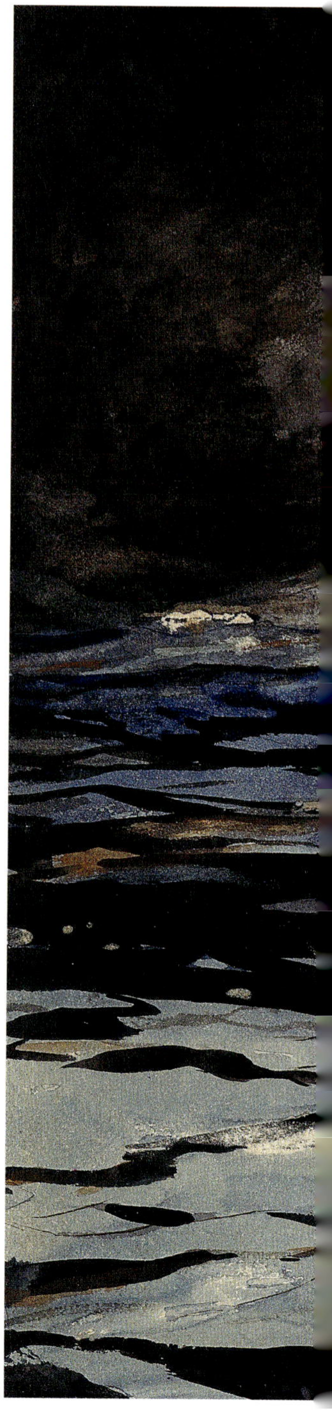

UNDER THE FALLS, THE GRAND DISCHARGE 1895

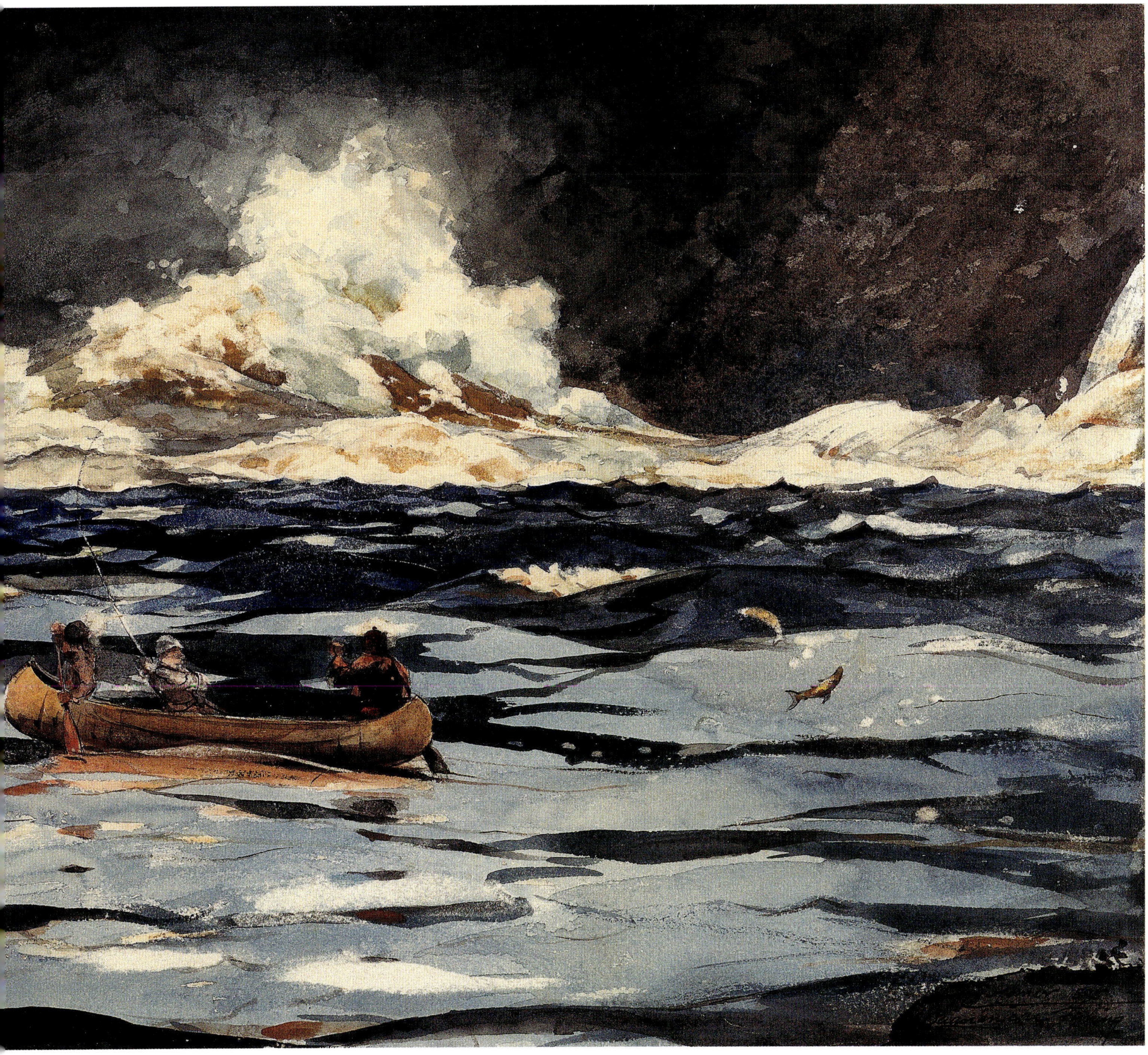

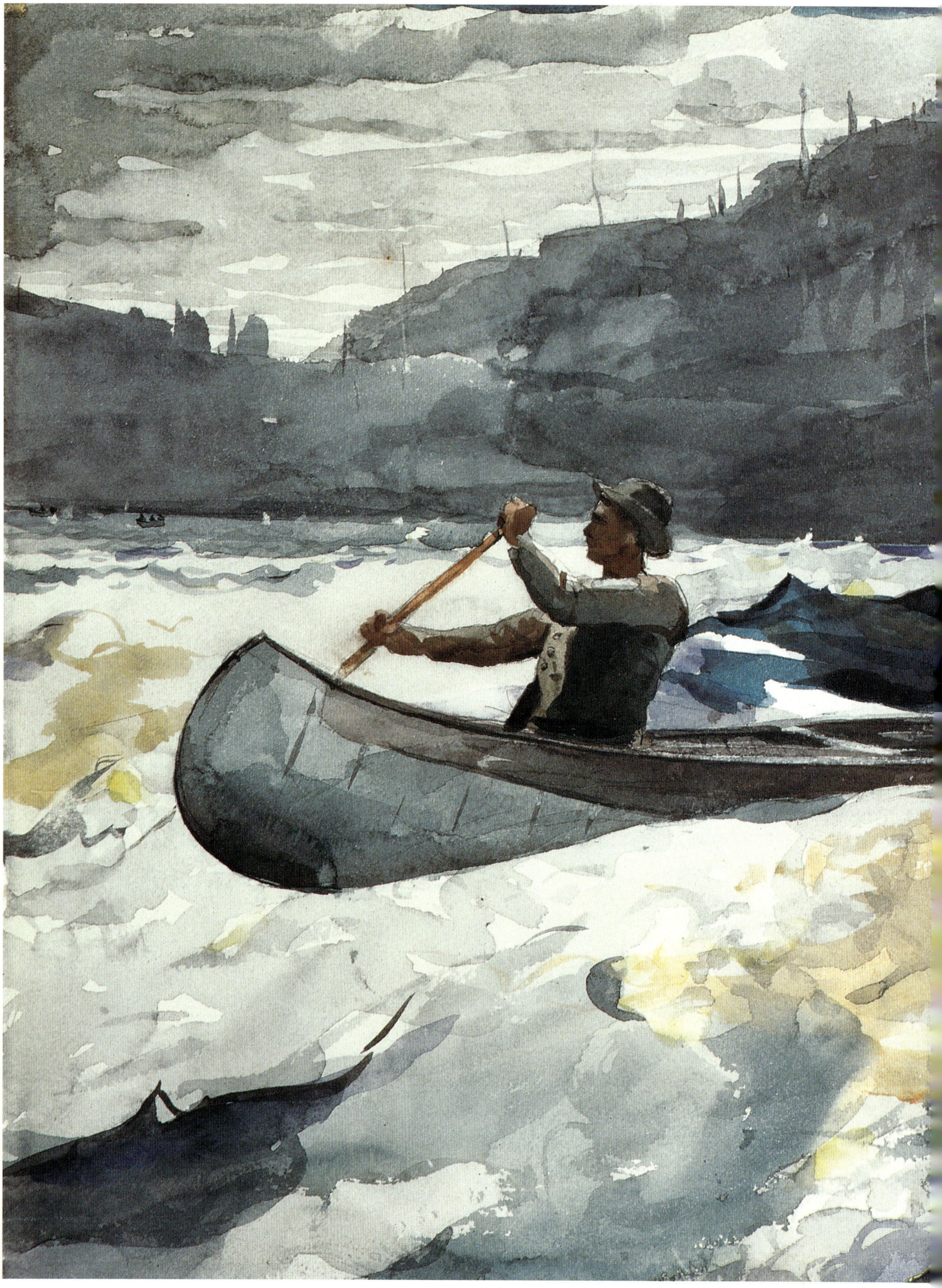

Shooting the Rapids 1902

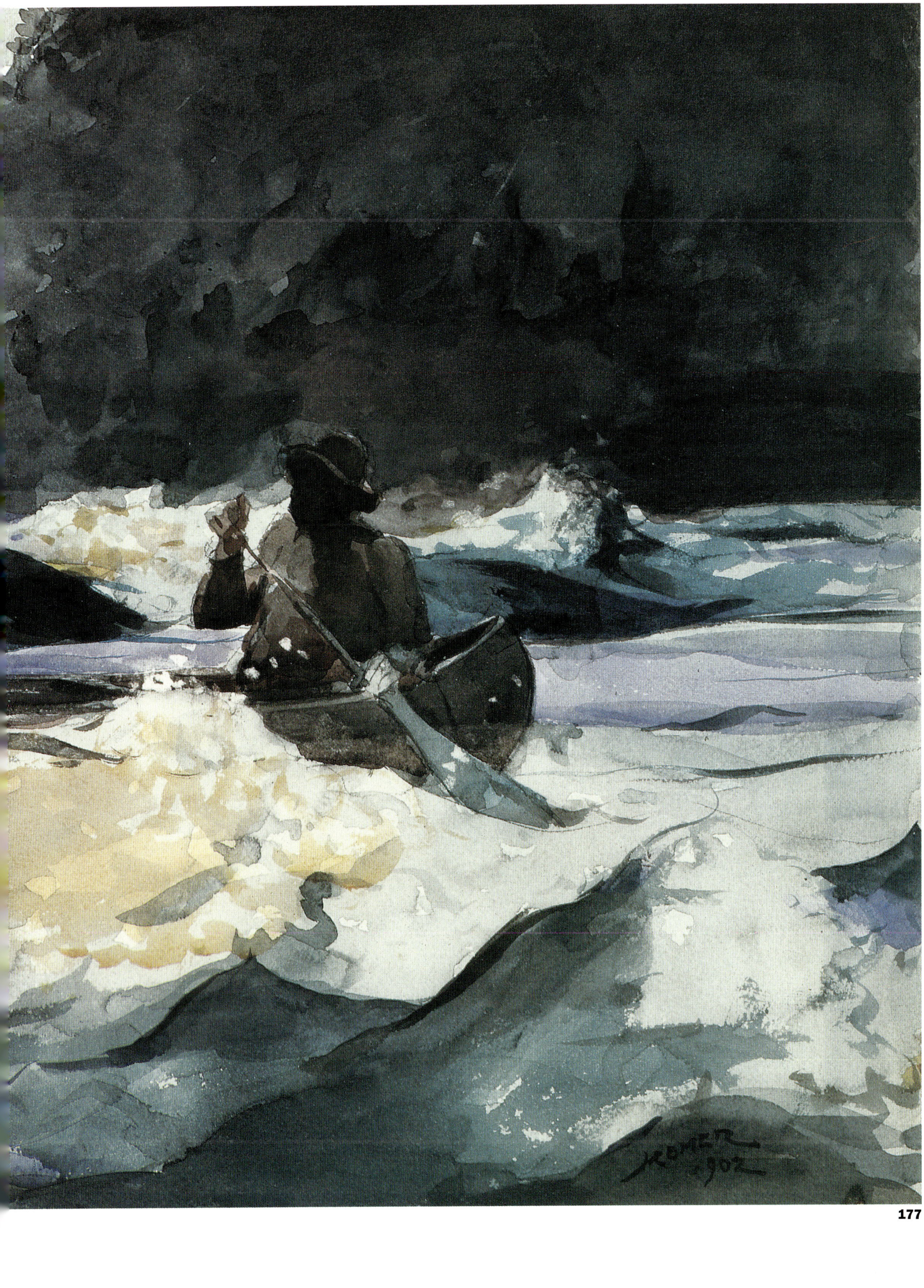

The Quebec watercolors employ a more limited palette than the Adirondacks paintings and are not as rich thematically. Gone are the subtle veils of color, replaced instead by choppy brushstrokes that capture the frenetic energy of the rushing river. Gone also are the deep shades with their subtle play of warm and cool tones. The Quebec watercolors are more extroverted, more obviously virile. They depict a world that, however wild in appearance, is set aside primarily for recreational purposes. Nature's raw power is very much in evidence, yet it is not the life-threatening fury of the ocean Homer so often depicted in his oil paintings but the thrill enjoyed by the sportsman in the great outdoors. Homer clearly knew his market, and tailored these works to appeal to fellow enthusiasts. It is a tribute to his genius that he could take into account potential buyers while losing none of the pulse-quickening excitement of the scenes he painted.

An exception to the energetic pace of the Quebec watercolors is a series of monochrome paintings Homer made on tinted gray paper. Stark, spare, and made without apparent labor, *Three Men in a Canoe* evokes the melancholy poetry of twilight in the wilderness. The quiet mood recalls such works as *Adirondack Lake* and *Sunrise, Fishing in the Adirondacks*, though here conveyed with even greater economy.

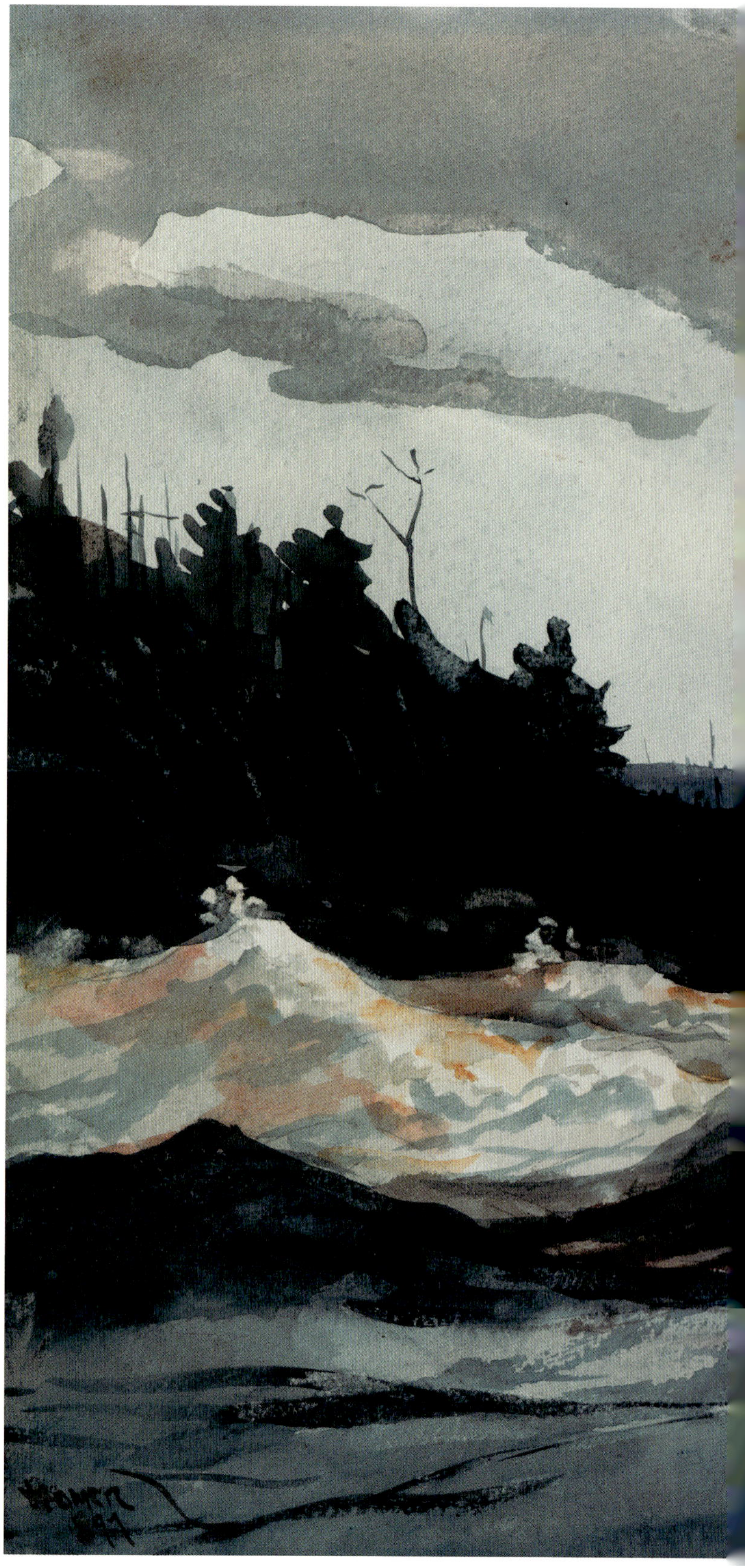

Canoe in Rapids 1897

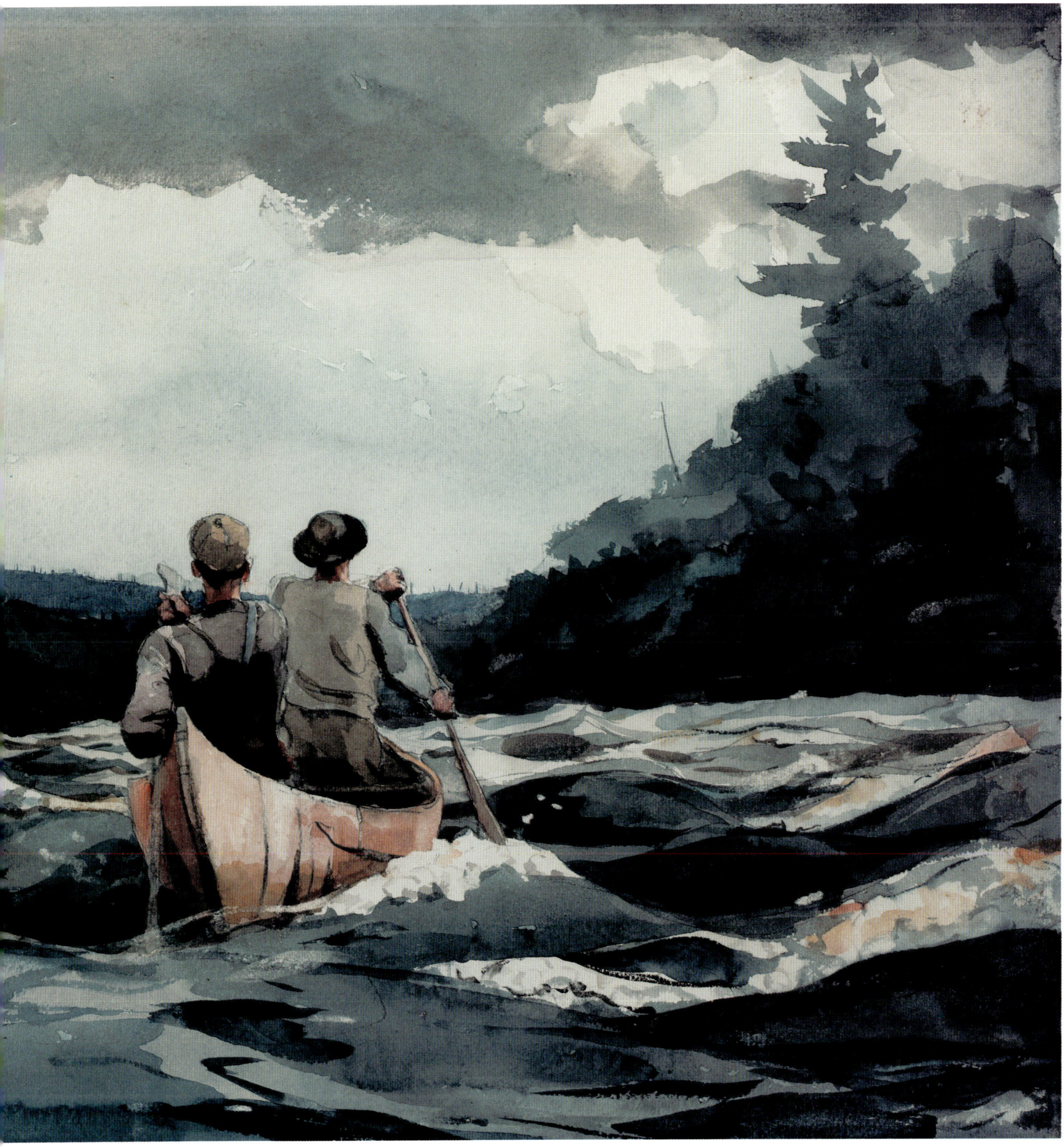

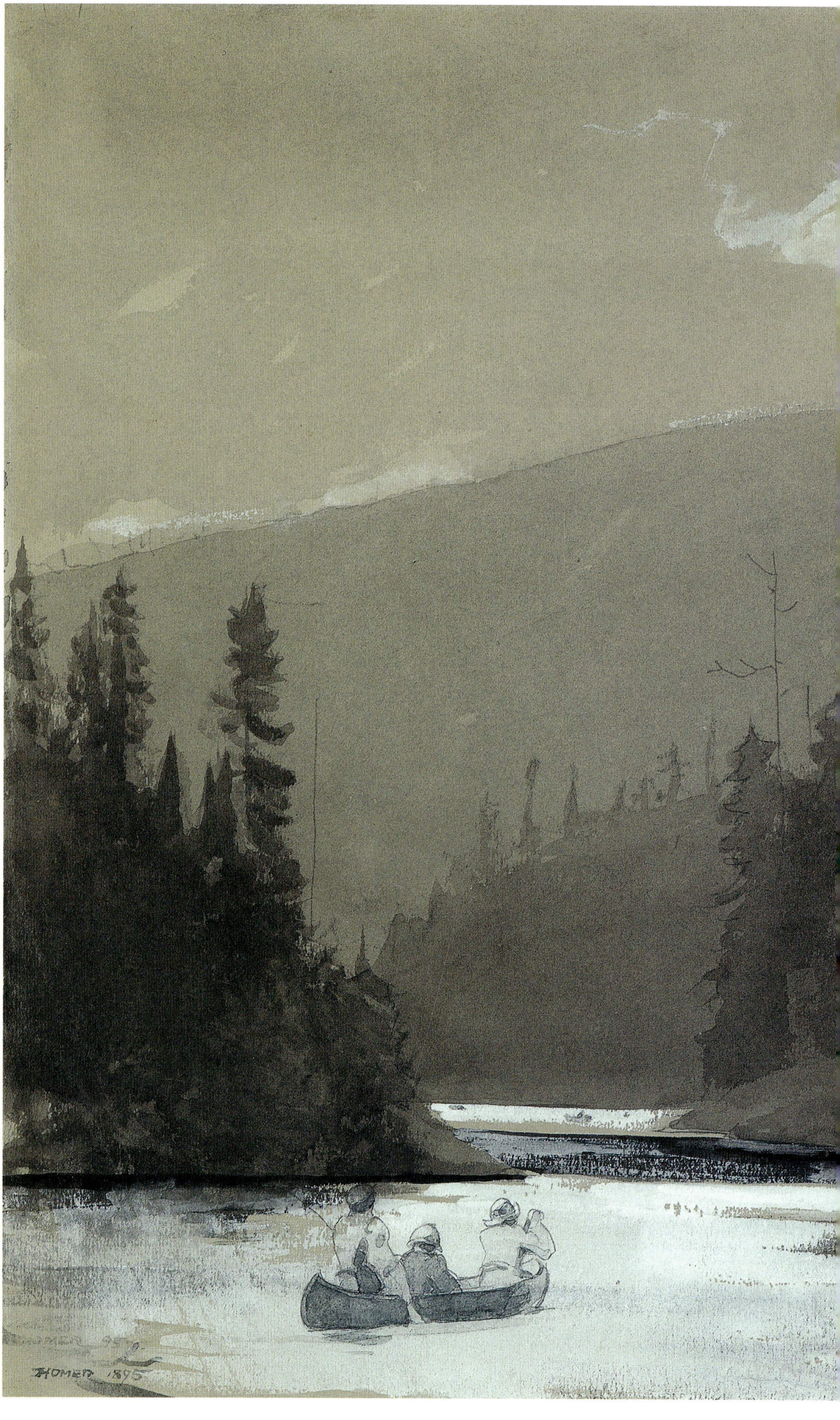

Three men in a Canoe 1895

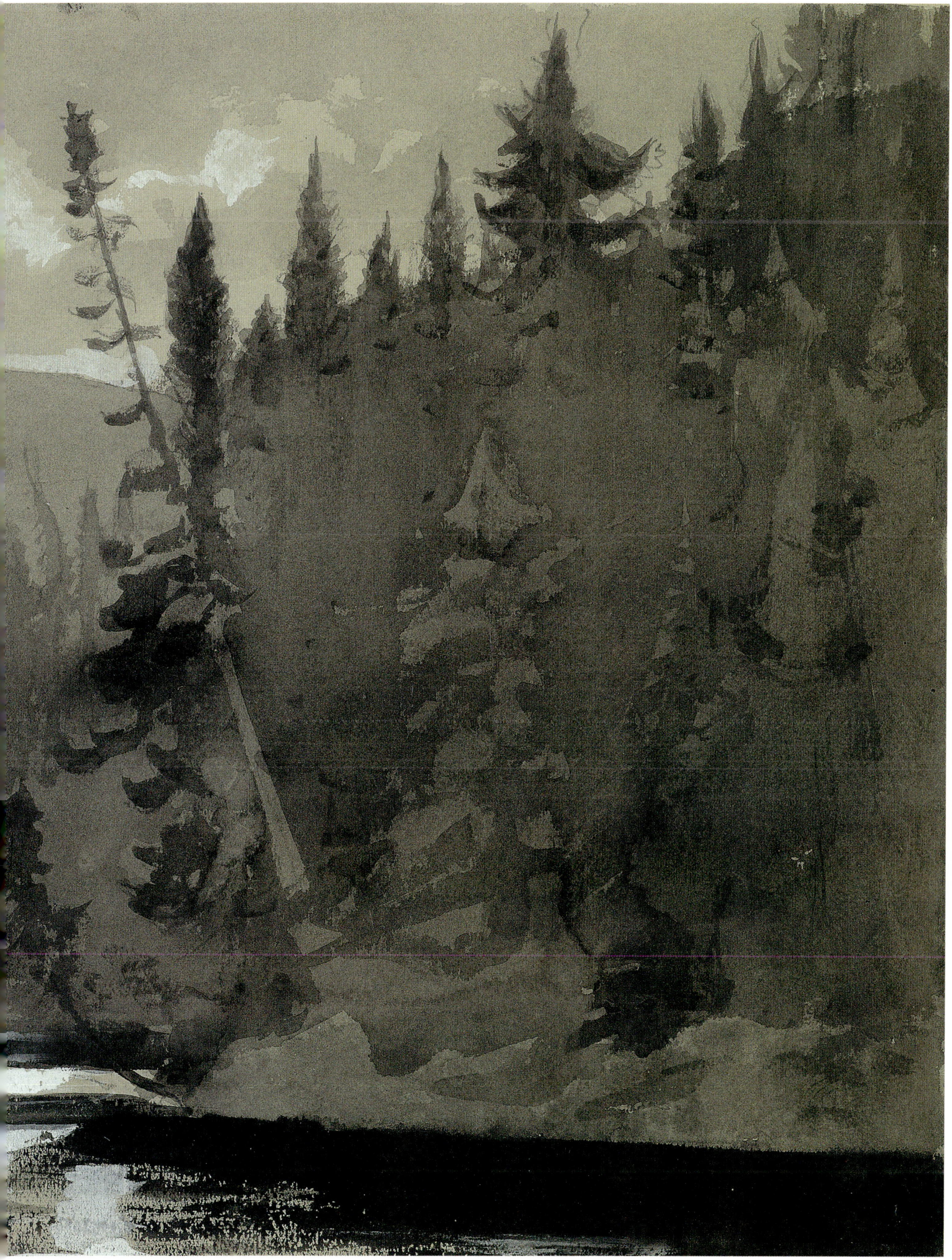

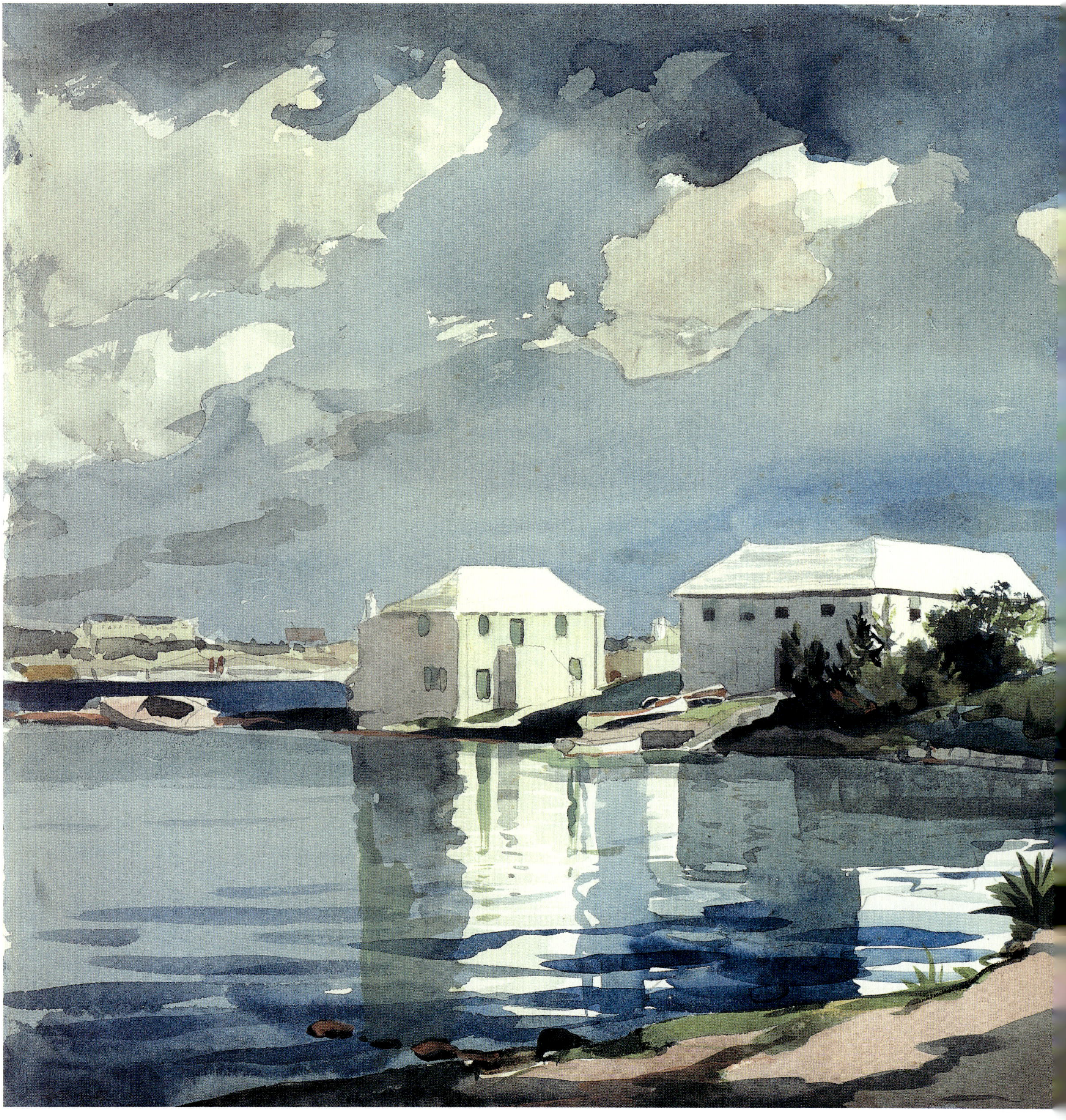

X.
Return to Paradise: Bermuda, the Bahamas, Florida, 1885–1904

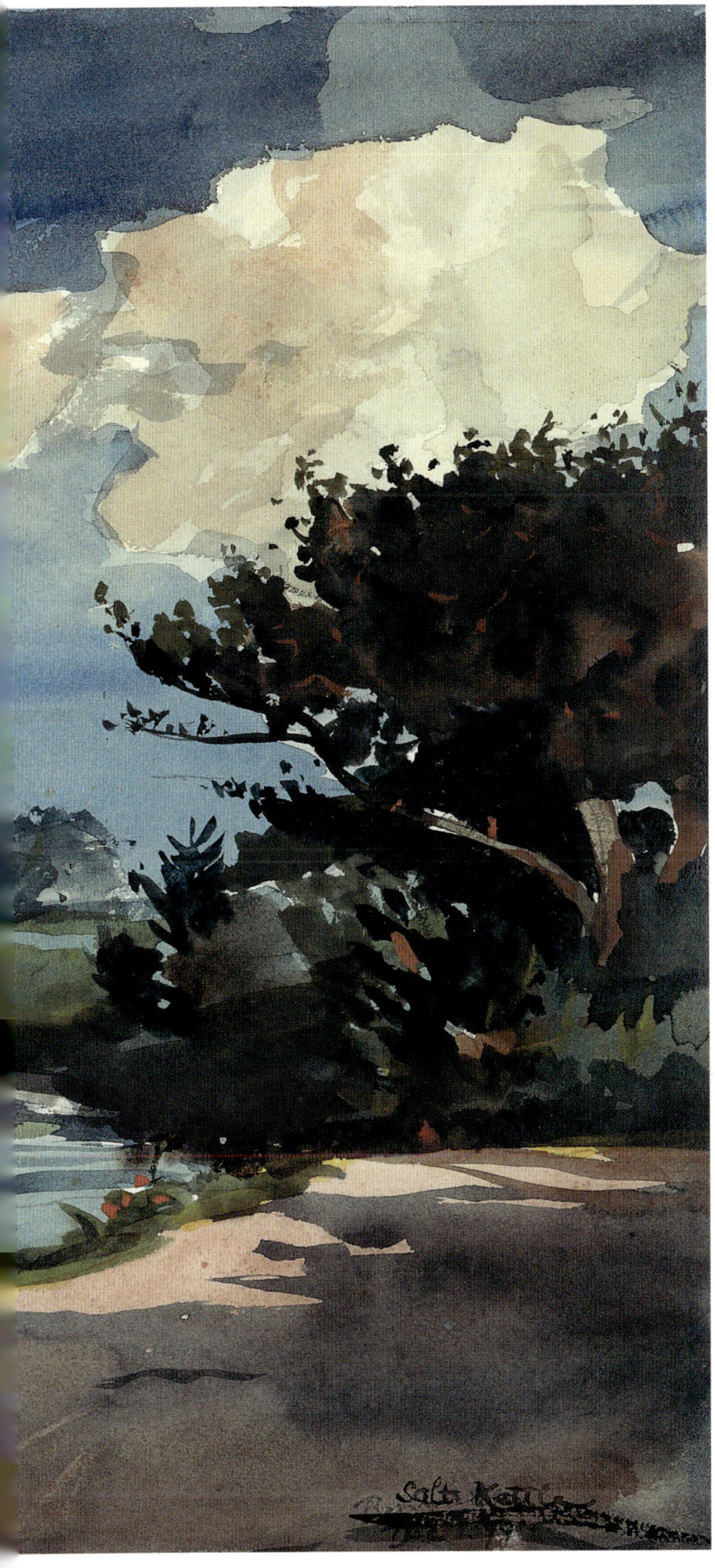

Salt Kettle, Bermuda 1899

During the last twenty-five years of his life, Homer continued to look to the Caribbean and Florida for relief from the harsh Maine winters. Florida, fast being developed as a haven for northern tourists, was his most frequent destination, though he also returned to the Bahamas in the winter of 1898–99 and added Bermuda to his itinerary, making his first trip in 1899 and returning in 1901.

Vacations in the Bahamas and Bermuda seemed calculated, at least in part, to provide him with subjects to paint in watercolor. The attractions of Florida for Homer included the warm climate of course but also ample opportunities to fish, as always his favorite pastime, and the itinerary usually included expeditions along the swampy rivers of northern part of the state. Of the seven trips to Florida he made between 1885 and 1909, he produced watercolors on only three of them: in 1885–86, 1890, and 1903.

The tropical watercolors completed between 1885 and 1905 demonstrate the undiminished power of the artist, now well into his sixties. The final watercolors are marked by a breadth of execution and fluency that reveals the full command of the medium won from years of experience. In their technical range and apparent effortlessness, these late watercolors remain unsurpassed.

They possess much of the sensuousness of the paintings Homer made in 1885 on his first trip to Nassau. Particularly in the Bermuda paintings from 1899, Homer indulged his love of color, reveling in the contrasts between whitewashed houses, bright blue sea, and vibrant blossoms. *Flower Garden and Bungalow, Bermuda* is as colorful as any image he ever painted. The tiny figure, framed by the bright yellow of the house, seems dwarfed by lush vegetation that sprouts with almost unnatural fecundity. A new intensity of color is also apparent in *Coral Formation*, where the accents of the red-coated soldiers stand out against the deep blue of the water and ocher highlights in the rocks. *Salt Kettle, Bermuda* is built around the contrast between the white of the houses and clouds—articulated by reserved areas of paper tinted with washes of gray and ocher—and the saturated blues of sky and water. The color is vivid, the brushstrokes confident and apparently effortless. There is none of the labored quality visible in some of the earlier watercolors, particularly from the Cullercoats period. Gone also are the subtly graded neutral tones with which he once carved out sculptural volumes. Homer now

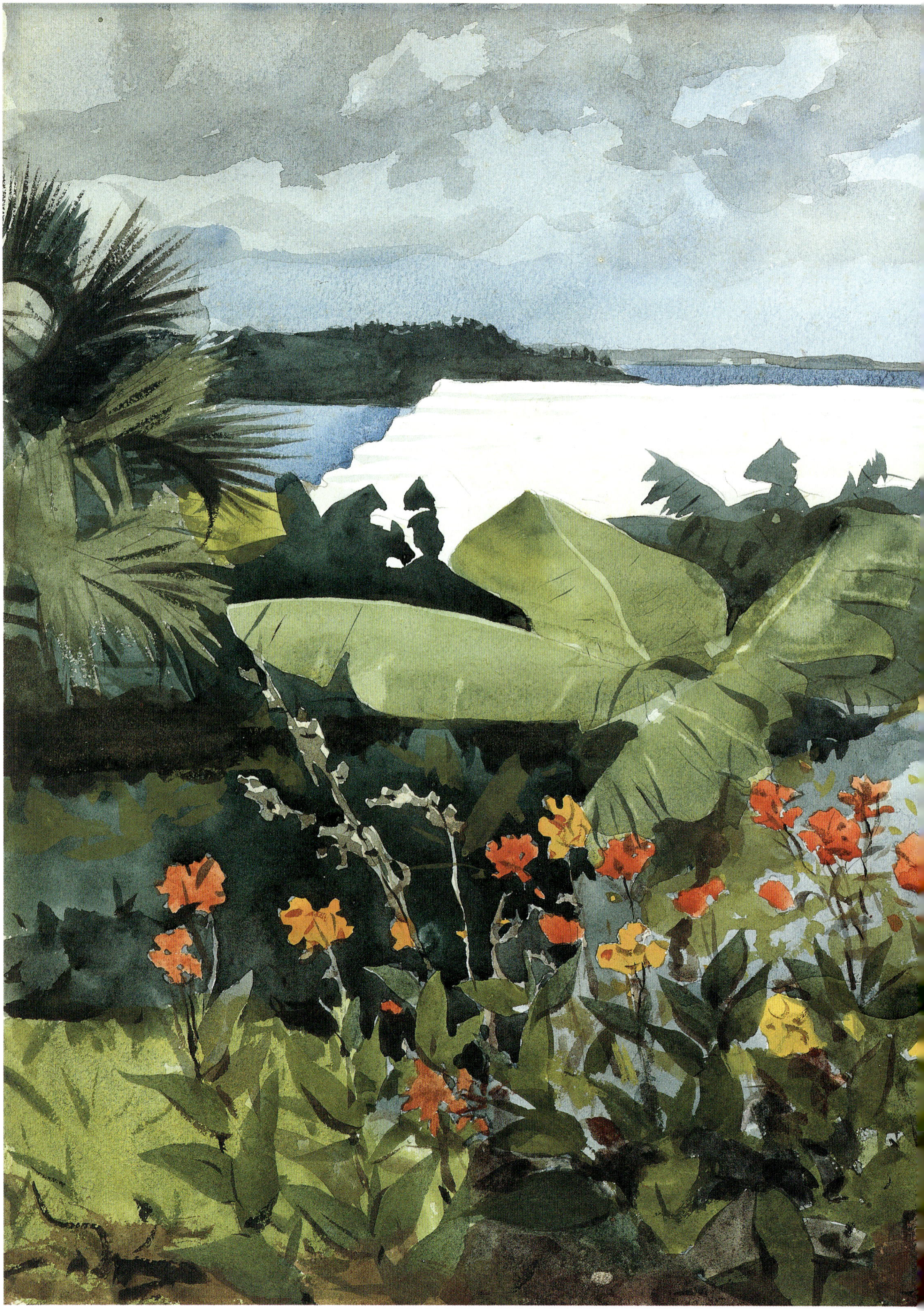

Flower Garden and Bungalow, Bermuda 1899

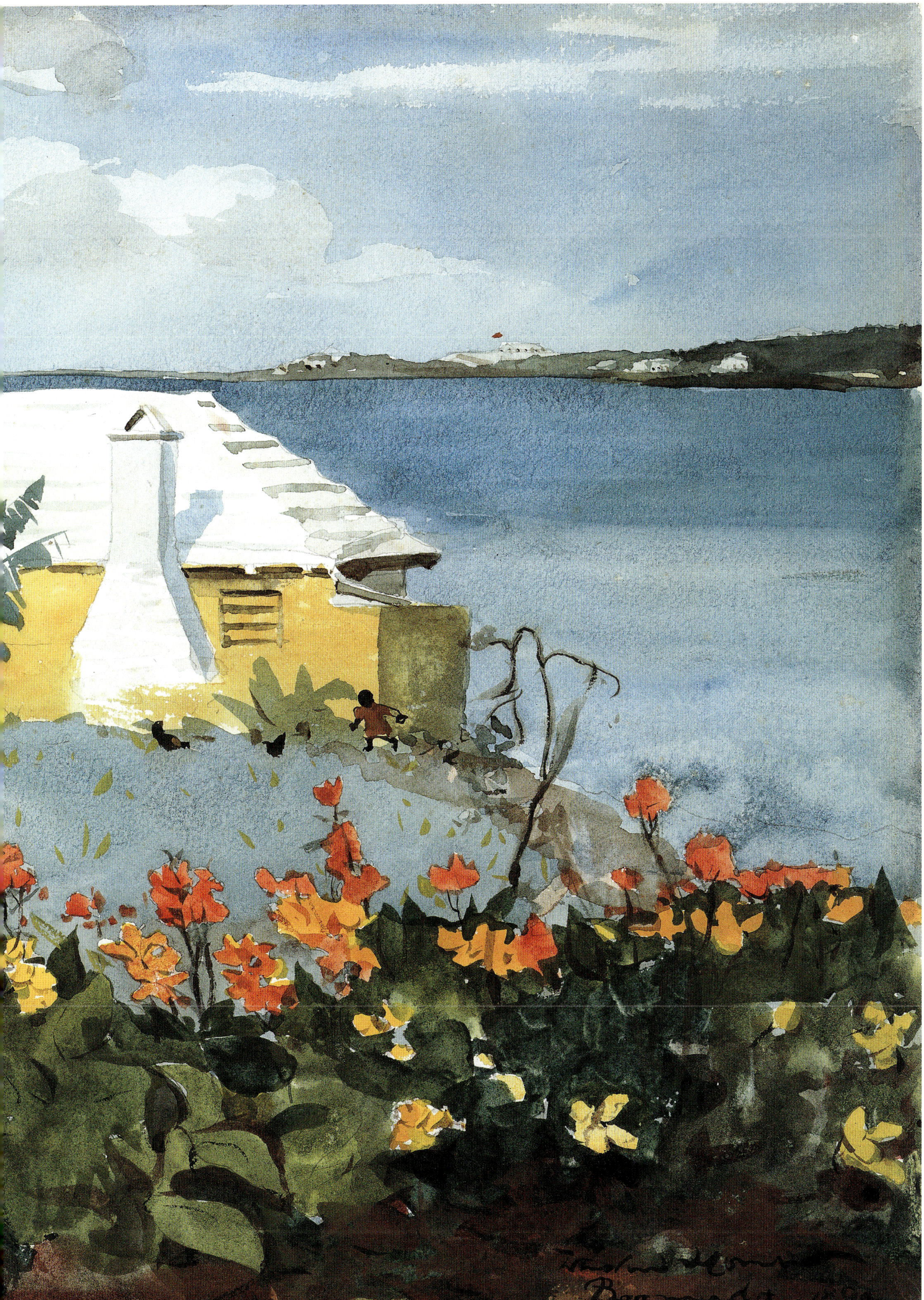

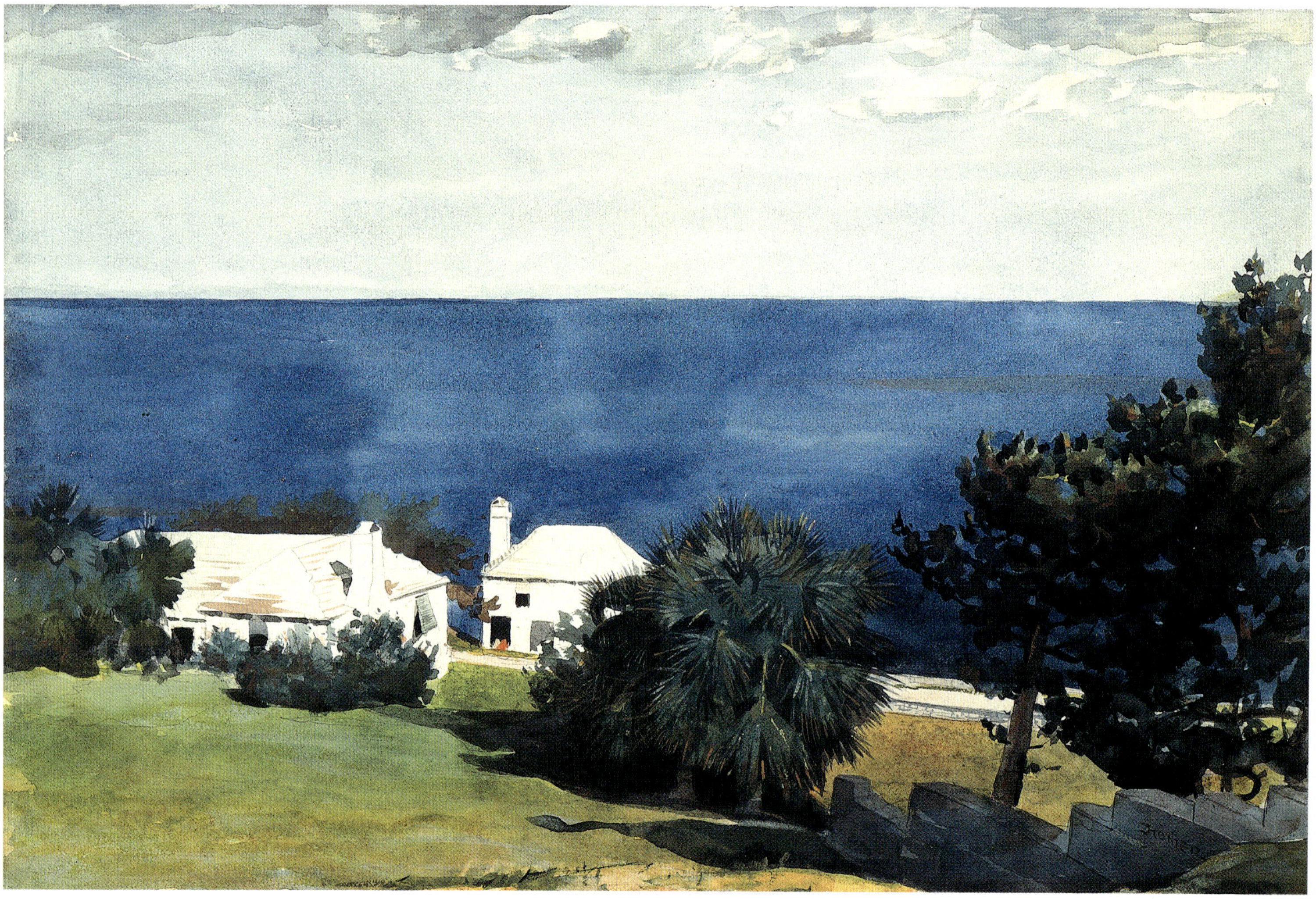

SHORE AT BERMUDA c. 1899

creates solid sculptural masses with one or two tones applied with a light but deft touch. Despite the almost garish palette, there is an element of cool abstraction in these Bermuda works, a formality of design undisturbed by any real human narrative.

The Nassau paintings of 1898–99 continue to show the sensual delight of a northerner basking in the warm winter sun. But Homer's brush has become more selective. He focuses less in these later works on picturesque scenes of native women in colorful costumes, ramshackle cabins, and tropical gardens, and concentrates instead on monumental figure compositions, mostly featuring young men of statuesque proportions. *West India Divers* picks up one theme of his earlier visit, depicting again the divers who made their living by bringing to the surface coral, sponge, and seashells. Homer found in the contrast of dark skin and blue water an endlessly rich pictorial motif.

Among the masterpieces of his oeuvre is the watercolor *The Sponge Diver* [pp. 190–191], later inscribed by Homer himself with the date to 1889, but actually painted on his return to Nassau in 1898. Homer invests this ordinary task with heroic grandeur, modeling the diver's muscular back in a few well-chosen strokes. The figure's

CORAL FORMATION 1901

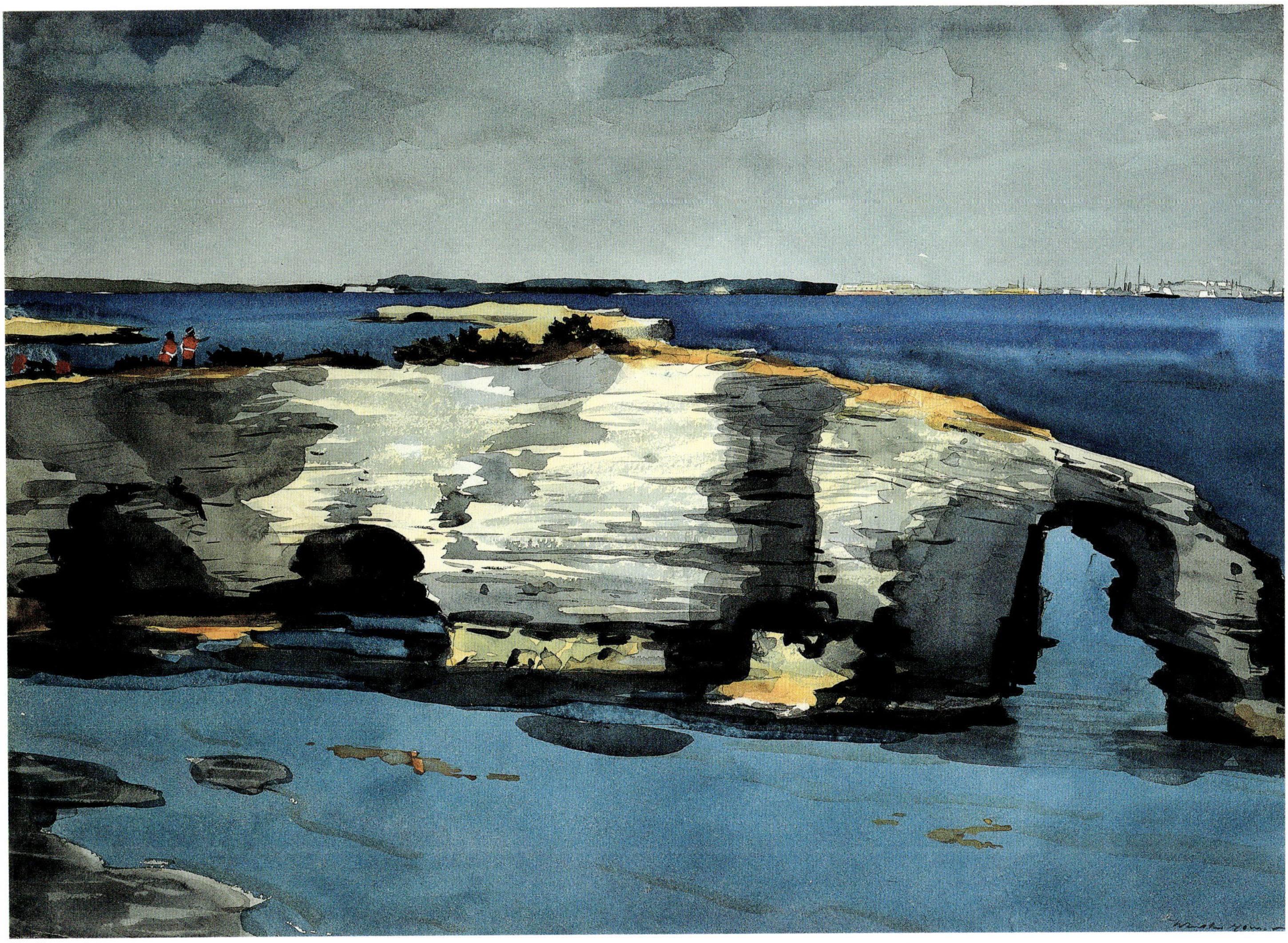

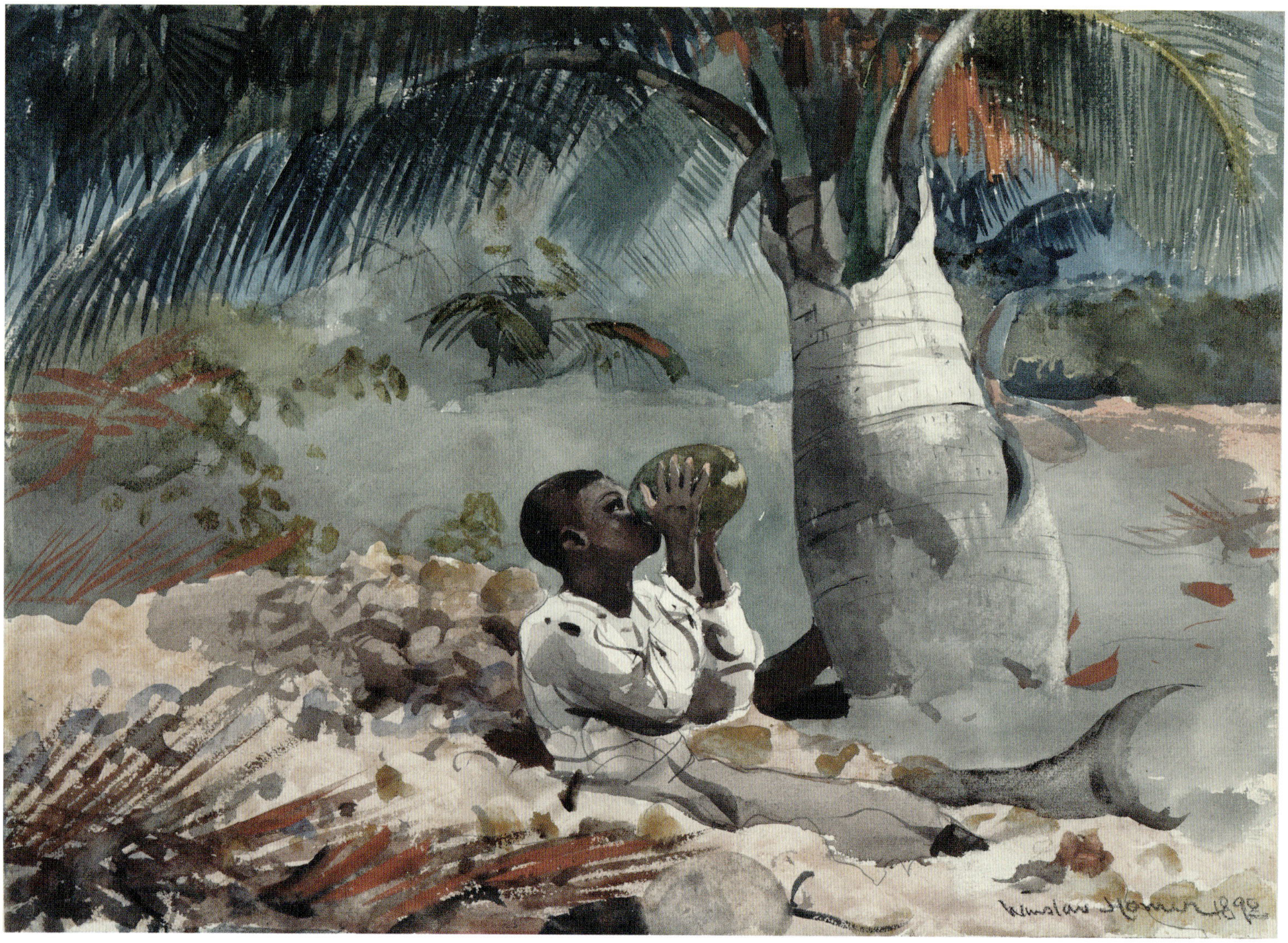

UNDER THE COCO PALM 1898

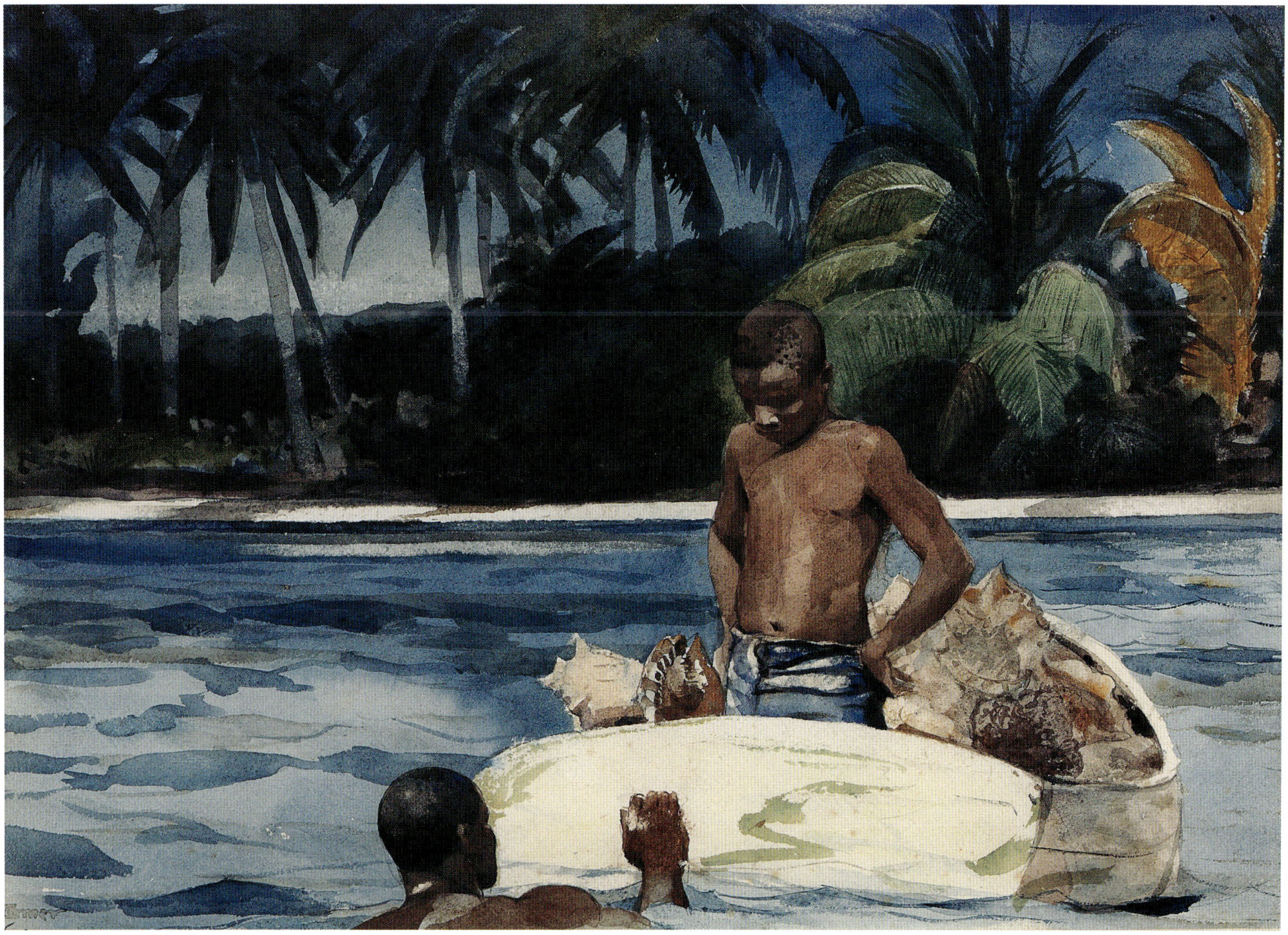

West India Divers 1899

air of effortless command and the simple, almost abstract shapes of the boat and oar create a composition of classical repose reminiscent of ancient Greek sculpture and the work of Michelangelo. Here Homer has achieved the monumentality of his Cullercoats watercolors, but with a brighter palette that conjures the heat and light of the Caribbean. It is with such works, timeless and yet exquisitely attuned to a precise moment in nature, that one sees the full flowering of Homer's genius as a painter in watercolor.

Under the Coco Palm is a work that seems to promise delights of an almost supernatural order. The boy who tilts his head up to drink the sweet milk of a coconut is lost in sensual bliss; the palm frond that lies beside him and continues the line of his hidden legs resembles the tail of a fish, so that this youth appears to be transformed into a mythical creature of the sea. Such a possibility hardly seems out of place where nature is so profligate with its gifts.

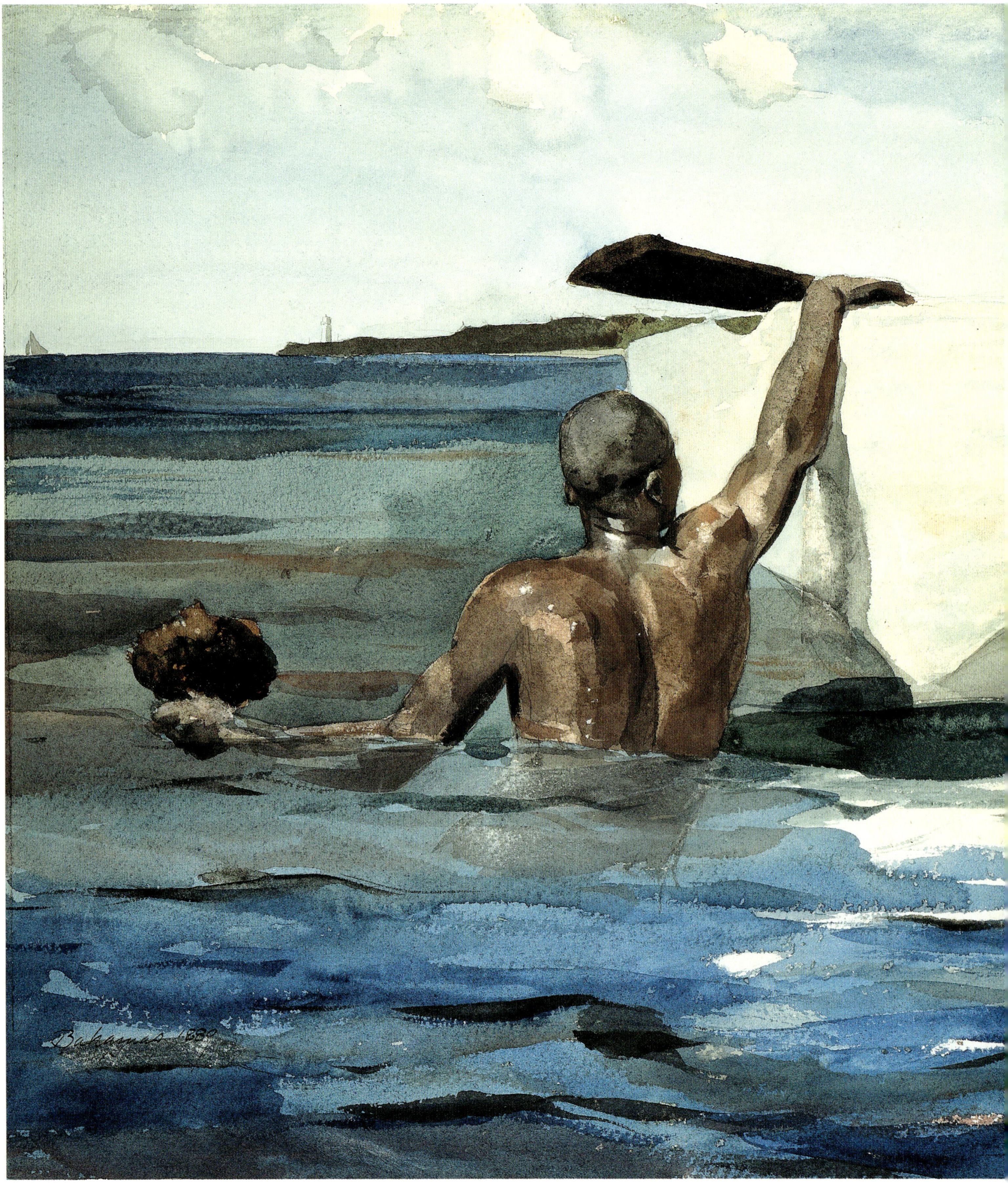

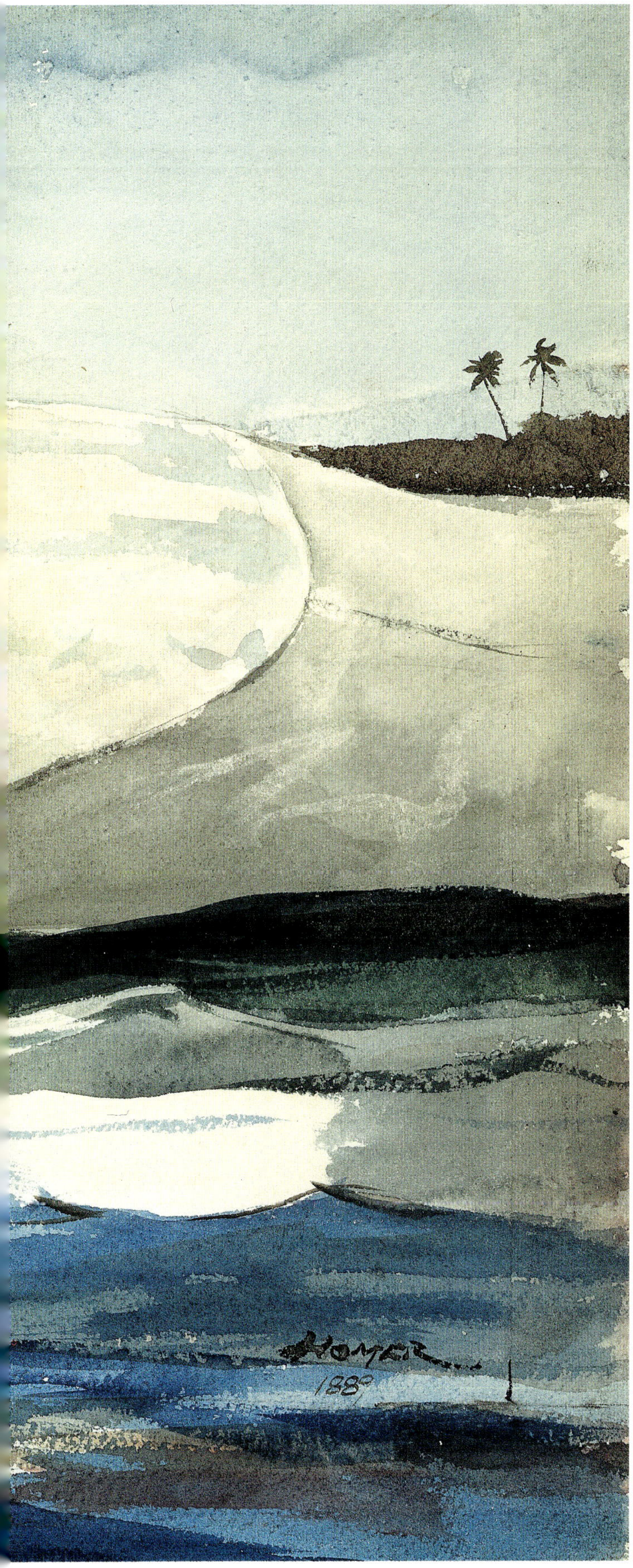

But a slightly more threatening tone has crept into these works, as if after the initial seduction Homer looked at this paradise with a more suspicious eye. A new mood can be detected in Homer's handling of water, which shows a greater vigor that perhaps reflects the experience of painting the turbulent Saguenay River. *The Turtle Pound* [pp. 196–197] echoes the monumental composition of *The Sponge Diver*, but here deeper, more varied hues of blue and green applied in bolder strokes animate the water and give the work a greater urgency. While *The Sponge Diver* possesses a sense of dignity and classical repose, *The Turtle Pound* seethes with barely suppressed energy.

As in the Quebec paintings, large swatches of reserved paper create bold highlights and reflections. The climate too seems more temperamental in these works. In *After the Hurricane, Bahamas*, Homer captures the aftermath of a storm through bold contrasts of light and dark laid in rapidly with a loaded brush. Natural violence is all the more ominous for being only implied. The skies are clearing and the sun has pierced the veil of clouds, but the foam-topped waves reveal the ocean's continued agitation. Though the worst is over, the man sprawled on the sands next to his shattered boat attests to the damage left in the storm's wake.

THE SPONGE DIVER 1898–1899

HURRICANE, BAHAMAS 1898/1899

AFTER THE HURRICANE, BAHAMAS 1899

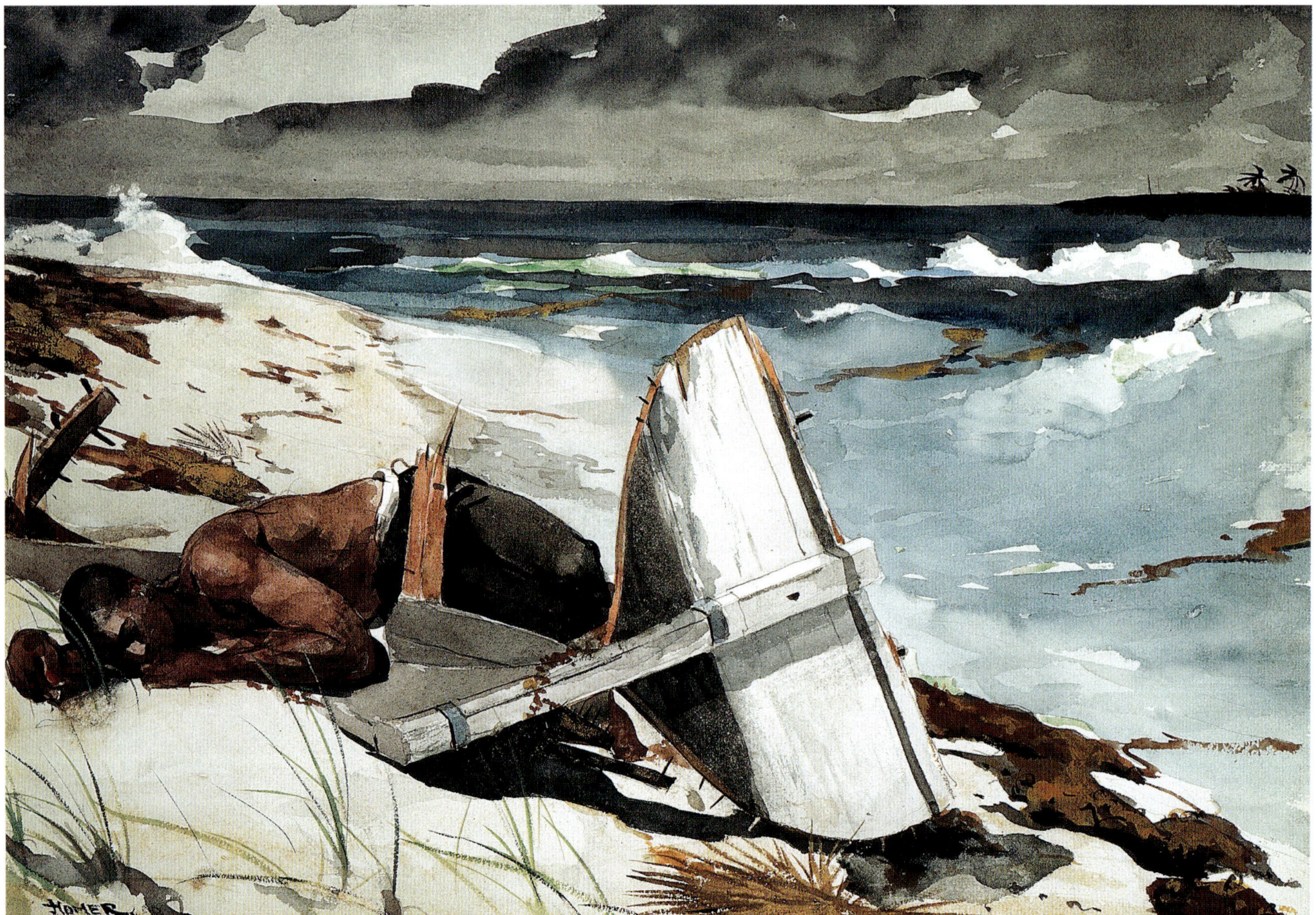

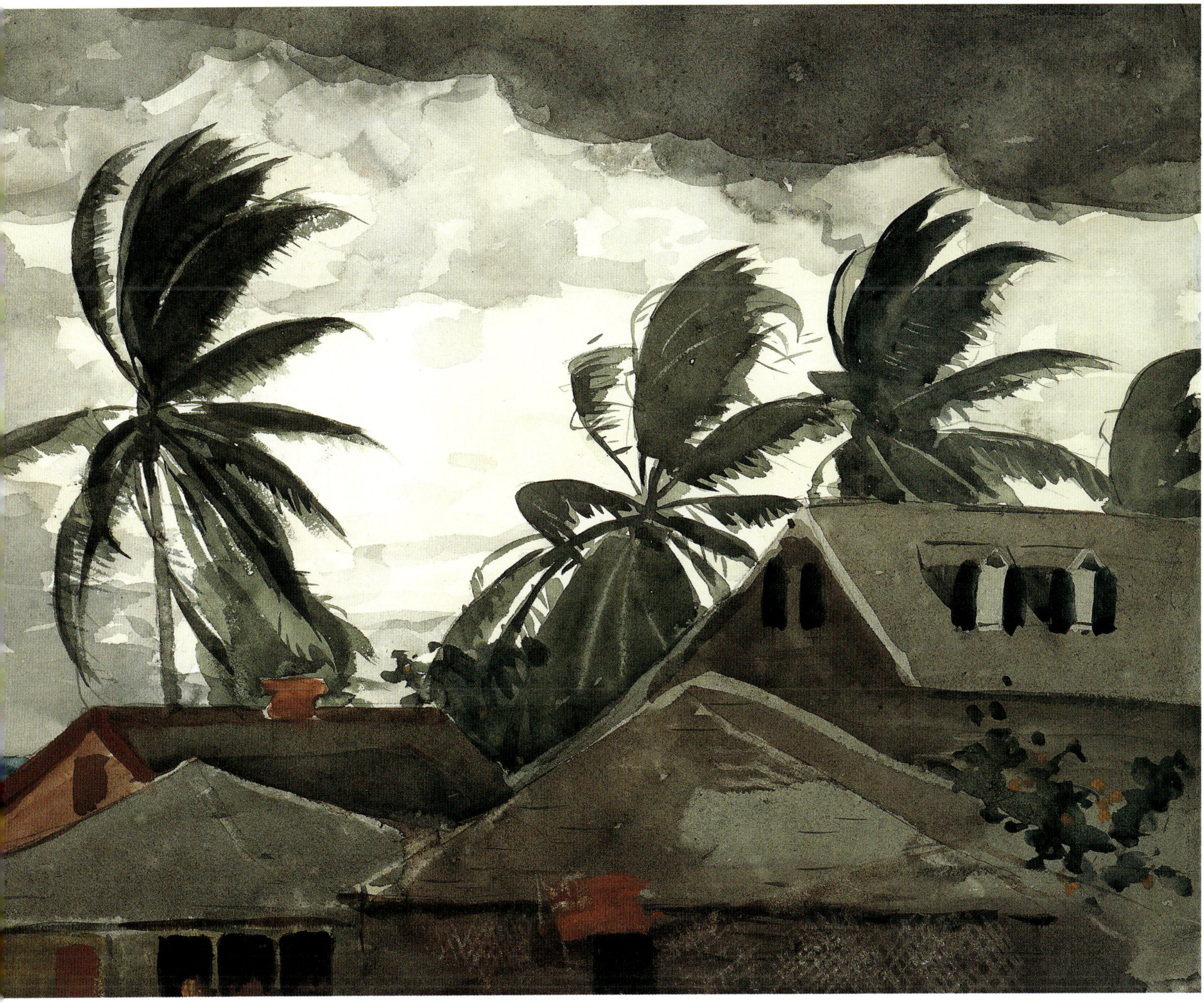

It is the eerie contrast between the dark clouds and returning sun that gives *After the Hurricane, Bahamas* its narrative power. In *Hurricane, Bahamas*, Homer uses line to tell a similar story, contrasting the arched backs of the palm fronds as they bend before the gale to the angular profile of the rooftops. Again, he does not place us in the middle of the storm, perhaps realizing that watercolor is too delicate a medium to capture the violence of a tropical hurricane. The somber palette, relieved only by a small patch of blue sea in the lower left, suggests that the storm is approaching or has just departed. The large area of white sky makes the dark clouds appear more threatening. Homer's vision of the tropics has come to embrace stronger contrasts. An earthly paradise this remains, but one whose turbulent undercurrents have risen closer to the surface.

Of all the tropical locales, Florida offered Homer the most varied field for his art. The Florida watercolors span almost twenty years and tackle a wide variety of scenery, from primeval jungle to the crowded harbor of Key West. *In a Florida Jungle* [pp. 198–199] is one of the most elaborate and carefully worked out watercolors Homer ever painted, revealing all the subtractive techniques and careful planning of his Cullercoats works. It is a richly detailed piece, elaborate in construction and in theme. The alligator emerging from the water, eyeing hungrily the unsuspecting spoonbill, provides an ominous narrative; buzzards fly overhead, ready to take advantage of the opportunity. Like *Mink Pond*, *In a Florida Jungle* shows the natural world at its most savage. The lush scenery cannot conceal the environment's basic cruelty. Similar feelings are evoked by *In the Jungle, Florida* [pp. 200–201], where a puma turns to snarl impotently at the red-winged bird in the upper-right-hand corner. Here, in keeping with the freedom of his last watercolors, the jungle is evoked more boldly, through overlapping washes and leaves rendered directly in thicker paint.

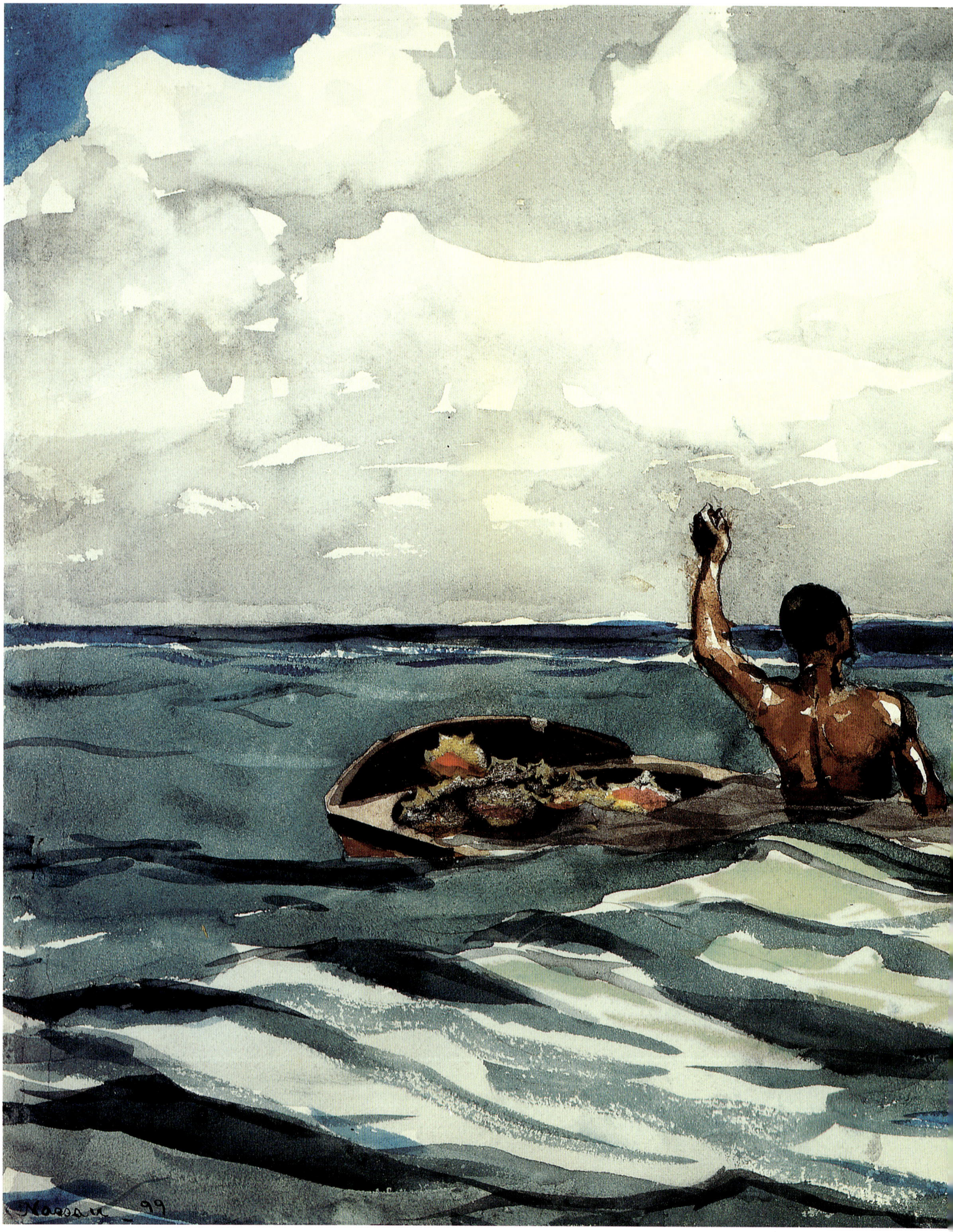
Nassau 99

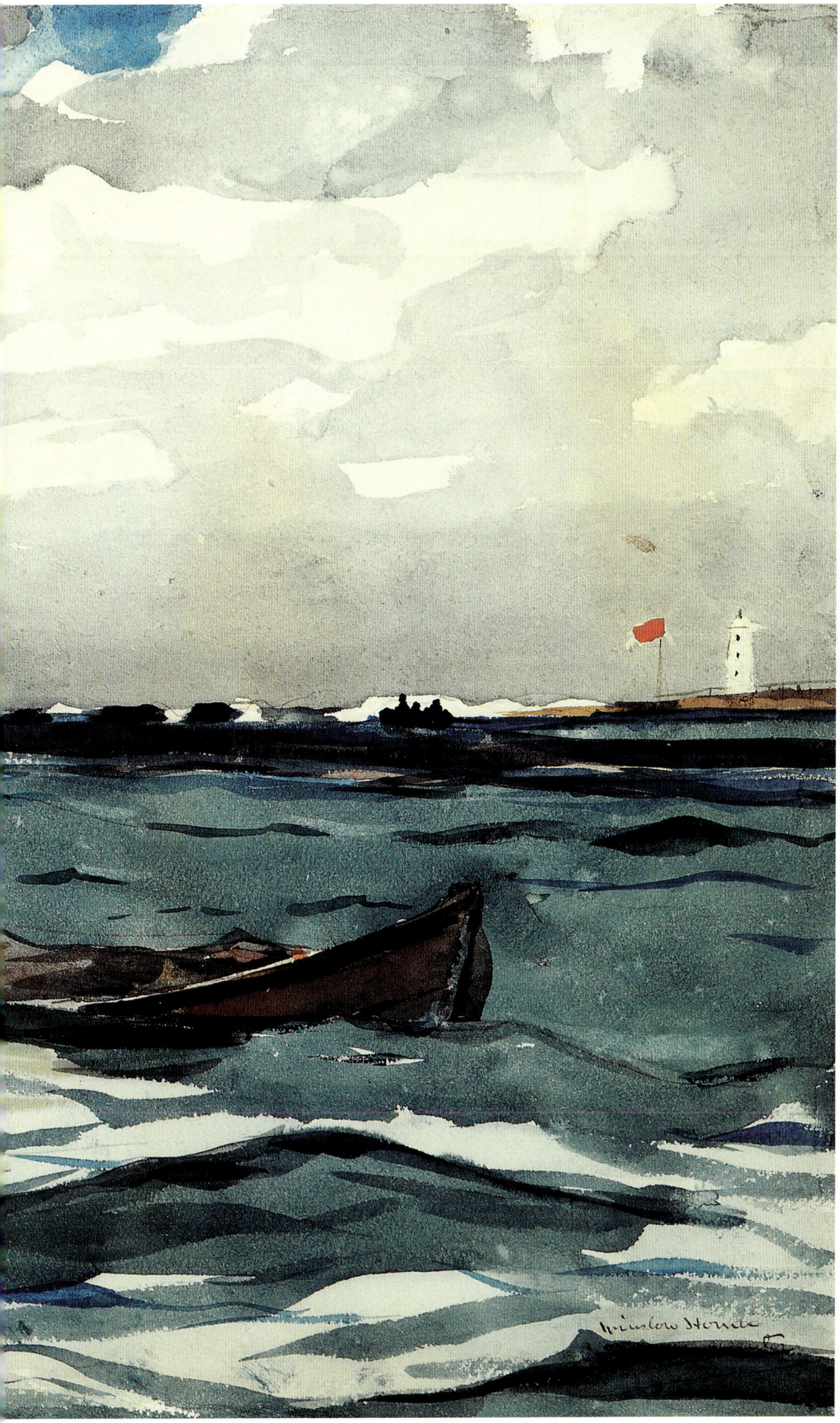

The Light House, Nassau 1899

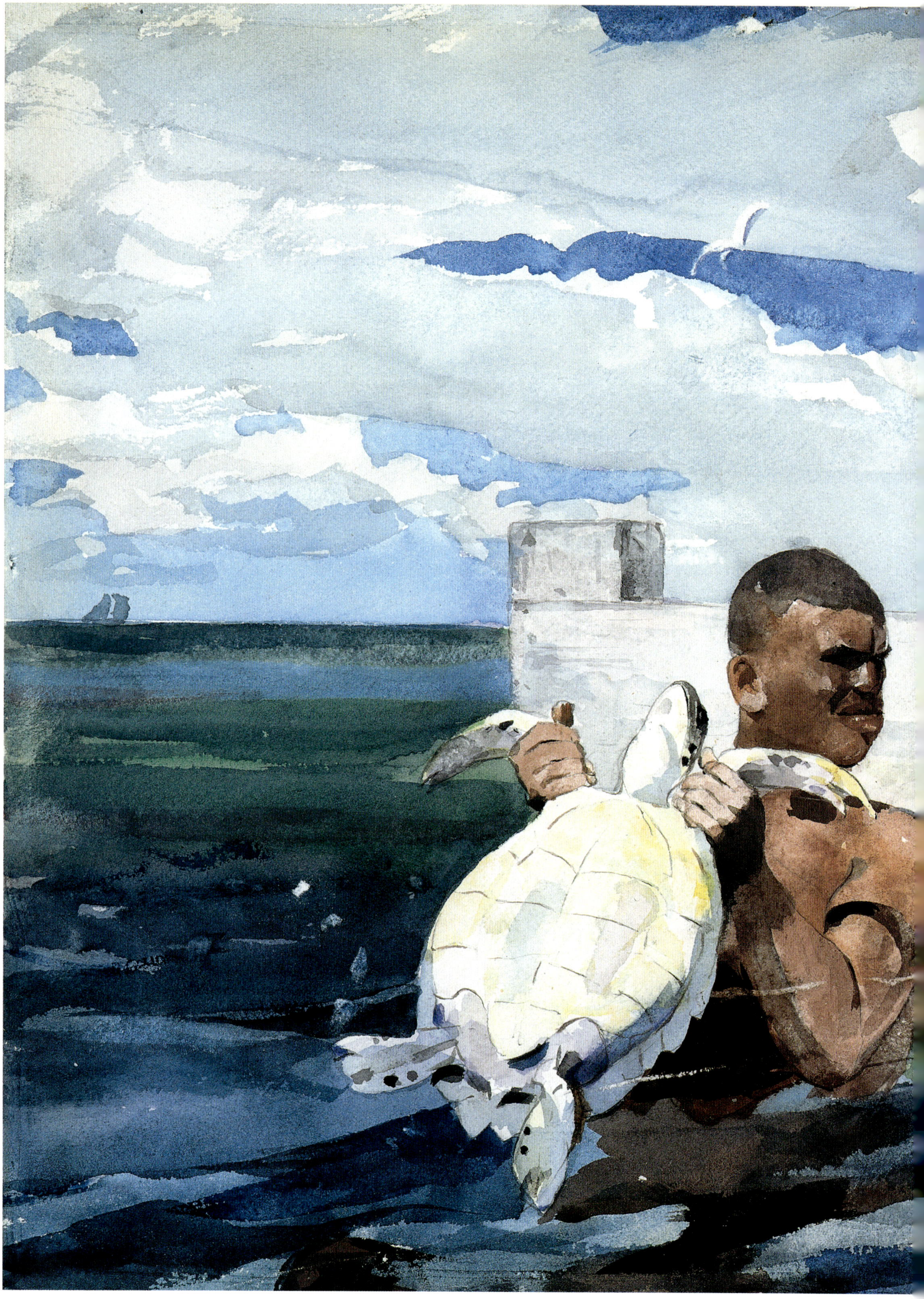

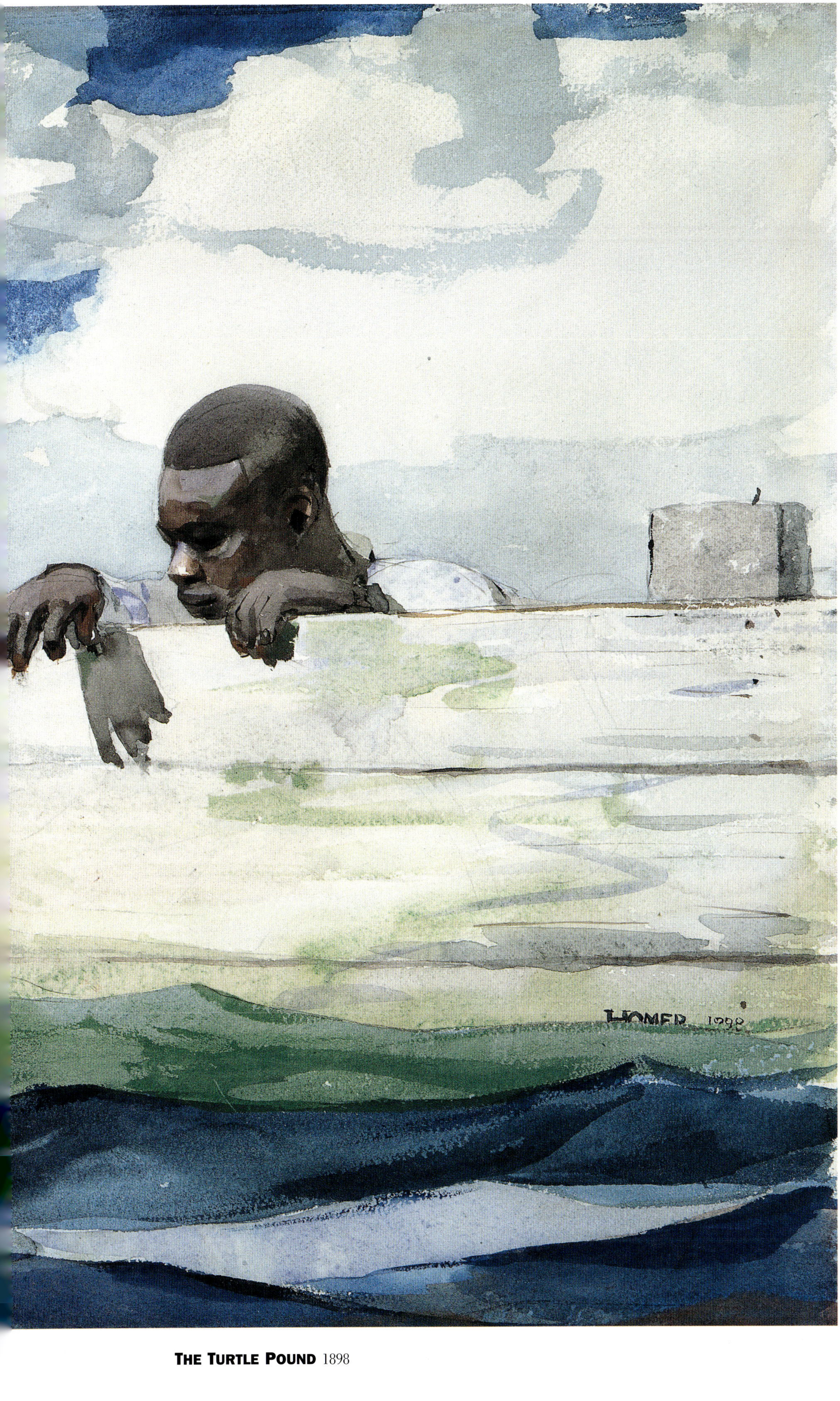

THE TURTLE POUND 1898

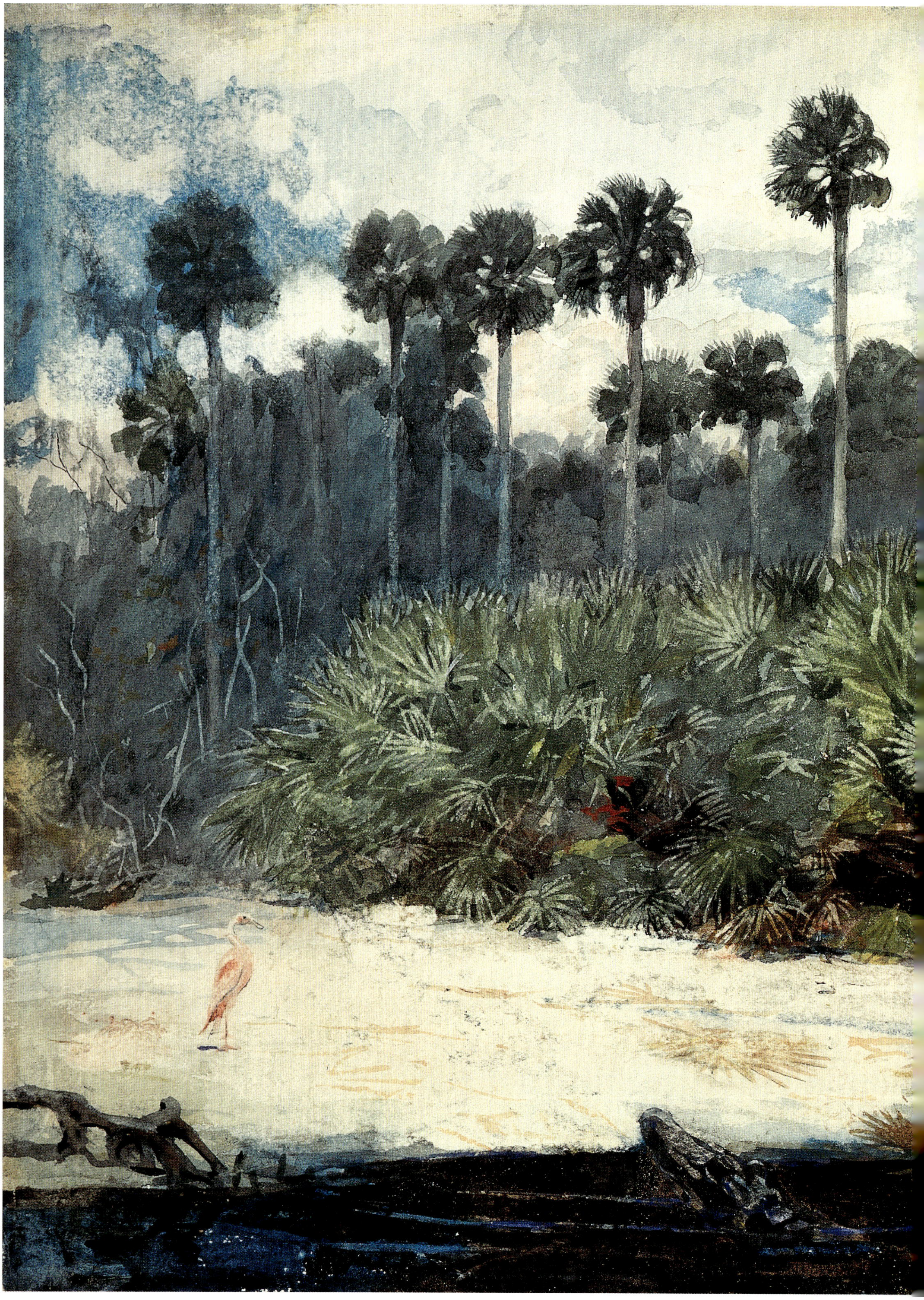

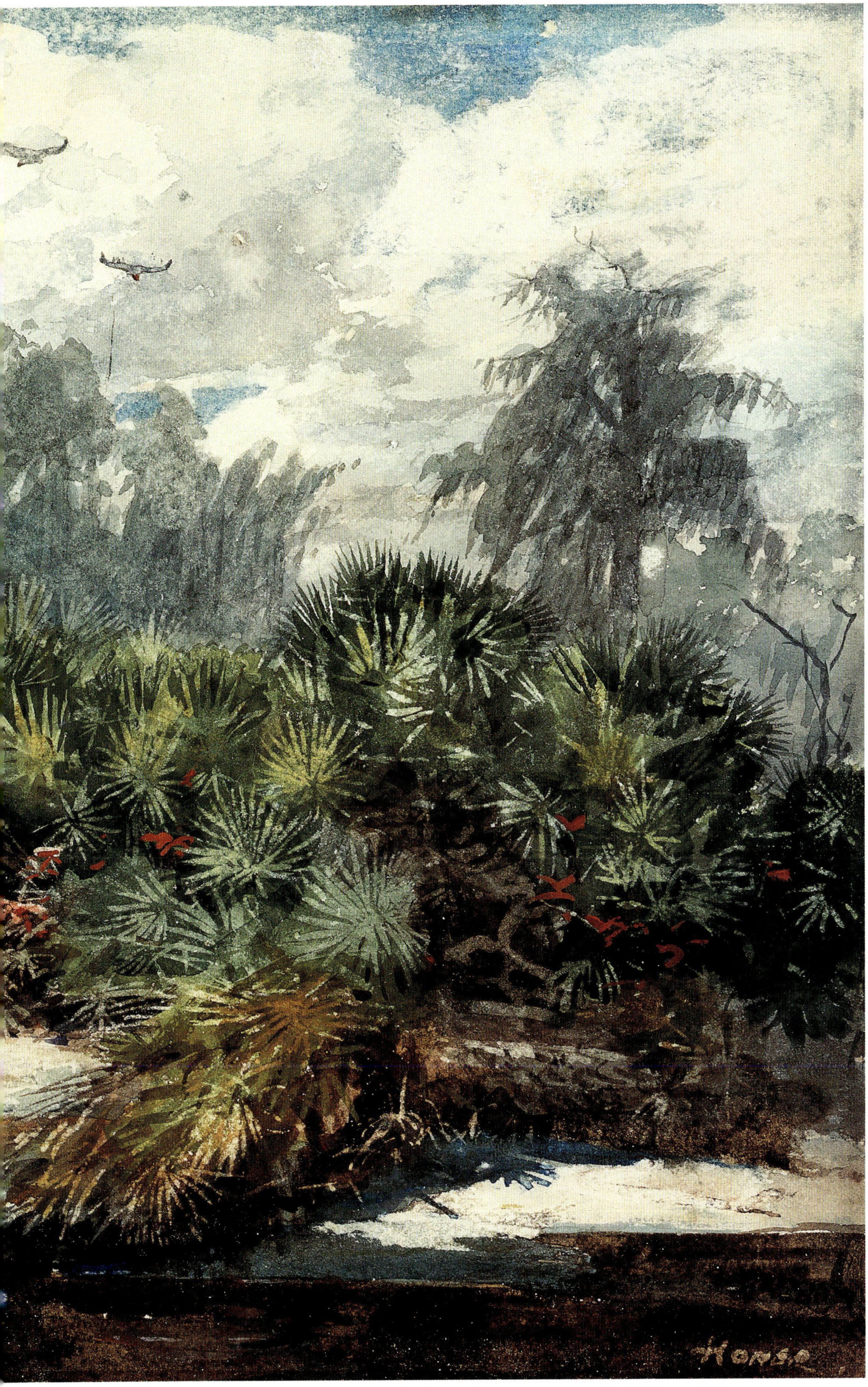

In a Florida Jungle c. 1885–1886

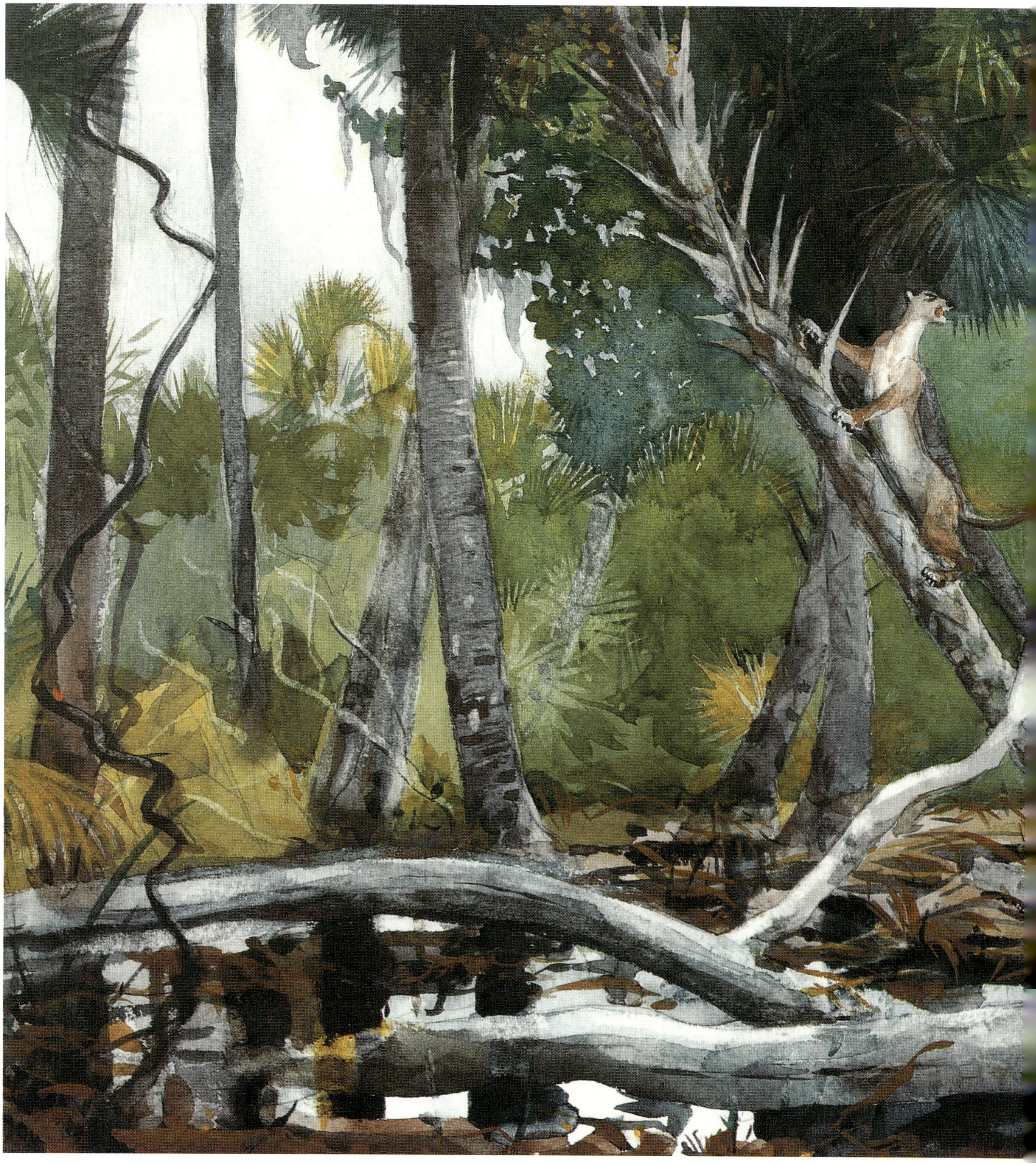

In the Jungle, Florida 1904

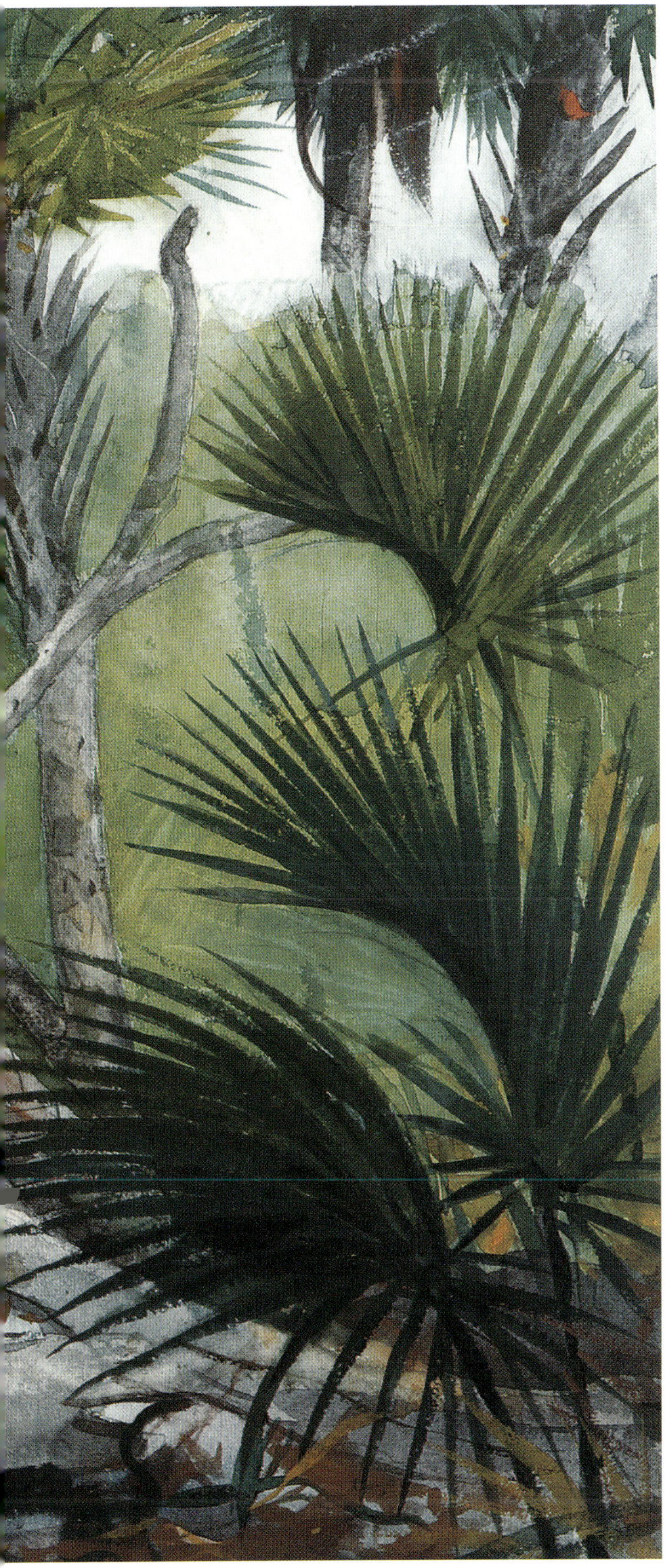

Also typical of his late style is *Key West, Negro Cabins and Palms* [pp. 204–205]. Instead of the carefully wrought details and subtractive techniques of *In a Florida Jungle*, Homer describes the scene in a few well-chosen brush-strokes. Color is reduced to a minimum, just a few bright accents in an otherwise monochrome painting. In its boldness and simplicity, *Key West, Negro Cabins & Palms* shows the artist paring down his watercolor technique to bare essentials. A lifetime of knowledge is distilled into a few fluid strokes of the brush.

The Florida watercolors from the winter of 1903–04 are Homer's last extended efforts in a medium in which he had worked with unparalleled brilliance for more than three decades. The trip included a fishing expedition up the Homosassa River in northern Florida and a journey by steamship to Key West. Here he painted a series of watercolors depicting boats at anchor in the harbor. As in the Nassau pictures, white-hulled boats against blue water form the basic compositional units. But the real subject of the Key West watercolors is the mercurial light and atmosphere of the humid tropics. There are few figures to lend drama to these works, only the changes wrought by the passage of the sun and the barometer's gyration. As Homer's understanding of the medium deepened, his approach became increasingly open-ended. Thin washes flow freely across the paper, puddling and bleeding one into another. The artist embraces these accidental effects, knowing just when and where to intervene. In *Fishing Boats, Key West* [pp. 214–215], he captures the ominous sky and choppy water preceding a storm with free-flowing washes that ripple across the paper. The briefest notations made with pencil and the tip of the brush are sufficient to indicate the arrayed masts of the fishing boats. Washes worked wet into wet capture clouds heavy with rain and agitated water. Homer finished the work by spattering the paper to create the effect of the first large raindrops hitting the surface of the water. In *Schooners at Anchor, Key West* [pp. 212–213], the temperamental nature of the water-drenched air lends a dramatic element to an otherwise placid scene; thickening clouds and fluttering canvas hint at turbulence to come.

The confidence of Homer's late style is well illustrated by images he painted along the Homosassa River. Homer clearly loved these swampy bayous with their lush vegetation. The power of his brush to suggest more than meets the eye is apparent in *Homosassa Jungle* [pp. 210–211], where overhanging palmettos and dark undergrowth

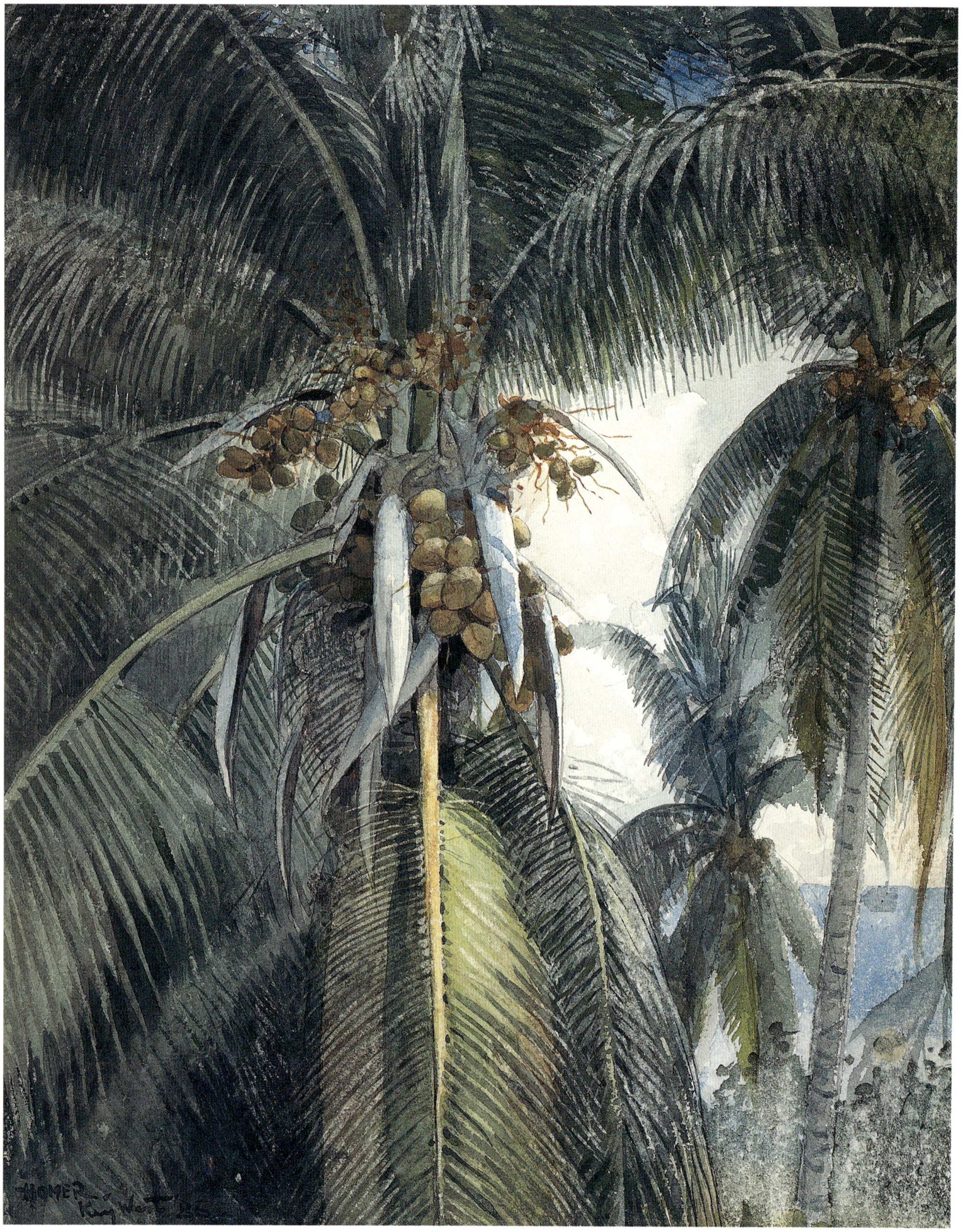

Coconut Palms, Key West 1886

Palm Trees, Florida 1904

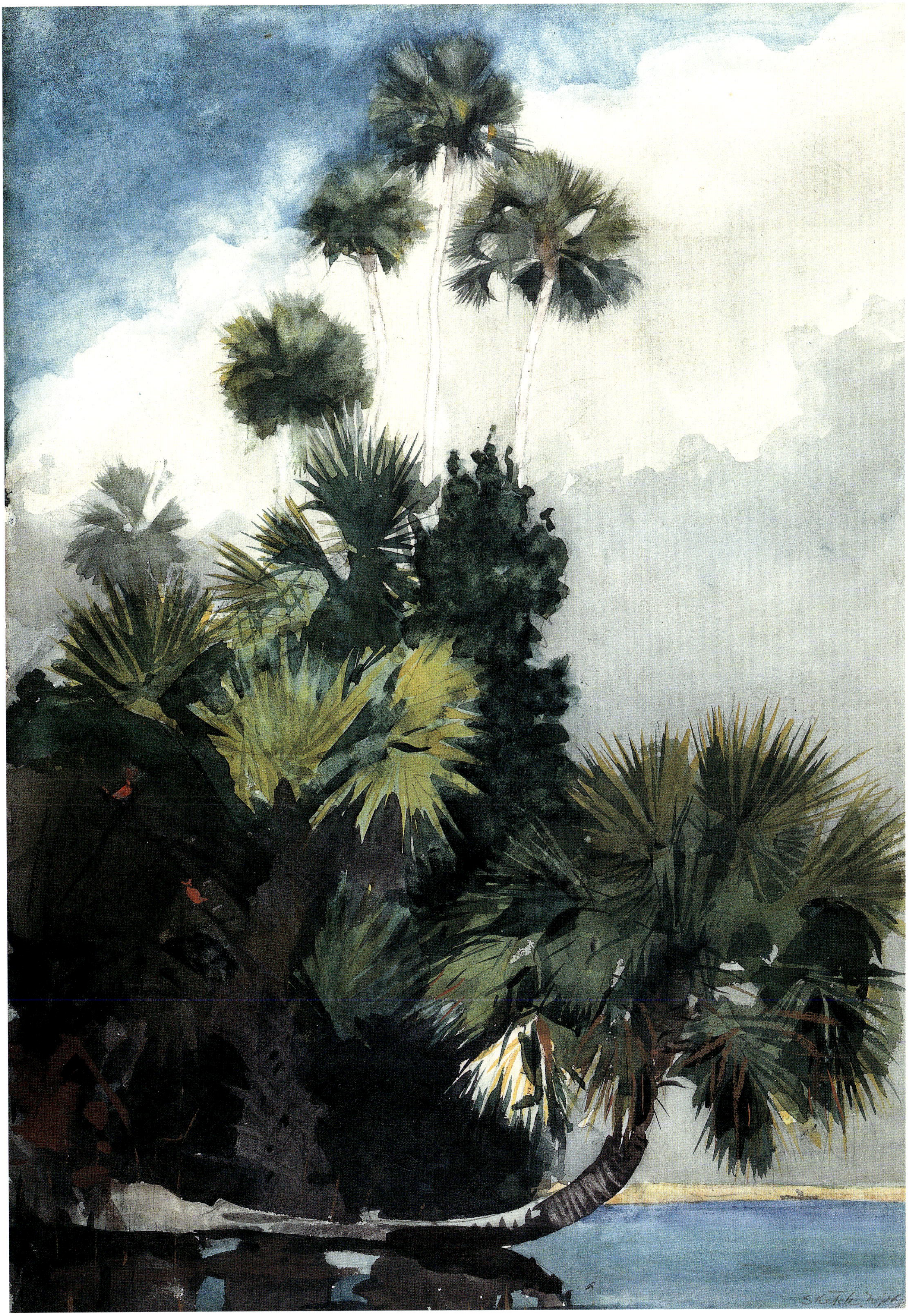

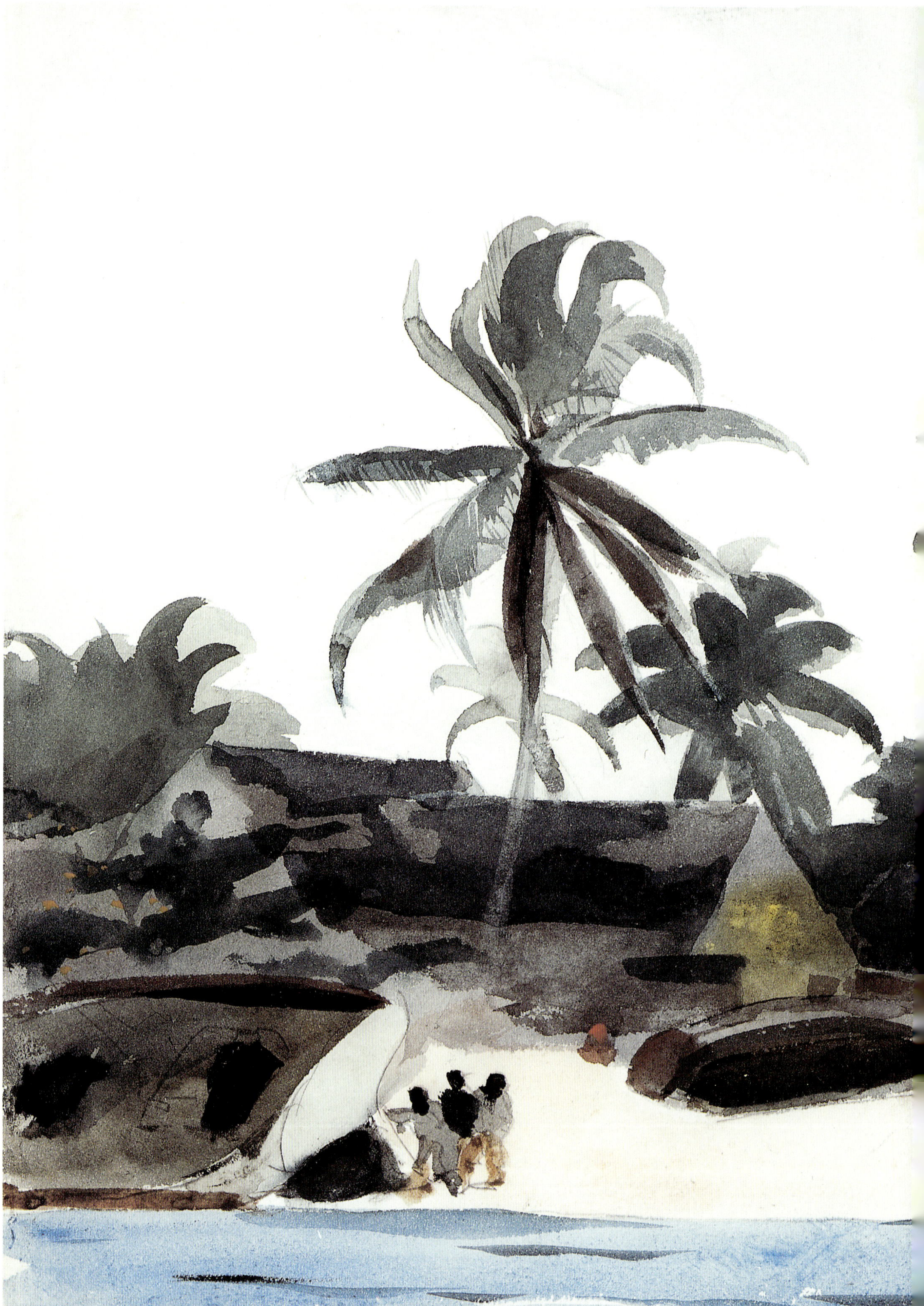

Key West, Negro Cabins & Palms 1898

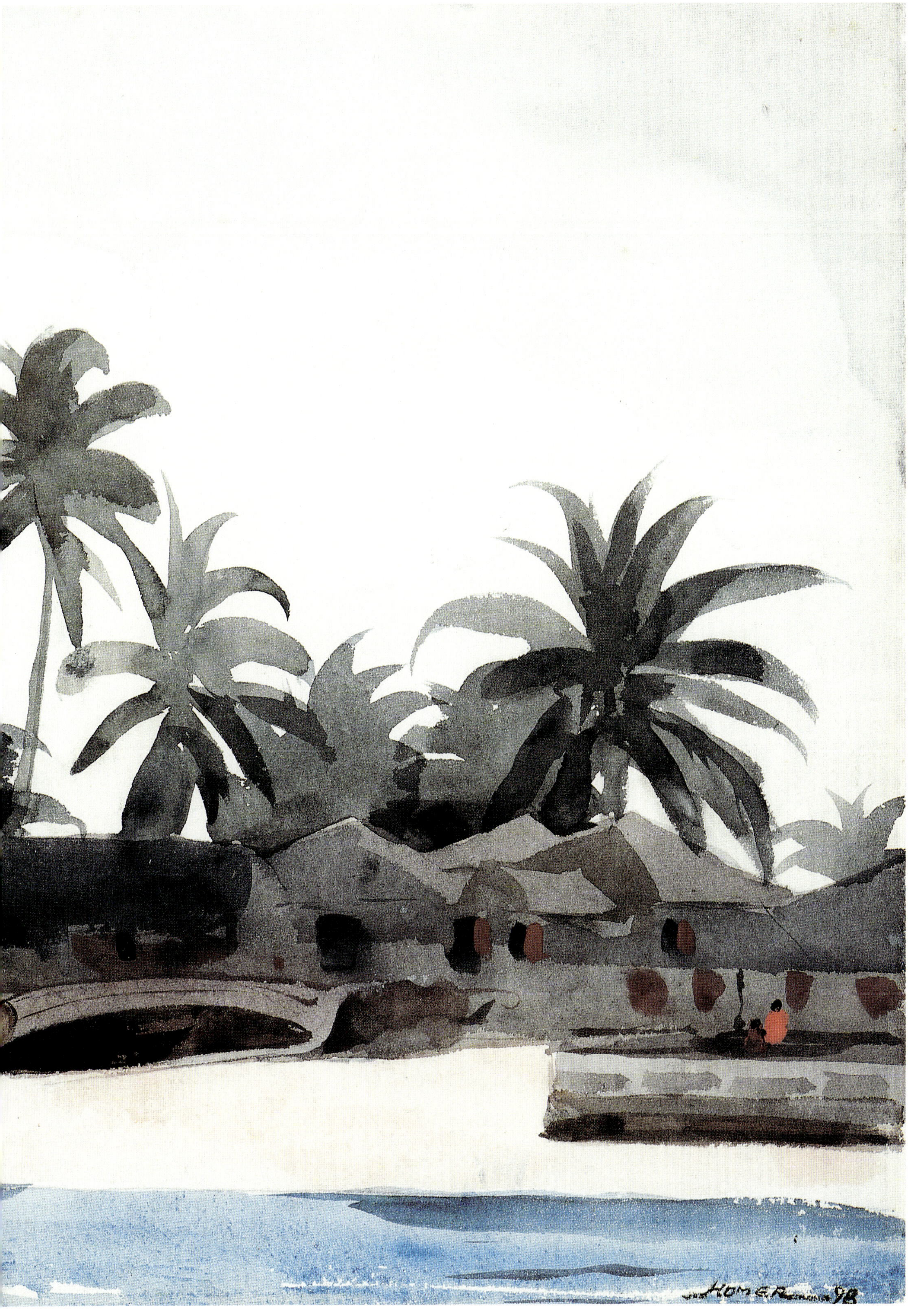
HOMER 98

are indicated in rapidly executed washes of warm and cool tones. Unlike the labored 1886 *In a Florida Jungle*, here Homer uses a minimum of detail, relying instead on the mottled splotches of wet color to suggest hazy, dappled sunshine filtering through thick leaves. The pictures of bass fishing that Homer painted in Florida are his most candid treatment of this subject, as if he were finally acknowledging the violence inherent in his own favorite sport. Works like *Foul Hooked Black Bass* leave us in no doubt as to the agony of the creature who struggles on the hook. Homer forces us to confront the reality of death up close. In the Adirondacks watercolors, scenes of fishing are characterized by serenity—it is the deer hunters who live by violence. In the Florida fishing scenes, the artist finally includes himself in the cycle of violence in which all creatures are caught.

Homer returned to Florida in December 1904. Only a single watercolor came out of this trip, his final work in a medium to which he had devoted over thirty years. *Diamond Shoal* [pp. 216–217] is an ambitious piece, depicting the storm-tossed boat that is a recurring theme in his late oil paintings. The watercolor actually depicts the

AT TAMPA 1885

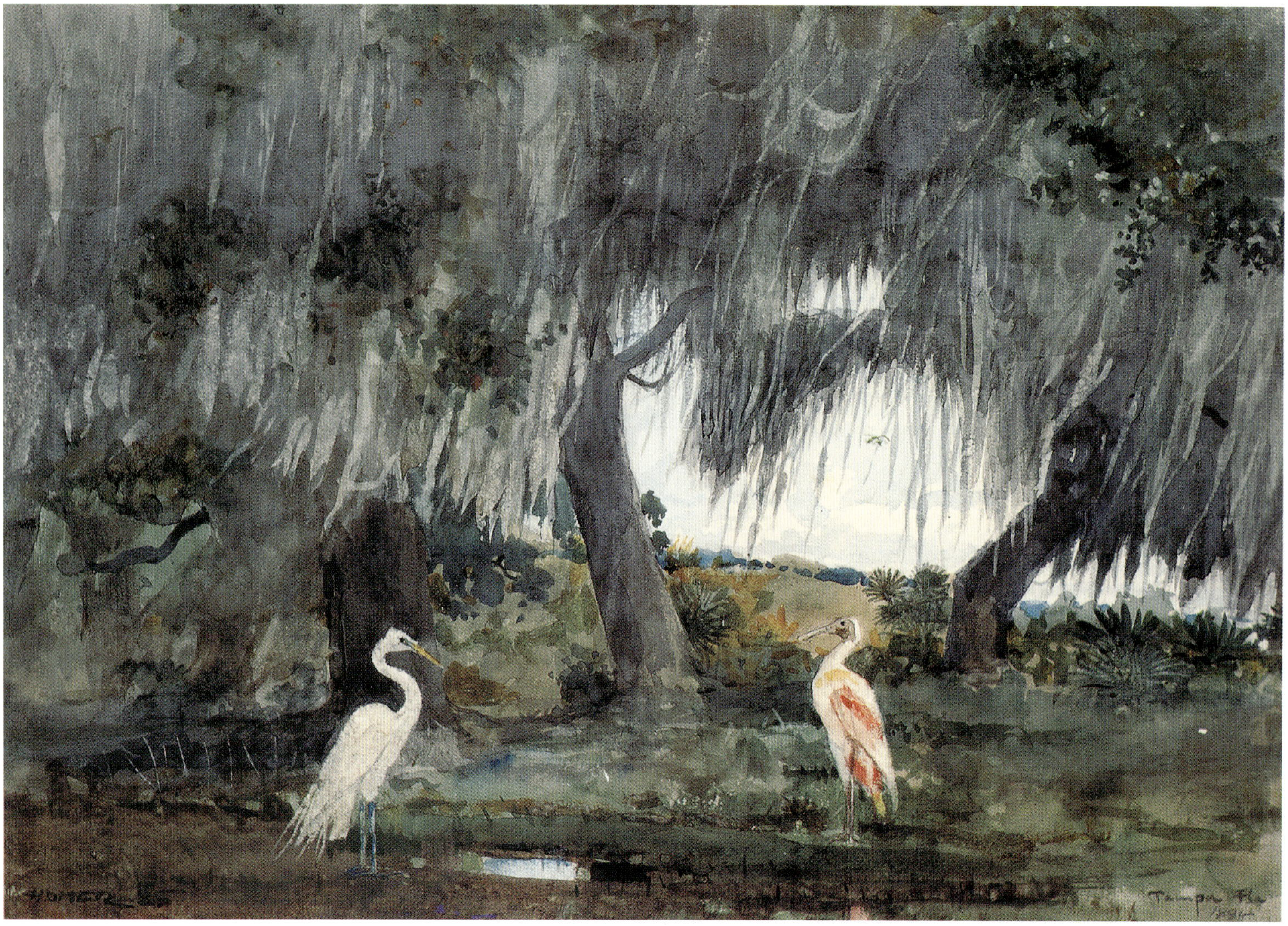

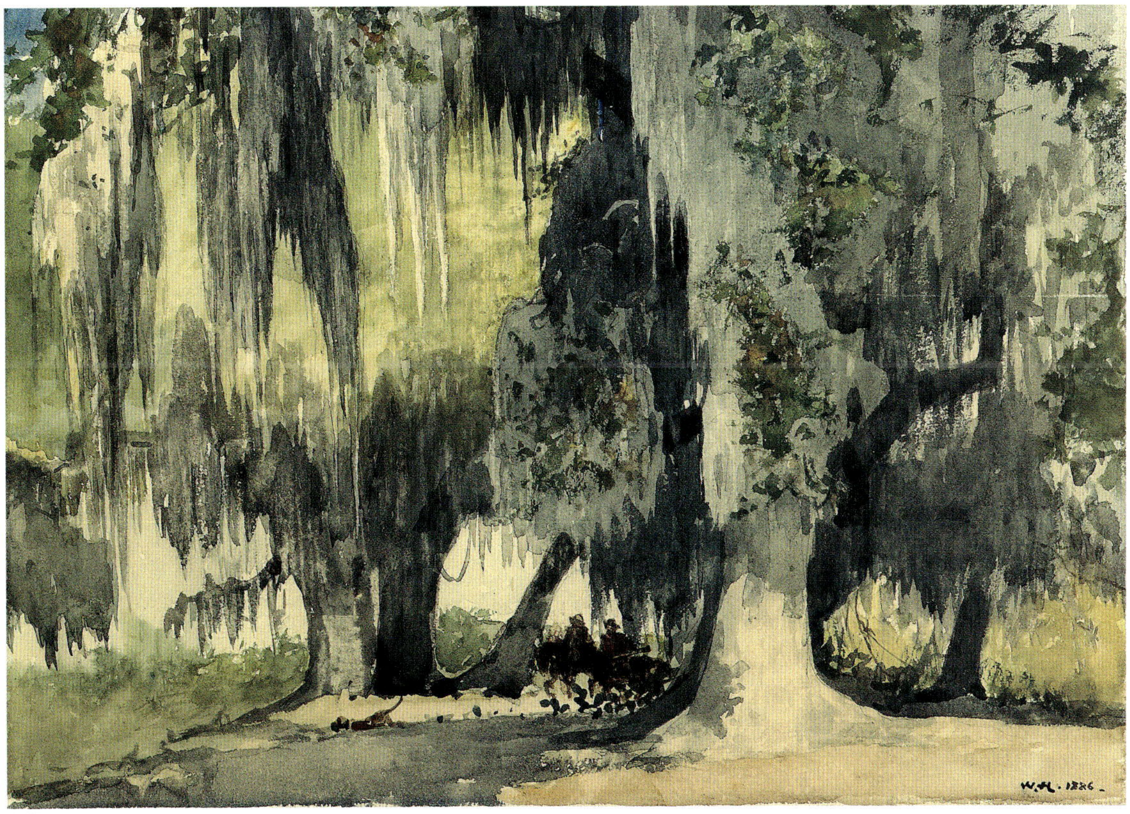

LIVE OAKS 1886

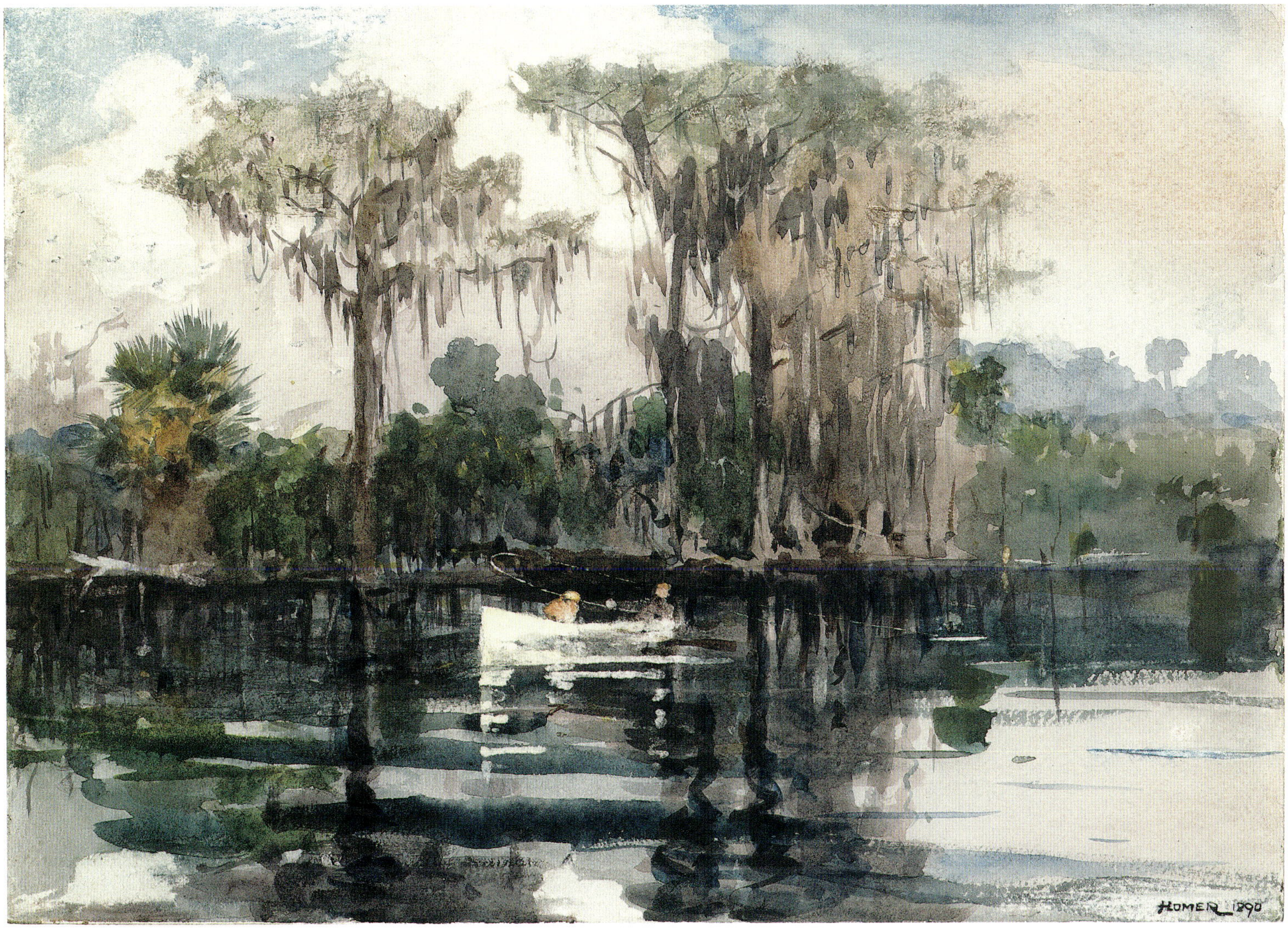

ST. JOHNS RIVER, FLORIDA 1890

dangerous shallows off Cape Hatteras, North Carolina—a region Homer must have observed from aboard a Florida-bound steamer—whose turbulent waters earned it the nickname "graveyard of the Atlantic." Homer captures the agitated water with brushwork that is both vigorous and varied. The white of the reserved paper here does not evoke warm sunlight but the ghastly, unnatural glow of a storm at sea. Though it feels like a studio creation, it is a far more dramatic piece than *The Wreck of the Iron Crown*, the watercolor it most closely resembles in subject. Homer now points the prow of the boat straight at the viewer for maximum impact. The two sailors who desperately trim the sail are shown only from the back, anonymous figures who pit their skill and courage against the fury of the sea.

Homer's career as a painter in watercolor concludes where it began: with the sea. *Diamond Shoal* forms a fitting bookend to works like *Gloucester Harbor* and *Sailing the Catboat.*. The boat whose prow once boldly pointed to distant horizons has now reversed tack and is heading for home. But the return journey is anything but placid. Those once certain they could navigate life's currents now struggle just to survive. This is the work of an artist nearing the end of his life, chastened by experience and less confident in the future.

FOUL HOOKED BLACK BASS 1904

HOMOSASSA RIVER 1904

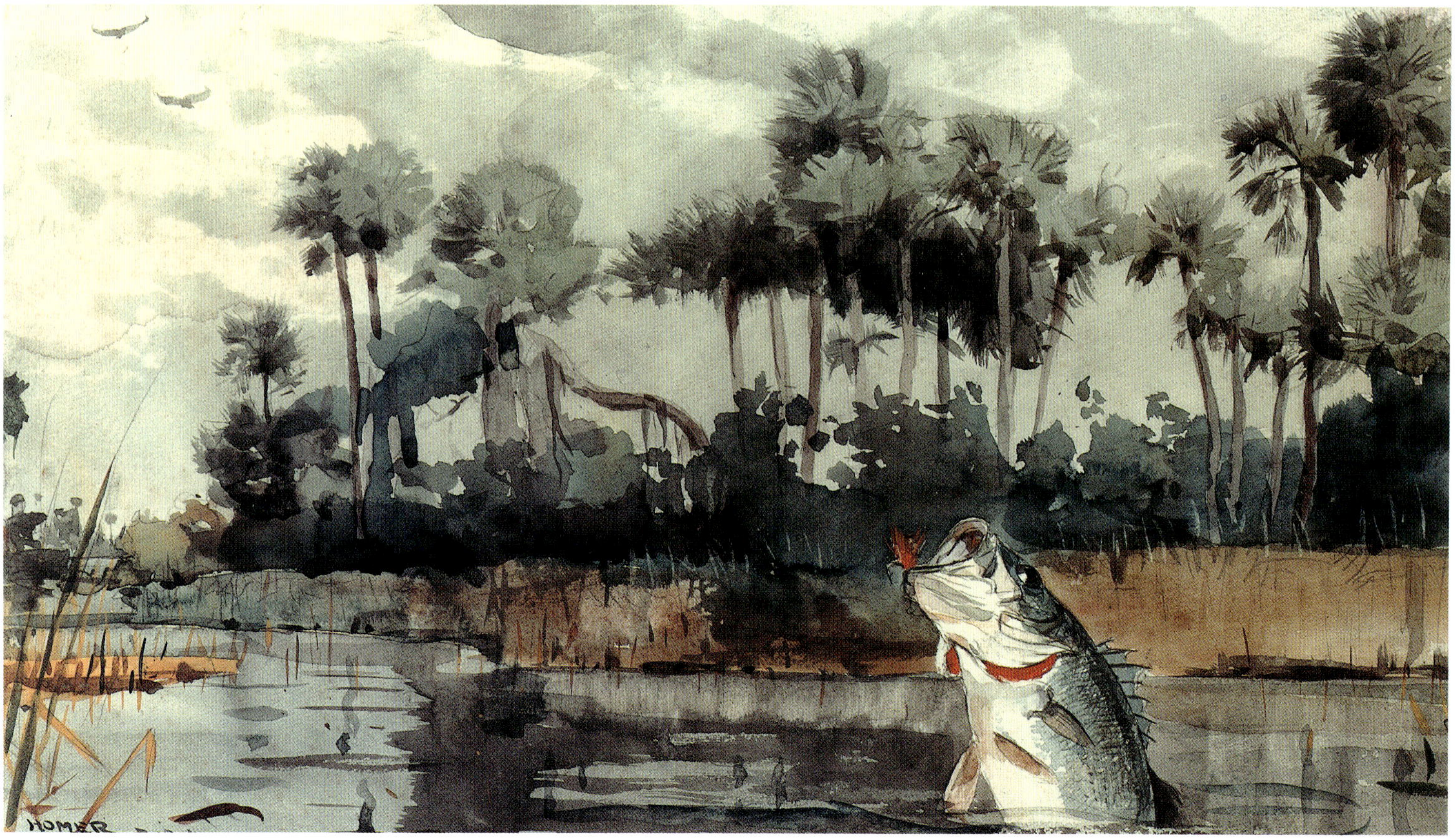

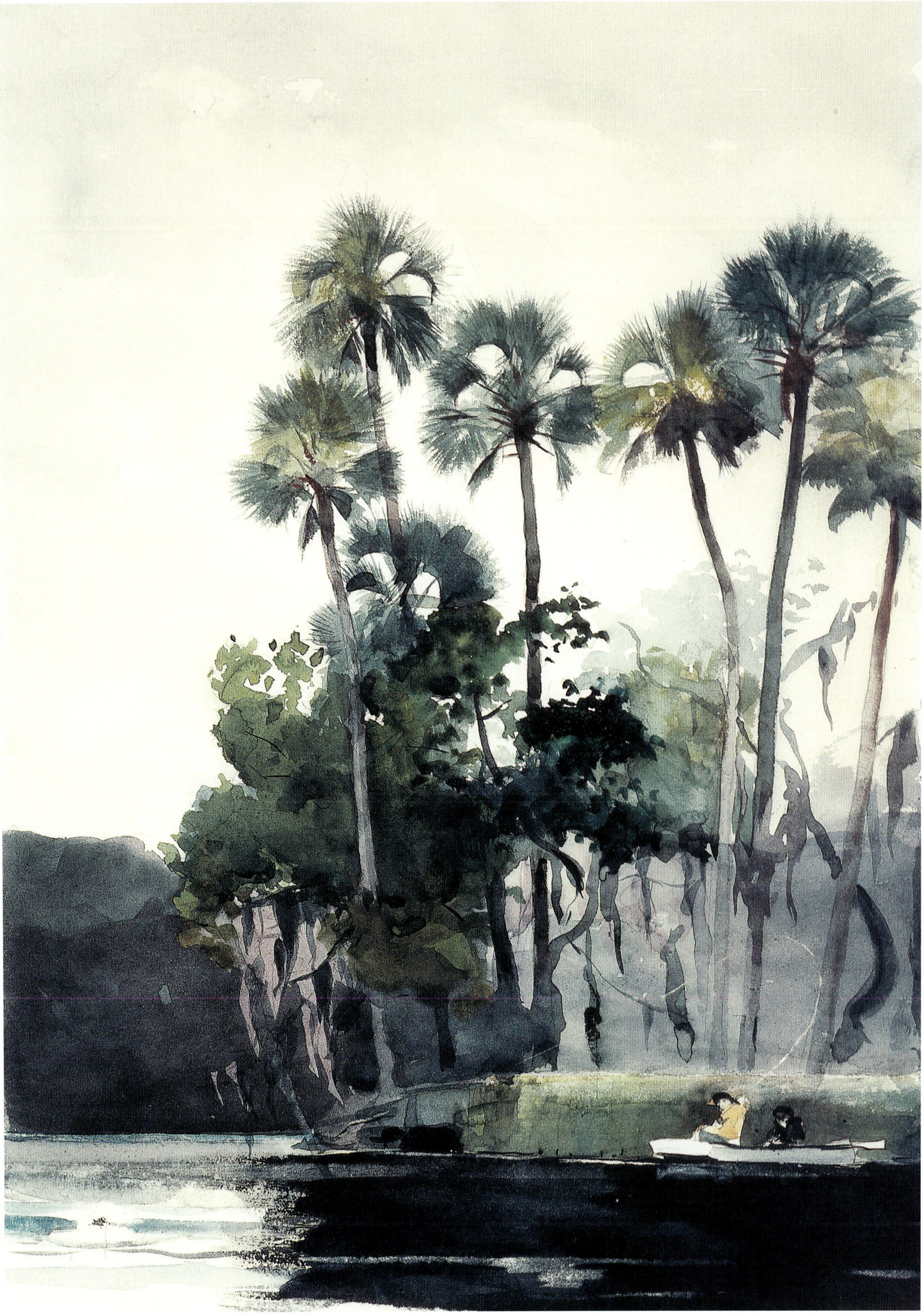

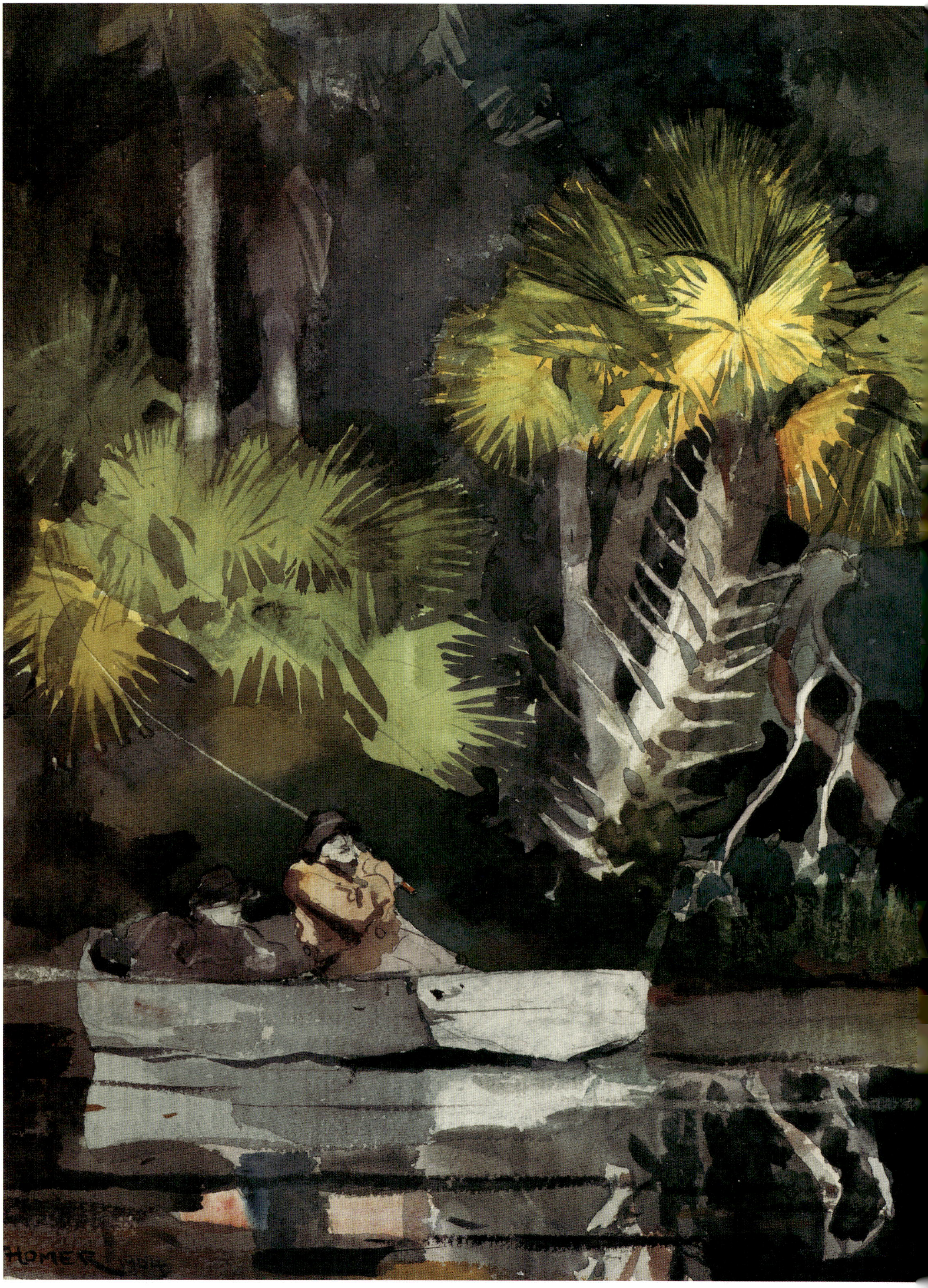

HOMOSASSA JUNGLE 1904

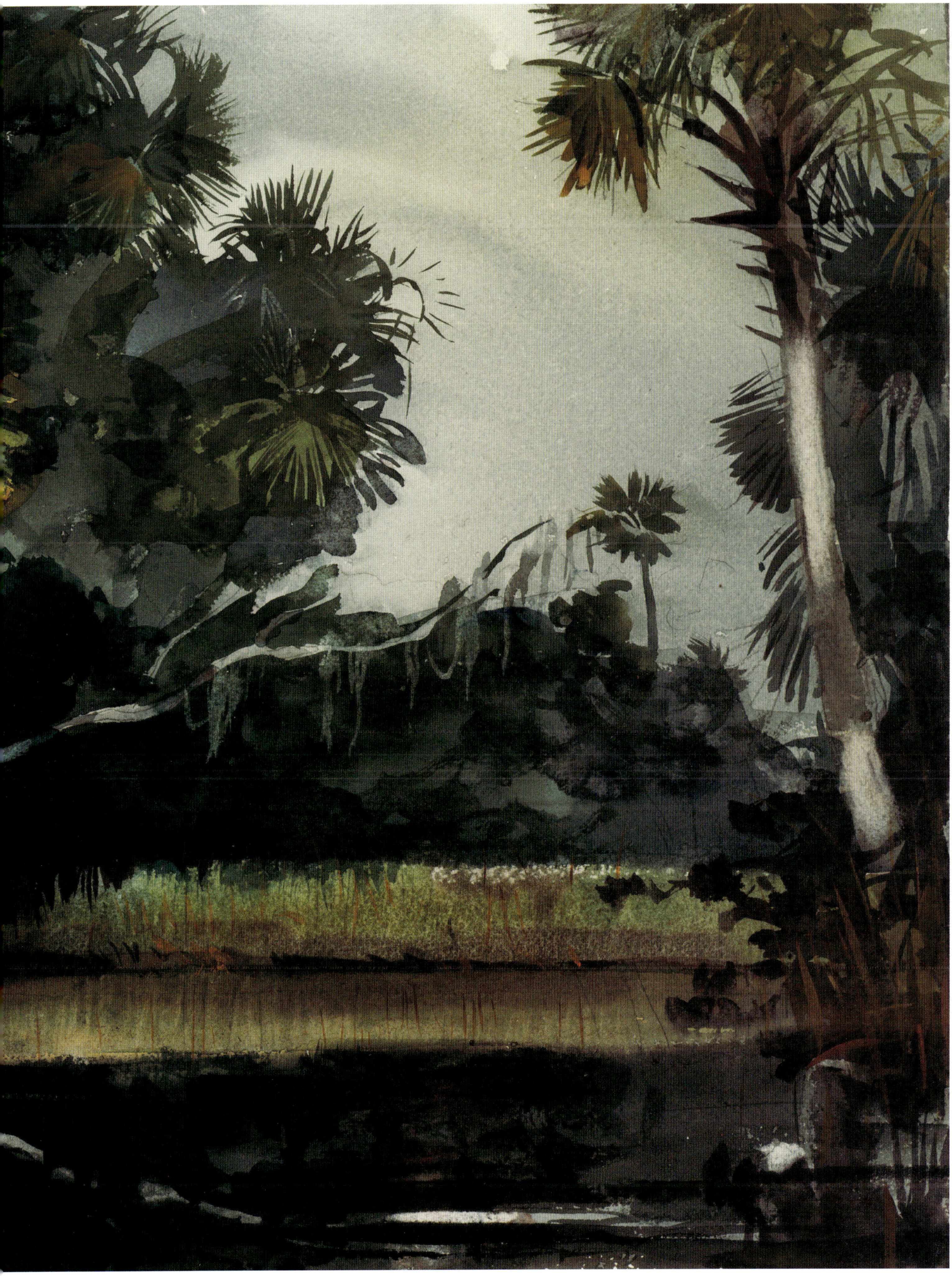

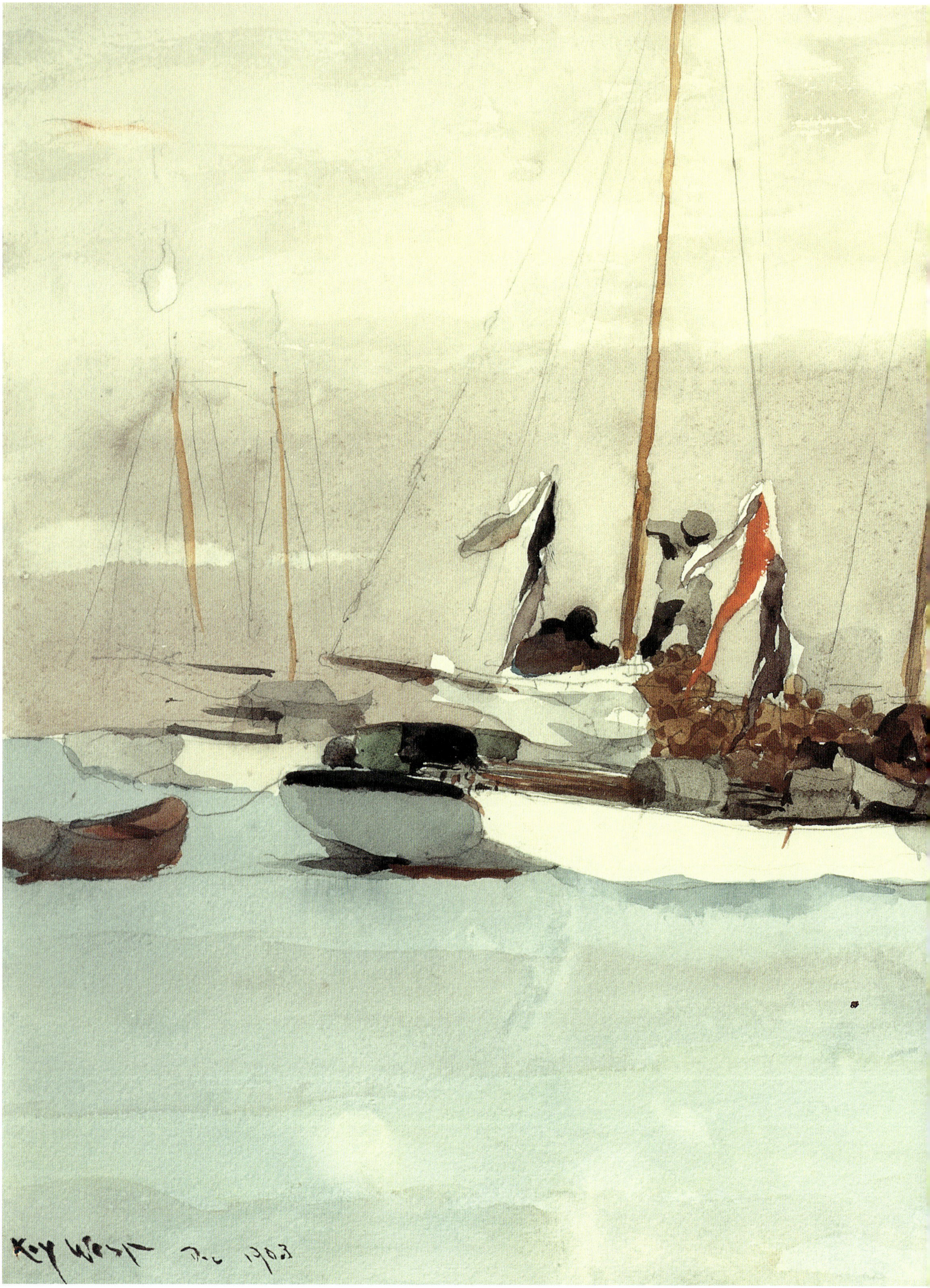
Key West Dec 1903

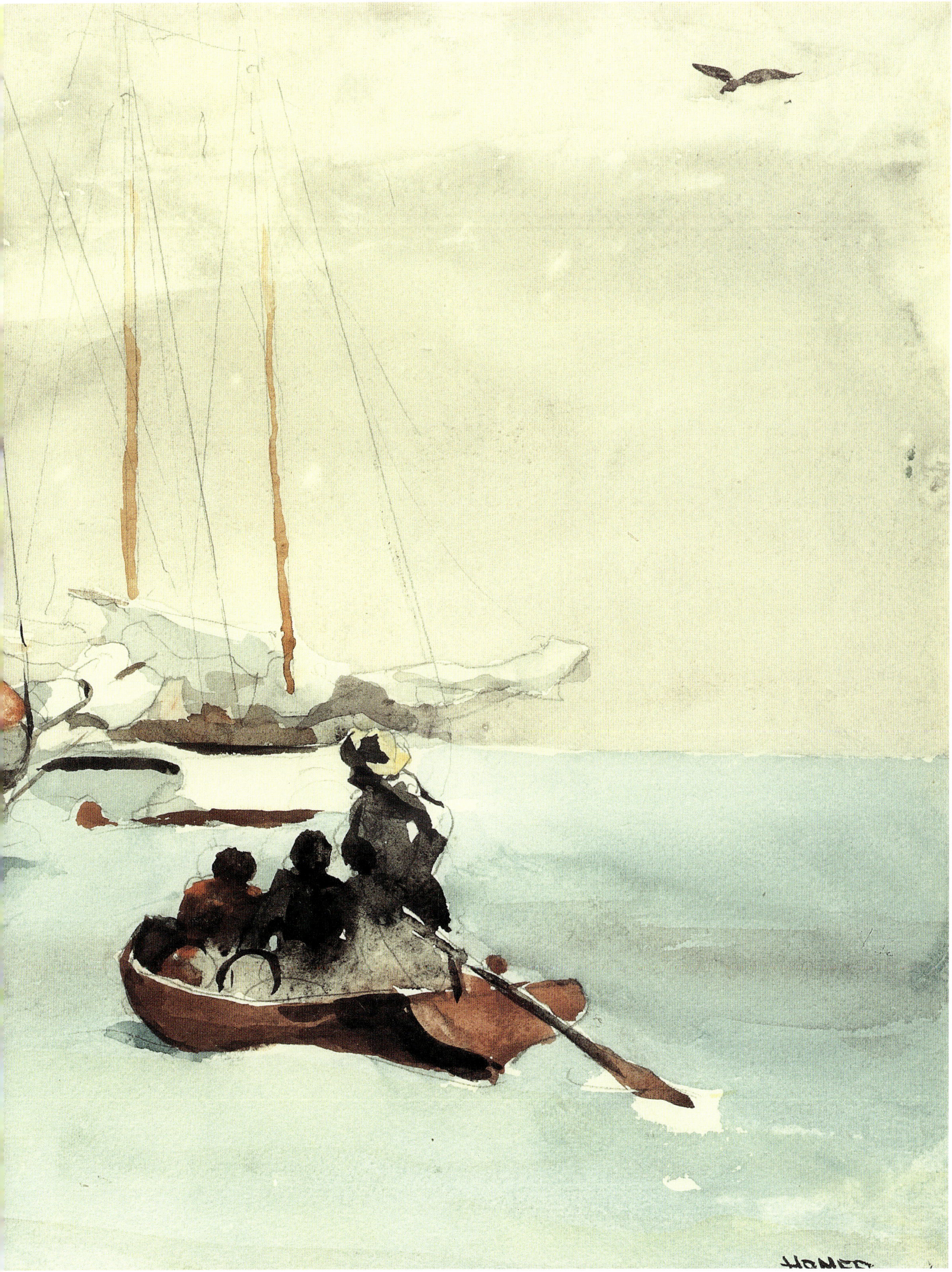

Schooners at Anchor, Key West 1903

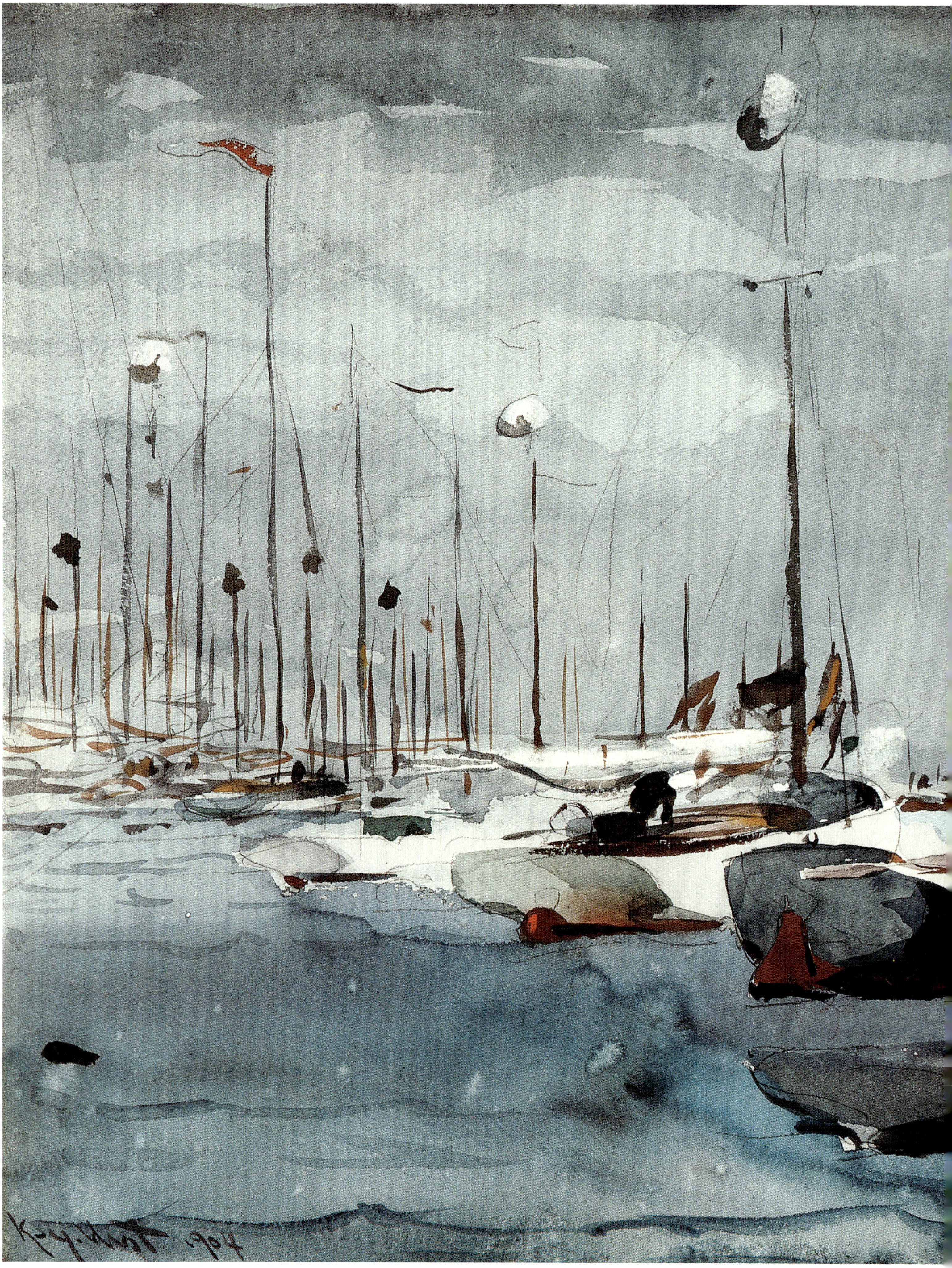

FISHING BOATS, KEY WEST 1904

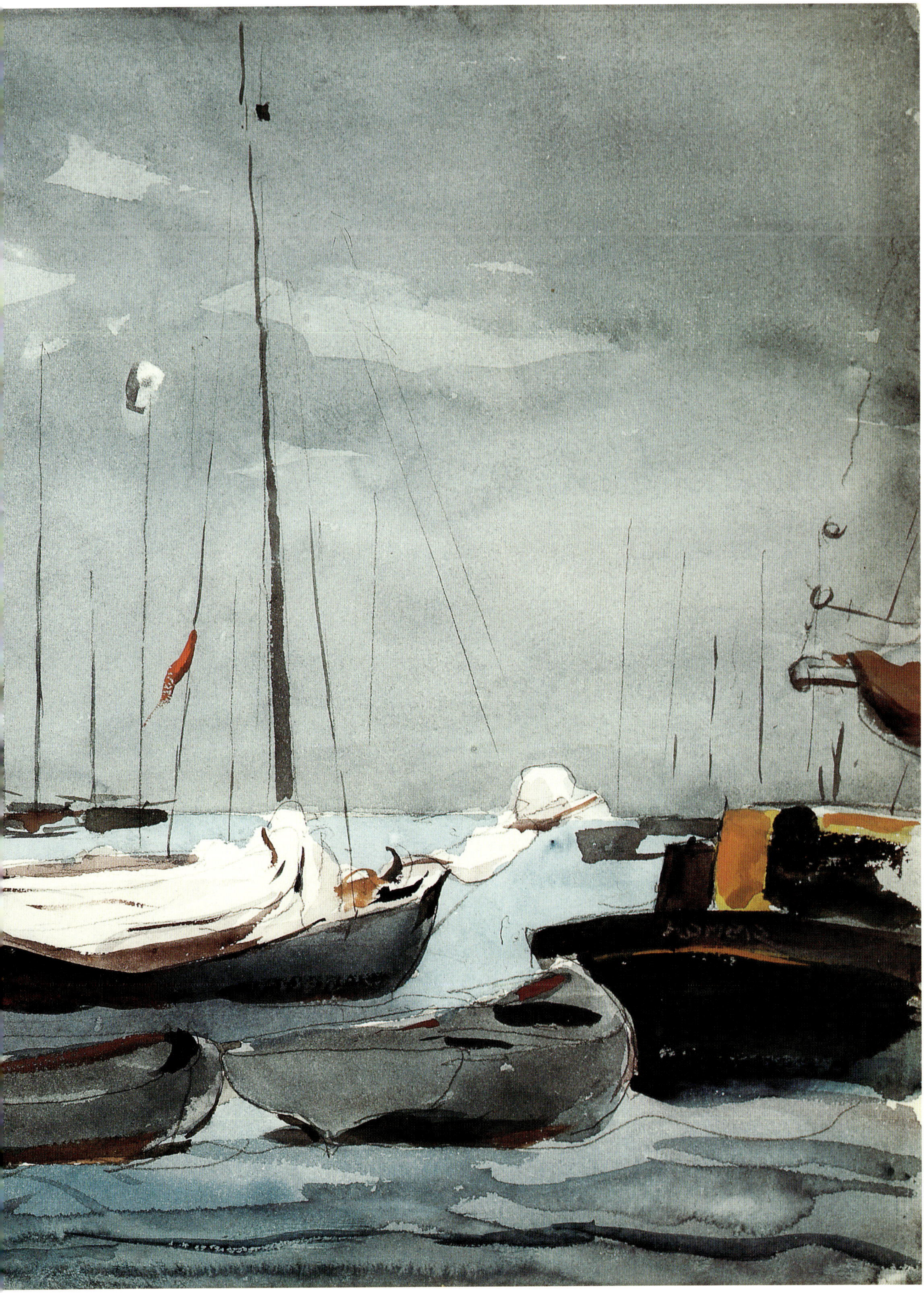

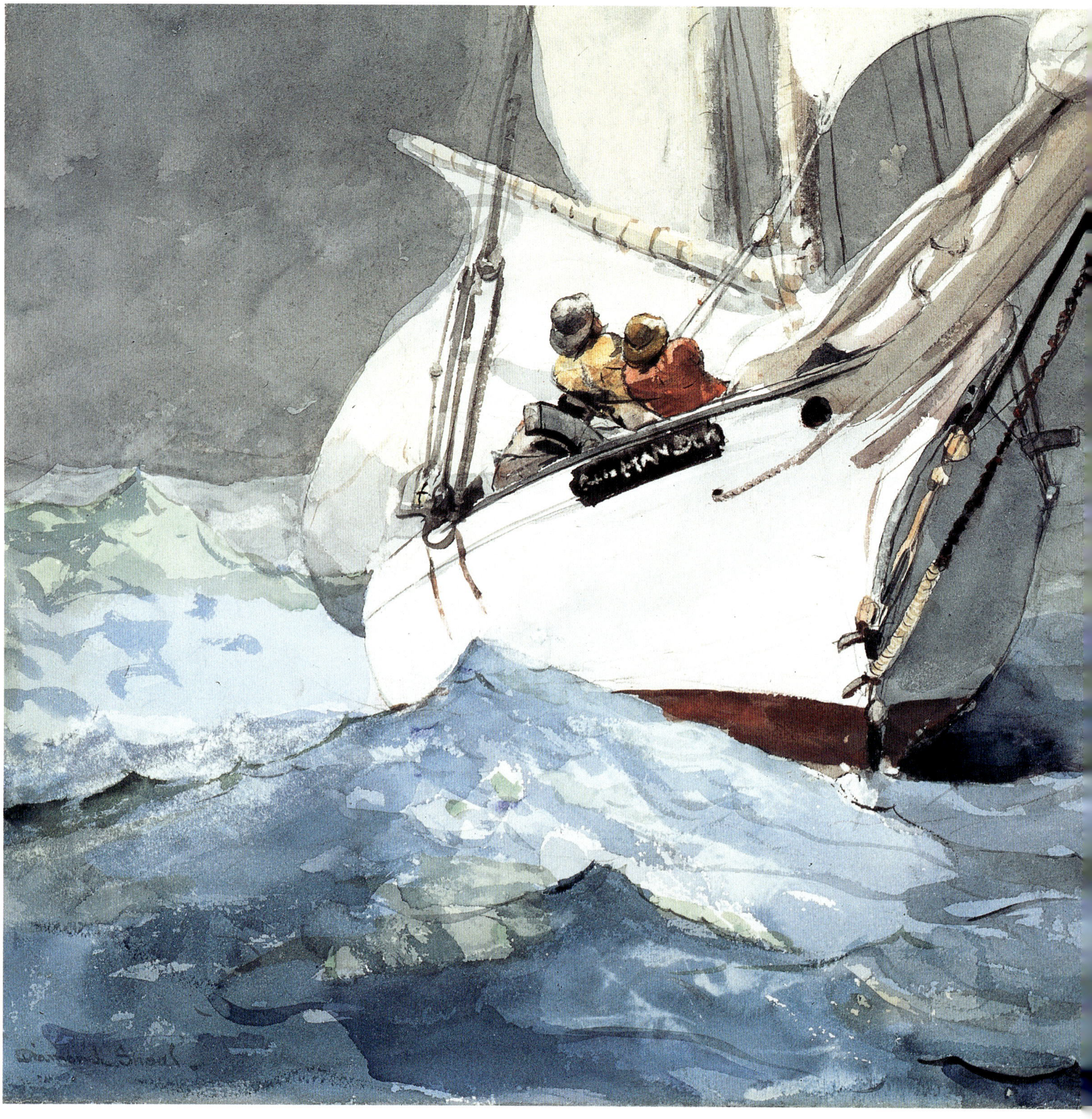

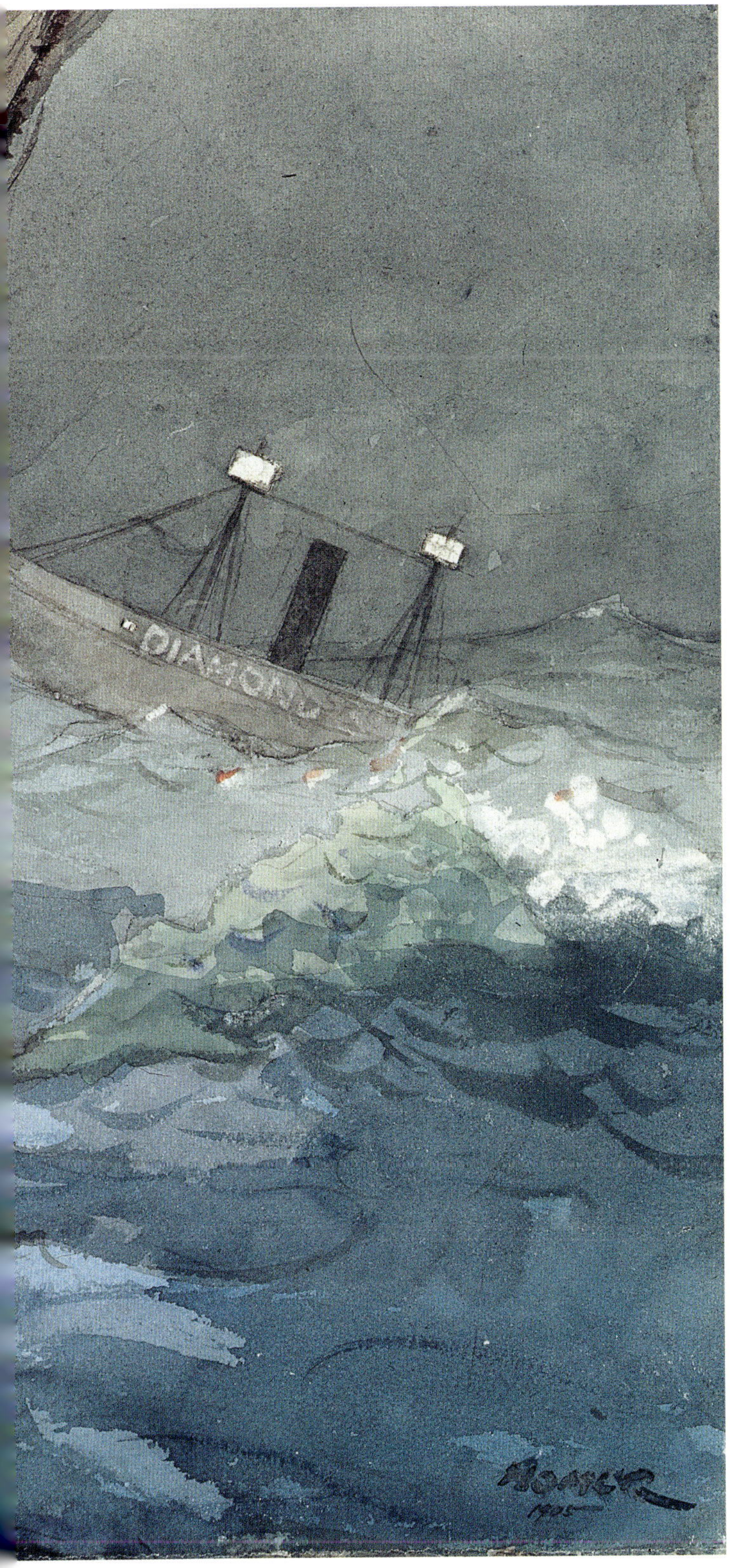

DIAMOND SHOAL 1905

Diamond Shoal is a work of astonishing power for an artist in his seventieth year. Homer completed a few more oil paintings after 1905, including the well-known images *Left and Right* (1909) and *Driftwood* (1909), his last work in any medium, but never again picked up his watercolor brushes. His retirement reflected perhaps his diminished energy, but certainly no loss of skill. Now a famous man, Homer could afford to rest on his laurels, painting only when the spirit moved him. A few years earlier, he had written to his friend John Beatty in his typically grumbling tone: "I only painted for pleasure, and now that it has ceased to give me pleasure there is no object left. I get lots more pleasure out of other things now; I would rather go fishing. Oh, I suppose if there was the hope of great financial gain, that would be an incentive." Before his trip to Key West, he wrote to his nephew Arthur: "I have an idea at present of doing some work but do not know how long that will last—at any rate I will once more have a good feed of goat flesh & smoke some good cigars & catch some red snappers." The tone is typical of Homer's letters toward the end of his life, reflecting a diminished commitment to doing serious work. But one also senses an artist at peace with himself, fully cognizant of his achievement and without the need to drive himself. It was late in his career when he wrote, "You will see, in the future I will live by my watercolors." These are the words of a man looking back on a life in art with justifiable pride in all he had accomplished and certain of his place in history.

Today, more than ninety years after his death, Homer's watercolors continue to attract the attention of scholars, writers, and curators. Hardly a month goes by without a new exhibition at a major museum featuring at least a few of his works in this medium. And over the years, whatever the fashion of the moment, they have continued to inspire other artists and capture the imagination of the broader artgoing public. The freshness and immediacy of the watercolors perhaps appeal more to contemporary eyes than the grander rhetoric of the oil paintings. Their focus on the relationship between the human and natural realms, their acute sensitivity to ecological issues, makes them seem particularly relevent at the beginning of the twenty-first century. Homer's prediction that his watercolors would earn him lasting fame has, it would seem, been amply confirmed.

CREDITS

The Adirondack Guide 1894
Watercolor over graphite on paper,
15 1/8 x 21 1/2 in. (38.4 x 54.6 cm.).
Museum of Fine Arts, Boston.
Bequest of Mrs. Anna H. Wadleigh, 47.268.
Courtesy, Museum of Fine Arts, Boston. Reproduced with permission.
© 2001, Museum of Fine Arts, Boston. All rights reserved.
136–137

Adirondack Lake 1889
Watercolor over graphite on paper,
14 x 20 in. (35.56 x 50.8 cm.).
Museum of Fine Arts, Boston.
Warren Collection, William Wilkins Warren Fund, 23.215.
Courtesy, Museum of Fine Arts, Boston. Reproduced with permission.
© 2001, Museum of Fine Arts, Boston. All rights reserved.
162–163

After the Hurricane, Bahamas 1899
Watercolor with touches of reddish-brown gouache and with traces of scraping over graphite on off-white wove paper, 15 x 21 3/8 in. (38 x 54.3 cm.).
The Art Institute of Chicago.
Mr. and Mrs. Martin A. Ryerson Collection, 1933.1235.
Photograph © 2001, The Art Institute of Chicago, All Rights Reserved.
192

An Afterglow 1883
Watercolor over graphite on thick, moderately textured, cream wove paper, 15 x 21 1/2 in. (38 x 54.7 cm.).
Museum of Fine Arts, Boston.
Bequest of William P. Blake in memory of his mother, Mary M. J. Dehon Blake, 22.606.
Courtesy, Museum of Fine Arts, Boston. Reproduced with permission.
© 2001, Museum of Fine Arts, Boston. All rights reserved.
94–95

Along the Road, Bahamas 1885
Watercolor and pencil on paper,
18 x 14 in. (45.7 x 35.6 cm.).
Courtesy of Christie's Images, Inc., New York.
126

Apple Picking 1878
Watercolor and gouache on paper,
7 x 8 3/8 in. (17.1 x 20.7 cm.).
Terra Foundation for the Arts.
Daniel J. Terra Collection, 1992.7.
Photography courtesy of Terra Foundation for the Arts, Chicago.
56

The Army of the Potomac—A Sharp-Shooter on Picket Duty 1862
Wood engraving, 9 1/16 x 13 5/8 in. (23 x 34.7 cm.).
14

The Artist's Brother, Charles Savage Homer, Jr. 1880
Watercolor, gouache and pencil on paper,
21 1/2 x 16 in. (54.5 x 40.6 cm.).
Courtesy of Christie's Images, Inc., New York.
20

Artists Sketching in the White Mountains 1868
Oil on panel, 9 7/16 x 15 13/16 in. (23.9 x 40.16 cm.).
Portland Museum of Art, Maine.
Bequest of Charles Shipman Payson, 1988.55.4.
Photo: Melville McLean
16

At Tampa 1885
Watercolor, 14 x 20 in. (35.6 x 50.8 cm.).
Courtesy of the Canajoharie Library and Art Gallery, Canajohairie, New York.
206

The Beach at Longbranch 1869
Wood engraving, 13 x 19 1/2 in. (33 x 49.6 cm.).
69

The Berry Pickers 1873
Pencil, watercolor and gouache,
9 3/4 x 13 7/8 in. (24.7 x 35.2 cm.).
Collection of Mr. and Mrs. Paul Mellon.
30–31

Blackboard 1877
Watercolor on wove paper,
19 3/4 x 12 3/4 in. (49 x 32 cm.).
National Gallery of Art, Washington.
Gift (partial and promised) of Jo Ann and Julian Ganz, Jr., in Honor of the 50th Anniversary of the National Gallery of Art.
65

Blown Away c. 1888
Watercolor over pencil,
10 1/8 x 19 1/16 in. (25.71 x 48.41 cm.).
The Brooklyn Museum of Art.
Museum Collection Fund and Special Subscription; 11.543.
108–109

The Blue Boat 1892
Watercolor over graphite on paper,
15 3/16 x 21 1/2 in. (38.57 x 54.6cm.).
Museum of Fine Arts, Boston.
Bequest of William Sturgis Bigelow, 26.764.
Courtesy, Museum of Fine Arts, Boston. Reproduced with permission.
© 2001, Museum of Fine Arts, Boston. All rights reserved.
140–141

Boy Fishing 1892
Watercolor, 14 5/8 x 21 in. (37.2 x 53.3 cm.).
San Antonio Museum of Art.
Purchased with funds provided by the Robert J. Kleberg, Jr., and Helen C. Kleberg Foundation and Friends of SAMA, 86.130.
160

Boy in a Boatyard 1873
Watercolor, tempera, and graphite on wove paper mounted on board, 7 7/16 x 13 5/8 in. (18.89 x 34.6 cm.).
Portland Museum of Art, Maine.
Bequest of Charles Shipman Payson, 1988.55.5.
Photo: Melville McLean
39

Boys and Kitten 1873
Watercolor and gouache over graphite on medium, textured cream wove paper,
9 5/8 x 13 5/8 in. (24.4 x 34.6 cm.).
Worcester Art Museum, Worcester, Massachusetts.
33

Boys in a Dory 1880
Watercolor and graphite on wove paper,
13 3/4 x 19 1/2 in. (34.9 x 49.5 cm.).
Addison Gallery of American Art,
Phillips Academy, Andover, Massachusetts.
Gift of anonymous donor, 1931.6.
75

Boys Wading 1873
Pencil, watercolor and gouache,
9 3/4 x 13 7/8 in. (24.76 x 35.22 cm.).
Collection of Mr. and Mrs. Paul Mellon.
38

Breezing Up (A Fair Wind) 1873–1876
Oil on canvas, 24 3/16 x 38 3/16 in. (61.5 x 97 cm.).
National Gallery of Art, Washington.
Gift of the W. L. and May T. Mellon Foundation.
© 2001 Board of Trustees, National Gallery of Art, Washington, 1943.13.1.
13

Canoe in Rapids 1897
Watercolor over graphite on white paper,
13 5/8 x 20 1/2 in. (34.6 x 52.1 cm.).
Courtesy of the Fogg Art Museum,
Harvard University Art Museums.
Louise E. Bettens Fund, 1924.30.
Photo: Katya Kallsen. © President and Fellows of Harvard College.
178–179

Children Playing Under a Gloucester Wharf 1880
Watercolor over graphite on paper,
8 1/16 x 13 1/2 in. (20.7 x 34.29 cm.).
Museum of Fine Arts, Boston.
Hayden Collection. Charles Henry Hayden Fund, 21.2554.
Courtesy, Museum of Fine Arts, Boston. Reproduced with permission.
© 2001, Museum of Fine Arts, Boston. All rights reserved.
74

Coconut Palms, Key West 1886
Watercolor on paper, 16 x 13 in. (40.6 x 33 cm.).
Private collection, Washington, D.C.
202

Contraband 1875
Watercolor, 8 3/4 x 7 7/8 in. (22.2 x 20 cm.).
Courtesy of the Canajoharie Library and Art Gallery, Canajoharie, New York.
55

Coral Formation 1901
Watercolor over graphite on medium, smooth, off-white wove paper, 14 x 21 in. (35.56 x 53.34 cm.).
Worcester Art Museum, Worcester, Massachusetts.
187

The Cotton Pickers 1876
Oil on canvas, 24 1/16 x 38 1/4 in. (89.23 x 125.1 cm.).
Los Angeles County Museum of Art.
Acquisition made possible through Museum Trustees: Robert O. Anderson, R. Stanton Avery, B. Gerald Cantor, Edward W. Carter, Justin Dart, Charles E. Ducommun, Camilla Chandler Frost, Julian Ganz, Jr., Dr. Armand Hammer, Harry Lenart, Dr. Franklin D. Murphy, Mrs. Joan Palevsky, Richard E. Sherwood, Maynard J. Toll, and Hal B. Wallis. M.77.68.
Photograph © 2001 Museum Associates / LACMA.
18

Deep Sea Fishing 1894
Watercolor on paper, 13 1/2 x 21 in. (34.29 x 53.34 cm.).
Courtesy of Vance Jordan Fine Art, Inc.
118

Deer Drinking 1892
Watercolor, 14 1/6 x 20 1/6 in. (35.7 x 51 cm.).
Yale University Art Gallery.
The Robert W. Carle, B.A. 1897, Fund, 1976.36.
156

Deer-Stalking in the Adirondacks in Winter 1871
Wood engraving, 9 1/4 x 12 in. (23.3 x 30.6 cm.).
17

Diamond Shoal 1905
Watercolor on paper, 13 7/8 x 21 3/4 in.
(35.2 x 55.3 cm.). Courtesy of Caldwell Gallery, Ltd.
216–217

Dog on a Log 1889
Watercolor and graphite on wove paper,
13 15/16 x 20 in. (34.9 x 50.2 cm.).
Addison Gallery of American Art,
Phillips Academy, Andover, Massachusetts.
Bequest of Miss Candace C. Stimson, 1946.120.
152

Driving Cows to Pasture 1879
Watercolor over graphite on paper,
8 1/2 x 13 1/2 in. (21.59 x 34.29 cm.).
Museum of Fine Arts, Boston.
Bequest of the estate of Katherine Dexter McCormick, 65.569.
Courtesy, Museum of Fine Arts, Boston. Reproduced with permission.
© 2001, Museum of Fine Arts, Boston. All rights reserved.
4–5

Eastern Point Light 1880
Watercolor over pencil,
9 5/8 x 13 3/8 in. (24.5 x 34 cm.).
The Art Museum, Princeton University.
Gift of Alastair B. Martin, Class of 1938, x1957.116.
78–79

End of the Portage 1897
Watercolor over pencil, 14 x 21 in. (35.6 x 53.3 cm.).
The Brooklyn Museum of Art.
Bequest of Helen B. Sanders, 78.151.1.
173

The Fallen Deer 1892
Watercolor over graphite on moderately thick, rough textured, dark cream wove paper,
13 3/4 x 19 3/4 in. (34.9 x 50.16 cm.).
Museum of Fine Arts, Boston.
Hayden Collection. Charles Henry Hayden Fund, 23.443.
Courtesy, Museum of Fine Arts, Boston. Reproduced with permission.
© 2001, Museum of Fine Arts, Boston. All rights reserved.
157

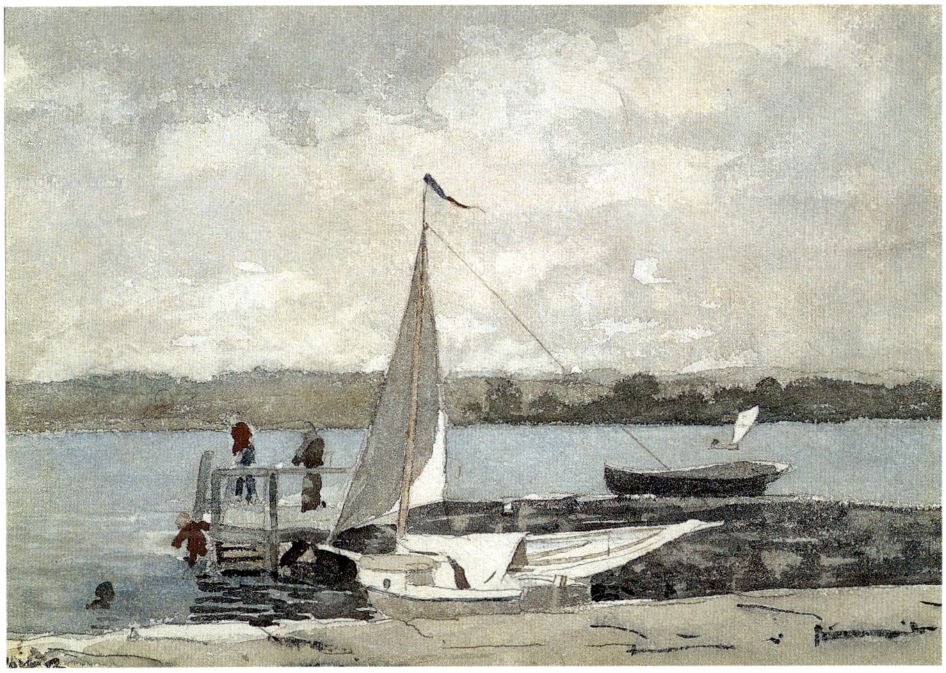

A Sloop at a Wharf, Gloucester 1880

Hudson River at Blue Ledge, Essex County (The Log Jam) 1889
Watercolor on paper,
14 1/2 x 21 in. (36.83 x 53.34 cm.),
Norton Museum of Art, West Palm Beach, Florida.
Bequest of R. H. Norton, 53.83.
144

Hudson River, Logging 1892
Watercolor over pencil,
14 x 20 3/4 in. (35.5 x 52.7 cm.).
The Corcoran Gallery of Art, Washington, DC.
Museum purchase, 03.4.
145

Hunter in the Adirondacks 1892
Watercolor over graphite on white paper,
13 7/8 x 19 15/16 in. (35.3 x 57.0 cm.).
Courtesy of the Fogg Art Museum, Harvard University Art Museums, Anonymous Gift, 1939.230.
Photo: Katya Kallgen © President and Fellows of Harvard College.
150–151

Hurricane, Bahamas 1898/1899
Watercolor and graphite on off-white wove paper,
14 1/2 x 21 1/8 in. (36.8 x 53.3 cm.).
The Metropolitan Museum of Art.
Amelia B. Lazarus Fund, 1910 (10.228.7.
Photograph © 1980 The Metropolitan Museum of Art.
193

In a Florida Jungle c. 1885–1886
Watercolor, 14 x 20 in. (35.8 x 51 cm.).
Worcester Art Museum,
Worcester, Massachusetts, 1911.19.
198–199

In Charge of Baby 1873
Watercolor on paper,
8 1/2 x 13 1/2 in. (21.6 x 34.3 cm.).
Mr. A. Alfred Taubman.
43

In the Garden 1874
Watercolor on paper,
9 1/16 x 6 11/16 in. (23 x 17 cm.).
Collection of Mr. and Mrs. Arthur G. Altschul.
58

In the Jungle, Florida 1904
Watercolor over pencil,
13 7/8 x 19 11/16 in. (35.2 x 24.6 cm.).
The Brooklyn Museum of Art.
Museum Collection Fund and Special Subscription; 11.547.
200–201

Inside the Bar, Cullercoats 1883
Watercolor, 15 3/8 x 28 1/2 in. (39.7 x 72.4 cm.).
The Metropolitan Museum of Art.
Gift of Louise Ryals Arkell, in memory of her husband, Bartlett Arkell, 1954 (54.183).
Photograph © 1996 The Metropolitan Museum of Art.
92–93

Key West, Negro Cabins & Palms 1898
Watercolor over pencil,
14 7/16 x 21 1/16 in. (36.6 x 53.5 cm.).
The Brooklyn Museum of Art.
Museum Collection Fund and Special Subscription; 11.538.
204–205

Leaping Trout 1889
Watercolor over graphite on moderately thick, slightly textured, dark cream wove paper,
14 x 20 in. (35.5 x 50.7 cm.).
Museum of Fine Arts, Boston.
William Wilkins Warren Fund, 99.24.
Courtesy, Museum of Fine Arts, Boston. Reproduced with permission.
© 2001, Museum of Fine Arts, Boston. All rights reserved.
166–167

The Life Line 1884
Oil on canvas, 28 3/4 x 44 5/8 in. (73 x 113.4 cm.).
Philadelphia Museum of Art.
The George W. Elkins Collection, E1924-4-15.
22

The Lighthouse, Nassau 1899
Watercolor over graphite on medium, smooth off-white wove paper, 14 1/2 x 21 in. (36.5 x 53.4 cm.).
Worcester Art Museum, Worcester, Massachusetts.
194–195

Live Oaks 1886
Watercolor, 12 1/2 x 19 1/2 in. (31.8 x 49.5 cm.).
Spencer Museum of Art, The University of Kansas.
William Bridges Thayer Memorial, 28.1796.
207

Looking Over the Cliff 1882
Watercolor, 20 1/2 x 13 1/2 in. (52.1 x 34.3 cm.).
Plainfield Public Library, Plainfield, New Jersey.
88

Maine Cliffs 1883
Watercolor over charcoal,
13 3/8 x 19 1/8 in. (34. x 48.7 cm.).
The Brooklyn Museum of Art.
Bequest of Sidney B. Curtis in Memory of S.W. Curtis; 50.184.
115

Man in a Punt, Fishing 1874
Watercolor over graphite on paper,
9 3/4 x 13 1/2 in. (24.8 x 34.3 cm.).
Private collection.
53

Mending the Nets 1882
Watercolor and gouache over graphite,
27 3/8 x 19 1/4 in. (69.5 x .48.9 cm.).
National Gallery of Art, Washington.
Bequest of Julia B. Engel, 1984.58.3.
Photograph © 2001 Board of Trustees, National Gallery of Art, Washington.
105

A Milkmaid 1874–1875
Chalk, gouache on wove paper,
13 3/4 x 7 1/8 in. (34.92 x 18.1 cm.).
Addison Gallery of American Art,
Phillips Academy, Andover, Massachusetts.
Gift of Mary D. and Arthur L. Williston, 1949.25.
58

The Milkmaid 1878
Watercolor over graphite,
19 3/4 x 14 3/16 in. (50.3 x 36 cm.).
National Gallery of Art, Washington.
Gift of Ruth K. Henschel in memory of her husband, Charles R. Henschel, 1975.92.11.
Photograph © 2001 Board of Trustees, National Gallery of Art, Washington.
59

Mink Pond 1891
Watercolor over graphite on heavy, white wove paper,
13 13/16 x 20 in. (35.2 x 50.8 cm.).
Courtesy of the Fogg Art Museum,
Harvard University Art Museums.
Bequest of Grenville L. Winthrop, 1943.304.
Photo: Allan Mcintyre, © President and Fellows of Harvard College.
168–169

Moonlight 1874
Watercolor and gouache, 14 x 20 in. (35.6 x 50.8 cm.).
Courtesy of the Canajoharie Library and Art Gallery, Canajoharie, New York.
70–71

Native Huts, Nassau 1885
Watercolor, gouache, and graphite on wove paper,
14 1/2 x 21 1/16 in. (36.8 x 53.5 cm.).
National Gallery of Art, Washington.
Collection of Mr. and Mrs. Paul Mellon, 1994.59.20.
Photograph © 2001 Board of Trustees, National Gallery of Art, Washington.
127

The New Novel 1877
Watercolor, 9 1/2 x 20 1/2 in. (24.1 x 52.1 cm.).
Museum of Fine Arts, Springfield, Massachusetts.
The Horace P. Wright Collection.
68–69

The Northeaster 1883
Watercolor, 14 1/8 x 19 3/4 in. (35.8 x 50.1 cm.).
The Brooklyn Museum of Art.
Bequest of Sidney B. Curtis in memory of S. W. Curtis; 50.185.
114

An October Day 1889
Watercolor, 13 7/8 x 19 3/4 in. (35.3 x 50.2 cm.).
Sterling and Francine Clark Art Institute,
Williamstown, Massachusetts, 1955.770.
154–155

Old Friends 1894
Watercolor over graphite on off-white wove paper,
21 3/8 x 15 1/8 in. (54.3 x 38.3 cm.).
Worcester Art Museum,
Worcester, Massachusetts, 1908.3.
149

Old Settlers 1892
Watercolor over graphite on paper,
21 1/2 x 15 1/8 in. (54.61 x 38.48 cm.).
Museum of Fine Arts, Boston.
Bequest of Nathaniel T. Kidder, 38.1412.
Courtesy, Museum of Fine Arts, Boston. Reproduced with permission.
© 2001, Museum of Fine Arts, Boston. All rights reserved.
148

On the Cliff 1881
Watercolor, 13 1/2 x 19 1/8 in. (34.2 x 48.5 cm.).
Courtesy of the Canajoharie Library and Art Gallery, Canajoharie, New York.
87

On the Trail c. 1892
Watercolor over graphite,
12 5/8 x 19 7/8 in. (32.1 x 50.5 cm.).
National Gallery of Art, Washington.
Gift of Ruth K. Henschel in memory of her husband, Charles R. Henschel, 1975.92.12.
Photograph © 2001 Board of Trustees, National Gallery of Art, Washington.
153

On the Way to Market, Bahamas 1885
Watercolor over pencil,
13 15/16 x 20 1/16 in. (35.4 x 51. cm.).
The Brooklyn Museum of Art.
Gift of Gunnar Maske in memory of
Elizabeth Treadway White Maske; 69.50.
(Title-page)

Oranges on a Branch 1885
Watercolor and pencil, 14 x 19 5/8 in.
(35.5 x 49.8 cm.), Private collection.
129

Osprey's Nest 1902
Watercolor and pencil,
21 1/2 x 13 5/8 in. (54.6 x 34.6 cm.).
Sterling and Francine Clark Art Institute,
Williamstown, Massachusetts, 1955.1502.
172

Our National Winter Exercise—Skating 1866
Wood engraving, 13 7/8 x 20 1/4 in. (35.4 x 21.4 cm.).
14

Paddling at Dusk 1892
Watercolor on paper,
15 1/8 x 21 3/8 in. (38.4 x 54.29 cm.).
Memorial Art Gallery of the University of Rochester, New York. Gift of Dr. and Mrs. James H. Lockhart, Jr., 84.50.
26

Palm Trees, Florida 1904
Watercolor over graphite on paper,
19 1/8 x 13 1/2 in. (48.64 x 34.29 cm.).
Museum of Fine Arts, Boston.
Bequest of John T. Spaulding, 48.731.
Courtesy, Museum of Fine Arts, Boston. Reproduced with permission.
© 2001, Museum of Fine Arts, Boston. All rights reserved.
203

Perils of the Sea 1881
Watercolor over light sketch in black chalk,
14 5/8 x 21 in. (37.2 x 53.3 cm.).
Sterling and Francine Clark Art Institute,
Williamstown, Massachusetts, 1955.774.
100–101

Prisoners from the Front 1866
Oil on canvas, 24 x 38 in. (61 x 96.5 cm.).
The Metropolitan Museum of Art.
Gift of Mrs. Frank B. Porter, 1922.22.207.
15

PROUT'S NECK, BREAKERS 1883
Watercolor, 14 7/8 x 21 5/16 in. (37.8 x 54.1 cm.).
The Art Institute of Chicago.
Mr. and Mrs. Martin A. Ryerson Collection, 1933.1247.

(Half-title, page 1)

PROUT'S NECK, LOOKING TOWARD OLD ORCHARD 1883
Watercolor and graphite on wove paper,
14 x 20 in. (35.56 x 50.8 cm.).
Addison Gallery of American Art,
Phillips Academy, Andover, Massachusetts.
Gift of anonymous donor, 1930.14.
120–121

PROUT'S NECK, SURF ON ROCKS 1895
Watercolor over graphite on off-white wove paper,
15 1/8 x 21 1/2 in. (38.4 x 54.5 cm.).
Worcester Art Museum,
Worcester, Massachusetts, 1911.20.
116–117

THE PUMPKIN PATCH 1878
Watercolor, 13 3/4 x 29 in. (34.9 x 73.7 cm.).
Courtesy of the Canajoharie Library and Art Gallery,
Canajoharie, New York.
50–51

REST 1885
Watercolor, 14 x 14 in. (35.6 x 35.6 cm.).
Private collection.
128

RETURNING FISHING BOATS 1883
Watercolor and white gouache over graphite on white paper, 15 7/8 x 24 3/4 in. (40.3 x 62.9 cm.).
Courtesy of the Fogg Art Museum,
Harvard University Art Museums. Anonymous gift.
Photo: Allan Mcintyre, © President and Fellows of Harvard College, 1939.233.
96–97

RUSTIC COURTSHIP 1874
Watercolor and gouache,
8 5/8 x 12 1/4 in. (22 x 31.1 cm.).
Collection of Mr. and Mrs. Paul Mellon.
46–47

SAGUENAY RIVER, LOWER RAPIDS 1897
Watercolor over graphite on moderately thick, smooth off white wove paper,
14 x 20 15/16 in. (35.3 x 53.1 cm.).
Worcester Art Museum,
Worcester, Massachusetts, 1911.20.
170–171

SAILBOAT AND FOURTH OF JULY FIREWORKS 1880
Watercolor on paper,
9 5/8 x 3 11/16 in. (24.5 x 34.7 cm.).
Courtesy of the Fogg Art Museum,
Harvard University Art Museums.
Bequest of Grenville L. Winthrop, 1943.305.
Photo: Allan Mcintyre, © President and Fellows of Harvard College.
82–83

SAILING THE CATBOAT c. 1873
Watercolor and gouache over pencil on paper,
7 1/2 x 13 3/4 in. (19.1 x 34.9 cm.).
Anonymous.
40–41

ST. JOHNS RIVER, FLORIDA 1890
Watercolor on paper,
13 1/2 x 19 7/8 in. (34.3 x 50.5 cm.).
The Hyde Collection, Glens Falls, New York, 1971.70.
207

SALT KETTLE, BERMUDA 1899
Watercolor over graphite,
13 15/16 x 21 in. (35.5 x 53.3 cm.).
National Gallery of Art, Washington.
Gift of Ruth K. Henschel in memory of her husband,
Charles R. Henschel, 1975.92.15.

182–183

SCHOONERS AT ANCHOR, KEY WEST 1903
Watercolor and pencil on paper,
14 x 21 3/4 in. (35.4 x 55.3 cm.).
Courtesy of Christie's Images, Inc., New York.
212–213

SHARKS; also **THE DERELICT** 1885
Watercolor over pencil,
14 1/2 x 20 15/16 in. (36.8 x 53.18 cm.).
The Brooklyn Museum of Art.
Bequest of Helen B. Sanders; 78.151.4.
132–133

THE SHIP'S BOAT 1883
Watercolor, 16 x 29 in. (40.6 x 73.7 cm.).
The New Britain Museum of American Art,
Connecticut, Charles F. Smith Fund.
110–111

SHOOTING THE RAPIDS 1902
Watercolor over pencil,
14 x 21 13/16 in. (35.6 x 53.3 cm.).
The Brooklyn Museum of Art.
Museum Collection Fund and Special Subscription; 11.537.
176–177

SHORE AT BERMUDA c. 1899
Watercolor over pencil, 14 x 21 in. (35.6 x 53.4 cm.).
The Brooklyn Museum of Art.
Museum Collection Fund and Special Subscription; 11.539.
186

THE SICK CHICKEN 1874
Watercolor, gouache, and graphite on wove paper,
9 3/4 x 7 3/4 in. (24.7 x 19.7 cm.).
National Gallery of Art, Washington.
Collection of Mr. and Mrs. Paul Mellon, 1994.59.21.

48

A SLOOP AT A WHARF, GLOUCESTER 1880
Watercolor, 9 x 13 1/2 in. (22.80 x 34.29 cm.).
Collection of Jean Pennau.
Courtesy, Questroyal Fine Art, New York.
219

SNAP THE WHIP 1872
Oil on canvas, 22 x 36 in. (55.9 x 91.4 cm.).
Butler Institute of American Art, Youngstown, Ohio.
Museum Purchase: 919-0-108.
19

THE SPONGE DIVER 1898–1899
Watercolor over graphite on paper,
15 x 21 3/8 in. (38.1 x 54.3 cm.).
Museum of Fine Arts, Boston.
Gift of Mrs. Robert B. Osgood, 1939, 621.

190–191

SPONGE FISHING, THE BAHAMAS 1885
Watercolor, 14 x 20 in. (35.6 x 50.8 cm.).
Courtesy of the Canajoharie Library and Art Gallery,
Canajoharie, New York.
130–131

STREET CORNER, SANTIAGO DE CUBA 1885
Watercolor over pencil on heavy, cream wove paper,
14 x 20 in. (35.5 x 50.8 cm.).
Museum of Fine Arts, Boston.
Anonymous gift in memory of Horace D. Chapin, 1978.300.

134

STUDY FOR THE HERRING NET 1884–1885
Black, brown and white chalk on paper,
16 5/8 x 20 9/16 in. (42.3 x 52.3 cm.).
Cooper-Hewitt, National Design Museum,
Smithsonian Institution, Gift of Charles Savage Homer, Jr. Photo: Art Resource, New York.
119

SUMMER CLOUD 1881
Watercolor on paper,
13 1/2 x 19 1/2 in. (34.3 x 49.5 cm.).
Mr. A. Alfred Taubman.
86

A SUMMER NIGHT 1890
Watercolor, 14 1/2 x 21 1/2 in. (36.8 x 54.6 cm.).
Wadsworth Atheneum, Hartford.
Gift of James J. Goodwin, 1923.82.
112–113

SUNRISE, FISHING IN THE ADIRONDACKS 1892
Watercolor, 13 1/2 x 20 1/2 in. (34.3 x 52.1 cm.).
The Fine Arts Museums of San Francisco,
Achenbach Foundation for Graphic Arts, Museum purchase, Mildred Anna Williams Collection, 1966.2.
164–165

SUNSET FIRES 1880
Watercolor, 9 3/4 x 13 5/8 in. (24.8 x 34.6 cm.).
The Westmoreland County Museum of Art,
Greensburg, Pennsylvania.
William A. Coulter Fund, 64.36.
72–73

TAKING A SUNFLOWER TO THE TEACHER 1875
Watercolor on paper,
7 x 5 7/8 in. (17.8 x 14.9 cm.).
Georgia Museum of Art, University of Georgia.
Eva Underhill Holbrook Memorial Collection of American Art. Gift of Alfred H. Holbrook, GMOA 45.50.
54

THREE BOYS ON THE SHORE 1873
Gouache and watercolor on paper mounted on board, 8 5/8 x 13 5/8 in. (21.9 x 34.6 cm.).
Terra Foundation for the Arts,
Daniel J. Terra Collection, 1999.75.
Photography courtesy of Terra Foundation for the Arts, Chicago.
34–35

THREE MEN IN A CANOE 1895
Watercolor and gouache over graphite,
13 3/4 x 19 3/8 in. (34.9 x 49.2 cm.).
Collection of Mrs. Wellington Henderson.
Photo: Benjamin Blackwell
180–181

TRAPPERS RESTING 1874
Watercolor, 9 3/4 x 13 3/4 in. (24.76 x 34.92 cm.).
Portland Museum of Art, Maine.
Gift of Charles Shipman Payson, 1988.55.6.
Photo: Melville McLean
138–139

TRAPPING IN THE ADIRONDACKS 1870
Wood engraving, 9 1/4 x 12 1/8 in. (23.7 x 31 cm.).
138

THE TRYSTING PLACE 1875
Watercolor, 12 x 8 1/6 in. (30.5 x 20.5 cm.).
The Art Museum, Princeton University.
Lent by the Department of Rare Books and Special Collections, Princeton University Library.
Gift of the estate of Lawrence Hutton in 1913, L.61.
Photo: Bruce M. White
63

THE TURTLE POUND 1898
Watercolor over pencil,
14 15/16 x 21 3/8 in. (38 x 54.2 cm.).
The Brooklyn Museum of Art.
Sustaining Membership Fund; A.T. White Memorial Fund; A. Augustus Healy Fund; 23.98.
196–197

TWO GIRLS ON THE BEACH, TYNEMOUTH 1881
Watercolor on paper, 14 x 20 in. (35.6 x 50.8 cm.).
Courtesy of Christie's Images, Inc., New York.
2–3

TWO WOMEN AND A CHILD AT A RAIL, OVERLOOKING THE BEACH AT CULLERCOATS 1881
Charcoal on paper,
8 3/8 x 11 3/4 in. (21.3 x 29.9 cm.).
Cooper-Hewitt, National Design Museum,
Smithsonian Institution,
Gift of Charles Savage Homer, Jr.
101

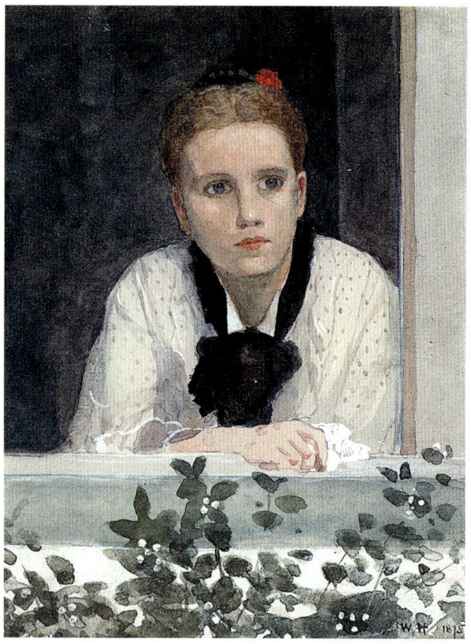

Young Girl at Window 1875

Tynemouth Priory, England 1881
Watercolor with reddish-brown gouache and traces of scraping over graphite on ivory wove paper,
10 1/4 19 7/8 x in. (26.2 x 50.5 cm.).
The Art Institute of Chicago.
Mr. and Mrs. Martin A. Ryerson Collection, 1933.1254.
Photograph © 2001, The Art Institute of Chicago, All Rights Reserved.
104

Under the Coco Palm 1898
Watercolor over graphite on white paper,
15 x 21 3/16 in. (38 x 53.8 cm.).
Courtesy of the Fogg Art Museum,
Harvard University Art Museums.
Louise E. Bettens Fund, ip, 1920.29
Photography courtesy of Yale University Art Gallery.
188

Under the Falls, the Grand Discharge 1895
Watercolor with pencil underdrawing on paper,
13 15/16 x 19 7/8 in. (35.4 x 50.5 cm.).
The Brooklyn Museum of Art.
Bequest of Helen Sanders, 78.151.2.
175

An Unexpected Catch 1890
Watercolor on paper,
11 1/2 x 19 3/4 in. (29.21 x 50.16 cm.).
Portland Museum of Art, Maine.
Bequest of Charles Shipman Payson, 1988.55.9.
Photo: Benjamin Magro
163

Waiting for a Bite c. 1874
Watercolor and graphite on wove paper,
7 5/16 x 13 5/16 in. (18.57 x 33.81 cm.).
Addison Gallery of American Art,
Phillips Academy, Andover, Massachusetts.
Gift of Mary D. and Arthur L. Williston, 1948.28.
52

Waiting for a Bite 1874
Oil on canvas, 11 15/16 x 20 1/8 in. (30.5 x 50.8 cm.).
Cummer Gallery of Art and Gardens,
Jacksonville, Florida.
16

Waiting for a Bite 1874
Wood engraving, 9 x 13 11/16 in. (23 x 35 cm.).
53

Waiting for Dad 1873
Watercolor and gouache on paper,
9 3/4 x 13 5/8 in. (24.8 x 34.6 cm.).
Mills College Art Museum, Oakland, California.
Gift of Jane Tolman, 1912.2.
39

Waiting for the Boats 1873
Watercolor, 8 1/2 x 13 1/2 in. (21.6 x 34.3 cm.).
Anonymous.
36–37

Watching the Harbor 1873
Watercolor, 8 1/4 x 13 1/4 in. (21 x 33.7 cm.).
Anonymous.
28–29

Watching the Tempest 1881
Watercolor over graphite on off-white paper,
13 15/16 x 19 7/8 in. (35.4 x 50.5 cm.).
Courtesy of the Fogg Art Museum,
Harvard University Art Museums.
Bequest of Grenville L. Winthrop, 1943.296.
Photo: Katya Kallsen, © President and Fellows of Harvard College.
98–99

Weary c. 1878
Watercolor and graphite on paper,
9 1/2 x 12 1/4 in. (22 x 28.6 cm.).
Terra Foundation for the Arts,
Daniel J. Terra Collection, 1992.41.
Photography courtesy of Terra Foundation for the Arts, Chicago.
57

West India Divers 1899
Watercolor, 14 7/8 x 21 3/8 in. (37.8 x 54.3 cm.).
Spencer Museum of Art, The University of Kansas.
William Bridges Thayer Memorial, 28.1785.
189

Windy Day, Cullercoats 1881
Graphite and gouache on paper,
11 3/16 x 20 1/4 in. (28.41 x 51.43 cm.).
Portland Museum of Art, Maine.
Bequest of Charles Shipman Payson, 1988.15.
Photo: Melville McLean
93

Woman and Elephant 1877
Watercolor on paper on linen,
11 3/4 x 8 3/4 in. (29.9 x 22.2 cm.).
Albright-Knox Art Gallery, Buffalo, New York.
Gift of Mrs. John W. Ames, 1959.
64

Woman Sewing 1878–1879
Watercolor over pencil,
9 3/4 x 7 7/8 in. (24.76 x 19.68 cm.).
The Corcoran Gallery of Art, Washington, DC.
Bequest of James Parmelee, 41.15.
66

Women in Autumn Woods c. 1887
Watercolor on paper, 11 x 20 in. (27.9 x 50.8 cm.).
Whereabouts unknown.
Courtesy of Kennedy Galleries, New York.
122

The Woodcutter 1891
Watercolor on paper,
13 3/4 x 19 7/8 in. (34.9 x 50.5 cm.).
Meredith Long & Company, Houston, Texas.
142–143

Wreck Near Gloucester 1880
Graphite on watercolor paper,
14 13/16 x 19 5/8 in. (37.6 x 50 cm.).
The Carnegie Institute Museum of Art, Pittsburg.
Museum Purchase, 17.3.2.
76–77

The Wreck of the Iron Crown 1881
Watercolor, 20 1/4 x 29 3/8 in. (51.4 x 74.7 cm.).
The Baltimore Museum of Art.
Private collection, on extended loan to
The Baltimore Museum of Art, R.8613.2.
102–103

Young Girl at Window 1875
Watercolor on paper mounted on masonite,
6 1/4 x 4 3/4 in. (15.8 x 11.11 cm.).
Collection of the New Britain Museum of
American Art, Connecticut.
Harriet Russell Stanley Fund. Photo: E. Irving Blumstrann
222

WORKS BY OTHER ARTISTS

John James Audubon
Black Guillemot, 1833
Watercolor, pastel, graphite, selective glazing, and gouache on paper,
14 3/4 x 21 5/16 in. (37.5 x 54.1 cm.).
The New York Historical Society.
23

Eastman Johnson
Negro Life in the South, 1859
Oil on canvas, 36 x 45 1/4 in. (91.44 x 114.93 cm.).
The New York Historical Society.
Robert L. Stuart Collection, on permanent loan from
The New York Public Library, S-225.
18

Eastman Johnson
The Old Stage Coach, 1871
Oil on canvas, 36 1/4 x 60 1/8 in. (92. 157.71 x cm.).
Milwaukee Art Museum, Layton Art Collection.
Gift of Frederick Layton, LI888.22.
19

John La Farge
Water-Lilies, Red and Green Pads.
Study from Nature, 1883
Watercolor and white gouache on thick wove paper,
7 3/8 x 11 1/4 in. (18.7 x 28.6 cm.).
Private collection.
Courtesy of Vance Jordan Fine Art, Inc.
23

John Singer Sargent
Violet Sleeping, c. 1907–1910
Watercolor and pencil on paperboard,
14 11/16 x 21 5/16 in. (37.3 x 54.2 cm.).
The Brooklyn Museum of Art.
Gift of Mrs. Lawrence B. Dunham; 77.145
24

PHOTOGRAPHS

The Charles Savage Homer House in Prout's Neck, Maine, with Winslow Homer's Studio, 1883
Bowdoin College Museum of Art, Brunswick, Maine.
Gift of the Homer Family, 1964.069.153.010.
22

Winslow Homer as a Young Man in Paris, 1867
Bowdoin College Museum of Art, Brunswick, Maine.
Gift of the Homer Family, 1964.069.179.001.
12

Winslow Homer Taken in New York, 1880
Albumen print.
Bowdoin College Museum of Art, Brunswick, Maine.
Gift of the Homer Family, 1964.069.179.003.
20

Winslow Homer with "The Gulf Stream" in His Painting Room at Prout's Neck, c. 1900
Albumen print.
Bowdoin College Museum of Art, Brunswick, Maine.
Gift of the Homer Family, 1964.069.179.009.
27

Winslow Homer's Watercolor Box
Tin, canvas, and kid cover, and stylus box,
2 13/16 x 8 3/8 in. (7.14 x 21.27 cm.).
Portland Museum of Art, Maine.
Gift of Robert Porteous, Jr., in honor of
Bennett C. Porteous, 1979.15.1.
25

SELECT BIBLIOGRAPHY

Beam, Philip Conway. *Winslow Homer*. New York, McGraw-Hill, 1975

——*Winslow Homer: Watercolors*. Exhibition Catalogue. Brunswick, ME: Bowdoin College Museum of Art, 1983.

——et al. *Winslow Homer in the 1890s: Prout's Neck Observed*. New York: Hudson Hills Press, 1990.

Bermingham, Peter. *American Art in the Barbizon Mood*. Washington, DC: Smithsonian Institution Press, 1975.

Brett, Bernard. *A History of Watercolor*. New York: Excalibur Books, 1984.

Carbone, Teresa A., and Patricia Hills. *Eastman Johnson: Painting America*. Brooklyn, NY: Brooklyn Museum of Art, 1999.

Cikovsky, Nicolai, Jr. *Winslow Homer*. New York: Rizzoli Books, 1992.

——, and Franklin Kelly. *Winslow Homer*. Washington, DC: National Gallery of Art, 1995.

Cohn, Marjorie B. *Wash and Gouache: A Study of the Development of the Materials of Watercolor*. Cambridge: Fogg Art Museum, 1977.

Conrads, Margaret C. *Winslow Homer and the Critics: Forging a National Art in the 1870s*. Princeton: Princeton University Press, 2001.

Cooper, Helen A. *Winslow Homer Watercolors*. Washington, DC: National Gallery of Art, 1986.

Downes, William Howe. *The Life and Work of Winslow Homer*. Boston: Houghton Mifflin, 1911.

Ferber, Linda S. *Masters of Color and Light: Homer, Sargent and the American Watercolor Movement*. Brooklyn, NY: Brooklyn Museum, 1988.

Finch, Christopher. *American Watercolors*. New York: Abbeville, 1986.

Gardner, Albert Ten Eyck. *History of Watercolor in America*. New York: Reinhold Publishing Corp., 1966.

——*Winslow Homer, American Artist: His World and His Work*. New York: Bramhall House, 1961.

Goodrich, Lloyd. *American Watercolor and Winslow Homer*. Exhibition Catalogue. Minneapolis: Walker Art Center, 1945.

——*Winslow Homer*. New York: Macmillan, 1944.

——*Winslow Homer*. Exhibition Catalogue. New York: Whitney Museum of American Art, 1973.

Hannaway, Patti. *Winslow Homer in the Tropics*. Richmond, VA: Westover Publishing Co., 1973.

Hoopes, Donelson F. *American Watercolor Painting*. New York: Watson-Guptill Publications, 1977.

——*Winslow Homer Watercolors*. New York: Watson-Guptill Publications, 1969.

Hendricks, Gordon. *The Life and Work of Winslow Homer*. New York: Harry N. Abrams, 1979.

Kushner, Marilyn S., Barbara Gallati, and Linda Ferber. *Winslow Homer: Illustrating America*. Brooklyn, NY: Brooklyn Museum of Art, 2000.

Little, Carl. *Winslow Homer and the Sea*. San Francisco: Pomegranate Artbooks, 1995.

——*Winslow Homer: His Art, His Light, His Landscapes*. Cobb, CA: First Glance Books, 1997.

Novak, Barbara. *American Painting of the Nineteenth Century: Realism, Idealism and the American Experience*. New York: Frederick Praeger, 1979.

——*Nature and Culture: American Landscape Painting 1825–1875*. New York: Oxford University Press, 1995.

Reed, Sue Welsh, and Carol Troyen. *Awash in Color: Homer, Sargent, and the Great American Watercolor*. Boston: Museum of Fine Arts, 1993.

Schneider, Paul. *The Adirondacks: A History of America's First Wilderness*. New York: H. Hold and Co., 1997.

Stebbins, Theodore. *American Master Drawings and Watercolors: A History of Works on Paper from Colonial Times to the Present*. New York: Harper & Row, 1976.

Strickler, Susan E. *American Traditions in Watercolor: The Worcester Art Museum Collection*. New York: Abbeville, 1987.

Tatham, David. "Trapper, Hunter, and Woodsman: Winslow Homer's Adirondack Figures", *American Art Journal*, 22 (1990), 41–67 [Tatham 1990b].

Wilmerding, John. *Audubon, Homer, Whistler and 19th-Century America*. New York: Lamplight Publishers, 1975.

——*Winslow Homer*. New York: Frederick Praeger, 1972.

CHRONOLOGY

1836 February 24 Winslow Homer born in Boston, Massachusetts, to Charles Savage Homer, Sr., and Henrietta Benson Homer

1842 The Homer family moves to Cambridge, Massachusetts

1854 Homer begins his apprenticeship at John H. Bufford's lithography shop, designing covers for sheet music

1857 Homer leaves Bufford's and begins to work as a freelance illustrator

June 13 Homer's first illustration, "Corner of Winter, Washington and Summer Streets, Boston," appears in *Ballou's Pictorial*

1859 Homer moves to New York City to pursue his career as a commercial illustrator

1861 October Homer travels with the Army of the Potomac on assignment from *Harper's Weekly*

1862 November 15 *Harper's Weekly* publishes Homer's *The Army of the Potomac—A Sharp-Shooter on Picket-Duty*. The work is inscribed, "From a painting by W. Homer," his first known work in oils

1865 May Elected a full academician of the National Academy of Design

1866–67

December 5 Homer leaves for France, where his *Prisoners from the Front* is included in the American section of the Exposition Universelle in Paris. He remains in France until the fall of 1867

1870 Homer makes his first trip to the Adirondacks, staying at the Baker family farm in Minerva, New York

1873 June Visits Gloucester, Massachusetts, where he makes his first watercolors

1874 Homer's second visit to the Adirondacks, where he makes such watercolors as *Waiting for a Bite*

1876 September First trip to Houghton Farm in Mountainville, New York, later the scene of watercolors like *Flock of Sheep, Houghton Farm* (1878) and *Feeding Time*

1877 Homer's only documented trip to the South, though earlier trips are surmised on the basis of paintings like *The Cotton Pickers* (1876) and *A Visit from the Old Mistress* (1876)

1878 Homer spends the summer months at Houghton Farm, home of his brother, Charles's, business partner, Lawson Valentine

1880 Summer Homer returns to Gloucester, lodging with the lighthouse keeper on Ten Pound Island. He produces such watercolors as *Eastern Point Light* and *Gloucester Sunset*

1881–82

March 15 Sails for Liverpool. He visits London, later settling in northern England, in the fishing village of Cullercoats. Here he begins such monumental watercolors as *An Afterglow* and *The Wreck of the Iron Crown*. Many of his Cullercoats watercolors are completed upon return to America in November 1882

1883 Charles purchases land in Prout's Neck, Maine, as a summer home for his parents

Summer Homer spend his first summer in Prout's Neck. By December a Boston newspaper notes that he has taken up permanent residence here. Work begins converting the carriage house next to the family house into a permanent home and studio

1884 April Homer exhibits *The Life Line* to widespread critical and popular acclaim

December With a commission from *Century Magazine* to provide illustrations, Homer makes his first trip to Nassau in the Bahamas. He makes his first tropical watercolors here. After a two-month stay, he sails for Santiago, Cuba

1885 December Homer makes his first trip to Florida, where he paints such watercolors as *At Tampa* and *In a Florida Jungle*

1888 With Charles he joins the North Woods Club on Mink Pond in the Adironracks. On fishing trips here, he makes many of his most important watercolors, staying for much of the spring and early summer. He returns for almost two months in the fall. These trips account for such masterpieces as *Leaping Trout* and *An October Day*

1893 Homer's first trip to Quebec. He and Charles join the Tourilli Fish and Game Club. He makes his first watercolors of the nearby Lake St. John in the summer of 1895

1898 Second trip to the Bahamas

1899 December First trip to Bermuda. Homer paints *Flower Garden and Bungalow, Bermuda*, and *Salt Kettle, Bermuda*

1903 December Travels to Key West, Florida, where he makes his last series of watercolors

1905 In January, Homer paints his last known watercolor, *Diamond Shoal*

1909 November Completes his final painting, *Driftwood*

1910 September 29 Homer dies in his Prout's Neck studio after suffering an internal hemorrhage

October 3 Homer is buried in Mount Auburn Cemetery in Cambridge, Massachusetts

INDEX